Exploring **LANGUAGE**

ELEVENTH EDITION

Gary Goshgarian

NORTHEASTERN UNIVERSITY

299
305
316

PEARSON
Longman

New York • San Francisco • Boston
London • Toronto • Sydney • Tokyo • Singapore • Madrid
Mexico City • Munich • Paris • Cape Town • Hong Kong • Montreal

This book is dedicated to my sons,
Nathan and David

Executive Editor: Lynn M. Huddon
Senior Supplements Editor: Donna Campion
Senior Marketing Manager: Sandra McGuire
Project Coordination, Text Design, and Electronic Page Makeup: Pre-Press Company, Inc.
Senior Cover Design Manager/Designer: Nancy Danahy
Cover Image: © Getty Images, Inc.
Photo Researcher: Chrissy McIntyre
Manufacturing Manager: Mary Fischer
Printer and Binder: R.R. Donnelley and Sons
Cover Printer: Phoenix Color Corporation

For permission to use copyrighted material, grateful acknowledgment is made to the copyright holders on pp. 596–601, which are hereby made part of this copyright page.

Library of Congress Cataloging-in-Publication Data

Exploring language / edited by Gary Goshgarian.—11th ed.
    p. cm.
    Includes bibliographical references and index.
    ISBN 0-321-45797-8
    1. College readers. 2. English language—Rhetoric—Problems, exercises, etc. 3.
    Critical thinking—Problems, exercises, etc. 4. English language. I. Goshgarian, Gary.
PE1417.E96 2006
808'.0427—dc22   2006025070

Please visit us at www.ablongman.com

ISBN 0-321-45797-8

1 2 3 4 5 6 7 8 9 10—DOC—09 08 07 06

Contents

Introduction: Thinking and Reading Critically   1

1 Language and History   23

BEGINNINGS: THE DEVELOPMENT OF LANGUAGE   25

Exploring the Language of Visuals: Tower of Babel   25

From Hand to Mouth   28
Michael C. Corballis

"What, then, are the advantages of a language that can operate autonomously through voice and ear, rather than hand and eye? Why speech?"

Language and Thought   34
Susanne K. Langer

"Language is the highest and most amazing achievement of the symbolistic human mind. The power it bestows is almost inestimable, for without it anything properly called 'thought' is impossible."

A Brief History of English   39
Paul Roberts

"In 1500 English was a minor language, spoken by a few people on a small island. Now it is perhaps the greatest language of the world. . . ."

2 The Power of Language 93

3 Writers Writing: Words in Context   154

5 Do You Know What I'm Saying?   297

HE SAYS, SHE SAYS: GENDER DIFFERENCES IN DISCOURSE   299

---

8 The English Language Debate 528

WHAT IS "STANDARD" ENGLISH? 530

Preface

I think that those instructors who have used earlier editions of *Exploring Language* will agree with me that this is, by far, the best edition to date. The eleventh edition provides a wide and diverse range of engaging and informative readings connected to language issues. It also aims to embrace changes in how we approach critical reading and writing in modern college classrooms.

Based on reviewer feedback, we kept the best readings from the previous edition. Almost half of the selections in the eleventh edition are new, many written since the last edition was published. Other sections have been updated to reflect current events, such as terrorism and America's war against it. This edition also features a new section on endangered languages. More than ever, movies and television have come under fire for celebrating dumb and crude use of language; the news media, for reporting news in slanted prose; nighttime television, for increased use of profanity; daytime talk shows, for rendering complex human issues in a sensational mixture of crude discourse and the latest psychobabble. Advertisers continue making bloated claims. Men and women still struggle to understand each other. Politicians are blasted for reducing intricate social issues to sound bites. Higher education is still locked in First Amendment debates over what to do about hate speech—racist, sexist, and other forms of offensive discourse—on American campuses. And "teenspeak" continues to make the older generation wince.

In spite of the many revisions to the eleventh edition, the original character and objective of *Exploring Language* remain the same: to bring together exciting and readable pieces that explore the various ways language and American society are interconnected. Once again, the aim is to lead students to a keener understanding of how language works: how it reconstructs the real world for us and how it can be used to lead, mislead, and manipulate us. Organized around eight major language areas, these selections demonstrate the subtle complexities and richness of English. They also invite students to debate current social and cultural issues that are inseparable from language. And they serve as models for composition, representing a diversity of expository techniques—narration, illustration, definition, process analysis, argumentation, persuasion, comparison, and contrast—and a diversity of genres—editorial essays, personal narratives, opinion columns, position papers, letters, memoirs, autobiographical musings, personal diaries, academic articles, humorous satires, interviews, and poetry.

The Eleventh Edition

A glance at the eight chapters' themes will give you a good idea of the breadth of coverage:

1. Language and History
2. The Power of Language
3. Writers Writing: Words in Context
4. Political Wordplay
5. Do You Know What I'm Saying?
6. Media Speak
7. Censorship and Free Speech
8. The English Language Debate

These themes reflect the wide spectrum of language issues that define our contemporary culture. Many new subtopics and readings were added to the already broad spectrum covered—essays that treat English in its present relation to race and ethnic identity, endangered languages, debates about "politically correct" bias-free language, political propaganda, bureaucratic doublespeak, advertising, journalism, text-messaging, sports mascots, ethnic prejudice, slang, so-called "gendered language," and other matters that suggest the endless potential of how language is used and abused.

A Wide Variety of Readings

In addition to updating a significant portion of the readings, this edition is infused with more variety and more genres than in any other edition of *Exploring Language*. Reflecting the wide range of expository modes and genres students are exposed to, this current text includes examples of personal narratives, objective reportage, newspaper opinion columns, position papers, various political arguments, editorials, op-ed essays, letters to the editor, memoirs, autobiographical musings, personal diaries, descriptive narratives, academic articles, pointed arguments, and even poems. This edition also includes several historical pieces and great speeches that influenced our culture and society.

Paired Essays and Debates

A key feature of *Exploring Language* since its first edition is the debate format. Each of the eight chapters contains essays on emotional or controversial topics paired with others presenting a scope of viewpoints. For instance, in the Chapter 1 subtheme "Preserving Voices: Defending Native Languages," James Geary describes the rapid loss of native languages across the globe, a phenomenon that concerns many linguists in "Speaking in Tongues." Kenan Malik, however, argues that language loss is simply the natural order of things in "Let Them Die." Some juxtaposed pieces might be indirect debates, such as advertising guru Charles O'Neill's defense of his craft, "The Language of Advertising," and William Lutz's condemnation of the weasel language of advertisers, "With These Words I Can Sell You

Anything." Other pieces delve into the nuances of an issue, such as in Chapter 4's subtheme, "Language and the Presidency," in which Renana Brooks postulates in "A Nation of Victims" that George W. Bush deliberately uses language to encourage Americans to feel a sense of helplessness in the face of terrorism. Her piece is followed by an actual speech by Bush on the "Global War on Terror" that allows students to analyze her argument. Or Charles R. Lawrence, III, who goes head-to-head with Alan Charles Kors over free speech versus censorship on college campuses in Chapter 7's case study, "Free Speech on Campus."

Updated Introduction to Critical Inquiry and Critical Reading

The premise of *Exploring Language* is that good writing grows out of good thinking, and good thinking grows out of good reading. Therefore, the text includes an introduction "Thinking and Reading Critically," which discusses what critical thinking and critical reading are, how to do each with step-by-step guidelines, and how each helps readers become better writers. The introduction illustrates the process in a detailed sample analysis of an essay addressing freedom of speech issues by *U.S. News & World Report* columnist John Leo. The sample not only illustrates a language issue that should appeal to students, but the analysis also gives them the tools to analyze the vast array of other language-based readings that follow.

Updated "Making Connections" Exercises

Each chapter subtheme is followed by several special writing and research exercises, "Making Connections." These exercises ask students to connect essays within the subtheme or chapter (and sometimes to other parts of the book) and research issues in greater depth. Many questions encourage Web-based research and direct students to additional online resources.

Revised Apparatus

All of the remaining apparatus in the book has been improved and updated to create penetrating and stimulating assignments. Each selection is preceded by a headnote containing useful thematic and biographical information, as well as clues to writing strategies. Each is followed by a series of review questions, "Thinking Critically," covering both thematic and rhetorical strategies as well as engaging writing assignments and other exercises. Specifically, we added more library and Internet research questions to the critical thinking exercises following each essay in the book.

Visuals

Recognizing the importance of visual communication, the last edition of *Exploring Language* integrated the text with a large number of different kinds of graphics for students to analyze and discuss. This eleventh edition includes updated visuals. In addition to the nine photographic chapter openers, we have included cartoons, print ads, comic strips, posters, poems, sign-language, photographs and more. Following each are "Thinking Critically" questions directing students to analyze the "language" of the images—the messages and commentary projected from the designs and layouts. More than ever before, students are making use of visual presentations in their writing, including their English essays. And the task is made easier because of the computer. Chapter 3 includes a discussion on the influence of fonts on reader's expectations.

Instructor's Manual

The *Instructor's Manual*, which is available to adopters, includes suggested responses to all the questions in the text. The *Instructor's Manual* also identifies questions that are particularly good for in-class discussion or collaborative student work.

Acknowledgments

Many people behind the scenes are, at the very least, deserving of thanks and acknowledgment for their help with this eleventh edition. It is impossible to thank all of them, but there are some for whose help I am particularly grateful. I would like, first, to thank those instructors who answered lengthy questionnaires on the effectiveness of the essays and supplied many helpful comments and suggestions: Darsie Bowden, DePaul University; Richard Follett, Los Angeles Pierce College; Gayle Fornataro, Los Angeles Valley College; Eileen A. Joy, Southern Illinois University; Elaine Richardson, Penn State University; David Sprunger, Concordia College; Rachel Wall, Kennesaw State University; Debbie J. Williams, Abilene Christian University.

To all the instructors and students who have used *Exploring Language* over the past ten editions, I am enormously grateful.

A very special thanks to Kathryn Goodfellow for her enormous assistance in locating material, writing the apparatus, and putting together the *Instructor's Manual*, all the while growing into first motherhood—this could not have been done without you. My thanks also to Amy Trumbull for her help in securing permissions for the text.

Finally to the people of Longman Publishers, especially my editor Lynn Huddon and her assistant Nicole Solano, thank you for your continuing support, understanding, and enthusiasm throughout the production process of this edition.

Gary Goshgarian

Introduction: Thinking and Reading Critically

What Is Critical Thinking?

Whenever you read a magazine article, newspaper editorial, or a piece of advertising and find yourself questioning the claims of the authors, you are exercising the basics of critical thinking. Instead of taking what you read at face value, you look beneath the surface of words and think about their meaning and significance. And you ask the authors questions such as:

- What did you mean by that?
- Can you back up that statement?
- How do you define that term?
- How did you draw that conclusion?
- Do all the experts agree?
- Is this evidence dated?
- So what?
- What is your point?
- Why do we need to know this?

You make statements such as:

- That's not true.
- You're contradicting yourself.
- I see your point, but I don't agree.
- That's not a good choice of words.
- You're jumping to conclusions.
- Good point. I never thought of that.
- That was nicely stated.
- This is an extreme view.

Whether conscious or unconscious, such responses indicate that you are thinking *critically* about what you read. You weigh claims, ask for definitions, evaluate information, look for proof, question assumptions, and make judgments. In short, you process another person's words, not just take them in.

Why Read Critically?

When you read critically, you think critically. And that means instead of simply accepting what's written on a page, you separate yourself from the text and decide for yourself what is or is not important or logical or right. And you do so because you bring to your reading your own perspective, experience, education, and personal values, as well as your powers of comprehension and analysis.

Critical reading is an active process of discovery. You discover an author's view on a subject; you enter a dialogue with the author; you discover the strengths and weaknesses of the author's thesis or argument; and you decide if you agree or disagree with the author's views. The end result is that you have a better understanding of the issue and the author. By asking questions of the author and analyzing where the author stands with respect to other experiences or views of the issue— including your own—you actively enter a dialogue or a debate. You seek out the truth on your own instead of accepting at face value what somebody else says.

In reality, that is how truth and meaning are achieved: through interplay. Experience teaches us that knowledge and truth are not static entities, but are the by-products of struggle and dialogue—of asking tough questions. We witness this phenomenon all the time, re-created in the media through dialogue and conflict. We've recognized it over the years as a force of social change. Consider, for example, how our culture has changed its attitudes with regard to race, its concepts of success, kinship, social groups, and class since the 1950s. Perhaps the most obvious example regards gender: were it not for people questioning old rigid conventions, most women would still be bound to the laundry and the kitchen stove.

The point is that critical reading is an active and reactive process—one that sharpens your focus on a subject and your ability to absorb information and ideas while encouraging you to question accepted norms, views, and myths. And that is both healthy and laudable, for it is the basis of social evolution.

Critical reading also helps you become a better writer, because critical reading is the first step to critical writing. Good writers look at another's writing the way a carpenter looks at a house: they study the fine details and how those details connect and create the whole. Likewise, they consider the particular slants and strategies of appeal. Good writers always have a clear sense of their audience— their readers' racial makeup, gender, and educational background; their political and/or religious persuasions; their values, prejudices, and assumptions about life; and so forth. Knowing one's audience helps writers determine nearly every aspect of the writing process: the kind of language to use; the writing style (casual or formal, humorous or serious, technical or philosophical); the particular slant to take (appealing to the readers' reason, emotions, or ethics, or a combination of these); what emphasis to give the essay; the type of evidence to offer; and the kinds of authorities to cite.

It's the same with critical reading. The better you become at analyzing and reacting to another's written work, the better you will analyze and react to your own. You will ask yourself: Is my analysis logical? Do my points come across clearly? Are my examples solid enough? Is this the best wording? Is my conclusion persuasive? Do I have a clear sense of my audience? What appeal strategy did I take—to logic, emotions, or ethics? In short, critical reading will help you to evaluate your own writing, thereby making you both a better reader and a better writer.

While you may already employ many strategies of critical reading, here are some techniques to make you an even better critical reader.

How to Read Critically

To help you read critically, use these six proven basic steps:

- Keep a journal on what you read.
- Annotate what you read.
- Outline what you read.
- Summarize what you read.
- Question what you read.
- Analyze what you read.

To demonstrate just how these techniques work, let's apply them to a sample essay. Reprinted below is the essay, "The Thought Police Keep Marching West," by John Leo, taken from his column posted online at the conservative Webzine *Townhall* on March 5, 2006. I chose this piece because, like all selections in this book, it addresses an interesting contemporary language issue, because it is accessible, and because the author raises some serious questions about free speech and censorship.

1   Law professor Eugene Volokh calls it "censorship envy." Muslims in Europe want the same sort of censorship that many nations now offer to other aggrieved groups. By law, eleven European nations can punish anyone who publicly denies the Holocaust. That's why the strange British historian David Irving is going to prison. Ken Livingstone, the madcap mayor of London, was suspended for four weeks for calling a Jewish reporter a Nazi. A Swedish pastor endured a long and harrowing prosecution for a sermon criticizing homosexuality, finally beating the rap in Sweden's Supreme Court.

2   Much of Europe has painted itself into a corner on the censorship issue. What can Norway say to pro-censorship Muslims when it already has a hate speech law forbidding, among other things, "publicly stirring up one part of the population against another," or any utterance that "threatens, insults, or subjects to hatred, persecution or contempt any person or group of persons because of their creed, race, colour or national or ethnic origin . . . or homosexual bent"? No insulting utterances at all? Since most strong opinions can be construed as insulting (hurting someone's feelings), no insults mean no free speech.

3   It's not just Europe. In Canada, a teacher drew a suspension for a letter to a newspaper arguing that homosexuality is not a fixed orientation, but a condition that can be treated. He was not accused of discrimination, merely of expressing thoughts that the state defines as improper. Another Canadian newspaper was fined $4,500 for printing an ad giving the citations—but not the text—of four biblical quotations against homosexuality. As David Bernstein writes in his book, *You Can't Say That!* "It has apparently become illegal in Canada to advocate traditional Christian opposition to homosexual sex."

4   Many nations have set themselves up for Muslim complaints by adopting the unofficial slogan of the West's chattering classes: multiculturalism trumps free speech. Sensitivity and equality are viewed as so important that the individual right to speak out is routinely eclipsed. Naturally enough, Muslims want to play the same

victim game as other aggrieved groups. The French Council of Muslims says it is considering taking *France Soir*, which reprinted the Danish cartoons, to court for provocation.

5   In truth, Muslims have been playing the game for some time. Michel Houellebecq, a French novelist, said some derogatory things about the Koran. Muslim groups hauled him into court, but the novelist was eventually exonerated. Actress Brigitte Bardot, an animal rights activist, criticized Muslim ritual slaughter and was fined 10,000 francs for the offense. Italian journalist Oriana Fallaci wrote an angry anti-Muslim book, meant to waken the west to the gravity of the threat posed by Islam. Muslims pressed for her prosecution in France. The case was thrown out of court on a technicality in 2002, but she is scheduled to go on trial again this coming June.

6   In Australia, a state tribunal found two pastors guilty of vilification of Muslims. They had argued that Islam is inherently a violent religion, and that Islam plans to take over Australia. To avoid up to a $7,000 fine or three months in jail, they were ordered to apologize and to promise not to repeat their remarks anywhere in Australia or over the Internet. The pastors refused to comply and are appealing to the Supreme Court. The case has become a major cause, with churches and Christian leaders fighting to overturn the law, and Muslims pushing for a broad hate-speech law.

7   An obvious thing to say about laws that limit speech is that we have no evidence that they work to meet their stated goal—reducing bigotry and increasing tolerance. Banning Holocaust denial, on grounds that it is inherently anti-Semitic, has no track record of improving respect for Jews. If anything, hatred of Jews appears to be on the rise in these nations. Setting up certain groups as beyond criticism is bound to increase resentment among those not similarly favored. (Yes, we know all groups are supposed to be treated alike, but that is not the way these laws work.). In real life, the creation of protected classes sharpens intergroup tensions and leads to competition for victim status.

8   An even more obvious point: We are very lucky to have the First Amendment. Without it, our chattering classes would be falling all over themselves to ban speech that offends sensitive groups, just like many Eurochatterers are doing now. We know this because our campus speech codes, the models for the disastrous hate-speech laws in Europe, Canada and Australia, were the inventions of our own elites. Without a First Amendment, the distortions and suppressions of campus life would likely have gone national. No more speech codes, please. In America, we get to throw rocks at all ideologies, religious and secular, and we get to debate issues, not have them declared off limits by sensitivity-prone agents of the state.

Keep a Journal on What You Read

Unlike writing an essay or a paper, keeping a journal is a personal exploration in which you develop your own ideas without set rules. It is a process of recording impressions and exploring feelings and ideas. It is an opportunity to write without restrictions and without judgment. You don't have to worry about breaking the rules—because in a journal, anything goes.

Reserve a special notebook just for your journal—not one that you use for class notes or homework. Also, date your entries and include the titles of the articles to which you are responding. Eventually, by the end of the semester, you should have a substantial number of pages to review so you can see how your ideas and writing style have developed over time.

What do you include in your journal? Although it may serve as a means to understanding an essay you're assigned, you are not required to write only about the essay itself. Perhaps the piece reminds you of something in your personal experience. Maybe it triggered an opinion you didn't know you had. Or perhaps it prompted you to explore a particular phrase or idea presented by the author.

Some students may find keeping a journal difficult because it is so personal. They may feel as if they're exposing their feelings too much. Or they may feel uncomfortable thinking that someone else—a teacher or another student—may read their writing. But such apprehensions shouldn't prevent you from exploring your impressions and feelings. Just don't share anything highly personal with your teachers or classmates. You may even consider keeping two journals—one for class and one for personal use.

Reprinted below is one student's journal entry on our sample essay, "The Thought Police Keep Marching West," by John Leo, *Townhall*, March 5, 2006:

> John Leo points out that freedom of speech, protected by the First Amendment in
>
> the United States, is being curtailed in many countries. His examples of how speech is
>
> being restricted in countries like France, Denmark, and even Canada are troubling. It
>
> seems as if freedom of speech applies only to very liberal viewpoints. You can speak in
>
> favor of homosexuality, but not against it. You can't say anything negative about
>
> Muslims or Islam despite current events in the Middle East. While Leo seems to lump
>
> all European Muslims together, he does make some interesting points about the state
>
> of free speech in Europe, and how it could threaten U.S. free speech in years to come.

Annotate What You Read

It's a good idea to underline (or highlight) key passages and make marginal notes when reading an essay. (If you don't own the publication in which the essay appears, or choose not to mark it up, it's a good idea to make a photocopy of the piece and annotate that.) I recommend annotating on the second or third reading, once you've gotten a handle on the essay's general ideas.

There are no specific guidelines for annotation. Use whatever technique suits you best, but keep in mind that in annotating a piece of writing, you are engaging in a dialogue with the author. As in any meaningful dialogue, you may hear things you may not have known, things that may be interesting and exciting to you, things that you may agree or disagree with, or things that give you cause to ponder. The other side of the dialogue, of course, is your response. In annotating a piece of writing, that response takes the form of underlining (or highlighting) key passages and jotting down comments in the margin. Such comments can take the form of full sentences or some shorthand codes. Sometimes "Why?" or "True" or "NO!" will be enough to help you respond to a writer's position or claim. If you come across a word or reference that is unfamiliar to you, underline or circle it. Once you've located the main thesis statement or claim, highlight or underline it and jot down "Claim" or "Thesis" in the margin.

Below is the Leo essay reproduced in its entirety with sample annotations.

1   Law professor Eugene Volokh calls it "censorship envy." Muslims in Europe want the same sort of censorship that many nations now offer to other aggrieved groups. By law, eleven European nations can punish anyone who publicly denies the Holocaust. That's why the strange British historian David Irving is going to prison. Ken Livingstone, the madcap mayor of London, was suspended for four weeks for calling a Jewish reporter a Nazi. A Swedish pastor endured a long and harrowing prosecution for a sermon criticizing homosexuality, finally beating the rap in Sweden's Supreme Court.

Is he an authority?

All Muslims? Generalization?

Which ones?

Look up these cases.

2   Much of Europe has painted itself into a corner on the censorship issue. What can Norway say to pro-censorship Muslims when it already has a hate speech law forbidding, among other things, "publicly stirring up one part of the population against another," or any utterance that "threatens, insults, or subjects to hatred, persecution or contempt any person or group of persons because of their creed, race, colour or national or ethnic origin . . . or homosexual bent"? No insulting utterances at all? Since most strong opinions can be construed as insulting (hurting someone's feelings), no insults mean no free speech.

Interesting point.

3   It's not just Europe. In Canada, a teacher drew a suspension for a letter to a newspaper arguing that homosexuality is not a fixed orientation, but a condition that can be treated. He was not accused of discrimination, merely of expressing thoughts that the state defines as improper. Another Canadian newspaper was fined $4,500 for printing an ad giving the citations—but not the text—of four biblical quotations against homosexuality. As David Bernstein writes in his book, *You Can't Say That!* "It has apparently become illegal in Canada to advocate traditional Christian opposition to homosexual sex."

Any other critics presenting the other side of the story?

4   Many nations have set themselves up for Muslim complaints by adopting the unofficial slogan of the West's chattering classes: multiculturalism trumps free speech. Sensitivity and equality are viewed as so important that the individual right to speak out is routinely eclipsed. Naturally enough, Muslims want to play the same victim game as other aggrieved groups. The French Council of Muslims says it is considering taking *France Soir*, which reprinted the Danish cartoons, to court for provocation.

look up definition for this.

Main Point

Author's bias?

Which cartoons? The ones of Muhammad?

5   In truth, Muslims have been playing the game for some time. Michel Houellebecq, a French novelist, said some derogatory things about the Koran. Muslim groups hauled him into court, but the novelist was eventually exonerated. Actress Brigitte Bardot, an animal rights activist, criticized Muslim ritual slaughter and was fined 10,000 francs for the offense. Italian journalist Oriana Fallaci wrote an angry anti-Muslim book, meant to waken the west to the gravity of the threat posed by Islam. Muslims pressed for her prosecution in France. The case was thrown out of court on a technicality in 2002, but she is scheduled to go on trial again this coming June.

Good use of examples in these two paragraphs

6   In Australia, a state tribunal found two pastors guilty of vilification of Muslims. They had argued that Islam is inherently a violent religion, and that Islam plans to take over Australia. To avoid up to a $7,000 fine or three months in jail, they were ordered to apologize and to promise not to repeat their remarks anywhere in Australia or over the Internet. The pastors refused to comply and are appealing to the Supreme Court. The case has become a major cause, with churches and Christian leaders fighting to overturn the law, and Muslims pushing for a broad hate-speech law.

7   An obvious thing to say about laws that limit speech is that we have no evidence that they work to meet their stated goal—reducing bigotry and increasing tolerance. Banning Holocaust denial, on grounds that it is inherently anti-Semitic, has no track record of improving respect for Jews. If anything, hatred of Jews appears to be on the rise in these nations. Setting up certain groups as beyond criticism is bound to increase resentment among those not similarly favored. (Yes, we know all groups are supposed to be treated alike, but that is not the way these laws

proof of this?

Major Idea

work.). In real life, the creation of protected classes sharpens intergroup tensions and leads to competition for victim status.

8   An even more obvious point: We are very lucky to have the First Amendment. Without it, our chattering classes would be falling all over themselves to ban speech that offends sensitive groups, just like many Eurochatterers are doing now. We know this because our campus speech codes, the models for the disastrous hate-speech laws in Europe, Canada and Australia, were the inventions of our own elites. Without a First Amendment, the distortions and suppressions of campus life would likely have gone national. No more speech codes, please. In America, we get to throw rocks at all ideologies, religious and secular, and we get to debate issues, not have them declared off limits by sensitivity-prone agents of the state.

Leading the reader with a bandwagon appeal?

Why introduce this issue now?

Outline What You Read

Briefly outlining an essay is a good way to see how writers structure their ideas. When you physically diagram the thesis statement, claims, and the supporting evidence, you can better assess the quality of the writing and decide how convincing it is. You may already be familiar with detailed, formal essay outlines in which structure is broken down into main ideas and subsections. However, a brief and concise breakdown of an essay's components provides a basic outline. Simply jot down a one-sentence summary of each paragraph. Sometimes brief paragraphs elaborating the same point can be lumped together:

- Point 1
- Point 2
- Point 3
- Point 4
- Point 5
- Point 6, etc.

Even though such outlines may seem rather primitive, they demonstrate at a glance how the various parts of an essay are connected—that is, the organization and sequence of ideas.

Below is a sentence outline of "The Thought Police Keep Marching West":

Point 1: European Muslims seek to censor anyone who speaks out against Muslims or Islam, similar to the type of censorship "benefiting" Jews and homosexuals.

Point 2: Leo cites Norway's hate-speech law, pointing out that it effectively prevents anyone from expressing a strong opinion.

Point 3: Leo explains that the censorship trend has crossed the Atlantic from Europe and has influenced Canadian law as well.

Point 4: Multiculturalist ideals are "eclipsing" the individual right to speak.

Point 5: In the next two paragraphs, Leo gives several more examples of how Muslim groups are encouraging censorship of anyone who speaks negatively of Muslims or Islam.

Point 6: Leo points out that banning speech, even hate-speech, does not improve respect for marginalized groups, and could in fact inflame negative sentiments.

Point 7: Leo praises the First Amendment, and notes that without it, "sensitive groups" would be able to censor negative viewpoints, similar to what is happening on college campuses.

At this point you should have a fairly good grasp of the author's stand on the issue. Now let's analyze the essay in its parts and as a whole.

Summarize What You Read

Summarizing is perhaps the most important technique to develop for understanding and evaluating what you read. This means boiling the essay down to its main points. In your journal or notebook, try to write a brief (about 100 words) synopsis of the reading in your own words. Note the claim or thesis of the discussion (or argument) and the chief supporting points. It is important to write these points down, rather than to highlight them passively with a pen or pencil, because the act of jotting down a summary helps you absorb the argument.

Now let's return to our sample essay. The brief paragraph below is a student summary of Leo's essay. To avoid plagiarism the author's words are paraphrased not copied. At times, it may be impossible to avoid using the author's own words in a summary, but if you do, remember to use quotation marks.

John Leo's article explores the issue of freedom of speech and censorship. In many European countries, marginalized groups have successfully used speech codes to censor opposing viewpoints, such as making it a crime to deny the Holocaust or to say homosexuality is sinful. Now Muslim groups are jumping on the bandwagon, suing newspapers and journalists for expressing negative viewpoints against Islam. Leo concludes that the First Amendment ensures that Americans may express themselves, but that this right is curtailed on college campuses. He calls for the end

of speech codes, in the interest of promoting debate and preserving our freedoms.

Although this paragraph seems to do a fairly good job of summarizing Leo's essay, it is difficult to reduce an essay to a hundred words. So, don't be too discouraged when trying to summarize a reading on your own.

Question What You Read

Although we break down critical reading into discrete steps, these steps will naturally overlap in the actual process. While reading the essay by John Leo you were simultaneously summarizing and evaluating Leo's points in your head, perhaps adding your own ideas or even arguing with him. If something strikes you as particularly interesting or insightful, make a mental note. Likewise, if something rubs you the wrong way, argue back. For beginning writers, a good strategy is to convert that automatic mental response into actual note taking.

In your journal (or, as suggested below, in the margins of the text), question and challenge the writer. Jot down any points in the essay that do not measure up to your expectations or personal views. Note anything you are skeptical about. Write down any questions you have about the claims, views, or evidence. If some point or conclusion seems forced or unfounded, record it and briefly explain why. The more skeptical and questioning you are, the better a reader you are. Likewise, note what features of the essay impressed you—outstanding points, interesting wording, clever or amusing phrases or allusions, particular references, the general structure of the piece. Record what you learn from the reading and what aspects of the issue you would like to explore.

Of course, you may not feel qualified to pass judgment on an author's views, especially if that author is a professional writer or an expert on a particular subject. Sometimes the issue discussed might be too technical, or you may not feel informed enough to make critical evaluations. Sometimes a personal narrative may focus on experiences completely alien to you. Nonetheless, you are an intelligent person with an instinct to determine if the writing impresses you or if an argument is sound, logical, and convincing. What you can do in such instances—and another good habit to get into—is think of other views on the issue. If you've read or heard of experiences different from the author's or arguments with opposing views, jot them down. Even if you haven't, the essay should contain some inference or reference to alternate experiences or opposing views (if it's an argument) from which you could draw a counterposition.

Let's return to Leo's essay, which, technically, is an argument. Although it's theoretically possible to question or comment on every sentence in the piece, let's select a couple of key points that may have struck you as presumptuous, overstated, or inconsistent with your own experience.

Paragraph 1: Leo groups all Muslim sentiment together, as in his comment,

"Muslims want the same sort of censorship that many nations now offer to other

aggrieved groups."

Paragraph 2: Leo raises the point that the Danish hate speech law could prevent anyone from expressing a strong opinion because "since most strong opinions can be construed as insulting (hurting someone's feelings), no insults mean no free speech."

Paragraph 4: Leo uses the phrase "chattering classes," which seems to be biased, and comments that Muslims want to play the "victim game."

Paragraph 5: Again, Leo makes a sweeping statement about Muslims, claiming that they have been "playing the game for some time."

Paragraph 7: Leo makes an interesting point that speech codes do not improve relations between opposing groups. But his proof is scanty.

Paragraph 8: Leo makes a broad jump from European censorship to campus speech codes. It seems a bit odd that the campus speech issue appears at the end of this essay, when no mention of it had been made before.

Analyze What You Read

To analyze something means breaking it down into its components, examining those components closely and evaluating their significance, and determining how they relate as a whole. In part, you already did this by briefly outlining the essay. But there is more, because analyzing what you read involves interpreting and evaluating the points of a discussion or argument as well as its presentation—that is, its language and structure. Ultimately, analyzing an essay after establishing its gist will help you understand what may not be evident at first. A closer examination of the author's words takes you beneath the surface and sharpens your understanding of the issue at hand.

Although there is no set procedure for analyzing a piece of prose, here are some specific questions you should raise when reading an essay, especially one that is trying to sway you to its view.

- What kind of audience is the author addressing?
- What are the author's assumptions?
- What are the author's purposes and intentions?
- How well does the author accomplish those purposes?
- How convincing is the evidence presented? Is it sufficient and specific? Relevant? Reliable? Not dated? Slanted?
- How good are the sources of the evidence used? Were they based on personal experience, scientific data, or outside authorities?
- Did the author address opposing views on the issue?
- Is the author persuasive in his or her perspective?

What Kind of Audience Is Being Addressed?

Before the first word is written, a good writer considers his or her audience—that is, the age group, gender, ethnic and racial makeup, educational background, socioeconomic status. Also considered are the values, prejudices, and assumptio of the readers, as well as their political and religious persuasions. Some writers, in- cluding several in this book, write for a "target" audience—readers who share the same interests, opinions, and prejudices. For example, many of the essays in Chap- ter 4, "Political Wordplay," were written for people familiar with current events and issues. Other writers write for a "general" audience. Although general audiences consist of very different people with diversified backgrounds, expectations, and standards, think of them as the people who read *Time, Newsweek,* and your local newspaper. That is, people whose average age is 35, whose educational level is high school plus two years of college, who make up the vast middle class of America, who politically stand in the middle of the road, and whose racial and ethnic origins span the world. You can assume they are generally informed about what is going on in the country, that they have a good comprehension of language and a sense of hu- mor, and that they are willing to listen to new ideas.

Because John Leo's essay appeared in his column on *Townhall.com,* he is clearly writing for a "general" but still "conservative" audience. A closer look tells us more:

- The language sounds like the essay is for a general audience with at least a high school education.

- The tone suggests that he is appealing to conservatives--someone who will agree that free speech is an important right.

- Leo comments on specific current events--the imprisonment of David Irving, the suspension of London mayor Ken Livingstone, the controversial cartoons depicting the prophet Muhammad--implying that the audience is likely to know about international people and news. He also expects his audience to know about the Holocaust.

- Leo expects us to understand certain religious principles, including why some Christian groups might be against homosexuality; and about Islamic dietary laws.

What Are the Author's Assumptions?

Having a sense of one's audience leads writers to certain assumptions. If a writer is writing to a general audience, as is Leo, then he or she can assume a certain level of awareness about language and current events, certain values about education and morality, and certain nuances of an argument. After going through Leo's essay, one might draw the following conclusions about the author:

- The examples supporting the thesis assume an audience familiar with current international events, and twentieth century world history.

- The reference to actress Bridgett Bardot assumes that readers will know who she is.

- Phrases such as "chattering classes" assume that the audience is conservative, and may believe that multiculturalism's influence on society is out of control.

What Are the Author's Purpose and Intentions?

A writer writes for a purpose beyond wanting to show up in print. Sometimes it is simply expressing how the writer feels about something; sometimes the intention is to convince others to see things in a different light; sometimes the purpose is to persuade readers to change their views or behavior. Of the Leo essay, it might be said that the author had the following intentions:

- To convince people that European and Canadian speech codes are a threat to freedom of expression.
- To raise awareness of how Muslim groups are using European speech codes to silence opposing viewpoints.
- To impress upon readers the threat of speech codes on U.S. freedom of speech.
- To call for the end of campus speech codes.

How Well Does the Author Accomplish Those Purposes?

Determining how well an author accomplishes such purposes may seem subjective, but in reality it comes down to how well the case is presented. Is the thesis clear? Is it well-laid out or argued? Are the examples sharp and convincing? Is the author's conclusion a logical result of what came before? Back to Leo's essay:

- He provides many examples of how journalists, politicians, and others have been censored for expressing unpopular viewpoints.
- He keeps to his point for most of his essay.
- He supports his assertions with many examples.
- He tends to lump Muslims together in a collective agenda.
- He introduces campus speech codes and the First Amendment only at the end of his essay, in his conclusion.

How Convincing Is the Evidence Presented? Is It Sufficient and Specific? Relevant? Reliable? Not Dated? Slanted?

Convincing writing depends on convincing evidence—that is, sufficient and relevant facts along with proper interpretations of facts. Facts are pieces of information that can be verified—such as statistics, examples, personal experience, expert testimony, and historical details. Proper interpretations of such facts must be logical and supported by relevant data. For instance, it is a fact that the SAT verbal scores in America went up in 2000. One interpretation might be that students are spending more time reading and less time watching TV than in the past. But without hard statistics documenting the viewing habits of a sample of students, that interpretation is shaky, the result of a writer jumping to conclusions.

Is the Evidence Sufficient and Specific? Writers use evidence on a routine basis, but sometimes it may not be sufficient. Sometimes the conclusions reached have too little evidence to be justified. Sometimes writers make hasty generalizations based solely on personal experience as evidence. How much evidence is enough? It's hard to say, but the more specific the details, the more convincing the argument. Instead of generalizations, good writers cite figures, dates, and facts; instead of paraphrases, they quote experts verbatim.

Is the Evidence Relevant? Good writers select evidence based on how well it supports the point being argued, not on how interesting, novel, or humorous it is. For instance, if you were arguing that Mark McGwire is the greatest living baseball player, you wouldn't mention that he was born in Pomona, California, and has a brother Dan who played quarterback for the Seattle Seahawks. Those are facts, but they have nothing to do with McGwire's athletic abilities. Irrelevant evidence distracts readers and weakens an argument.

Is the Evidence Reliable? Not Dated? Evidence should not be so vague or dated that it fails to support one's claim. For instance, it wouldn't be accurate to say that Candidate Jones fails to support the American worker because 15 years ago she purchased a foreign car. It's her current actions that are more important. Readers expect writers to be specific enough with data for them to verify. A writer supporting animal rights may cite cases of rabbits blinded in drug research, but such tests have been outlawed in the United States for many years. Another may point to medical research that appears to abuse human subjects, but not name the researchers, the place, or the year of such testing. Because readers may have no way of verifying evidence, suspicious claims will weaken an argument.

Is the Evidence Slanted? Sometimes writers select evidence that supports their case while ignoring evidence that doesn't. Often referred to as "stacking the deck," this practice is unfair and potentially self-defeating for a writer. Although some evidence may have merit, an argument will be dismissed if readers discover that evidence was slanted or suppressed. For example, suppose you heard a classmate claim that he would never take a course with Professor Sanchez because she gives surprise quizzes, assigns 50 pages of reading a night, and doesn't grade on a curve. Even if these reasons are true, that may not be the whole truth. You might discover that Professor Sanchez is a dynamic and talented teacher whose classes are stimulating. Withholding that information may make an argument suspect. A better strategy is to acknowledge counterevidence and to confront it—that is, to strive for a balanced presentation by raising views and evidence that may not be supportive of your own.

How Good Are the Sources of the Evidence Used? Were They Based on Personal Experience, Scientific Data, or Outside Authorities?

Writers enlist four basic kinds of evidence to support their views or arguments: personal experience (theirs and others'), outside authorities, factual references and examples, and statistics. In your own writing, you'll be encouraged to use combinations of these.

Personal testimony should not be underestimated. Think of the books you've read or movies you've seen based on word-of-mouth recommendations. (Maybe even the school you're attending!) Personal testimony provides eyewitness accounts not available to you or readers—and sometimes they are the most persuasive kind of evidence. Suppose you are writing about the rising alcohol abuse on college campuses. In addition to statistics and hard facts, quoting the experience of a first-year student who nearly died one night from alcohol poisoning would add dramatic impact. Although personal observations are useful and valuable, writers must not draw hasty conclusions from them. Because you and a couple of friends are in favor of replacing letter grades with a pass–fail system does not support the claim that the student body at your school is in favor of the conversion.

Outside authorities are people recognized as experts in a given field. The appeal to such authorities is a powerful tool in writing, especially for writers wanting to persuade readers of their views. We hear it all the time: "Scientists have found . . . ," "Scholars inform us that . . . ," "According to his biographer, Abraham Lincoln. . . ." Although experts try to be objective and fair-minded, sometimes their testimony is biased. You wouldn't turn to scientists working for tobacco companies for unbiased opinions on lung cancer.

Factual references and examples do as much to inform as to persuade. If somebody wants to sell you something, they'll pour on the details. Think of the television commercials that show sport utility vehicles climbing rocky mountain roads while a narrator lists all the great standard features—permanent four-wheel drive, alloy wheels, second-generation airbags, power brakes, cruise control, etc.—or, the cereal "infomercials" in which manufacturers explain how their new Yumm-Os now have 15 percent more fiber to help prevent cancer. Although readers may not have the expertise to determine which data are useful, they are often convinced by the sheer weight of the evidence—like courtroom juries judging a case.

Statistics impress people. Saying that 77 percent of your school's student body approves of women in military combat roles is much more persuasive than saying "a lot of people" do. Why? Because statistics have a no-nonsense authority. Batting averages, polling results, economic indicators, medical and FBI statistics, demographic percentages—they're all reported in numbers. If accurate, they are hard to argue with, though they can be used to mislead. If somebody claims that 139 people on campus protested the appearance of a certain controversial speaker, it would be a distortion of the truth not to mention that another 1,500 attended the talk and gave the speaker a standing ovation. Likewise, the manufacturer who claims that its potato chips are 100 percent cholesterol free misleads the public, because no potato chips cooked in vegetable oil contain cholesterol—which is found only in animal fats. That is known as the "bandwagon" use of statistics—in other words, appealing to crowd-pleasing, healthy eating awareness.

Now let's examine briefly Leo's sources of evidence:

- Leo presents many examples of how speech codes have been used to silence opposing viewpoints in countries such as Canada, England, Norway, France, and Australia.
- Leo may skew some of his evidence in that he lumps Muslims together, saying "Muslims in Europe," and "Muslims have been playing the game . . .".
- Leo supports his points with several authoritative references; however, these references do not consider alternative points of view.
- Leo makes references to facts but does not provide the details, such as when he states "by law, eleven nations can punish anyone who publicly denies the Holocaust." He does not say which nations, or provide details.

Did the Author Address Opposing Views on the Issue?

Many of the essays in this book will, in varying degrees, try to persuade you to agree with the author's position or argument. But, of course, any slant on a topic can have multiple points of view. In developing their ideas, good writers will antic-ipate different and opposing views. They will cite contrary opinions, maybe even evidence unsupportive of their own position. Not to do so leaves their own stand open to counterattack, as well as to claims of naiveté and ignorance. This is particularly damaging when arguing some controversial issue. Returning to the Leo essay:

- Leo does not introduce alternative points of view into his editorial. It is, after all, an editorial article and thus, is based on his opinion as he can best support it.

Is the Author's Perspective Persuasive?

Style and content make for persuasive writing. Important points are how well a paper is composed—the organization, the logic, the quality of thought, the presentation of evidence, the use of language, the tone of discussion—and the details and evidence. Turning to Leo's essay, we might make the following observation:

- Leo is very persuasive in convincing his audience that the European speech codes should be taken seriously. He does not, however, effectively persuade his readers that this trend is threatening American freedom of speech.

Logical Fallacies—What They Are and How to Avoid Them

Sometimes writers make errors in logic. In fact, we've already pointed out a few of them above. Such errors are called *logical fallacies,* a term derived from the Latin *fallere,* meaning, "to deceive." Used unintentionally, these fallacies deceive writers into feeling that what they're saying is more persuasive than it really is. Even though an argument may be well developed and contain evidence, a fallacy creates a flaw in logic, thereby weakening the structure and persuasiveness.

Not all logical fallacies are unintentional. Sometimes a fallacy is deliberately employed—for example when the writer's goal has more to do with persuading than arriving at the truth. Every day we are confronted with fallacies in commercials and advertisements. Likewise, every election year the airwaves are full of candidates' bloated claims and pronouncements rife with logical fallacies of all sorts.

Recognizing logical fallacies when they occur in a reading is an important step in critical thinking—assessing the effectiveness of the writer's argument. Following are some of the most common logical fallacies to look for.

LOGICAL FALLACIES

Ad Hominem Argument: Attacks the opponent rather than the opponent's views.

Of course she supports bilingual education. She's a bleeding-heart liberal.

PROBLEM: Name-calling makes us question the writer's real motives or credibility.

Ad Misericordium Argument (or so-called *pity appeal*): Appeals to reader's emotions rather than reason.

It makes no difference if he was guilty of Nazi war crimes. This man is eighty years old and in frail health, so he should not be made to stand trial.

PROBLEM: Pity appeal feels like manipulation and distraction from the real issue.

The Bandwagon Appeal: Plays on our fears of being left out or different.

Everybody knows he's the best candidate for the office.

PROBLEM: We're asked to "get with it" without weighing the evidence.

Begging the Question:

Assumes that something is a fact when it really has yet to be proven.

That judge will probably go easy on that defendant because they are both women.

PROBLEM: Assumes that because the judge is female she will be more compassionate to another female which in itself assumes that women are more compassionate than men.

Circular Reasoning:

Where the conclusion of an argument is hidden in the argument's premise.

Steroids are dangerous because they ruin your health.

PROBLEM: Steroids are dangerous because they're dangerous. Repetition of key terms or ideas is not evidence.

False Analogy:

An analogy is a comparison. False analogies compare two things that seem alike but really are not.

The 2001 attack on the World Trade Center was the Pearl Harbor of the 21st Century.

PROBLEM: Although the two have similarities, they are also very different events. For example, the attack on Pearl Harbor was a military attack on a naval base while the attack on the World Trade Center was committed by terrorists on a civilian target.

False Dilemma:

A claim or solution that presents only two extremes, when a possible or practical middle ground exists.

I stumbled on my way up the aisle. My wedding was a disaster.

PROBLEM: A single incident doesn't necessarily ruin the entire event. The rest of the wedding could have been quite satisfactory and enjoyable.

Hasty Generalization:

A conclusion that is based on too little evidence, or reached when the evidence itself is too broad, not factual, or not substantiated.

Television has caused a significant increase in violence and sexual promiscuity in America's youth.

PROBLEM: This oversimplifies the relationship between television and violence and promiscuity in youth, and discounts other factors that may be connected to the issue.

Non Sequitur: Draws a conclusion that does not follow logically from the premise or previous statement leading to an error in deduction.

Mrs. Marshall is a fabulous tennis player and knows how to dress with style. She comes from money.

PROBLEM: The ability to play tennis or dress well has nothing to do with one's financial background.

Faulty Cause-and-Effect Reasoning: (Also known as *post hoc, ergo propter hoc* reasoning, from the Latin "after this, therefore because of this.") Establishes a questionable cause-and-effect relationship between chronological events. It assumes that because one event happened before another, the first influenced the second.

Every time Bill goes with me to Jacobs Field, the Cleveland Indians lose.

PROBLEM: Although the Indians lose whenever Bill joins you at Jacobs Field, his presence does not cause the team to lose. It's just coincidence.

Slippery Slope: Presumes one event will inevitably lead to a chain of other events that ends in a catastrophe—as one slip on a mountain will cause a climber to tumble down and bring with him or her all those in tow.

Censorship of obscene material will spell the end of freedom of speech and freedom of the press.

PROBLEM: This domino-effect reasoning is fallacious because it depends more on presumption than on hard evidence.

Stacking the Deck: Offers only the evidence that supports the premise while disregarding or withholding contrary evidence.

Our Wonder Wieners all-beef hot dogs now contain 10 percent less fat."

PROBLEM: Sounds like good news, but what the ad doesn't tell us is that Wonder Wieners still contain 30 percent fat.

Red Herring: A fact that is thrown into an argument in order to distract the reader from the real issue.

Jennifer isn't the sort of girl who shoplifts; she is on the girl's lacrosse team, the honor society, and she volunteers at the retirement home twice a month.

PROBLEM: Simply because Jennifer is athletic, a good student, and a volunteer doesn't mean she isn't capable of shoplifting.

Exploring the Language of Visuals

We have all heard the old saying, "a picture is worth a thousand words." In addition to many insightful and interesting articles on language, this edition of *Exploring Language* features selected visuals to help illustrate the nonverbal ways we use and process language. We constantly react to nonverbal cues in our daily lives. Symbols, images, gestures, and graphics all communicate information instantly that we process as language.

To better understand how such "visual language" works, we have interspersed throughout this text various cartoons, posters, and photographs that highlight the different ways we communicate without using words. For example, a cartoon communicates a certain set of expectations before a reader even begins to examine it closely. We know instantly that it is a cartoon, and that, as such, it is supposed to convey some form of humor. In well-known cartoons, we may even recall the personalities of the characters depicted and expect certain reactions or attitudes from them. In advertisements, cultural cues of imagery, symbolism, the use of light and dark, and the product's purpose are all used by advertisers to tap into our presumed set of expectations. Sometimes it is the symbolic representation of an action—such as the image of an Afghan woman's eyes and mouth scratched out in Chapter 2—that instantly conveys meaning. The photo of Sanger's gag, also in that chapter, immediately tells us that she is being silenced against her will, and our common sense of the sanctity of freedom of speech reacts to her predicament.

As you review the various visual presentations throughout the text, consider the ways symbolism, brand recognition, stereotyping, and cultural expectations contribute to how such illustrations communicate their ideas. Try to think abstractly, taking into account the many different levels of consciousness that visuals use to communicate. Consider also the way shading, lighting, and subject placement in the photos all converge to make a point. "Read" them as you would any text, as part of the overall purpose of this book to "explore language."

In the chapters that follow, you will discover more than one hundred different selections—both written and visual—that range widely across contemporary language matters that we hope you will find exciting and thought-provoking. Arranged thematically into eight chapters, the writings represent widely diverse language topics—from the evolution of English to tribal dialects and cybernetic slang; from the dangers of political gobbledygook to the pleasures of language that make us laugh; from the way TV influences our general discourse to gender differences in language; from arguments against the use of Indian names and mascots by sports teams to arguments for and against campus speech codes. Some of the topics will be familiar; others will be first-time exposure. Regardless of how these language issues touch your experience, critical thinking, critical reading, and critical writing will open you up to a deeper understanding of our language, our culture, and yourself as a vital member of that language community.

SOME USEFUL URLS ON WRITING AND LANGUAGE

Search Engines

- Google: http://google.com
- Alta Vista: http://altavista.com
- Lycos: http://lycos.cs.cmu.edu/
- Yahoo: www.yahoo.com/
- Dogpile: www.dogpile.com

Online Writing Resources

- *The Modern Language Association (MLA) Guide to Style*
  www.wilpaterson.edu/wpcpages/library/mla.htm
- *The American Psychological Association (APA) Guide to Style*
  www.wilpaterson.edu/wpcpages/library/apa.htm
- *Roget's Thesaurus*
  www.thesaurus.com
- *Merriam-Webster Dictionary*
  www.m-w.com
- *Merriam Webster Slang Dictionary*
  www.m-w.com/lighter/flap.htm
- *Quotations*
  www.starlingtech.com/quotes/
- *Bartletts Familiar Quotations*
  www.bartlettquotations.com
- *The Internet Public Library's Online Literary Criticism Collection* contains more than one thousand critical and biographical Web sites about authors and works that can be referenced by author, title, or literary period.
  www.ipl.org/ref/litcrit/
- *Project Gutenberg* provides a huge library of electronically sorted books that can be downloaded for free and viewed offline.
  www.promo.net/pg/
- *The University of California, Santa Barbara,* maintains a Web site on general English literature resources, as well as categories for time period and genre.
  www.ucsb.edu/shuttle/english.html
- *The Academy of American Poet's Web* site features an online poet database and critical essays on writing about poetry.
  www.poets.org

• *The Write Way* contains one of the best lists of Web site links for students of writing on the Internet. Included here are links to dictionaries, style guides, professional writers associations, leading newspapers, encyclope- dias, movie reviews, and so forth. www.mailbag.com/users/lrjohnson/Writing.html

Language and History

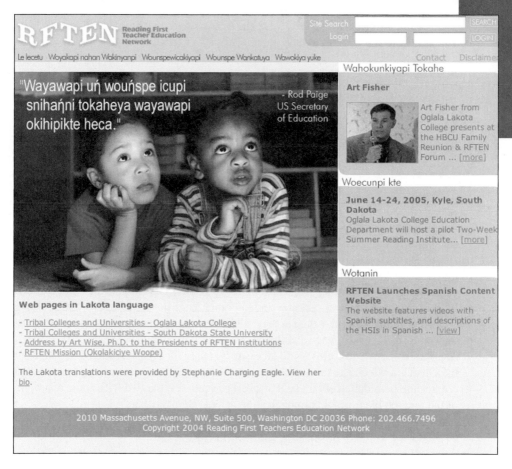

1

Web pages in Lakota language

- Tribal Colleges and Universities - Oglala Lakota College
- Tribal Colleges and Universities - South Dakota State University
- Address by Art Wise, Ph.D. to the Presidents of RFTEN institutions
- RFTEN Mission (Okolakiciye Woope)

The Lakota translations were provided by Stephanie Charging Eagle. View her bio.

■ While many ancient languages fade and die out, some are successfully brought back from the brink of extinction. Here, a Web site provides resources and links for students learning the endangered Lakota language.

Language is the basis of thought and the highest intellectual activity we practice. It is also the way we define ourselves—who we are as a species, as individuals, as a society, and as a culture. How we use language—our word choice, style of expression, tone—can convey much about our background, education, personality, even values. Likewise, the success of communication between individuals tells much about the health of a society and its culture. In many ways, we are our language. The readings in this section examine the origins and history of language ands its importance to human culture and identity.

Beginnings: The Development of Language

We begin this chapter with a look at some fundamental aspects of language—from a biblical exploration of how the world's many languages came to be, to how our brains are hardwired to construct grammar instinctively. The opening discussion of the famed ancient Tower of Babel gives the Bible's explanation for the diversity of language, and through three famous Renaissance paintings, we see how artists interpreted this legendary story of the origins of the world's languages. Michael C. Corballis then presents his theory on the evolution of language from gesture to spoken words in "From Hand to Mouth." Linguist Susanne K. Langer discusses the uniquely human phenomenon of language symbolism. In "Language and Thought" she explores the relationship between word and thought and the difference between symbols and signs—differences that separate humans from the rest of the animal kingdom. In "A Brief History of English," Paul Roberts discusses the evolution of our native language beginning with the tongue of obscure Germanic tribes that invaded England in the sixth century to the contemporary English spoken by over 700 million people around the world. Linguist Steven Pinker explores the connection between the way children learn language and the origins of language in "Horton Heared a Who!" The section comes to a close with an essay by Margalit Fox, "Another Language for the Deaf," in which she takes a close look at a new type of pictographic writing that crosses the boundaries of language itself. The section is capped with some examples of the remarkable form of communication called "SignWriting."

Preserving Voices: Defending Ancient Languages

There are an estimated six thousand (some estimates go as high as seven thousand) languages spoken throughout the world. Linguists estimate that over the next few decades at least half of these languages will be lost. For many of us who speak one of the world's primary languages, such as English, Spanish, or Mandarin Chinese, this loss may seem relatively insignificant. But for the millions who speak endangered languages, it means the loss of their culture and historical identity. In a broader sense, linguists argue that when a language dies, we lose the unique local and cultural knowledge of the region in which it was spoken, as well as a window into the human mind. The second part of this chapter takes a look at ancient and endangered languages—including what happens when languages die, how some Native American tribes are trying to save their indigenous tongues, and how these languages connect the past with the present.

BEGINNINGS: THE DEVELOPMENT OF LANGUAGE

Exploring the Language of **VISUALS**

The Tower of Babel: Artistic Interpretations

The tale of the Tower of Babel provides an explanation of why there are so many different languages in the world. The historical Tower of Babel was probably a stepped pyramid known as a ziggurat with a temple to the Babylonian god Marduk at the top. Chapter 11 in the book of Genesis describes the building of the Tower of Babel to reach the heavens. At the time of its construction, the tale tells us, humans spoke only one language. Angered by man's arrogance, God confused their speech so that the builders each spoke a different language. As a result of this "confusion of tongues" (languages) work ceased, and the people were scattered about the face of the earth. The tower, various nonbiblical sources tell us, was destroyed by a great wind.

■ The Tower of Babel, 1587, by unknown artist, Kurpfalzisches Museum, Heidelberg

■ The Little Tower, mid–16th century, by Pieter Brueghel the Elder, Museum Bojimans van Beuningen, Rotterdam

There are many other ancient stories about the origins of diverse languages that are similar to the biblical tale. It does not mention the tower by name, but the Qur'an has a story with similarities to the biblical story of the Tower of Babel, although it is set during the time Moses was in Egypt. There is also a similar story in Sumerian mythology called "Enmerkar and the Lord of Aratta," in which two rival gods, Enki and Enlil, as a result of their fighting, confuse the language of humans.

Historical linguistics has long wrestled with the idea of a single original language. Current scholarship points to a branching of languages from a single Indo-European tongue. The main issue of dispute is *when* this branching occurred, and *why*, which in any case, would have happened several thousand years before the biblical date of the fall of the Tower of Babel.

The following reading is from the book of Genesis, Chapter 11 verses 1-9, from the King James Version of the Bible.

Now the whole earth had one language and few words. And as men migrated from the east, they found a plain in the land of Shinar and settled there. And they said to one another, 'Come, let us make bricks, and burn them thoroughly.' And they had brick for stone, and bitumen for mortar. Then they said, 'Come, let us build ourselves a city, and a tower with its top in the heavens, and let us make a name for ourselves, lest we be scattered abroad upon the face of the whole earth.' And the Lord came down to see the city and the tower, which the sons of men had built. And the Lord said, 'Behold, they are one people, and they have all one language; and this is only the beginning of what they will do; and nothing that they propose to do

■ Construction of the Tower of Babel, 16th century, by Hendrick III van Cleve, Kroller-Muller Museum, Otterio

will now be impossible for them. Come, let us go down, and there confuse their language, that they may not understand one another's speech.' So the Lord scattered them abroad from there over the face of all the earth, and they left off building the city.' Therefore its name was called Babel, because there the Lord confused the language of all the earth; and from there the Lord scattered them abroad over the face of all the earth. (Genesis 11:1-9)

THINKING CRITICALLY

1. These three pictures were all painted during the 1500s by different Flemish artists. What similarities and differences do you see among the paintings?

2. What message, if any, do you think each artist was trying to convey with his interpretation of the Tower of Babel tale? Explain.

3. Do you think language began with a single tongue spoken by everyone, or did it evolve in different locations spoken by different groups of people? Explain your viewpoint.

From Hand to Mouth

Michael C. Corballis

> You have probably heard the phrase "actions speak louder than words." In this essay, linguist Michael C. Corballis explores the connection between gestures and spoken language. Human language, he conjectures, evolved from gestures—a form of sign language that predated spoken speech. Drawing on evidence from anthropology, animal behavior, neurology, anatomy, linguistics, and evolutionary psychology, Corballis describes a few of the reasons why he believes language probably developed from gestures to a signed language, punctuated with grunts and other vocalizations, which eventually developed into the spoken word. While his hypothesis is still the subject of debate, anyone who also "speaks with their hands" is likely to understand his logic.
>
> Michael Corballis is a professor of psychology and a member of the Research Center for Cognitive Science at the University of Auckland, in Australia. He is the author of several books, including *The Lopsided Ape: The Evolution of the Generative Mind* (1993) and *From Hand to Mouth* (revised in 2003) from which this essay is excerpted. His work has appeared in *Science*, *Nature*, *Scientific American*, and *American Scientist.*

1 Imagine trying to teach a child to talk without using your hands or any other means of pointing or gesturing. The task would surely be impossible. There can be little doubt that bodily gestures are involved in the development of language, both in the individual and in the species. Yet, once the system is up and running, it can function entirely on vocalizations, as when two friends chat over the phone and create in each other's minds a world of events far removed from the actual sounds that emerge from their lips. My contention is that the vocal element emerged relatively late in hominid evolution. If the modern chimpanzee is to be our guide, the common ancestor of 5 or 6 million years ago would have been utterly incapable of a telephone conversation but would have been able to make voluntary movements of the hands and face that could at least serve as a platform upon which to build a language.

2 Evidence suggests that the vocal machinery necessary for autonomous speech developed quite recently in hominid evolution. Grammatical *language* may well have begun to emerge around 2 million years ago but would at first have been primarily gestural, though no doubt punctuated with grunts and other vocal cries that were at first largely involuntary and emotional. The complex adjustments necessary to produce speech as we know it today would have taken some time to evolve, and may not have been complete until some 170,000 years ago, or even later, when *Homo sapiens* emerged to grace, but more often disgrace, the planet. These adjustments may have been incomplete even in our close relatives the Neanderthals; arguably, it was this failure that contributed to their demise.

3 The question now is what were the selective pressures that led to the eventual dominance of speech? On the face of it, an acoustic medium seems a poor way to convey information about the world; not for nothing is it said that a picture is worth a thousand words. Moreover, signed language has all the lexical and grammatical complexity of spoken language. Primate evolution is itself a grammatical complexity of spoken language. Primate evolution is itself a testimony to the primacy of the

visual world. We share with monkeys a highly sophisticated visual system, giving us three-dimensional information in color about the world around us, and an intricate system for exploring that world through movement and manipulation. Further, in a hunter-gatherer environment, where predators and prey are of major concern, there are surely advantages in silent communication since sound acts as a general alert. And yet we came to communicate about the world in a medium that in all primates except ourselves is primitive and stereotyped—and noisy.

4   Before we consider the pressures that may have favored vocalization over gestures, it bears repeating that the switch from hand to mouth was almost certainly not an abrupt one. In fact, manual gestures still feature prominently in language; even as fluent speakers gesture almost as much as they vocalize, and of course deaf communities spontaneously develop signed languages. It has also been proposed that speech itself is in many respects better conceived as composed of gestures rather than sequences of those elusive phantoms called phonemes. In this view, language evolved as a system of gestures based on movements of the hands, arms and face, including movements of the mouth, lips, and tongue. It would not have been a big step to add voicing to the gestural repertoire, at first as mere grunts, but later articulated so that invisible gestures of the oral cavity could be rendered accessible, but to the ear rather than the eye. There may therefore have been a continuity from a language that was almost exclusively manual and facial, though perhaps punctuated by involuntary grunts, to one in which the vocal component has a much more extensive repertoire and is under voluntary control. The essential feature of modern expressive language is not that it is purely vocal, but rather that the vocal component can function autonomously and provide the grammar as well as the meaning of linguistic communication.

5   What, then, are the advantages of a language that can operate autonomously through voice and ear, rather than hand and eye? Why speech?

Advantages of Arbitrary Symbols

6 One possible advantage of vocal language is its arbitrariness. Except in rare cases of onomatopoeia, spoken words cannot be iconic, and they therefore offer scope for creating symbols that distinguish between objects or actions that look alike or might otherwise be confusable. The names of similar animals, such as cats, lions, tigers, cheetahs, lynxes, and leopards, are all rather different. We may be confused as to which animal is which, but at least it is clear which one we are talking about. The shortening of words over time also makes communication more efficient, and some of us have been around long enough to see this happen: *television* has become *TV* or *telly*, *microphone* has been reduced to *mike* (or *mic*), and so on. The fact that more frequent words tend to be shorter than less frequent ones was noted by the American philologist George Kingsley Zipf, who related it to a principle of "least effort." So long as signs are based on iconic resemblance, the signer has little scope for these kinds of calibration.

7   It may well have been very important for hunter-gatherers to identify and name a great many similar fruits, plants, trees, animals, birds, and so on, and attempts at iconic representation would eventually only confuse. Jared Diamond observes that people living largely traditional lifestyles in New Guinea can name hundreds of

birds, animals, and plants, along with details about each of them. These people are illiterate, relying on word of mouth to pass on information, not only about potential foods, but also about how to survive dangers, such as crop failures, droughts, cyclones, and raids from other tribes. Diamond suggests that the main repository of accumulated information is the elderly. He points out that humans are unique among primates in that they can expect to live to a ripe old age, well beyond the age of child bearing (although perhaps it was not always so). A slowing down of senescence may well have been selected in evolution because the knowledge retained by the elderly enhanced the survival of their younger relatives. An elderly, knowledgeable granny may help us all live a little longer, and she can also look after the kids.

8   In the naming and transmission of such detailed information, iconic representation would almost certainly be inefficient; edible plants or berries could be confused with poisonous ones, and animals that attack confused with those that are benign. This is not to say that gestural signs could not do the trick. Manual signs readily become conventionalized and convey abstract information. Nevertheless, there may be some advantage to using spoken words, since they have virtually no iconic content to begin with, and so provide a ready-made system for abstraction.

9   I would be on dangerous ground, however, if I were to insist too strongly that speech is linguistically superior to signed language. After all, students at Gallaudet University seem pretty unrestricted in what they can learn; signed language apparently functions well right through to university level—and still requires students to learn lots of vocabulary from their suitably elderly professors. It is nevertheless true that many signs remain iconic, or at least partially so, and are therefore somewhat tethered with respect to modifications that might enhance clarity or efficiency of expression. But there may well be a trade-off here. Signed languages may be easier to learn than spoken ones, especially in the initial stages of acquisition, in which the child comes to understand the linking of objects and actions with their linguistic representations. But spoken languages, once acquired, may relay messages more accurately, since spoken words are better calibrated to minimize confusion. Even so, the iconic component is often important, and as I look over the quadrangle outside my office I see how freely the students there are embellishing their conversations with manual gestures.

In the Dark

10 Another advantage of speech over gesture is obvious: we can use it in the dark! This enables us to communicate at night, which not only extends the time available for meaningful communications but may also have proven decisive in the competition for space and resources. We of the gentle species *Homo sapiens* have a legacy of invasion, having migrated out of Africa into territories inhabited by other hominins who migrated earlier. Perhaps it was the newfound ability to communicate vocally, without the need for a visual component, that enabled our forebearers to plan, and even carry out, invasions at night, and so vanquish the earlier migrants.

11   It is not only a question of being able to communicate at night. We can also speak to people when objects intervene and you can't see them, as when you yell to your friend in another room. All this has to do, of course, with the nature of sound

itself, which travels equally well in the dark as in the light and wiggles its way around obstacles. The wall between you and the base drummer next door may attenuate the sound but does not completely block it. Vision, on the other hand, depends on light reflected from an external source, such as the sun, and is therefore ineffective when no such source is available. And the light reflected from the surface of an object to your eye travels in rigidly straight lines, which means that it can provide detailed information about shape but is susceptible to occlusion and interference. In terms of the sheer ability to reach those with whom you are trying to communicate, words speak louder than actions.

Listen to Me!

12 Speech does have one disadvantage, though: it is generally accessible to those around you and is therefore less convenient for sending confidential or secret messages or for planning an attack on enemies within earshot. To some extent, we can overcome this impediment by whispering. And sometimes, people resort to signing. But the general alerting function of sound also has its advantages. When Mark Antony cried, "Friends, Romans, countrymen, lend me your ears," he was trying to attract attention as well as deliver a message.

13   In the evolution of speech, the alerting component of language might have consisted at first simply of grunts that accompany gestures to give emphasis to specific actions or encourage reluctant offspring to attend while a parent lays down the law. It is also possible that nonvocal sounds accompanied gestural communication. Russell Gray has suggested to me that clicking one's fingers, as children often do when putting their hands up in class to answer a question, may be a sort of "missing link" between gestural and vocal language. I know of no evidence that chimpanzees or other nonhuman primates are able to click their fingers as humans can, although lip smacking, as observed in chimpanzees, may have played a similar role. Sounds may therefore have played a similar and largely alerting role in the early evolution of language, gradually assuming more prominence in conveying the message itself.

14   For humans, visual signals can only attract attention if they occur within a fairly restricted region of space, whereas the alerting power of sound is more or less independent of where its source is located relative to the listener. And sound is a better alerting medium in other respects as well. No amount of gesticulation will wake a sleeping person, whereas a loud yell will usually do the trick. The alerting power of sound no doubt explains why animals have evolved vocal signals for sending messages of alarm. Notwithstanding the peacock's tail or the parrot's gaudy plumage, even birds prefer to make noises to attract attention, whether in proclaiming territory or warning of danger. Visual signals are relatively inefficient because they may elude our gaze, and in any case we can shut them out by closing our eyes, as we do automatically when we sleep. Our ears, in contrast, remain open and vulnerable to auditory assault.

15   Speech has another, and subtler, attentional advantage. Manual gesture is much more demanding of attention, since you must keep your eyes fixed on the gesturer in order to extract her meaning, whereas speech can be understood regardless of where you are looking. There are a number of advantages in being able to

communicate with people without having to look at them. You can effectively divide attention, using speech to communicate with a companion while visual attention is deployed elsewhere, perhaps to watch a football game or to engage in some joint activity, like building a boat. Indeed, the separation of visual and auditory attention may have been critical in the development of pedagogy.

Three Hands Better Than Two?

16   Another reason why vocal language may have arisen is that it provides an extra medium. We have already seen that most people gesture with their hands, and indeed their faces, while they talk. One might argue then, that the addition of a vocal channel provides additional texture and richness to the message.

17   But it is perhaps not simply a matter of being better. Susan Goldin-Meadow and David McNeill suggest that speech may have evolved because it allowed the vocal and manual components to serve different and complementary purposes. Speech is perfectly adequate to convey syntax, which has no iconic or mimetic aspect, and can relieve the hands and arms of this chore. The hands and arms are, of course, well adapted to providing the mimetic aspect of language, indicating in analogue fashion the shapes and sizes of things, or the direction of movement, as in the gesture that might accompany the statement "he went that-a-way." By allowing the voice to take over the grammatical component, the hands are given free rein, as it were, to provide the mimetic component.

18   But speech may have evolved, not because it gave the hands freer rein for mimetic expression, but rather because it freed the hands for other activities. Charles Darwin, who seems to have thought of almost everything, wrote, "We might have used our fingers as efficient instruments, for a person with practice can report to a deaf man every word of a speech rapidly delivered at a public meeting; but the loss of our hands, while thus employed, would have been a serious inconvenience." It would clearly be difficult to communicate manually while holding an infant, or driving a car, or carrying the shopping, yet we can and do talk while doing these things.

19   Speech also has the advantage over manual gesture in that it can be accomplished in parallel with manual demonstrations. Demonstrations might themselves be considered gestures, of course, but the more explanatory aspects of pedagogy, involving grammatical structure and symbolic content, would interfere with manual demonstration if they too were conveyed manually. Clearly, it is much easier and more informative to talk while demonstrating than to try to mix linguistic signs in with the demonstrations. This is illustrated by any good TV cooking show, where the chef is seldom at a loss for either words or ingredients. It may not be far-fetched to suppose that the selective advantages of vocal communication emerged when the homimins began to develop a more advanced tool technology, and they could eventually verbally explain what they were doing while they demonstrated tool-making techniques. Moreover, if vocal language did not become autonomous until the emergence of *Homo sapiens*, this might explain why tool manufacture did not really begin to develop true diversity and sophistication, and indeed to rival language itself in these respects, until within the last 100,000 years.

20   Thus, it was not the emergence of language itself that gave rise to the evolutionary explosion that has made our lives so different from our near relatives, the great apes. Rather, it was the invention of autonomous speech, freeing the hands for more sophisticated manufacture and allowing language to disengage from other manual activities, so that people could communicate while changing the baby's diaper, and even explain to a novice what they were doing. The idea that language may have evolved relatively slowly, seems much more in accord with biological reality than the notion of a linguistic "big bang" within the past 200,000 years. Language and manufacture also allowed cultural transmission to become the dominant mode of inheritance in human life. That ungainly bird, the jumbo jet, could not have been created without hundreds, perhaps thousands, of years of cultural evolution, and the brains that created it were not biologically superior to the brains that existed 100,000 years ago in Africa. The invention of speech may have merely been the first of many developments that have put us not only on the map, but all over it.

THINKING CRITICALLY

1. Corballis begins his essay by asking his readers to "imagine trying to teach a child to talk without using your hands, or any other means of pointing or gesturing." Why do you think he opens his piece with this scenario? How does it set up the argument that follows? Explain.

2. In paragraph 4, Corballis notes "manual gestures still feature prominently in language." What communication role do gestures play in language? Are gestures essential to communication? Are they the natural precursor to language? Why or why not?

3. Corballis's argument is that gesture preceded spoken language. Do you agree with his premise? Why or why not?

4. What advantages, according to Corballis, does spoken language have over gestured communication? List the examples he provides and evaluate the logic of each one.

5. What assumptions does Corballis make about his readers/audience in this essay in order for his argument to be effective? What objections, if any, could his readers raise against his theory of "from hand to mouth"?

WRITING ASSIGNMENTS

1. Corballis notes that spoken language allows us to come up with many different words for similar things, especially things occurring in nature. Write a short essay applying this aspect of language in a more modern sense. What advantages does spoken language provide over gesture that is essential to our survival in the 21st century?

2. Corballis notes that he would be "on dangerous ground" if he were to insist that spoken language is linguistically superior to signed language (paragraph 9). What do you think? The signing skills of teachers at Gallaudet University (an undergraduate institution of higher learning for the deaf and hard-of-hearing) notwithstanding could higher learning, or education in general, be possible without any spoken language as part of our human evolution? Why or why not? Write a short essay explaining your viewpoint, using examples from this essay and from outside research.

3. In paragraph 9, Corballis observes students outside his office "embellishing their conversations with manual gestures." Repeat this exercise on your own. Watch two or more friends engage in a conversation and note how often and in what ways they use their hands to enhance the discussion. Are they merely waving their hands, or unconsciously making more deliberate gestures? Would the conversation lose something—clarity, vibrancy, etc.—if the speakers did not gesture? Write an essay based on your observations on the connection between hand and mouth in communication.

Language and Thought
Susanne K. Langer

Language is the highest intellectual activity we practice. It is the way we define ourselves—who we are as a species, as a society, as a culture, and as individuals. It is the basis of thought because it contains the symbols of thought. How are thought and language connected? How do signs, which even some animals respond to, differ from the symbols that constitute language? The following essay by Susanne Langer answers these and many other questions about language and thought.

Susanne Langer was one of the twentieth century's most influential philosophers. A graduate of Radcliffe and Harvard, she is the author of *Philosophy in a New Key: A Study in the Symbolism of Reason, Rite and Art* (1942) and *Language and Myth* (1946). She died in 1985, a few years after completing the culmination of her life's work, the three-volume *Mind: An Essay on Human Feeling* (1982).

1 A symbol is not the same thing as a sign; that is a fact that psychologists and philosophers often overlook. All intelligent animals use signs; so do we. To them as well as to us sounds and smells and motions are signs of food, danger, the presence of other beings, or of rain or storm. Furthermore, some animals not only attend to signs but produce them for the benefit of others. Dogs bark at the door to be let in; rabbits thump to call each other; the cooing of doves and the growl of a wolf defending his kill are unequivocal signs of feelings and intentions to be reckoned with by other creatures.

2   We use signs just as animals do, though with considerably more elaboration. We stop at red lights and go on green; we answer calls and bells, watch the sky for coming storms, read trouble or promise or anger in each other's eyes. That is animal intelligence raised to the human level. Those of us who are dog lovers can probably all tell wonderful stories of how high our dogs have sometimes risen in the scale of clever sign interpretation and sign using.

3   A sign is anything that announces the existence or the imminence of some event, the presence of a thing or a person, or a change in the state of affairs. There are signs of the weather, signs of danger, signs of future good or evil, signs of what the past has been. In every case a sign is closely bound up with something to be noted or expected in experience. It is always a part of the situation to which it refers, though the reference may be remote in space and time. Insofar as we are led

to note or expect the signified event we are making correct use of a sign. This is the essence of rational behavior, which animals show in varying degrees. It is entirely realistic, being closely bound up with the actual objective course of history— learned by experience, and cashed in or voided by further experience.

4   If man had kept to the straight and narrow path of sign using, he would be like the other animals, though perhaps a little brighter. He would not talk, but grunt and gesticulate the point. He would make his wishes known, give warnings, perhaps develop a social system like that of bees and ants, with such a wonderful efficiency of communal enterprise that all men would have plenty to eat, warm apartments—all exactly alike and perfectly convenient—to live in, and everybody could and would sit in the sun or by the fire, as the climate demanded, not talking but just basking, with every want satisfied, most of his life. The young would romp and make love, the old would sleep, the middle-aged would do the routine work almost unconsciously and eat a great deal. But that would be the life of a social, superintelligent, purely sign-using animal.

5   To us who are human, it does not sound very glorious. We want to go places and do things, own all sorts of gadgets that we do not absolutely need, and when we sit down to take it easy we want to talk. Rights and property, social position, special talents and virtues, and above all our ideas, are what we live for. We have gone off on a tangent that takes us far away from the mere biological cycle that animal generations accomplish; and that is because we can use not only signs but also symbols.

6   A symbol differs from a sign in that it does not announce the presence of the object, the being, condition, or whatnot, which is its meaning, but merely *brings this thing to mind.* It is not a mere "substitute sign" to which we react as though it were the object itself. The fact is that our reaction to hearing a person's name is quite different from our reaction to the person himself. There are certain rare cases where a symbol stands directly for its meaning: in religious experience, for instance, the Host is not only a symbol but a Presence. But symbols in the ordinary sense are not mystic. They are the same sort of thing that ordinary signs are; only they do not call our attention to something necessarily present or to be physically dealt with—they call up merely a conception of the thing they "mean."

7   The difference between a sign and a symbol is, in brief, that a sign causes us to think or act *in the face* of the thing signified, whereas a symbol causes us to think *about* the thing symbolized. Therein lies the great importance of symbolism for human life, its power to make this life so different from any other animal biography that generations of men have found it incredible to suppose that they were of purely zoological origin. A sign is always embedded in reality, in a present that emerges from the actual past and stretches to the future; but a symbol may be divorced from reality altogether. It may refer to what is not the case, to a mere idea, a figment, a dream. It serves, therefore, to liberate thought from the immediate stimuli of a physically present world; and that liberation marks the essential difference between human and nonhuman mentality. Animals think, but they think *of* and *at* things; men think primarily *about* things. Words, pictures, and memory images are symbols that may be combined and varied in a thousand ways. The result is a symbolic structure whose meaning is a complex of all their respective meanings, and this

kaleidoscope of *ideas* is the typical product of the human brain that we call the "stream of thought."

8   The process of transforming all direct experience into imagery or into that supreme mode of symbolic expression, language, has so completely taken possession of the human mind that it is not only a special talent but a dominant, organic need. All our sense impressions leave their traces in our memory not only as signs disposing our practical reactions in the future but also as symbols, images representing our *ideas* of things; and the tendency to manipulate ideas, to combine and abstract, mix and extend them by playing with symbols, is man's outstanding characteristic. It seems to be what his brain most naturally and spontaneously does. Therefore his primitive mental function is not judging reality, but *dreaming his desires.*

9   Dreaming is apparently a basic function of human brains, for it is free and unexhausting like our metabolism, heartbeat, and breath. It is easier to dream than not to dream, as it is easier to breathe than to refrain from breathing. The symbolic character of dreams is fairly well established.

10   Symbol mongering, on this ineffectual, uncritical level, seems to be instinctive, the fulfillment of an elementary need rather than the purposeful exercise of a high and difficult talent.

11   The special power of man's mind rests on the evolution of this special activity, not on any transcendently high development of animal intelligence. We are not immeasurably higher than other animals; we are different. We have a biological need and with it a biological gift that they do not share.

12   Because man has not only the ability but also the constant need of *conceiving* what has happened to him, what surrounds him, what is demanded of him—in short, of symbolizing nature, himself, and his hopes and fears—he has a constant and crying need of *expression.* What he cannot express, he cannot conceive; what he cannot conceive is chaos, and fills him with terror.

13   If we bear in mind this all-important craving for expression, we get a new picture of man's behavior; for from this trait spring his powers and his weaknesses. The process of symbolic transformation that all our experiences undergo is nothing more nor less than the process of *conception,* underlying the human faculties of abstraction and imagination.

14   When we are faced with a strange or difficult situation, we cannot react directly, as other creatures do, with flight, aggression, or any such simple instinctive pattern. Our whole reaction depends on how we manage to conceive the situation—whether we cast it in a definite dramatic form, whether we see it as a disaster, a challenge, a fulfillment of doom, or a fiat of the Divine Will. In words or dreamlike images, in artistic or religious or even in cynical form, we must *construe* the events of life. There is great virtue in the figure of speech, "I can *make* nothing of it," to express a failure to understand something. Thought and memory are processes of *making* the thought content and the memory image; the pattern of our ideas is given by the symbols through which we express them. And in the course of manipulating those symbols we inevitably distort the original experience, as we abstract certain features of it, embroider and reinforce those features with other ideas, until the conception we project on the screen of memory is quite different from anything in our real history.

15   Conception is a necessary and elementary process; what we do with our conceptions is another story. That is the entire history of human culture—of intelligence and morality, folly and superstition, ritual, language, and the arts—all the phenomena that set man apart from, and above, the rest of the animal kingdom. As the religious mind has to make all human history a drama of sin and salvation in order to define its own moral attitudes, so a scientist wrestles with the mere presentation of "the facts" before he can reason about them. The process of *envisaging* facts, values, hopes, and fears underlies our whole behavior pattern; and this process is reflected in the evolution of an extraordinary phenomenon found always, and only, in human societies—the phenomenon of language.

16   Language is the highest and most amazing achievement of the symbolistic human mind. The power it bestows is almost inestimable, for without it anything properly called "thought" is impossible. The birth of language is the dawn of humanity. The line between man and beast—between the highest ape and the lowest savage—is the language line. Whether the primitive Neanderthal man was anthropoid or human depends less on his cranial capacity, his upright posture, or even his use of tools and fire, than on one issue we shall probably never be able to settle—whether or not he spoke.

17   In all physical traits and practical responses, such as skills and visual judgments, we can find a certain continuity between animal and human mentality. Sign using is an ever evolving, ever improving function throughout the whole animal kingdom, from the lowly worm that shrinks into his hole at the sound of an approaching foot, to the dog obeying his master's command, and even to the learned scientist who watches the movements of an index needle.

18   This continuity of the sign-using talent has led psychologists to the belief that language is evolved from the vocal expressions, grunts and coos and cries, whereby animals vent their feelings or signal their fellows; that man has elaborated this sort of communion to the point where it makes a perfect exchange of ideas possible.

19   I do not believe that this doctrine of the origin of language is correct. The essence of language is symbolic, not signific; we use it first and most vitally to formulate and hold ideas in our own minds. Conception, not social control, is its first and foremost benefit.

20   Watch a young child that is just learning to speak play with a toy; he says the name of the object, e.g.: "Horsey! Horsey! Horsey!" over and over again, looks at the object, moves it, always saying the name to himself or to the world at large. It's quite a time before he talks to anyone in particular; he talks first of all to himself. This is his way of forming and fixing the *conception* of the object in his mind, and around this conception all his knowledge of it grows. *Names* are the essence of language; for the *name* is what abstracts the conception of the horse from the horse itself, and lets the mere idea recur at the speaking of the name. This permits the conception gathered from one horse experience to be exemplified again by another instance of a horse, so that the notion embodied in the name is a general notion.

21   To this end, the baby uses a word long before he *asks* for the object; when he wants his horsey he is likely to cry and fret, because he is reacting to an actual environment, not forming ideas. He uses the animal language of *signs* for his wants; talking is still a purely symbolic process—its practical value has not really impressed him yet.

22   Language need not be vocal; it may be purely visual, like written language, or even tactual, like the deaf-mute system of speech; but it *must be denotative.* The sounds, intended or unintended, whereby animals communicate do not constitute a language because they are signs, not names. They never fall into an organic pattern, a meaningful syntax of even the most rudimentary sort, as all language seems to do with a sort of driving necessity. That is because signs refer to actual situations, in which things have obvious relations to each other that require only to be noted; but symbols refer to ideas, which are not physically there for inspection, so their connections and features have to be represented. This gives all true language a natural tendency toward growth and development, which seems almost like a life of its own. Languages are not invented; they grow with our need for expression.

23   In contrast, animal "speech" never has a structure. It is merely an emotional response. Apes may greet their ration of yams with a shout of "Nga!" But they do not say "Nga" between meals. If they could *talk about* their yams instead of just saluting them, they would be the most primitive men instead of the most anthropoid of beasts. They would have ideas, and tell each other things true or false, rational or irrational; they would make plans and invent laws and sing their own praises, as men do.

THINKING CRITICALLY

1. Langer's opening statement is "A symbol is not the same thing as a sign." In your own words, what is the difference between signs and symbols? Give some examples from your own experience.

2. What would human beings be like if they used only signs? What would be the state of human communications?

3. According to Langer, how did language develop?

4. Langer says that symbols cause us to think about the thing symbolized. What do the following symbols make us think about, or what messages are communicated by them: clothes with the Tommy Hilfiger trademark on them; a dorm windowsill stacked with beer cans; a Coach handbag; an American flag pin; a peace sign window decal; a Harley-Davidson motorcycle; a swastika; a rainbow sticker?

5. In the opening paragraphs, Langer uses comparison to clarify the differences between signs and symbols. What comparisons does she specifically use? How effective are they in helping the reader understand her points?

6. In paragraph 2, Langer gives some examples of signs, yet she waits until paragraph 3 to define *sign.* Why do you think she uses this strategy? Is it effective for her purpose?

WRITING ASSIGNMENTS

1. Write a paper entitled "A Sign of the Times" in which you choose and discuss an appropriate sign of the state of today's world.

2. Write an essay describing all the different symbols and signs to which you responded on your way to class today.

3. What are some of the signs and symbols of the Internet? Write an essay in which you describe how Internet symbols have changed our world.

4. The very clothes we wear convey symbolic messages of some sort—socioeconomic status, awareness, worldliness, sometimes even political statements. Describe some of the messages you like to project through your choice of clothing, boots, shoes, jewelry, and so on.

A Brief History of English
Paul Roberts

While nobody knows exactly how languages began, Paul Roberts explains in this famous essay that language development is best understood if we examine its historical transformations. With engaging storytelling flair, Roberts makes accessible the long and complicated evolution of the English language. Tracing over 1,400 turbulent years from its Anglo-Saxon roots to the contemporary utterances of over 700 million people around the world, Roberts's brief history makes clear that language is in a constant state of change. Every day the English language adds new words to its lexicon, redefines old ones, and grows in dialectical diversity.

Paul Roberts was a well-known linguist and author of several books on English history and grammar including *Patterns of English* (1956) and *Understanding English* (1958), from which this essay was excerpted.

1 No understanding of the English language can be very satisfactory without a notion of the history of the language. But we shall have to make do with just a notion. The history of English is long and complicated, and we can only hit the high spots.

2 The history of our language begins a little after 600 C.E. Everything before that is pre-history, which means that we can guess at it but can't prove much. For a thousand years or so before the birth of Christ our linguistic ancestors were savages wandering through the forests of northern Europe. Their language was a part of the Germanic branch of the Indo-European family.

3 At the time of the Roman Empire—say, from the beginning of the Christian Era to around 400 C.E.—the speakers of what was to become English were scattered along the northern coast of Europe. They spoke a dialect of Low German. More exactly, they spoke several different dialects, since they were several different tribes. The names given to the tribes who got to English are *Angles, Saxons,* and *Jutes.* For convenience, we can refer to them all as Anglo-Saxons.

4 Their first contact with civilization was a rather thin acquaintance with the Roman Empire on whose borders they lived. Probably some of the Anglo-Saxons wandered into the Empire occasionally, and certainly Roman merchants and traders traveled among the tribes. At any rate, this period saw the first of our many borrowings from Latin. Such words as *kettle, wine, cheese, butter, cheap, plum, gem, bishop, church* were borrowed at this time. They show something of the relationship of the Anglo-Saxons with the Romans. The Anglo-Saxons were learning, getting their first taste of civilization.

5 They still had a long way to go, however, and their first step was to help smash the civilization they were learning from. In the fourth century the Roman power

weakened badly. While the Goths were pounding away at the Romans in the Mediterranean countries, their relatives, the Anglo-Saxons, began to attack Britain.

6   The Romans had been the ruling power in Britain since 43 C.E. They had subjugated the Celts whom they found living there and had succeeded in setting up a Roman administration. The Roman influence did not extend to the outlying parts of the British Isles. In Scotland, Wales, and Ireland the Celts remained free and wild, and they made periodic forays against the Romans in England. Among other defense measures, the Romans built the famous Roman Wall to ward off the tribes in the north.

7   Even in England the Roman power was thin. Latin did not become the language of the country as it did in Gaul and Spain. The mass of people continued to speak Celtic, with Latin and the Roman civilization it contained in use as a top dressing.

8   In the fourth century, troubles multiplied for the Romans in Britain. Not only did the untamed tribes of Scotland and Wales grow more and more restive, but also the Anglo-Saxons began to make pirate raids on the eastern coast. Furthermore, there was growing difficulty everywhere in the Empire, and the legions in Britain were siphoned off to fight elsewhere. Finally, in 410 C.E., the last Roman ruler in England, bent on becoming emperor, left the islands and took the last of the legions with him. The Celts were left in possession of Britain but almost defenseless against the impending Anglo-Saxon attack.

9   Not much is surely known about the arrival of the Anglo-Saxons in England. According to the best early source, the eighth-century historian Bede, the Jutes came in 449 in response to a plea from the Celtic king, Vortigern, who wanted their help against the Picts attacking from the north. The Jutes subdued the Picts but then quarreled and fought with Vortigern, and, with reinforcements from the Continent, settled permanently in Kent. Somewhat later the Angles established themselves in eastern England and the Saxons in the south and west. Bede's account is plausible enough, and these were probably the main lines of the invasion.

10   We do know, however, that the Angles, Saxons, and Jutes were a long time securing themselves in England. Fighting went on for as long as a hundred years before the Celts in England were all killed, driven into Wales, or reduced to slavery. This is the period of King Arthur, who was not entirely mythological. He was a Romanized Celt, a general, though probably not a king. He had some success against the Anglo-Saxons, but it was only temporary. By 550 or so the Anglo-Saxons were finally established. English was in England.

11   All this is pre-history, so far as the language is concerned. We have no record of the English language until after 600, when the Anglo-Saxons were converted to Christianity and learned the Latin alphabet. The conversion began, to be precise, in the year 597 and was accomplished within thirty or forty years. The conversion was a great advance for the Anglo-Saxons, not only because of the spiritual benefits but also because it reestablished contact with what remained of Roman civilization. This civilization didn't amount to much in the year 600, but it was certainly superior to anything in England up to that time.

12   It is customary to divide the history of the English language into three periods: Old English, Middle English, and Modern English. Old English runs from the ear-

liest records—i.e., seventh century—to about 1100; Middle English from 1100 to 1450 or 1500; Modern English from 1500 to the present day. Sometimes Modern English is further divided into Early Modern, 1500–1700, and Late Modern, 1700 to the present.

13   When England came into history, it was divided into several more or less autonomous kingdoms, some of which at times exercised a certain amount of control over the others. In the century after the conversion the most advanced kingdom was Northumbria, the area between the Humber River and the Scottish border. By 700 C.E. the Northumbrians had developed a respectable civilization, the finest in Europe. It is sometimes called the Northumbrian Renaissance, and it was the first of the several renaissances through which Europe struggled upward out of the ruins of the Roman Empire. It was in this period that the best of the Old English literature was written, including the epic poem *Beowulf.*

14   In the eighth century, Northumbrian power declined, and the center of influence moved southward to Mercia, the kingdom of the Midlands. A century later the center shifted again, and Wessex, the country of the West Saxons, became the leading power. The most famous king of the West Saxons was Alfred the Great, who reigned in the second half of the ninth century, dying in 901. He was famous not only as a military man and administrator but also as a champion of learning. He founded and supported schools and translated or caused to be translated many books from Latin into English. At this time also much of the Northumbrian literature of two centuries earlier was copied in West Saxon. Indeed, the great bulk of Old English writing which has come down to us is in the West Saxon dialect of 900 or later.

15   In the military sphere, Alfred's great accomplishment was his successful opposition to the Viking invasions. In the ninth and tenth centuries, the Norsemen emerged in their ships from their homelands in Denmark and the Scandinavian peninsula. They traveled far and attacked and plundered at will and almost with impunity. They ravaged Italy and Greece, settled in France, Russia, and Ireland, colonized Iceland and Greenland, and discovered America several centuries before Columbus. Nor did they overlook England.

16   After many years of hit-and-run raids, the Norsemen landed an army on the east coast of England in the year 866. There was nothing much to oppose them except the Wessex power led by Alfred. The long struggle ended in 877 with a treaty by which a line was drawn roughly from the northwest of England to the southeast. On the eastern side of the line Norse rule was to prevail. This was called the Danelaw. The western side was to be governed by Wessex.

17   The linguistic result of all this was a considerable injection of Norse into the English language. Norse was at this time not so different from English as Norwegian or Danish is now. Probably speakers of English could understand, more or less, the language of the newcomers who had moved into eastern England. At any rate, there was considerable interchange and word borrowing. Examples of Norse words in the English language are *sky, give, law, egg, outlaw, leg, ugly, scant, sly, crawl, scowl, take, thrust.* There are hundreds more. We have even borrowed some pronouns from Norse—*they, their,* and *them.* These words were borrowed first by the eastern and northern dialects and then in the course of hundreds of years made their way into English generally.

18   It is supposed also—indeed, it must be true—that the Norsemen influenced the sound structure and the grammar of English. But this is hard to demonstrate in detail.

19   We may now have an example of Old English. The favorite illustration is the Lord's Prayer, since it needs no translation. This has come to us in several different versions. Here is one:

> Fæder ure [thorn]u[eth]e eart on heofonum si [thorn]in nama gehalgod. Tobe-cume [thorn]in rice. Gewur[eth]e [thorn]in willa on eor[eth]an swa swa on he-ofonum. Urne gedæghwamlican hlaf syle us to dæg. And forgyf us ure gyltas swa swa we forgyfa[thorn] urum glytendum. And ne gelæd [thorn]u us on cost-nunge ac alys us of yfele. So[eth]lice.

20   Some of the differences between this and Modern English are merely differences in orthography. For instance, the sign *æ* is what Old English writers used for a vowel sound like that in modern *hat* or *and*. The *th* sounds of modern *thin* or *then* are represented in Old English by [thorn] or [eth]. But of course there are many differences in sound too. *Ure* is the ancestor of modern *our*, but the first vowel was like that in *too* or *ooze*. *Hlaf* is modern *loaf*; we have dropped the *h* sound and changed the vowel, which in *half* was pronounced something like the vowel in *father*. Old English had some sounds which we do not have. The sound represented by *y* does not occur in Modern English. If you pronounce the vowel in *bit* with your lips rounded, you may approach it.

21   In grammar, Old English was much more highly inflected than Modern English is. That is, there were more case endings for nouns, more person and number endings for verbs, a more complicated pronoun system, various endings for adjectives, and so on. Old English nouns had four cases—nominative, genitive, dative, accusative. Adjectives had five—all these and an instrumental case besides. Present-day English has only two cases for nouns—common case and possessive case. Adjectives now have no case system at all. On the other hand, we now use a more rigid word order and more structure words (prepositions, auxiliaries, and the like) to express relationships than Old English did.

22   Some of this grammar we can see in the Lord's Prayer. *Heofonum*, for instance, is a dative plural; the nominative singular was *heofon*. *Urne* is an accusative singular; the nominative is *ure*. In *urum glytendum* both words are dative plural. *Forgyfaþ* is the third person plural form of the verb. Word order is different: "urne gedæghwamlican hlaf syle us" in place of "Give us our daily bread." And so on.

23   In vocabulary Old English is quite different from Modern English. Most of the Old English words are what we may call native English: that is, words which have not been borrowed from other languages but which have been a part of English ever since English was a part of Indo-European. Old English did certainly contain borrowed words. We have seen that many borrowings were coming in from Norse. Rather large numbers had been borrowed from Latin, too. Some of these were taken while the Anglo-Saxons were still on the continent (*cheese, butter, bishop, kettle*, etc.); a large number came into English after Conversion (*angel, candle, priest, martyr, radish, oyster, purple, school, spend*, etc.). But the great majority of Old English words were native English.

24   Now, on the contrary, the majority of words in English are borrowed, taken mostly from Latin and French. Of the words in *The American College Dictionary* only about 14 percent are native. Most of these, to be sure, are common, high-frequency words—*the, of, I, and, because, man, mother, road,* etc.; of the thousand most common words in English, some 62 percent are native English. Even so, the modern vocabulary is very much Latinized and Frenchified. The Old English vocabulary was not.

25   Sometime between the year 1000 and 1200 various important changes took place in the structure of English, and Old English became Middle English. The political event which facilitated these changes was the Norman Conquest. The Normans, as the name shows, came originally from Scandinavia. In the early tenth century they established themselves in northern France, adopted the French language, and developed a vigorous kingdom and a very passable civilization. In the year 1066, led by Duke William, they crossed the Channel and made themselves masters of England. For the next several hundred years, England was ruled by kings whose first language was French.

26   One might wonder why, after the Norman Conquest, French did not become the national language, replacing English entirely. The reason is that the Conquest was not a national migration, as the earlier Anglo-Saxon invasion had been. Great numbers of Normans came to England, but they came as rulers and landlords. French became the language of the court, the language of the nobility, the language of polite society, the language of literature. But it did not replace English as the language of the people. There must always have been hundreds of towns and villages in which French was never heard except when visitors of high station passed through.

27   But English, though it survived as the national language, was profoundly changed after the Norman Conquest. Some of the changes—in sound structure and grammar—would no doubt have taken place whether there had been a Conquest or not. Even before 1066 the case system of English nouns and adjectives was becoming simplified; people came to rely more on word order and prepositions than on inflectional endings to communicate their meanings. The process was speeded up by sound changes which caused many of the endings to sound alike. But no doubt the Conquest facilitated the change. German, which didn't experience a Norman Conquest, is today rather highly inflected compared to its cousin English.

28   But it is in vocabulary that the effects of the Conquest are most obvious. French ceased, after a hundred years or so, to be the native language of very many people in England, but it continued—and continues still—to be a zealously cultivated second language, the mirror of elegance and civilization. When one spoke English, one introduced not only French ideas and French things but also their French names. This was not only easy but socially useful. To pepper one's conversation with French expressions was to show that one was well-bred, elegant, *au courant.* The last sentence shows that the process is not yet dead. By using *au courant* instead of, say, *abreast of things,* the writer indicates that he is no dull clod who knows only English but an elegant person aware of how things are done in *le haut monde.*

29   Thus French words came into English, all sorts of them. There were words to do with government: *parliament, majesty, treaty, alliance, tax, government;* church

words: *parson, sermon, baptism, incense, crucifix, religion;* words for foods: *veal, beef, mutton, bacon, jelly, peach, lemon, cream, biscuit;* colors: *blue, scarlet, vermilion;* household words: *curtain, chair, lamp, towel, blanket, parlor;* play words: *dance, chess, music, leisure, conversation;* literary words: *story, romance, poet, literary;* learned words: *study, logic, grammar, noun, surgeon, anatomy, stomach;* just ordinary words of all sorts: *nice, second, very, age, bucket, gentle, final, fault, flower, cry, count, sure, move, surprise, plain.*

30   All these and thousands more poured into the English vocabulary between 1100 and 1500, until at the end of that time many people must have had more French words than English at their command. This is not to say that English became French. English remained English in sound structure and in grammar, though these also felt the ripples of French influence. The very heart of the vocabulary, too, remained English. Most of the high-frequency words—the pronouns, the prepositions, the conjunctions, the auxiliaries, as well as a great many ordinary nouns and verbs and adjectives—were not replaced by borrowings.

31   Middle English, then, was still a Germanic language, but it differed from Old English in many ways. The sound system and the grammar changed a good deal. Speakers made less use of case systems and other inflectional devices and relied more on word order and structure words to express their meanings. This is often said to be a simplification, but it isn't really. Languages don't become simpler; they merely exchange one kind of complexity for another. Modern English is not a simple language, as any foreign speaker who tries to learn it will hasten to tell you.

32   For us, Middle English is simpler than Old English just because it is closer to Modern English. It takes three or four months at least to learn to read Old English prose and more than that for poetry. But a week of good study should put one in touch with the Middle English poet Chaucer. Indeed, you may be able to make some sense of Chaucer straight off, though you would need instruction in pronunciation to make it sound like poetry. Here is a famous passage from the *General Prologue to the Canterbury Tales,* fourteenth century:

> Ther was also a Nonne, a Prioresse.
> That of hir smyling was ful symple and coy;
> Hir gretteste ooth was but by Seinte Loy;
> And she was cleped madame Eglentyne.
> Ful weel she soong the service dyvyne,
> Entuned in hir nose ful semely,
> And Frenshe she spak ful faire and fetisly,
> After the scole of Stratford-atte-Bowe,
> For Frenshe of Parys was to hirse unknowe.

33   Sometime between 1400 and 1600 English underwent a couple of sound changes which made the language of Shakespeare quite different from that of Chaucer. Incidentally, these changes contributed much to the chaos in which English spelling now finds itself.

34   One change was the elimination of a vowel sound in certain unstressed positions at the end of words. For instance, the words *name, stone, wine, dance* were

pronounced as two syllables by Chaucer but as just one by Shakespeare. The *e* in these words became, as we say, "silent." But it wasn't silent for Chaucer; it represented a vowel sound. So also the words *laughed, seemed, stored* would have been pronounced by Chaucer as two-syllable words. The change was an important one because it affected thousands of words and gave a different aspect to the whole language.

35   The other change is what is called the Great Vowel Shift. This was a systematic shifting of half a dozen vowels and diphthongs in stressed syllables. For instance, the word *nam* had in Middle English a vowel something like that in the modern word *father; wine* had the vowel of modern *mean; he* was pronounced something like modern *hey; mouse* sounded like *moose; moon* had the vowel of *moan*. Again, the shift was thoroughgoing and affected all the words in which these vowel sounds occurred. Since we still keep the Middle English system of spelling these words, the differences between Modern English and Middle English are often more real than apparent.

36   The vowel shift has meant also that we have come to use an entirely different set of symbols for representing vowel sounds than is used by writers of such languages as French, Italian, or Spanish, in which no such vowel shift occurred. If you come across a strange word—say, *bine*—in an English book, you will pronounce it according to the English system, with the vowel of *wine* or *dine*. But if you read *bine* in a French, Italian, or Spanish book, you will pronounce it with the vowel of *mean* or *seen*.

37   These two changes, then, produced the basic differences between Middle English and Modern English. But there were several other developments that had an effect upon the language. One was the invention of printing, an invention introduced into England by William Caxton in the year 1475. Where before books had been rare and costly, they suddenly became cheap and common. More and more people learned to read and write. This was the first of many advances in communication which have worked to unify languages and to arrest the development of dialect differences, though of course printing affects writing principally rather than speech. Among other things it hastened the standardization of spelling.

38   The period of Early Modern English—that is, the sixteenth and seventeenth centuries—was also the period of the English Renaissance, when people developed, on the one hand, a keen interest in the past and, on the other, a more daring and imaginative view of the future. New ideas multiplied, and new ideas meant new language. Englishmen had grown accustomed to borrowing words from French as a result of the Norman Conquest; now they borrowed from Latin and Greek. As we have seen, English had been raiding Latin from Old English times and before, but now the floodgates really opened, and thousands of words from the classical languages poured in. *Pedestrian, bonus, anatomy, contradict, climax, dictionary, benefit, multiply, exist, paragraph, initiate, scene, inspire* are random examples. Probably the average educated American today has more words from French in his vocabulary than from native English sources, and more from Latin than from French.

39   The greatest writer of the Early Modern English period is of course Shakespeare, and the best-known book is the King James Version of the Bible, published in 1611. The Bible (if not Shakespeare) has made many features of Early Modern

English perfectly familiar to many people down to present times, even though we do not use these features in present-day speech and writing. For instance, the old pronouns *thou* and *thee* have dropped out of use now, together with their verb forms, but they are still familiar to us in prayer and in Biblical quotation: "Whither thou goest, I will go." Such forms as *hath* and *doth* have been replaced by *has* and *does;* "Goes he hence tonight?" would now be "Is he going away tonight?"; Shakespeare's "Fie on't, sirrah" would be "Nuts to that, Mac." Still, all these expressions linger with us because of the power of the works in which they occur.

40   It is not always realized, however, that considerable sound changes have taken place between Early Modern English and the English of the present day. Shakespearean actors putting on a play speak the words, properly enough, in their modern pronunciation. But it is very doubtful that this pronunciation would be understood at all by Shakespeare. In Shakespeare's time, the word *reason* was pronounced like modern *raisin; face* had the sound of modern *glass;* the *l* in *would, should, palm* was pronounced. In these points and a great many others, the English language has moved a long way from what it was in 1600.

41   The history of English since 1700 is filled with many movements and counter-movements, of which we can notice only a couple. One of these is the vigorous attempt made in the eighteenth century, and the rather halfhearted attempts made since, to regulate and control the English language. Many people of the eighteenth century, not understanding very well the forces which govern language, proposed to polish and prune and restrict English, which they felt was proliferating too wildly. There was much talk of an academy which would rule on what people could and could not say and write. The academy never came into being, but the eighteenth century did succeed in establishing certain attitudes which, though they haven't had much effect on the development of the language itself, have certainly changed the native speaker's feeling about the language.

42   In part a product of the wish to fix and establish the language was the development of the dictionary. The first English dictionary was published in 1603; it was a list of 2,500 words briefly defined. Many others were published with gradual improvements until Samuel Johnson published his *English Dictionary* in 1755. This, steadily revised, dominated the field in England for nearly a hundred years. Meanwhile in America, Noah Webster published his dictionary in 1828, and before long dictionary publishing was a big business in this country. The last century has seen the publication of one great dictionary: the twelve-volume *Oxford English Dictionary,* compiled in the course of seventy-five years through the labors of many scholars. We have also, of course, numerous commercial dictionaries which are as good as the public wants them to be if not, indeed, rather better.

43   Another product of the eighteenth century was the invention of "English grammar." As English came to replace Latin as the language of scholarship it was felt that one should also be able to control and dissect it, parse and analyze it, as one could Latin. What happened in practice was that the grammatical description that applied to Latin was removed and superimposed on English. This was silly, because English is an entirely different kind of language, with its own forms and signals and ways of producing meaning. Nevertheless, English grammars on the Latin model

were worked out and taught in the schools. In many schools they are still being taught. This activity is not often popular with school children, but it is sometimes an interesting and instructive exercise in logic. The principal harm in it is that it has tended to keep people from being interested in English and has obscured the real features of English structure.

44   But probably the most important force in the development of English in the modern period has been the tremendous expansion of English-speaking peoples. In 1500 English was a minor language, spoken by a few people on a small island. Now it is perhaps the greatest language of the world, spoken natively by over a quarter of a billion people and as a second language by many millions more. When we speak of English now, we must specify whether we mean American English, British English, Australian English, Indian English, or what, since the differences are considerable. The American cannot go to England or the English-man to America confident that he will always understand and be understood. The Alabaman in Iowa or the Iowan in Alabama shows himself a foreigner every time he speaks. It is only because communication has become fast and easy that English in this period of its expansion has not broken into a dozen mutually unintelligible languages.

THINKING CRITICALLY

1. Roberts states in the opening of his essay that there can be no real understanding of the English language without an understanding of its history. Discuss some of the ways, as outlined by Roberts, in which history has had a bearing on the development of the English language since the time of the Roman Empire.

2. In paragraph 4, Roberts lists English words borrowed from Latin, noting that in their nature these words "show something of the relationship of the Anglo-Saxons with the Romans." What kind of relationship do you suppose these two peoples had, based on the list of words given by Roberts?

3. In terms of grammar, Roberts says that Old English was much more highly inflected than Modern English (paragraph 21). What does he mean by this statement?

4. What political event facilitated the change from Old to Middle English? How did this change occur? Do you think that political events still play a part in language development? Explain your answer.

5. Characterize the style and tone of this essay. To what audience do you suppose Roberts is aiming this piece?

6. Is Roberts successful in demonstrating the connection between history and language development? Locate one or two passages in which you find that connection to be especially strong.

WRITING ASSIGNMENTS

1. Roberts's piece is based on the idea that English has been affected by historical events. Choose a recent event—White House politics, the terrorist attacks of September 11, 2001, the violence in Israel, or the American war with Iraq—and write a paper exploring how English has been influenced by it.

2. Choose a short passage of modern prose. Using a dictionary, look up a dozen of the words in the passage, paying special attention to the origins of the words. Write a paragraph in which you detail your findings, noting whether or not they reflect Roberts's claims about the historical development of the English language.

3. Write a paper on how the Internet and computers in general have influenced our current language. What words have been "invented" or reappropriated by our use of this medium? How do Internet-influenced words cross the boundaries between computers and our common tongue?

4. What was the position of the French language after the Norman Conquest? What remnants of this class-split society are still reflected in our language today? Write a short essay exploring a contemporary society in which there is a class split along language lines. How does this language split affect this country.

Horton Heared a Who!

Steven Pinker

What can the grammatical slips of children as they learn to speak tell us about language, history, and the human mind? In this essay, linguist Steven Pinker explains that language acquisition follows regular, predictable patterns. Children are able to instinctually develop grammatical rules—not merely by imitating the language of adults—but they also can produce new words that they never heard before. How they do this, says Pinker, can give us a glimpse into the early origins of language.

Steven Pinker is a psychology professor at Harvard University. Until 2003, he taught in the Department of Brain and Cognitive Sciences at Massachusetts Institute of Technology (MIT). He is internationally recognized for his research on language and cognition. In addition to being published in scholarly journals, his essays have appeared in popular media including the *New York Times*, *Time*, and *Slate*. He is author of several books, including *The Language Instinct* (1994), *How the Mind Works* (1999), *Words and Rules* (2000), and *The Blank Slate* (2002). This essay first appeared in the November 1, 1999 issue of *Time* magazine.

1   Kids say the darnedest things. "We holded the baby rabbits." "The alligator goed kerplunk." "Horton heared a Who!" These lapses, you might dimly recall, have something to do with irregular verbs. But please don't stop reading just yet. Children's errors are not just anecdotes for grandparents or reminders of long forgotten grammar lessons. They are windows into the workings of language, history, and the human mind.

2   Verbs in English come in two flavors. Regular verbs like *walk* and *smell* form the past tense by adding *–ed*: Today I walk, yesterday I walked. English has thousands of them, and new ones arise every day, thanks to our ability to apply rules instinctively. When people first heard *to spam*, *to mosh*, and *to diss*, they did not run to the dictionary to look up their past tenses; they knew they were spammed, moshed, and dissed.

3   Even children do it. Told that a man likes to wug, they will say that yesterday he wugged. Children are not sponges; they are constantly creating new sentences and words, and never more clearly or charmingly than when they run into the second flavor of verb, the quirky irregulars. The past of *spring* is *sprang*, but the past of *cling*

is not *clang* but *clung*, and the past of *bring* is neither *brang* nor *brung* but *brought*. English has only 180 irregulars, a rag-tag list that children simply have to memorize.

4 But when an irregular word is still fresh in the mind, it is fragile. If a child's memory cannot cough up *held* quickly enough, he or she adds *–ed* by default and says heared or holded instead.

5 Irregular and regular verbs embody the two underlying tricks behind the gift of articulate speech: words and rules. A word is a memorized link between a sound and a meaning. The word *duck* does not look, walk, or quack like a duck. But we can use it to convey the idea of a duck because we all once learned to connect the sound with the idea.

THE FAMILY CIRCUS.   By Bil Keane

6-2
©1994 Bil Keane, Inc.
Dist. by Cowles Synd., Inc.

"Mommy, Dolly hitted me."
"Dolly HIT me."
"You too?! Boy, she's in trouble!"

6 We also combine words into bigger words and sentences, using the second trick of language, rules. Journalists say that when a dog bites a man, that isn't news, but when a man bites a dog, that is news. Rules let us convey news, by reshuffling words in systematic ways.

7 Today's regular and irregular verbs have their roots in old border disputes between the word module and the rule module. Many irregulars can be traced back over 5,500 years, to a mysterious tribe that came to dominate Europe, western Asia, and northen India. Their language, Indo-European, is the ancestor of Hindi, Persian, Russian, Greek, Latin, Gaelic, and English. It had rules that replaced vowels: the past of *senkw-* (sink) was *sonkw-*.

8 Language as it evolves over the centuries is like the game of Broken Telephone, where a whispered phrase gets increasingly distorted as it passes from lip to ear to lip. Eventually speakers can no longer discern the rule behind a motley set of mangled verbs. They just memorize them as a list, as do subsequent generations. These are the irregulars, the fossils of dead rules.

9 The irregulars are vulnerable, too, because they depend on fallible human memory. If a verb declines in popularity, speakers may not hear its irregular form often enough to stamp it securely in memory. They fall back on *–ed*, changing the language for following generations. That is why forms from Chaucer's time such as *chide-chid* and *writhe-wrothe* disappeared, replaced by *chided* and *writhed*.

10 You can feel that force of history acting today. *Smote, slew, bade, rent*, and *forsook* sound odd, and few people would use them in casual speech. In a century, they will probably go the way of *chid* and *wrothe*.

11   Do irregular and regular verbs really come out of a dictionary in one part of the brain and a grammar in another? Perhaps. Some neurological patients seem to have damaged dictionaries: they strain to retrieve words, but speak in fluent sentences. As expected, they have trouble producing irregular verbs, and like children (whose memory for words is also fragile), they make errors like heared and holded. New techniques in cognitive neuroscience have found that irregular and regular forms trigger signals in different parts of the brain, perhaps from the systems for memory and for computation.

12   Why pay so much attention to the lowly irregular verb? I see these studies as part of a trend in intellectual life that biologist E. O. Wilson calls "consilience": the bridging of the two cultures of science and humanities through an understanding of how the mind works. The link connecting the migrations of great prehistoric tribes to the brain-imaging technologies of the next millennium may lie in the slip of the child's tongue.

THINKING CRITICALLY

1. How, according to Pinker, can young children's grammar lapses serve as "windows into the workings of language, history, and the human mind"? Explain.

2. In paragraph 2, Pinker observes that we are able to conjugate new verbs "instinctively." Do you think grammar is instinctual? Why or why not?

3. Pinker notes that when words fall out of regular use (such as *smote, slew, bade,* and *forsook*) we forget their irregular conjugations and fall back on the *–ed* of regular verbs. Can you think of any additional verbs besides the ones Pinker names that are undergoing this change now?

4. Why does Pinker think irregular verbs are worthy of study? Explain.

WRITING ASSIGNMENTS

1. Create a list of irregular verbs (a Google search should make compiling this list easy) and ask a child between the ages of 3 and 4 to use them in a present and past-tense sentence. How often do they use the *–ed* ending? Do they use any words correctly? If so, which ones? Write a short essay on children's language acquisition or irregular and regular verbs based on your observations.

2. Write a personal narrative of your own recollections of learning language as a child. Did you use words like *brang* or *brung*? Did irregular verbs confuse you? Speak to people who knew you as a young child for their memories of any language "slips" you may have made as you learned to speak. When, if ever, did you become *aware* of language?

Another Language for the Deaf
Margalit Fox

While sign language opened the doors of language to the deaf, the thousands of people who use it still must learn two languages to communicate in their world: the language of signing and the alphabet of the general population. For years, the primary language of the deaf—signing—could not be written down. SignWriting hopes to change this situation. In the next piece, Margalit Fox explains how SignWriting, a system of graphic symbols based on dance notation, aims to capture the world's signed languages in written form. But as Fox explains, the concept faces many challenges.

Margalit Fox is a reporter for the *New York Times* and an editor for that paper's *Book Review*. This article first appeared in the April 14, 2002 edition of the *New York Times*.

1 Imagine a language that can't be written. Hundreds of thousands of people speak it, but they have no way to read a newspaper or study a schoolbook in the language they use all day long.

2   That is the situation of the quarter-million or more deaf people in North America whose primary language is American Sign Language. Although they form a vast linguistic minority, their language, as complex as any spoken one, has by its very nature defied most attempts to write it down. In recent years, however, a system of graphic symbols based on dance notation has allowed the world's signed languages to be captured on paper. What's more, the system's advocates say, it may furnish deaf children with a long-sought bridge to literacy in English and other spoken languages, often a great struggle for signers.

3   But despite its utility, the system, called SignWriting, has yet to be widely adopted by deaf people: for many, the issue of whether signed languages need to be written at all remains an open question. "The written form is used by a small number of educated people," Valerie Sutton, the creator of SignWriting, said in a telephone interview from her office in La Jolla, Calif.

4   Little by little, though, SignWriting is gaining footholds in individual homes and classrooms in America and abroad. Disseminated by Ms. Sutton's nonprofit organization <www.signwriting.org>, it can now be found in 27 countries, including Italy, South Africa, Nicaragua, Japan, and Saudi Arabia.

5   American Sign Language is not English. Spoken in the United States and parts of Canada, it uses word orders and grammatical constructs not found in English (in certain respects it resembles Navajo).

6   For a deaf child whose first language is A.S.L., English—that is, written English—must be learned as a foreign language, just as a hearing person might study Sanskrit. But there is a catch: "The letters of the alphabet are based on sounds they can't hear," Ms. Sutton explained. For this reason, many deaf students never become fully literate in English, a perennial concern of educators. According to a long-term study by the Gallaudet Research Institute in Washington, deaf high school seniors score, on average, just below the fourth-grade level on standardized reading tests.

7   Dawn McReynolds of Clinton Township, MI, ran into the problem three years ago, when she discovered her 12-year-old did not know what "bread" meant. Born deaf, and fluent in A.S.L., Nicole McReynolds, then a sixth-grader in public school, was clearly bright. But standardized tests put her academic skills at a first- to second-grade level. As her stunned mother discovered after she pulled Nicole from the classroom and began home schooling, though Nicole had learned by rote to spell simple English words—"bread," "map," "yell"—she had little idea what they actually meant.

8   "Anything I could draw a picture for, she was O.K. with," Mrs. McReynolds said. "But things like 'what,' 'where,' 'when,' 'who'—she had no idea. It was horrible. It was as if she'd never been educated."

9   Advocates of SignWriting hope the system can help bridge the literacy gap. Though no formal studies have been published, anecdotal evidence from parents and teachers suggests its potential. "It's made English come alive for her," said Mrs. McReynolds, who introduced Nicole to SignWriting two and a half years ago, after seeing it on local television.

10   Where spoken languages operate acoustically, signed languages work spatially. Each sign is a compact bundle of data, conveying linguistic information by three primary means at once: the shape of the signer's hands, the location of the hands in space, and the direction in which the hands move. (Facial expression also matters.)

11   Devising a writing system that can capture this blizzard of data for each of A.S.L.'s thousands of signs is no simple task. "When you write English, we're using two-dimensional paper to represent a one-dimensional language, because English is just a series of sounds in a sequence, and we write down the sounds in the order we say them," said Karen van Hoek, a linguist who helped develop Sign-Writing. "But with sign language, it's the reverse: we're trying to get a three-dimensional language compressed down onto two-dimensional, flat paper."

12   Other writing systems have been created for A.S.L. during its century-and-a-half-long history. Some, used by linguists, are too abstract for everyday communication. Another, developed recently at the University of Arizona, is meant to help teach written English but not to handle literary traffic, like novel-writing, entirely in A.S.L.

13   SignWriting, which grew out of a system for transcribing movement that Ms. Sutton developed in the 1970s to notate choreography, can be handwritten, or typed using special software. Written vertically, it uses simple geometric forms to collapse a sign's three basic parameters—hand shape, location, and movement—into a streamlined icon, topped by a stylized face.

14   Few embraced the system at first. Many signers, mindful of a long paternalistic history of hearing people tampering with A.S.L., questioned Ms. Sutton's motives. Educators feared it would deter the deaf from learning English.

15   Though hostility has subsided, SignWriting is used today by only a small fraction of the deaf population, between 5,000 and 8,000 people worldwide, Ms. Sutton estimates. As Jane Fernandes, the provost of Gallaudet University, the prestigious school for the hearing impaired, said in an e-mail interview: "There are many deaf adults who were raised with Sign Language in their homes and schools and who have learned to read and write English quite fluently. They were able to navigate between Sign Language and English, without a system for writing their signs down."

16   While acknowledging SignWriting's potential usefulness in teaching English, Dr. Fernandes, who is deaf, expressed doubt about the larger need for written A.S.L. "English is the language of society," she wrote. "It works well for us and I believe English will remain the language in which we write in America."

17   Nicole McReynolds mastered SignWriting fairly easily, and the English words that eluded her began gradually to fall into place. Now 15 and a ninth-grader, she is back in public school, maintaining a B average in a program for hearing-impaired students conducted in English.

18   Before SignWriting, Mrs. McReynolds said, "I didn't think she would be able to live an independent life." These days, Nicole talks of college. "We believe that SignWriting is going to accompany her through her life," her mother said. "There is so much more hope for the future for her because she has this ability now."

THINKING CRITICALLY

1. How is sign language different from "spoken" languages? What challenges does sign language face in order to transition into written form? Explain.

2. In what ways is learning written English for a deaf child much like learning a foreign language? What literacy obstacles must deaf children address when trying to learn written English?

3. Why does SignWriting hold promise over other forms of ASL writing systems? Explain.

4. Sign languages are true languages, with vocabularies of thousands of words and complex and sophisticated grammars. Attend a speech or watch a program that has an ASL interpreter present and focus your attention on the interpreter. If you could not hear, could you understand the context of the speech based on the signing? How does the interpreter augment his/her signing to complement the meaning of the speech? Explain.

5. Fox explains that when Sutton first developed SignWriting, it was met with suspicion by many members of the deaf world "mindful of a long paternalistic history of hearing people tampering with ASL." What does Fox mean? Why would deaf people question Sutton's motives?

6. In what ways did SignWriting represent a "coming into language" for Nicole McReynolds? Explain.

WRITING ASSIGNMENTS

1. Visit the Web site for SignWriting maintained by Sutton at www.signwriting.org and review how the system works. Prepare an analysis of the written system explaining its basic premise, how to read it, and its ease of use.

2. Interview at least one deaf person on campus and discuss his or her knowledge and opinions of SignWriting. Ask them to explain, if possible, Fox's statement that when SignWriting was first introduced, the deaf community viewed it with suspicion. Based on your interview, develop an essay on some of the social implications of SignWriting.

3. Explore the challenges of conveying a gestured language, such as ASL, into a written form. Try to tell a simple story, such as "The Three Little Pigs" or "Goldilocks and the Three Bears" without using a phonetic alphabet (heard sounds), but with pictograms (visual depictions) instead. Describe your experience and how it connects to your understanding of language and communication in general in an exploratory essay.

Exploring the Language of Visuals

SignWriting

To hearing individuals, the disconnect between written English and American Sign Language (ASL) is hard to understand. But imagine trying to learn a language that you cannot hear. How would you know what "sh," "oo," or "ch" or any phonetic sound actually meant? In the preceding piece, Margalit Fox describes how SignWriting, developed by Valerie Sutton, is attempting to bridge the literacy gap between ASL and written English.

SignWriting is a visually designed set of symbols that records sign language. It aims to capture the visual subtleties of sign language by recording body movement. Because it records sign language rather than spoken languages such as English or Spanish, SignWriting can be used internationally to communicate.

Valerie Sutton is the inventor of Sutton Movement Writing, a visual alphabet for writing the movements of the human body. Her system includes DanceWriting, used to record dance choreography, and SignWriting—which she developed in 1974—used to communicate sign languages used by the deaf. She is the author of several books on dance choreography, including *DanceWriting Shorthand for Modern and Jazz Dance* (1982), and *The Bournonville School* (1975, 1976). The article that follows, "SignWriting: A Deaf Perspective" employs Sutton's SignWriting alphabet. The article is written by born-deaf, native American Sign Language instructor Lucinda O'Grady Batch, who wrote her thoughts directly in ASL in SignWriting. The English translation of the ASL was done after the ASL article was written. SignWriting gives the Deaf the opportunity to write directly in their own language.

THINKING CRITICALLY

1. Visit Sutton's Web site and read the section "What is SignWriting?" at www.signwriting.org. Then review some of the lessons on SignWriting featured on the Web site. Does the system seem easy to follow and understand? In your opinion, could the system forge stronger language connections between hearing and nonhearing people? Explain.

2. After reviewing the SignWriting alphabet featured at the SignWriting Web site, www.signwriting.org, write a short message using the SignWriting system. Exchange your message with a classmate, and try to translate. How easy or difficult did you find the system to use? Explain.

3. In your opinion, is SignWriting a language or merely a system of symbols? What constitutes "language"? What is an alphabet? Explain.

4. Sutton states on her Web site that SignWriting can be used to read, write, and learn sign language. Explore how SignWriting and sign language are connected. Using two or three examples, compare the movements of ASL for certain words to their SignWriting counterparts.

SignWriting®

A Deaf Perspective...

by Lucinda O'Grady Batch

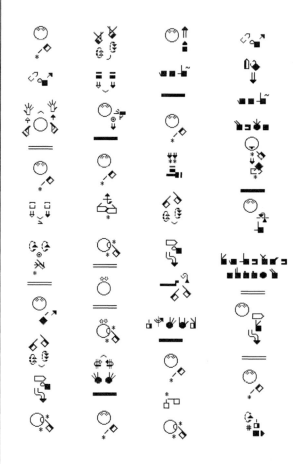

I am writing to tell you how strongly I feel about SignWriting and how much it can benefit Deaf people.

I was born Deaf to a Deaf family and I am a native American Sign Language (ASL) user. I have been working with Sign Writing since 1982. I was the first Deaf person to write articles in ASL, in SignWriting, for the SignWriter Newspaper. Later, Valerie Sutton and I established....

the Deaf Action Committee For SignWriting (the DAC) in 1988.

I think it is very important to spread the word about SignWriting. ASL is a language in its own right, yet until the development of SignWriting, it was a language without a written form. When I found out about Sign Writing I was thrilled to think that at last we would have a way to write our language.

Deaf Americans are one of the very few linguistic minorities that are unable to get books teaching English in

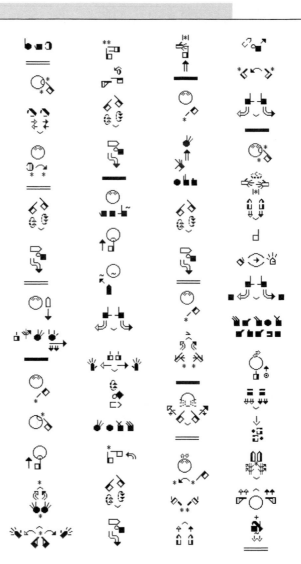

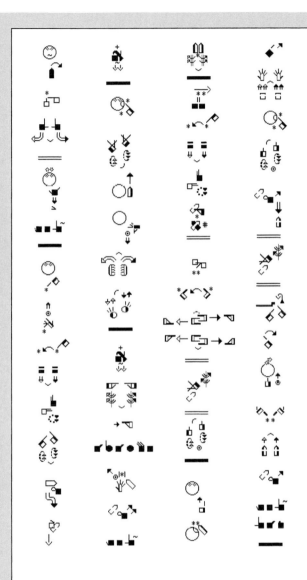

their native language. I feel that we can use SignWriting in order to learn English. Deaf people will benefit greatly from books explaining English grammar and idioms in written ASL.

We can also use it to write down and preserve our stories, poetry and plays. As you know, there are many Deaf playwrights and poets, and up until now, they have not had a way to write the ASL in their literature.

No matter what the
project, SignWriting
encourages us to read
and write and I feel
that is important.

All of us hope that you
will enjoy learning
SignWriting. Your in-
terest and support is a
great help to our Deaf
community.

Lucinda
O'Grady
Batch

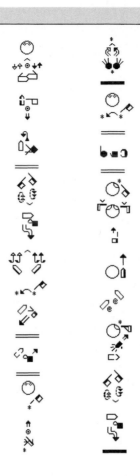

PRESERVING VOICES: DEFENDING ANCIENT LANGUAGES

Speaking in Tongues
James Geary

The Internet, global economics, tourism, and communications continue to shrink the world. While a smaller world may seem to have many benefits, it has put hundreds of languages at risk. The next essay provides an overview of the plight of many languages, how some linguists are trying to save endangered tongues before they die out completely, and the cultural implications of the death of languages.

James Geary serves as the European editor for *Time* magazine. He is the author of *The World in a Phrase (2005),* and the popular science book *The Body Electric: An Anatomy of the New Bionic Senses (2002).* This essay appeared in the July 7, 1997 issue of *Time.*

1 Sitting in a circle with a dozen other members of the native American Tlingit (pronounced klink-it) tribe, Jon Rowan, a 33-year-old schoolteacher, mutters in frustration: "We're babies. All we speak is baby gibberish." The group is gathered at the community center in Klawock, a town of some 800 people on the eastern fringe of Prince of Wales Island. In the Gulf of Alaska, some 40 km off the Alaskan coast, Prince of Wales Island still survives in a state of pristine natural beauty. But this idyllic stretch of land is home to at least one endangered species: the Tlingit language.

2 Rowan and his fellow tribesmen meet every other week in sessions like this to learn their native tongue before the last fluent tribal elder dies. But as Rowan's frustration indicates, the task is made more difficult because Tlingit is becoming extinct. Forty years ago, the entire tribe was fluent in the language, a guttural tongue that relies heavily on accompanying gesture for its meaning. Now it is spoken by only a handful of people throughout southern Alaska and portions of Canada, nearly all of whom are over the age of 60. Since Tlingit was not originally a written language, Rowan and company are trying to record as much of it as possible by translating just about anything they can get their hands on into Tlingit, from Christmas carols like "*Jingle Bells*" to nursery rhymes such as Hickory Dickory Dock.

3 The plight of Tlingit is a small page in the modern version of the Tower of Babel story—with the plot reversed. The Old Testament describes the first, mythical humans as "of one language and of one speech." They built a city on a plain with a tower whose peak reached unto heaven. God, offended by their impudence in building something to rival His own creation, punished them by shattering their single language into many tongues and scattering the speakers. "Therefore is the name of it called Babel," the Bible says, "because the Lord did there confound the language of all the earth."

4 Today, this diaspora of languages is being pulled back. Mass tourism is shrinking the world, bringing once-distant peoples face to face. Telecommunications technology and the Internet are providing people from Peru to Pennsylvania with access to identical information and entertainment, while consumers from Bangkok to Brussels go to the same shops to purchase the same products from the same multinational corporations. All are conversant in the universal language of popular culture and commercial advertising. Much of the world, it seems, is coming to resemble a kind of new Babel, a cozy little global village of common understanding.

5 And there is hard evidence that the number of languages in the world is shrinking: of the roughly 6,500 languages now spoken, up to half are already endangered or on the brink of extinction. Linguists estimate that a language dies somewhere in the world every two weeks. "More conflicts have been created between the world's languages than ever before, causing languages to disappear at an increasing rate," says Stephen Wurm, professor emeritus at the Australian National University in Canberra and editor of UNESCO's *Atlas of the World's Languages in Danger of Disappearing*.

6 Languages, like all living things, depend on their environment to survive. When they die out, it is for reasons analogous to those that cause the extinction

of plant and animal species: they are consumed by predator tongues, deprived of their natural habitats or displaced by more successful competitors. In this type of linguistic natural selection, though, the survival of the fittest is not determined by intrinsic merits and adaptability alone; the economic might, military muscle, and cultural prestige of the country in which a language is spoken play a decisive role. A language's star rises and falls with the fortunes of its speakers. As the only remaining superpower, the United States is now at the zenith of its economic and cultural hegemony. English therefore thrives as the world's lingua franca while minority languages—like Tlingit—succumb to pressure from mightier competitors.

7   But the death of a language such as Tlingit means more than simply the loss of another obscure, incomprehensible tongue. It marks the loss of an entire culture. "Just as the extinction of any animal species diminishes our world, so does the extinction of any language," argues Michael Krauss, an expert on endangered languages at the University of Alaska at Fairbanks. "Any language is as divine and endless a mystery as a living organism. Should we mourn the loss of [a language] any less than the loss of the panda or the California condor?" He says that "Unless we wake up to the problem, we stand to lose up to 95% of our languages in the coming century." Indigenous peoples are not waiting for the slow death of linguistic extinction. They are speaking out to try to save their endangered tongues.

Instruments of Empire

8 In 1492, when Columbus set sail for the New World, medieval linguist Antonio de Nebrija compiled a book of Spanish grammar, the first work of its kind for a European language. When he presented the volume to Queen Isabella, the monarch was puzzled. "What is it for?" she asked. "Your Majesty," the Bishop of Avila replied, "language is the perfect instrument of empire."

9   The European empire-building expeditions of the 16th and 17th centuries heralded the beginning of the end for thousands of languages in North and South America. As the continents were colonized by the European powers and their original inhabitants marginalized, indigenous languages vanished along with their native speakers. In Brazil, for example, an estimated 75 percent of all the languages once spoken in the country have perished since the arrival of the Portuguese in 1500. Of the 180 native tongues that remain, only one is spoken by more than 10,000 people, out of a population of 160 million. "The world is a mosaic of visions," says Aryon Dall'Igna Rodrigues, Brazil's leading authority on native languages. "With each language that disappears, a piece of that mosaic is lost."

10   Among the Krenak in southeastern Brazil, only a handful of elders among the 70 or so tribesmen still speak their mother tongue. Originally a tribe of hunter-gatherers, the Krenak were expelled from their land and herded into reserves by government agents intent on making more space for farming. Up until the 1950s, Catholic missionaries forbade them to perform rituals or speak their own language. The linguistic ban, combined with the tribe's expulsion from its traditional lands, devastated the oral transmission of tribal culture. "Oral traditions are constantly renovated as they're passed on," says Ailton Krenak, 42,

tribal member and head of the Nucleus of Indian Culture, a Sao Paulo–based organization that promotes Brazil's cultural diversity. "When a language is no longer spoken, it's like pinning a dead butterfly on a board—you've interrupted the chain of life."

11   But languages can be remarkably resilient. When empires crumble, suppressed tongues have a way of sprouting up again through the cracks. The dissolution of the Soviet Union in 1991 provided the Krenak with an unexpected opportunity to mend some of the broken links in their oral tradition—and restore a missing piece to the world's mosaic. In 1993, during the period of glasnost begun by Russian President Mikhail Gorbachev, Hungarian linguist Eva Sebastien stumbled across the manuscripts of Henrikh Henrikhovich Maniser, a Russian anthropologist who trekked across Brazil at the turn of the century, in the archives of the Ethnography Institute of the Russian Academy of Sciences in St. Petersburg. During his travels, Maniser recorded traditional Krenak narratives, rituals, and songs in both Russian and the native Krenak, thereby preserving a trove of words, expressions and stories the Krenak believed were gone for good. By translating from Russian into Portuguese, and then cross-checking with Maniser's Krenak, Ailton is working to recover more of the tribe's lost language and return it to his people. "Discovering these words, stories [and] songs is to recover the path of our being," he says, "the path of our dream."

Wealth of Nations

12 Examples of linguistic imperialism are not confined to the 16th and 17th centuries. In the 20th century, political repression has often combined with rapid industrialization to drive a language under. In the former Soviet Union, the country's program of "Russification" for indigenous populations scattered along the southern, northern, and Pacific borders intensified in the 1950s. To inculcate native children with Russian culture, boarding schools, or internats, were established, where children as young as two years old lived in a completely Russian environment for nine months of the year. Internat students routinely lost interest—and proficiency—in their native tongues. This policy of linguistic and cultural repression created a generation estranged from its own language and traditional way of life.

13   One branch of the Nenets tribe, a group of some 20,000 reindeer herders living in the Yamal-Nenets Autonomous Region on the coast of the Kara Sea in the Arctic Circle, has been luckier than most. Although they were subjected to the internat regime and lost their pasture lands on Novaya Zemlya to the Soviet nuclear testing program in 1950s, they were spared the first Siberian oil and gas boom in 1970s, which ravaged the lands and traditions of neighboring tribes.

14   In the treeless expanse beyond the wooden barracks of Salekhard, a town founded by Russian fur traders 400 years ago, the Nentsi lifestyle hasn't changed much for hundreds of years. Their language embodies the rites and rituals of a life set to the rhythms of the tundra. The year begins in November with "the hunt for the polar fox"; spring's advent is marked by the birth of the first reindeer fawns; summer's start is known as nyarkanze iriy, "the month of the flowering grasses." But with the discovery in the late 1980s of huge natural gas

beds on the Yamal Peninsula, the Nentsi way is threatened. Foreign companies are lining up to exploit the fabulous wealth lying below what has come to be known as the "Nentsi Emirates." How can the Nentsi preserve their language if their way of life is lost?

15   "Our language has the smell of smoke," says Valentina Nyarui, a Nentsi educator who is leading the effort to maintain her tribal tongue. Nyarui is convinced the Nentsi must cling to their centuries-old patterns of herding and hunting. "Children need to see the flocks of geese rising from the lakes," she says, "the herds of reindeer with their massive horns." To this end, she is collecting and composing folk songs and lullabies to encourage language transmission from parent to child.

16   Meanwhile, development plans for the region are being vetted by the Committee for the Protection of the Environment and Natural Resources in Moscow to ensure that the economy and the ecosystem are given equal consideration. The Russian Duma is also debating the establishment of "ethnic nature parks," a policy that would guarantee indigenous peoples the right to pursue their traditional lifestyles in areas being developed. But even if ecological destruction is averted, many Nentsi might be tempted to trade their traditional lifestyles and language for jobs with the gas companies. Why should young Nentsi bother with their mother tongue when their futures will depend on being able to speak Russian? Nyarui says this linguistic and cultural erosion has already begun. "The Nentsi in towns are losing their language," she explains. "They live in Russian homes. They don't wear their traditional clothes. They don't tell their traditional stories." The challenge facing the Nentsi—and the Russian government—is how to exploit the natural wealth of the Yamal Peninsula without destroying the cultural wealth of the Nentsi people.

The Smell of Rain

17 With just over one-fifth of all existing languages, the Pacific basin is one of the most linguistically diverse regions in the world. Since European colonization though, the number of native languages has dwindled considerably. When white settlers first arrived in Australia in 1788, the continent supported some 250 Aboriginal tongues. Today, only 20 are considered still viable.

18   Australian Aborigines endured a policy of cultural and linguistic assimilation similar to that of the Nentsi. For many Aboriginal people, the disappearance of their traditional language still leaves a painful gap in their sense of self. "You feel lost without it," says Rhonda Inkamala, 36, a language coordinator at the bilingual Yapirinya school in Alice Springs. "You feel left out." To make sure Aboriginal children are not deprived of their linguistic heritage, Inkamala helps organize a program through which students at the Yapirinya school spend two days a week on cultural excursions into the surrounding area with local tribal elders.

19   Aboriginal languages are distinctive for the rich vocabularies they use to describe the natural world. The evocative imagery they contain expresses how closely Aboriginal clans are linked to the land. One traditional song in the threatened Ngiyampaa language of New South Wales, for example, describes a bird whose tail twitches like a walu. The closest English approximation to walu is "a strip of bark

dangling from a tree." In the Eastern Arrernte language of Central Australia the simple, sensual word nyimpe denotes "the smell of rain."

20   But the value of Aboriginal languages does not lie in their poetic beauty alone. Nicholas Evans, head of linguistics at Melbourne University and a specialist in Aboriginal languages, credits these little-known tongues with advances in science. Botanists are discovering new species of flora by researching the different Aboriginal names given to seemingly identical plants. The study of these languages can also shed new light on the migrations of early populations and the origins of cultural innovations. "The process has just begun of correlating linguistic with archaeological facts," says Evans. "But we can infer a lot about Australia's ancient past through looking at information furnished by languages. This is lost when the language goes."

A War of Words

21 Linguistic revival is often associated with a resurgence of ethnic or national identity. Northern Ireland is a classic example of how language can become bound up with the struggle for this type of cultural and political recognition. After conquering Ireland during the middle of the 16th century, the English virtually eliminated the Irish-speaking ruling classes and their cultural institutions. English displaced Irish as the lingua franca of government and public life, while Irish became associated with economic and cultural backwardness. When Northern Ireland was founded in 1921, the new political establishment favored the Protestant, English-speaking Unionists, relegating Irish to the Catholic Nationalist community.

22   But when the current Troubles began in Northern Ireland in 1968, Irish became a badge of cultural and national identity. Sinn Fein (Irish for "Ourselves Alone"), the political wing of the Irish Republican Army, is still run in a loosely bilingual fashion. Many members of the republican movement, including current Sinn Fein President Gerry Adams, first learned Irish in prison. A gesture of defiance and a boost to self-esteem, knowledge of Irish also had an enormous practical advantage: prisoners could converse in a language that their guards didn't understand. There are now two Irish-only wings in the Maze prison 20 km southwest of Belfast. "Sinn Fein has no monopoly on the Irish language," says West Belfast Sinn Fein councillor Mairtin O Muilleoir. "But we believe that, in creating a new Ireland, we need a strong Irish identity. The Irish language can help create that."

23   While language activists claim Irish is above politics, its close association with the I.R.A. and Sinn Fein does little to garner acceptance by Unionists. But the language is nevertheless winning a lively following among the general population, mainly in the nationalist areas of Belfast and Londonderry. On the Falls Road in nationalist West Belfast alone, there are more than 60 Irish language classes.

24   This new-found popularity is exemplified south of the border as well by the first Irish-language television channel, Teilifis na Gaeilge (TnaG). Launched last year, the station broadcasts music, documentary, dramatic, sports, and news programs aimed primarily at young people. "The largest group of fluent Irish speakers

WORLD'S TOP TEN LANGUAGES	
First-language speaker estimates given in millions	
1. Mandarin Chinese	726
2. English	427
3. Spanish	266
4. Hindi	182
5. Arabic	181
6. Portuguese	165
7. Bengali	162
8. Russian	158
9. Japanese	124
10. German	121

Source: *The Cambridge Encyclopedia of Language*

is the under-25s," says TnaG spokesman Padhraic O. Ciardha. "There has been a huge upsurge in interest in Irish culture, and TnaG is reflecting that. We've been able to prove that something indigenous doesn't have to be backward-looking."

Leaving the Nest

25 The most serious indication of a language's imminent demise is when it is no longer spoken by children. Cut the cords of linguistic transmission between the generations and when the elders die, their language dies with them. For much of this century in New Zealand, the decline in fluent Maori speakers was drastic and seemingly irreversible. From an estimated 64,000 in the early 1970s, the number fell to around 10,000 in 1995. There was almost no language transmission from Maori parents to their children during the 1960s and 1970s. But since the first Kohanga Reo (language nests)—a nationwide network of early childhood centers that nurture a knowledge of the Maori language among children—were established in 1982, this downward spiral has been halted.

26 Language nests provide a fun, home-like environment for children under the age of five, where they are intensively exposed to the Maori language. Paid staff are a mix of elderly Maori speakers, usually grandparents, and younger teachers. There are now over 800 language nests across the country, which have introduced more than 100,000 Maori children to their native tongue.

27 Maori was made an official language of New Zealand, alongside English, in 1987. Some Maori leaders are now petitioning the government to restore the country's original Maori name, Aotearoa, meaning Land of the Long White Cloud. Today, almost 60 percent of all New Zealand schoolchildren—Maori and non-Maori alike— study the language to some extent. But an even surer sign of Maori's renewed vigor is the fact that New Zealand English is dotted with Maori words and expressions. The most common, kia ora, an all-purpose salutation, is increasingly used instead of

"hello" both in general conversation and when answering the telephone. "Language is absolutely important to cultural integrity and survival," says Timoti Karetu, 60, head of the Maori Language Commission. "The more Maori is used to pepper New Zealand speech, the more it becomes a unique language to New Zealand."

28   That uniqueness is plain to see before each match played by New Zealand's national rugby team, the All Blacks. The haka, a fierce traditional Maori dance, is intended to intimidate the opposition. Players line up on the field and make a series of aggressive gestures with their hands and feet while beginning to chant "Ka mate! Ka mate! Ka ora! Ka ora!" The Ka Mate haka tells the story of the great Maori warrior Te Rauparaha's daring escape from his enemies. It translates roughly as: "It is death! It is life! . . . One last upward step, then step forth into the sun that shines!"

29   For many of the world's indigenous tongues, a very thin line separates the new dawn of language revival from the black hole of extinction. But the efforts of communities as diverse as the Tlingit and the Krenak show that it is still possible for small groups of determined individuals to confound the forces of globalization and mass culture that are the prime architects of today's Tower of Babel. In the coming struggle for linguistic survival, native peoples like the Maori may yet have the last word.

THINKING CRITICALLY

1. What obstacles do Rowan and his fellow tribesman face in saving their language?

2. Why does Geary compare the plight of Tlingit to a modern version of the Tower of Babel story, with the plot reversed? (If necessary, review the Tower of Babel story at the beginning of this chapter.)

3. How is modern technology threatening ancient languages such as Tlingit? What role has globalization in general had on language?

4. What is linguistic imperialism? In what ways have governments tried to control native languages? Why do some governments seek to suppress them?

5. What can aboriginal languages tell us about the culture of a people? Why are their vocabularies important?

WRITING ASSIGNMENTS

1. What are the ramifications of the death of a language, both for the people who speak it and society as a whole? Write an essay exploring what it means to lose an ancient tongue.

2. Geary's essay focuses on what is lost when a language dies. Write an essay in which you either support the preservation of obscure native languages or encourage the globalization movement towards fewer languages.

3. Write a personal narrative exploring how your own language has helped shaped your personal and cultural identity. Include in your evaluation any local words that identify you as from a particular region of the U.S. What could a linguist learn about you from the way you speak?

Lost In Translation

Soo Ji Min

Linguists estimate that over half of the thousands of languages currently spoken across the globe are endangered. When the last speaker of an ancient tongue dies, the language is considered "dead." Linguists are racing to document these languages before they are lost from the historical record forever—along with the cultural and social history that connected a people to their language. The next article details how linguist K. David Harrison from Swarthmore College is trying to preserve the history of the Chulym language in Siberia.

Soo Ji Min is a journalist and social activist. This article first appeared in the November 2004 issue *of Science and Sprit* magazine.

1   Vassilij Gabov leans forward to address the ninety-six-year-old woman on the other side of the couch. In gravelly Russian, the native Siberian asks Varvara Budeeva where she's from. There's no answer. Gabov repeats the question. Still unable to provoke a response, the heavy-set man moves across the couch and sits directly beside Budeeva. Seamlessly switching to a different language, he shouts into her ear: "Where were you born? What clan are you from?"

2   Had Gabov been wearing a black suit, dark sunglasses, and shiny wingtip shoes, he might be mistaken for a mobster interrogating a recalcitrant witness. But his weathered face and soft eyes convey only the best of intentions. In reality, Gabov lives in Tegul'det, a remote village in central Siberia. The former truck driver has been hired as a guide and translator for American linguists spending ten days on a pilot language expedition in southwestern Siberia. K. David Harrison, a specialist in Tuvan and other Siberian languages, is searching for native speakers of Middle Chulym (chew-LIM), a language on the brink of extinction.

3   Harrison is having trouble getting started. The first Chulym speaker he and Gabov located was completely deaf; the second was incoherent. Budeeva was next on the list, and while she never does answer Gabov's questions—because, as luck would have it, she too is totally deaf—she becomes the fourth recorded speaker of Middle Chulym when she steps outside to wave goodbye to her visitors and speaks the Chulym word for "dog" while pointing at her pet.

4   But it is Gabov, whose shift from Russian to Chulym surprises everyone in the room, who reveals himself as the third, and most intriguing, of thirty-five native speakers Harrison will find concentrated in six isolated villages in southwestern Siberia. Just two days earlier, Gabov spoke only Russian to Harrison. Fearing that his Chulym was deficient, Gabov kept his knowledge of his native tongue hidden, leading Harrison to a pair of older Chulym speakers instead. But spurred as much by Harrison's quest as by the researcher's video camera and voice recorder, Gabov reached out to Budeeva, and made a connection through a shared language that had retreated as much from his mind as from his tongue. And in that instant he became, at fifty-two years old, the youngest known speaker of Middle Chulym.

5   "The way you talk identifies the group you belong to," says David Lightfoot, dean of Georgetown University's Graduate School of Arts and Sciences and a professor of linguistics. "A language essentially disappears because people choose at some level of consciousness to adopt another group's language . . . it's an act of allegiance to one culture and a rejection of another culture."

6   But more than the rejection of a culture, the death of a language can be a step toward the death of the culture it expresses and embodies. Encoded in Middle Chulym, and in every language, are clues to how people lived—kinship systems, economies, livelihood, and leisure. "Language conveys evidence of cultural phenomena," says Lightfoot. "If a language disappears then the cultural evidence disappears also, because it was only embedded in the language."

7   Nearly 3,500 of the world's languages are at risk of extinction in one lifetime—roughly half the world's total. And there's little stopping the dissolution of the Turkic language that originated on the upper reaches of the Chulym River in the district of Tomsk. In a community of 426, only thirty-five elders are fluent speakers. The rest speak Russian only. "It's a moribund language," says Harrison.

8   Until he arrived last summer, Harrison, who spends the school year teaching at Swarthmore College in Pennsylvania, says the Chulym people had not been visited by a scientist since a group of Soviet linguists came through in 1972. Even then, their language had only been written down by the scientists in a few notebooks and locked away in an archive. Unless something is done to revive the language and cultivate it within the younger generation, Chulym, and much of the culture it reflects, will completely vanish over the next thirty to forty years.

9   "A working language conveys so much about a culture—ethics, history, love, family dynamics—in short: the whole life of a people," says Diane Ackerman, a visiting professor at Cornell University and author of *An Alchemy of the Mind: The Marvel and Mystery of the Brain*. "To lose a single language is like watching a species of animal go extinct and know it will never occur again on the planet."

10   Already starting to fade from the Chulym cultural landscape are ancestral hunting stories that once were verbally shared, retold, and embellished. Tales about bears, for example, never mentioned the word "bear" directly, explains Harrison. "They would say 'furry one' or 'brown animal.'" For the Chulym, the bear is a mystical animal to be both feared and respected. It is a powerful symbol, one that demands special rituals be performed to assuage the bear's spirit. These rituals formed part of an animistic belief system, which holds that spirits inhabit inanimate objects—rocks, trees, bodies of water—as well as living creatures.

11   But these same tales, told in Russian, are mere skeletons of the originals. As the Russian language absorbed the Chulym speakers, these stories were relegated to the recesses of the Chylum minds and culture, weakening their animistic religious beliefs. At one time, special practitioners called *qam* were prevalent in traditional society. Similar to shamans, they functioned as experts at interacting with the spirit world, and were called upon in dire situations, such as serious illness or death. Harrison discovered that at most, only two people still alive in the community might actually have seen a shamanic ritual with their own eyes—one of them being Varvara Budeeva. Shamans disappeared long ago from Chulym society because

native Siberians and Russians were converted to Orthodox Christianity, which forbade Shamanic practices. "We feel that [animism and Shamanism] are two really essential elements in their culture and even though they've mostly been forgotten, there are little scraps left that you can look at," says Harrison.

12   Recording these ancient tales on paper, however, may produce nothing more than additional cultural remnants. Lost in the transition from the spoken word to the written word is the vibrant history and oral traditions encoded in the Middle Chulym language. These codes, according to Harrison, survive only through speech. "The great majority of the world's languages have no writing system at all, and they do just fine without it," he says. "No writing system has ever been devised that is capable of capturing the full complexity and richness of language." So when a language draws its last breath and disappears, Harrison worries that a unique way of seeing the world dies with it—an extinction of ideas. How the mind produces, processes, and understands language is severely compromised as languages wither and fade. In order for linguists to answer the question posed by Noam Chomsky: "What is a possible human language?" they must examine *all* human languages. To many linguists, the question is simply unanswerable if one looks only at major world languages like Chinese, Russian, or Spanish. Smaller, local languages often provide evidence of new types of linguistic structures or typologies. In all languages, for example, a sentence may contain a subject, object, and a verb—of which six possible configurations exist. Until recently, Harrison says, linguists had found only five of the six combinations employed in human language. The discovery of the missing link—object, verb, *then* subject—was made by Desmond Derbyshire, who found this usage in the endangered Amazonian language Hixkaryana.

13   "The languages that are disappearing are most unusual in their structures compared to the majority languages that are displacing them," says Doug Whalen, president of the Connecticut-based Endangered Language Fund. "There is a global tendency for [majority languages] to be less complicated than [smaller languages] morphologically. English has been simplifying its morphology for centuries . . . 'Thou,' for example, has disappeared from modern usage."

14   If these smaller languages go extinct without being documented, warns Harrison, "we simply will never know the full range of human cognitive capacity because many of the less likely and rarer types of complex structures will have disappeared."

15   Some language experts offer translation as a modern antidote to language loss. "After all, we can translate pretty well from one language to another," says Steven Pinker, a linguist and the Johnstone Family Professor in the Department of Psychology at Harvard University. "During World War II, the Navajo Code Talkers managed to transfer pretty arcane modern military secrets using the Navajo language."

16   But, argues Harrison, specialized knowledge encoded in a native language and used in a particular context or setting can be lost when speakers shift from one language to another, more dominant tongue. The Middle Chulym, for example, once relied on fishing as their primary means of subsistence. Their language would have reflected this—using detailed words to describe fishing nets and traps, a fish's lifecycle, behaviors, body parts—and would have had a fairly complex classification

system. "When the Middle Chulym switch over to speaking Russian, they lose some of this knowledge," argues Harrison. "It's very hard to prove, but that's my starting hypothesis—that there are complex knowledge systems in any language, but especially in languages where people live very closely to the land and are dependent on it."

17   Even in situations where a language's structure remains, the way the native language is used changes, often taking on the speaking style and attitudes of the more dominant language. "The way we experience language is not through its structure directly, but the way its structure gets used in making continuous discourse," explains Michael Silverstein, Charles F. Grey Distinguished Service Professor in the departments of anthropology, linguistics, and psychology at the University of Chicago. As a native language group shifts to acquiring a more dominant one, the replacing language can, over time, wreak havoc on the weaker language. "It's the subtle ways in which a culturally distinctive communicative perspective emerges in the process of actually using language that gets very much transformed and frequently destroyed over a couple of generations."

18   After recording a Chulym bear story, for example, Harrison played it back to a sixteen-year-old with some knowledge of Chulym. The young listener understood that the story had something to do with a bear, but nothing more. The key to accessing the rich meaning and history locked behind a simple tale was lost with the demise of the Chulym language.

19   "The kids know their grandparents speak some funny other language, but they don't know what it is," Harrison says, noting he found just four "passive speakers" of the language—all in their mid-thirties—in addition to the thirty-five fluent speakers. "It's hard to imagine what it would take exactly to get them interested enough to learn it."

20   Once marginalized, a language often struggles to survive, but bringing a language back from the brink of extinction takes intensive effort, money, and community support. Because the Chuylm community is impoverished and small, the chances are good that its native language will die. "When that particular mode of communication disappears, they will be completely deprived of their own history and culture," says Naoki Sakai, a professor of Japanese history and literature at Cornell University.

21   The Soviet Union's role in the gradual demise of the Chulym language began in the 1940s when Joseph Stalin ordered Chulym and other Siberian children to attend boarding schools and prohibited the instruction of any non-Russian language. As children, Gabov and other Chulym speakers were effectively forced to abandon their mother tongue. "Chulym was viewed as a gutter language," explains Gabov, reverting back to the Russian he is more comfortable speaking. Chulym, if spoken at all, was confined to the privacy of individual homes. Ashamed and afraid to speak Chulym in public, many hid their knowledge of their native tongue, as Gabov did when he first met Harrison.

22   The plight of the language worsened in the 1970s as the Soviet government implemented its "village consolidation program," forcibly relocating the Chulym into larger, Russian-speaking settlements—further diluting the population base and thinning the concentration of native speakers.

23   To some linguists, the shift from Chulym to Russian is as much evidence of a natural evolution as it is a result of sociopolitical pressure. While lamenting the potential loss of subject matter and culture, Lightfoot maintains a scholarly distance. "I don't think linguists are in a position to say to people, 'You should do all you can to preserve your language.' It's an individual choice and a Darwinian process. There's not much we [as linguists] should do about it."

24   But sometimes the true preferences of native speakers are not readily apparent to the linguistic community at large. When he found Gabov last summer, Harrison not only located a driver and a guide, he discovered a living reminder that language may be banished from the tongue, but not necessarily from the mind. Growing up in the shadow of the linguistic repression imposed by the Soviet Union, Gabov had every reason to completely discard his native tongue—fully and finally forgetting that part of his heritage. But for a three-year period in the late 1980s, he did just the opposite. Each day during the winter hunting season, Gabov made entries into a journal. A *written* journal. Developing an orthography adapted from the Russian alphabet, the same man who for days hid his knowledge of the language Harrison was seeking actually devised a system of writing it down.

25   Sadly, the linguistic insecurities Gabov displayed when Harrison first met him are deep-seated. When Gabov shared his creation with a Russian acquaintance, he was promptly ridiculed for his attempts. At that point, Gabov says, he threw away his journal and did not write again. Any possibility of a written record of the fading language would likely have died with Gabov's entries had it not been for his chance meeting with Harrison. Gabov was able to reproduce his system for Harrison, who, in turn, plans to publish both a children's storybook and an elementary primer—both written in Middle Chulym, and both at the request of the Chulym tribal council.

26   When the storybook is printed next year, it will include an encounter between Gabov and a moose, along with a bear-hunting story and a tale of a Shamaness, as told by Varvara Budeeva. The text will be augmented with illustrations drawn by Middle Chulym children who listened to the stories as read to them in Russian.

27   While it may be too late to preserve the Chulym language as a medium for daily communication and repository of traditional knowledge among the Chulym people, it is not too late to record it, and in so doing make at least some small part of the knowledge available to future generations—particularly the young Chulym.

28   "These languages need to be documented for science," Harrison says, "and for the native community itself."

THINKING CRITICALLY

1. Why does Vassilij Gabov speak Russian to Varvara Budeeva before he switches to Chulym? What does his hesitation to speak Chulym reveal about how we use language? What accounts for his "linguistic insecurity"?

2. David Lightfoot observes that "the way you talk identifies the group you belong to" (paragraph 5). What does the way you talk reveal about your group?

3. Why do linguists believe it is important to document endangered languages?

4. Paragraphs 10–12 describe some Chulym legends. What is lost in the translation of these legends into Russian?

5. What insights do human languages offer to our understanding of the human mind? Provide some examples from the essay.

6. Why did the Soviet Union forbid Siberian children from speaking Chulym? What role does politics play in the extinction or preservation of a language?

WRITING ASSIGNMENTS

1. Visit Dr. K. David Harrison's research Web site at www.swarthmore.edu/SocSci/dharris2/. Evaluate what he is doing to raise awareness about language endangerment and extinction. Review his research and write a short essay explaining his research, focus, efforts to preserve language, and the likelihood of success.

2. Imagine that you are one of only a handful of speakers of your native language in a small area of the world. What steps, if any, would you take to preserve your language, and why? If you would likely choose not to save your native tongue, explain your reasons for not doing so.

Tribal Talk
Michelle Nijhuis

The survival of a language depends not just on the people who currently speak it, but on passing it to the next generation. Dominant languages used for commerce, politics, and education make it difficult for many languages to survive, with children learning and using a native tongue only at home. In this essay, Michelle Nijhuis describes how some immersion schools are trying to revive and preserve Native American languages, such as the Blackfeet language.

Michelle Nijhuis is a contributing editor of the environmental journal *High Country News,* and her work has appeared in many publications including *Smithsonian, Salon.com, The Christian Science Monitor, The San Francisco Chronicle, Mother Jones, Sierra, Orion,* and *Audubon.* She is the winner of the Walter Sullivan Award for scientific journalism. This article was first published in the November 2003 issue of *Smithsonian Magazine.*

1 Jesse DesRosier begins each school day like lots of kids. The eighth grader hangs up his coat, pulls off his muddy boots and lopes into his classroom, raising a hand in greeting. Then he opens his mouth, and out comes a small miracle.

2 "*Oki, aahsaapinakos!*"

3 Hello, good morning! Bantering easily in the drawn-out vowels and clipped endings of a nearly extinct language, Jesse and his 35 classmates are the first fluent Blackfoot speakers in more than two generations. Here at the Nizipuhwahsin, or RealSpeakSchool, on the Blackfeet Reservation in far northwestern Montana, the kids spend all day speaking their ancestral tongue. From kindergarten through eighth grade, they study math, reading, history and other subjects in Blackfoot.

4 "Some people think our language is dead, but it's not," says DesRosier, a lanky teenager with a ready grin and dark, narrow braids that reach the middle of his back. "We still have our language and we're bringing it back."

5   What's at stake is more than words. Filled with nuance and references to Blackfeet history and traditions, the language embodies a culture. "The language allows kids to unravel the mysteries of their heritage," says Darrell Kipp, director of the school and one of its founders.

6   The Blackfoot language, also known as Piegan, has been in danger of disappearing for nearly a century. From the late 1800s through the 1960s, the Bureau of Indian Affairs forced tens of thousands of Native Americans into English-only government boarding schools. Taken hundreds of miles from the reservations, the children were often beaten for speaking native languages and sent home ashamed of them. As adults, they cautioned their own children to speak English only.

7   "We were told, 'You'd be better off learning only English, so what happened to us won't happen to you,' " says 68-year-old Cynthia Kipp, whose grandchildren attend Real Speak.

8   Over the decades, many tribal languages fell silent. Of the 300 languages spoken in North America at the time of European settlement, 150 have disappeared completely, and only a handful of the survivors are acquiring new speakers. By 1980, the remaining Blackfoot speakers were more than 50 years old, and Blackfoot was headed down the well-worn road to oblivion.

9   But in 1982, Darrell Kipp, now 59, a Harvard graduate and technical writer (and distant cousin of Cynthia Kipp), moved back to the reservation's windblown plains after a 20-year absence. He met up with Dorothy Still Smoking, who had also returned, in 1979, after earning a master's from the University of South Dakota, to become a dean at the reservation's community college. Both wanted to learn the language they'd occasionally heard but rarely spoke as children. "There was always a missing piece in my life," says Still Smoking, 54, "and that was the cultural component. The language contains everything—our values and wisdom, our outlook on the world."

10   In 1987, Kipp, Still Smoking, and a fluent Blackfoot speaker named Edward Little Plume, 73, founded the nonprofit Piegan Institute, dedicated to restoring Blackfoot and other tribal languages. Because many people on the reservation still associated their language with humiliating experiences at boarding school, the institute was controversial. "We met people who could not only not speak the language but also had a negative view of it," says Kipp.

11   To calm the waters, Kipp, Still Smoking and Little Plume made a video about tribal elders' experiences with the language and distributed 2,000 copies among the reservation's 7,000 residents. The video did the trick. "People realized we didn't give up the language by choice," says Kipp. "Our parents and grandparents didn't pass it on to us because they didn't want us to be abused."

12   Now Kipp and his colleagues had to figure out the best way to teach fluency. Though some local high schools had offered tribal language classes for years, these brief encounters taught familiarity, not fluency. "I'd teach the numbers up to five, and by the next week they'd have forgotten them," says Arthur Westwolf, a Real Speak teacher who worked in the reservation's public schools for 18 years.

13   In the early 1980s, the Maori of New Zealand and native Hawaiian Islanders had pioneered a different strategy by creating immersion centers called language nests, in which students hear and speak their ancestral language all day.

14   Intrigued by this approach, Kipp and the others raised private foundation grants sufficient to start classes at day care centers in 1995. Four years later, they finished construction of Real Speak, a one-story, three-classroom school in Browning, Montana.

15   Today, demand for the few openings at the school, where tuition is $100 a month, has parents signing up their toddlers, and the school's large, airy classrooms explode with activity. While younger students review their numbers or sing a Blackfoot version of "Frère Jacques," older students present illustrated short stories they've written in Blackfoot, work on math problems, or visit the local senior center.

16   Though students may have heard no more than a few words of Blackfoot before entering, they are soon chatting and joking in the language. They also use it outside the classroom: one second grader, Leo John Bird III, plans to say a prayer in Blackfoot at a rodeo in memory of his grandfather, while other students rehearse a play about the Lewis and Clark expedition that they plan to perform at the University of Montana.

17   The school has received visitors from other tribes, including the Tlingit of Alaska and the Pechanga of Southern California. The Washoe recently opened an immersion school in Nevada, and the Ojibwa have established several such programs in Minnesota and Wisconsin. In Montana, two other tribes have started their own immersion programs. Supporters say the impact runs deep. "This is a way to heal the identity confusion that so many of our students go through," says Joyce Silverthorne, a tribal education director and member of the Montana Board of Public Education. Through immersion, she says, students "become well grounded in who they are." In Indian Country, where the frequency of suicide among adolescents is more than double the national rate, such confidence can be, literally, a lifesaver.

18   "It makes kids proud to be Blackfeet," says Jesse DesRosier, who recently graduated from Real Speak but returns for language classes. "When I have kids, I want to try and put them in this school." And that's not all. "We beat the public school in flag football. We did all our plays in Indian, and the other team didn't know what we were saying. That's how we won."

THINKING CRITICALLY

1. Why does Nijhuis describe Jesse's greeting to his classmates as "a small miracle"?

2. Why have over 150 tribal languages spoken in North America disappeared completely? In what ways have native speakers themselves contributed to the death of their language?

3. This essay describes how immersion programs are being used to save ancestral tongues such as the Blackfeet and Maori languages. Do you think such programs are a good idea? Would you participate in such a program if your native language were endangered? Why or why not?

4. What is the opinion of the author towards immersion schools? Identify areas in her essay in which she reveals her position.

WRITING ASSIGNMENTS

1. Research more about the Blackfeet language online at www.native_languages_ blackfoot.htm and www.omniglot.com/writing/blackfoot.htm. Write a short informational essay about the language, its history, and the effort to save it.

2. Find out if there are any endangered languages spoken in your area, including local tribes or immigrant populations. Contact your school's linguistic department (if it has one) for more information on endangered languages in your area. Are any efforts underway to preserve or document these languages?

3. Many ancient North American languages have died or are dying because of the marginalization of Native American culture. Prepare a research report on the languages or one particular language lost in the United States or Canada as a result of western immigration and industrialization.

Say No More
Jack Hitt

> While many languages survived in isolation, they now struggle, and often die out when a more widely spoken language encroaches on their territory. Such is the case of Kawesqar, a language spoken in an isolated area of southern Chile. With Spanish the dominant language of commerce and education, few people bother to speak the language, and children are failing to learn it at all. The next article, by journalist Jack Hitt, explores the human meaning of language loss.
>
> Jack Hitt is contributing editor to *Harper's*, *GQ*, *Lingua Franca*, and *This American Life* and a contributing writer to the *New York Times*, in which this article was first published on February 29, 2004.

1 Languages die the way many people do—at home, in silence, attended by loved ones straining to make idle conversation.

2   "Did you sell any baskets?" Gabriela Paterito asks her neighbor Francisco Arroyo in her vowelly Spanish. She's in her two-room shack in Puerto Eden, a tiny fishing village on Wellington Island in the Patagonia region of southern Chile. There is a long, long silence. She's a short woman, dense from some 70 years of life, but with a girl's head of beautiful black hair. In the room are Francisco and a few others, among the last six speakers of Kawesqar, the language native to these parts since the last ice age.

3   Linguists now estimate that half of the more than 6,000 languages currently spoken in the world will become extinct by the end of this century. In reaction, there are numerous efforts to slow the die-off—from graduate students heading into the field to compile dictionaries; to charitable foundations devoted to the cause, like the Endangered Language Fund; to transnational agencies, some with melancholic names appropriate to the task, like the European Bureau for Lesser Used Languages. Chile started a modest program, not long after the ugly debates surrounding Christopher Columbus in 1992, to save Kawesqar (Ka-WES-kar) and Yaghan, the last two native languages of southern Chile. But how does one salvage an ailing language when the economic advantages of, say, Spanish are all around you? And is it

possible to step inside a dying language to learn whether it can be saved and, more rudely, whether it should be? |

4   Gabriela crams another stick into her wood stove to keep us dry and warm. The rain is coming now like nails, as it does most days. The silence stretches out. You begin to feel it, like a cold draft. Three or four aching minutes of it. My boots need some examining.

5   "Canastos," mutters Francisco, repeating the Spanish word for baskets, his grunting tone suggesting a bad day. When languages die under the pressure of a dominant tongue like Spanish, there is a familiar path of retreat. The language will withdraw from the public sphere first, hiding out in the living rooms and kitchens of the fluent, where it becomes increasingly private and intimate and frail. Francisco takes a two-foot length of reedy grass and softens it by rubbing it against the stove. All around weaving begins—the distinctive Kawesqar baskets, small with long grassy handles.

6   "It's been raining all day," Francisco adds, again in Spanish. Juan Carlos, who is 39 and my guide, motions me to give him a cigarette. Juan Carlos was born and grew up here but left at 15 for school. Now college-educated, he has devoted his life and work to helping the Kawesqar community. (He has just finished a documentary film about the Kawesqar.) He doesn't smoke, he told me, except here. For the last few days, smoking and enduring long silences have pretty much accounted for our social life. I haven't smoked seriously for 15 years. I'm blowing through two packs a day.

7   Every window here frames a magnificent photo op. Outside Gabriela's is a curving line of shacks hugging the shore of a small bay, bright red-and-yellow fishing boats beached in front, and behind, a dramatic ascent of mountains capped in white—gushing here and there with little snow-melt waterfalls. Full-spectrum rainbows break out so frequently that no one notices but me and the tourists. They, too, are visible out the window, all wearing their orange cruise-ship-issue rain slickers, their cameras aimed aloft. To get here, it's a three-day chug by boat through the cold, uninhabited island channels of Patagonia. Once a week, the tourists come. They have less than an hour onshore to feel the intensity of its remote beauty—and maybe buy a native basket—before motoring out to the anchored cruise ship and a night of pisco sours.

8   "A lot of rain," announces Juan Carlos. The fire crackles and hisses. The rain continues, staccato.

9   "Rain," Gabriela adds.

10   I sit quietly, smoking my way through their Samuel Beckett dialogue.

11   "Not many baskets," Francisco says, offering his full report.

12   I wonder if I should ask them to speak Kawesqar, but I don't want to intrude. I want to get a sense of when they naturally converse in their language. Later, Juan Carlos tells me that the elder Kawesqar feel awkward speaking their moribund language around me. It's a combination of embarrassment and a sense that they don't want to make me feel uncomfortable. As the rain pours down, I light up a cigarette. My very presence here to observe this thing, difficult to see, has made it disappear.

13   The Kawesqar are famous for their adaptation to this cold, rainy world of islands and channels. The first Europeans were stunned. The Kawesqar and the other natives

of the region traveled in canoes, naked, oiled with blubber, occasionally wearing an animal skin. The men sat at the front and hunted sea lions with spears. The women paddled. The children stayed in the sanctuary between their parents, maintaining fire in a sand pit built in the middle of the canoe. Keeping fire going in a land of water was the most critical and singular adaptation of the Kawesqar. As a result, fire blazed continuously in canoes and at the occasional landfall. The first European explorers marveled at the sight of so much fire in a wet and cold climate, and the Spanish named the southernmost archipelago the land of fire, Tierra del Fuego.

14   When Charles Darwin first encountered the Kawesqar and the Yaghans, years before he wrote *The Origin of Species,* he is said to have realized that man was just another animal cunningly adapting to local environmental conditions. But that contact and the centuries to follow diminished the Kawesqar, in the 20th century, to a few dozen individuals. In the 1930's, the remaining Kawesqar settled near a remote military installation—Puerto Eden, now inhabited mostly by about 200 Chileans from the mainland who moved here to fish.

15   The pathology of a dying language shifts to another stage once the language has retreated to the living room. You can almost hear it disappearing. There is Grandma, fluent in the old tongue. Her son might understand her, but he also learned Spanish and grew up in it. The grandchildren all learn Spanish exclusively and giggle at Grandma's funny chatter.

16   ⫽ In two generations, a healthy language—even one with hundreds of thousands of speakers—can collapse entirely, sometimes without anyone noticing. This process is happening everywhere.⫽In North America, the arrival of Columbus and the Europeans who followed him whittled down the roughly 300 native languages to only about 170 in the 20th century. According to Marianne Mithun, a linguist at the University of California at Santa Barbara, the recent evolution of English as a global language has taken an even greater toll. "Only one of those 170 languages is not officially endangered today," Mithun said. "Greenlandic Eskimo."

17   ⫽Without the revitalization of youth, a language can go from being alive to endangered (declining speakers among the young), then moribund (only elderly speakers left alive), then dead (the last known speaker dies)—all linguistic terms of art.⫽William Sutherland, the author of a study in *Nature* magazine last spring, compared the die-off to an environmental catastrophe. According to Sutherland, 438 languages are in the condition of Kawesqar, that is, with fewer than 50 speakers, making them "critically endangered"—a category that in the animal world includes 182 birds and 180 mammals. Languages "seem to follow the same patterns" as animals, Sutherland told a reporter for *Bloomberg News.* "Stability and isolation seem to breed abundance in the number of bird and animal species, and they do the same for languages." Conversely, the instability and homogenization of the global economy is creating a juggernaut of monoculture, threatening plants and animals. But, Sutherland makes clear, the one life form even more endangered is human culture.

18   According to Daniel Nettle and Suzanne Romaine, authors of *Vanishing Voices,* the last time human language faced such a crisis of collapse was when we invented farming, around 8000 B.C., during the switch-over from highly mobile hunting and gathering to sedentary agriculture. Then the multitude of idioms developed on the run cohered into language families, like Indo-European, Sino-Tibetan

and Elamo-Dravidian. The difference this time is that with each language gone, we may also lose whatever knowledge and history were locked up in its stories and myths, along with the human consciousness embedded in its grammatical structure and vocabulary.

19   One often hears the apocryphal story about the Inuit and their 40 words for "snow." True or not, it acknowledges the inherent human sense that each language, developed over a certain time and geography, is a revelation of what we call "a sense of place." To let languages die out, en masse, is to permit the phrase "terra incognita" to creep back onto our environmental maps. One organization of linguists, biologists, and anthropologists, known as Terralingua, is working to keep languages alive by highlighting what gets lost when they fade away. "I remember when I was doing fieldwork in Mexico," said Luisa Maffi, Terralingua's president. She encountered a man whose native Mayan was already blurred with Mexican Spanish. He had traveled with his 2-year-old daughter to a health clinic because she was sick with serious diarrhea. "He no longer knew the word for yakan k'ulub wamal," she said, using the Mayan term for a plant long known to cure the problem. "It was probably growing in his backyard."

20   A handful of linguists dismiss salvage efforts like Terralingua's as futile exercises. They say languages just die, as spoken Latin did, and then are reborn as French, Spanish, and Italian. No big deal. Or more bluntly, all this sentimentality about dying languages is just another symptom of academe's mewling, politically correct minority-mongering. In the magazine *Prospect*, the writer Kenan Malik summarized this position in an essay titled "Let Them Die." "There is nothing noble or authentic about local ways of life; they are often simply degrading and backbreaking," Malik argued. "What if half the world's languages are on the verge of extinction? Let them die in peace."

21   Linguists counter that yes, there is a natural process of language death; but the order of magnitude of the current die-off is what should create concern. What's happening with human culture now, they say, should shock people the way the Cuyahoga River catching fire in 1969 radically changed how many thought about the environment.

22   To general linguists, the dismissive position is just deliberate ignorance. But they also argue that the utilitarian case is too narrow. In peril is not just knowledge but also the importance of diversity and the beauty of grammar. They will tell you that every language has its own unique theology and philosophy buried in its very sinews. For example, because of the Kawesqar's nomadic past, they rarely use the future tense; given the contingency of moving constantly by canoe, it was all but unnecessary. The past tense, however, has fine gradations. You can say, "A bird flew by." And by the use of different tenses, you can mean a few seconds ago, a few days ago, a time so long ago that you were not the original observer of the bird (but you know the observer yourself) and, finally, a mythological past, a tense the Kawesqar use to suggest that the story is so old that it no longer possesses fresh descriptive truth but rather that other truth which emerges from stories that retain their narrative power despite constant repetition.

23   "There was once a man and a woman who killed a sacred deer," Gabriela began, translating into Spanish a Kawesqar tale told in the mythological tense.

"Afterward a great flood came. The waters rose until they were standing in it up to their waist. Everyone died but the man and the woman." Then, in time, she went on, from just these last two Kawesqar, they figured out a way to endure, repopulate the land and revive the life of the Kawesqar among the channel islands.

24   Outside, the rain kept coming down.

25   The rhythm of Puerto Eden became easier after a few days. The fishermen headed out in the morning, and the rest of us made social calls. In time, I got to hear some actual Kawesqar spoken, and it sounded a lot like Hollywood's generic Apache, but with a few unique and impossible sounds. I learned to say "Æs ktæl sa Jack, akuókat cáuks ktæl?" ("My name is Jack, what's yours?") That second word, ktæl, means "name" and is (sort of) pronounced ka-tull. It happens entirely in the back of the mouth, in a really challenging way. But during these visits, always and constantly, dominant-culture television hollered at us from a corner. Besides meeting the Kawesqar in Puerto Eden, I have to say, I caught up on a lot of missed episodes of "MacGyver" and "Baywatch."

26   Later in the week, Juan Carlos and I spent more time at his sister's house, and there the evidence of European culture insinuating itself deeply into the minds and habits of the Kawesqar was everywhere.

27   Maria Isabel is a few years older than her brother. She was sick as a child and was raised in Punta Arenas, on the Chilean mainland. She studied and lived in metropolitan Santiago. She never had a Kawesqar youth and can't speak the language.

28   "I am Kawesqar," she told me in Spanish, as if to acknowledge the inexplicable tug identity has on all of us. When I asked her if she intended to learn her mother's language, she insisted that she would. "I hope next year," she said, unconvincingly.

29   I spent a lot of time with Maria Isabel because her husband, Luis, was installing their first flushable toilet. When we weren't talking about Kawes-qar, we were measuring holes, figuring out how to run a sewer pipe into the bay, and reading the toilet-assembly instructions (helpfully printed in five dominant languages). Eventually, the hole was properly centered, so we set down the beeswax ring, lifted the porcelain carefully and pressed it into its permanent location.

30   Does anything say Western dominance quite like the flush of a private john?

31   Well, maybe one other thing. In our intimate chats and smokes, Juan Carlos told me about his own three children. He lives with them back on the mainland, in a house where two other adults speak some Kawesqar. One is Juan Carlos's brother, José, a professor of anthropology at the Universidad Arcis Magallanes in Punta Arenas. And the other is Oscar Aguilera, a linguist at the university. He's of Spanish descent, but he has devoted his life's work to the language of the Kawesqar.

32   Aguilera arrived in Puerto Eden from Santiago in 1975 with the simple intention of "describing" the language as a linguist. There he met a people nearly cut off from the outside world. Among the little contact they'd had, oddly, was with NASA. The space agency came to the village in 1959 to conduct experiments on the ability of humans to withstand extremely cold temperatures. An elderly villager told Aguilera that the NASA scientists asked one Kawesqar man to sit naked in a cold tent with his feet in a bucket of water. He fled in the middle of the night.

33   Aguilera befriended Gabriela's in-laws and knew Gabriela's husband well. He got to know her two young boys, and when they were teenagers, Aguilera took them to Santiago, where they finished school and went to college. Now they all live together in Punta Arenas with Juan Carlos's three young children, who use the affectionate term for "grandfather" with Aguilera.

34   When I visited the home for dinner one night, the three children ran up to greet me. They attend the local British school—and so were taught in Spanish and English. One little girl proudly read me last night's homework: "I played in the yard," and "I rode my bicycle." She beamed. It's cool speaking the dominant language.

35   Later, I asked Juan Carlos why they didn't speak Kawesqar at home. Wouldn't it make sense, since the children were at that magic language-acquisition stage of youth?

36 |"We are going to teach them later," he said. Juan Carlos added that they needed the proper books. Of course, Aguilera is the man who compiled the grammar and teaching manual for Kawesqar and is working on a dictionary with José. But government funds for these projects are spotty, and Aguilera admits it will be years before they are completed.|

37   Their answers revealed just how difficult language resurrection is. Learning a language, even your mother's, requires enormous motivation. Plus, Juan Carlos and José say they are "semi-speakers"—in part because they were taken away from home so young to be educated in Spanish-dominated schools. Even the fluent Kawesqar speakers in Puerto Eden have occasionally asked Aguilera, the lexicographer, to remind them of a certain word.

38   "Some days," Aguilera told me when we were alone for a while, "I think that I might be the last speaker of Kawesqar."

39   Among linguists, the sorrowful story of the "last speaker" is practically a literary genre. The names ring out, like a Homeric catalog. Ned Maddrell, the last speaker of Manx, died in the village of Cregneash on the Isle of Man in 1974. Tevfik Esenc, the last speaker of Ubykh, died in Turkey in 1992. Red Thunder Cloud, the last speaker of Catawba, died in 1996. More are coming. Marie Smith-Jones in Alaska, the last speaker of Eyak, is 83 years old.

40   Farther south from the Kawesqar, I learned, lived the last speaker of Yaghan. Many people urged me to visit Puerto Williams and its native settlement, called Ukika, because of that intriguing notion—that all of Yaghan now dwells entirely in the mind of one elderly woman, Cristina Calderón.

41   Right away, though, I discovered that the "last speaker" of Yaghan is accustomed to charging passengers from the cruise ship that arrives each week for the privilege of taking her picture or hearing a few of the last words in her unusual-sounding language. From me she wanted impossible sums of money. When I tried to sneak in early one morning for a quick interview, word traveled in the village so fast that within minutes her granddaughter/booking agent was through the door and a screaming match broke out (not in Yaghan).

42   That night, Aguilera and I decided to pursue a rumor that there was in fact another Yaghan, a penultimate speaker named Emelinda, who hadn't mastered the

cruise-ship racket. We managed to get inside Emelinda's house without attracting attention.

43   She was a kind old woman whose Yaghan, according to Aguilera, was authentic. Our conversation was brief and brittle. When I asked Emelinda what could be done to keep Yaghan alive, she said she was already doing it, as if a formal program were under way.

44   "I talk to myself in Yaghan," Emelinda explained in Spanish. "When I hang up my clothes outside, I say the words in Yaghan. Inside the house, I talk in Yaghan all day long."

45   I asked her if she ever had a conversation with the only other person in the world who could easily understand her, Cristina Calderón, the official "last speaker" of Yaghan.

46   "No," Emelinda said impatiently, as if I'd brought up a sore topic. "The two of us don't talk."

47   After returning from Chile, I learned that the last-speaker hustle isn't new. Remember Red Thunder Cloud, the last Catawba speaker? Actually, he was Cromwell Ashbie Hawkins West, the son of an African-American druggist in Newport, R.I. According to Ives Goddard of the Smithsonian, West was "a great mimic and fast learner." He quickly mastered the language, donned some turquoise jewelry and, until his death in 1996, worked the last-speaker circuit. Usually, he could be found at county fairs, hawking Red Thunder Cloud's Accabonac Princess American Indian Tea—"fresh from the American forest to you."

48   There's a paradox in those last-speaker stories. After all, what is driving these languages off the cliff but sheer economics? It only makes a kind of poetic sense that in their death throes their speakers would resort to economic ploys. But this is also where the environmental metaphor of endangered languages falls apart. Getting down to a few in number is irreversibly the end of, say, a fern or a tiger. For humans, it's often the beginning of politics.

49   The very success of English as a global language is prompting a revival of ancestral tongues. Compared to the die-off now in progress, it's a drop in the bucket. Still, many native American languages have reacted against these near-death experiences. The Miami in Oklahoma and the Mohawk straddling the Canadian border have full-scale programs for language revival. Native Hawaiian, also written off only a few decades ago, has 18 schools teaching a new generation in the original language of the islands.

50   Partly with money from government lawsuits—the Catawba received $50 million in 1993 after suing over land claim disputes dating to 1760—and partly with revenue from casinos, many of these tribes are rushing to get the programs up and running before the last of the speaking elders die. The Tuscarora tribe near Niagara Falls, N.Y., is down to Howdy Hill, the last speaker who grew up learning the language at home. But now a revival program claims as many as 25 new speakers.

51   Other languages are long past the last speaker, yet revival is still not out of the question. Stephanie Fielding is the great-great-niece of Fidelia Fielding, the last speaker of Mohegan, who died in 1908. Fielding is currently enrolled in M.I.T.'s

linguistics program. She is 58 and devoted to resurrecting her ancestors' language, largely from her aunt's diaries. The academic degree to which she aspires has not yet been accredited. A master's with a concentration in "language reclamation" will be available from M.I.T. at the earliest by 2005 or 2006, according to Norvin Richards, an associate professor of linguistics.

52   "The number of people who contacted us in the last year is about 20, which in linguistics is a bit largish," Richards said. M.I.T. will have to compete with the University of Arizona and the University of Alaska Fairbanks, which already offer reclamation degrees.

53   Most of these language-revival movements model themselves on the national language of Israel. For more than two millenniums, Hebrew was found almost exclusively in Scripture and rabbinical writings. Its retreat was nearly complete—out of the public square, into the house and finally into the scrolls of the Torah. But the early pioneers of what would become Israel faced a politically charged question: which of their languages should dominate? Ashkenazi Yiddish? Russian? German? Sephardic Ladino? The commonly agreed-upon answer was supplied by Eliezer Ben-Yehuda, the Jewish linguist who used the stiff, formal language of the Bible to conjure into existence a modern version—now the main language of 3.6 million people. (Of course, Hebrew's comeback has helped drive Yiddish and Ladino into "endangered" status.)

54   Language revival as a means of identity politics may well be the way of the future. The big fight in linguistics over the past two decades has been about English First. But first is no longer the question. Now the question is, What will be your second language? In America, the drift in high-school curriculums has always been toward a second dominant language—French, Spanish, German, maybe Chinese if you're a rebel. But what if the second language could be that of your ancestors?

55   That possibility is already proving to be quite popular with many people. As their initiatives succeed and become more visible, they will drive into the open a question for English-speaking Americans, the owner-operators of the dominant linguistic ecosystem. Do we want to dwell in a society that encourages linguistic revival and cultural diversity, knowing that with it may come a lot of self-righteous minority-pitying? Or, shall we just sit contentedly amid a huge cultural die-off, harrumphing like some drunk uncle at the family reunion angrily spilling his beer and growling, "Let 'em die"? Keep in mind that if the actuarial tables are correct, it means that once the languages start to die off in earnest, there will be a "death of the last speaker" article in the papers, on average, every 12 days.

56   ❘The other paradox of this gathering twilight is that while the grown-ups are having their arguments about what we should and shouldn't do—and after the linguists have compiled their dictionaries and put together their grammars—the future of all these resurrections will depend on teenagers.❘

57   Will it become cool to speak and live and sing and groove in, say, Mohegan? It depends.

58   Twenty years ago, the distinct language of Welsh was in intensive care, destined to die. Now 21 percent of the people in Wales speak it regularly. Gaelic in Ireland has failed, by comparison. Maybe 3 percent of the people in Ireland speak Gaelic regularly today. Some argue that Wales needed something extra to distinguish itself

from the English up the road, while the Irish live on an island. But other observers, like the author David Crystal, point to the influence of the kids. In his book *Language Death*, he cites a small scandal that broke out in 1998. The Welsh band Manic Street Preachers promoted a new album in Cardiff by hanging an enormous banner written in the old tongue. When he saw it, Peter Hughes Griffiths, a professor at Trinity College in Carmathen who teaches the language, condemned the banner for using slang.

59 "You would have thought the group would have made the effort to make sure the poster was grammatically correct," he fumed to an English newspaper. "Standards are not being kept up."

60 The professor was quickly hooted down by newspapers and by the Welsh Language Board. He had missed the point: kids would propel the language, not him. Kids—with their mistakes, bastardizations, slang, import words and poor syntax—will be the ones who breathe new casual life into old formal syntax. That said, there always remains the other possibility—that the next generation will decide that the native tongue is preposterous, and poof.

61 On my last day in Puerto Eden, we didn't have the proper glue to connect the lengths of PVC pipe. So we improvised, building small fires beneath each end until the plastic softened enough to slip one pipe over the other. Problem solved, we went inside for a celebratory cup of tea. Luis and Maria Isabel have one child, a daughter, Maria José, 15. She was visiting her parents from the mainland, where she's in school.

62 "I am Kawesqar," she said, just like her mom. But where Mom made solemn promises that one day she'll learn the language, Maria José swears to it while laughing. She had on a tight sweater and elephant bell-bottoms, and she had attached the bottom of each pant leg to the sole of her shoe, with tacks, to create a perfect flare on each leg. While we spoke, she watched the television set where a top-hits show blasted techno music beamed in from dominant-culture HQ some 10,000 miles away. She danced along. I lighted my last cigarette.

63 "Fire!" she shouted in perfect English, pointing to my match. She burst out laughing. "I speak Kawesqar!" Her mother laughed and leaned over to tell me that the Kawesqar word for "match" is precisely the English word "fire"—dating back to when the first British explorer handed a Kawesqar nomad a box of matches. Maybe it was Darwin himself; maybe that moment was the beginning of the end for this old language.

64 Or the beginning of a new Kawesqar. Maria José looked directly at the TV, carefully mimicking the latest moves, dancing and giggling out of control. "Fire! Fire! Fire!"

THINKING CRITICALLY

1. What do you think is Hitt's objective in this essay? What is he trying to achieve? Explain.

2. What accounts for the quick demise of Kawesqar in only two generations?

3. What is "terra incognita"? How does it relate to linguistics and the death of a language?

4. What examples does Hitt provide that demonstrate the ramifications of language loss? What do these examples reveal about his personal position on the issue of endangered languages?

5. Why does Hitt feel that economic ploys used by "last speakers" possess a certain poetic justice?

6. On what will language resurrection depend? In your opinion what endangered languages are more likely to survive and why?

WRITING ASSIGNMENTS

1. Jack Hitt notes that some linguists believe that we should let some languages die—because language death and growth is part of linguistic evolution. Prepare a survey on the issue of endangered languages. (The Endangered Language Fund Web site may provide some background resources for your survey.) Ask students for their opinion on the issue of endangered languages—including awareness of impending extinction, the value of saving languages, and the possible impact of language loss. Write a short essay evaluating your results.

2. Several authors in this section, including Hitt, note that English as a global language is taking a "toll" on other languages driving them to extinction. Write an essay expressing your own viewpoint on this assertion. Is English to blame for the extinction of so many languages? How should English-speakers respond?

3. Hitt observes that many young people on whom the survival of their native language depends are not interested in making the effort to learn the tongue of their ancestors. What would you do in the same situation? Respond realistically, considering your life and activities today. Would you have the time or the inclination to try and save your native tongue? Are linguists holding youth to unreasonable expectations?

Let Them Die
Kenan Malik

In the previous article, Jack Hitt noted that some academics, such as Kenan Malik in this essay, have argued that language loss is a natural progression of the human experience. Rather than seeking to preserve dying languages, we should accept their loss as a part of linguistic evolution. Are linguists fighting the wrong battle? Should we stop trying to preserve languages on the brink of extinction and, as Malik asserts in this article, "let them die in peace"?

Kenan Malik is a writer and lecturer. His articles have appeared in many newspapers and magazines including the *Guardian, Financial Times, The Prospect, TLS,* and *Nature.* He is the author of two books: *The Meaning of Race: Race, History and Culture in Western Society* (1996) and *Man, Beast and Zombie* (2000). This essay first appeared in the *Prospect* in November 2000.

1 There are around 6000 languages in the world today. Shortly there will be one less. Eighty-one-year-old Marie Smith Jones is the last living speaker of Eyak, an Alaskan language. When she dies, so will her language. Over the past few decades a huge number of languages have died in this fashion. When Ned Madrell died on

the Isle of Man in 1974, he also took the ancient Manx language to the grave. The death in 1992 of Tefvic Escenc, a farmer from the Turkish village of Haci Osman, killed off Ubykh, a language once spoken in the northern Caucasus. Laura Somersal died in 1990, the last speaker of a Native American tongue, Wappo. Six years later another Native American language, Catawba, passed away with the death of Carlos Westez, more popularly known as Red Thunder.

2   At least half of the world's 6,000 languages are expected to disappear over the next century; some pessimists suggest that by the year 3000 just 600 languages will be left. According to the American Summer Institute of Linguistics, there are 51 languages with only one speaker left—28 of them in Australia alone. A further 500 languages are spoken by fewer than 100 speakers, and another 1,500 by fewer than 1,000 speakers. Most will be lucky to survive the next decade. Such accelerated disappearance has galvanized into action an increasingly vocal campaign to preserve "linguistic diversity." In an obituary to Carlos Westez, the writer Peter Popham warned that "when a language dies" we lose "the possibility of a unique way of perceiving and describing the world." Despairing of the "impact of a homogenizing monoculture upon our way of life," Popham worried about the "spread of English carried by American culture, delivered by Japanese technology and the hegemony of a few great transnational languages: Chinese, Spanish, Russian, Hindi." The linguist David Crystal echoed these sentiments in a Prospect essay last year. "We should care about dying languages," he argued, "for the same reason that we care when a species of animal or plant dies. It reduces the diversity of our planet."

3   Now a new book, *Vanishing Voices*, by the anthropologist Daniel Nettle and linguist Suzanne Romaine, links the campaign to preserve languages to the campaign for fundamental human rights, and for the protection of minority groups, in the face of what they regard as aggressive globalisation and cultural imperialism. "Linguistic diversity," they argue, "is a benchmark of cultural diversity." Language death "is symptomatic of cultural death: a way of life disappears with the death of a language." "Every people," Nettle and Romaine conclude, "has a right to their own language, to preserve it as a cultural resource, and to transmit it to their children."

4   Campaigners for linguistic diversity portray themselves as liberal defenders of minority rights, protecting the vulnerable against the nasty forces of global capitalism. Beneath the surface rhetoric, however, their campaign has much more in common with reactionary, backward-looking visions, such as William Hague's campaign to "save the pound" as a unique expression of British identity, or Roger Scruton's paean to a lost Englishness. All seek to preserve the unpreservable, and all are possessed of an impossibly nostalgic view of what constitutes a culture or a "way of life."

5   The whole point of a language is to enable communication. As the renowned Mexican historian and translator Miguel Leon-Portilla has put it, "In order to survive, a language must have a function." A language spoken by one person, or even a few hundred, is not a language at all. It is a private conceit, like a child's secret code. It is, of course, enriching to learn other languages and delve into other cultures. But it is enriching not because different languages and cultures are unique, but because making contact across barriers of language and culture allows us to expand our own horizons and become more universal in our outlook.

6   In bemoaning "cultural homogenization," campaigners for linguistic diversity fail to understand what makes a culture dynamic and responsive. It is not the fracturing of the world with as many different tongues as possible; it is rather the overcoming of barriers to social interaction. The more universally we can communicate, the more dynamic our cultures will be, because the more they will be open to new ways of thinking and doing. It is not being parochial to believe that were more people to speak English—or Chinese, Spanish, Russian or Hindi—the better it would be. The real chauvinists are surely those who warn darkly of the spread of "American culture" and "Japanese technology."

7   At the core of the preservers' argument is the belief that a particular language is linked to a particular way of life and a particular vision of the world. "Each language has its own window on the world," write Nettle and Romaine. "Every language is a living museum, a monument to every culture it has been vehicle to." It's an idea that derives from nineteenth century Romantic notions of cultural difference. "Each nation speaks in the manner it thinks," wrote the German critic and poet Johann Gottfried von Herder, "and thinks in the manner it speaks." For Herder, the nature of a people was expressed through its volksgeist—the unchanging spirit of a people. Language was particularly crucial to the delineation of a people, because "in it dwell the entire world of tradition, history, religion, principles of existence; its whole heart and soul."

8   The human capacity for language certainly shapes our ways of thinking. But particular languages almost certainly do not. Most linguists have long since given up on the idea that people's perceptions of the world, and the kinds of concepts they hold, is constrained by the particular language they speak. The idea that French speakers view the world differently from English speakers, because they speak French, is clearly absurd. It is even more absurd to imagine that all French speakers have a common view of the world, thanks to a common language.

9   But if the Romantic idea of language has little influence, the Romantic idea of human differences certainly does. The belief that different peoples have unique ways of understanding the world became, in the nineteenth century, the basis of a racial view of the world. Herder's volksgeist developed into the notion of racial makeup, an unchanging substance, the foundation of all physical appearance and mental potential, and the basis for division and difference within humankind. Today, biological notions of racial difference have fallen into disfavor, largely as a result of the experience of Nazism and the Holocaust. But while racial science has been discredited, racial thinking has not. It has simply been re-expressed in cultural rather than biological terms. Cultural pluralism has refashioned the idea of race for the post-Holocaust world, with its claim that diversity is good in itself and that humanity can be parceled up into discrete groups, each with its own particular way of life, mode of expression, and unique "window upon the world."

10   The contemporary argument for the preservation of linguistic diversity, liberally framed though it may be, draws on the same philosophy that gave rise to ideas of racial difference. That is why the arguments of Popham, Crystal, Nettles, and Romaine, on this issue if not on anything else, would have found favor with the late Enoch Powell. "Every society, every nation is unique," he wrote. "It has its own past, its own story, its own memories, its own ways, its own languages or ways of

speaking, its own—dare I use the word—culture." Language preservers may be acting on the best of intentions, but they are treading on dangerous ground, and they carry with them some unpalatable fellow-travellers.

11   The linguistic campaigners' debt to Romanticism has left them, like most multiculturalists, with a thoroughly confused notion of rights. When Nettle and Romaine suggest, in *Vanishing Voices*, that "the right of people to exist, to practice and produce their own language and culture, should be inalienable," they are conflating two kinds of rights—individual rights and group rights. An individual certainly has the right to speak whatever language he or she wants, and to engage in whatever cultural practices they wish to in private. But it is not incumbent on anyone to listen to them, nor to provide resources for the preservation of either their language or their culture. The reason that Eyak will soon be extinct is not because Marie Smith Jones has been denied her rights, but because no one else wants to, or is capable of, speaking the language. This might be tragic for Marie Smith Jones—and frustrating for professional linguists—but it is not a question of rights. Neither a culture, nor a way of life, nor yet a language, has a God-given "right to exist."

12   Language campaigners also confuse political oppression and the loss of cultural identity. Some groups—such as Turkish Kurds—are banned from using their language as part of a wider campaign by the Turkish state to deny Kurds their rights. But most languages die out, not because they are suppressed, but because native speakers yearn for a better life. Speaking a language such as English, French or Spanish, and discarding traditional habits, can open up new worlds and is often a ticket to modernity. But it is modernity itself of which Nettles and Romaine disapprove. They want the peoples of the Third World, and minority groups in the West, to follow "local ways of life" and pursue "traditional knowledge" rather than receive a "Western education." This is tantamount to saying that such people should live a marginal life, excluded from the modern mainstream to which the rest of us belong. There is nothing noble or authentic about local ways of life; they are often simply degrading and backbreaking. "Nobody can suppose that it is not more beneficial for a Breton or a Basque to be a member of the French nationality, admitted on equal terms to all the privileges of French citizenship . . . than to sulk on his own rocks, without participation or interest in the general movement of the world." So wrote John Stuart Mill more than a century ago. It would have astonished him that in the twenty-first century there are those who think that sulking on your own rock is a state worth preserving.

13   What if half the world's languages are on the verge of extinction? Let them die in peace.

THINKING CRITICALLY

1. What is the position of the author on language extinction? Why does he feel that linguists are wasting their time in efforts to revive dying languages?

2. Why does Malik refer to the campaign to preserve linguistic diversity as surface rhetoric?

3. In paragraph 5 Malik states that "the whole point of a language is to enable communication." When a language fails in its primary function it becomes obsolete. Do you agree or disagree with this position?

4. Evaluate the author's tone in this essay. How do you think other writers in this section would respond to his argument?

WRITING ASSIGNMENTS

1. Write a response to Malik's argument that endangered languages should be "left to die in peace." Refer to specific points made in his essay and others in this chapter in your response.

2. Write an essay in which you identify the primary function(s) of a language. How does your description compare to Malik's definition in paragraph 5?

3. At the end of his essay, Malik notes that some linguists would rather impede the progress of a group than lose an ancient language. In other words, the interests of the linguists are not necessarily in the best interests of the native speakers of an endangered language. Respond to this idea with your own opinion.

Exploring the Language of V I S U A L S

International Mother Language Day

International Mother Language Day was created by the United Nations Educational, Scientific and Cultural Organization (UNESCO) to promote linguistic and cultural diversity and multilingualism. UNESCO considers language to be one of the most powerful instrument for preserving and developing cultural and social heritage. Measures taken to preserve and promote mother tongues promote both linguistic diversity and cultural awareness. Vigdis Finnbogadottir, UNESCO's Goodwill Ambassador for Languages, and a former President of Iceland explains, "Everyone loses if one language is lost because then a nation and culture lose their memory, and so does the complex tapestry from which the world is woven and which makes the world an exciting place." This poster was created to celebrate and increase awareness of International Mother Language Day 2006, which addressed the topic of languages and cyberspace.

THINKING CRITICALLY

1. What can you determine about International Mother Language Day based upon this poster alone? Can you guess the thematic topic of the 2006 event? Would this poster encourage you to find out more about International Mother Language Day? Why or why not?

2. Visit the United Nations Educational, Scientific and Cultural Organization's Web site addressing the topic of multilingualism in cyberspace at www. unesco.org/webworld/multilingualism and learn more about *Initiative B@bel*. What is the position of UNESCO on language and cyberspace? What is the objective of *Initiative B@bel*?

3. Research the history of International Mother Language Day online. What other themes has UNESCO covered for this day? Which ones seem particularly compelling, and why?

4. UNESCO observes "Ensuring that languages can continue in use alongside the major international languages of communication is a genuine challenge to countries worldwide." What are the major languages of communication? How are these languages used, and what has made them "major"?

5. Do you think language diversity is important on the Web? Why or why not? Explain your position.

MAKING CONNECTIONS

1. Several essays in this section mention Marie Smith Jones, the last living speaker of the Alaskan language Eyak, and other "last speakers" such as Ned Maddrell (Manx). Research one of these last speakers, (the June 2005 issue of *The New Yorker* has an excellent article on Smith Jones, "Last Words: A Language Dies," by Elizabeth Kolbert), and prepare a report on factors that contributed to the demise of his or her language.

2. The National Association of Tribal Historic Preservation Officers site, www.nathpo.org/News/newswire-language.htm, lists many articles connected to the preservation of Native American languages. Read some of these articles and write a short report on current efforts some tribes are undertaking to save their native languages.

3. Some endangered languages, such as Hawaiian, Welsh, Gaelic, and even Hebrew, have been brought back from the brink of extinction. Research one of these languages and write an essay about how they were preserved.

4. Should we be concerned that so many ancient languages are disappearing? Write an essay in which you argue for or against saving endangered languages to preserve linguistic diversity. In your response, refer to points made by authors in this section.

5. Most Americans came to the United States from outside the country, speaking languages other than English. Immigrants were encouraged to speak English, especially outside the home, and as a result, the mother tongue was often lost within a generation. In what ways is this circumstance similar, and in what ways is it different, to the loss of endangered languages? Present your perspective in a short essay, considering the cultural, social, religious, and economic connections between language, history, and identity.

The Power of Language

2

■ In 1948, Eleanor Roosevelt addressed the United Nations General Assembly at the Sorbonne on "The Struggles for the Rights of Man." Later that year, *The Human Rights Declaration* was passed by the United Nations.

Language is such an intricate part of culture that we often lose sight of its power: how language leads and misleads us, how it educates and informs us, and how it shapes our perception of the world and even our personal identity. We may also take for granted how language empowers us, and how it can forge understanding, break silences, and inspire action. In this chapter, we will explore the ways we "come into language" and how it can be used to "break silences"—that is, how the power of language moves us as individuals, as social beings, and as leaders.

Personal Recollections: Coming into Language

As individuals, we come to language in different ways, yet we share in the magic that opens the world to us and us to it. The next five essays explore how people from diverse backgrounds discovered the power of the word in shaping the world and the self within it. In "Homemade Education," the influential black leader Malcolm X explains how as a young man he was possessed by words. He did not discover the power of words in a school library or the cozy confines of a bedroom, but in a prison cell, where he taught himself how to read and write, liberating his mind while his body was behind bars. "A Word for Everything" describes how the blind and deaf Helen Keller literally broke her silence when she discovered "the key to all language" and connected the concept of words to the things around her. Leonard Michaels, after experiencing an epiphany while walking in Paris, ponders the connection between language and personal and cultural identity in "My Yiddish." Next, Christine Marín provides an equally dramatic account of her discovery of the power of language to shape one's identity in "Spanish Lessons." The final essay in this section, by Maxine Hong Kingston, the daughter of Chinese immigrants, describes her traumatizing introduction to the English language. The section ends with a visual exploration of the way preschool and early elementary school children learn the elements of language and writing through an exercise called "independent writing" in which they are encouraged to write unhindered by spelling and grammar rules.

Speaking Out: Inspiring Change

The second section of this chapter examines how language can be used to challenge convention and fuel movements that inspire social change. Many of the people featured in these essays took great personal risk in using their voices to confront issues connected to racism, sexism, personal liberty, or inequality. Often speaking for a powerless or silenced segment of society, these speakers incited social change through the power of language. First, Elizabeth Cady Stanton's "Seneca Falls Declaration" on women's suffrage demands equal political representation for women. The matter of civil rights is addressed by Martin Luther King, Jr. in "A Letter from Birmingham Jail," in which he argues compellingly that nonviolent protest can end racist hatred and bigotry. Sojourner Truth lends her voice to this issue as both a woman and a former slave in "Ain't I a Woman?" Eleanor Roosevelt defines basic human rights and freedoms for people of all nations in a speech presented to the United Nations in "The Struggle for Human Rights." Two visuals in the section feature the "silencing" of women—one at the beginning of the twentieth century, and another at the beginning of the twenty-first. As you read the articles and inspect the visuals in this section, consider how words and actions challenge us to think and how the power of language can change the world.

PERSONAL RECOLLECTIONS: COMING INTO LANGUAGE

Homemade Education
Malcolm X

It was said that he was the only man in America who could start a race riot—or stop one. A one-time street hustler, Malcolm X was born Malcolm Little in 1925. He rose to become one of the most articulate, fiery, and powerful leaders of black America during the 1960s. His writings and lectures taught African-Americans that by taking action, they could take control over their own destiny. In 1946, Malcolm X was arrested for robbery. While in prison, Malcolm became a follower of Elijah Muhammad, the leader of the Nation of Islam (which was sometimes called the Black Muslim Movement). He rescinded his "slave name," Little, and was assigned the new name "X." It was during this time that he discovered the world of language and became obsessed with the written word and books, which he called "intellectual vitamins." After his release, he quickly rose through the ranks of the Nation of Islam and became one of its top administrators. In 1964, Malcolm X left the Nation of Islam to form his own organization, the Muslim Mosque, that articulated a more secular black nationalism. After a trip to Mecca, however, he began to change his views towards whites, considering the possibility that some whites could contribute to the struggle for racial equality. A year later, on February 21, 1965, Malcolm X was assassinated in the Audubon Ballroom in New York City while addressing a full house.

The following article is Malcolm X's account of coming to language—an inspiring glimpse of one man's struggle to find self-expression in the power of words. This excerpt comes from *The Autobiography of Malcolm X* (1965), an absorbing personal narrative written with the assistance of *Roots* author Alex Haley.

1 I've never been one for inaction. Everything I've ever felt strongly about, I've done something about. I guess that's why, unable to do anything else, I soon began writing to people I had known in the hustling world, such as Sammy the Pimp, John Hughes, the gambling house owner, the thief Jumpsteady, and several dope peddlers.

I wrote them all about Allah and Islam and Mr. Elijah Muhammad. I had no idea where most of them lived. I addressed their letters in care of the Harlem or Roxbury bars and clubs where I'd known them.

2   I never got a single reply. The average hustler and criminal was too uneducated to write a letter. I have known many slick sharp-looking hustlers, who would have you think they had an interest in Wall Street; privately, they would get someone else to read a letter if they received one. Besides, neither would I have replied to anyone writing me something as wild as "the white man is the devil."

3   What certainly went on the Harlem and Roxbury wires was that Detroit Red was going crazy in stir, or else he was trying some hype to shake up the warden's office.

4   During the years that I stayed in the Norfolk Prison Colony, never did any official directly say anything to me about those letters, although, of course, they all passed through the prison censorship. I'm sure, however, they monitored what I wrote to add to the files which every state and federal prison keeps on the conversation of Negro inmates by the teachings of Mr. Elijah Muhammad.

5   But at that time, I felt that the real reason was that the white man knew that he was the devil.

6   Later on, I even wrote to the Mayor of Boston, to the Governor of Massachusetts, and to Harry S. Truman. They never answered; they probably never even saw my letters. I handscratched to them how the white man's society was responsible for the black man's condition in this wilderness of North America.

7   It was because of my letters that I happened to stumble upon starting to acquire some kind of a homemade education.

8   I became increasingly frustrated at not being able to express what I wanted to convey in letters that I wrote, especially those to Mr. Elijah Muhammad. In the street, I had been the most articulate hustler out there—I had commanded attention when I said something. But now, trying to write simple English, I not only wasn't articulate, I wasn't even functional. How would I sound writing in slang, the way I would *say* it, something such as, "Look, daddy, let me pull your coat about a cat. Elijah Muhammad—"

9   Many who today hear me somewhere in person, or on television, or those who read something I've said, will think I went to school far beyond the eighth grade. This impression is due entirely to my prison studies.

10   It had really begun back in the Charlestown Prison, when Bimbi first made me feel envy of his stock of knowledge. Bimbi had always taken charge of any conversation he was in, and I had tried to emulate him. But every book I picked up had few sentences which didn't contain anywhere from one to nearly all of the words that might as well have been in Chinese. When I just skipped those words, of course, I really ended up with little idea of what the book said. So I had come to the Norfolk Prison Colony still going through only book-reading motions. Pretty soon, I would have quit even these motions, unless I had received the motivation that I did.

11   I saw that the best thing I could do was get hold of a dictionary—to study, to learn some words. I was lucky enough to reason also that I should try to improve my penmanship. It was sad. I couldn't even write in a straight line. It was both ideas together that moved me to request a dictionary along with some tablets and pencils from the Norfolk Prison Colony school.

12   I spent two days just riffling uncertainly through the dictionary's pages. I'd never realized so many words existed! I didn't know *which* words I needed to learn. Finally, just to start some kind of action, I began copying.

13   In my slow, painstaking, ragged handwriting, I copied into my tablet everything printed on that first page, down to the punctuation marks.

14   I believe it took me a day. Then, aloud, I read back, to myself, everything I'd written on the tablet. Over and over, aloud, to myself, I read my own handwriting.

15   I woke up the next morning, thinking about those words—immensely proud to realize that not only had I written so much at one time, but I'd written words that I never knew were in the world. Moreover, with a little effort, I also could remember what many of these words meant. I reviewed the words whose meanings I didn't remember. Funny thing, from the dictionary's first page right now, that "aardvark" springs to my mind. The dictionary had a picture of it, a long-tailed, long-eared, burrowing African mammal, which lives off termites caught by sticking out its tongue as an anteater does for ants.

16   I was so fascinated that I went on—I copied the dictionary's next page. And the same experience came when I studied that. With every succeeding page, I also learned of people and places and events from history. Actually the dictionary is like a miniature encyclopedia. Finally the dictionary's A section had filled a whole tablet—and I went on into the B's. That was the way I started copying what eventually became the entire dictionary. It went a lot faster after so much practice helped me pick up handwriting speed. Between what I wrote in my tablet, and writing letters, during the rest of my time in prison I would guess I wrote a million words.

17   I suppose it was inevitable that as my word-base broadened, I could for the first time pick up a book and read and now begin to understand what the book was saying. Anyone who has read a great deal can imagine the new world that opened. Let me tell you something: from then until I left that prison, in every free moment I had, if I was not reading in the library, I was reading on my bunk. You couldn't have gotten me out of books with a wedge. Between Mr. Muhammad's teachings, my correspondence, my visitors . . . and my reading of books, months passed without my even thinking about being imprisoned. In fact, up to then, I never had been so truly free in my life.

THINKING CRITICALLY

1. What exactly motivates Malcolm X to "get a hold of a dictionary—to study, to learn some words"?

2. Explain how Malcolm X could be the "most articulate hustler" on the street, yet be unable to write simple English that was articulate and functional.

3. In your own words, summarize what Malcolm X means when he says, "In fact, up to then, I never had been so truly free in my life." Can you in any way relate to his sense of freedom here? Have you ever had a similarly intense learning experience? If so, what was it like?

4. Would this essay be likely to inspire an illiterate person to learn to read? Why or why not?

5. Having read this essay, do you feel that studying a dictionary is or is not an effective way to improve language skills?

6. Consider the introductory paragraph. What would you say is its function? Does it establish the thesis and controlling idea of the essay? Did it capture your attention and make you want to read on? Explain.

WRITING ASSIGNMENTS

1. Think of a situation in which you lacked the language skills you needed to communicate effectively. It may have been in a college interview, writing a letter to a friend, or expressing your ideas in class. Write an essay explaining the circumstances—how it made you feel and how you solved or coped with the problem. The tone of the piece may be serious, dramatic, or even humorous.

2. Do a little research to find out what kinds of services your community offers to adults who want to learn to read. You might start by contacting town hall, the department of education, and reading clinics. After gathering information, write an essay outlining what is available and whether or not you feel these services are adequate.

3. Access the CMG Web site on Malcolm X at www.cmgww.com/historic/malcolm/index.html. Write an essay connecting his background to the excerpt from his autobiography. How did his determination to read lead to his success as a great orator? Would Malcolm X have been as successful if he had not had this experience in jail?

A Word for Everything

Helen Keller

Most of us take for granted the ability to acquire language and communication skills. We develop these skills from infancy. As young children, we are constantly bombarded with visual and verbal stimuli, from which we begin to acquire language. But for Helen Keller (1880–1968), deaf and blind from the age of 19 months, a silent and dark world was her reality. She was unable to effectively communicate her needs and desires and to connect with the people around her.

When Helen was almost seven years old, her parents sought the help of Anne Mansfield Sullivan, a teacher familiar with communicating with the blind and deaf. Anne Sullivan changed Helen's world forever. The following excerpt is from Helen Keller's autobiography, *The Story of My Life*. In this essay, Keller remembers the arrival of her teacher and how Sullivan introduced her to the wonders of language. Specifically, Keller recalls the exact moment when she realized that everything had a name, and her joyous realization that she was connected to the world and the people around her.

1 The most important day I remember in all my life is the one on which my teacher, Anne Mansfield Sullivan, came to me. I am filled with wonder when I consider the immeasurable contrasts between the two lives which it connects. It was the third of March, 1887, three months before I was seven years old.

2 On the afternoon of that eventful day, I stood on the porch, dumb, expectant. I guessed vaguely from my mother's signs and from the hurrying to and fro in the house that something unusual was about to happen, so I went to the door and waited

on the steps. The afternoon sun penetrated the mass of honeysuckle that covered the porch, and fell on my upturned face. My fingers lingered almost unconsciously on the familiar leaves and blossoms which had just come forth to greet the sweet southern spring. I did not know what the future held of marvel or surprise for me. Anger and bitterness had preyed upon me continually for weeks and a deep languor had succeeded this passionate struggle.

3   Have you ever been at sea in a dense fog, when it seemed as if a tangible white darkness shut you in, and the great ship, tense and anxious, groped her way toward the shore with plummet and sounding-line, and you waited with beating heart for something to happen? I was like that ship before my education began, only I was without compass or sounding-line, and had no way of knowing how near the harbor was. "Light! Give me light!" was the wordless cry of my soul, and the light of love shone on me in that very hour.

4   I felt approaching footsteps. I stretched out my hand as I supposed to my mother. Some one took it, and I was caught up and held close in the arms of her who had come to reveal all things to me, and, more than all things else, to love me.

5   The morning after my teacher came she led me into her room and gave me a doll. The little blind children at the Perkins Institution had sent it and Laura Bridgman had dressed it; but I did not know this until afterward. When I had played with it a little while, Miss Sullivan slowly spelled into my hand the word "d-o-l-l." I was at once interested in this finger play and tried to imitate it. When I finally succeeded in making the letters correctly I was flushed with childish pleasure and pride. Running downstairs to my mother I held up my hand and made the letters for doll. I did not know that I was spelling a word or even that words existed; I was simply making my fingers go in monkey-like imitation. In the days that followed I learned to spell in this uncomprehending way a great many words, among them *pin, hat, cup* and a few verbs like *sit, stand* and *walk.* But my teacher had been with me several weeks before I understood that everything has a name.

6   One day, while I was playing with my new doll, Miss Sullivan put my big rag doll into my lap also, spelled "d-o-l-l" and tried to make me understand that "d-o-l-l" applied to both. Earlier in the day we had had a tussle over the words "m-u-g" and "w-a-t-e-r." Miss Sullivan had tried to impress it upon me that "m-u-g" is *mug* and that "w-a-t-e-r" is *water,* but I persisted in confounding the two. In despair she had dropped the subject for the time, only to renew it at the first opportunity. I became impatient at her repeated attempts and, seizing the new doll, I dashed it upon the floor. I was keenly delighted when I felt the fragments of the broken doll at my feet. Neither sorrow nor regret followed my passionate outburst. I had not loved the doll. In the still, dark world in which I lived there was no strong sentiment or tenderness. I felt my teacher sweep the fragments to one side of the hearth, and I had a sense of satisfaction that the cause of my discomfort was removed. She brought me my hat, and I knew I was going out into the warm sunshine. This thought, if a wordless sensation may be called a thought, made me hop and skip with pleasure.

7   We walked down the path to the well-house, attracted by the fragrance of the honeysuckle with which it was covered. Some one was drawing water and my teacher placed my hand under the spout. As the cool stream gushed over one hand

she spelled into the other the word *water,* first slowly, then rapidly. I stood still, my whole attention fixed upon the motions of her fingers. Suddenly I felt a misty consciousness as of something forgotten—a thrill of returning thought; and somehow the mystery of language was revealed to me. I knew then that "w-a-t-e-r" meant the wonderful cool something that was flowing over my hand. That living word awakened my soul, gave it light, home, joy, set it free! There were barriers still, it is true, but barriers that could in time be swept away.

8   I left the well-house eager to learn. Everything had a name and each name gave birth to a new thought. As we returned to the house every object which I touched seemed to quiver with life. That was because I saw everything with the strange, new sight that had come to me. On entering the door I remembered the doll I had broken. I felt my way to the hearth and picked up the pieces. I tried vainly to put them together. Then my eyes filled with tears; for I realized what I had done, and for the first time I felt repentance and sorrow.

9   I learned a great many new words that day. I do not remember what they all were; but I do know that *mother, father, sister, teacher* were among them—words that were to make the world blossom for me, "like Aaron's rod, with flowers." It would have been difficult to find a happier child than I was as I lay in my crib at the close of that eventful day and lived over the joys it had brought me, and for the first time longed for a new day to come.

10   I had now the key to all language, and I was eager to learn to use it. Children who hear acquire language without any particular effort; the words that fall from others' lips they catch on the wing, as it were, delightedly, while the little deaf child must trap them by a slow and often painful process. But whatever the process, the result is wonderful. Gradually, from naming an object we advance step by step until we have traversed the vast distance between our first stammered syllable and the sweep of thought in a line of Shakespeare.

11   At first, when my teacher told me about a new thing I asked very few questions. My ideas were vague, and my vocabulary was inadequate; but as my knowledge of things grew, and I learned more and more words, my field of inquiry broadened, and I would return again and again to the same subject, eager for further information. Sometimes a new word revived an image that some earlier experience had engraved on my brain. I remember the morning that I first asked the meaning of the word "love." This was before I knew many words. I had found a few early violets in the garden and brought them to my teacher. She tried to kiss me; but at that time I did not like to have any one kiss me except my mother. Miss Sullivan put her arm gently round me and spelled into my hand, "I love Helen."

12   "What is love?" I asked.

13   She drew me closer to her and said, "It is here," pointing to my heart, whose beats I was conscious of for the first time. Her words puzzled me very much because I did not then understand anything unless I touched it.

14   I smelt the violets in her hand and asked, half in words, half in signs, a question which meant, "Is love the sweetness of flowers?"

15   "No," said my teacher.

16   Again I thought. The warm sun was shining on us.

17   "Is this not love?" I asked, pointing in the direction from which the heat came, "Is this not love?"

18   It seemed to me that there could be nothing more beautiful than the sun, whose warmth makes all things grow. But Miss Sullivan shook her head, and I was greatly puzzled and disappointed. I thought it strange that my teacher could not show me love.

19   A day or two afterward I was stringing beads of different sizes in symmetrical groups—two large beads, three small ones, and so on. I had made many mistakes, and Miss Sullivan had pointed them out again and again with gentle patience. Finally I noticed a very obvious error in the sequence and for an instant I concentrated my attention on the lesson and tried to think how I should have arranged the beads. Miss Sullivan touched my forehead and spelled with decided emphasis, "Think."

20   In a flash I knew that the word was the name of the process that was going on in my head. This was my first conscious perception of an abstract idea.

21   For a long time I was still—I was not thinking of the beads in my lap, but trying to find a meaning for "love" in the light of this new idea. The sun had been under a cloud all day, and there had been brief showers; but suddenly the sun broke forth in all its southern splendor.

22   Again I asked my teacher, "Is this not love?"

23   "Love is something like the clouds that were in the sky before the sun came out," she replied. Then in simpler words than these, which at that time I could not have understood, she explained: "You cannot touch the clouds, you know; but you feel the rain and know how glad the flowers and the thirsty earth are to have it after a hot day. You cannot touch either; but you feel the sweetness that it pours into everything. Without love you would not be happy or want to play."

24   The beautiful truth burst upon my mind—I felt that there were invisible lines stretched between my spirit and the spirits of others.

25   From the beginning of my education Miss Sullivan made it a practice to speak to me as she would speak to any hearing child; the only difference was that she spelled the sentences into my hand instead of speaking them. If I did not know the words and idioms necessary to express my thoughts she supplied them, even suggesting conversation when I was unable to keep up my end of the dialogue.

26   This process was continued for several years; for the deaf child does not learn in a month, or even in two or three years, the numberless idioms and expressions used in the simplest daily intercourse. The little hearing child learns these from constant repetition and imitation. The conversation he hears in his home stimulates his mind and suggests topics and calls forth the spontaneous expression of his own thoughts. This natural exchange of ideas is denied to the deaf child. My teacher, realizing this, determined to supply the kinds of stimulus I lacked. This she did by repeating to me as far as possible, verbatim, what she heard, and by showing me how I could take part in the conversation. But it was a long time before I ventured to take the initiative, and still longer before I could find something appropriate to say at the right time.

27   The deaf and the blind find it very difficult to acquire the amenities of conversation. How much more this difficulty must be augmented in the case of those who are both deaf and blind! They cannot distinguish the tone of the voice or, without

assistance, go up and down the gamut of tones that give significance to words; nor can they watch the expression of the speaker's face, and a look is often the very soul of what one says.

THINKING CRITICALLY

1. Helen Keller was almost seven years old before her teacher Anne Sullivan began to teach her language. Would her experience have been different if she had been younger or older? Explain.

2. How do young children understand words such as think, know, or feel that have no physical or visual representation? How does Helen Keller begin to understand these terms?

3. Why doesn't the young Helen feel sorry for breaking her new doll? What accounts for her later remorse? What made the difference in Helen's emotional perspective? How are emotions connected to language?

4. What are the "amenities of conversation" that Keller alludes to in her final paragraph? Why are they important to communication? How can a look be "the very soul of what one says"?

5. How does Keller describe things that she has never seen nor heard? How do her descriptions help her connect to her audience?

6. Evaluate Keller's tone in this essay. How does her tone help her audience relate to her essay? Who do you think her audience is, and what is she hoping to convey to them?

7. How does Keller use simile and metaphor in her writing? Why do you think she employs this literary convention?

WRITING ASSIGNMENTS

1. How would you describe sound and sight to a person who could experience neither? Describe some everyday events such as a sunset or an ocean wave to a person who has never had sight or hearing. What descriptive alternatives would you use? After writing, explain the rationale behind your description.

2. Sit down with a friend and try to communicate using the Anne Sullivan and Helen Keller method of tracing letters into the palm of the hand. You may wish to use blindfolds for this exercise; do not speak throughout the exercise. Write an essay about your experience. Did it make you view your own method of communication differently?

3. Keller describes the moment when she first made the connection between Sullivan's palm tracings and the object described. She identifies this moment as the moment her soul was awakened and given "light, hope, [and] joy." Write about an experience of your own in which you had a moment of awakening that forever changed the way you understood your world. Following Keller's format, relate the events leading up to this moment. How did it change your life?

4. Read more about the life of Helen Keller. For a brief biographical sketch, try the Great Women Hall of Fame at www.greatwomen.org or read the autobiography from which this essay was taken. The American Foundation for the Blind's archives features more information about Keller, her teacher Anne Sullivan, and Keller's early experiences with language acquisition at www.afb.org/default.asp. Write a paper on how this remarkable woman became one of the most well-known and respected women in America. What role did language play in her fame?

Exploring the Language of **V I S U A L S**

American Sign Language Alphabet

Many of us take for granted the ability to verbally communicate—to shout a greeting across a courtyard, to hear a warning of imminent danger, to cluck baby talk to a giggling infant, or to whisper a secret in a friend's ear. However, many Americans who are hearing impaired must find alternative ways to communicate to others. Although sign language is one way of addressing this obstacle, it presents its own challenges. Few hearing people know sign language well enough to use it to communicate effectively. Moreover, it requires face-to-face contact between signers. The American Sign Language Alphabet is a manual alphabet that augments the vocabulary of American Sign Language by allowing the speaker to sign the individual letters of a word such as with names, book titles, or when clarification is needed. Letters should be signed with the palm facing the viewer.

As you study this alphabet and answer the questions that follow, consider the ways you communicate verbally with others around you. What would happen if you could not verbally express yourself and, instead, had to rely on sign language to be understood? What advantages and disadvantages might you experience? For example, would sign language be more freeing—allowing you to communicate from distances or in loud areas where you may not be understood?

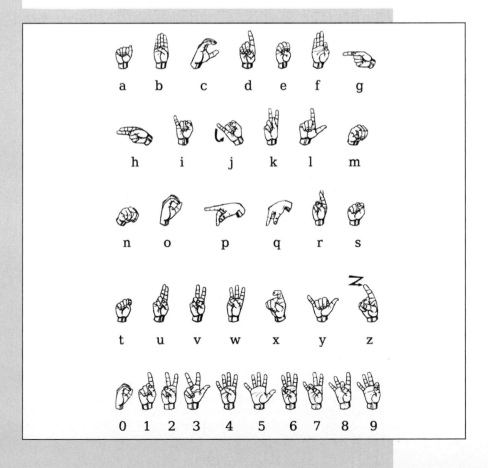

THINKING CRITICALLY

1. Study and learn the ASL alphabet with a classmate or friend and spell out some names or titles. How easily are you understood? How quickly were you able to use the signed alphabet?

2. American Sign Language (ASL) is taught in many colleges and universities to hearing students. Contrary to popular assumption, ASL is not a signed form of English, but a language in its own right that developed gradually and still evolves, as many languages do. Find out if your school offers courses in ASL. If so, ask permission to attend a class and write about the experience. Try to apply some of the things you have learned about language in this class to your assessment of ASL.

3. If you have a hearing or speech impairment, discuss how this challenge affects your daily life and your communication with others. If you do not have any unique hearing or speech difficulties, discuss how you communicate with people who do. What issues do you confront, and how do you deal with them? Explain.

4. Sign languages are true languages, with vocabularies of thousands of words and complex and sophisticated grammars. Attend a speech or watch a program that has an ASL interpreter present. Focus your attention on the interpreter. If you could not hear, could you understand the context of the speech based on the interpreter's signing? How does the interpreter augment his or her signing to complement the meaning of the speech? Explain.

5. Although many people do not know American Sign Language (ASL), they do rely on some form of sign language to express themselves, such as by nodding or shaking their heads or through waving and other hand gestures. Discuss the ways you use sign language to convey meaning.

6. How could sign language improve the lives of hearing people? What advantages could signed languages offer over spoken ones? Explain.

My Yiddish

Leonard Michaels

> While language is mostly an unconscious activity, there are times when we focus on it intently—such as when we speak carefully for emphasis, or when we are trying to communicate in or understand another language. When Leonard Michaels overhears a conversation in Paris, he is at first thrilled to think that he has finally reached the point where he can understand—without effort—French. His heart sinks when he realizes that the conversation is not in French, but in Yiddish. Nevertheless the experience inspires him to reflect on the role of language in his life, its importance to his personal identity, and the identity of entire cultures.
>
> Leonard Michaels (1933–2003) was an American writer of short stories, novels, and essays. He is the author of *I Would Have Saved Them If I Could* (1975), *The Men's Club* (1981), and *Girl with a Monkey* (2000). Michaels, the son of immigrant Polish Jews, grew up on New York's Lower East Side and spoke only Yiddish until he was five years old. He wrote "My Yiddish" for an anthology called *The Genius of Language* (2004), abridged here.

1 In Paris one morning in the 1970s, walking along Rue Mahler, I saw a group of old men in an argument, shouting and gesticulating. I wanted to know what it was about, but my graduate-school French was good enough only to read great writers, not good enough for an impassioned argument or even conversation with the local grocer. But then, as I walked by the old men, I felt a shock and a surge of exhilaration. I did understand them. My god, I possessed the thing-spoken French! Just as suddenly, I crashed. The old men, I realized, were shouting in Yiddish.

2 Like a half-remembered dream, the incident lingered. It seemed intensely personal, yet impersonal. Meaning had come alive in me. I hadn't translated what the old men said. I hadn't done anything. A light turned on. Where nothing had been, there was something.

3 Philosophers used to talk about "The Understanding" as if it were a distinct mental function. Today they talk about epistemology or cognitive science. As for The Understanding, it's acknowledged in IQ tests, the value of which is subject to debate. It's also acknowledged in daily life in countless informal ways. You're on the same wave length with others or you are not. The Paris incident, where I rediscovered The Understanding, made me wonder if Descartes's remark, "I think, therefore I am," might be true in his case, but not mine. I prefer to say, "I am, therefore I think." And also, therefore, I speak.

4 Until I was five, I spoke only Yiddish. It did much to permanently qualify my thinking. Eventually I learned to speak English, then to imitate thinking as it transpires among English speakers. To some extent, my intuitions and my expression of thoughts remain basically Yiddish. I can say only approximately how this is true. For example this joke:

> The rabbi says, "What's green, hangs on the wall, and whistles?"
>
> The student says, "I don't know."
>
> The rabbi says, "A herring."

The student says, "Maybe a herring could be green and hang on the wall, but it absolutely doesn't whistle."

The rabbi says, "So it doesn't whistle."

The joke is inherent in Yiddish, not any other language. It's funny, and, like a story by Kafka, it isn't funny. I confess that I don't know every other language. Maybe there are such jokes in Russian or Chinese, but no other language has a history like Yiddish which, for ten centuries, has survived the dispersion and murder of its speakers.

5   As the excellent scholar and critic Benjamin Harshav points out, in *The Meaning of Yiddish*, the language contains many words that don't mean anything—*nu, epes, tokeh, shoyn*. These are fleeting interjections, rather like sighs. They suggest, without meaning anything, "so," "really," "well," "already." Other Yiddish words and phrases, noticed by Harshav, are meaningful but defeat translation. Transparent and easy to understand, however, is the way Yiddish serves speech—between you and me—rather than the requirements of consecutive logical discourse; that is, between the being who goes by your name and who speaks to others objectively and impersonally. For example, five times five is twenty-five, and it doesn't whistle.

6   Yiddish is probably at work in my written English. This moment, writing in English, I wonder about the Yiddish undercurrent. If I listen, I can almost hear it: "This moment"—a stress followed by two neutral syllables—introduces a thought which hangs like a herring in the weary droop of "writing in English," and then comes the announcement, "I wonder about the Yiddish undercurrent." The sentence ends in a shrug. Maybe I hear the Yiddish undercurrent, maybe I don't. The sentence could have been written by anyone who knows English, but it probably would not have been written by a well-bred Gentile. It has too much drama, and might even be disturbing, like music in a restaurant or an elevator. The sentence obliges you to abide in its staggered flow, as if what I mean were inextricable from my feelings and required a lyrical note. There is a kind of enforced intimacy with the reader. A Jewish kind, I suppose. In Sean O'Casey's lovelier prose you hear an Irish kind.

7   Wittgenstein says in his *Philosophical Investigations*, "Aren't there games we play in which we make up the rules as we go along, including this one." Nu. Any Yiddish speaker knows that. A good example of playing with the rules might be Montaigne's essays, the form that people say he invented. *Shoyn*, a big inventor. Jews have always spoken essays. The scandal of Montaigne's essays is that they have only an incidental relation to a consecutive logical argument but they are cogent nonetheless. Their shape is their sense. It is determined by motions of his mind and feelings, not by a pretension to rigorously logical procedure. Montaigne literally claims his essays are himself. Between you and him nothing intervenes. A Gentile friend used to say, in regard to writing she didn't like, "There's nobody home." You don't have to have Jewish ancestors, like those of Montaigne and Wittgenstein, to understand what she means.

8   I didn't speak English until I was five because my mother didn't speak English. My father had gone back to Poland to find a wife. He returned with an attractive seventeen-year-old who wore her hair in a long black braid. Men would hit on her, so my father wouldn't let her go take English classes. She learned English by doing my elementary-school homework with me. As for me, before and after the age of

five, I was susceptible to lung diseases and spent a lot of time in a feverish bed, in a small apartment on the Lower East Side of Manhattan, where nobody spoke anything but Yiddish. Years passed before I could ride a bike or catch a ball. In a playground fight, a girl could have wiped me out. I was badly coordinated and had no strength or speed, only a Yiddish mouth.

9   For a long time, Yiddish was my whole world. In this world, family didn't gather before dinner for cocktails and conversation. There were no cocktails, but conversation was daylong and it included criticism, teasing, opinionating, gossiping, joking. It could also be very gloomy. To gather before dinner for conversation would have seemed unnatural. I experienced the pleasure of such conversation for the first time at the University of Michigan, around 1956. It was my habit to join a friend at his apartment after classes. He made old-fashioneds and put music on the phonograph, usually chamber music. By the time we left for dinner, I felt uplifted by conversation and splendid music. Mainly, I was drunk, also a new experience. Among my Jews, conversation had no ritual character, no aesthetic qualities. I never learned to cultivate the sort of detachment that allows for the always potentially offensive personal note. Where I came from, everything was personal. . . .

10   The first time I went to a baseball game, the great slugger Hank Greenberg, during warm-up, casually tossed a ball into the stands, a gift to the crowd of pre-adolescent kids among whom I sat. My hand, thrusting up in a blossom of hands, closed on that baseball. I carried it home, the only palpable treasure I'd ever owned. I never had toys. On Christmas nights I sometimes dreamed of waking and finding toys in the living room. *Tokeh*? Yes, really. If there is a support group for Christmas depressives, I will be your leader. The baseball made me feel like a real American. It happened to me long before I had a romance with the mythical blonde who grants citizenship to Jews. By then I was already fifteen. I had tasted *traif* and long ago stopped speaking Yiddish except when I worked as a waiter in Catskills hotels. What Yiddish remained was enough to understand jokes, complaints, insults, and questions. As guests entered the dining room, a waiter might say, "Here come the *vildeh chayes*," or wild animals. One evening in the Catskills I went to hear a political talk, given in Yiddish. I understood little except that Yiddish could be a language of analysis, spoken by intellectuals. I felt alienated and rather ashamed of myself for not being like them.

11   Family members could speak Polish as well as Yiddish, and some Hebrew and Russian. My father worked for a short while in Paris and could manage French. My mother had gone to high school in Poland and was fluent in Polish, but refused to speak the language even when I asked her to. Her memory of pogroms made it unspeakable. In Yiddish and English I heard about her father, my grandfather, a tailor who made uniforms for Polish army officers. Once, after he'd worked all night to finish a uniform, the officer wouldn't pay. My grandfather, waving a pair of scissors, threatened to cut the uniform to pieces. The officer paid. The Germans later murdered my grandfather, his wife, and one daughter. Polish officers imprisoned in Katyn forest and elsewhere were massacred by Stalin. This paragraph, beginning with the first sentence and concluding with a moral, is in the form of a *geshichte*, or Yiddish story, except that it's in English and merely true. . . .

12   Family was uncles and aunts who escaped from Poland and immigrated to the United States. They stayed with us until they found their own apartments. I'd wake in the morning and see small Jews sleeping on the living room floor. My aunt Molly, long after she had a place of her own, often stayed overnight and slept on the floor. She was very lonely. Her husband was dead, her children had families of their own. A couch with a sheet, blanket, and pillow was available, but she refused such comforts. She wanted to be less than no trouble. She wore two or three dresses at once, almost her entire wardrobe. She slept on the floor in her winter coat and dresses. To see Molly first thing in the morning, curled against a wall, didn't make us feel good. She was the same height as my mother, around five feet, and had a beautiful intelligent melancholy face. I never saw her laugh, though she might chuckle softly, and she smiled when she teased me. She used to krotz (scratch) my back as I went to sleep, and she liked to speak to me in rhymes. First they were entirely Yiddish. Then English entered the rhymes.

> *Label, gay fressen.*
> *A fish shtayt on de tish.*
>
> Lenny, go eat.
> A fish is on the table.

13   "Shtayt" doesn't exactly mean "is." "Stands on the table" or "stays on the table" or "exists on the table" would be somewhat imprecise, though I think "A fish exists on the table" is wonderful. I once brought a girlfriend home, and Aunt Molly said, very politely, "You are looking very fit." Her "fit" sounded like "fet," which suggested "fat." My girlfriend squealed in protest. It took several minutes to calm her down. The pronunciation of "fet" for "fit" is typical of Yiddishified English, which is almost a third language. I speak it like a native when telling jokes. The audience for such jokes has diminished over the years because most Jews now are politically liberal and have college degrees and consider such jokes undignified or racist. A joke that touches on this development tells of Jewish parents who worry about a son who studies English literature at Harvard. They go to see Kittredge, the great Shakespeare scholar, and ask if he thinks their son's Yiddish accent is a disadvantage. Kittredge booms, "Vot ekcent?" . . .

14   What I have retained of Yiddish, I'm sorry to say, isn't much above the level of my Aunt Molly's poems. But what good to me is Yiddish? Recently, in Rome, during the High Holidays, a cordon was established around the synagogue in the ghetto, guarded by the police and local Jews. As I tried to pass I was stopped by a Jew. I was amazed. Couldn't he tell? I said, "Ich bin a yid. Los mir gayen arein." He said, "Let me see your passport." *La mia madrelingua* wasn't his. This happened to me before with Moroccan Jews in France. I've wondered about Spinoza. His Latin teacher was German, and the first Yiddish newspaper was published in Amsterdam around the time of his death. Did he know Yiddish?

15   I'm sure of very little about what I know except that the Yiddish I can't speak is more natural to my being than English, and partly for that reason I've studied English poets. There is a line in T. S. Eliot where he says words slip, slide, crack, or something. "Come off it, Tom," I think. "With words you never had no problem."

Who would suspect from his hateful remark about a Jew in furs that Eliot's family, like my mother's ancestors in Vienna, was up from the fur business? Eliot liked Groucho Marx, a Jew, but did he wonder when writing Four Quartets, with its striking allusions to Saint John of the Cross, that the small dark brilliant mystical monk might have been a Jew?

16   "Let there be light" are the first spoken words in the Old Testament. This light is understanding, not merely seeing. The Yiddish saying, "To kill a person is to kill a world," means the person is no longer the embodiment, or a mode of the glorious nothing that is the light, or illuminated world. This idea, I believe, is elaborated in Spinoza's *Ethics*. Existence—or being—entails ethics. Maybe the idea is also in Wittgenstein, who opens the Tractatus this way: "The world is everything that is the case." So what is the case? If it's the case that facts are bound up with values, it seems Yiddish or Spinozist. Possibly for this reason Jewish writers in English don't write about murder as well as Christians. Even Primo Levi, whose great subject is murder, doesn't offer the lacerating specificity one might expect. . .

17   My mother sometimes switches in midsentence, when talking to me, from English to Yiddish. If meaning can leave English and reappear in Yiddish, does it have an absolutely necessary relation to either language? Linguists say, "No. Anything you can say in German you can say in Swahili which is increasingly Arabic." But no poet could accept the idea of linguistic equivalence, and a religious fanatic might want to kill you for proposing it. Ultimately, I believe, meaning has less to do with language than with music, a sensuous flow that becomes language only by default, so to speak, and by degrees. In great fiction and poetry, meaning is obviously close to music. Writing about a story by Gogol, Nabokov says it goes la, la, do, la la la etc. The story's meaning is radically musical. I've often had to rewrite a paragraph because the sound was wrong. When at last it seemed right, I discovered—incredibly—the sense was right. Sense follows sound. Otherwise we couldn't speak so easily or quickly. If someone speaks slowly, and sense unnaturally precedes sound, the person can seem too deliberative; emotionally false, boring. I can tell stories all day, but to write one that sounds right entails labors of indefinable innerness until I hear the thing I must hear before it is heard by anyone else. A standard of rightness probably exists for me in my residual subliminal Yiddish. Its effect is to inhibit as well as to liberate. An expression, popular not long ago, "I hear you," was intended to assure you of being understood personally, as if there were a difference in comprehension between hearing and really hearing. In regard to being really heard, there are things in Yiddish that can't be heard in English. *Hazar fisl kosher*. "A pig has clean feet." It is an expression of contempt for hypocrisy. The force is in Yiddish concision. A pig is not clean. With clean feet it is even less clean. Another example: I was talking to a friend about a famous, recently deceased writer. The friend said, "He's *ausgespielt*." Beyond dead. He's played out. So forget it. Too much has been said about him.

18   Cultural intuitions, or forms or qualities of meaning, dancing about in language, derive from the unique historical experience of peoples. The intuitions are not in dictionaries but carried by tones, gestures, nuances effected by word order, etc. When I understood the old men in Paris I didn't do or intend anything. It wasn't a moment of romantic introspection. I didn't know what language I heard. I didn't

understand that I understood. What comes to mind is the assertion that begins the Book of John: "In the beginning was the word." A sound, a physical thing, the word is also mental. So this monism can be understood as the nature of everything. Like music that is the meaning of stories, physical and mental are aspects of each other. Yiddish, with its elements of German, Hebrew, Aramaic, Latin, Spanish, Polish, Russian, Rumanian, is metaphorically everything. A people driven hither and yon, and obliged to assimilate so much, returned immensely more to the world. How they can become necessary to murder is the hideous paradox of evil.

19   When I was five years old, I started school in a huge gloomy Victorian building where nobody spoke Yiddish. It was across the street from Knickerbocker Village, the project in which I lived. To cross that street meant going from love to hell. I said nothing in the classroom and sat apart and alone, and tried to avoid the teacher's evil eye. Eventually, she decided that I was a moron, and wrote a letter to my parents saying I would be transferred to the "ungraded class" where I would be happier and could play ping-pong all day. My mother couldn't read the letter so she showed it to our neighbor, a woman from Texas named Lynn Nations. A real American, she boasted of Indian blood, though she was blond and had the cheekbones, figure, and fragility of a fashion model. She would ask us to look at the insides of her teeth, and see how they were cupped. To Lynn this proved descent from original Americans. She was very fond of me, though we had no conversation, and I spent hours in her apartment looking at her art books and eating forbidden foods. I could speak to her husband, Arthur Kleinman, yet another furrier, and a lefty union activist, who knew Yiddish.

20   Lynn believed I was brighter than a moron and went to the school principal, which my mother would never have dared to do, and demanded an intelligence test for me. Impressed by her Katharine Hepburn looks, the principal arranged for a school psychologist to test me. Afterwards, I was advanced to a grade beyond my age with several other kids, among them a boy named Bonfiglio and a girl named Estervez. I remember their names because we were seated according to our IQ scores. Behind Bonfiglio and Estervez was me, a kid who couldn't even ask permission to go the bathroom. In the higher grade I had to read and write and speak English. It happened virtually overnight so I must have known more than I knew. When I asked my mother about this she said, "Sure you knew English. You learned from trucks." She meant: while lying in my sickbed I would look out the window at trucks passing in the street; studying the words written on their sides, I taught myself English. Unfortunately, high fevers burned away most of my brain, so I now find it impossible to learn a language from trucks. A child learns any language at incredible speed. Again, in a metaphorical sense, Yiddish is the language of children wandering for a thousand years in a nightmare, assimilating languages to no avail.

21   I remember the black shining print of my first textbook, and my fearful uncertainty as the meanings came with all their exotic Englishness and devoured what had previously inhered in my Yiddish. Something remained indigestible. What it is can be suggested, in a Yiddish style, by contrast with English. A line from a poem by Wallace Stevens, which I have discussed elsewhere, seems to me quintessentially goyish, or antithetical to Yiddish:

It is the word *pejorative* that hurts.

22   Stevens affects detachment from his subject, which is the poet's romantic heart, by playing on a French construction: "word *pejorative*," like *mot juste*, makes the adjective follow the noun. Detachment is further evidenced in the rhyme of "word" and "hurts." The delicate resonance gives the faint touch of hurtful impact without obliging the reader to suffer the experience. The line is ironically detached even from detachment. In Yiddish there is plenty of irony, but not so nicely mannered or sensitive to a reader's experience of words. Stevens's line would seem too self-regarding; and the luxurious subtlety of his sensibility would seem unintelligible, if not ridiculous. He flaunts sublimities here, but it must be said that elsewhere he is as visceral and concrete as any Yiddish speaker.

23   I've lost too much of my Yiddish to know exactly how much remains. Something remains. A little of its genius might be at work in my sentences, but this has nothing to do with me personally. The pleasures of complexity and the hilarity of idiocy, as well as an idea of what's good or isn't good, are in Yiddish. If it speaks in my sentences, it isn't I, let alone me, who speaks.

24   When asked what he would have liked to be if he hadn't been born an Englishman, Lord Palmerston said, "An Englishman." The answer reminds me of a joke. A Jew sees himself in a mirror after being draped in a suit by a high-class London tailor. The tailor asks what's wrong. The Jew says, crying, "Vee lost de empire." The joke assimilates the insane fury that influenced the nature of Yiddish and makes it apparent that identity for a Jew is not, as for Palmerston, a witty preference.

THINKING CRITICALLY

1. What impression did Michaels's experience on the rue Mahler have on him? Why does he describe the incident as both "intensely personal, yet impersonal"?

2. What does Michaels mean by "The Understanding" (paragraph 3)?

3. In what ways is Yiddish, as Michaels describes it, different from other languages? How does the language itself reflect the culture and history of the people who speak it? Explain.

4. Michaels uses some interesting expressions in his essay, such as in paragraph 6 when he says "The sentence ends in a shrug." Identify several areas of his essay where Michaels uses language in an interesting or unexpected way.

5. What influence has Yiddish had on Michaels? How does he feel about its role in his writing and his sense of identity? Explain.

6. Evaluate Michaels's use of examples in his essay to demonstrate his points.

WRITING ASSIGNMENTS

1. Consider the role your native language has had on your sense of personal and cultural identity. Does it serve to connect you in more ways than simply a means of communication? If you are bilingual, does your native language seem more a part of your core identity, as Yiddish is for Leonard Michaels? Write an essay exploring the role of language in your life in both a cultural and personal sense.

2. Michaels describes a language epiphany he had while in Paris, France. Write a personal narrative in which you describe a particularly poignant moment connected to language you experienced yourself, perhaps in a foreign country. You could also write about a moment when you realized the importance of language in your life.

3. Michaels notes that much of the humor in Yiddish jokes depends upon an inherent understanding of the language. Yiddish jokes may not be funny in Russian, English, or other languages that do not share a similar history.

Spanish Lessons

Christine Marín

Christine Marín was born to bilingual Mexican-American parents in Globe, Arizona. Remembering the discrimination they encountered during their own childhoods, the elder Maríns determined that their children would speak English in their home. Her parents recognized the power of language—they told their children to "speak better English than the gringo, so that he could not ridicule [them] the way they had been ridiculed in school and work." In this environment, Christine Marín began to encounter some mixed messages. On the one hand, she was encouraged to be proud of her heritage and cultural background; on the other, she was discouraged from speaking Spanish. It was not until high school that she began to recognize the power of the Spanish tongue. The essay that follows describes Marín's gradual awakening to the power of her cultural language, her emerging respect for this language, and how it ultimately shaped her identity.

Christine Marín is the curator for the Chicano Research Collection at the University of Arizona, where she also teaches in the Women's Studies program. She is the author of *Latinos in Museums: Heritage Reclaimed* (1998).

1 The reality of being a Mexican-American whose mother tongue was English and who did not speak Spanish came in the form of a 1958 high school band trip and the song "La Bamba" by Ritchie Valens (I didn't even know he was Mexican-American!), which was quite popular. I wasn't any different from the other high school kids who learned the words of popular songs we heard on the radio. Anglo and Mexican-American kids would sit together in the back of the bus and sing loudly and attempt to drown out the singing of those kids who sat toward the front of the bus. The game was to see who could sing the best and the loudest, and consequently drown out the singing of those in front.

2 On one band trip we sang "La Bamba." I didn't realize we were singing so loudly and in Spanish! My "voice" came out in the form of Spanish lyrics, although I was unaware of it. My Mexican-American identity shone through. I remember how proud I was for singing in Spanish, even though I didn't understand all the words of the song. I didn't know what a *bamba* was or what a *marinero* was. I hadn't heard those words before, and I wondered if my Mexican-American girlfriends knew the meaning of the song. I stumbled over the words, mispronouncing many of them. Suddenly, one popular Anglo girl sitting toward the front of the bus stood up in the middle of the aisle and shouted out loud so that everyone could hear: "Hey, you Mexicans! This is America! Stop singing in Spanish!" She proceeded to loudly sing "God Bless America" and "My Country 'Tis of Thee." To my surprise, her Anglo friends joined her in singing those patriotic songs. Well, our group of Mexican-American girls was not to be outdone. We sang

the words to "La Bamba" even louder, and this infuriated her even more! Eventually, our band director jumped up from his seat and demanded that we all shut up. That stopped the singing. I could see that our band director was agitated, but I wasn't sure if it was because of that stupid, racist remark from that little twerp or because of all the noise throughout the bus.

3   It didn't take me long to figure out what had happened. I realized that the girl and her friends did not resent being outsung but resented the fact that we were singing in Spanish, using words that weren't even a part of my everyday vocabulary! All I was doing was singing a song. I felt like getting up out of my seat and beating up that insensitive, stupid girl—and good! But I didn't. I learned the power of both the English and Spanish languages on that band trip. And what a lesson it was! The Spanish language posed a threat to that girl, and it made me feel proud of being a Mexican-American despite the fact that I didn't speak Spanish. I felt superior to her because I knew two languages and I could understand both English and Spanish, while she could only understand English.

4   In high school, I was an above-average student but certainly not one who made straight A's. I excelled in English and writing assignments, and my work was noticed by my English teachers, especially Mrs. Ethel Jaenicke. She hoped I would attend college after high school, something I hadn't thought was possible. She spent extra time with me and encouraged me to continue my writing. Unfortunately, my father's pay didn't stretch far enough to pay for a college education. My parents, however, knew the value and importance of a good education and wanted their children to continue on to college. They made great sacrifices to help all of us begin our college education and were encouraging, nurturing, and understanding about our struggles to stay in school. It was ultimately up to us to somehow find the money to stay in school and continue our education.

5   After graduation from Globe High School in 1961, I moved to Phoenix, where I lived with my older brother and his wife. A friend of his helped me get a job as a salesgirl at Jay's Credit Clothing, a Jewish-owned clothing store in downtown Phoenix. Customers bought their goods on credit. The clothing lines were fashionable, stylish, and overpriced. Most of the customers were African-Americans, Mexicans, Mexican-Americans, and some Anglos. Mexican-American saleswomen were paid a small weekly salary but earned most of their money through sales commissions. Making those sales was very competitive, and I didn't do so well. I couldn't speak Spanish well enough to assist Spanish-speaking customers who came into the store, which left me frustrated and embarrassed. One of the senior Mexican-American saleswomen felt sorry for me; she noticed how desperately I struggled with the language. She often gave me her own sales after she had assisted Spanish-speaking customers by putting my name on her sales tickets. She knew I would be attending Arizona State University in August and needed to save money for school. She took me under her wing and spoke to me of her childhood wishes of going to college, though her family couldn't afford to send her. This woman worked in that clothing store for many years. She taught me another lesson about the power of language: bilingualism paid well—monetarily well! I decided to recapture my lost native tongue and consciously worked on speaking more Spanish so that I could earn more money.

6   At ASU, I enrolled in liberal arts courses and had many interests. I took classes in psychology, sociology, history, and English, to name but a few. One college adviser even suggested that I major in Spanish because "Mexicans make good Spanish teachers and you could always find a job teaching it." If he only knew how badly I spoke the language! I didn't want to major in Spanish. Chalk up two more lessons learned about the power of language. First, someone assumed I spoke Spanish simply because of my surname and brown-colored skin. Second, by knowing the Spanish language, I would always be guaranteed a teaching job. However, I didn't want to be a teacher. . . .

7   During my freshman year, an English professor insulted my character and intelligence when she accused me of taking credit for a writing assignment she believed was written by someone else. According to her, the essay was extremely well written, but I couldn't have written it because "Mexicans don't write that well." "You people don't even speak the language correctly." Another hard lesson to learn about the power of language! This time the lesson was that my skin color and Spanish surname—not my language proficiency and ability in English—served as criteria to discriminate against me. My English ability was questioned and discredited. The academy had silenced my English voice. No matter how hard I tried, I couldn't convince her I had written that essay and that I had not paid someone to write it for me, as she presumed. This incident angered me. I had done what my parents said—be better than the gringo through language. But since this gringa professor had power and status, she felt she could accuse me of cheating. Needless to say, I dropped the class and never spoke to her again. I didn't care whether she believed me or not. . . .

8   In 1970, I applied for and was hired for a bibliographer position, where I learned all aspects of verifying English-language bibliographic entries and citations for monographs, serials, periodicals, and government documents, among others. I learned the intricacies of checking and verifying library holdings and how to use bibliographic tools and sources. I grew intellectually in my work. Because of my knowledge of library-related information, I became the "expert" and "voice" for my classmates and their friends who either were unfamiliar with the library system or found learning how to use book or serial catalogs confusing. I taught them how to use the library's catalogs and reference tools and encouraged them to enjoy the library setting. My job empowered me. I had learned a new code—the library code.

9   The year 1970 was an important one for Mexican-American students at ASU in other ways. My friends were beginning to call themselves "Chicanos" as a term of self-identification and tossed aside the term "Mexican Americans." For them, the term "Chicano" meant empowerment, and they found a new identity as Chicanos. But it was not a new word to me. I had heard it used by my parents and their friends when I was growing up in Globe. My father called himself a Chicano, and so did his friends from his military service days in World War II. For them the word "Chicano" was used in friendship—as a term of endearment, as a term of identity.

10   Now my college friends were using the word "Chicano" differently and in a defiant manner, with the word "power" after it: "Chicano Power!" For them and for me, it became a term of self-identity. The word was an assertion of ethnic and cultural pride, a term heard in a new form of social protests and associated with student activism and civil rights militancy. Chicanos throughout the Southwest were caught up in the Chicano Movement, a civil rights movement. They made new

demands—that they become visible rather than invisible on their college and university campuses—and wanted a voice. They demanded courses that described the history, culture, and experiences of Chicanos in the Southwest. They wanted Chicano counselors and professors to teach bilingual-bicultural education courses and courses in social work on their campuses. Arizona State University was going to be at the forefront in making these changes. Two scholars, Dr. Manuel Patricio Servín and Dr. H. William Axford, played in integral role in this demand for change. Hayden Library was to be the setting that allowed students to legitimize history, culture, art, language, and literature by acknowledging the presence of Mexican-Americans, Chicanos, and Mexicans. . . .

11   Servín and Axford quickly became my friends; the scholar and the librarian took me under their wings. They anticipated what Chicano students were going to do: demand that their library have books *by* and *about* them. They were right, and they gave students their voice. This is where I came in. Not long after his arrival, Dr. Axford came to the bibliography department and asked if anyone was familiar with Chicano materials. Being the only Chicana in the department, I was the one who spoke up.

12   In 1969, my friends had organized the Mexican-American Students Organization (MASO) on the ASU campus, and I attended the meetings. MASO students came from various Arizona places, including mining towns, cities, and rural towns. The majority spoke English, so meetings were conducted in English; the MASO newsletter was written in English, with a few slogans in Spanish thrown in for effect, such as *¡Basta Ya!, ¡Viva La Raza!, Con Safos,* and *¡Viva La Huelga!* By 1970, I had attended Chicano Movement–related meetings, had participated in United Farmworker rallies in Phoenix, and had leafleted pro-union literature urging the boycott of lettuce sold at Safeway stores. I became well acquainted with Chicano Movement ideologies and with the events of the times.

13   I met with Drs. Axford and Servín and listened to a new idea that they proposed to me. Dr. Axford suggested that I become the bibliographer for the Chicano Studies Collection, with my first task being to conduct an inventory of the library's holdings of Chicano-related materials. Dr. Servín provided me with various bibliographies listing the Chicano Studies' holdings of university libraries in California. I kept a record of the library's strengths and weaknesses in Chicano Studies by searching publishers' catalogs, listing the titles we didn't have, and marking them as available for purchasing. In that meeting with Drs. Axford and Servín, I learned that it was their intent to build a Chicano Studies Collection that would support Servín's teaching and research needs in Chicano Studies and the needs of those students who would enroll in the American Studies program. Dr. Axford wanted to strengthen the library's holding in Chicano Studies so that he would be prepared to justify those holdings to Chicano students when they demanded that the library have them. I agreed to become the bibliographer for the Chicano Studies Collection. I was the staff of one. In essence, Axford and Servín empowered me to take over the Chicano Studies Collection. I became the expert, the liaison for scholars, students, and researchers. The Chicano Studies Collection became another means by which my voice was heard. I now had the opportunity to tell others of my culture, of which I was proud. . . .

14   Dr. Axford was open to the idea of meeting with MASO. I agreed to work with MASO representatives in selecting books for the Chicano Studies Collection. It was a

positive relationship, reflective of Dr. Axford's philosophy of open access to library materials and sources. Chicano students began to utilize the library, and brown faces were now appearing in greater numbers in the study areas in and around the collection. Soon I was collecting and saving MASO newsletters, leaflets, minutes from meetings, membership lists, and other Chicano movement materials for my own interest. Dr. Servín encouraged me to collect these materials for the library and planted the seed in my mind to someday build a Chicano Studies archives. What a great idea! He also encouraged me to return to school and enroll in his courses to familiarize myself with the historical literature of the Southwest. It was my fate and destiny to encounter Drs. Servín and Axford and to find a new direction that would satisfy my intellectual growth and development. I learned more about Chicano history from Dr. Servín's classes, where I was exposed to the writings, research, and thought of Chicano scholars and writers. He also gave me the opportunity to do research and helped me publish my first article about the Chicano Movement in a scholarly journal that he edited. In 1974, my scholarly voice came through.

15   Outside the classroom, I continued to be exposed to Chicano Movement ideas and activities, and I easily made friends and contacts who would lead me to those elusive materials that are archival prizes in academic libraries today. I was challenged to improve my Spanish language skills by those individuals who were community activists. They spoke in both English and Spanish, and I learned what the term "codeswitching" meant. As a reflection of the times, MASO students changed their name in 1971 to MECHA, which stands for Movimiento Estudiantil Chicano de Aztlán.

16   I've continued working at Hayden Library, where I am now the curator/archivist for the Chicano Research Collection. I have built the Chicano Studies Collection into an important archival repository. During the last ten years, I've been an adjunct faculty associate in the Women's Studies program, where I have taught the courses "La Chicana" and "Women in the Southwest." I have assigned my students to write about the history of Chicanas in their families, to become curious about their family histories, and to incorporate oral history into their research. Through this assignment, they give voice to their own family histories, and they acquire their own voices in the discovery of their identities. Their manuscripts, as well as those of others, are in the Chicano Research Collection. These materials provide information about the past. Students, researchers, and scholars from all over the world have access to records, documents, oral histories, photographs, diaries, correspondence, videos, pamphlets, leaflets, and posters about the history, culture, and heritage of Chicanos, Chicanas, and Mexican-Americans in the United States. I am proud and honored to preserve these records for future Chicana and Chicano scholars. It is these materials that transmit the voices of *nuestra raza* vis-à-vis the printed page.

17   As I conclude my journey and the sharing of my story of growing up in an Arizona mining town, I have come to discover the many voices and modes of communication I had available to me and how they have contributed to the formation of self and identity. These voices have empowered me, educated me, sensitized me. Empowerment came through my work as an archivist and MASO/MECHA student, my scholarship, and my work in academe. My English voices as a young child, in

school, and throughout ring clear: the discrimination in academe that I encountered in my English class and also my knowledge of the intricacies of library language. My Spanish voices are also evident: in the back of the band bus in high school; when, for economic survival, I was a salesclerk; and when, through activism, I worked for change in the Chicano community. My empowerment coming full circle is evident through the sharing of my voice in my scholarship and my roles as teacher, lecturer, and historian. From the back of the bus to the ivory tower, I have learned the power of language.

THINKING CRITICALLY

1. What is the catalyst for Christine Marín's awareness of the power of Spanish in her life? How does she react to this event? How does it connect to her identity and her growing consciousness of the power of language?

2. How does Marín's physical appearance conflict with the expectations of the "Anglos" around her? Cite some examples in which her ethnic appearance causes cultural confusion and how she deals with this.

3. How does Marín learn to appreciate her heritage? Having been raised in an English-only household as an American, how does her ancestry begin to blend with her identity? Review the changes described by Marín to the term *Chicano*. What did the word mean to her when she was a child in a Mexican-American household? How did the word change in the early 1970s while she was in college? What do you think accounts for this transition?

4. Until college, Marín says that she did not really feel that her Mexican heritage made her any different from her peers. What event does Marín experience as a freshman that changes her perspective? How does she react to it?

5. How does the Chicano Studies Collection at the University of Arizona become a means by which Marín's voice can be heard? What is this voice? How does it empower her?

6. What do you think is the meaning of the author's last sentence? Does it connect to her essay as a whole? Explain.

WRITING ASSIGNMENTS

1. Marín details some of the experiences that contributed to her awareness of the power of her ancestral language and its connection to her identity. Can you recall any events in your life that made you realize the connections between your language and your sense of self? Write about your experience.

2. When Marín was a freshman, she encountered a teacher who refused to believe that she was capable of writing well because of her physical appearance. Have you ever experienced a similar situation in which someone judged you by your looks and not by your verbal or intellectual skills? Alternatively, have you ever made assumptions about another person's abilities based on what they looked like? Explain.

3. Is the way you personally use language something that you take for granted? Write an essay in which you explore the power of your own language. As you write, consider how language contributes to your identity and how you fit into your culture. How does your language empower you?

The Language of Silence
Maxine Hong Kingston

Maxine Hong Kingston, born in 1940, was raised in a Chinese immigrant community in Stockton, California. As a first-generation American, she found herself having to adjust to two distinctly contrasting cultures. For a young girl, this was confusing and difficult, as she recalls in this selection from her highly praised and popular autobiography, *The Woman Warrior: Memoirs of a Girlhood Among Ghosts* (1976). To the Chinese immigrant, white Americans are "ghosts"—pale, threatening, and at times, comical specters who speak an incomprehensible tongue. For Kingston, becoming American meant adopting new values, defining a new self, and finding a new voice.

Before the publication of her award-winning autobiography, Kingston taught in several high schools and business schools. Since then, she has published *China Men* (1980) a novel, *The Tripmaster Monkey: His Fake Book* (1989), and reflections on writing, *To Be the Poet* (2002). She currently teaches English at the University of California, Berkeley.

1 Long ago in China, knot-makers tied string into buttons and frogs, and rope into bell pulls. There was one knot so complicated that it blinded the knot-maker. Finally an emperor outlawed this cruel knot, and the nobles could not order it anymore. If I had lived in China, I would have been an outlaw knot-maker.

2 Maybe that's why my mother cut my tongue. She pushed my tongue up and sliced the frenum. Or maybe she snipped it with a pair of nail scissors. I don't remember her doing it, only her telling me about it, but all during childhood I felt sorry for the baby whose mother waited with scissors or knife in hand for it to cry—and then, when its mouth was wide open like a baby bird's, cut. The Chinese say "a ready tongue is an evil."

3 I used to curl up my tongue in front of the mirror and tauten my frenum into a white line, itself as thin as a razor blade. I saw no scars in my mouth. I thought perhaps I had had two frena, and she had cut one. I made other children open their mouths so I could compare theirs to mine. I saw perfect pink membranes stretching into precise edges that looked easy enough to cut. Sometimes I felt very proud that my mother committed such a powerful act upon me. At other times I was terrified—the first thing my mother did when she saw me was to cut my tongue.

4 "Why did you do that to me, Mother?"

5 "I told you."

6 "Tell me again."

7 "I cut it so that you would not be tongue-tied. Your tongue would be able to move in any language. You'll be able to speak languages that are completely different from one another. You'll be able to pronounce anything. Your frenum looked too tight to do those things, so I cut it."

8 "But isn't 'a ready tongue an evil'?"

9 "Things are different in this ghost country."

10 "Did it hurt me? Did I cry and bleed?"

11 "I don't remember. Probably."

12   She didn't cut the other children's. When I asked cousins and other Chinese children whether their mothers had cut their tongues loose, they said "What?"

13   "Why didn't you cut my brothers' and sisters' tongues?"

14   "They didn't need it."

15   "Why not? Were theirs longer than mine?"

16   "Why don't you quit blabbering and get to work?"

17   If my mother was not lying she should have cut more, scraped away the rest of the frenum skin, because I have a terrible time talking. Or she should not have cut at all, tampering with my speech. When I went to kindergarten and had to speak English for the first time, I became silent. A dumbness—a shame—still cracks my voice in two, even when I want to say "hello" casually, or ask an easy question in front of the check-out counter, or ask directions of a bus driver. I stand frozen, or I hold up the line with the complete, grammatical sentence that comes squeaking out at impossible length. "What did you say?" says the cab driver, or "Speak up," so I have to perform again, only weaker the second time. A telephone call makes my throat bleed and takes up that day's courage. It spoils my day with self-disgust when I hear my broken voice come skittering out into the open. It makes people wince to hear it. I'm getting better, though. Recently I asked the postman for special-issue stamps; I've waited since childhood for postmen to give me some of their own accord. I am making progress, a little every day.

18   My silence was thickest—total—during the three years that I covered my school paintings with black paint. I painted layers of black over houses and flowers and suns, and when I drew on the background, I put a layer of chalk on top. I was making a stage curtain, and it was the moment before the curtain parted or rose. The teachers called my parents to school, and I saw they had been saving my pictures, curling and cracking, all alike and black. The teachers pointed to the pictures and looked serious, talked seriously too, but my parents did not understand English. ("The parents and teachers of criminals were executed," said my father.) My parents took the pictures home. I spread them out (so black and full of possibilities) and pretended the curtains were swinging open, flying up, one after another, sunlight underneath, mighty operas.

19   During the first silent year I spoke to no one at school, did not ask before going to the lavatory, and flunked kindergarten. My sister also said nothing for three years, silent in the playground and silent at lunch. There were other quiet Chinese girls not of our family, but most of them got over it sooner than we did. I enjoyed the silence. At first it did not occur to me I was supposed to talk or to pass kindergarten. I talked at home and to one or two of the Chinese kids in class. I made motions and even made some jokes. I drank out of a toy saucer when the water spilled out of the cup, and everybody laughed, pointing at me, so I did it some more. I didn't know that Americans don't drink out of saucers.

20   I liked the Negro students (Black Ghosts) best because they laughed the loudest and talked to me as if I were a daring talker too. One of the Negro girls had her mother coil braids over her ears Shanghai-style like mine; we were Shanghai twins except that she was covered with black like my paintings. Two Negro kids enrolled in Chinese school, and the teachers gave them Chinese names. Some Negro kids walked me to school and home, protecting me from the Japanese kids, who hit me and chased me and stuck gum in my ears. The Japanese kids were noisy and tough.

They appeared one day in kindergarten, released from concentration camp, which was a tic-tac-toe mark, like barbed wire, on the map.

21   It was when I found out I had to talk that school became a misery, that the silence became a misery. I did not speak and felt bad each time that I did not speak. I read aloud in first grade, though, and heard the barest whisper with little squeaks come out of my throat. "Louder," said the teacher, who scared the voice away again. The other Chinese girls did not talk either, so I knew the silence had to do with being a Chinese girl.

22   Reading out loud was easier than speaking because we did not have to make up what to say, but I stopped often, and the teacher would think I'd gone quiet again. I could not understand "I." The Chinese "I" has seven strokes, intricacies. How could the American "I," assuredly wearing a hat like the Chinese, have only three strokes, the middle so straight? Was it out of politeness that this writer left off strokes the way a Chinese has to write her own name small and crooked? No, it was not politeness; "I" is a capital and "you" is a lower-case. I stared at that middle line and waited so long for its black center to resolve into tight strokes and dots that I forgot to pronounce it. The other troublesome word was "here," no strong consonant to hang on to, and so flat, when "here" is two mountainous ideographs. The teacher, who had already told me every day how to read "I" and "here," put me in the low corner under the stairs again, where the noisy boys usually sat.

23   When my second grade class did a play, the whole class went to the auditorium except the Chinese girls. The teacher, lovely and Hawaiian, should have understood about us, but instead left us behind in the classroom. Our voices were too soft or nonexistent, and our parents never signed the permission slips anyway. They never signed anything unnecessary. We opened the door a crack and peeked out, but closed it again quickly. One of us (not me) won every spelling bee, though.

24   I remember telling the Hawaiian teacher, "We Chinese can't sing 'Land where our fathers died.'" She argued with me about politics, while I meant because of curses. But how can I have that memory when I couldn't talk? My mother says that we, like ghosts, have no memories.

25   After American school, we picked up our cigar boxes, in which we had arranged books, brushes, and an inkbox neatly, and went to Chinese school, from 5:00 to 7:30 P.M. There we chanted together, voices rising and falling, loud and soft, some boys shouting, everybody reading together, reciting together and not alone with one voice. When we had a memorization test, the teacher let each of us come to his desk and say the lesson to him privately, while the rest of the class practiced copying or tracing. Most of the teachers were men. The boys who were so well behaved in the American school played tricks on them and talked back to them. The girls were not mute. They screamed and yelled during recess, when there were no rules; they had fistfights. Nobody was afraid of children hurting themselves or of children hurting school property. The glass doors to the red and green balconies with the gold joy symbols were left wide open so that we could run out and climb the fire escapes. We played capture-the-flag in the auditorium, where Sun Yat-sen and Chiang Kai-shek's pictures hung at the back of the stage, the Chinese flag on their left and the American

flag on their right. We climbed the teak ceremonial chairs and made flying leaps off the stage. One flag headquarters was behind the glass door and the other on stage right. Our feet drummed on the hollow stage. During recess, the teachers locked themselves up in their office with the shelves of books, copybooks, inks from China. They drank tea and warmed their hands at a stove. There was no play supervision. At recess we had the school to ourselves, and also we could roam as far as we could to— downtown, Chinatown stores, home—as long as we returned before the bell rang.

26   At exactly 7:30 the teacher again picked up the brass bell that sat on his desk and swung it over our heads, while we charged down the stairs, our cheering magnified in the stairwell. Nobody had to line up.

27   Not all of the children who were silent at American school found voice at Chinese school. One new teacher said each of us had to get up and recite in front of the class, who was to listen. My sister and I had memorized the lesson perfectly. We said it to each other at home, one chanting, one listening. The teacher called on my sister to recite first. It was the first time a teacher had called on the second-born to go first. My sister was scared. She glanced at me and looked away; I looked down at my desk. I hoped that she could do it because if she could, then I would have to. She opened her mouth and a voice came out that wasn't a whisper, but it wasn't a proper voice either. I hoped that she would not cry, fear breaking up her voice like twigs underfoot. She sounded as if she were trying to sing through weeping and strangling. She did not pause or stop to end the embarrassment. She kept going until she said the last word, and then she sat down. When it was my turn, the same voice came out, a crippled animal running on broken legs. You could hear splinters in my voice, bones rubbing jagged against one another. I was loud, though. I was glad I didn't whisper. There was one little girl who whispered. . . .

28   How strange that the emigrant villagers are shouters, hollering face to face. My father asks, "Why is it I can hear Chinese from blocks away? Is it that I understand the language? Or is it they talk loud?" They turn the radio up full blast to hear the operas, which do not seem to hurt their ears. And they yell over the singers that wail over the drums, everybody talking at once, big arm gestures, spit flying. You can see the disgust on American faces looking at women like that. It isn't just the loudness. It is the way Chinese sounds, ching-chong ugly, to American ears, not beautiful like Japanese sayonara words with the consonants and vowels as regular as Italian. We make guttural peasant noise and have Ton Duc Thang names you can't remember. And the Chinese can't hear Americans at all; the language is too soft and western music unhearable. I've watched a Chinese audience laugh, visit, talk-story, and holler during a piano recital, as if the musician could not hear them. A Chinese-American, somebody's son, was playing Chopin, which has no punctuation, no cymbals, no gongs. Chinese piano music is five black keys. Normal Chinese women's voices are strong and bossy. We American-Chinese girls had to whisper to make ourselves American-feminine. Apparently, we whispered even more softly than the Americans. Once a year the teachers referred my sister and me to speech therapy, but our voices would straighten out, unpredictably normal, for the therapists. Some of us gave up, shook our heads, and said nothing, not one word. Some of us could not even shake our heads. At times, shaking my head no is more self-assertion than I

can manage. Most of us eventually found some voice, however faltering. We invented an American-feminine speaking personality.

THINKING CRITICALLY

1. Kingston employed silence rather than language in the early grades. What accounts for the difference in attitude between kindergarten, where she "employed the silence," and first grade, where "silence became a misery"?

2. Kingston's teacher punished her for failing to read "I" and "here." How does this episode demonstrate the clash between Chinese and American cultures? Are there other episodes in the essay that also demonstrate this struggle?

3. How did Kingston's Chinese school differ from the American one? What impact did the former school have on her language development?

4. What do you make of Kingston's paintings? What was Kingston's personal view of her work? How do they relate to her "language of silence"?

5. Examine the conclusion of the essay. Would you say this is a moment of triumph or defeat for Kingston? Explain.

6. At what point in the essay do you know Kingston's focus? What are the clues to her purpose? Does this lead capture your attention? Explain.

7. Kingston writes this essay using the first person. How is this ironic in light of what she writes in the piece? Would this essay be as effective if it were told from a third-person point of view? Explain.

WRITING ASSIGNMENTS

1. Assume that you are a teacher with Kingston as a pupil. How would you handle her? What different tactics would it take to get her to come out of herself? Write a paper in which you describe your role.

2. Did you have difficulties "coming to language" as a child? Do you remember resorting to protective silence because of your accent, a different primary language, or a different cultural identity? Did you feel fear and/or embarrassment because of your difference, and did you carry the results of your experience into your adult life? If so, in what way? In a personal narrative, describe your experience.

3. Kingston admits that even as an adult, she has "a terrible time talking." She says that she still freezes with shame, that she can hardly be heard, that her voice is broken and squeaky. What about her writing style? Do you see any reflection of her vocal difficulties—any signs of hesitation or uncertainty? In a paper, consider these questions as you try to describe her style as it relates to her experiences as a young girl.

4. Bilingual education is a controversial form of education designed to instill educational confidence in school children, allowing them to learn using the language spoken in their homes. See the National Clearinghouse for Bilingual Education's Web site maintained by George Washington University for more information on this form of education at www.ncela.gwu.edu/. Kingston relates that she had to go to a separate Chinese school after her regular school day. Do you think Kingston's educational experience would have been different had she been taught in a bilingual classroom?

Exploring the Language of VISUALS

A Child's First Story

Independent writing is a pedagogical approach to language that allows children to express themselves through writing without the restrictions of spelling and grammar. Designed to promote confidence and comfort with the written word, this type of writing exercise is becoming popular in kindergartens and first-grade classrooms nationwide. Here is a sample of a kindergartener's first attempts at writing about two girls who lost their puppy.

THINKING CRITICALLY

1. Could you understand Cassie's story without the teacher's "translation" under her sentences? What can we deduce about the way children sound out and process language based on Cassie's story?

2. What strikes you about Cassie's writing? What letters does she leave out? How does she construct her words? What words is Cassie unlikely to *ever* spell correctly without formal academic instruction and why?

3. Recall your own early writing experiences. Were you encouraged, like Cassie, to simply use language comfortably, without rules, or were you given strict instruction on spelling and grammar? Were you penalized for incorrect use of language? What do you think of this particular technique as a means to facilitate writing and comfort with the written word?

4. Repeat this exercise with a child under the age of 6 and see how it compares to Cassie's piece. Remember to tell the child that spelling doesn't matter. Do they ask for help? If so, what sort of help? Do they seem at ease or uncomfortable with the exercise? Can you make any observations about children and language based on watching a child do this exercise? Explain.

MAKING CONNECTIONS

1. Most students probably take literacy for granted. Imagine that you were illiterate—that is, you could not read or write. Brainstorm and make a list of all the things you could not do. Select one or two of the items on your list and write in your journal about what it might be like to be illiterate. You might try adopting the point of view of an illiterate young parent or a successful salesperson who has kept his or her illiteracy a secret.

2. Recall any communication difficulties you had as a child. Perhaps you are bilingual or had difficulty pronouncing certain words, or maybe an older sibling prevented you from expressing yourself. Explain how your experience made you feel, recalling, if possible, any particularly telling experiences. Can you identify with any of the authors in this section? If so, which ones and why?

3. Did your parents or grandparents come to America from another country? If not, are you acquainted with anyone who did? Conduct an interview with this person about his or her language choices. What is his or her view about the importance of language? What happened to his or her language after moving America? Provide a brief biographical sketch of the person you interviewed and present your research to the class.

4. Helen Keller writes that the acquisition of language "set her free." Malcolm X expresses similar views on the freeing power of language. In your journal, record your own feelings about the different ways that language provides freedom. In addition to drawing from some of the essays in this section, you may wish to add an experience of your own.

5. Each of the authors in this section recollects a moment in which they realized the power of language. For Malcolm X, It was when he realized how language could set him free. For Helen Keller, it was when she first connected words to abstract concepts. For Christine Marín, it was when she connected ethnic pride to the language of her ancestors. Write about a defining moment in your life when you felt the power of language.

6. Research the origins and development of American Sign Language. How does this system of communication qualify as "a language"? How has this language changed the lives of nonhearing people? Explain.

SPEAKING OUT: INSPIRING CHANGE

Seneca Falls Declaration
Elizabeth Cady Stanton

Elizabeth Cady Stanton (1815–1902) was one of the first activists for women's rights in America. Born in Johnstown, New York, she was educated at Johnstown Academy, an all-male school to which she was admitted under special arrangement. After a few years of study at the Troy Female Seminary, she turned to law but was denied admission to the New York Bar because of her gender. Following her marriage to abolitionist Henry B. Stanton, she was denied recognition as a delegate at London's World Anti-Slavery Convention in 1840 because she was a woman. Incensed by such prejudice, Stanton dedicated the rest of her life to the abolition of laws that restricted the freedom and denied the civil rights of women.

In 1848, Stanton helped organize the Seneca Falls Convention, which inaugurated the movement for women's suffrage. In 1869, she was elected the first president of the National Woman's Suffrage Association, a post she held until 1890. Her writings include the three-volume *History of Woman's Suffrage* (1896), *A Woman's Bible* (1895), and her autobiographical *Eighty Years and More* (1898). The following speech, enumerating women's grievances and demanding equal rights, is modeled after Thomas Jefferson's Declaration of Independence. Stanton delivered this speech at the 1848 Seneca Falls Convention held in New York state.

1 When in the course of human events, it becomes necessary for one portion of the family of man to assume among the people of the earth a position different from that which they have hitherto occupied, but one to which the laws of nature and of nature's God entitle them, a decent respect to the opinions of mankind requires that they should declare the causes that impel them to such a course.

2 We hold these truths to be self-evident: that all men and women are created equal; that they are endowed by their Creator with certain inalienable rights; that among these are life, liberty, and the pursuit of happiness; that to secure these rights governments are instituted, deriving their just powers from the consent of the governed. Whenever any form of government becomes destructive of these ends, it is the right of those who suffer from it to refuse allegiance to it, and to insist upon the institution of a new government, laying its foundation on such principles, and organizing its powers in such form, as to them shall seem most likely to effect their safety and happiness. Prudence, indeed, will dictate that governments long established should not be changed for light and transient causes; and accordingly all experience hath shown that mankind are more disposed to suffer, while evils are sufferable, then to right themselves by abolishing the forms to which they were accustomed. But when a long train of abuses and usurpations, pursuing invariably the same object evinces a design to reduce them under absolute despotism, it is their duty to throw off such government, and to provide new guards for their future security. Such has been the patient sufferance of the women under this government, and such is now the necessity which constrains them to demand the equal station to which they are entitled.

3 The history of mankind is a history of repeated injuries and usurpations on the part of man toward woman, having in direct object the establishment of an absolute tyranny over her. To prove this, let facts be submitted to a candid world.

4 He has never permitted her to exercise her inalienable right to the elective franchise.

5 He has compelled her to submit to laws, in the formation of which she had no voice.

6 He has withheld from her rights which are given to the most ignorant and degraded men—both natives and foreigners.

7 Having deprived her of this first right of a citizen, the elective franchise, thereby leaving her without representation in the halls of legislation, he has oppressed her on all sides.

8   He has made her, if married, in the eye of the law, civilly dead.

9   He has taken from her all right in property, even to the wages she earns.

10   He has made her, morally, an irresponsible being, as she can commit many crimes with impunity, provided they be done in the presence of her husband. In the covenant of marriage she is compelled to promise obedience to her husband, he becoming, to all intents and purposes, her master—the law giving him power to deprive her of her liberty, and to administer chastisement.

11   He has so framed the laws of divorce, as to what shall be the proper causes, and in case of separation, to whom the guardianship of the children shall be given, as to be wholly regardless of the happiness of women—the law, in all cases, going upon a false supposition of the supremacy of man, and giving all power into his hands.

12   After depriving her of all rights as a married woman, if single, and the owner of property, he has taxed her to support a government which recognizes her only when her property can be made profitable to it.

13   He has monopolized nearly all the profitable employments, and from those she is permitted to follow, she receives but a scanty remuneration. He closes against her all the avenues to wealth and distinction which he considers most honorable to himself. As a teacher of theology, medicine, or law, she is not known.

14   He has denied her the facilities for obtaining a thorough education, all colleges being closed against her.

15   He allows her in Church, as well as State, but a subordinate position, claiming Apostolic authority for her exclusion from the ministry, and, with some exceptions, from any public participation in the affairs of the Church.

16   He has created a false public sentiment by giving to the world a different code of morals for men and women, by which moral delinquencies which exclude women from society, are not only tolerated, but deemed of little account in man.

17   He has usurped the prerogative of Jehovah himself, claiming it as his right to assign for her a sphere of action, when that belongs to her conscience and to her God.

18   He has endeavored, in every way that he could, to destroy her confidence in her own powers, to lessen her self-respect, and to make her willing to lead a dependent and abject life.

19   Now, in view of this entire disfranchisement of one-half the people of this country, their social and religious degradation—in view of the unjust laws above mentioned, and because women do feel themselves aggrieved, oppressed, and fraudulently deprived of their most sacred rights, we insist that they have immediate admission to all the rights and privileges which belong to them as citizens of the United States.

20   In entering upon the great work before us, we anticipate no small amount of misconception, misrepresentation, and ridicule; but we shall use every instrumentality without our power to effect our object. We shall employ agents, circulate tracts, petition the State and National legislatures, and endeavor to enlist the pulpit and the press on our behalf. We hope this Convention will be followed by a series of Conventions embracing every part of the country.

Resolutions

21 Whereas, The great precept of nature is conceded to be, that "man shall pursue his own true and substantial happiness." Blackstone in his Commentaries remarks, that this law of Nature being coeval with mankind, and dictated by God himself, is of course superior in obligation to any other. It is binding over all the globe, in all countries and at all times; no human laws are of any validity if contrary to this, and such of them as are valid, derive all their force, and all their validity, and all their authority, mediately and immediately, from this original; therefore,

22 *Resolved,* That such laws as conflict, in any way, with the true and substantial happiness of woman, are contrary to the great precept of nature and of no validity, for this is "superior in obligation to any other."

23 *Resolved,* That all laws which prevent woman from occupying such a station in society as her conscience shall dictate, or which place her in a position inferior to that of man, are contrary to the great precept of nature, and therefore of no force or authority.

24 *Resolved,* That woman is man's equal—was intended to be so by the Creator, and the highest good of the race demands that she should be recognized as such.

25 *Resolved,* That the women of this country ought to be enlightened in regard to the laws under which they live, that they may no longer publish their degradation by declaring themselves satisfied with their present position, nor their ignorance, by asserting that they have all the rights they want.

26 *Resolved,* That inasmuch as man, while claiming for himself intellectual superiority, does accord to woman moral superiority, it is preeminently his duty to encourage her to speak and teach, as she has an opportunity, in all religious assemblies.

27 *Resolved,* That the same amount of virtue, delicacy, and refinement of behavior that is required of woman in the social state, should also be required of man, and the same transgressions should be visited with equal severity on both man and woman.

28 *Resolved,* That the objection of indelicacy and impropriety, which is so often brought against woman when she addresses a public audience, comes with a very ill-grace from those who encourage, by their attendance, her appearance on the stage, in the concert, or in feats of the circus.

29 *Resolved,* That woman has too long rested satisfied in the circumscribed limits which corrupt customs and a perverted application of the Scriptures have marked out for her, and that it is time she should move in the enlarged sphere which her great Creator has assigned her.

30 *Resolved,* That it is the duty of the women of this country to secure to themselves their sacred right to the elective franchise.

31 *Resolved,* That the equality of human rights results necessarily from the fact of the identity of the race in capabilities and responsibilities.

32 *Resolved, therefore,* That, being invested by the Creator with the same capabilities, and the same consciousness of responsibility for their exercise, it is demonstrably the right and duty of woman, equally with man, to promote every righteous cause by every righteous means; and especially in regard to the great subjects of morals and religion, it is self-evidently her right to participate with her brother in teaching them, both in private and in public, by writing and by speak-

ing, by any instrumentalities proper to be used, and in any assemblies proper to be held; and this being a self-evident truth growing out of the divinely implanted principles of human nature, any custom or authority adverse to it, whether modern or wearing the hoary sanction of antiquity, is to be regarded as a self-evident falsehood, and at war with mankind.

33   [At the last session Lucretia Mott offered and spoke to the following resolution:] *Resolved,* That the speedy success of our cause depends upon the zealous and untiring efforts of both men and women, for the overthrow of the monopoly of the pulpit, and for the securing to women an equal participation with men in the various trades, professions, and commerce.

THINKING CRITICALLY

1. Why did Elizabeth Cady Stanton model her "Declaration of Sentiments and Resolutions" after the United States' Declaration of Independence? Do you think her strategy was effective? Why or why not? What statements does she make concerning the equality of men and women?

2. Which of the "repeated injuries and usurpation on the part of man toward woman" are still going on today?

3. What is the "great precept of nature" that Stanton refers to in paragraph 21? How does Stanton use this argument to provide a foundation for her resolutions? Where in the resolutions does she qualify her evidence from a higher authority when she refers to "a perverted application of the Scriptures"?

4. What do you think Stanton means when she urges women to be as responsible as men in promoting "every righteous cause by every righteous means" (paragraph 32)?

5. List the ways in which Stanton attempts to break down the social limitations placed upon women of her time. How does she attack these boundaries?

WRITING ASSIGNMENTS

1. Review the Seneca Falls Declaration and rewrite the resolutions that you feel have not yet been achieved. Use the same form employed by Stanton. You may update the diction.

2. You are a newspaper reporter covering the Seneca Falls Convention in New York in 1848, for a front-page story. Write a newspaper article addressing the social and political implications of the rally. Be sure to include a title for your article.

3. Access the Library of Congress's photo archive of the Women's Suffrage Movement at www.memory.loc.gov/ammem/today/jan11.html. Drawing from the information gathered from this site and its many useful links, write a letter inviting one of the political activists from this era such as Alice Paul, Lucy Burns, Susan B. Anthony, Julia Ward Howe, Lucy Stone, or Carrie Chapman Catt to a twenty-first-century discussion on women's rights. Include some things about women's rights today that might provoke their interest.

Exploring the Language of **VISUALS**

Afghanistan Woman

Women in Afghanistan face many challenges as they navigate the complex political, economic, and social systems left after the fall of the Taliban. The country is still deeply conservative and holds women to strict social rules of conduct. Most women still wear burkas—some are fearful of retaliation if they don't and others prefer the protection of anonymity a burka can provide in a volatile environment. But clothing, while a visual reminder of oppression, is one of the lesser challenges Afghan women must address. Life under the Taliban created a social and economic climate in which women were completely dependent on men—they were not allowed to hold jobs, go to school, or even drive a car. Today, women in Afghanistan, who make up over 60 percent of the country's population, are trying to learn how to be members of society again—in less than ideal conditions.

The New Courier, no. 1. © Reza/Webistan, Paris.

This picture, taken in Kabul, the capital of Afghanistan, depicts the defaced image of a woman with her head covered, but not wearing a burka. The photo appeared in the fall 2002 issue of *The New Courier*, a magazine published by the United Nations Educational, Scientific and Cultural Organization (UNESCO). UNESCO "serves as a clearinghouse—for the dissemination and sharing of information and knowledge— while helping to build their human and institutional capacities in diverse fields."

THINKING CRITICALLY

1. What can you determine about attitudes toward women in Afghanistan based on what you see in the photo?

2. Would this photo have less impact if only the woman's mouth had been scratched over? What is the symbolism of having both the eyes and the mouth defaced? Explain.

3. How does this photo make you feel, and why? Explore the implications of this image—the various responses it may elicit from different viewers, such as a woman or man walking on the streets of Kabul, or as a reader of a magazine published by the United Nations.

4. Read more about the situation of women in Afghanistan at www.rawa.us/ rawa.html. The Revolutionary Association of the Women of Afghanistan (RAWA) is "the oldest political/social organization of Afghan women struggling for peace, freedom, democracy and women's rights" in Afghanistan. How does the information on the Web site reflect the image in the photo? What cultural and social forces must women in Afghanistan face?

Letter from Birmingham Jail

Martin Luther King, Jr.

> In 1963, Martin Luther King, Jr. was arrested at a sit-in demonstration in Birmingham, Alabama. Written from a jail cell, the famous letter reprinted here was addressed to King's fellow clergy, who were critical of his activities in the name of social justice. The letter, however, has a second audience in mind—the collective conscience of the American people. As such, the letter functions much like one of King's speeches, in which he applies both emotion and logic to strategically make his point.
>
> Martin Luther King, Jr. was one of the most prominent and charismatic leaders for black civil rights in America. An ordained minister with a doctorate in theology, King organized the Southern Christian Leadership Conference in 1957 to promote justice and equality for African-Americans. Under King's leadership, the civil rights movement eventually eliminated racist laws that prohibited blacks from using restaurants, public swimming pools, and seats in the front sections of buses. For his efforts, King was awarded the Nobel Peace Prize in 1964. Four years later, while supporting striking sanitation workers in Memphis, Tennessee, King was assassinated.

My Dear Fellow Clergymen:

1 While confined here in the Birmingham city jail, I came across your recent statement calling my present activities "unwise and untimely." Seldom do I pause to answer criticism of my work and ideas. If I sought to answer all the criticisms that cross my desk, my secretaries would have little time for anything other than such correspondence in the course of the day, and I would have no time for constructive work. But since I feel that you are men of genuine good will and that your criticisms are sincerely set forth, I want to try to answer your statement in what I hope will be patient and reasonable terms.

2 I think I should indicate why I am here in Birmingham, since you have been influenced by the view which argues against "outsiders coming in." I have the honor of serving as president of the Southern Christian Leadership Conference, an organization operating in every southern state, with headquarters in Atlanta, Georgia. We have some eighty-five affiliated organizations across the South, and one of them is the Alabama Christian Movement for Human Rights. Frequently we share staff, educational and financial resources with our affiliates. Several months ago the affiliate here in Birmingham asked us to be on call to engage in a nonviolent direct-action program if such were deemed necessary. We readily consented, and when the hour came we lived up to our promise. So I, along with several members of my staff, am here because I was invited here, I am here because I have organizational ties here.

3 But more basically, I am in Birmingham because injustice is here. Just as the prophets of the eighth century B.C. left their villages and carried their "thus saith the Lord" far beyond the boundaries of their home towns, and just as the Apostle Paul left his village of Tarsus and carried the gospel of Jesus Christ to the far corners of the Greco-Roman world, so am I compelled to carry the gospel of freedom beyond my own home town. Like Paul, I must constantly respond to the Macedonian call for aid.

4 Moreover, I am cognizant of the interrelatedness of all communities and states. I cannot sit idly by in Atlanta and not be concerned about what happens in Birmingham. Injustice anywhere is a threat to justice everywhere. We are caught in an inescapable network of mutuality, tied in a single garment of destiny. Whatever affects one directly, affects all indirectly. Never again can we afford to live with the narrow, provincial "outside agitator" idea. Anyone who lives inside the United States can never be considered an outsider anywhere within its bounds.

5 You deplore the demonstrations taking place in Birmingham. But your statement, I am sorry to say, fails to express a similar concern for the conditions that brought about the demonstrations. I am sure that none of you would want to rest content with the superficial kind of social analysis that deals merely with effects and does not grapple with underlying causes. It is unfortunate that demonstrations are taking place in Birmingham, but it is even more unfortunate that the city's white power structure left the Negro community with no alternative.

6 In any nonviolent campaign there are four basic steps: collection of the facts to determine whether injustices exist; negotiation; self-purification; and direct action. We have gone through all these steps in Birmingham. There can be no gainsaying the fact that racial injustice engulfs this community. Birmingham is probably the most thoroughly segregated city in the United States. Its ugly record of brutality is widely known. Negroes have experienced grossly unjust treatment in the courts. There have been more unsolved bombings of Negro homes and churches in Birmingham than in any other city in the nation. These are the hard, brutal facts of the case. On the basis of these conditions, Negro leaders sought to negotiate with the city fathers. But the latter consistently refused to engage in good-faith negotiation.

7 Then, last September, came the opportunity to talk with leaders of Birmingham's economic community. In the course of the negotiations, certain promises were made by the merchants—for example, to remove the stores' humiliating racial signs. On the basis of these promises, the Reverend Fred Shuttlesworth and the leaders of the

Alabama Christian Movement for Human Rights agreed to a moratorium on all demonstrations. As the weeks and months went by, we realized that we were the victims of a broken promise. A few signs, briefly removed, returned; the others remained.

8 As in so many past experiences, our hopes had been blasted, and the shadow of deep disappointment settled upon us. We had no alternative except to prepare for direct action, whereby we would present our very bodies as a means of laying our case before the conscience of the local and the national community. Mindful of the difficulties involved, we decided to undertake a process of self-purification. We began a series of workshops on nonviolence, and we repeatedly asked ourselves: "Are you able to accept blows without retaliating?" "Are you able to endure the ordeal of jail?" We decided to schedule our direct-action program for the Easter season, realizing that except for Christmas, this is the main shopping period of the year. Knowing that a strong economic-withdrawal program would be the by-product of direct action, we felt that this would be the best time to bring pressure to bear on the merchants for the needed change.

9 Then it occurred to us that Birmingham's mayoralty election was coming up in March, and we speedily decided to postpone action until after election day. When we discovered that the Commissioner of Public Safety, Eugene "Bull" Connor, had piled up enough votes to be in the run-off, we decided again to postpone action until the day after the run-off so that the demonstrations could not be used to cloud the issues. Like many others, we waited to see Mr. Connor defeated, and to this end we endured postponement after postponement. Having aided in this community need, we felt that our direct-action program could be delayed no longer.

10 You may well ask: "Why direct action? Why sit-ins, marches and so forth? Isn't negotiation a better path?" You are quite right in calling for negotiation. Indeed, this is the very purpose of direct action. Nonviolent direct action seeks to create such a crisis and foster such a tension that a community which has constantly refused to negotiate is forced to confront the issue. It seeks so to dramatize the issue that it can no longer be ignored. My citing the creation of tension as part of the work of the nonviolent-resister may sound rather shocking. But I must confess that I am not afraid of the word "tension." I have earnestly opposed violent tension, but there is a type of constructive, nonviolent tension which is necessary for growth. Just as Socrates felt that it was necessary to create a tension in the mind so that individuals could rise from the bondage of myths and half-truths to the unfettered realm of creative analysis and objective appraisal, so must we see the need for nonviolent gadflies to create the kind of tension in society that will help men rise from the dark depths of prejudice and racism to the majestic heights of understanding and brotherhood.

11 The purpose of our direct-action program is to create a situation so crisis-packed that it will inevitably open the door to negotiation. I therefore concur with you in your call for negotiation. Too long has our beloved Southland been bogged down in a tragic effort to live in monologue rather than dialogue.

12 One of the basic points in your statement is that the action that I and my associates have taken in Birmingham is untimely. Some have asked: "Why didn't you give the

new city administration time to act?" The only answer that I can give to this query is that the new Birmingham administration must be prodded about as much as the outgoing one, before it will act. We are sadly mistaken if we feel that the election of Albert Boutwell as mayor will bring the millennium to Birmingham. While Mr. Boutwell is a much more gentle person than Mr. Connor, they are both segregationists, dedicated to maintenance of the status quo. I have hope that Mr. Boutwell will be reasonable enough to see the futility of massive resistance to desegregation. But he will not see this without pressure from devotees of civil rights. My friends, I must say to you that we have not made a single gain in civil rights without determined legal and nonviolent pressure. Lamentably, it is an historical fact that privileged groups seldom give up their privileges voluntarily. Individuals may see the moral light and voluntarily give up their unjust posture; but, as Reinhold Niebuhr has reminded us, groups tend to be more immoral than individuals.

13 We know through painful experience that freedom is never voluntarily given by the oppressor; it must be demanded by the oppressed. Frankly, I have yet to engage in a direct-action campaign that was "well timed" in the view of those who have not suffered unduly from the disease of segregation. For years now I have heard the word "Wait!" It rings in the ear of every Negro with piercing familiarity. This "Wait" has almost always meant "Never." We must come to see, with one of our distinguished jurists, that "justice too long delayed is justice denied."

14 We have waited for more than 340 years for our constitutional and God-given rights. The nations of Asia and Africa are moving with jet-like speed toward gaining political independence, but we still creep at horse-and-buggy pace toward gaining a cup of coffee at a lunch counter. Perhaps it is easy for those who have never felt the stinging darts of segregation to say, "Wait." But when you have seen vicious mobs lynch your mothers and fathers at will and drown your sisters and brothers at whim; when you have seen hate-filled policemen curse, kick, and even kill your black brothers and sisters; when you see the vast majority of your twenty million Negro brothers smothering in an airtight cage of poverty in the midst of an affluent society; when you suddenly find your tongue twisted and your speech stammering as you seek to explain to your six-year-old daughter why she can't go to the public amusement that has just been advertised on television, and see tears welling up in her eyes when she is told that Funtown is closed to colored children, and see ominous clouds of inferiority beginning to form in her little mental sky, and see her beginning to distort her personality by developing an unconscious bitterness toward white people; when you have to concoct an answer for a five-year-old son who is asking: "Daddy, why do white people treat colored people so mean?"; when you take a cross-country drive and find it necessary to sleep night after night in the uncomfortable corners of your automobile because no motel will accept you; when you are humiliated day in and day out by nagging signs reading "white" and "colored"; when your first name becomes "nigger," your middle name becomes "boy" (however old you are) and your last name becomes "John," and your wife and mother are never given the respected title "Mrs."; when you are harried by day and haunted by night by the fact that you are Negro, living constantly at tiptoe stance, never quite knowing what to expect next, and are plagued with inner fears and outer

resentments; when you are forever fighting a degenerating sense of "nobodiness"—then you will understand why we find it difficult to wait. There comes a time when the cup of endurance runs over, and men are no longer willing to be plunged into the abyss of despair. I hope, sirs, you can understand our legitimate and unavoidable impatience.

15 You express a great deal of anxiety over our willingness to break laws. This is certainly a legitimate concern. Since we so diligently urge people to obey the Supreme Court's decision of 1954 outlawing segregation in the public schools, at first glance it may seem rather paradoxical for us consciously to break laws. One may well ask: "How can you advocate breaking some laws and obeying others?" The answer lies in the fact that there are two types of laws: just and unjust. I would be the first to advocate obeying just laws. One has not only a legal but a moral responsibility to obey just laws. Conversely, one has a moral responsibility to disobey unjust laws. I would agree with St. Augustine that "an unjust law is no law at all."

16 Now, what is the difference between the two? How does one determine whether a law is just or unjust? A just law is a man-made code that squares with the moral law or the law of God. An unjust law is a code that is out of harmony with the moral law. To put it in the terms of St. Thomas Aquinas: An unjust law is a human law that is not rooted in eternal law and natural law. Any law that uplifts human personality is just. Any law that degrades human personality is unjust. All segregation statutes are unjust because segregation distorts the soul and damages the personality. It gives the segregator a false sense of superiority and the segregated a false sense of inferiority. Segregation, to use the terminology of the Jewish philosopher Martin Buber, substitutes an "I-it" relationship for an "I-thou" relationship and ends up relegating persons to the status of things. Hence segregation is not only politically, economically and sociologically unsound, it is morally wrong and sinful. Paul Tillich has said that sin is separation. Is not segregation an existential expression of man's tragic separation, his awful estrangement, his terrible sinfulness? Thus it is that I can urge men to obey the 1954 decision of the Supreme Court, for it is morally right; and I can urge them to disobey segregation ordinances, for they are morally wrong.

17 Let us consider a more concrete example of just and unjust laws. An unjust law is a code that a numerical or power majority group compels a minority group to obey but does not make binding on itself. This is *difference* made legal. By the same token, a just law is a code that a majority compels a minority to follow and that it is willing to follow itself. This is *sameness* made legal.

18 Let me give another explanation. A law is unjust if it is inflicted on a minority that, as a result of being denied the right to vote, had no part in enacting or devising the law. Who can say that the legislature of Alabama which set up that state's segregation laws was democratically elected? Throughout Alabama all sorts of devious methods are used to prevent Negroes from becoming registered voters, and there are some counties in which, even though Negroes constitute a majority of the population, not a single Negro is registered. Can any law enacted under such circumstances be considered democratically structured?

19 Sometimes a law is just on its face and unjust in its application. For instance, I have been arrested on a charge of parading without a permit. Now, there is nothing wrong in having an ordinance which requires a permit for a parade. But such an ordinance becomes unjust when it is used to maintain segregation and to deny citizens the First Amendment privilege of peaceful assembly and protest.

20 I hope you are able to see the distinction I am trying to point out. In no sense do I advocate evading or defying the law, as would the rabid segregationist. That would lead to anarchy. One who breaks an unjust law must do so openly, lovingly, and with a willingness to accept the penalty. I submit that an individual who breaks a law that conscience tells him is unjust, and who willingly accepts the penalty of imprisonment in order to arouse the conscience of the community over its injustice, is in reality expressing the highest respect for law.

21 Of course, there is nothing new about this kind of civil disobedience. It was evidenced sublimely in the refusal of Shadrach, Meshach, and Abednego to obey the laws of Nebuchadnezzar, on the grounds that a higher moral law was at stake. It was practiced superbly by the early Christians, who were willing to face hungry lions and the excruciating pain of chopping blocks rather than submit to certain unjust laws of the Roman Empire. To a degree, academic freedom is a reality today because Socrates practiced civil disobedience. In our own nation, the Boston Tea Party represented a massive act of civil disobedience.

22 We should never forget that everything Adolf Hitler did in Germany was "legal" and everything the Hungarian freedom fighters did in Hungary was "illegal." It was "illegal" to aid and comfort a Jew in Hitler's Germany. Even so, I am sure that, had I lived in Germany at the time, I would have aided and comforted my Jewish brothers. If today I lived in a Communist country where certain principles dear to the Christian faith are suppressed, I would openly advocate disobeying that country's antireligious laws.

23 I must make two honest confessions to you, my Christian and Jewish brothers. First, I must confess that over the past few years I have been gravely disappointed with the white moderate. I have almost reached the regrettable conclusion that the Negro's great stumbling block in his stride toward freedom is not the White Citizen's Counciler or the Ku Klux Klanner, but the white moderate, who is more devoted to "order" than to justice; who prefers a negative peace which is the absence of tension to a positive peace which is the presence of justice; who constantly says: "I agree with you in the goal you seek, but I cannot agree with your methods of direct action"; who paternalistically believes he can set the timetable for another man's freedom; who lives by a mythical concept of time and who constantly advises the Negro to wait for a "more convenient season." Shallow misunderstanding from people of good will is more frustrating than absolute misunderstanding from people of ill will. Lukewarm acceptance is much more bewildering than outright rejection.

24 I had hoped that the white moderate would understand that law and order exist for the purpose of establishing justice and that when they fail in this purpose they become the dangerously structured dams that block the flow of social progress. I had hoped

that the white moderate would understand that the present tension in the South is a necessary phase of the transition from an obnoxious negative peace, in which the Negro passively accepted his unjust plight, to a substantive and positive peace, in which all men will respect the dignity and worth of human personality. Actually, we who engage in nonviolent direct action are not the creators of tension. We merely bring to the surface the hidden tension that is already alive. We bring it out in the open, where it can be seen and dealt with. Like a boil that can never be cured so long as it is covered up but must be opened with all its ugliness to the natural medicines of air and light, injustice must be exposed, with all the tension its exposure creates, to the light of human conscience and the air of national opinion before it can be cured.

25 In your statement you assert that our actions, even though peaceful, must be condemned because they precipitate violence. But is this a logical assertion? Isn't this like condemning a robbed man because his possession of money precipitated the evil act of robbery? Isn't this like condemning Socrates because his unswerving commitment to truth and his philosophical inquiries precipitated the act by the misguided populace in which they made him drink hemlock? Isn't this like condemning Jesus because his unique God-consciousness and never-ceasing devotion to God's will precipitated the evil act of crucifixion? We must come to see that, as the federal courts have consistently affirmed, it is wrong to urge an individual to cease his efforts to gain his basic constitutional rights because the quest may precipitate violence. Society must protect the robbed and punish the robber.

26 I had also hoped that the white moderate would reject the myth concerning time in relation to the struggle for freedom. I have just received a letter from a white brother in Texas. He writes: "All Christians know that the colored people will receive equal rights eventually, but it is possible that you are in too great a religious hurry. It has taken Christianity almost two thousand years to accomplish what it has. The teachings of Christ take time to come to earth." Such an attitude stems from a tragic misconception of time, from the strangely irrational notion that there is something in the very flow of time that will inevitably cure all ills. Actually, time itself is neutral; it can be used either destructively or constructively. More and more I feel that the people of ill will have used time much more effectively than have the people of good will. We will have to repent in this generation not merely for the hateful words and actions of the bad people but for the appalling silence of the good people. Human progress never rolls in on wheels of inevitability; it comes through the tireless efforts of men willing to be co-workers with God, and without this hard work, time itself becomes an ally of the forces of social stagnation. We must use time creatively, in the knowledge that the time is always ripe to do right. Now is the time to make real the promise of democracy and transform our pending national elegy into a creative psalm of brotherhood. Now is the time to lift our national policy from the quicksand of racial injustice to the solid rock of human dignity.

27 You speak of our activity in Birmingham as extreme. At first, I was rather disappointed that fellow clergymen would see my nonviolent efforts as those of an extremist. I began thinking about the fact that I stand in the middle of two opposing forces in the Negro Community. One is a force of complacency, made up in part of

Negroes who, as a result of long years of oppression, are so drained of self-respect and a sense of "somebodiness" that they have adjusted to segregation; and in part of a few middle-class Negroes who, because of a degree of academic and economic security and because in some ways they profit by segregation, have become insensitive to the problems of the masses. The other force is one of bitterness and hatred, and it comes perilously close to advocating violence. It is expressed in the various black nationalist groups that are springing up across the nation, the largest and best known being Elijah Muhammad's Muslim movement. Nourished by the Negro's frustration over the continued existence of racial discrimination, this movement is made up of people who have lost faith in America, who have absolutely repudiated Christianity, and who have concluded that the white man is an incorrigible "devil."

28 I have tried to stand between these two forces, saying that we need emulate neither the "do-nothingism" of the complacent nor the hatred and despair of the black nationalist. For there is the more excellent way of love and nonviolent protest. I am grateful to God that, through the influence of the Negro church, the way of nonviolence became an integral part of our struggle.

29 If this philosophy had not emerged, by now many streets of the South would, I am convinced, be flowing with blood. And I am further convinced that if our white brothers dismiss as "rabble-rousers" and "outside agitators" those of us who employ nonviolent direct action, and if they refuse to support our nonviolent efforts, millions of Negroes will, out of frustration and despair, seek solace and security in black-nationalist ideologies—a development that would inevitably lead to a frightening racial nightmare.

30 Oppressed people cannot remain oppressed forever. The yearning for freedom eventually manifests itself, and that is what has happened to the American Negro. Something within has reminded him of his birthright of freedom, and something without has reminded him that it can be gained. Consciously or unconsciously, he has been caught up by the *Zeitgeist,* and with his black brothers of Africa and his brown and yellow brothers of Asia, South America and the Caribbean, the United States Negro is moving with a sense of great urgency toward the promised land of racial justice. If one recognizes this vital urge that has engulfed the Negro community, one should readily understand why public demonstrations are taking place. The Negro has many pent-up resentments and latent frustrations, and he must release them. So let him march; let him make prayer pilgrimages to the city hall; let him go on freedom rides—and try to understand why he must do so. If his repressed emotions are not released in nonviolent ways, they will seek expression through violence; this is not a threat but a fact of history. So I have not said to my people: "Get rid of your discontent." Rather, I have tried to say that this normal and healthy discontent can be channeled into the creative outlet of nonviolent direction action. And now this approach is being termed extremist.

31 But though I was initially disappointed at being categorized as an extremist, as I continue to think about the matter I gradually gained a measure of satisfaction from the label. Was not Jesus an extremist for love: "Love your enemies, bless them that curse you, do good to them that hate you, and pray for them which despitefully use

you, and persecute you." Was not Amos an extremist for justice: "Let justice roll
down like waters and righteousness like an everflowing stream." Was not Paul an
extremist for the Christian gospel: "I bear in my body the marks of the Lord Jesus."
Was not Martin Luther an extremist: "Here I stand; I cannot do otherwise, so help
me God." And John Bunyan: "I will stay in jail to the end of my days before I make
a butchery of my conscience." And Abraham Lincoln: "This nation cannot survive
half slave and half free." And Thomas Jefferson: "We hold these truths to be self-
evident, that all men are created equal. . . ." So the question is not whether we will
be extremists, but what kind of extremists we will be. Will we be extremists for hate
or for love? Will we be extremists for the preservation of injustice or for the existence of justice? In that dramatic scene on Calvary's hill, three men were crucified.
We must never forget that all three were crucified for the same crime—the crime of
extremism. Two were extremists for immorality, and thus fell below their environment. The other, Jesus Christ, was an extremist for love, truth, and goodness, and
thereby rose above his environment. Perhaps the South, the nation and the world
are in dire need of creative extremists. . . .

32   If I have said anything in this letter that overstates the truth and indicates an unreasonable impatience, I beg you to forgive me. If I have said anything that understates
the truth and indicates my having a patience that allows me to settle for anything
less than brotherhood, I beg God to forgive me.

33   I hope this letter finds you strong in the faith. I also hope that circumstances will
soon make it possible for me to meet each of you, not as an integrationist or a civil-
rights leader but as a fellow clergyman and a Christian brother. Let us all hope that
the dark clouds of racial prejudice will soon pass away and the deep fog of misunderstanding will be lifted from our fear-drenched communities, and in some not too
distant tomorrow the radiant stars of love and brotherhood will shine over our great
nation with all their scintillating beauty.

Yours for the cause of Peace and Brotherhood,
Martin Luther King, Jr.

THINKING CRITICALLY

1. King states in paragraph 26, "We will have to repent in this generation not
   merely for the hateful words and actions of the bad people but for the appalling
   silence of the good people." What does this statement mean to you? Do you
   agree? In what situations might silence be appalling?

2. Describe the voice and tone King uses in this letter. What does his voice reveal
   about his personality, and how does it affect his argument? How does he establish credibility, authority, and personality in his letter? Explain.

3. In paragraph 12, King states that the Birmingham officials at the time were
   "dedicated to maintenance of the status quo." What was the status quo in the
   Birmingham of 1963? What is the status quo today?

4. In paragraph 14, King provides a "catalogue" of reasons why the civil rights
   movement cannot wait any longer. Analyze this technique in terms of King's argument. What effect does this cataloguing have on the reader?

5. Martin Luther King, Jr. was first and foremost a preacher. How does the language in his letter reveal his profession? Would this letter be as effective as a speech? Would it be better? How does the medium (letter or speech) affect the choice of language used?

6. In paragraphs 15 through 20, King provides "proof" regarding the differences between just and unjust laws. Examine the language in this section and decide whether his logic is effective. Explain your conclusions.

WRITING ASSIGNMENTS

1. Some critics have commented that King was considered a great leader by the white status quo because he preached a program of nonviolence and used a rhetoric that reflected "acceptable American values." Explore this idea further by researching some additional speeches made by King. Then, drawing from your research, write an essay addressing this issue expressing your opinion.

2. Using the language techniques employed by King in his letter, write your own letter directed toward people you respect protesting an injustice that you feel they may not entirely understand. Consider the concerns of your audience as you explain the nature of the injustice, the history/sociology behind it, and why you feel your argument is valid and should be accepted by your readers.

3. In his letter, King justifies civil disobedience by arguing that the established laws are unjust. Are there any current laws that seem unjust to you? Would you demonstrate to protest a current unjust law or practice? Why or why not?

Ain't I a Woman?

Sojourner Truth

Sojourner Truth was born into slavery with the name Isabella Baumfree around 1797. In 1826, she escaped to freedom with her infant daughter Sophia. In 1843, she changed her name to Sojourner Truth, which some biographers attribute to her intention to travel the country "telling the truth." Other historians report that her name change was connected to a religious experience. During her lifetime, she spoke for women's rights and prison reform and even addressed the Michigan Legislature speaking against capital punishment. She was highly respected among abolitionists and met Abraham Lincoln in 1864 at the White House. She also met Elizabeth Cady Stanton in 1867, while traveling through the South. After a long life fighting for human rights, Sojourner Truth died at her home in Battle Creek, Michigan, in 1883.

In May of 1851, Sojourner Truth attended a women's rights convention held in Akron, Ohio. The only black woman in attendance, on the second day of the convention, Truth rose from her seat and approached the podium. Nearly six-feet tall, with a deep clear voice, Truth systematically refuted the claims of some of the male speakers that day. What follows is a transcription of that speech as recorded by Frances D. Gage, who presided at the convention.

1 Well, children, where there is so much racket there must be something out o' kilter. I think that 'twixt the negroes of the South and the women of the North all a-talking

about rights, the white man will be in a fix pretty soon. But what's all this here talking about?

2   That man over there says that women need to be helped into carriages, and lifted over ditches, and to have the best place everywhere. Nobody ever helps me into carriages, or over mud puddles, or gives me any best place *(and raising herself to her full height and her voice to a pitch like rolling thunder, she asked),* and ain't I a woman? Look at me! Look at my arm! *(And she bared her right arm to the shoulder, showing her tremendous muscular power.)* I have ploughed, and planted, and gathered into barns, and no man could head me—and ain't I a woman? I could work as much and eat as much as a man (when I could get it), and bear the lash as well—and ain't I a woman? I have borne thirteen children and seen them almost all sold off to slavery, and when I cried out with my mother's grief, none but Jesus heard—and ain't I a woman?

3   Then they talk about this thing in the head—what's this they call it? *("Intellect," whispered someone near.)* That's it honey. What's that got to do with woman's rights or Negroes' rights? If my cup won't hold but a pint and yours holds a quart, wouldn't you be mean not to let me have my little half-measure full? *(And she pointed her significant finger and sent a keen glance at the minister who had made the argument. The cheering was long and loud.)*

4   Then that little man in black there, he says women can't have as much rights as man, 'cause Christ wasn't a woman. Where did your Christ come from? *(Rolling thunder could not have stilled that crowd as did those deep, wonderful tones, as she stood there with outstretched arms and eye of fire. Raising her voice still louder, she repeated,)* Where did your Christ come from? From God and a woman. Man had nothing to do with Him. *(Oh! what a rebuke she gave the little man.)*

5   *(Turning again to another objector, she took up the defense of mother Eve. I cannot follower [sic] her through it all. It was pointed, and witty, and solemn, eliciting at almost every sentence deafening applause; and she ended [sic] by asserting that)* If the first woman God ever made was strong enough to turn the world upside down, all alone, these together *(and she glanced her eye over us),* ought to be able to turn it back and get it right side up again; and now they are asking to do it, the men better let them. *(Long-continued cheering.)*

6   'Bliged to you for hearing on me, and now old Sojourner hasn't got anything more to say.

THINKING CRITICALLY

1. How does Truth prefix each of her "answers" to the male dissenters? Can you figure out what the men said from Truth's words? Explain.

2. What is the biblical argument against the equality of women? How does Truth address this argument?

3. According to historians, the women at the Akron convention asked Frances Gage to prevent Truth from speaking, fearing that it would "mix and confuse" causes. What do you think was the basis of their fear? How do you think they felt about Truth after she spoke?

4. What kind of courage did it take for Truth to speak at this convention, both as a woman and as an ex-slave? How does she use her background to assert her convictions? Is she effective in making her point? Explain.

WRITING ASSIGNMENTS

1. Visit the Sojourner Truth Institute at www.sojournertruth.org and read more about this remarkable woman. Write an essay on how her achievements as a woman and as a former slave left their mark on our history. How do you think Truth would react to our society today?

2. Both Stanton and Truth address the "biblical" argument made against women's rights. Stanton calls this argument "perverted," and Truth likewise challenges it. To what argument are they referring? Evaluate this "biblical argument" against women's rights. Then write an essay in which you address this issue. How does the biblical argument factor into our modern ideology?

3. Compare the general status of American women with that of women in other countries in order to demonstrate the wide range of women's rights and roles. Using library research and, if possible, personal testimony from people from other countries, develop your findings in a paper. A good Web site on international women's rights is at www.wld.org/org.html, which provides links to other Internet Web sites addressing women's rights.

The Struggle for Human Rights
Eleanor Roosevelt

Anna Eleanor Roosevelt was the wife of Franklin D. Roosevelt, the thirty-second president of the United States. As first lady during her husband's presidency from 1933 to 1945, Roosevelt served as her husband's political right arm. She expanded the role of the president's wife into a position involving political action and public service. Their marriage is considered one of the "greatest political partnerships in history." After her husband's death while still in office in 1945, Roosevelt remained active in international politics. In 1946, she was elected head of the United Nation's Human Rights Division, and she played a central role in the adoption of the Declaration of Human Rights by the United Nations in 1948. She remained a member of the UN delegation until 1953, but she continued to participate in international human rights issues until her death in 1962.

Roosevelt delivered the following speech on September 28, 1948, at the Sorbonne during a meeting of the United Nation's General Assembly in Paris. Several months later, on December 10, 1948, the Human Rights Declaration was passed by the UN.

1 I have come this evening to talk with you on one of the greatest issues of our time—that is the preservation of human freedom. I have chosen to discuss it here in France, at the Sorbonne, because here in this soil the roots of human freedom have long ago struck deep and here they have been richly nourished. It was here the Declaration of the Rights of Man was proclaimed, and the great slogans of the French

Revolution—liberty, equality, fraternity—fired the imagination of men. I have chosen to discuss this issue in Europe because this has been the scene of the greatest historic battles between freedom and tyranny. I have chosen to discuss it in the early days of the General Assembly because the issue of human liberty is decisive for the settlement of outstanding political differences and for the future of the United Nations.

2   The decisive importance of this issue was fully recognized by the founders of the United Nations at San Francisco. Concern for the preservation and promotion of human rights and fundamental freedoms stands at the heart of the United Nations. Its Charter is distinguished by its preoccupation with the rights and welfare of individual men and women. The United Nations has made it clear that it intends to uphold human rights and to protect the dignity of the human personality. In the preamble to the Charter the keynote is set when it declares: "We the people of the United Nations determined . . . to reaffirm faith in fundamental human rights, in the dignity and worth of the human person, in the equal rights of men and women and of nations large and small, and . . . to promote social progress and better standards of life in larger freedom." This reflects the basic premise of the Charter that the peace and security of mankind are dependent on mutual respect for the rights and freedoms of all.

3   One of the purposes of the United Nations is declared in article 1 to be: "to achieve international cooperation in solving international problems of an economic, social, cultural, or humanitarian character, and in promoting and encouraging respect for human rights and for fundamental freedoms for all without distinction as to race, sex, language, or religion."

4   This thought is repeated at several points and notably in articles 55 and 56 the Members pledge themselves to take joint and separate action in cooperation with the United Nations for the promotion of "universal respect for, and observance of, human rights and fundamental freedoms for all without distinction as to race, sex, language, or religion."

5   The Human Rights Commission was given as its first and most important task the preparation of an International Bill of Rights. The General Assembly, which opened its third session here in Paris a few days ago, will have before it the first fruit of the Commission's labors in this task, that is the International Declaration of Human Rights.

6   The Declaration was finally completed after much work during the last session of the Human Rights Commission in New York in the spring of 1948. The Economic and Social Council has sent it without recommendation to the General Assembly, together with other documents transmitted by the Human Rights Commission.

7   It was decided in our Commission that a Bill of Rights should contain two parts:

1. A Declaration which could be approved through action of the Member States of the United Nations in the General Assembly. This declaration would have great moral force, and would say to the peoples of the world "this is what we hope human rights may mean to all people in the years to come." We have put down here the rights that we consider basic for individual human beings the world over to have. Without them, we feel that the full development of individual personality is impossible.

2. The second part of the bill, which the Human Rights Commission has not yet completed because of the lack of time, is a covenant which would be in the form of a treaty to be presented to the nations of the world. Each nation, as it is prepared to do so, would ratify this covenant and the covenant would then become binding on the nations which adhere to it. Each nation ratifying would then be obligated to change its laws wherever they did not conform to the points contained in the covenant.

8   This covenant, of course, would have to be a simpler document. It could not state aspirations, which we feel to be permissible in the Declaration. It could only state rights which could be assured by law and it must contain methods of implementation, and no state ratifying the covenant could be allowed to disregard it. The methods of implementation have not yet been agreed upon, nor have they been given adequate consideration by the Commission at any of its meetings. There certainly should be discussion on the entire question of this world Bill of Human Rights and there may be acceptance by this Assembly of the Declaration if they come to agreement on it. The acceptance of the Declaration, I think, should encourage every nation in the coming months to discuss its meaning with its people so that they will be better prepared to accept the covenant with a deeper understanding of the problems involved when that is presented, we hope, a year from now and, we hope, accepted.

9   The Declaration has come from the Human Rights Commission with unanimous acceptance except for four abstentions—the U.S.S.R., Yugoslavia, Ukraine, and Byelorussia. The reason for this is a fundamental difference in the conception of human rights as they exist in these states and in certain other Member States in the United Nations.

10   In the discussion before the Assembly, I think it should be made crystal clear what these differences are and tonight I want to spend a little time making them clear to you. It seems to me there is a valid reason for taking the time today to think carefully and clearly on the subject of human rights, because in the acceptance and observance of these rights lies the root, I believe, of our chance of peace in the future, and for the strengthening of the United Nations organization to the point where it can maintain peace in the future.

11   We must not be confused about what freedom is. Basic human rights are simple and easily understood: freedom of speech and a free press; freedom of religion and worship; freedom of assembly and the right of petition; the right of men to be secure in their homes and free from unreasonable search and seizure and from arbitrary arrest and punishment.

12   We must not be deluded by the efforts of the forces of reaction to prostitute the great words of our free tradition and thereby to confuse the struggle. Democracy, freedom, human rights have come to have a definite meaning to the people of the world which we must not allow any nation to so change that they are made synonymous with suppression and dictatorship.

13   There are basic differences that show up even in the use of words between a democratic and a totalitarian country. For instance "democracy" means one thing to the U.S.S.R. and another to the U.S.A. and, I know, in France. I have served since the first meeting of the nuclear commission on the Human Rights Commission, and I think this point stands out clearly.

14   The U.S.S.R. Representatives assert that they already have achieved many things which we, in what they call the "bourgeois democracies" cannot achieve because their government controls the accomplishment of these things. Our government seems powerless to them because, in the last analysis, it is controlled by the people. They would not put it that way—they would say that the people in the U.S.S.R. control their government by allowing their government to have certain absolute rights. We, on the other hand, feel that certain rights can never be granted to the government, but must be kept in the hands of the people.

15   For instance, the U.S.S.R. will assert that their press is free because the state makes it free by providing the machinery, the paper, and even the money for salaries for the people who work on the paper. They state that there is no control over what is printed in the various papers that they subsidize in this manner, such, for instance, as a trade-union paper. But what would happen if a paper were to print ideas which were critical of the basic policies and beliefs of the Communist government? I am sure some good reason would be found for abolishing the paper.

16   It is true that there have been many cases where newspapers in the U.S.S.R. have criticized officials and their actions and have been responsible for the removal of those officials, but in doing so they did not criticize anything which was fundamental to Communist beliefs. They simply criticized methods of doing things, so one must differentiate between things which are permissible, such as criticism of any individual or of the manner of doing things, and the criticism of a belief which would be considered vital to the acceptance of Communism.

17   What are the differences, for instance, between trade-unions in the totalitarian states and in the democracies? In the totalitarian state a trade-union is an instrument used by the government to enforce duties, not to assert rights. Propaganda material which the government desires the workers to have is furnished by the trade-unions to be circulated to their members.

18   Our trade-unions, on the other hand, are solely the instrument of the workers themselves. They represent the workers in their relations with the government and with management and they are free to develop their own opinions without government help or interference. The concepts of our trade-unions and those in totalitarian countries are drastically different. There is little mutual understanding.

19   I think the best example one can give of this basic difference of the use of terms is "the right to work." The Soviet Union insists that this is a basic right which it alone can guarantee because it alone provides full employment by the government. But the right to work in the Soviet Union means the assignment of workers to do whatever task is given to them by the government without an opportunity for the people to participate in the decision that the government should do this. A society in which everyone works is not necessarily a free society and may indeed be a

slave society; on the other hand, a society in which there is widespread economic insecurity can turn freedom into a barren and vapid right for millions of people.

20   We in the United States have come to realize it means freedom to choose one's job, to work or not to work as one desires. We, in the United States, have come to realize, however, that people have a right to demand that their government will not allow them to starve because as individuals they cannot find work of the kind they are accustomed to doing and this is a decision brought about by public opinion which came as a result of the Great Depression in which many people were out of work, but we would not consider in the United States that we had gained any freedom if we were compelled to follow a dictatorial assignment to work where and when we were told. The right of choice would seem to us an important, fundamental freedom.

21   I have great sympathy with the Russian people. They love their country and have always defended it valiantly against invaders. They have been through a period of revolution, as a result of which they were for a time cut off from outside contact. They have not lost their resulting suspicion of other countries and the great difficulty is today that their government encourages this suspicion and seems to believe that force alone will bring them respect.

22   We, in the democracies, believe in a kind of international respect and action which is reciprocal. We do not think others should treat us differently from the way they wish to be treated. It is interference in other countries that especially stirs up antagonism against the Soviet government. If it wishes to feel secure in developing its economic and political theories within its territory, then it should grant to others that same security. We believe in the freedom of people to make their own mistakes. We do not interfere with them and they should not interfere with others.

23   The basic problem confronting the world today, as I said in the beginning, is the preservation of human freedom for the individual and consequently for the society of which he is a part. We are fighting this battle again today as it was fought at the time of the French Revolution and at the time of the American Revolution. The issue of human liberty is as decisive now as it was then. I want to give you my conception of what is meant in my country by freedom of the individual.

24   Long ago in London during a discussion with Mr. Vyshinsky, he told me there was no such thing as freedom for the individual in the world. All freedom of the individual was conditioned by the rights of other individuals. That of course, I granted. I said: "We approach the question from a different point of view/we here in the United Nations are trying to develop ideals which will be broader in outlook, which will consider first the rights of man, which will consider what makes man more free; not governments, but man."

25   The totalitarian state typically places the will of the people second to decrees promulgated by a few men at the top.

26   Naturally, there must always be consideration of the rights of others; but in a democracy this is not a restriction. Indeed, in our democracies we make our freedoms secure because each of us is expected to respect the rights of others and we are free to make our own laws. Freedom for our peoples is not only a right, but also a tool. Freedom of speech, freedom of the press, freedom of information, freedom

of assembly—these are not just abstract ideals to us; they are tools with which we create a way of life, a way of life in which we can enjoy freedom.

27   Sometimes the processes of democracy are slow, and I have known some of our leaders to say that a benevolent dictatorship would accomplish the ends desired in a much shorter time than it takes to go through the democratic processes of discussion and the slow formation of public opinion. But there is no way of insuring that a dictatorship will remain benevolent or that power once in the hands of a few will be returned to the people without struggle or revolution. This we have learned by experience and we accept the slow processes of democracy because we know that shortcuts compromise principles on which no compromise is possible.

28   The final expression of the opinion of the people with us is through free and honest elections, with valid choices on basic issues and candidates. The secret ballot is an essential to free elections but you must have a choice before you. I have heard my husband say many times that a people need never lose their freedom if they kept their right to a secret ballot and if they used that secret ballot to the full. Basic decisions of our society are made through the expressed will of the people. That is why when we see these liberties threatened, instead of falling apart, our nation becomes unified and our democracies come together as a unified group in spite of our varied backgrounds and many racial strains.

29   In the United States, we have a capitalistic economy. That is because public opinion favors that type of economy under the conditions in which we live. But we have imposed certain restraints; for instance, we have antitrust laws. These are the legal evidence of the determination of the American people to maintain an economy of free competition and not to allow monopolies to take away the people's freedom.

30   Our trade unions grow stronger because the people come to believe that this is the proper way to guarantee the rights of the workers and that the right to organize and to bargain collectively keeps the balance between the actual producer and the investor of money and the manager in industry who watches over the man who works with his hands and who produces the materials which are our tangible wealth.

31   In the United States, we are old enough not to claim perfection. We recognize that we have some problems of discrimination but we find steady progress being made in the solution of these problems. Through normal democratic processes we are coming to understand our needs and how we can attain full equality for all our people. Free discussion on the subject is permitted. Our Supreme Court has recently rendered decisions to clarify a number of our laws to guarantee the rights of all.

32   The U.S.S.R. claims it has reached a point where all races within her borders are officially considered equal and have equal rights and they insist that they have no discrimination where minorities are concerned.

33   This is a laudable objective but there are other aspects of the development of freedom for the individual which are essential before the mere absence of discrimination is worth much, and these are lacking in the Soviet Union. Unless they are being denied freedoms which they want and which they see other people have,

people do not usually complain of discrimination. It is these other freedoms—the basic freedoms of speech, of the press, of religion and conscience, of assembly, of fair trial and freedom from arbitrary arrest and punishment, which a totalitarian government cannot safely give its people and which give meaning to freedom from discrimination.

34   It is my belief, and I am sure it is also yours, that the struggle for democracy and freedom is a critical struggle, for their preservation is essential to the great objective of the United Nations to maintain international peace and security. Among free men the end cannot justify the means. We know the patterns of totalitarianism—the single political party, the control of schools, press, radio, the arts, the sciences, and the church to support autocratic authority; these are the age-old patterns against which men have struggled for three thousand years. These are the signs of reaction, retreat, and retrogression.

35   The United Nations must hold fast to the heritage of freedom won by the struggle of its people; it must help us to pass it on to generations to come.

36   The development of the ideal of freedom and its translation into the everyday life of the people in great areas of the earth is the product of the efforts of many peoples. It is the fruit of a long tradition of vigorous thinking and courageous action. No one race or one people can claim to have done all the work to achieve greater dignity for human beings and greater freedom to develop human personality. In each generation and in each country there must be a continuation of the struggle and new steps forward must be taken since this is preeminently a field in which to stand still is to retreat.

37   The field of human rights is not one in which compromises on fundamental principles are possible. The work of the Commission on Human Rights is illustrative. The Declaration of Human Rights provides: "Everyone has the right to leave any country, including his own." The Soviet representative said he would agree to this right if a single phrase was added to it—"in accordance with the procedure laid down in the laws of that country." It is obvious that to accept this would be not only to compromise but to nullify the right stated. This case forcefully illustrates the importance of the proposition that we must ever be alert not to compromise fundamental human rights merely for the sake of reaching unanimity and thus lose them.

38   As I see it, it is not going to be easy to attain unanimity with respect to our different concepts of government and human rights. The struggle is bound to be difficult and one in which we must be firm but patient. If we adhere faithfully to our principles I think it is possible for us to maintain freedom and to do so peacefully and without recourse to force.

39   The future must see the broadening of human rights throughout the world. People who have glimpsed freedom will never be content until they have secured it for themselves. In a truest sense, human rights are a fundamental object of law and government in a just society. Human rights exist to the degree that they are respected by people in relations with each other and by governments in relations with their citizens.

40   The world at large is aware of the tragic consequences for human beings ruled by totalitarian systems. If we examine Hitler's rise to power, we see how the chains

are forged which keep the individual a slave and we can see many similarities in the way things are accomplished in other countries. Politically men must be free to discuss and to arrive at as many facts as possible and there must be at least a two-party system in a country because when there is only one political party; too many things can be subordinated to the interests of that one party and it becomes a tyrant and not an instrument of democratic government.

41   The propaganda we have witnessed in the recent past, like that we perceive in these days, seeks to impugn, to undermine, and to destroy the liberty and independence of peoples. Such propaganda poses to all peoples the issue whether to doubt their heritage of rights and therefore to compromise the principles by which they live, or try to accept the challenge, redouble their vigilance, and stand steadfast in the struggle to maintain and enlarge human freedoms.

42   People who continue to be denied the respect to which they are entitled as human beings will not acquiesce forever in such denial.

43   The Charter of the United Nations is a guiding beacon along the way to the achievement of human rights and fundamental freedoms throughout the world. The immediate test is not only to the extent to which human rights and freedoms have already been achieved, but the direction in which the world is moving. Is there a faithful compliance with the objectives of the Charter if some countries continue to curtail human rights and freedoms instead of to promote the universal respect for an observance of human rights and freedoms for all as called for by the Charter?

44   The place to discuss the issue of human rights is in the forum of the United Nations. The United Nations has been set up as the common meeting ground for nations, where we can consider together our mutual problems and take advantage of our differences in experience. It is inherent in our firm attachment to democracy and freedom that we stand always ready to use the fundamental democratic procedures of honest discussion and negotiation. It is now as always our hope that despite the wide differences in approach we face in the world today, we can with mutual good faith in the principles of the United Nations Charter, arrive at a common basis of understanding.

45   We are here to join the meetings of this great international Assembly which meets in your beautiful capital of Paris. Freedom for the individual is an inseparable part of the cherished traditions of France. As one of the Delegates from the United States I pray Almighty God that we may win another victory here for the rights and freedoms of all men.

THINKING CRITICALLY

1. How does Roosevelt connect to her audience at the beginning of her speech? Who is her audience? Would her speech be as effective without her introductory remarks? Identify other areas in her speech where she reaches out to her audience in a distinctly personal way.

2. What countries abstained from ratifying the International Declaration of Human Rights? What reasons does Roosevelt give for this abstention? How does she feel about their abstention?

3. Evaluate the overall strengths and weaknesses of this speech. Identify specific parts of her oration, and explain why you think they are effective or ineffective.

4. What, according to Roosevelt, is the definition of freedom? Do you agree with her definition? Is there anything you would add or change? Explain.

5. In paragraph 15, Roosevelt discusses the word "free" as it applies to the idea of freedom of the press. How is the word "free" interpreted by the U.S.S.R. (Russia)? How does their interpretation differ from that of the U.S.? In what ways can different interpretations of the same word cause political dissent? Explain.

6. In paragraph 20, Roosevelt notes that a vital human right is the "right of choice." Yet she does not include this right in her definition of freedom at the beginning of her speech. Was this an oversight, or a deliberate omission? Is there a difference between freedom and human rights? Explain.

7. Roosevelt ends her speech with a plea to God. Why does she make this appeal? How does it contribute to her speeches? What thoughts and ideas does it leave with her audience? Explain.

8. Evaluate Roosevelt's use of the word "our" in paragraph 10, and "we" in paragraph 24. How does she use these words? How does her rhetorical use of language make what she has to say more powerful and compelling? Explain.

WRITING ASSIGNMENTS

1. Research the Declaration of the Rights of Man (France), the document which Roosevelt mentions in her opening remarks. How does this document compare to the Declaration of Independence (U.S.)? Why do you think Roosevelt references one document and not the other? Evaluate and discuss the two documents considering the language used in each.

2. Eleanor Roosevelt was a highly respected woman, but was still participating in a distinctly male-dominated political arena. Does gender play a role in her speech and her mission? Explore the way gender does, or does not affect her speech, her audience's reception of her words, and her subject matter.

3. Write an essay in which you create your own declaration of inalienable human rights. If you wish, you may compare your version to that ratified by the United Nations in 1948, at www.un.org/rights/ and discuss how your version is similar and/or different, and why.

Exploring the Language of VISUALS

Margaret Sanger Silenced

Social change doesn't happen through silence and inaction. Throughout history, some voices broke the silence to speak out against discrimination and oppression. One such woman was Margaret Sanger (1879–1966) who championed women's rights, especially the right to use birth control. This image from 1929 shows Sanger satirizing how she was silenced by lawmakers for speaking out about birth control. Although Sanger wasn't allowed to speak out (she was arrested for doing so in 1914 and again after opening a birth control clinic in 1916), consider how this photograph does, in fact, serve as an expression of speech.

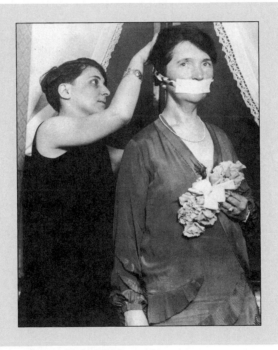

THINKING CRITICALLY

1. How does the photograph make you feel, and why? Explore the implications of the photograph and the ways it is designed to elicit a response from the viewer.

2. Freedom of speech is a fundamental right that many Americans hold dear. Does it surprise you that as recently as 1929 you could be arrested for speaking out on something such as birth control? Does such control exist today? Explore this issue and then discuss the results of your research in class.

3. Research the career of Margaret Sanger at www.nyu.edu/projects/sanger/. In what ways did Sanger "break a silence" by challenging the status quo? What was she fighting for? What did her fight represent? Explain.

MAKING CONNECTIONS

1. Write a letter to the editor expressing your opinion about one of the "speeches" included in this section as if it had been recently delivered. Write your letter as if you were living in the historical period of the selection. For example, you could be a man from 1848 commenting on the Seneca Falls Convention or a woman expressing her opinion of Eleanor Roosevelt's speech to the United Nations.

2. In paragraph 26 in his "Letter from Birmingham Jail," Martin Luther King, Jr. states, "We will have to repent in this generation not merely for the hateful words and actions of the bad people but for the appalling silence of the good people." Compare the implications of his statement to a speech given on April 22, 1999, by Nobel Peace Prize winner, Elie Weisel, *The Perils of Indifference*, at www.historyplace.com/speeches/wiesel.htm, given as part of the White House Millennium lecture series. Write an essay exploring the ideas expressed by each man, as well as your own perspective on "indifference" and "silence."

3. Select a current (within the last two years) photo, essay, or article that you think represents an example of someone challenging the status quo. Explain why you think your selection fits within the overall theme of this section. How does your photo or article compare/contrast with the selections featured in this section? What do you think will be the long-term implications of your example of broken silence?

4. Martin Luther King, Jr.'s most famous speech, "I Have a Dream," was delivered on the steps of the Lincoln Memorial in Washington, D.C., in 1963. Review the text of his speech at www.americanrhetoric.com/speeches/ihaveadream.htm. How is this speech an example of "language that inspired change"? Consider the symbolism of his choice of venue. How does the location of his speech connect to the speech itself? Would a different location have served his purpose as well? Why or why not? Write an essay in which you address how this speech changed (or did not change) the way people thought about civil rights.

5. Compare the use of repetition in Martin Luther King, Jr.'s "I Have a Dream" speech to that of Sojourner Truth's "Ain't I a Woman?" In what ways do they employ similar linguistic devices? How do you think each would respond to the other's oratory style? Subject matter? Explain.

■ Often ambiguous, political language carries tremendous power to influence national policy, laws, and social mores. What are our expectations of political language? How do we filter the fluff from the substance?

Each of the essays in this text explores how language constructs reality for us: how it can be used to communicate, inform, lead, mislead, and even manipulate us. Although many pieces celebrate the joys of language, others lament its woes—that politicians and bureaucrats talk gobbledygook, that advertisers torture language to sell their goods, and that the ability of students to write clearly is deteriorating. In short, you hear a lot about bad writing.

This chapter offers insights and advice about good writing. From a practical point of view, the essays in this chapter are intended to help prepare you for the writing projects featured in this book and in your academic studies. The readings in this chapter also aim to provide the foundations of basic rhetorical principles and strategies so that you can participate with confidence in lively and informed debates about language.

Most college writing is an exercise in persuasion—an attempt to influence readers' attitudes about the subject matter. This is true whether you're discussing tragic irony in *Oedipus Rex,* analyzing the causes of World War I, writing a lab report on the solubility of salt, protesting next year's tuition increase, or explaining the joys of bungee jumping. How successful you are at persuading your readers will have a lot to do with the words you choose.

The Writing Process

Our opening piece, "Writing for an Audience" by Linda Flower, offers some key points of advice on establishing common ground with one's readers. The next two articles are by writers who are also writing instructors. Anne Lamott explains how she helps her students find their muse in "Getting Started." Pamela Childers shares her classroom and writing center insights in "What My Students Have Taught Me About Writing." The section closes with a humorous essay on the process of writing verses the product, in "Forget Ideas, Mr. Author. What Kind of Pen Do You Use?" by Stephen J. Fry.

Finding the Right Words

The second section features essays providing advice and suggestions on how to choose the right words to effectively express your message, and how to formulate that message so that your reader will be receptive and open to your ideas. Beginning writers often opt for cluttered expressions, empty jargon, and convoluted constructions to make what they say sound "smarter." However, all they achieve with this approach is poor writing. Richard Lederer explains in the section's first essay, "The Case for Short Words," that often the best way to say something is with short, clear, pure words that are rich with meaning. Patricia T. O'Conner builds on his tips by adding thirteen more of her own in "Saying Is Believing" in which she explains that the best writers are the ones who are easily understood—ones you can read, "without breaking a sweat." And nobody could agree more than popular novelist,

Kurt Vonnegut, who gives eight friendly tips on writing with style. Marjorie Agosin explains why she must always write in Spanish—to preserve both her childhood, her identity, and the beauty of expression that is sometimes lost in translation. James Isaacs explains how *not* to communicate in his parody of what nearly every high school and college graduate must endure—the commencement speech in "Clichés, Anyone?" The section closes with an amusing insert featured in the business newspaper *The Wall Street Journal*, "The Financial Media's 25 Worst Clichés," which pokes fun at phrases used often by financial journalists.

THE WRITING PROCESS

Writing for an Audience
Linda Flower

One of the most important tasks an educated person does is manage information. And writing is an important part of managing information. We write to keep track of things (lists, inventories, databases), to organize materials (outlines, tables of contents, indexes), and to develop ideas too complex to manage in our heads. We also write to tell people what we know, what conclusions we've drawn about a situation, and how we'd like them to proceed. In the next essay, Linda Flower tells us that to be successful managers of information we need to know how our audience will see the information we present, so that we can choose and shape information to help them understand our perspective.

Linda Flower is a professor of English at Carnegie-Mellon University and is, through her many books and articles, a prominent voice in the field of composition and rhetoric. She is the author of several textbooks, including *Problem Solving Strategies for Writing in College and the Community* (1985) and *The Construction of Negotiated Meaning: A Social Cognitive Theory of Writing* (1994). Her suggestions on creating common ground with your audience should be useful in writing situations you encounter in your college and professional career.

1   The goal of the writer is to create a momentary common ground between the reader and the writer. You want the reader to share your knowledge and your attitude toward that knowledge. Even if the reader eventually disagrees, you want him or her to be able for the moment to *see things as you see them.* A good piece of writing closes the gap between you and the reader.

Analyze Your Audience

2   The first step in closing that gap is to gauge the distance between the two of you. Imagine, for example, that you are a student writing your parents, who have always lived in New York City, about a wilderness survival expedition you want to go on

over spring break. Sometimes obvious differences such as age or background will be important, but the critical differences for writers usually fall into three areas: the reader's *knowledge* about the topic; his or her *attitude* toward it, and his or her personal or professional *needs*. Because these differences often exist, good writers do more than simply express their meaning; they pinpoint the critical differences between themselves and their reader and design their writing to reduce those differences. Let us look at these three areas in more detail.

Knowledge

3 This is usually the easiest difference to handle. What does your reader need to know? What are the main ideas you hope to teach? Does your reader have enough background knowledge to really understand you? If not, what would he or she have to learn?

Attitudes

4 When we say a person has knowledge, we usually refer to his conscious awareness of explicit facts and clearly defined concepts. This kind of knowledge can be easily written down or told to someone else. However, much of what we "know" is not held in this formal, explicit way. Instead it is held as an attitude or image—as a loose cluster of associations. For instance, my image of lakes includes associations many people would have, including fishing, water skiing, stalled outboards, and lots of kids catching night crawlers with flashlights. However, the most salient or powerful parts of my image, which strongly color my whole attitude toward lakes, are thoughts of cloudy skies, long rainy days, and feeling generally cold and damp. By contrast, one of my best friends has a very different cluster of associations: to him a lake means sun, swimming, sailing, and happily sitting on the end of a dock. Needless to say, our differing images cause us to react quite differently to a proposal that we visit a lake. Likewise, one reason people often find it difficult to discuss religion and politics is that terms such as "capitalism" conjure up radically different images.

5 As you can see, a reader's image of a subject is often the source of attitudes and feelings that are unexpected and, at times, impervious to mere facts. A simple statement that seems quite persuasive to you, such as "Lake Wampago would be a great place to locate the new music camp," could have little impact on your reader if he or she simply doesn't visualize a lake as a "great place." In fact, many people accept uncritically any statement that fits in with their own attitudes—and reject, just as uncritically, anything that does not.

6 Whether your purpose is to persuade or simply to present your perspective, it helps to know the image and attitudes that your reader already holds. The more these differ from your own, the more you will have to do to make him or her *see* what you mean.

Needs

7 When writers discover a large gap between their own knowledge and attitudes and those of the reader, they usually try to change the reader in some way. Needs,

however, are different. When you analyze a reader's needs, it is so that you, the writer, can adapt to him. If you ask a friend majoring in biology how to keep your fish tank from clouding, you don't want to hear a textbook recitation on the life processes of algae. You expect the friend to adapt his or her knowledge and tell you exactly how to solve your problem.

8   The ability to adapt your knowledge to the needs of the reader is often crucial to your success as a writer. This is especially true in writing done on a job. For example, as producer of a public affairs program for a television station, 80 percent of your time may be taken up planning the details of new shows, contacting guests, and scheduling the taping sessions. But when you write a program proposal to the station director, your job is to show how the program will fit into the cost guidelines, the FCC requirements for relevance, and the overall programming plan for the station. When you write that report your role in the organization changes from producer to proposal writer. Why? Because your reader needs that information in order to make a decision. He may be interested in your scheduling problems and the specific content of the shows, but he reads your report because of his own needs as station director of that organization. He has to act.

9   In college, where the reader is also a teacher, the reader's needs are a little less concrete but just as important. Most papers are assigned as a way to teach something. So the real purpose of a paper may be for you to make connections between two historical periods, to discover for yourself the principle behind a laboratory experiment, or to develop and support your own interpretation of a novel. A good college paper doesn't just rehash the facts; it demonstrates what your reader, as a teacher, needs to know—that you are learning the thinking skills his or her course is trying to teach.

10   Effective writers are not simply expressing what they know, like a student madly filling up an examination bluebook. Instead they are *using* their knowledge: reorganizing, maybe even rethinking their ideas to meet the demands of an assignment or the needs of their reader.

THINKING CRITICALLY

1. Who does Flower assume to be her audience for this essay on audience? What evidence can you point to in the text that supports this answer?

2. Flower speaks of three areas of difference between a writer and his or her audience. List these three areas and, for each area, find two places in the text where Flower's writing seems designed to reduce those differences, or to close the gap.

3. What is Flower's position on persuasiveness in writing? How is this attitude important to her point overall?

4. Do you find her discussion persuasive? Has she effectively closed the gaps between you, as audience, and herself, as writer? Discuss places in this text where she has been successful. Can you find places where she has not been successful? Or where you think she might have done a better job? Write out any suggestions you have where you think she might have done a better job.

5. Make a list of different writing situations you have recently encountered or might expect to encounter in your work or profession. Identify a specific audience,

then think very specifically about the knowledge, attitude, and needs of that audience and brainstorm a list of adjustments you'll have to make in order to bridge any gaps between you and your audience. Be ready to compare your answers with those of other students in the class.

6. Flower does not directly address what happens when an audience is comprised of different kinds of people. Can you think of instances where this has happened or might happen? What kinds of choices might an author make in order to meet the needs of many different kinds of people at one time? What happens when the writer fails to establish common ground with some part of her/his audience?

WRITING ASSIGNMENTS

1. Flower is an expert in writing. Think of something you know really well and write an essay in which you explain it (or some element of it) to an audience that does not have your expertise.

2. Find samples of text (in the broadest sense of the word) on the same topic, but which are focused on different audiences. For your samples, you might look at an encyclopedia, news article, biography, textbook, expert opinion/testimonial, video clip, photograph or drawing, instruction manual, and so on. Consider differences in age, gender, culture, and educational backgrounds. Once you've gathered a range of materials, choose three that offer the most variety. Write an essay in which you describe the audience intended by the author(s) or creator(s) of each text; also discuss the strategies each author employed to bridge the presumed gaps in knowledge, attitude, and needs. Finally, draw conclusions about the relevance of these differences. Your focus should be on choices made with regard to language; organization; visual elements, including layouts; visual aids; and rhetorical elements such as narrative, exemplification, definition, comparison/contrast, exposition, and anything else that seems important.

3. Find a piece of text that is intended for an audience other than yourself. Perhaps find a journal from your major area that is targeted at professors/scholars; or find a discussion on a subject matter in which you have little or no background. Discuss the places where you have trouble and/or the different kinds of trouble you have. Explain what the author has done to meet the needs of his or her presumed audience. Then, talk about different strategies that might be employed in a revised version of the text aimed at you rather than at the intended audience. Append a one-page rewrite of this text (or some portion of it) to illustrate how the rewrite could be accomplished.

Getting Started

Anne Lamott

For many students, the biggest writing challenge is simply getting started. In the next essay, writer and creative writing instructor Anne Lamott gives advice on how to get the ball rolling. The task of getting started, and feeling comfortable with what to write, is a challenge to students and published writers alike.

Anne Lamott is the author of several novels and memoirs, including *Hard Laughter* (1980), *All New People* (1989), *Operating Instructions* (1993), and

Crooked Little Heart (1997). A past recipient of a Guggenheim fellowship, she has been a book review columnist for *Mademoiselle* magazine, and a restaurant critic for *California* magazine. She teaches writing at the University of California, Davis, and is a featured instructor at writing seminars throughout the state. The following piece is an excerpt from her 1995 book on writing, *Bird by Bird: Some Instructions on Writing and Life.*

1   The very first thing I tell my new students on the first day of a workshop is that good writing is about telling the truth. We are a species that needs and wants to understand who we are. Sheep lice do not seem to share this longing, which is one reason they write so very little. But we do. We have so much we want to say and figure out. Year after year my students are bursting with stories to tell, and they start writing projects with excitement and maybe even joy—finally their voices will be heard, and they are going to get to devote themselves to this one thing they've longed to do since childhood. But after a few days at the desk, telling the truth in an interesting way turns out to be about as easy and pleasurable as bathing a cat. Some lose faith. Their sense of self and story shatters and crumbles to the ground. Historically they show up for the first day of the workshop looking like bright goofy ducklings who will follow me anywhere, but by the time the second class rolls around, they look at me as if the engagement is definitely off.

2   "I don't even know where to start," one will wail.

3   Start with your childhood, I tell them. Plug your nose and jump in, and write down all your memories as truthfully as you can. Flannery O'Connor said that anyone who survived childhood has enough material to write for the rest of his or her life. Maybe your childhood was grim and horrible, but grim and horrible is okay if it is well done. Don't worry about doing it well yet, though. Just start getting it down.

4   Now, the amount of material may be so overwhelming that it can make your brain freeze. When I had been writing food reviews for a number of years, there were so many restaurants and individual dishes in my brainpan that when people asked for a recommendation, I couldn't think of a single restaurant where I'd ever actually eaten. But if the person could narrow it down to, say, Indian, I might remember one lavish Indian palace, where my date had asked the waiter for the Rudyard Kipling sampler and later for the holy-cow tartare. Then a number of memories would come to mind, of other dates and other Indian restaurants.

5   So you might start by writing down every single thing you can remember from your first few years in school. Start with kindergarten. Try to get the words and memories down as they occur to you. Don't worry if what you write is no good, because no one is going to see it. Move on to first grade, to second, to third. Who were your teachers, your classmates? What did you wear? Who and what were you jealous of? Now branch out a little. Did your family take vacations during those years? Get these down on paper. Do you remember how much more presentable everybody else's family looked? Do you remember how when you'd be floating around in an inner tube on a river, your own family would have lost the little cap that screws over the airflow valve, so every time you got in and out of the inner tube, you'd scratch new welts in your thighs? And how other families never lost the caps?

6   If this doesn't pan out, or if it does but you finish mining this particular vein, see if focusing on holidays and big events helps you recollect your life as it was. Write down everything you can remember about every birthday or Christmas or Seder or Easter or whatever, every relative who was there. Write down all the stuff you swore you'd never tell another soul. What can you recall about your birthday parties—the disasters, the days of grace, your relatives' faces lit up by birthday candles? Scratch around for details: what people ate, listened to, wore—those terrible petaled swim caps, the men's awful trunks, the cocktail dress your voluptuous aunt wore that was so slinky she practically needed the Jaws of Life to get out of it. Write about the women's curlers with the bristles inside, the garters your father and uncles used to hold up their dress socks, your grandfathers' hats, your cousins' perfect Brownie uniforms, and how your own looked like it had just been hatched. Describe the trench coats and stoles and car coats, what they revealed and what they covered up. See if you can remember what you were given that Christmas when you were ten, and how it made you feel inside. Write down what the grown-ups said and did after they'd had a couple of dozen drinks, especially that one Fourth of July when your father made Fish House punch and the adults practically had to crawl from room to room.

7   Remember that you own what happened to you. If your childhood was less than ideal, you may have been raised thinking that if you told the truth about what really went on in your family, a long bony white finger would emerge from a cloud and point at you, while a chilling voice thundered, "We *told* you not to tell." But that was then. Just put down on paper everything you can remember now about your parents and siblings and relatives and neighbors, and we will deal with libel later on.

8   But how?" my students ask. "How do you actually do it?"

9   You sit down, I say. You try to sit down at approximately the same time every day. This is how you train your unconscious to kick in for you creatively. So you sit down at, say, nine every morning, or ten every night. You put a piece of paper in the typewriter, or you turn on your computer and bring up the right file, and then you stare at it for an hour or so. You begin rocking, just a little at first, and then like a huge autistic child. You look at the ceiling, and over at the clock, yawn, and stare at the paper again. Then, with your fingers poised on the keyboard, you squint at an image that is forming in your mind—a scene, a locale, a character, whatever—and you try to quiet your mind so you can hear what that landscape or character has to say above the other voices in your mind. The other voices are banshees and drunken monkeys. They are the voices of anxiety, judgment, doom, guilt. Also, severe hypochondria. There may be a Nurse Ratched–like listing of things that must be done right this moment: foods that must come out of the freezer, appointments that must be canceled or made, hairs that must be tweezed. But you hold an imaginary gun to your head and make yourself stay at the desk. There is a vague pain at the base of your neck. It crosses your mind that you have meningitis. Then the phone rings and you look up at the ceiling with fury, summon every ounce of noblesse oblige, and answer the call politely, with

maybe just the merest hint of irritation. The caller asks if you're working, and you say yeah, because you are.

10   Yet somehow in the face of all this, you clear a space for the writing voice, hacking away at the others with machetes, and you begin to compose sentences. You begin to string words together like beads to tell a story. You are desperate to communicate, to edify or entertain, to preserve moments of grace or joy or transcendence, to make real or imagined events come alive. But you cannot will this to happen. It is a matter of persistence and faith and hard work. So you might as well just go ahead and get started.

11   I wish I had a secret I could let you in on . . . some code word that has enabled me to sit at my desk and land flights of creative inspiration like an air-traffic controller. But I don't. All I know is that the process is pretty much the same for almost everyone I know. The good news is that some days it feels like you just have to keep getting out of your own way so that whatever it is that wants to be written can use you to write it. It is a little like when you have something difficult to discuss with someone, and as you go to do it, you hope and pray that the right words will come if only you show up and make a stab at it. And often the right words do come, and you—well—"write" for a while; you put a lot of thoughts down on paper. But the bad news is that if you're at all like me, you'll probably read over what you've written and spend the rest of the day obsessing, and praying that you do not die before you can completely rewrite or destroy what you have written, lest the eagerly waiting world learn how bad your first drafts are.

12   The obsessing may keep you awake, *or* the self-loathing may cause you to fall into a narcoleptic coma before dinner. But let's just say that you do fall asleep at a normal hour. Then the odds are that you will wake up at four in the morning, having dreamed that you have died. Death turns out to feel much more frantic than you had imagined. Typically you'll try to comfort yourself by thinking about the day's work—the day's excrementitious work. You may experience a jittery form of existential dread, considering the absolute meaninglessness of life and the fact that no one has ever really loved you; you may find yourself consumed with a free-floating shame, and a hopelessness about your work, and the realization that you will have to throw out everything you've done so far and start from scratch. But you will not be able to do so. Because you suddenly understand that you are completely riddled with cancer.

13   And then the miracle happens. The sun comes up again. So you get up and do your morning things, and one thing leads to another, and eventually, at nine, you find yourself back at the desk, staring blankly at the pages you filled yesterday. And there on page four is a paragraph with all sorts of life in it, smells and sounds and voices and colors and even a moment of dialogue that makes you say to yourself, very, very softly, "Hmmm." You look up and stare out the window again, but this time you are drumming your fingers on the desk, and you don't care about those first three pages; those you will throw out, those you needed to write to get to that fourth page, to get to that one long paragraph that was what you had in mind when you started, only you didn't know that, couldn't know that,

until you got to it. And the story begins to materialize, and another thing is happening, which is that you are learning what you aren't writing, and this is helping you to find out what you *are* writing. Think of a fine painter attempting to capture an inner vision, beginning with one corner of the canvas, painting what he thinks should be there, not quite pulling it off, covering it over with white paint, and trying again, each time finding out what his painting isn't, until finally he finds out what it is.

14   And when you do find out what one corner of your vision is, you're off and running. And it really is like running. It always reminds me of the last lines of *Rabbit, Run:* "his heels hitting heavily on the pavement at first but with an effortless gathering out of a kind of sweet panic growing lighter and quicker and quieter, he runs. Ah: runs. Runs."

15   I wish I felt that kind of inspiration more often. I almost never do. All I know is that if I sit there long enough, something will happen.

THINKING CRITICALLY

1. What does Lamott mean when she says, ". . . writing is about the truth"? Although she describes a creative writing workshop, how do you think this principle of truth could apply to other types of writing? Explain.

2. Who is "Nurse Ratched," and how can "she" interfere with your writing? What recommendations does Lamott give for stilling the voice of Nurse Ratched and other anxieties that may interfere with your writing?

3. Evaluate Lamott's style and tone in this essay. Does her writing reflect the lessons she teaches in this piece? How does her style connect with her audience? Do you think you would like to have her as a writing instructor? Why or why not?

4. Lamott observes that her class begins eager to begin writing, but soon grows frustrated with the actual mechanics of the process. Think about your own writing process. How do you write? Why do you write? Have you experienced frustrations similar to the students in Lamott's class? Explain.

5. What audience do you think Lamott is writing for? Support your answer by citing examples from her essay.

6. Lamott comments that one challenge many writers—including herself—face is dealing with a sense of "self-loathing" toward what they have written. Can you relate to this feeling? Why or why not?

WRITING ASSIGNMENTS

1. Follow Lamott's advice to her class on getting started. Recall an incident from your childhood and write about it each day for a week. Focus on recalling memories, feelings, and impressions of the event. Return each day to add to and rework what you have written. At the end of the week, describe the experience of writing this way. Turn in both the creative writing piece you wrote and your analysis of the exercise to your instructor.

2. Have you ever had writer's block? How did you overcome it? What suggestions could you add to Lamott's advice for "getting started"?

3. The next time you have an essay assigned, keep a log or diary in which you can write about your own writing process. Include comments about how you approach and think about the assignment, how you prepare and actually write the piece, and how you revise and edit your essay. Be sure to include commentary on your feelings and impressions of the process as well as the actual mechanics of writing.

What My Students Have Taught Me About Writing
Pamela Childers

In the preceding essay, Anne Lamott describes the advice she gave her creative writing students. In the next piece, another writing instructor, Pamela Childers, discusses what her students have taught *her* about writing. As the director of a secondary school writing center, Childers is often reminded that writing is a constantly evolving process of discovery. Through freewriting and collaborative writing exercises, students develop and polish their skills. But collaboration, as Childers explains, can be as illuminating for the instructor as it is for the student writer.

Pamela Childers is director of the McCallie Writing Center at the McCallie School in Chattanooga, Tennessee. She is the author of many articles on writing and the teaching of writing. She would like to thank her students, Tripp Grant, Wesley Bell, Matt Lockaby, Evan Miller, and Chad Littleton for their advice and assistance in preparing this essay.

1 I'm a writer, but I am a better writer than I was when I started teaching because of my students. They have taught me how to improve my own writing by writing with them, getting feedback on my writing from them and listening to their questions about writing. Evan Miller took an independent study course with me his senior year, and I asked him to describe his writing process as I have with many students. Although an experienced writer who probably had not reflected upon his own writing process before, Evan has clearly practiced writing for years. Other students are not necessarily as motivated as Evan, but over the years they teach us, their teachers, many lessons about writing. Here are a few:

Lesson #1 - You Need to Be Able to Write for a Variety of Purposes and Audiences

2 The purpose of an essay for class is to demonstrate knowledge of information in a formal, well-written format, and the audience is usually the teacher who will grade the paper. The purpose of other writing may be to gain acceptance to college, to learn information, to inform, to discover or to entertain. Linda Flower reminds us to know who the audience is for our writing, and often it may just be ourselves.

3 Listen to the voice of Tripp in a freewrite assignment to describe his writing process:

4 Writing to me is an expression. My earliest memories of writing are when I was very young. I used to write stories of my friends and I going on fictional

adventures that were fun to write. Then it was a pleasure. Now it is a burden. Now my days are filled with papers of cell division, the life of John Donne, and the typical existentialist. The fond memories of fictional stories and eighth grade journal writing are rapidly being taken over by the typical school research project.

5   The reason that I don't like the typical paper is because I never mastered the language. When it comes to grammar and vocabulary, I am on the level of an eighth grader. I cannot write from the heart on what I feel and I feel very restricted. Pleasure writing comes from the heart; it is very relieving to be able to write about anything.

6   The process I use is pretty simple. I write what I think will get me the best grade and not what comes from what I feel for a lot of projects. I don't plan out some fancy outline. I usually just come up with a good opening paragraph and then support it with crummy paragraphs and then bring it all together at the end. It is what every teacher tells you to do. I am just not good at it because of the language. I don't know how to express my thoughts in a persuasive form.

7   Tripp's experiences in secondary school probably continued through college as well. With some luck, he might have encountered some real-life writing experiences and some that allowed him to write about what "comes from the heart." Tripp has learned to write for his audience—what most of us do for publication because the "grade" is acceptance of our article, chapter or book, for instance. It is sheer joy when what we care about can be presented in a form that is acceptable for the particular audience that will publish the piece of writing.

8   In Tripp's case, his audiences so far have been teachers of science, history, and English, and he has learned the "formula" for those papers. However, is Tripp not writing from the heart in this freewrite? Is he not persuasive? Again and again, college writing teachers who have read Tripp's piece say, "I want him in my class because he clearly has his own voice." Notice that they do not say, "That student really has a problem with mechanics; he does have trouble with language."

Lesson #2 - Keep That Editor Inside Your Head Until the Last Possible Moment

9 Donald Murray talks about all the revisions one must make, but he focuses on information, form, structure, development, dimension, and voice. There are revision processes before the final edit for grammar, spelling, and punctuation. He is focusing on the content of a piece of writing that is never done. If Murray looked at Tripp's paper, he wouldn't talk about the spelling, run-on sentences, or incorrect pronoun usage. The writing was clearly written for Tripp alone (or possibly to share with me); but Murray would encourage Tripp's strong voice and use of detail. What made Tripp think he was not good with language?

10   This year I have been working with John, an honors student who needs some guidance in writing timed essays. Since I read Advanced Placement Language and Composition essays, I thought I might be able to work with John on improving his writing to respond to a prompt not previously seen. We discovered in talking about his writing process that John was trying to write precisely the perfect sentence for

each and every line of his written response. It was taking him forever, and he never had time left to look at what he had written before the paper had to be submitted. We decided to try some practice freewrites on the computer with the monitor turned off. John loved the freedom to just let ideas flow through his hands on the keyboard without looking at them on the monitor. Now we both know that John had been allowing the editor in his head to critique each sentence as he wrote it. We will continue to do freewrites, some by hand and some on the computer, keeping the editor in the back of his head until he is ready to read through the final draft of the whole paper. I find myself doing this exercise, too, just to help me focus more on ideas and less on format on timed writings, which essentially are organized, timed early drafts.

Lesson #3 - Write About What You Know

11   Writer and educator Stephen Tchudi says, "To write well, one must know something well." It becomes obvious to readers who knows what they are talking about and who does not. It is easier to have the dilemma of knowing too much about something than not knowing enough to write about it intelligently. For the former, the problem is explaining one's knowledge clearly to the audience who does not know what you know; for the latter, the problem is finding anything specific to say. As in battle, when you are preparing, you want all the reinforcements you can gather. In writing, those reinforcements are specific details or primary and secondary sources in research to back up your knowledge.

12   During the semester that I taught Tripp, he began to work with an eighth-grade physics class on their portfolios. He had to read about writing, about portfolios, about evaluating writing, and actually work with students on creating an assessment tool for their portfolios. Students wrote letters to him and the other seniors in his class, explaining a physics concept to them. Tripp had to evaluate the students' understanding of the concept as part of his evaluation of their portfolios. In the process, he learned a great deal about his own writing.

Lesson #4 - Collaboration and a Real Audience Make a Difference

13   Tripp and two of his classmates had conducted the sessions with the eighth graders and gathered documentation from their experiences. A friend was editing a collection on assessment for *The Clearing House*, a national educational journal; so I suggested that he consider an article written by these three students. Tripp was scared; he felt confident that he could not write well. When the three of them each wrote a first draft, they were amazed at how much they could add to each other's writing with details. Through many drafts, they helped each other develop the article. During this process, I would ask them questions to help get them closer to a finished product. After they sent it to the editor, he phoned and each of them had a chance to take notes on the feedback he gave them. That was a real audience who would determine whether their article would be published! Tripp wrote a note at the end of the year in which he said, "I now think I might be a writer who has his own

voice for the first time." Now for the first time Tripp realized he had a writing style of his own! The three students were college freshmen at Samford, Wake Forest, and Madison when they received their copies of the publication. I wish I could have been there for their reaction to seeing their article published in a national professional journal.

14   Collaboration on a publication helps students gain confidence in their ability to write and also helps them discover new ways of thinking from a trusted colleague. Throughout the years, I have written numerous articles and chapters with students, teachers of other subjects and colleagues at other institutions. Each collaboration makes me work harder on my own writing, reevaluate my thinking in drafts, and appreciate the writing and thinking of others. It creates a supportive and critical environment, one with respected peers.

Lesson #5 - If You Are Comfortable with Your Writing You Will Take Risks to Write Better

15 Wes has always been an A student; however, when it came time to work on his college application essays, he had writer's block. In fact, his writing about himself became stilted, formal, without humor. Having known Wes for several years, I had heard his corny jokes and puns quite often. After four or five drafts of his essays, I would ask him what he might do to demonstrate who he really was that did not appear on the application form. We took a phrase or sentence from one of the other drafts and started again. Granted, these were still not the real voice of Wes, but the final drafts he submitted gave the picture of a humanistic, well-rounded individual who was academically and physically talented. However, when Wes had to write scholarship essays, he started taking some big risks, using irony, satire, and allusions to literature, history, current events, and science. I asked him why his voice had changed in these papers and he responded, "I know that I have been accepted into the school; now I can truly be myself without the danger of not being able to go to the college of my choice." The difference in style was amazing, and he was pleased with the results.

16   As we become more comfortable with writing for a particular audience, whether known or unknown, we may become more willing to experiment with writing. A few years back a senior came to me saying, "Doc, I know the formula for getting a good grade on essays, but I want to learn how to write well." After I recovered, I asked him, "Are you willing to take some risks with your thinking and writing?" For an entire semester we played with language, including the writing of his college application essay for early decision. On Christmas Eve, I received a phone call from this student saying he had been accepted to the college of his choice. The success of his writing involved his commitment to improving and his willingness to experiment with his own writing.

Lesson #6 - You Need to Allow Time to Write More Than One Draft

17 When I first started teaching, it was common practice for most students to turn in something they had written the night before. In the 1980s, real writers began

talking about drafts, pre-writing, peer response and feedback, more pre-writing, drafts, revision, and editing; they called it the writing process. As much as English language arts teachers tried to encourage a real process for their students' writing, students resisted. Teachers were still putting red marks on their papers and making the corrections for the students on the graded papers. For the most part, that has changed; students now have class activities that help them prepare for the writing of a paper, and they have a chance to get feedback from classmates before they write and submit a final draft. However, the students who do well with their writing have started early, allowed time to distance themselves from their own writing, and actually "re-visioned" their own papers. A dozen years ago students would come to the writing center, type in and print one draft to submit to their teachers. Now, they start earlier, bounce ideas off others, allow themselves time to rethink, and reread materials before they start writing a final draft.

Lesson #7 - Don't Take Yourself Too Seriously: Be Open to Criticism

18 I have directed two secondary school writing centers at public and private institutions and found that the atmosphere of mutual respect and humor in a low-risk environment makes a big difference in long-term writing improvement. I listen to the soft laughter, sometimes uproars, that emerge from various corners of the room and know that learning is occurring. Students are reading their papers aloud, and others are listening intently and jotting notes or questions. The reader will say something and realize how absurd it is with a word missing or an illogical conclusion, and the two of them will laugh.

19 Matt had been a regular in the writing center; however, it wasn't until he started working on college application essays that he felt comfortable coming to ask for some feedback. When a student writes well enough to get good grades in high school, he seldom sees the need for any input from someone else. This was Matt, my friend who came to talk with me quite regularly but not someone who "needed help" at least not until he had to write application essays. The help that Matt needed focused on continuity and consistency in the use of metaphors or the precise tone he wished to convey to his audience—the people who would determine his academic future. Through a series of 15 drafts for one essay and multiple drafts of other ones, Matt and I spent many hours laughing. Sometimes other students would look at us as if we could not possibly be doing serious work, but what they did not know was that we were talking about expanding his metaphor of cooking pasta for assimilation in America or his use of irony in defining freedom. It was delightful to be part of Matt's experience with important assignments that allowed him to enjoy the process because he did not take himself too seriously.

20 When I have to write something to be sent to their parents, I hand it to a group of students and laughter invariably results. They know the intended audience much better than I do, so they set me straight on phrases that would make no sense to their parents. If I am proposing a new course, I run the proposal by the current seniors who tell me that no one would sign up for this course the way I have described it. "Help

me out here," I say, and they do! Last year, one student wrote on our writing center flyer: "We poke fun at your papers in a supportive way." Not really, but the message indicates the humorous environment we create to allow someone to say that.

21   Each day as I leave the writing center or the classroom, I think about the lessons I have learned from my students. Some come from students who are now returning as alumni, many reminding me of specific lessons we have learned together. When I had lunch with Matt, I asked if he was doing okay meeting deadlines in college. He began telling me about a research project that he loved because it was creative, required much more research than he would normally have done and took the form of a proposal for a real course. I asked him if he would read my essay for college students and critique it for me; once again, he was teaching me about his writing process, but this time we were collaborating on *my* paper.

THINKING CRITICALLY

1. Childers uses many examples of her own students' writing to support her essay. Is this an effective technique? Did you find the examples helpful? Explain.

2. When Childers first introduces Tripp, we learn that while he writes for his audience, he doesn't seem to enjoy writing. Why? What advice do you think Anne Lamott would give him? What would you suggest, and why?

3. What have Childers's students taught her about writing? Explain.

4. Has fear, like the fears Wes faces when writing his college entrance essays, ever affected or restricted your own writing? Explain.

5. Why is it important for students to find their own voice and style and be comfortable with writing?

WRITING ASSIGNMENTS

1. Childers describes how a collaborative writing effort helped Tripp and two other classmates find their own voice and prepare a paper for publication. Repeat this exercise with two other students in your writing class. Prepare a short essay together, and then edit the piece as individuals, asking questions to draw out each other's points, voice, and style. How does the final piece compare to essays you have written without the benefit of collaboration? Explain.

2. Freewriting has helped many of Childers's students find their own voice. Conduct a freewriting assignment in which you explore and discuss your own writer's voice. What is your voice? How do you know it is yours? What makes it different or unique? Is voice important to your writing? Why or why not?

3. Write about a personal experience in which you realized how important effective communication skills really were. It could be from a college application process, a job or school experience, or a miscommunication between family members or friends. In your answer, be sure to address how using language effectively helped solve the problem.

4. If your school has one, interview instructors at your school's writing lab or writing resource center and ask them for their own observations on effective writing

and if they have learned anything about writing from the students who come to the lab/center. Share the results of your interview with the rest of the class for group discussion on effective writing practices.

Forget Ideas, Mr. Author. What Kind of Pen Do You Use?

Stephen J. Fry

As writers, we are deeply interested in the *process* of writing, not just in the end product. It may surprise students to learn that many famous writers ask themselves the same, self-doubting questions students ask: Am I doing this right? Do other writers get writer's block the way I do? Is my writing clear? Am I getting my point across? Will my readers even care? Writer Joyce Carol Oates once said, "When writers ask each other what time they start working and when they finish and how much time they take for lunch, they're actually trying to find out 'Is he as crazy as I am?'" In the next essay, comedian, actor, and prolific writer Stephen Fry takes a humorous look at the questions people ask writers and the challenges even highly successful writers face.

Stephen Fry is an English comedian, author, actor, and filmmaker. His vast span of work includes roles in television in the BBC series *Blackadder* and *The Young Ones*, and movie appearances in *Peter's Friends* and *A Fish Called Wanda*. Most recently, he was the narrator for the 2005 film, *The Hitchhiker's Guide to the Galaxy*. He has authored numerous scripts and screenplays for television and cinema, and is the author of many novels and books, including *The Liar* (1992) and *The Ode Less Traveled* (2005). This essay was printed in the July 29, 2002, edition of the *New York Times*.

1 Here is a truth to which all writers can attest: Readers are more interested in process than in product.

2 Authors know this for certain, because authors undergo Trial By Event, "event" being publisher-speak for anything from a chilly book signing in a half-empty general store with one paperback carousel next to the soda cabinet to a grand festival colloquium held before an audience of readers so literary that you just know they have terriers called Scott and Zelda and a parrot called Trilling.

3 No matter how well read the audience may be, when it comes to the Q&A, it is always the same. After a few polite interrogatory skirmishes for form's sake come the only questions that matter to the reader.

4 Do you write in longhand or on a computer?"

5 If longhand: "Pencil, ballpoint or old-fashioned ink pen?"

6 If computer: "PC or Mac? Which font do you prefer?"

7 No doubt if you were to reveal that you dictated your work, there would come a fresh slew of questions. "Into a machine or to a secretary?" "Sony or Panasonic?" "Male or female?"

8   As it happens I have never heard an author say that he did use dictation; this seems to be a method of the Erle Stanley Gardner generation that has fallen into desuetude. Perhaps the rise of computer speech recognition will change this. But if I did happen to be sharing a festival stage with a literary dictator, I would be fascinated by his answer. You see, writers (perhaps especially writers) want to know how to write, too.

9   Musicians tend not to face these questions because it is not generally held that everyone has a symphony in him somewhere. Language however belongs to us all. Is there a hint of resentment in readers? "We all speak English. We all write e-mails and letters every day. What's your secret? Just give us enough detail, and we can be inducted into the coterie, too." It is almost as if some people feel that they were off sick or at the dentist's the day the rest of the class was told how to write a book, and that it isn't fair of authors to keep the mystery to themselves.

10   I exaggerate for effect. Not every reader wants to be a writer, and literary festival audiences are hardly the most reliable sample group from which to extrapolate.

11   I once shared a stage with Gore Vidal in Manchester, England, which was a very great honor indeed, although he did not appear to appreciate it. No, but, tush. Mr. Vidal was asked if he felt there had ever been an age in recent history that could boast so few good writers as the present. "There are as many good writers as ever there were," he replied, and I wish I could reproduce on the page the trademark patrician Gore-drawl that transforms his lightest remark into a marmoreal epigram. "The problem is that there are so few good readers."

12   The rise of digital cameras and desktop editing software is starting to create the same effect with filmmaking, by the way. A director is now as likely to be asked by a film fan, "Do you prefer anamorphic or super-35?" or "Do you favor the bleach bypass process?" as once he would be asked, "What's Robert Redford really like?" or "Does Clint do his own stunts?'

13   A loss of innocence or a thrilling indication that soon we will all be artists? I don't know. I do know that, as I suggested earlier, writers are just as interested as readers in the trivial detail of another writer's day.

14   For example, I read somewhere that Graham Greene used to leave his last sentence of the writing day unfinished. In this way, he always had something straightforward to do the next morning. I have copied this idea and find that something as simple as completing a sentence works very well as a way of priming the pump at the start of the day. Such a technique doesn't transform one into a literary master any more than growling bad-temperedly, beetling your brows and using an ear trumpet will enable you to write great symphonies, but every little helps.

15   My latest novel, *Revenge*, caused me a very specific hair-raising and sleep-depriving problem. I had planned it out in my head, which is about as much planning as I ever do, not being an index-card, scenario, or flow-chart sort of a person. It was to be a story of wrongful imprisonment and subsequent vengeance. As I thought the narrative through, a little voice started whispering wicked thoughts into my ear.

16   "This isn't very original," it would say. "I've heard it before."

17   At first I didn't pay much attention. When did any of us last read an original story? Original writing is the issue. Treatment is all. But then one night I sat bolt upright in bed and screamed in horror. The truth had suddenly exploded into my consciousness.

18   The story, the plot I had been working out with such pleasure, was not just un-original, it was a straight steal, virtually identical in all but period and style to Alexandre Dumas's *Count of Monte Cristo*.

19   What does a writer do on such occasions? Abandon his narrative and embark upon another? I was already three chapters in, and those authorial juices that take so long to summon up were flowing nicely. Should I rely on the fact that *The Count of Monte Cristo* is one of those novels that few (myself included at that point) have actually read? I was in one heck of a pickle, let me tell you.

20   I arose early next day and drove into the medieval university town of Cambridge, where there are more bookshops than people, and bought every copy of the Dumas original I could find, for now a new, more benign voice was whispering in my ear.

21   "I bet Dumas pinched the story, too."

22   And sure enough, in an introduction to one of the editions I found came the welcome news that the story of a wrongly imprisoned sailor who escapes the Chateau d'If was, in Dumas's day, a kind of urban legend that he had gratefully lifted.

23   If we're talking process incidentally, Dumas's publishers paid him by the line. Can you imagine anything so foolish? This is why his work is crammed with dialogue.

24   "Pass the mustard."

25   "Eh?"

26   "I said, 'Pass the mustard.'"

27   "You want some custard?"

28   "No, mustard."

29   "Oh."

30   Each carriage return a happy ring on the cash register.

31   Anyway, once I was assured in my own mind that the outline of the story was not original to Dumas, I continued with the book, deciding that a "literary rework-ing" or "homage" was perfectly acceptable, and that I could not in all seriousness be charged with that most unforgivable of literary crimes, plagiarism.

32   As a further safeguard I changed the names of my protagonists to anagrams of the originals. Thus Edmond Dantès, who reinvents himself as Monte Cristo, be-comes in my story Ned Maddstone, who reinvents himself as Simon Cotter. Baron Danglars is turned into Barson-Garland and so on. Edmond's affianced Mercedes transforms herself (in an unforgivable example of automobile paronomasia) into Portia.

33   Interestingly, and I had not meant in any way to trap or test, my French transla-tors were the only people to pick up on the story's similarity to Monte Cristo. Since then, in new editions, including the current American one, we have proudly announced the book's connection to Dumas. No one, however, has noticed the jeu d'esprit of anagrams and awful puns. All that work for nothing. If you have an hour

or so to kill, you might like to pick up a copy (you can read it on a bookshop sofa, far be it from me vulgarly to hawk for business) and see how many you can spot.

34   Oh, I use a Mac, by the way. Times Roman, 14 point. Very traditional.

THINKING CRITICALLY

1. What type of questions do Fry's readers ask him? Why does he find these questions humorous? What sorts of questions would you ask when meeting a famous author?

2. Fry wonders if his readers believe that if they get the right details they can be writers too. Do you think there is a writer in everyone? Why or why not?

3. Fry uses some unusual and uncommon words in his essay. What does his word choice reveal about the assumptions he makes regarding the audience for this essay? Identify some of these unusual words. How do they color his writing?

4. What surprising predicament did Fry face when writing his novel *Revenge*? How did he solve his dilemma? What personal imprint did he make on the novel?

WRITING ASSIGNMENTS

1. In this essay, Stephen Fry described his personal approach to writing. Write your own narrative on how you write. Include any unique challenges you have faced.

2. Contact your local bookstore or library and attend a "meet the author" reading or book signing. Note what questions members of the audience ask the author. Are they more interested in the process of writing, the details, or in the final product? Write a short essay based on your observations.

Exploring the Language of **V I S U A L S**

The Secret Lives of Fonts

Phil Renaud

Despite the abundance of choices, most students don't give much thought to the fonts they use when writing their essays and term papers. Or if they do, it is often to stretch or shrink papers to meet a required page-count. Research indicates that certain fonts are better for reading than others. For example, serif fonts, such as Times New Roman and Garamond cause less eye strain when used as body text than sans serif fonts, such as Arial and Trebuchet. But can font choice influence how teachers grade papers? In the next essay, one student explains why he thinks students might want to consider carefully the fonts they use.

Phil Renaud is a philosophy major at the University of Windsor in Ontario, Canada. He posted these observations on the influence of fonts on term-paper grading on Fad.tastic, a multiauthor online journal/blog site that explores trends in Web design in March 2006.

1   I'm nearing the end of my sixth semester of university, and things are going pretty well. I'm clearing a decent grade point average, enjoying my major, and just having wrapped up my semester's "essay alley," wherein all my courses require a term paper or two, getting my results back telling me that I'm doing much better than usual.

2   At first, I'm just relieved to be doing so well. Still, ever the skeptic, I start to wonder: what exactly am I doing differently now to be getting all these A-range paper grades all of the sudden?

3   I haven't drastically changed the amount of effort I'm putting into my writing. I'm probably even spending less time with them now than I did earlier in my studies, and while I guess you could argue that I'm probably just being a great example of practice making perfect, I've got my doubts; I even used to take courses concentrating on writing better essays, and in the time surrounding that, my grades were pretty low.

4   Then it hits me: the only thing I've really changed since I've been getting these grades is . . . **my essay font.**

5   Long story short, this throws me into something of a panic: I keep all my essays' final copies in storage, so I go through every scholarly paper I've written for the past few years in hopes of garnering some sort of makeshift empirical results with regards to my essay styles. Here's what I'm working with:

Total Number of Essays Written: 52
Fonts Used: Times New Roman, Trebuchet MS, Georgia

Let me explain what I found; I think the results might be a little bit surprising.

1. Times New Roman

The Emergence of Consciousness
in Hegel's *Phenomenology*

PART A: EXEGESIS

Total *Times New Roman* styled essays: 11
Average Grade: A-

6   Everybody starts out using Times New Roman, I think. It's the default in most text editors, and the natural tendency of first-year college students being lazy; it's unlikely too many of them bothered messing around with the fonts until at least later in their studies. I was in the same boat. Anyway, the A- average is pretty close to where my GPA stands, and assuming that the professor marking the papers generally sees a few hundred in *Times* font every semester, I imagine he/she really just marked the paper on the basis of its integrity.

7   However, I don't think I can say the same about the next two fonts . . .

2. Trebuchet MS

Social Political Philosophy: Critical Theory
Marcuse and One-Dimensional Culture

Total *Trebuchet MS* styled essays: 18
Average Grade: B-

8   Ouch! Nobody likes to see a B- on papers that they put serious effort into. Unfortunately, these guys made up more than a third of my total essay output. So what gives? Was I just neglecting my papers around this time? Personal crises bogging me down? Partying a little too hard?

9   Actually, none of the above. I wrote most of these in second-third year, where I had a good bit more free time to study than usual, and as it turns out, I got some of my best overall marks. I checked my exam/non-essay grades from around that time, and they were through the roof! "A"-range grades on pretty much *everything that didn't give me the option of styling my font*.

10   Well, before I start chanting "Academic Objectivity" is a myth, there's still one more font to investigate.

3. Georgia

Mind Design and Android

Epistemology
On Pollock and Cruz's Naturalized Epistemology

Total *Georgia* styled essays: 23
Average Grade: A

11   Well, would you believe it? My essays written in Georgia did the best overall. This got me thinking as to why that might be: *maybe fonts speak a lot louder than we think they do.* Especially to a professor who has to wade through a collection of them; *Times* seems to be the norm, so it really doesn't set off any subconscious triggers. *Georgia* is enough like *Times* to retain its academic feel, and is different enough to be something of a relief for the grader. *Trebuchet* seems to set off a negative trigger, maybe just based on the fact that it's not as easy to read in print, maybe on the fact that it looks like something off a blog rather than an academic journal. Who knows.

12 So, What Are You Trying to Say?

13   I want to say that serifs appeal to academics more than sans serifs do. I even briefly hypothesized that potential students would be innately drawn towards the [Web]site of a college with a serif font more than one with a sans serif.

14   I didn't go into this hoping to try and make any claims against academic integrity here; I can't imagine this is something that a professor would do knowingly.

15   What I'm not opposed to saying, however, is that the style used in an essay certainly seems to influence grading tendencies, even if that is at an unconscious level. I think that it's possible that a person sees a serif font and thinks "proper, academic," and sees a sans serif font and thinks "focus is on the style, not the substance; must lack integrity." Maybe.

16   But, it's hard to deny this, evidenced over 52 papers. Within each of the three fonts I used, there wasn't terribly much variance, either. It's not like these were just written for one subject, either: a wide range of disciplines were included, from philosophy to economics to marketing to political science to computer science, even having paper on computational neuromodeling thrown in there.

17   So, be mindful of your target audience when you're making a document, whether it's a university essay or a commercial Web site. You never know just how loudly a font speaks.

THINKING CRITICALLY

1. Renaud proposes that font choice subconsciously influences how instructors grade papers. How persuasive is his evidence?

2. Do you think about font choice when writing your own essays and term papers? If so, what factors influence your choice of font?

3. Research the difference between serif and sans serif fonts. What fonts are recommended for what purposes? After researching font faces, do you think you will be more thoughtful in choosing a font face for your essays?

4. Select 10 different font faces (5 serif and 5 sans serif) and ask at least 12 people to react to them. Are some fonts more serious then others? Academic? Frivolous? Childlike? Explain.

MAKING CONNECTIONS

1. The authors in this section all describe different aspects of the writing process—from audience identification, to finding your inspiration, to editing the final product. During your next essay assignment, keep a journal of your impressions of each step of the writing process as you compose your essay. In your journal, consider your approach to the writing process during each step and the feedback you received from teachers and peers.

2. Many writing instructors encourage freewriting exercises that promote the unencumbered flow of ideas as a way to develop writing skills. Try to write about a topic—for example, teenage use of alcohol or a particular type of controversial music—for two different audiences. Keep your audience in mind as you write, but remain mindful of simply allowing your ideas to flow freely. After you complete this writing exercise, consider how freewriting compares to more structured methods of writing.

3. After reading the work of the authors featured in this section, do you have a better sense of the writing process? Explain why or why not.

4. In your own opinion, which stage of the writing process is the most important? Support your answer by drawing from material provided in this section as well as from your personal writing experiences.

5. What common advice and/or suggestions do the authors in this section make? Identify similarities and differences in their essays.

FINDING THE RIGHT WORDS

The Case for Short Words
Richard Lederer

Sometimes students pull out the dictionary or thesaurus in an effort to find words that seem more "academic." We seem to think that the longer or more difficult the word is to pronounce, the more intelligent the writer must be. But this isn't necessarily the case. In many situations, short words do the job better than long or complicated ones. In this essay, writer and former high school teacher Richard Lederer explains why small, short words can be the most powerful words of all.

Richard Lederer is the author of several best-selling books on words and language, including *Get Thee to a Punnery* (1988), *Crazy English* (1989), and *Fractured English* (1996). Lederer, who holds a PhD in linguistics, is a regular contributor to *Writer's Digest*, and a language commentator on National Public Radio (NPR). The following essay was published in the August 1999 issue of the San Diego *Writers Monthly* and was featured in Lederer's 1991 book, *The Miracle of Language*.

1   When you speak and write, there is no law that says you have to use big words.
Short words are as good as long ones, and short, old words—like sun and grass and
home—are best of all. A lot of small words, more than you might think, can meet
your needs with a strength, grace, and charm that large words do not have.

2   Big words can make the way dark for those who read what you write and hear
what you say. Small words cast their clear light on big things—night and day, love
and hate, war and peace, and life and death. Big words at times seem strange to the
eye and the ear and the mind and the heart. Small words are the ones we seem to
have known from the time we were born, like the hearth fire that warms the home.

3   Short words are bright like sparks that glow in the night, prompt like the dawn
that greets the day, sharp like the blade of a knife, hot like salt tears that scald the
cheek, quick like moths that flit from flame to flame, and terse like the dart and
sting of a bee.

4   Here is a sound rule: Use small, old words where you can. If a long word says
just what you want to say, do not fear to use it. But know that our tongue is rich in
crisp, brisk, swift, short words. Make them the spine and the heart of what you
speak and write. Short words are like fast friends. They will not let you down.

5   The title of this essay and the four paragraphs that you have just read are
wrought entirely of words of one syllable. In setting myself this task, I did not feel
especially cabined, cribbed, or confined. In fact, the structure helped me to focus
on the power of the message I was trying to put across.

6   One study shows that twenty words account for twenty-five percent of all
spoken English words, and all twenty are monosyllabic. In order of frequency they
are: *I, you, the, a, to, is, it, that, of, and, in, what, he, this, have, do, she, not, on,* and
they. Other studies indicate that the fifty most common words in written English are
each made of a single syllable.

7   For centuries our finest poets and orators have recognized and employed the
power of small words to make a straight point between two minds. A great many of
our proverbs punch home their points with pithy monosyllables: "Where there's a
will, there's a way," "A stitch in time saves nine," "Spare the rod and spoil the
child," "A bird in the hand is worth two in the bush."

8   Nobody used the short word more skillfully than William Shakespeare, whose
dying King Lear laments:

> And my poor fool is hang'd! No, no, no life!
> Why should a dog, a horse, a rat have life,
> And thou no breath at all? . . .
> Do you see this? Look on her, look, her lips.
> Look there, look there!

9   Shakespeare's contemporaries made the King James Bible a centerpiece of short
words—"And God said, Let there be light: and there was light. And God saw the
light, that it was good." The descendants of such mighty lines live on in the twentieth
century. When asked to explain his policy to parliament, Winston Churchill
responded with these ringing monosyllables: "I will say: it is to wage war, by sea,
land, and air, with all our might and with all the strength that God can give us." In his

"Death of the Hired Man" Robert Frost observes that "Home is the place where, when you have to go there, They have to take you in." And William H. Johnson uses ten two-letter words to explain his secret of success: "If it is to be, It is up to me."

10   You don't have to be a great author, statesman, or philosopher to tap the energy and eloquence of small words. Each winter I asked my ninth graders at St. Paul's School to write a composition composed entirely of one-syllable words. My students greeted my request with obligatory moans and groans, but, when they returned to class with their essays, most felt that, with the pressure to produce high-sounding polysyllables relieved, they had created some of their most powerful and luminous prose. Here are submissions from two of my ninth graders:

> What can you say to a boy who has left home? You can say that he has done wrong, but he does not care. In spite of the breeze that made the vines sway, we all wished we could hide from the glare in a cool, white house. But, as there was no one to help dock the boat, we had to stand and wait.
>
> At last the head of the crew leaped from the side and strode to a large house on the right. He shoved the door wide, poked his head through the gloom, and roared with a fierce voice. Five or six men came out, and soon the port was loud with the clank of chains and creak of planks as the men caught ropes thrown by the crew; pulled them taut, and tied them to posts. Then they set up a rough plank so we could cross from the deck to the shore. We all made for the large house while the crew watched, glad to be rid of us.

THINKING CRITICALLY

1. What, according to Lederer, are the "big things" that small words describe? Can you think of additional small words that describe "big things"?

2. In paragraph 7, Lederer points out several proverbs that use small words. Identify at least three or four more and test his observation. Do short words predominate? If so, what explains the high proportion of small words in proverbs?

3. Review the examples of student writing Lederer cites in his essay. What seems special about their writing? Does it seem constrained by the requirements of his assignment? Why or why not?

4. Why do so many students feel pressured to use long or complicated words instead of smaller ones? Do teachers reinforce the idea that big words are better? Do you think your grades would suffer if you opted for smaller words in your essays and homework assignments? Explain.

5. Evaluate Lederer's introductory paragraphs (1–4), which only use one-syllable words. Did you realize that he was using only short words when you first read these paragraphs? What impression did you have of his writing in these first four paragraphs? Explain.

WRITING ASSIGNMENTS

1. Duplicate Lederer's assignment to his class. Write a full paragraph describing an everyday event, idea, or scene (getting up in the morning, viewing a sunrise, looking up at a night sky, a visit with your parents, how you feel about a

significant other, etc.). After writing your paragraph and checking that it is indeed written using only one-syllable words, describe the challenges you faced and impressions you had of the composition processes.

2. Find a paragraph or two from an essay or freewriting assignment that you think is a good representation of your academic voice. Try rewriting the paragraph(s) using only short words. In addition to comparing the two from your own perspective, give the two pieces to a friend or family member and ask them to evaluate each. Ask your reviewer to explain what makes the piece they prefer better in their opinion. Describe the results in a short essay, drawing your own conclusions from your experiment.

Saying Is Believing

Patricia T. O'Conner

In the preceding piece, Richard Lederer made his case for short words. In this essay, grammarian and writer Patricia T. O'Conner explains how to avoid some of the pitfalls facing many college writers by embracing the principles of "plain English." Too often, complexity, confusion, wordiness, and redundancy sidetrack writers. Her solution is a list of 13 points that will improve your writing, and guide you through the writing blunders many students make.

A former editor of the *New York Times Book Review*, Patricia O'Conner is the author of three books on writing and has published articles on grammar and writing in many newspapers and journals including the *New York Times* and *Newsweek*. She is the author of *Words Fail Me: What Everyone Who Writes Should Know About Writing* (2000) and of *You Send Me* (2002), written with husband Stewart Kellerman. This essay was first published in her grammar guidebook, *Woe Is I: The Grammarphobe's Guide to Better English in Plain English* (1996).

1 A good writer is one you can read without breaking a sweat. If you want a workout, you don't lift a book—you lift weights. Yet we're brainwashed to believe that the more brilliant the writer, the tougher the going.

2 The truth is that the reader is always right. Chances are, if something you're reading doesn't make sense, it's not your fault—it's the writer's. And if something you write doesn't get your point across, it's probably not the reader's fault—it's yours. Too many readers are intimidated and humbled by what they can't understand, and in some cases that's precisely the effect the writer is after. But confusion is not complexity; it's just confusion. A venerable tradition, dating back to the ancient Greek orators, teaches that if you don't know what you're talking about, just ratchet up the level of difficulty and no one will ever know.

3 Don't confuse simplicity, though, with simplemindedness. A good writer can express an extremely complicated idea clearly and make the job look effortless. But such simplicity is a difficult thing to achieve, because to be clear in your writing you have to be clear in your thinking. This is why the simplest and clearest writing has the greatest power to delight, surprise, inform, and move the reader.

You can't have this kind of shared understanding if writer and reader are in an adversary relationship.

4   Now, let's assume you know what you want to say, and the idea in your head is as clear as a mountain stream. (I'm allowed a cliché once in a while.) How can you avoid muddying it up when you put it into words?

5   There are no rules for graceful writing, at least not in the sense that there are rules for grammar and punctuation. Some writing manuals will tell you to write short sentences, or to cut out adjectives and adverbs. I disagree. The object isn't to simulate an android. When a sentence sounds nice, reads well, and is easy to follow, its length is just right. But when a sentence is lousy, you can take steps to make it more presentable. These are general principles, and you won't want to follow all of them all of the time (though it's not a bad idea).

1. Say what you have to say

6 Unless you're standing at a lectern addressing an audience, there's no need to clear your throat. Your listeners aren't finding their seats, putting down their forks, wrapping up a conversation, or whatever. Your audience—the reader—is ready. So get to it.

7   These are the kinds of throat-clearing phrases you can usually ditch:

> *At this juncture I thought you might be interested in knowing . . .*
> *Perhaps it would be valuable as we arrive at this point in time to recall. . .*
> *I can assure you that I'm sincere when I say . . .*
> *In light of recent developments the possibility exists that . . .*

8   (Of course, some messages could do with a bit of cushioning: *We at the bank feel that under the circumstances you would want us to bring to your attention as soon as possible the fact that . . . your account is overdrawn.*)

2. Stop when you've said it

9 Sometimes, especially when you're on a roll and coming up with your best stuff, it's hard to let go of a sentence (this one, for example), so when you get to the logical end you just keep going, and even though you know the reader's eyes are glazing over, you stretch one sentence thinner and thinner—with a semicolon here, a *however* or *nevertheless* there—and you end up stringing together a whole paragraph's worth of ideas before you finally realize it's all over and you're getting writer's cramp and you have to break down and use a period.

10   When it's time to start another sentence, start another sentence.

11   How do you know when it's time? Well, try breathing along with your sentences. Allow yourself one nice inhalation and exhalation per sentence as you silently read along. If you start to turn blue before getting to the end, either you're reading too slowly (don't move your lips) or the sentence is too long.

3. Don't belabor the obvious

12 Some writers can't make a point without poking you in the ribs with it. A voice isn't just pleasing; it's pleasing *to the ear*. You don't just give something away; you give

it away *for free*. The reader will get the point without the unnecessary prepositional phrases (phrases that start with words like *by, for, in, of*, and *to*): pretty *in appearance*, tall *of stature*, blue *in color*, small *in size*, stocky *in build*, plan *in advance*, drive *by car*, assemble *in a group*. You get the picture.

4. Don't tie yourself in knots to avoid repeating a word

13 It's better to repeat a word that fits than to stick in a clumsy substitute that doesn't. Just because you've called something a spider once doesn't mean that the next time you have to call it an arachnid or a predaceous eight-legged creepy-crawly.

14   Editors sometimes call this attempt at elegant variation the Slender Yellow Fruit Syndrome. It is best explained by example: *Freddie was offered an apple and a banana, and he chose the slender yellow fruit.*

5. Be direct

15 Too many writers back into what they have to say. A straightforward statement like *He didn't intend to ruin your flower bed* comes out *His intention was not to ruin your flower bed.*

16   Don't mince words. If what you mean is, *Mom reorganized my closet brilliantly*, don't water it down by saying, *Mom's reorganization of my closet was brilliant.*

17   Here are a couple of other examples:

> *Their house was destroyed in 1993. Not: The destruction of their house occurred in 1993.*
> *We concluded that Roger's an idiot. Not: Our conclusion was that Roger's an idiot.*

18   If you have something to say, be direct about it. As in geometry, the shortest distance between two points is a straight line.

6. Don't make yourself the center of the universe

19 Of course we want to know what happened to you. Of course we care what you think and feel and do and say. But you can tell us without making every other word *I* or *me* or *my*. (Letter writers, who are fast becoming an endangered species, are often guilty of this. Next time you write a letter or memo, look it over and see how many sentences start with *I*.)

20   You can prune phrases like *I think that*, or *in my opinion*, or *let me emphasize that* out of your writing (and your talking, for that matter) without losing anything. Anecdotes can be told, advice given, opinions opined, all with a lot fewer first-person pronouns than you think.

21   This doesn't mean we don't love you.

7. Put descriptions close to what they describe

22 A television journalist in the Farm Belt once said this about a suspected outbreak of hoof-and-mouth disease: *The pasture contained several cows seen by news reporters that were dead, diseased, or dying.*

23   Do you see what's wrong? The words *dead, diseased, or dying* are supposed to describe the cows, but they're so far from home that they seem to describe the reporters. What the journalist should have said was: *Reporters saw a pasture containing several cows that were dead, diseased, or dying.*

24   When a description strays too far, the sentence becomes awkward and hard to read. Here's an adjective (*bare*) that has strayed too far from the noun (*cupboard*) it describes: *Ms. Hubbard found her **cupboard,** although she'd gone shopping only a few hours before, **bare**.* Here's one way to rewrite it: *Although she'd gone shopping only a few hours before, Ms. Hubbard found her **cupboard bare**.*

25   And here's an adverb (*definitely*) that's strayed too far from its verb (*is suing*): *She **definitely,** if you can believe what all the papers are reporting and what everyone is saying, **is suing**.* Put them closer together: *She **definitely is suing**, if you can believe what all the papers are reporting and what everyone is saying.*

26   The reader shouldn't need a map to follow a sentence.

8. Put the doer closer to what's being done

27 Nobody's saying that sentences can't be complex and interesting; they can, as long as they're easy to follow. But we shouldn't have to read a sentence twice to get it. Here's an example that takes us from Omaha to Sioux City by way of Pittsburgh:

> *The **twins**, after stubbornly going to the same high school despite the advice of their parents and teachers, chose different colleges.*

28   Find a way to say it that puts the doer (the subject, *twins*) closer to what's being done (the verb, *chose*): *The **twins chose** different colleges, after stubbornly going to the same high school despite the advice of their parents and teachers.*

29   If you need a compass to navigate a sentence, take another whack at the writing.

9. Watch out for pronounitis

30 A sentence with too many pronouns (*he, him, she, her, it, they, them*, and other words that substitute for nouns) can give your reader hives: *Fleur thinks that Judy told **her** boyfriend about **their** stupid little adventure and that **she** will come to regret it.*

31   Whose boyfriend? Whose stupid little adventure? Who'll regret what?

32   When you write things like this, of course, you know the cast of characters. It won't be so clear to somebody else. Don't make the reader guess.

10. Make sure there's a time and place for everything

> *While the merger specialist was vacationing in Aspen, she said she secretly put the squeeze on Mr. Buyout by threatening to go public with candid photos of him in one of those foil helmets, getting his hair streaked at Frederic Fekkai.*

33   Did the merger specialist tell this story when she was vacationing in Aspen, or is that where she put the squeeze on Mr. Buyout? Were the photos taken earlier? And where is Frederic Fekkai? This calls for two sentences:

> *While vacationing in Aspen, the merger specialist faxed us her secret. She had put the squeeze on Mr. Buyout in New York the week before by threatening to*

go public with candid photos of him in one of those foil helmets, getting his hair streaked at Frederic Fekkai.

34 Where are we? What's going on? What time is it? These are questions the reader shouldn't have to ask.

11. Imagine what you're writing

35 Picture in your mind any images you've created.

Are they unintentionally funny, like this one? *The bereaved family covered the mirrors as a reflection of its grief.* If you don't see what's wrong, reflect on it for a moment.

36 Are there too many of them, as in this sentence? *The remaining bone of contention is a thorn in his side and an albatross around his neck:* Give the poor guy a break. One image at a time, please.

12. Put your ideas in order

37 Don't make the reader rearrange your messy sentences to figure out what's going on. The parts should follow logically. This doesn't mean they should be rattled off in chronological order, but the sequence of ideas should make sense. Here's how Gracie Allen might have talked about a soufflé recipe, for instance:

> *It is possible to make this soufflé with four eggs instead of eight. But it will collapse and possibly even catch fire in the oven, leaving you with a flat, burned soufflé. Now, you wouldn't want that, would you? So if you have only four eggs, reduce all the other ingredients in the recipe by half.*

38 Rearrange the ideas:

> *This soufflé recipe calls for eight eggs. If you want to use fewer, reduce the other ingredients accordingly. If the proportions aren't maintained, the soufflé could flatten or burn.*

13. Read with a felonious mind

39 Forget the details for a minute. Now step back and take a look at what you've written. Have you said what you wanted to say? After all, leaving the wrong impression is much worse than making a couple of grammatical boo-boos. Get some perspective.

40 Assuming you've made your point, ask yourself whether you could make it more smoothly. Somebody once said that in good writing, the sentences hold hands. See if you can give yours a helping hand. It may be that by adding or subtracting a word here or there, you could be even clearer. Or you could switch two sentences around, or begin one of them differently.

41 There's no easy way to raise your writing from competence to artistry. It helps, though, to read with a felonious mind. If you see a letter or memo or report that you admire, read it again. Why do you like it, and what makes it so effective? When you find a technique that works, steal it. Someday, others may be stealing from you.

THINKING CRITICALLY

1. O'Conner comments in her first sentence, "A good writer is one you can read without breaking a sweat." Do you agree with this observation? Why or why not? What makes a writer "good"?

2. Evaluate O'Conner's tips as they compare to your own writing challenges. Which ones seem to be particularly helpful, and why? If none of them seem relevant, explain why you hold this point of view.

3. O'Conner observes that many people are "brainwashed into believing that the more brilliant the writer, the tougher the going." What does she mean by this statement? Do you agree? Explain.

4. Which items in O'Conner's list endorse the use of "active voice"? What are the merits of active voice? How can using the active voice help writers and readers?

5. In paragraph 3, O'Conner warns, "don't confuse simplicity . . . with simplemindedness." Clear writing is the result of clear thinking. Think about your own writing process. How do you perceive the connection between your own thought process and your writing? Explain.

WRITING ASSIGNMENTS

1. In her introduction, O'Conner comments that readers are "brainwashed" into thinking that brilliant writers are difficult to understand. Select two or three writers who you consider to be "brilliant," and evaluate how difficult their writing is to understand by analyzing a few pages of their writing. Based on your analysis, write an essay in which you agree or disagree with O'Conner's viewpoint.

2. Write with a "felonious mind." Pick two or three writers whose prose you admire and analyze their writing styles. Pick one writer to imitate, and, using that writer's particular style, write three or four paragraphs of your own. How does it "feel" to write like another writer? Did it make your writing stronger? Was it strange to write in another writer's voice? Explain.

3. Using an essay you have recently written, compare your writing to the 13 points O'Conner outlines in her article. Identify areas where you meet her recommendations, and where you fall into some of the writing pitfalls she describes.

How to Write With Style

Kurt Vonnegut

Kurt Vonnegut is one of America's most popular contemporary novelists and humorists. He is the author of such favorite and critically acclaimed novels as *Sirens of Titan* (1959), *Cat's Cradle* (1963), *Slaughterhouse Five* (1969), *Breakfast of Champions* (1973), *Hocus Pocus* (1990), and *Timequake* (1993). Vonnegut has also written short stories for many magazines and journals, and has occasionally made cameo appearances in popular films. The enormous success of his writing can be attributed to his imagination, his satiric voice, and his writing style. In the next piece, Vonnegut gives his own practical advice on writing well, and on how to approach writing with style and a sense of self.

1 Newspaper reporters and technical writers are trained to reveal almost nothing about themselves in their writings. This makes them freaks in the world of writers, since

almost all of the other ink-stained wretches in that world reveal a lot about themselves to readers. We call these revelations, accidental and intentional, elements of style.

2   These revelations tell us as readers what sort of person it is with whom we are spending time. Does the writer sound ignorant or informed, stupid or bright, crooked or honest, humorless or playful—? And on and on.

3   Why should you examine your writing style with the idea of improving it? Do so as a mark of respect for your readers, whatever you're writing. If you scribble your thoughts any which way, your readers will surely feel that you care nothing about them. They will mark you down as an egomaniac or a chowderhead—or worse, they will stop reading you.

4   The most damning revelation you can make about yourself is that you do not know what is interesting and what is not. Don't you yourself like or dislike writers mainly for what they choose to show you or make you think about? Did you ever admire an empty-headed writer for his or her mastery of the language? No.

5   So your own winning style must begin with ideas in your head.

1. Find a Subject You Care About

6 Find a subject you care about and which you in your heart feel others should care about. It is this genuine caring, and not your games with language, which will be the most compelling and seductive element in your style.

7   I am not urging you to write a novel, by the way—although I would not be sorry if you wrote one, provided you genuinely cared about something. A petition to the mayor about a pothole in front of your house or a love letter to the girl next door will do.

2. Do Not Ramble, Though

8 I won't ramble on about that.

3. Keep It Simple

9 As for your use of language: Remember that two great masters of language, William Shakespeare and James Joyce, wrote sentences which were almost childlike when their subjects were most profound. "To be or not to be?" asks Shakespeare's Hamlet. The longest word is three letters long. Joyce, when he was frisky, could put together a sentence as intricate and as glittering as a necklace for Cleopatra, but my favorite sentence in his short story "Eveline" is this one: "She was tired." At that point in the story, no other words could break the heart of a reader as those three words do.

10   Simplicity of language is not only reputable, but perhaps even sacred. The *Bible* opens with a sentence well within the writing skills of a lively fourteen-year-old: "In the beginning God created the heaven and the earth."

4. Have the Guts to Cut

11 It may be that you, too, are capable of making necklaces for Cleopatra, so to speak. But your eloquence should be the servant of the ideas in your head. Your rule might be this: If a sentence, no matter how excellent, does not illuminate your subject in some new and useful way, scratch it out.

5. Sound Like Yourself

12 The writing style which is most natural for you is bound to echo the speech you heard when a child. English was the novelist Joseph Conrad's third language, and much that seems piquant in his use of English was no doubt colored by his first language, which was Polish. And lucky indeed is the writer who has grown up in Ireland, for the English spoken there is so amusing and musical. I myself grew up in Indianapolis, where common speech sounds like a band saw cutting galvanized tin, and employs a vocabulary as unornamental as a monkey wrench.

13 In some of the more remote hollows of Appalachia, children still grow up hearing songs and locutions of Elizabethan times. Yes, and many Americans grow up hearing a language other than English, or an English dialect a majority of Americans cannot understand.

14 All these varieties of speech are beautiful, just as the varieties of butterflies are beautiful. No matter what your first language, you should treasure it all your life. If it happens not to be standard English, and if it shows itself when you write standard English, the result is usually delightful, like a very pretty girl with one eye that is green and one that is blue.

15 I myself find that I trust my own writing most, and others seem to trust it most, too, when I sound most like a person from Indianapolis, which is what I am. What alternatives do I have? The one most vehemently recommended by teachers has no doubt been pressed on you, as well: to write like cultivated Englishmen of a century or more ago.

6. Say What You Mean to Say

16 I used to be exasperated by such teachers, but am no more. I understand now that all those antique essays and stories with which I was to compare my own work were not magnificent for their datedness or foreignness, but for saying precisely what their authors meant them to say. My teachers wished me to write accurately, always selecting the most effective words, and relating the words to one another unambiguously, rigidly, like parts of a machine. The teachers did not want to turn me into an Englishman after all. They hoped that I would become understandable—and therefore understood. And there went my dream of doing with words what Pablo Picasso did with paint or what any number of jazz idols did with music. If I broke all the rules of punctuation, had words mean whatever I wanted them to mean, and strung them together higgledy-piggledy, I would simply not be understood. So you, too, had better avoid Picasso-style or jazz-style writing, if you have something worth saying and wish to be understood.

17 Readers want our pages to look very much like pages they have seen before. Why? This is because they themselves have a tough job to do, and they need all the help they can get from us.

7. Pity the Readers

18 They have to identify thousands of little marks on paper, and make sense of them immediately. They have to *read*, an art so difficult that most people don't really master it even after having studied it all through grade school and high school—twelve long years.

19   So this discussion must finally acknowledge that our stylistic options as writers are neither numerous nor glamorous, since our readers are bound to be such imperfect artists. Our audience requires us to be sympathetic and patient teachers, even willing to simplify and clarify—whereas we would rather soar high above the crowd, singing like nightingales.

20   That is the bad news. The good news is that we Americans are governed under a unique Constitution, which allows us to write whatever we please without fear of punishment. So the most meaningful aspect of our styles, which is what we choose to write about, is utterly unlimited.

8. For Really Detailed Advice

21 For a discussion of literary style in a narrower sense, in a more technical sense, I commend to your attention *The Elements of Style*, by William Strunk, Jr., and E. B. White (Allyn & Bacon, 2000). E. B. White is, of course, one of the most admirable literary stylists this country has so far produced.

22   You should realize, too, that no one would care how well or badly Mr. White expressed himself, if he did not have perfectly enchanting things to say.

THINKING CRITICALLY

1. Examine one of your essays that was recently corrected by your English instructor. On the basis of the corrections, do you think your instructor agrees or disagrees with Vonnegut's advice?

2. According to Vonnegut, what is the advantage of reading "all those antique essays and stories" (paragraph 16)?

3. This article was originally published as an advertisement sponsored by the International Paper Company. Do you feel the average reader would enjoy and profit from the essay?

4. Why do you think Vonnegut chose Shakespeare and Joyce from the hundreds of great writers of the past to demonstrate the value of simplicity?

5. A key piece of advice Vonnegut gives is, "Sound like yourself." Do you think he follows his own advice? Give examples to support your answer.

6. Occasionally Vonnegut uses a simile or metaphor to make a point. Cite some examples from the essay. How do they contribute to the piece?

WRITING ASSIGNMENTS

1. Select an essay you have studied in this book—one that is considerably more formal than Vonnegut's. Rewrite a paragraph the way you think Vonnegut would have written it. Which style do you prefer, and why?

2. Write an essay showing how Vonnegut's essay embodies his own advice.

3. If you have read any of Vonnegut's novels, write a paper in which you try to demonstrate how Vonnegut the essayist sounds like Vonnegut the novelist.

4. Compose a letter to Kurt Vonnegut, providing your personal observations about one or more of his works of fiction. In your letter, employ the writing advice he gives in this essay.

Always Living in Spanish

Marjorie Agosin

Finding the right words is a challenge for any writer. It can be even more daunting, however, when trying to express yourself in a another language. For Marjorie Agosin, who was raised in Chile until political upheaval forced her family to move to Georgia, something was lost for her when she tried to write in English instead of her beloved Spanish. She had difficulty in finding the right words to convey the depth and breath of meaning. She decided to "always write in Spanish." In this essay, Agosin explains how and why she arrived at this decision.

Marjorie Agosin is a professor of Spanish at Wellesley College and the author of over 20 books of poetry. Well-known for her human rights activities, and the recipient of a United Nations Leadership Award for Human Rights, Agosin's own background is peppered with political struggle. The descendant of European Jews who escaped the Holocaust and settled in Chile, her family was forced by Pinochet's dictatorship to flee to the United States in the early 1970s. Her most recent book of poetry is *Mother, Speak to Us About War/Madre, Hablanos De La Guerra* (2006). This essay was first published in *The Literary Life* in 1999.

1 In the evenings in the northern hemisphere, I repeat the ancient ritual that I observed as a child in the southern hemisphere: going out while the night is still warm and trying to recognize the stars as it begins to grow dark silently. In the sky of my country, Chile, that long and wide stretch of land that the poets blessed and dictators abused, I could easily name the stars: the three Marias, the Southern Cross, and the three Lilies, names of beloved and courageous women.

2 But here in the United States, where I have lived since I was a young girl, the solitude of exile makes me feel that so little is mine, that not even the sky has the same constellations, the trees and the fauna the same names or sounds, or the rubbish the same smell. How does one recover the familiar? How does one name the unfamiliar? How can one be another or live in a foreign language? These are the dilemmas of one who writes in Spanish and lives in translation.

3 Since my earliest childhood in Chile I lived with the tempos and the melodies of a multiplicity of tongues: German, Yiddish, Russian, Turkish, and many Latin songs. Because everyone was from somewhere else, my relatives laughed, sang, and fought in a Babylon of languages. Spanish was reserved for matters of extreme seriousness, for commercial transactions, or for illnesses, but everyone's mother tongue was always associated with the memory of spaces inhabited in the past: the shtetl, the flowering and vast Vienna avenues, the minarets of Turkey, and the Ladino whispers of Toledo. When my paternal grandmother sang old songs in Turkish, her voice and body assumed the passion of one who was there in the city of Istanbul, gazing by turns toward the west and the east.

4 Destiny and the always ambiguous nature of history continued my family's enforced migration, and because of it I, too, became one who had to live and speak in translation. The disappearances, torture, and clandestine deaths in my country in the early seventies drove us to the United States, that other America that looked with suspicion at those who did not speak English and especially those who came

from the supposedly uncivilized regions of Latin America. I had left a dangerous place that was my home, only to arrive in a dangerous place that was not: a high school in the small town of Athens, Georgia, where my poor English and my accent were the cause of ridicule and insult. The only way I could recover my usurped country and my Chilean childhood was by continuing to write in Spanish, the same way my grandparents had sung in their own tongues in diasporic sites.

5   The new and learned English language did not fit with the visceral emotions and themes that my poetry contained, but by writing in Spanish I could recover fragrances, spoken rhythms, and the passion of my own identity. Daily I felt the need to translate myself for the strangers living all around me, to tell them why we were in Georgia, why we ate differently, why we had fled, why my accent was so thick, and why I did not look Hispanic. Only at night, writing poems in Spanish, could I return to my senses, and soothe my own sorrow over what I had left behind.

6   This is how I became a Chilean poet who wrote in Spanish and lived in the southern United States. And then, one day, a poem of mine was translated and published in the English language. Finally, for the first time since I had left Chile, I felt I didn't have to explain myself. My poem, expressed in another language, spoke for itself . . . and for me.

7   Sometimes the austere sounds of English help me bear the solitude of knowing that I am foreign and so far away from those about whom I write. I must admit I would like more opportunities to read in Spanish to people whose language and culture is also mine, to join in our common heritage and in the feast of our sounds. I would also like readers of English to understand the beauty of the spoken word in Spanish, that constant flow of oxytonic and paraoxytonic syllables (*Verde que te quiero verdo*), the joy of writing—of dancing—in another language. I believe that many exiles share the unresolvable torment of not being able to live in the language of their childhood.

8   I miss that undulating and sensuous language of mine, those baroque descriptions, the sense of being and feeling that Spanish gives me. It is perhaps for this reason that I have chosen and will always choose to write in Spanish. Nothing else from my childhood world remains. My country seems to be frozen in gestures of silence and oblivion. My relatives have died, and I have grown up not knowing a young generation of cousins and nieces and nephews. Many of my friends disappeared, others were tortured, and the most fortunate, like me, became guardians of memory. For us, to write in Spanish is to always be in active pursuit of memory. I seek to recapture a world lost to me on that sorrowful afternoon when the blue electric sky and the Andean cordillera bade me farewell. On that, my last Chilean day, I carried under my arm my innocence recorded in a little blue notebook I kept even then. Gradually that diary filled with memoranda, poems written in free verse, descriptions of dreams and of the thresholds of my house surrounded by cherry trees and gardenias. To write in Spanish is for me a gesture of survival. And because of translation, my memory has now become a part of the memory of many others.

9   Translators are not traitors, as the proverb says, but rather splendid friends in this great human community of language.

THINKING CRITICALLY

1. In what ways is Agosin's decision to always write in Spanish a reflection of her family's history?

2. Why does Agosin have trouble expressing herself adequately in English? What challenges did she face in expressing herself when her family moved to Georgia?

3. Why is the first of her poems that was translated into English particularly important to Agosin?

4. Do you think Agosin believes Spanish is a language superior to English? Why or why not?

WRITING ASSIGNMENTS

1. Agosin must write in Spanish because she identifies it as part of her creative soul and her personal identity. What would you do if faced with the same situation as Agosin? Write a personal narrative exploring the connection between your native language and your creativity.

2. Agosin ends her essay with a reference to the saying *translators are traitors* ("I traduttori sono traditori"). What challenges do translators face when translating one language to another? Can the power of a original poem in another language such as French or Spanish be truly captured as it is translated into English, and vice versa?

Clichés, Anyone?

James Isaacs

Clichés are trite or overused expressions, and most writing books will tell you to avoid them. The problem with clichés is that they fail to have real substance—they are weakened by overuse. And because they are phrases on tap, users don't bother to come up with their own ideas or fresh wording. In this essay, James Isaacs presents a commencement speech; such speeches tend to serve as venues of packaged oratory. As you read this parody, try to identify the clichés and their intended meanings. You might even hear echoes of your own high school commencement!

James Isaacs is a writer, musician, and music critic for Microsoft's Sidewalk Boston Web site. He was nominated for a Grammy in 1986 for coproducing the reissue of Frank Sinatra's work. For the past 15 years, Isaacs has hosted and produced jazz, soul, and pop-music programs for National Public Radio. This piece first appeared in the *Boston Globe* on May 8, 1998.

1 *Commencement fast approaches. On college campuses and in high school auditoriums and gymnasiums across the land, a parade of orators will loft the traditional airballs of homespun homilies, peppy locker room bromides, and windbaggery under many sails.*

2 *In recent years I have picked up extra income writing graduation addresses for a few locally based notables, including a second-string television news anchor, several lieutenants of industry, and a minor pol or two.*

3   *The only instruction I received was that I should write in their voices, and this I think I did. However, as this spring finds me happily and inordinately busy at work on a made-for-community-access-TV musical "The Alchemy of Opie and Anthony," I hereby offer the following to any and all commencement speakers:*

4 Good morning (afternoon, evening), members of the Class of 1998 at (name of institution of learning) and your families and friends.

5 At this point in time, as we near the dawn of the new millennium and each of us seeks some sort of defining moment, it has never been more important to send a message, big time. Two words: "Work ethic." Or "speed bump." Or "role model." Whatever, as you young folks put it so succinctly.

6 That we're all on the same page and bring something to the table is the post-modern buzz that's on the cutting edge, you know what I'm saying? And in order to deconstruct the spin control, to be some kind of player—an icon, if you will—you will at some time in your life have to draw a line in the sand, even if your agenda is granularly challenged. So, do the math. Right there in the sand, go figure! It ain't rocket science.

7 It is then, and only then, once you step up to the plate, no matter how much you may have on your plate, that you'll get over it and start turning your life around by taking it to the next level. I know because I've been there, done that, while on my watch. And a fine Swiss watch it was until an 800-pound gorilla with in-your-face attitude hurled it almost over-the-top of Fenway Park's famous Green Monster.

8 So much for quality time.

9 And as you know, it ain't over till it's over. Or until the fat lady sings. But that's a story for another day.

10 To the young women among this year's graduates: Going out into the world can be a no-brainer, no problem, provided, of course, you have all your ducks in a row and they're in a full attack mode feeding frenzy, ready to push the envelope and deliver an awesome slam dunk that's in the zone.

11 It's also imperative that you keep this in mind: In order to distance yourself from every victim, enabler, and co-dependent on your radar screen, you might have to go right off the charts to reinvent yourself. And when it's time to move on, well, you go, girl! Hey, even if it's on my dime, never forget that it's your call as to who will carry your water, no matter what he said or, for that matter, she said.

12 As for you young men, I recall that many years ago when I first expressed interest in a career in photojournalism, my father said, "Read my lips: Get a 'Life.'"

13 "Dad," I replied, "you just don't get it." Which certainly was true at the time, since we subscribed to *Collier's*. But when I also mentioned that I wanted to move to New York, his advice was equally blunt: "Don't go there." To which I answered: "Dad, even though you da man, you don't have a clue. But thanks for sharing."

14 So at the end of the day, life is face time. But it's also about show-me-the-money. And that's a good thing. First and foremost, however, I cannot stress strongly enough the notion that if you don't ask, don't tell, you will begin the healing process, get over it, and come to closure. It doesn't get any better than this.

15 End of story. To coin a phrase.

THINKING CRITICALLY

1. Give your own definition of a cliché. How often do you use clichés in your own speech? How does Isaacs tap into our common knowledge of clichés in this commencement speech spoof?

2. Would this article be funny to a non-American audience? For example, would German- or Chinese-speaking people understand its humor? What about an English or Irish audience? Explain.

3. Although Isaacs pokes fun at the overuse of clichés during commencement speeches, clichés do enable speakers to connect to their audience. Identify some situations where clichés would be useful linguistic devices.

4. What is Isaacs's message in this article? What point is he trying to convey? Explain.

5. Recall your own commencement speech. Do you remember what was said? How does the memory of your commencement speech compare to your classmates' memories of it? As a group, how do the speeches compare in style and content?

6. What is Isaacs saying about the basic substance of the commencement speech? Do you agree with his perspective? Why or why not?

WRITING ASSIGNMENTS

1. Write your own commencement speech. What would you say to connect to your audience? Would you use common linguistic conventions? Would you use clichés?

2. Write a letter to a friend using as many clichés as you can as long as they are appropriate to your message. Evaluate what you have written. Was this exercise easy or difficult? Explain.

3. Evaluate a political speech made by a politician. You may find it useful to record the speech or obtain a transcript of it. Did the official use any clichés? If so, identify and analyze them. Are some expressions more noticeable than others? Did any escape your notice the first time you heard the speech? Explain.

The Financial Media's 25 Worst Clichés
Jonathan Clements

This item appeared in the *Wall Street Journal* on March 19, 2002.

1   Cigarettes come with health warnings. Maybe financial journalists should, too.

2   In recent years, I have done a handful of columns where I took phrases frequently heard on Wall Street and then offered my translation for what those comments really mean. Along the way, I have poked fun at brokers, market strategists, money managers, and ordinary investors.

3   But why stop there? Often, financial journalists also fail to say what they really mean. Examples? Consider the 25 comments below, variations of which often appear in the media. The list was put together with help from investment experts William Bernstein, Kevin Bernzott, Meir Statman, and Alan Weiss.

- *"The banking community is divided"*: We called two sources and got different opinions.
- *"A spokesman for the state securities commission declined to comment, citing its ongoing investigation"*: Which got started when we called the agency and asked whether investigators were looking at the issue.
- *"Ms. Smith, who isn't involved in the lawsuit, says the late-day announcement is good news for the plaintiff"*: We were on deadline, and nobody was picking up the phone, so we called Ms. Smith instead.
- *"A company spokeswoman declined to comment"*: But off the record, we got an earful from the executive vice president.
- *"Experts are still trying to untangle the legal issues involved"*: We talked to three lawyers, and we still don't understand what's going on.
- *"The euro set new lows for the session on signs of a U.S. economic rebound"*: We haven't the slightest inkling what the connection is between the euro and the U.S. economy. But there has to be some explanation for the currency's tumble.
- *"Stocks are expected to open lower on Monday"*: Sure, we're right only half the time. But Sammy Sosa would kill for that sort of batting average.
- *"Considered one of Wall Street's most iconoclastic strategists, Mr. Wharton predicts the Dow Jones Industrial Average will plunge below 5000"*: Sure, the guy is off his rocker. But he makes great copy.
- *"Bond prices fell in anticipation of higher interest rates"*: Or maybe interest rates rose in anticipation of lower bond prices. How could we possibly know? We majored in English.
- *"Many investors fear there's more stock-market carnage to come"*: Everybody in the newsroom is totally freaked out.
- *"Want to become a millionaire? Try our five-step program"*: With enough time, a high savings rate and outsize investment returns, we can assume our way to anything.
- *"Looking for big gains in the year ahead? Here are seven stocks that are set to sizzle"*: Reader amnesia is our best friend.
- *"While many small investors have suffered big losses recently, few can rival the dismal record of Mr. Warren, who owns just three stocks—Kmart, Enron, and Global Crossing"*: Can you believe this guy agreed to speak to us? It's amazing what people will tell the press.
- *"Jim and Betty Hancock, shown in the accompanying photograph, began diligently saving for college soon after their first child was born"*: Actually, the Hancocks seem to spend most of their spare time at the local mall. But they sure photograph well.
- *"Like thousands of other investors, Wendy Evans was badly burned by last month's partnership debacle"*: You wouldn't believe how many calls we had to make and how many Internet bulletin boards we had to scour before we found this woman.
- *"Here are our 10 funds to buy now"*: One will be a great performer, seven will be mediocre, and two will be total dogs. But which is which? You will have to figure that out on your own.

- "*See our list of last year's top-performing mutual funds*": Which may be useful if you are the kind of person who drives using only the rearview mirror.
- "*Many investors ignore costs when picking mutual funds. But that can be a big mistake*": First, we make an unsubstantiated claim about investor behavior. Then, we argue that these folks are foolish. Ah, sometimes there's no sweeter scent than a straw man burning.
- "*Indeed, if you had blindly bought into the prior year's hottest sector, you wouldn't have made any money over the past decade, once you figure in inflation, taxes, and trading costs*": We tortured the data base until it confessed.
- "*The fund's risk-adjusted performance is among the best in the growth-and-income category*": Its raw performance stinks.
- "*Despite the fund's dazzling record, analysts say it should account for only a small portion of your portfolio*": If you stick any money in this fund, don't blame us.
- "*The fund's recent performance reads like a chapter out of a Stephen King novel*": When we were kids, we used to pull the legs off spiders.
- "*Last quarter's top-performing fund manager thinks further gains lie ahead*": Remember what we said about ignoring short-term performance? Scratch that.
- "*The fund's manager avoids swinging for the fences, instead aiming to hit singles and doubles*": Maybe the sports page has some openings.
- "*Today's boardroom Sturm und Drang left many observers with a sense of déjà vu*": And if the foreign editor asks, tell her our Italian is also pretty good.

MAKING CONNECTIONS

1. Select an essay you have already written and apply some of the principles of writing described by Lederer and Vonnegut in their articles. Identify the parts of your essay that you changed and how the altered sections employ the techniques described in the two essays. How does your revised essay compare to its first version? Explain.

2. Find two magazine or newspaper articles covering the same event or person—maybe a movie star or political figure or athlete. How do they differ? How do they use the facts? How do they change and use language?

3. Which of the authors in this section provided you with the most useful information for improving your own writing—and why? Use examples from the article to support your response.

4. Several of the writers in this section provided lists of advice designed to improve your personal writing style. Create a list of your own in which you provide advice to less experienced writers, such as students just beginning junior high school. You may draw from the advice of the writers in this chapter, your own experience, and points made during class discussion. Remember to "write to your audience" when composing your list.

5. All writers put their personal stamp on their work. Write a short essay about how the words you chose—and how you express them—influence your audience's opinion of your message.

4 Political Wordplay

■ Speaking over 6,500 different languages worldwide, human beings are social creatures who depend on language to survive. Consider the ways you use language to communicate. What social, biological, and intellectual influences affect the way you communicate with different people?

P olitical language is a language of power. It influences government policy and action, identifies the dominant values of the moment, and wins votes. Likewise, it is a language that is capable of making war, establishing peace, and electing presidents. However, political language also reflects the political needs of its users at a particular time. Thus, it has a reputation for being flexible and ambiguous, or worse, evasive and irresponsible as politicians shift the language to achieve their personal agendas. It is this "shifty" nature of political language that has contributed to the traditional American distrust of politicians and their promises. The essays in this chapter explore the various ways in which political language persuades the masses, manipulates words and meanings, promotes or supports certain value systems, and influences public opinion.

Politically Speaking

The first section of this chapter examines how political language persuades the public by tapping into its common beliefs, fears, anxieties, hopes, and expectations. This political wordplay comes in many forms, some more damaging than others. If the fundamental objective of political wordplay is to bend minds, its misuse may have dangerous implications. That misuse of language is the subject of the first selection, "How to Detect Propaganda," composed in 1937 by members of the former Institute for Propaganda Analysis—a group that monitored the various kinds of political propaganda circulating before and during World War II. This famous, timeless piece examines the particular rhetorical devices that constitute propaganda and serves as a tool to understanding the language of political manipulation—a concept further explored by George Orwell in the next article, "Politics and the English Language." In this classic attack on politicians, Orwell reminds us that those who control language—the double-talk, pious platitudes, and hollow words—hold the power to twist the native tongue to political advantage. Hugh Rank describes how to understand these common patterns of persuasion in political language in "Pep Talk." Professional word watcher William Lutz defines the different kinds of "doublespeak" used by government bureaucrats in "Doubts About Doublespeak." And rounding out the section, Trudy Lieberman urges journalists to stop playing so nicely with politicians who avoid tough questions in "Answer the &$%#* Question!"

Warspeak: Language and Conflict

The next section in this chapter considers the relationship between language, terrorism, and the political developments in the Middle East. Jon Hooten opens with a discussion of the language of war in "Fighting Words: The War Over Language." Then, Deroy Murdock challenges us to chose our words carefully when describing terrorism in "Terrorism and the English Language." Amir Taheri and Jim Guirard express their views on the language used to justify terrorist acts in editorials that discuss the disparity between what Islam proclaims and what much of the Islamic world is willing to permit. The collection closes with "Selling America" by Sandra Silberstein, a review of the public relations effort to promote the war on terror.

Language and the Presidency

The last section of chapter 4 examines the relationship between language and the presidency. How is the public's perception of the president connected to his command of language? How is a presidential speech written, and how does the president shape the finished product? Political communications analysts Robert E. Denton Jr. and Dan F. Hahn explore the ways the president serves as the mouthpiece of the nation in "The Rhetorical Presidency." Following these general observations, the next authors focus more specifically on the language of George W. Bush. First, psychologist Renana Brooks describes the ways Bush uses language to emotionally appeal to his audience and even create a sense of dependency in "A Nation of Victims." Then D. T. Max describes the etymology of the speech that "changed a presidency," given on September 20, 2001, in response to the attacks on the World Trade Center and the Pentagon. Following Max's essay is a speech on terrorism given to an assembly of college students at Kansas State University in 2006. The section ends with a review of what many people consider one of the greatest presidential speeches of all time: John F. Kennedy's inaugural address. Thurston Clarke first examines the nuances of this landmark speech in "Why JFK's Inaugural Succeeded," which is then followed by the text of Kennedy's actual speech delivered on January 20, 1961.

┃ POLITICALLY SPEAKING

How to Detect Propaganda
Institute for Propaganda Analysis

> During the late 1930s, like today, political propaganda was rife, both in the United States and abroad. In 1937, Clyde R. Miller of Columbia University founded the Institute for Propaganda Analysis to expose propaganda circulating at the time. With the backing of several prominent businesspeople, the Institute continued its mission for nearly five years, publishing various pamphlets and monthly bulletins to reveal its findings. The following essay is a chapter from one of its pamphlets. It presents a specific definition of propaganda, with an analysis of seven common devices necessary to bend truth—and minds—to political causes.

1 If American citizens are to have clear understanding of present-day conditions and what to do about them, they must be able to recognize propaganda, to analyze it, and to appraise it.

2 But what is propaganda?

3 As generally understood, *propaganda is expression of opinion or action by individuals or groups deliberately designed to influence opinions or actions of other individuals or groups with reference to predetermined ends.* Thus propaganda differs from scientific analysis. The propagandist is trying to "put something

across," good or bad, whereas the scientist is trying to discover truth and fact. Often the propagandist does not want careful scrutiny and criticism; he wants to bring about a specific action. Because the action may be socially beneficial or socially harmful to millions of people, it is necessary to focus upon the propagandist and his activities using the searchlight of scientific scrutiny. Socially desirable propaganda will not suffer from such examination, but the opposite type will be detected and revealed for what it is.

4   We are fooled by propaganda chiefly because we don't recognize it when we see it. It may be fun to be fooled but, as the cigarette ads used to say, it is more fun to know. We can more easily recognize propaganda when we see it if we are familiar with the seven common propaganda devices. These are:

1. The Name Calling Device

2. The Glittering Generalities Device

3. The Transfer Device

4. The Testimonial Device

5. The Plain Folks Device

6. The Card Stacking Device

7. The Band Wagon Device

5   Why are we fooled by these devices? Because they appeal to our emotions rather than to our reason. They make us believe and do something we would not believe or do if we thought about it calmly, dispassionately. In examining these devices, note that they work most effectively at those times when we are too lazy to think for ourselves; also, they tie into emotions which sway us to be "for" or "against" nations, races, religions, ideals, economic and political policies and practices, and so on through automobiles, cigarettes, radios, toothpastes, presidents, and wars. With our emotions stirred, it may be fun to be fooled by these propaganda devices, but it is more fun and infinitely more to our own interests to know how they work.

6   Lincoln must have had in mind citizens who could balance their emotions with intelligence when he made this remark ". . . but you can't fool all of the people all of the time."

Name Calling

7 "Name Calling" is a device to make us form a judgment without examining the evidence on which it should be based. Here the propagandist appeals to our hate and fear. He does this by giving "bad names" to those individuals, groups, nations, races, policies, practices, beliefs, and ideals which he would have us condemn and reject. For centuries the name "heretic" was bad. Thousands were oppressed, tortured, or put to death as heretics. Anybody who dissented from popular or group belief or practice was in danger of being called a heretic. In the light of today's knowledge, some heresies were bad and some were good. Many of the pioneers of modern science were called heretics; witness the cases of Copernicus, Galileo,

Bruno. Today's bad names include: Fascist, demagogue, dictator, Red, financial oligarchy, Communist, muckraker, alien, outside agitator, economic royalist, Utopian, rabble-rouser, trouble-maker, Tory, Constitution-wrecker.

8   "Al" Smith called Roosevelt a Communist by implication when he said in his Liberty League speech, "There can be only one capital, Washington or Moscow." When "Al" Smith was running for the presidency many called him a tool of the Pope, saying in effect, "We must choose between Washington and Rome." That implied that Mr. Smith, if elected President, would take his orders from the Pope. Likewise Mr. Justice Hugo Black has been associated with a bad name, Ku Klux Klan. In these cases some propagandists have tried to make us form judgments without examining essential evidence and implications. "Al Smith is a Catholic. He must never be President." "Roosevelt is a Red. Defeat his program." "Hugo Black is or was a Klansman. Take him out of the Supreme Court."

9   Use of "bad names" without presentation of their essential meaning, without all their pertinent implications, comprises perhaps the most common of all propaganda devices. Those who want to *maintain the status quo* apply bad names to those who would change it. . . . Those who want to *change the status quo* apply bad names to those who would maintain it. For example, the *Daily Worker* and the *American Guardian* apply bad names to conservative Republicans and Democrats.

Glittering Generalities

10   "Glittering Generalities" is a device by which the propagandist identifies his program with virtue by use of "virtue words." Here he appeals to our emotions of love, generosity, and brotherhood. He uses words like truth, freedom, honor, liberty, social justice, public service, the right to work, loyalty, progress, democracy, the American way, Constitution-defender. These words suggest shining ideals. All persons of good will believe in these ideals. Hence the propagandist, by identifying his individual group, nation, race, policy, practice, or belief with such ideals, seeks to win us to his cause. As Name Calling is a device to make us form a judgment to *reject and condemn* without examining the evidence, Glittering Generalities is a device to make us *accept and approve* without examining the evidence.

11   For example, use of the phrases, "the right to work" and "social justice," may be a device to make us accept programs for meeting labor-capital problems which, if we examined them critically, we would not accept at all.

12   In the Name Calling and Glittering Generalities devices, words are used to stir up our emotions and to befog our thinking. In one device "bad words" are used to make us mad; in the other "good words" are used to make us glad.

13   The propagandist is most effective in the use of these devices when his words make us create devils to fight or gods to adore. By his use of the "bad words," we personify as a "devil" some nation, race, group, individual, policy, practice, or ideal; we are made fighting mad to destroy it. By use of "good words," we personify as a godlike idol some nation, race, group, etc. Words which are "bad" to some are "good" to others, or may be made so. Thus, to some the New Deal is "a prophecy of social salvation" while to others it is "an omen of social disaster."

14   From consideration of names, "bad" and "good," we pass to institutions and symbols, also "bad" and "good." We see these in the next device.

Transfer

15 "Transfer" is a device by which the propagandist carries over the authority, sanction, and prestige of something we respect and revere to something he would have us accept. For example, most of us respect and revere our church and our nation. If the propagandist succeeds in getting church or nation to approve a campaign in behalf of some program, he thereby transfers its authority, sanction, and prestige to that program. Thus we may accept something which otherwise we might reject.

16   In the Transfer device, symbols are constantly used. The cross represents the Christian Church. The flag represents the nation. Cartoons like Uncle Sam represent a consensus of public opinion. Those symbols stir emotions. At their very sight, with the speed of light, is aroused the whole complex of feelings we have with respect to church or nation. A cartoonist by having Uncle Sam disapprove a budget for unemployment relief would have us feel that the whole United States disapproves relief costs. By drawing an Uncle Sam who approves the same budget, the cartoonist would have us feel that the American people approve it. Thus the Transfer device is used both for and against causes and ideas.

Testimonial

17 The "Testimonial" is a device to make us accept anything from a patent medicine or a cigarette to a program of national policy. In this device the propagandist makes use of testimonials. "When I feel tired, I smoke a Camel and get the grandest 'lift.' " "We believe the John L. Lewis plan of labor organization is splendid; C.I.O. should be supported." This device works in reverse also; counter-testimonials may be employed. Seldom are these used against commercial products like patent medicines and cigarettes, but they are constantly employed in social, economic, and political issues. "We believe that the John L. Lewis plan of labor organization is bad; C.I.O. should not be supported."

Plain Folks

18 "Plain Folks" is a device used by politicians, labor leaders, businessmen, and even by ministers and educators to win our confidence by appearing to be people like ourselves—"just plain folks among the neighbors." In election years especially do candidates show their devotion to little children and the common, homey things of life. They have front porch campaigns. For the newspaper men they raid the kitchen cupboard, finding there some of the good wife's apple pie. They go to country picnics; they attend service at the old frame church, they pitch hay and go fishing; they show their belief in home and mother. In short, they would win our votes by showing that they're just as common as the rest of us—"just plain folks"—and, therefore, wise and good. Businessmen often are "plain folks" with the factory hands. Even distillers use the device. "It's our family's whiskey, neighbor; and neighbor, it's your price."

Card Stacking

19 "Card Stacking" is a device in which the propagandist employs all the arts of deception to win our support for himself, his group, nation, race, policy, practice, belief, or ideal. He stacks the cards against the truth. He uses under-emphasis and over-emphasis to dodge issues and evade facts. He resorts to lies, censorship, and distortion. He omits facts. He offers false testimony. He creates a smoke screen of clamor by raising a new issue when he wants an embarrassing matter forgotten. He draws a red herring across the trail to confuse and divert those in quest of facts he does not want revealed. He makes the unreal appear real and the real appear unreal. He lets half-truth masquerade as truth. By the Card Stacking device, a mediocre candidate, through the "build-up," is made to appear an intellectual titan; an ordinary prize fighter, a probable world champion; a worthless patent medicine, a beneficent cure. By means of this device propagandists would convince us that a ruthless war of aggression is a crusade for righteousness. Some member nations of the Non-Intervention Committee send their troops to intervene in Spain. Card Stacking employs sham, hypocrisy, effrontery.

The Band Wagon

20 The "Band Wagon" is a device to make us follow the crowd, to accept the propagandist's program en masse. Here his theme is: "Everybody's doing it." His techniques range from those of medicine show to dramatic spectacle. He hires a hall, fills a great stadium, marches a million men in parade. He employs symbols, colors, music, movement, all the dramatic arts. He appeals to the desire, common to most of us, to "follow the crowd." Because he wants us to "follow the crowd" in masses, he directs his appeal to groups held together by common ties of nationality, religion, race, environment, sex, vocation. Thus propagandists campaigning for or against a program will appeal to us as Catholics, Protestants, or Jews; as members of the Nordic race or as Negroes; as farmers or as school teachers; as housewives or as miners. All the artifices of flattery are used to harness the fears and hatreds, prejudices, and biases, convictions and ideals common to the group; thus emotion is made to push and pull the group on to the Band Wagon. In newspaper articles and in the spoken word this device is also found. "Don't throw your vote away. Vote for our candidate. He's sure to win." Nearly every candidate wins in every election—before the votes are in.

Propaganda and Emotion

21 Observe that in all these devices our emotion is the stuff with which propagandists work. Without it they are helpless; with it, harnessing it to their purposes, they can make us glow with pride or burn with hatred, they can make us zealots in behalf of the program they espouse. As we said at the beginning, propaganda as generally understood is expression of opinion or action by individuals or groups with reference to predetermined ends. Without the appeal to our emotion—to our fears and to our courage, to our selfishness and unselfishness, to our loves and to our hates—propagandists would influence few opinions and few actions.

22 To say this is not to condemn emotion, an essential part of life, or to assert that all predetermined ends of propagandists are "bad." What we mean is that the intelligent citizen does not want propagandists to utilize his emotions, even to the

attainment of "good" ends, without knowing what is going on. He does not want to be "used" in the attainment of ends he may later consider "bad." He does not want to be gullible. He does not want to be fooled. He does not want to be duped, even in a "good" cause. He wants to know the facts and among these is included the fact of the utilization [of] his emotions.

23   Keeping in mind the seven common propaganda devices, turn to today's newspapers and almost immediately you can spot examples of them all. At election time or during any campaign, Plain Folks and Band Wagon are common. Card Stacking is hardest to detect because it is adroitly executed or because we lack the information necessary to nail the lie. A little practice with the daily newspapers in detecting these propaganda devices soon enables us to detect them elsewhere—in radio, newsreel, books, magazines, and in expression[s] of labor unions, business groups, churches, schools, and political parties.

THINKING CRITICALLY

1. Look at the definition of the word *propaganda* in paragraph 3. How many sets of people are involved—how many parties does it take to make propaganda? What are the roles or functions of each set of people?

2. Supply an example of the way emotion overrides reason for each of the seven common propaganda devices the authors identify.

3. Can you supply "bad names" from your own experience as a student? Some examples to get you started might include "geek," "nerd," and "teacher's pet" to refer to students; you can probably think of some generic terms for teachers as well. Compare these terms to the definition of propaganda. Do you think these terms qualify as propaganda?

4. How are name-calling and glittering generalities similar devices? How are they different? What do the authors of the document say? What additional features can you find?

5. How do transfer, testimonial, and plain folks devices all make use of power or prestige to influence our thinking? Can you think of something or someone you respect that could be used as a propaganda device—for example, a major sporting event, such as the Super Bowl, or a football hero?

6. Give examples of times in your life when you have used the card stacking or band wagon devices to try to get something you wanted—such as permission from a parent, or an excused absence from a teacher.

7. What is the difference between "the propagandist" and "the scientist" in paragraph 3? What is their relationship to "truth and fact"? What is their relationship to each other? What is their relationship to the language they use?

8. What is "socially desirable propaganda"? Can you give examples from your own experience? Do you think that socially desirable propaganda uses the same devices that the authors of this article identify? Consider the "safe-sex" campaigns you've been exposed to.

WRITING ASSIGNMENTS

1. Based on your understanding of the whole article, and on class discussion, develop your own definition of propaganda. Make sure you define each key term that you use.

2. Following the suggestions set down in the final paragraph of this essay, collect examples of propaganda from at least five different sources. Examine them, then describe in a paper what devices they use. How do the creators of each kind of propaganda show that they are aware of their audience's emotions? What emotions do they appeal to? How much "truth and fact" do they seem to rely on?

3. Research and collect newspaper articles on an election—a race for student government on your campus, a recent town or state proposition, or even a national election. Be sure to collect a handful of articles from at least two major candidates, or from two sides of the issue. What propaganda devices did each side use? Which side won? How much of a role do you think propaganda played in deciding the outcome?

4. Do you think the authors of this article would advocate getting rid of all propaganda? Why, or why not? Be sure to include a discussion of what propaganda is, and what function or role it serves.

Politics and the English Language
George Orwell

In this essay, George Orwell explains how the language of politics, especially what is known as "political rhetoric," is designed to cloud the public's perception of political issues. Like the propaganda examined in the previous essay, political rhetoric disguises real issues behind a mask of political mottoes, character assassinations, and catchphrases, all designed to confuse the public. There are many reasons to use such evasive tactics: to garner support, to get votes, to dodge political responsibility, and to discredit political opponents. As in his novel *1984*, in this essay Orwell confronts the social forces that endanger free thought and truth. Political rhetoric, he explains, is the enemy of truth and the cause of linguistic degeneration.

George Orwell was a novelist, an essayist, and one of the most important social critics of the twentieth century. In 1945, he wrote the acclaimed political satire, *Animal Farm* and in 1949, his famous nightmare vision of a totalitarian state, *1984*, first appeared. "Politics and the English Language" was included in one of his essay collections, *Shooting an Elephant* (1946). Although the essay was written in 1945, the targets still exist, and the criticism is still valid, making it as poignant today as it was over half a century ago.

1 Most people who bother with the matter at all would admit that the English language is in a bad way, but it is generally assumed that we cannot by conscious action do anything about it. Our civilization is decadent and our language—so the argument runs—must inevitably share in the general collapse. It follows that any struggle against the abuse of language is a sentimental archaism, like preferring candles to electric light or hansom cabs to aeroplanes. Underneath this lies the half-conscious belief that language is a natural growth and not an instrument which we shape for our own purposes.

2   Now, it is clear that the decline of a language must ultimately have political and economic causes: it is not due simply to the bad influence of this or that individual writer. But an effect can become a cause, reinforcing the original cause and producing the same effect in an intensified form, and so on indefinitely. A man may take to drink because he feels himself to be a failure, and then fail all the more

completely because he drinks. It is rather the same thing that is happening to the English language. It becomes ugly and inaccurate because our thoughts are foolish, but the slovenliness of our language makes it easier for us to have foolish thoughts. The point is that the process is reversible. Modern English, especially written English, is full of bad habits which spread by imitation and which can be avoided if one is willing to take the necessary trouble. If one gets rid of these habits one can think more clearly, and to think clearly is a necessary first step towards political regeneration: so that the fight against bad English is not frivolous and is not the exclusive concern of professional writers. I will come back to this presently, and I hope that by that time the meaning of what I have said here will have become clearer. Meanwhile, here are five specimens of the English language as it is now habitually written.

3   These five passages have not been picked out because they are especially bad—I could have quoted far worse if I had chosen—but because they illustrate various of the mental vices from which we now suffer. They are a little below the average, but are fairly representative samples. I number them so that I can refer back to them when necessary:

> 1. I am not, indeed, sure whether it is not true to say that the Milton who once seemed not unlike a seventeenth-century Shelley had not become, out of an experience ever more bitter in each year, more alien [*sic*] to the founder of that Jesuit sect which nothing could induce him to tolerate.
> Professor Harold Laski (Essay in *Freedom of Expression*)

> 2. Above all, we cannot play ducks and drakes with a native battery of idioms which prescribes such egregious collocations of vocables as the Basic *put up with* for *tolerate* or *put at a loss* for *bewilder*.
> Professor Lancelot Hogben (*Interglossa*)

> 3. On the one side we have the free personality: by definition it is not neurotic, for it has neither conflict nor dream. Its desires, such as they are, are transparent, for they are just what institutional approval keeps in the forefront of consciousness; another institutional pattern would alter their number and intensity, there is little in them that is natural, irreducible, or culturally dangerous. But *on the other side,* the social bond itself is nothing but the mutual reflection of these self-secure integrities. Recall the definition of love. Is not this the very picture of a small academic? Where is there a place in this hall of mirrors for either personality or fraternity?
> Essay on Psychology in *Politics* (New York)

> 4. All the "best people" from the gentlemen's clubs, and all the frantic fascist captains, united in common hatred of Socialism and bestial horror of the rising tide of the mass revolutionary movement, have turned to acts of provocation, to foul incendiarism, to medieval legends of poisoned wells, to legalize their own destruction of proletarian organizations, and rouse the agitated petty-bourgeoisie to chauvinistic fervor on behalf of the fight against the revolutionary way out of the crisis.
> Communist Pamphlet

5. If a new spirit is to be infused into this old country, there is one thorny and contentious reform which must be tackled, and that is the humanization and galvanization of the B.B.C. Timidity here will bespeak canker and atrophy of the soul. The heart of Britain may be sound and of strong beat, for instance, but the British lion's roar at present is like that of Bottom in Shakespeare's *Midsummer Night's Dream*—as gentle as any sucking dove. A virile new Britain cannot continue indefinitely to be traduced in the eyes, or rather ears, of the world by the effete languors of Langham Place, brazenly masquerading as "standard English." When the Voice of Britain is heard at nine o'clock, better far and infinitely less ludicrous to hear aitches honestly dropped than the present priggish, inflated, inhibited, school-ma'amish arch braying of blameless bashful mewing maidens!

Letter in *Tribune*

4   Each of these passages has faults of its own, but, quite apart from avoidable ugliness, two qualities are common to all of them. The first is staleness of imagery; the other is lack of precision. The writer either has a meaning and cannot express it, or he inadvertently says something else, or he is almost indifferent as to whether his words mean anything or not. This mixture of vagueness and sheer incompetence is the most marked characteristic of modern English prose, and especially of any kind of political writing. As soon as certain topics are raised, the concrete melts into the abstract and no one seems able to think of turns of speech that are not hackneyed: prose consists less and less of *words* chosen for the sake of their meaning, and more and more of *phrases* tacked together like the sections of a prefabricated hen-house. I list below, with notes and examples, various of the tricks by means of which the work of prose-construction is habitually dodged:

Dying Metaphors

5 A newly invented metaphor assists thought by evoking a visual image, while on the other hand a metaphor which is technically "dead" (e.g., *iron resolution*) has in effect reverted to being an ordinary word and can generally be used without loss of vividness. But in between these two classes there is a huge dump of worn-out metaphors which have lost all evocative power and are merely used because they save people the trouble of inventing phrases for themselves. Examples are: *Ring the changes on, take up the cudgels for, toe the line, ride roughshod over, stand shoulder to shoulder with, play into the hands of, no axe to grind, grist to the mill, fishing in troubled waters, on the order of the day, Achilles' heel, swan song, hotbed.* Many of these are used without knowledge of their meaning (what is a "rift," for instance?), and incompatible metaphors are frequently mixed, a sure sign that the writer is not interested in what he is saying. Some metaphors now current have been twisted out of their original meaning without those who use them even being aware of the fact. For example, *toe the line* is sometimes written *tow the line.* Another example is the hammer and the anvil, now always used with the implication that the anvil gets the worst of it. In real life it is always the anvil that breaks the hammer, never the other way about: a writer who stopped to think what he was saying would be aware of this, and would avoid perverting the original phrase.

Operators or Verbal False Limbs

6 These save the trouble of picking out appropriate verbs and nouns, and at the same time pad each sentence with extra syllables which give it an appearance of symmetry. Characteristic phrases are *render inoperative, militate against, make contact with, be subjected to, give rise to, give grounds for, have the effect of, play a leading part (role) in, making itself felt, take effect, exhibit a tendency to, serve the purpose of,* etc., etc. The keynote is the elimination of simple verbs. Instead of being a single word, such as *break, stop, spoil, mend, kill,* a verb becomes a *phrase,* made up of a noun or adjective tacked on to some general-purpose verb such as *prove, serve, form, play, render.* In addition, the passive voice is wherever possible used in preference to the active, and noun constructions are used instead of gerunds (*by examination* of instead of *by examining*). The range of verbs is further cut down by means of the *-ize* and *de-* formations, and the banal statements are given an appearance of profundity by means of the *not un-* formation. Simple conjunctions and prepositions are replaced by such phrases as *with respect to, having regard to, the fact that, by dint of, in view of, in the interests of, on the hypothesis that;* and the ends of sentences are saved from anticlimax by such resounding common places as *greatly to be desired, cannot be left out of account, a development to be expected in the near future, deserving of serious consideration, brought to a satisfactory conclusion,* and so on and so forth.

Pretentious Diction

7 Words like *phenomenon, element, individual* (as noun), *objective, categorical, effective, virtual, basic, primary, promote, constitute, exhibit, exploit, utilize, eliminate, liquidate,* are used to dress up simple statements and give an air of scientific impartiality to biased judgments. Adjectives like *epoch-making, epic, historic, unforgettable, triumphant, age-old, inevitable, inexorable, veritable,* are used to dignify the sordid processes of international politics, while writing that aims at glorifying war usually takes on an archaic color, its characteristic words being: *realm, throne, chariot, mailed fist, trident, sword, shield, buckler, banner, jackboot, clarion.* Foreign words and expressions such as *cul de sac, ancien régime, deus ex machina, mutatis mutandis, status quo, gleichschaltung, weltanschauung,* are used to give an air of culture and elegance. Except for the useful abbreviations i.e., e.g., and *etc.,* there is no real need for any of the hundreds of foreign phrases now current in English. Bad writers, and especially scientific, political and sociological writers, are nearly always haunted by the notion that Latin or Greek words are grander than Saxon ones, and unnecessary words like *expedite, ameliorate, predict, extraneous, deracinated, clandestine, subaqueous* and hundreds of others constantly gain ground from their Anglo-Saxon opposite numbers.[1] The jargon peculiar to Marxist

---

[1] An interesting illustration of this is the way in which the English flower names which were in use till very recently are being ousted by Greek ones, *snapdragon* becoming *antirrhinum, forget-me-not* becoming *myosotis,* etc. It is hard to see any practical reason for this change of fashion; it is probably due to an instinctive turning-away from the more homely word and a vague feeling that the Greek is scientific.

writing (*hyena, hangman, cannibal, petty bourgeois, these gentry, lacquey, flunkey, mad dog, White Guard,* etc.) consists largely of words and phrases translated from Russian, German, or French; but the normal way of coining a new word is to use a Latin or Greek root with the appropriate affix and, where necessary, the *-ize* formation. It is often easier to make up words of this kind (*deregionalize, impermissible, extramarital, non-fragmentary* and so forth) than to think up the English words that will cover one's meaning. The result, in general, is an increase in slovenliness and vagueness.

Meaningless Words

8 In certain kinds of writing, particularly in art criticism and literary criticism, it is normal to come across long passages which are almost completely lacking in meaning.[2] Words like *romantic, plastic, values, human, dead, sentimental, natural, vitality,* as used in art criticism, are strictly meaningless, in the sense that they not only do not point to any discoverable object, but are hardly ever expected to do so by the reader. When one critic writes, "The outstanding feature of Mr. X's work is its living quality," while another writes, "The immediately striking thing about Mr. X's work is its peculiar deadness," the reader accepts this as a simple difference of opinion. If words like *black* and *white* were involved, instead of the jargon words *dead* and *living,* he would see at once that language was being used in an improper way. Many political words are similarly abused. The word *Fascism* has now no meaning except in so far as it signifies "something not desirable." The words *democracy, socialism, freedom, patriotic, realistic, justice,* have each of them several different meanings which cannot be reconciled with one another. In the case of a word like *democracy,* not only is there no agreed definition, but the attempt to make one is resisted from all sides. It is almost universally felt that when we call a country democratic we are praising it: consequently the defenders of every kind of regime claim that it is a democracy, and fear that they might have to stop using the word if it were tied down to any one meaning. Words of this kind are often used in a consciously dishonest way. That is, the person who used them has his own private definition, but allows his hearer to think he means something quite different. Statements like *Marshal Pétain was a true patriot, The Soviet Press is the freest in the world, The Catholic Church is opposed to persecution,* are almost always made with intent to deceive. Other words used in variable meanings, in most cases more or less dishonestly, are: *class, totalitarian, science, progressive, reactionary, bourgeois, equality.*

9   Now that I have made this catalogue of swindles and perversions, let me give another example of the kind of writing that they lead to. This time it must of its

---

[2]Example: "Comfort's catholicity of perception and images, strangely Whimanesque in range, almost the exact opposite in aesthetic compulsion, continues to evoke that trembling atmospheric accumulative hinting at a cruel, an inexorably serene timelessness . . . Wrey Gardiner scores by aiming at simple bull's-eyes with precision. Only they are not so simple, and through this contended sadness runs more than the surface bittersweet of resignation." (*Poetry Quarterly*)

nature be an imaginary one. I am going to translate a passage of good English into modern English of the worst sort. Here is a well-known verse from *Ecclesiastes*:

> I returned and saw under the sun, that the race is not to the swift, nor the battle to the strong, neither yet bread to the wise, nor yet riches to men of understanding, nor yet favour to men of skill; but time and chance happeneth to them all.

10   Here it is in modern English:

> Objective consideration of contemporary phenomena compels the conclusion that success or failure in competitive activities exhibits no tendency to be commensurate with innate capacity, but that a considerable element of the unpredictable must invariably be taken into account.

11   This is a parody, but not a very gross one. Above, for instance, contains several patches of the same kind of English. It will be seen that I have not made a full translation. The beginning and ending of the sentence follow the original meaning fairly closely, but in the middle the concrete illustrations—race, battle, bread—dissolve into the vague phrase "success or failure in competitive activities." This had to be so, because no modern writer of the kind I am discussing—no one capable of using phrases like "objective consideration of contemporary phenomena"—would ever tabulate his thoughts in that precise and detailed way. The whole tendency of modern prose is away from concreteness. Now analyse these two sentences a little more closely. The first contains forty-nine words but only sixty syllables, and all its words are those of everyday life. The second contains thirty-eight words of ninety syllables; eighteen of its words are from Latin roots, and one from Greek. The first sentence contains six vivid images, and only one phrase ("time and chance") that could be called vague. The second contains not a single fresh, arresting phrase, and in spite of its ninety syllables it gives only a shortened version of the meaning contained in the first. Yet without a doubt it is the second kind of sentence that is gaining ground in modern English. I do not want to exaggerate. This kind of writing is not yet universal, and outcrops of simplicity will occur here and there in the worst-written page. Still, if you or I were told to write a few lines on the uncertainty of human fortunes, we should probably come much nearer to my imaginary sentence than to the one from *Ecclesiastes*.

12   As I have tried to show, modern writing at its worst does not consist in picking out words for the sake of their meaning and inventing images in order to make the meaning clearer. It consists in gumming together long strips of words which have already been set in order by someone else, and making the results presentable by sheer humbug. The attraction of this way of writing is that it is easy. It is easier— even quicker, once you have the habit—to say *In my opinion it is not an unjustifiable assumption that* than to say *I think*. If you use ready-made phrases, you not only don't have to hunt about for words; you also don't have to bother with the rhythms of your sentences, since these phrases are generally so arranged as to be more or less euphonious. When you are composing in a hurry—when you are dictating to a stenographer, for instance, or making a public speech—it is natural to fall into a pretentious, Latinized style. Tags like *a consideration which we should*

do well to bear in mind or a conclusion to which all of us would readily assent will save many a sentence from coming down with a bump. By using stale metaphors, similes and idioms, you save much mental effort, at the cost of leaving your meaning vague, not only for your reader but for yourself. This is the significance of mixed metaphors. The sole aim of a metaphor is to call up a visual image. When these images clash—as in *The Fascist octopus has sung its swan song, the jackboot is thrown into the melting pot*—it can be taken as certain that the writer is not seeing a mental image of the objects he is naming; in other words he is not really thinking. Look again at the examples I gave at the beginning of this essay: Professor Laski (1) uses five negatives in fifty-three words. One of these is superfluous, making nonsense of the whole passage, and in addition there is the *slip alien* for *akin,* making further nonsense, and several avoidable pieces of clumsiness which increase the general vagueness. Professor Hogben (2) plays ducks and drakes with a battery which is able to write prescriptions, and, while disapproving of the everyday phrase *put up with,* is unwilling to look *egregious* up in the dictionary and see what it means; (3), if one takes an uncharitable attitude towards it, is simply meaningless; probably one could work out its intended meaning by reading the whole of the article in which it occurs. In (4), the writer knows more or less what he wants to say, but an accumulation of stale phrases chokes him, like tea leaves blocking a sink. In (5), words and meaning have almost parted company. People who write in this manner usually have a general emotional meaning—they dislike one thing and want to express solidarity with another—but they are not interested in the detail of what they are saying. A scrupulous writer, in every sentence that he writes, will ask himself at least four questions, thus: What am I trying to say? What words will express it? What image or idiom will make it clearer? Is this image fresh enough to have an effect? And he will probably ask himself two more: Could I put it more shortly? Have I said anything that is avoidably ugly? But you are not obliged to go to all this trouble. You can shirk it by simply throwing your mind open and letting the ready-made phrases come crowding in. They will construct your sentences for you—even think your thoughts for you, to a certain extent—and at need they will perform the important service of partially concealing your meaning even from yourself. It is at this point that the special connection between politics and the debasement of language becomes clear.

13   In our time it is broadly true that political writing is bad writing. Where it is not true, it will generally be found that the writer is some kind of rebel, expressing his private opinions and not a "party line." Orthodoxy, of whatever color, seems to demand a lifeless, imitative style. The political dialects to be found in pamphlets, leading articles, manifestos, White Papers and the speeches of undersecretaries do, of course, vary from party to party, but they are all alike in that one almost never finds in them a fresh, vivid, home-made turn of speech. When one watches some tired hack on the platform mechanically repeating the familiar phrases—*bestial atrocities, iron heel, bloodstained tyranny, free peoples of the world, stand shoulder to shoulder*—one often has a curious feeling that one is not watching a live human being but some kind of dummy: a feeling which suddenly becomes stronger at moments when the light catches the speaker's spectacles and turns them into blank discs which seem to have no eyes behind them. And this is not altogether fanciful.

A speaker who uses that kind of phraseology has gone some distance towards turning himself into a machine. The appropriate noises are coming out of his larynx, but his brain is not involved as it would be if he were choosing his words for himself. If the speech he is making is one that he is accustomed to make over and over again, he may be almost unconscious of what he is saying, as one is when one utters the responses in church. And this reduced state of consciousness, if not indispensable, is at any rate favorable to political conformity.

14   In our time, political speech and writing are largely the defense of the indefensible. Things like the continuance of British rule in India, the Russian purges and deportations, the dropping of the atom bombs on Japan, can indeed be defended, but only by arguments which are too brutal for most people to face, and which do not square with the professed aims of political parties. Thus political language has to consist largely of euphemism, question-begging and sheer cloudy vagueness. Defenseless villages are bombarded from the air, the inhabitants driven out into the countryside, the cattle machine-gunned, the huts set on fire with incendiary bullets: this is called *pacification*. Millions of peasants are robbed of their farms and sent trudging along the roads with no more than they can carry: this is called *transfer of population or rectification of frontiers*. People are imprisoned for years without trial, or shot in the back of the neck or sent to die of scurvy in Arctic lumber camps; this is called *elimination of unreliable elements*. Such phraseology is needed if one wants to name things without calling up mental pictures of them. Consider for instance some comfortable English professor defending Russian totalitarianism. He cannot say outright, "I believe in killing off your opponents when you can get good results by doing so." Probably, therefore, he will say something like this:

15   "While freely conceding that the Soviet régime exhibits certain features which the humanitarian may be inclined to deplore, we must, I think, agree that a certain curtailment of the right to political opposition is an unavoidable concomitant of transitional periods, and that the rigors which the Russian people have been called upon to undergo have been amply justified in the sphere of concrete achievement."

16   The inflated style is itself a kind of euphemism. A mass of Latin words falls upon the facts like soft snow, blurring the outlines and covering up all the details. The great enemy of clear language is insincerity. When there is a gap between one's real and one's declared aims, one turns as it were instinctively to long words and exhausted idioms, like a cuttlefish squirting out ink. In our age there is no such thing as "keeping out of politics." All issues are political issues, and politics itself is a mass of lies, evasions, folly, hatred and schizophrenia. When the general atmosphere is bad, language must suffer. I should expect to find—this is a guess which I have not sufficient knowledge to verify—that the German, Russian and Italian languages have all deteriorated in the last ten or fifteen years, as a result of dictatorship.

17   But if thought corrupts language, language can also corrupt thought. A bad usage can spread by tradition and imitation, even among people who should and do know better. The deposed language that I have been discussing is in some ways very convenient. Phrases like *a not unjustifiable assumption, leaves much to be desired, would serve no good purpose, a consideration which we should do well to bear in mind,* are a continuous temptation, a packet of aspirins always at one's elbow. Look back through this essay, and for certain you will find that I have again and again

committed the very faults I am protesting against. By this morning's post I have received a pamphlet dealing with conditions in Germany. The author tells me that he "felt impelled" to write it. I open it at random and here is almost the first sentence that I see: "[The Allies] have an opportunity not only of achieving a radical transformation of Germany's social and political structure in such a way as to avoid a nationalistic reaction in Germany itself, but at the same time of laying the foundations of a co-operative and unified Europe." You see, he "feels impelled" to write—feels, presumably, that he has something new to say—and yet his words, like cavalry horses answering the bugle, group themselves automatically into the familiar dreary pattern. This invasion of one's mind by ready-made phrases (*lay the foundations, achieve a radical transformation*) can only be prevented if one is constantly on guard against them, and every such phrase anaesthetizes a portion of one's brain.

18   I said earlier that the decadence of our language is probably curable. Those who deny this would argue, if they produced an argument at all, that language merely reflects existing social conditions, and that we cannot influence its development by any direct tinkering with words and constructions. So far as the general tone or spirit of a language goes, this may be true, but it is not true in detail. Silly words and expressions have often disappeared, not through any evolutionary process but owing to the conscious action of a minority. Two recent examples were *explore every avenue* and *leave no stone unturned*, which were killed by the jeers of a few journalists. There is a long list of flyblown metaphors which could similarly be got rid of if enough people would interest themselves in the job, and it should also be possible to laugh the *not un-* formation out of existence,[3] to reduce the amount of Latin and Greek in the average sentence, to drive out foreign phrases and strayed scientific words, and, in general, to make pretentiousness unfashionable. But all these are minor points. The defense of the English language implies more than this, and perhaps it is best to start by saying what it does *not* imply.

19   To begin with it has nothing to do with archaism, with the salvaging of obsolete words and turns of speech, or with the setting up of a "standard English" which must never be departed from. On the contrary, it is especially concerned with the scrapping of every word or idiom which has outworn its usefulness. It has nothing to do with correct grammar and syntax, which are of no importance so long as one makes one's meaning clear, or with the avoidance of Americanisms, or with having what is called a "good prose style." On the other hand it is not concerned with fake simplicity and the attempt to make written English colloquial. Nor does it even imply in every case preferring the Saxon word to the Latin one, though it does imply using the fewest and shortest words that will cover one's meaning. What is above all needed is to let the meaning choose the word, and not the other way about. In prose, the worst thing one can do with words is to surrender to them. When you think of a concrete object, you think wordlessly, and then, if you want to describe the thing you have been visualizing

---

[3]One can cure oneself of the *not un-* formation by memorizing this sentence: *A not unblack dog was chasing a not unsmall rabbit across a not ungreen field.*

you probably hunt about till you find the exact words that seem to fit it. When you think of something abstract you are more inclined to use words from the start, and unless you make a conscious effort to prevent it, the existing dialect will come rushing in and do the job for you, at the expense of blurring or even changing your meaning. Probably it is better to put off using words as long as possible and get one's meaning as clear as one can through pictures or sensations. Afterwards one can choose—not simply *accept*—the phrases that will best cover the meaning, and then switch round and decide what impression one's words are likely to make on another person. This last effort of the mind cuts out all stale or mixed images, all prefabricated phrases, needless repetitions, and humbug and vagueness generally. But one can often be in doubt about the effect of a word or a phrase, and one needs rules that one can rely on when instinct fails. I think the following rules will cover most cases:

1. Never use a metaphor, simile or other figure of speech which you are used to seeing in print.

2. Never use a long word where a short one will do.

3. If it is possible to cut a word out, always cut it out.

4. Never use the passive where you can use the active.

5. Never use a foreign phrase, a scientific word or a jargon word if you can think of an everyday English equivalent.

6. Break any of these rules sooner than say anything outright barbarous.

20   These rules sound elementary, and so they are, but they demand a deep change of attitude in anyone who has grown used to writing in the style now fashionable. One could keep all of them and still write bad English, but one could not write the kind of stuff that I quoted in those five specimens at the beginning of this article.

21   I have not here been considering the literary use of language, but merely language as an instrument for expressing and not for concealing or preventing thought. Stuart Chase and others have come near to claiming that all abstract words are meaningless, and have used this as a pretext for advocating a kind of political quietism. Since you don't know what Fascism is, how can you struggle against Fascism? One need not swallow such absurdities as this, but one ought to recognize that the present political chaos is connected with the decay of language, and that one can probably bring about some improvement by starting at the verbal end. If you simplify your English, you are freed from the worst follies of orthodoxy. You cannot speak any of the necessary dialects, and when you make a stupid remark its stupidity will be obvious, even to yourself. Political language—and with variations this is true of all political parties, from Conservatives to Anarchists—is designed to make lies sound truthful and murder respectable, and to give an appearance of solidity to pure wind. One cannot change this all in a moment, but one can at least change one's own habits, and from time to time one can even, if one jeers loudly enough, send some worn-out and useless phrase—some jackboot, Achilles' heel,

hotbed, melting pot, acid test, veritable inferno or other lump of verbal refuse—into the dustbin where it belongs.

THINKING CRITICALLY

1. Orwell argues that modern writers are destroying the English language. Explain some of the ways in which they are doing so.

2. What is a *euphemism*? Orwell cites "pacification" as an example from World War II (paragraph 14). Try to find some euphemisms that came out of the 2003 war with Iraq. Name and explain some of the euphemisms common in business today.

3. Orwell lists six rules at the end of the essay (paragraph 19). What does he mean by the last rule?

4. Toward the end of the essay, Orwell writes, "Look back through this essay, and for certain you will find that I have again and again committed the very faults I am protesting against." (paragraph 17). Where in the essay has he broken his own rules?

5. Does Orwell seem to criticize one end of the political spectrum more than the other? Support your answer with references to Orwell's essay.

6. Reread the first four paragraphs. What kind of personality does Orwell project—reasonable, honest, condescending, cynical? Explain.

7. Orwell begins his arguments by citing five writers. How does he use these references throughout the essay?

8. Is there any emotional appeal in this essay? If so, what is it and how is it created?

9. Exactly where in the essay does Orwell begin to talk about politics and the English language? Why does he start his discussion there?

WRITING ASSIGNMENTS

1. Orwell gives five examples of bad writing from his own day. Have things changed much since then? Compile your own list from current newspapers, magazines, and books. How do your findings compare with Orwell's?

2. Orwell takes a passage from *Ecclesiastes* and "translates" it to illustrate bad writing by his contemporaries. Do the same with a different passage from the Bible or an excerpt from a poem or novel. Use some of the same techniques Orwell employs.

3. Have you ever been the victim of political propaganda? Have you ever voted for something or someone (or would have were you not underage) because of a campaigner's persuasive political language, or given to a cause for the same reason? Write an account of your experience, and try to explain how the language influenced you.

4. Read (or reread) one of the political satires mentioned in the headnote to this article: either *Animal Farm* or *1984*. How does language create power for the rulers in the novel? What kinds of power does Orwell think language can have? Examine what literary critics have said by researching articles about the novel with reference tools such as the *Modern Language Association Bibliography*, *Contemporary Literary Criticism*, or the *Dictionary of Literary Biography*.

The Pep Talk: Patterns of Persuasion in Political Language

Hugh Rank

> Many people have negative impressions of political language because so much of it seems to be doublespeak or lofty rhetoric. Hugh Rank agrees that negative stereotypes of politicians and the language they use are based on some "kernels of truth." He also believes that as responsible citizens we must be able to critically analyze political language. In the next essay, Rank explains how the "pep talk," a high-pressure, emotional appeal designed to persuade audiences, is used by politicians to influence and encourage voters to support political goals and agendas.
>
> Hugh Rank is the author of *Teaching about Public Persuasion: Rationale and a Schema* (1976). Rank won the 1976 Orwell Award presented by the Committee on Public Doublespeak for his essay "Intensifying/Downplaying Schema," in which he observed that all acts of public persuasion are variations of intensifying or downplaying. The following piece is an excerpt from his 1984 book, *The Pep Talk: How to Analyze Political Language.*

1   The term "pep talk" is most commonly associated with the pep rallies before the big football games, or the coach's inspiring speech at half-time in the locker room, or the sales manager's enthusiastic meetings instilling a competitive spirit encouraging the staff to greater efforts to sell more, to do more, or to beat their rivals. But in this essay, the term "pep talk" is going to be used more broadly and metaphorically to suggest a very common pattern in a great deal of social and political persuasion.

2   Political, as used here, suggests not only our domestic party politics (Democrat, Republican; national, state, and local politics) and international political issues (Communism, etc.), but also, in the broadest sense, any grouping together for a goal, a purpose, a cause. Thus, this pattern can usefully help to analyze civil rights and environmental issues, party politics and neighborhood citizen's groups, union strikes and company sales meetings, picket lines and protestors, special interest groups and "single issue" candidates, and often rumors and "junk mail."

3   The "pep talk," as used here, is that pattern of persuasion used to organize and direct the energy of a group toward *committed collective action:* commonly a sequence of (1) the Threat, (2) the Bonding, (3) the Cause, (4) the Response.

4   Whether the cause or the group is "good" or "bad," important or trivial, the pattern will be basically the same. The *intent* of a "pep talk" may be the persuader's malicious exploitation of the naive, or it may be the most genuine altruism and benevolence, but the pattern will be basically the same. The *content* of the "pep talk" may be true or false, accurate or erroneous, but the pattern will be basically the same. The *consequences* may be beneficial or harmful, to the individual or to others, but the pattern will be basically the same.

5   In reality, the "pep talk" is not as tidy, nor as sequential as this 1, 2, 3, 4 pattern. Observers come in at different times, or hear only brief fragments. On one hand, we're probably accustomed to the bonding efforts of our own group (nationality,

religious, ethnic, etc.), on the other hand, watching the TV news, we're apt to see only a brief exposure of some other group's "cause" without really knowing much about their whole set of beliefs and attitudes, hopes and fears. Typically, we see bits and fragments of the "pep talk," odds and ends.

6   Here's a basic structure to help sort out these fragments of political language and relate them to their part in a process of purposeful communication. Consider first some of the possible benefits and dangers involved in such "pep talks," then note the qualifications and variations: for example, the differences and overlaps between "the pitch" and "the pep talk."

7   Using simple terms such as "pep talk," (and later, "horror stories" and "atrocity pictures") helps to clarify a complex process. Some people may feel that this informal language is flippant or frivolous. But the intent here is not to minimize the genuine human pain and suffering often related to such "pep talks" in the past, but to innoculate for the future. If, by the use of a simple pattern and memorable phrases, it is possible to clarify and to simplify these basic techniques for large audiences, especially younger audiences, then it would be cynical *not* to do so, or to restrict such information to an elite few.

8   For the past few generations, for the first time in human history, broadcasting can link persuaders with a mass audience. Not only do many corporations seek after this audience, using the "pitch" to sell their products, but also many political groups and "causes" would like to organize and direct the energies of this large audience.

9   In the future, as in the past, people will be asked to join in a good cause, or to fight for God and country, or to defend themselves and to protect others from an evil threat. A "cause" can involve mankind's most noble sentiments. But, our altruistic impulses can also be exploited, manipulated, abused by others.

10   Young people are always the prime target for such a "pep talk": they have a great deal of idealism, enthusiasm—and inexperience. It's useful to know some patterns of persuasion, and to teach them to the young. It helps to clarify choice and decisions. There are times when we may wish to commit ourselves to a cause. If we are aware of some patterns, our decisions may be more based on the merit of the cause rather than on the slick delivery, the skill, the cleverness or the charisma of the persuader. If we know the form, we can concentrate on the substance.

11   The propagandist does not want our thought, our contemplation, our analysis, our advance awareness of the techniques; the propagandist wants a response, action.

12   Some persuasion emphasizes the positive or upbeat: some conservative persuasion, for example, would stress joy, contentment, and satisfaction for the "good" possessed, for the blessings received, as we often hear on Thanksgiving Day, Christmas, Fourth of July; some progressive persuasion, for example, might stress growth, progress, and achievement, the optimistic hopes and dreams of a situation getting better ("I have a dream . . ."). There's a great deal of such ceremonial rhetoric, appropriate to many situations, and we expect it and hear it in many instances in which the audience is to be inspired or praised, calmed or consoled. Similarly, in religious persuasion, some preachers might focus on the glory of God, the beauty of the universe, or heavenly delights. But, other preachers have been known to talk about hellfire and damnation. Perhaps the "pep talk" might be the

secular equivalent of such hellfire preaching: starting with a problem, working on the emotions, and leading to solutions being suggested.

13   If there are varieties of religious experience, so also there are varieties of secular experience. Some people would prefer hearing "good news" all the time; others would object to such a thing as being unrealistic and Pollyannish. Some people may not like a "pep talk"—some may object to its negative emphasis, others to its emotional intensity, others to its seeming artificiality. Without denying the virtues of positive inspirational rhetoric, the emphasis in this book is on the negative: the conservative rhetoric stressing anxiety and fear of losing the "good" and the progressive rhetoric stressing anger, resentment, and frustration about not having the "good" or seeking relief from the "bad." The attempt here is not to endorse or condemn what persuaders do, but to observe and describe it.

Good Results, Good Intentions

14   "Pep talks" can be beneficial, can be the means to good effects. There are, genuinely, many "good causes." Many things which need to be done in order to make this a better society can only be done by organized group effort. Individuals working alone simply cannot do some things which people can do collectively. Various methods of organizing people are possible: a business corporation can offer financial rewards, for example; or a powerful government can simply command by force. Yet, even without such inducements as money or guns, human energies can be organized toward collective action simply by skillful combination of words and images, a "pep talk."

15   Assume that all or most "pep talks" are made with *good intentions*, that is, the speakers are sincere believers in the merits of their "good cause." (Some persuaders may not be so; some may be manipulators or con men.) However, "good intentions" do not necessarily guarantee good results. But, if it is assumed that everyone (even scoundrels and rascals) can justify their actions as being based on "good intentions," one need not waste effort trying to establish the persuader's motives; be concerned instead with the *consequences*. More specifically, be aware of the potentially *bad* effects of "pep talks."

16   "Pep talks" can cause harm to great numbers of people. In a world with very real danger of wars among nations, terrorist assaults by individuals and small groups, and sophisticated weapons easily available, it's very risky to stimulate fears or incite quick responses based on emotional feelings. The obvious, overt danger is that of stirring up hatreds and triggering off the Crazies. The more subtle danger is the general conditioning within a wider society in preparation for officially-sanctioned wars.

17   "Pep talks" can be harmful to individuals. What may benefit the group, may harm the individual. All of us owe some debt of loyalty to the many groups to which we belong because we inherit or share in their benefits. Yet, any time a person gives up responsibility to any group, the person risks a loss of self. Yet, it happens. Some people with low self-esteem find their comfort in belonging to a group, identifying with it, and following it with unquestioning loyalty.

18   Self-righteousness is another danger. People who are "true believers" in the absolute virtue of their own "cause" are, at best, obnoxious; at worst, dangerous. The world has seen too many wars, slaughters and massacres carried out in the

name of God or the cause of Justice. The "pep talk" encourages polarized thinking, dichotomies, the "good guys/bad guys" mentality; it encourages people who are narrow and rigid authoritarians to believe that they are the "good guys," the Truth-Possessors with an authority to impose the "right way" on others.

19   Individuals can be harmed emotionally by a constant repetition of the "threats" and warnings given in "pep talks." Just as some young people, for example, can be overstimulated by the acquisitive demands ("buy this . . . get that") of commercial advertising, and end up being always dissatisfied and frustrated, so also some people can be overstimulated by a constant repetition of threats, warnings, bad news, and urgent pleas. A sensitive young person, for example, encountering a daily dose of environmentalist pleas (pictures of dead seals, dead whales, dead birds, dead dogs, etc.) can be overwhelmed by this depressing sight.

20   Often these are undue fears, unreasonable anxieties, because the degree, proportion, or relationship of the harm has been exaggerated out of context. Even though any single ad or any single "pep talk" could be defended as being tolerable, the *cumulative impact* of thousands of single-issue "cause" group ads, each intensifying their own warnings and problems, can be harmful to the sensibilities of the audience which receives them all. Our children grow up not only blitzed by commercial advertising pleasantly promising dreams of the good life, but also saturated with horrible warnings and nightmare images.

21   Cynicism is one result. Sometimes young people completely accept a "pep talk" at face value, literally, without reservations. Later, they may feel that they had been deceived, duped, or exploited. Such disillusionment often causes a bitter reaction: cynicism, apathy, a total rejection of previous beliefs. Problems of credibility also exist when so many extreme warnings are made about so many things that some people simply overload and discount everything. Many people scoff at FDA warnings about cancer-causing chemicals ("next thing they'll say is that *everything* causes cancer" is the cliché) without recognizing the real complexity. Many people simply disregard, block out, any warnings about nuclear war as being either unthinkable or unbelievable.

22   We not only live in an age of real problems and real threats, but we also live in an age in which the professional persuaders are right with us, daily and constantly, often to warn us about these problems and ask us to do something about them. A hundred years ago, even sixty years ago, the average citizen would seldom experience a skillfully constructed "pep talk" during the course of a lifetime. Today, the average citizen is likely to see bits and fragments of one every time the TV is turned on, and is likely to get a complete "pep talk" daily in the mailbox.

The Pitch, the Pep Talk, and Other Persuasive Attempts

23 Both the "pitch" and the "pep talk" seek a response, but the basic difference between the two is that the "pep talk" seeks a *committed collective action*. That is, the "pitch" leads to a simple response (usually, to buy); the "pep talk" asks a person to *join with others, for a cause.*

24   To relate these techniques with other persuasive attempts, consider first the *timing* of the response, using the terms *Command* propaganda which seeks an immediate response *(Now!)* and *Conditioning* propaganda which seeks to mold

public opinions, assumptions, beliefs, attitudes on a long-term basis as the necessary climate or atmosphere for a future response *(Later!)*

25   Both the "pitch" and the "pep talk" are *Command* propagandas, seeking immediate actions. The chart (opposite) relates these two concepts with terms used by others to describe other kinds of persuasive attempts.

	"Command propaganda" is the easiest to recognize. Here both the "pitch" and the "pep talk" are types of such persuasions seeking an immediate response.	"Conditioning propaganda" is more subtle, harder to analyze or limit; many different names have been used to describe persuasion which seeks to create, shape, mold basic opinions, assumptions, beliefs, attitudes, myths, worldviews.
Timing of Response	NOW!	LATER
	(Command)	(Conditioning)
Kind of Response		"soft sell"
		"public relations" (PR)
		"publicity"
action	"THE PITCH"	"institutional advertising"
		"corporate advertising"
		"image building"
		"promotion"
		"goodwill advertising"
		"political education" (Lenin)
		"basic propaganda" (Goebbels)
		"sub-propaganda" (Ellul)
		"pre-propaganda"
committed		"education"
collective	"THE PEP TALK"	"indoctrination"
action		"awareness"
		"consciousness raising"

The persuader's goals are to get others . . . *to do* the "right" acts . . . and *to think* the "right" way.

26   In reality, such neat categories do not exist. Borderline cases are common, between command and conditioning propagandas, and between the "pitch" and the "pep talk." Adding to the complexity of any real situation are some common basic factors which can be described in terms of *multiples, mixtures,* and *mistakes.*

27   *Multiples.* Multiple persuasion attempts are usually made at the same time, either to the same audience using different pitches, or to different audiences using the same pitch. In auto ads, for example, there may be a dozen different sets of ads prepared for different audiences: some ads stressing a "safety" angle for old folks,

"sporty" for young folks; some ads with urban backgrounds, some with rural; some emphasizing economy, others stressing prestige, and all could be talking about the same car. In such an advertising campaign, a basic premise is that most people only notice ads directed at "them" in such smaller sub-categories, and ignore the ads directed at other sub-categories.

28   Multiple association devices are also used in politics. In a typical political campaign, for example, the major parties will create and fund a whole host of various committees and "front organizations" and sub-groups (such as Farmers For Reagan, Polish-Americans For Reagan, Italian-Americans For Reagan, Union Members for Reagan, etc.) not only to give the illusion of widespread support, but also to appeal to those specific ethnic, occupational, or interest groups. Political protest movements also have a multiplicity of propagandas going on at the same time (e.g., Vietnam Veterans Against the War, Another Mother for Peace, Clergy and Laity United for Peace, Students for Peace, etc.); such diversity is sometimes a genuine grassroots movement, sometimes manipulated by others.

29   *Mixtures.* In any political campaign, there's likely to be a mixture of the "pitch" directed at an outside public, and the "pep talk" directed at an insider audience—the party regulars. In religious persuasion, there's likely to be one kind of evangelizing, spreading the good news, to others, and another kind of preaching to the saved. In both of these examples, we are likely to see a "recruiting sequence": first, the "pitch" to bring in new members, converts; then, the "pep talk" to keep them bonded and to direct them toward a new action. Or we might find a re-directing sequence; first, a "pep talk" to bond for one cause; then, once bonded, re-directed to another cause. Or we might find an escalation sequence: a series of "pep talks" leading to increasingly more difficult actions, "raising the ante."

30   Thus far, we've been assuming that these patterns and variations can be applied to *truthful* and *sincere* attempts at persuasion; but they can also be applied to *deceitful* and *insincere* "pitches" and "pep talks." A scoundrel, for example, may use a "pep talk" to bond people for a political or religious cause, simply as a prelude to a "pitch" to get the audience to buy something or donate money. Sometimes this is obvious and recognizable—if the politician or minister walks away with bulging pockets stuffed with money. But, more likely, it's difficult to detect, and the real borderline cases will be between clever scoundrels and true believers.

31   Mixed motives are common in almost every human action. Multiple goals are possible, simultaneously, in almost every human endeavor. Consider, for example, the many *reasons* for, and the *results* sought in, "corporate advertising" in such organizations as Mobil, U.S. Steel, Dow Chemical, IBM, Xerox, Union Carbide, and other corporate giants. Such "corporate advertising" (*not* ads for specific consumer products) is also called, by various writers, "public relations," "institutional advertising," "image building," "goodwill advertising," and other related synonyms.

32   Note that all four general purposes (above the line) could exist at the same time; most corporations defend their expenditures (to their stockholders and to the general public) with such explanations. In actual practice, there are no problems with the overlaps among these four categories. Serious "borderline" problems occur however in that vague area between *command* propaganda and *conditioning* propaganda, between "advocacy advertising" and "corporate advertising." Just where is

Mixed Motives in Corporate Advertising

Label	Purpose	Audience
synonyms: "corporate advertising"	to sell, indirectly, consumer products by building awareness (Hi!) and reputation (Trust Me) of parent corporation, brand names, logos.	consumers
"institutional advertising" "public relations"	to encourage new stockholders to invest money, existing stockholders to retain stock.	investors; financial community
"image advertising" "goodwill" "publicity"	to increase employee morale, higher productivity and work quality; to attract good new employees.	employees; potential employees
	to influence, indirectly, legislation and regulation; to get citizens and their representatives friendly and favorably disposed toward the corporation; to ward off taxes, controls, regulations, limits, etc.	citizens: voters, legislators & regulators
"advocacy advertising" is the closely related *Command* propaganda here seeking a specific immediate response.	to influence, directly, legislation or regulation: seeking specific actions, explicit directives: "Write your Senator . . . Vote for . . ."	citizens: voters, legislators & regulators

the boundary between spending money to have the public "like" (tolerate, accept) the corporation (or the policies, the goals of the corporation) and spending money to have the public "advocate" (support, endorse) the goals and policies of the corporation. Clarifying the issues at this borderline involves high stakes because of the tax laws and the problems of corporate influence—complex legal problems which do not fit neatly into any existing jurisdiction, but are overlapping concerns of the FTC, FCC, and IRS. (As the first step in approaching this problem, the Senate's Subcommittee on Administrative Practice has published a whopping, 2133 pp., *Sourcebook on Corporate Image and Corporate Advocacy Advertising.*)

33   Another factor which makes it difficult to deal with the borderline between command propaganda, seeking an immediate response, and conditioning propaganda, preparing the way for a future response, is that all of this is an *ongoing process*, constantly in motion. Any particular piece of information may be "news" to the *receivers* or may call for an urgent action, but the *sender* may know months or years ahead about the content and timing of a long-term propaganda campaign.

34   The "pitch" and the "pep talk" may be useful to help understand some of the persuasive messages we receive, but we must be prepared to see the variations and the "surface texture." In the United States alone, for example, there are literally several hundred thousand commercial products which advertise, and there are probably more than that number of sources of political, religious, ethnic, and social propagandas. We live in this environment of competing propagandas, and the hubbub of this marketplace of ideas can get confusing at times.

35   *Mistakes.* Because of all of this complexity, persuaders can make mistakes. Every persuader seeks to be effective, but this is not always the result. Sometimes ads come "too close" to us, get palsy-walsy, treating us as if we were already friendly, assuming our interest and involvement, taking our assent for granted. This kind of error in persuasion causes the audience to back off, to reject the over-friendly advances as being offensive, cloying, too saccharine. Sometimes this is caused by a mishandling of the "confidence" (Trust Me) part of the "pitch." Sometimes it's caused by using a "pep talk" instead of a "pitch," in a situation which is not appropriate. Sometimes, in a "pep talk," errors in persuasion can occur because of an incomplete bonding or a premature "response" plea.

36   *Delivery.* Although this book concentrates on patterns and the structure underneath, the "surface" tactics of delivery or execution are equally important. Simply to point out the pattern doesn't mean that everyone has the skill to do it well. Effectiveness varies with the speaker, the audience, and the situation. Sometimes an attempt at a "pep talk" falls flat; the audience may not be moved or may react against it as being too "gung ho" or too "rah-rah" or as "laying it on too thick."

37   If the bonding is incomplete, if the audience doesn't genuinely feel a part of the group, feel threatened by the outside, then the pep talk may be ineffective or backfire.

A Borderline Case: The "Scare-and-Sell" Ad

38 In contrast to most advertising which deals with our dreams, promises, and hopes, some health and safety products (such as fire and life insurance, travelers' checks, burglar alarms, over-the-counter medicines, deodorants, etc.) often start from our nightmares, threats, and fears: the *"scare-and-sell"* approach.

39   Thus, the ad may begin with a "threat," and in this way is similar to the beginning of the "pep talk." But the "scare-and-sell" approach *does not* ask for bonding or commitment to a cause. It's a pitch, a simple sales transaction: "You have a problem; here's the solution."

40   The problem is emphasized, then the solution is offered ("anxiety arousal and satisfaction"), but there is no demand on us to give anything other than our money. It's easiest to recognize this in ads which dramatize physical fears (death, fire, loss of money, etc.), but we also have emotional fears (loneliness, rejection, etc.) that are stirred by many ads. The basic "translation" of many ads might read: "You'll be unloved, unwanted, rejected . . . unless you buy our soap, toothpaste, deodorant, hairspray, etc."

A Borderline Case: The Selling of the Candidates

41 Following the lead of books such as Daniel Boorstin's *The Image* and Joe McGinnis' *The Selling of the President*, and movies such as *The Candidate,* there has been increasing criticism about the packaging or marketing or selling of modern political candidates as if they were commercial products: bars of soap, tubes of toothpaste. Critics cry that "Madison Avenue" has taken over: slick professionals, crass manipulators, PR specialists and media technicians who know how to create and manipulate an "image," a "television personality," a "plastic person" who looks like and talks like what the polls say the voters want. There has been a great deal of commentary about these media mercenaries or rented rhetoricians.

42   Usually such complaints about modern political campaigns are set in contrast to romanticized images of old-time party politics—of Fourth of July speeches, political rallies, orators on the gazebos, friendly waving crowds, torchlight parades and bandwagons, hand-printed homemade signs, and all the hoopla and ballyhoo which we associate with political campaigns in the days before radio and television. Most of this old time politicing can best be described in terms of the *"pep talk"*: the great emphasis was on the bonding of the group, for a cause. Party politics emphasized the group; later, "issue politics" of the 1960s also could be described in terms of the "pep talk" because of its emphasis on "principles," on the "cause."

43   But the approach of those who are creating the "image" candidates can best be described in terms of the *"pitch."* Most of these ads are *not* asking the voters to join the party, work for the party, commit themselves to a cause, but are simply asking for a one-shot "purchase"—a vote. (And if that purchase isn't satisfactory, there'll be a new improved model for the next election.)

44   We are likely to see more of the "pitch" in future political campaigns because of the decline in political party membership, party loyalty; the increase in uncommitted "Independent" voters; and because it is ultimately cheaper and easier to use the technology of the mass media than to sustain an ongoing organization.

45   In the future, we're still likely to see the "pep talk" given to insiders (usually by means of meetings; rallies, letter mailings, in-house publications), but the use of the "pitch" will increase in messages directed to outsiders—to the uncommitted public—seeking only their vote on election day.

46   However, this new kind of "image" campaigning may always be considered a borderline case between a "pitch" and a "pep talk," because it is likely such "pitches" will have the surface appearance of a "pep talk" by using such *commitment words* ("dedicate yourself . . . join us . . . in our noble cause"), but in fact seeking or specifying *no other response than voting.* When somebody asks us to canvas a neighborhood, ring doorbells, fold envelopes, work hard and give time for the cause, we are likely to be hearing part of a "pep talk"; but when we see the 30-second-spot on TV, we're likely to be seeing the "pitch."

Hired Hands and True Believers

47 No one yet knows the full implications of this new "image" campaigning. Those who use the "pitch" in political advertising are open to charges of being cynical, calculating manipulators; those who use the "pep talk" are feared as zealots, fanatics, extremists. But some political observers are saying that we have passed the era of

conflicts between political parties, and of conflicts between opposing ideologies, and now are witnessing the conflict between technicians: which team of specialists can best package the product and sell it.

48   *To recap:* The "pep talk" is used here to label a common pattern of persuasion used to organize and direct the energy of a group toward committed collective action; commonly, the sequence: (1) the Threat; (2) the Bonding; (3) the Cause; (4) the Response. Regardless of intent, consequences, significance, or content, the pattern is basically the same, albeit we often see only bits and fragments as reported and edited by others. "Pep talks" can be beneficial as aids to directing human effort; but "pep talks" can also be harmful to society (inciting hatreds, wars) and to the individual (irresponsibility, self-righteousness, undue fears, cynicism). The "pep talk" is similar to the "pitch" in that both are *command* propagandas seeking a response; but the "pitch" leads to a simple transaction while the "pep talk" asks a person to join with others for a good cause. A static diagram is limited in suggesting the reality of multiple and mixed persuasion techniques and motives (illustrated by the mixed motives of "corporate ads") and in the reality of mistakes in planning and in delivery. Borderline cases exist: some commercial products using ads stressing fears, the "scare-and-sell" technique; some slick political ads "selling candidates" as if they were commercial products.

THINKING CRITICALLY

1. What is the "pep talk"? Who uses it and why?

2. How does Rank's analysis of the "pep talk" as a form of public persuasion provide insight into the dynamics of what makes a speech compelling to an audience? Explain.

3. Describe the basic pattern of the "pep talk." How does dissecting its patterns help us understand its benefits and dangers? Explain.

4. In what ways can the "pep talk" be beneficial? How can it be used to support good causes? Conversely, how can it be abused?

5. What is the difference between the "pitch" and the "pep talk"? Can you identify examples of each used recently? Explain.

6. Evaluate Rank's own use of language as he describes the structure of the "pep talk." Is he persuasive? Critical? Unbiased and fair? Explain.

7. What similarities exist between political "pep talks" and advertising? Discuss how you think they are similar, or different, drawing from the information outlined by Rank in his essay.

WRITING ASSIGNMENTS

1. Locate a recent speech given by a politician and analyze it using Rank's guidelines for understanding the "pep talk."

2. Describe a situation in which you were deceived or inspired by a "pep talk." What compelled you to believe the speaker? What made the speech effective? Describe the experience and its influence on you.

3. Write your own "pep talk." Prepare a short speech for a political or social cause. After you prepare the speech, deliver it to the class. Be prepared to explain why you chose certain persuasive tactics, and to discuss the effectiveness of the speech as part of a peer review.

Doubts About Doublespeak

William Lutz

It has been said that the only sure (or certain) things we cannot change are death and taxes. Well, that's not exactly right. We can call them "terminal living" and "revenue enhancement" to make people feel better about them. And that, in part, is the nature of what William Lutz rails against here: doublespeak. It is language intended not to reveal but to conceal, not to communicate but to obfuscate. In this essay, Lutz categorizes four kinds of doublespeak, distinguishing annoying though relatively harmless professional jargon from ruthlessly devious coinages such as "ethnic cleansing," which attempt to mask barbaric acts.

William Lutz is a professor of English at Rutgers University. He is the editor of the *Quarterly Review of Doublespeak* as well as author of *Beyond Nineteen Eighty-Four: Doublespeak in a Post-Orwellian Age* (1989) and *Doublespeak: From Revenue Enhancement to Terminal Living* (1990). "Doubts About Doublespeak" first appeared in *State Government News*, in July 1993.

1   During the past year, we learned that we can shop at a "unique retail biosphere" instead of a farmers' market, where we can buy items made of "synthetic glass" instead of plastic, or purchase a "high velocity, multipurpose air circulator," or electric fan. A "waste-water conveyance facility" may "exceed the odor threshold" from time to time due to the presence of "regulated human nutrients," but that is not to be confused with a sewage plant that stinks up the neighborhood with sewage sludge. Nor should we confuse a "resource development park" with a dump. Thus does doublespeak continue to spread.

2   Doublespeak is language which pretends to communicate but doesn't. It is language which makes the bad seem good, the negative seem positive, the unpleasant seem attractive, or at least tolerable. It is language which avoids, shifts or denies responsibility; language which is at variance with its real or purported meaning. It is language which conceals or prevents thought.

3   Doublespeak is all around us. We are asked to check our packages at the desk "for our convenience" when it's not for our convenience at all but for someone else's convenience. We see advertisements for "preowned," "experienced" or "previously distinguished" cars, not used cars and for "genuine imitation leather," "virgin vinyl" or "real counterfeit diamonds." Television offers not reruns but "encore telecasts." There are no slums or ghettos, just the "inner city" or "substandard housing" where the "disadvantaged" or "economically nonaffluent" live and where there might be a problem with "substance abuse." Nonprofit organizations don't make a profit, they have "negative deficits" or experience "revenue excesses." With doublespeak it's not dying but "terminal living" or "negative patient care outcome."

4   There are four kinds of doublespeak. The first kind is the euphemism, a word or phrase designed to avoid a harsh or distasteful reality. Used to mislead or deceive, the euphemism becomes doublespeak. In 1984 the U.S. State Department's annual reports on the status of human rights around the world ceased using the word "killing." Instead the State Department used the phrase "unlawful or arbitrary deprivation of life," thus avoiding the embarrassing situation of government-sanctioned killing in countries supported by the United States.

to not deal w/ emotions or people

5   A second kind of doublespeak is jargon, the specialized language of a trade, profession or similar group, such as doctors, lawyers, plumbers or car mechanics. Legitimately used, jargon allows members of a group to communicate with each other clearly, efficiently and quickly. Lawyers and tax accountants speak to each other of an "involuntary conversion" of property, a legal term that means the loss or destruction of property through theft, accident or condemnation. But when lawyers or tax accountants use unfamiliar terms to speak to others, then the jargon becomes doublespeak.

6   In 1978 a commercial 727 crashed on takeoff, killing three passengers, injuring 21 others and destroying the airplane. The insured value of the airplane was greater than its book value, so the airline made a profit of $1.7 million, creating two problems: the airline didn't want to talk about one of its airplanes crashing, yet it had to account for that $1.7 million profit in its annual report to its stockholders. The airline solved both problems by inserting a footnote in its annual report which explained that the $1.7 million was due to "the involuntary conversion of a 727."

7   A third kind of doublespeak is gobbledygook or bureaucratese. Such doublespeak is simply a matter of overwhelming the audience with words—the more the better. Alan Greenspan, a polished practitioner of bureaucratese, once testified before a Senate committee that "it is a tricky problem to find the particular calibration in timing that would be appropriate to stem the acceleration in risk premiums created by falling incomes without prematurely aborting the decline in the inflation-generated risk premiums."

8   The fourth kind of doublespeak is inflated language, which is designed to make the ordinary seem extraordinary, to make everyday things seem impressive, to give an air of importance to people or situations, to make the simple seem complex. Thus do car mechanics become "automotive internists," elevator operators become "members of the vertical transportation corps," grocery store checkout clerks become "career associate scanning professionals," and smelling something becomes "organoleptic analysis."

9   Doublespeak is not the product of careless language or sloppy thinking. Quite the opposite. Doublespeak is language carefully designed and constructed to appear to communicate when in fact it doesn't. It is language designed not to lead but mislead. Thus, it's not a tax increase but "revenue enhancement" or "tax-base broadening." So how can you complain about higher taxes? Those aren't useless, billion dollar pork barrel projects; they're really "congressional projects of national significance," so don't complain about wasteful government spending. That isn't the Mafia in Atlantic City; those are just "members of a career-offender cartel," so don't worry about the influence of organized crime in the city.

10   New doublespeak is created every day. The Environmental Protection Agency once called acid rain "poorly-buffered precipitation" then dropped that term in favor of "atmospheric deposition of anthropogenically-derived acidic substances," but recently decided that acid rain should be called "wet deposition." The Pentagon, which has in the past given us such classic doublespeak as "hexiform rotatable surface compression unit" for steel nut, just published a pamphlet warning soldiers that exposure to nerve gas will lead to "immediate permanent incapacitation." That's almost as good as the Pentagon's official term "servicing the target," meaning to kill

the enemy. Meanwhile, the Department of Energy wants to establish a "monitored retrievable storage site," a place once known as a dump for spent nuclear fuel.

11   Bad economic times give rise to lots of new doublespeak designed to avoid some very unpleasant economic realities. As the "contained depression" continues so does the corporate policy of making up even more new terms to avoid the simple, and easily understandable, term "layoff." So it is that corporations "reposition," "restructure," "reshape," or "realign" the company and "reduce duplication" through "release of resources" that involves a "permanent downsizing" or a "payroll adjustment" that results in a number of employees being "involuntarily terminated."

12   Other countries regularly contribute to doublespeak. In Japan, where baldness is called "hair disadvantaged," the economy is undergoing a "severe adjustment process," while in Canada there is an "involuntary downward development" of the work force. For some government agencies in Canada, wastepaper baskets have become "user friendly, space effective, flexible, deskside sortation units." Politicians in Canada may engage in "reality augmentation," but they never lie. As part of their new freedom, the people of Moscow can visit "intimacy salons," or sex shops as they're known in other countries. When dealing with the bureaucracy in Russia, people know that they should show officials "normal gratitude," or give them a bribe.

13   The worst doublespeak is the doublespeak of death. It is the language, wrote George Orwell in 1946, that is "largely the defense of the indefensible . . . designed to make lies sound truthful and murder respectable, and to give an appearance of solidity to pure wind." In the doublespeak of death, Orwell continued, "defenseless villages are bombarded from the air, the inhabitants driven out into the countryside, the cattle machine-gunned, the huts set on fire with incendiary bullets. This is called pacification. Millions of peasants are robbed of their farms and sent trudging along the roads with no more than they can carry. This is called transfer of population or rectification of frontiers." Today, in a country once called Yugoslavia, this is called "ethnic cleansing."

14   It's easy to laugh off doublespeak. After all, we all know what's going on, so what's the harm? But we don't always know what's going on, and when that happens, doublespeak accomplishes its ends. It alters our perception of reality. It deprives us of the tools we need to develop, advance and preserve our society, our culture, our civilization. It breeds suspicion, cynicism, distrust and, ultimately, hostility. It delivers us into the hands of those who do not have our interests at heart. As Samuel Johnson noted in 18th century England, even the devils in hell do not lie to one another, since the society of hell could not subsist without the truth, any more than any other society.

THINKING CRITICALLY

1. What is doublespeak, according to Lutz? What is its purpose?

2. Lutz divides doublespeak into four types. What are they? Give some of your own examples of each type. As best you can, rank these four types according to which are most offensive or harmful. Explain your choices.

3. In paragraph 4, Lutz classifies euphemisms as a form of doublespeak. In your opinion, are there instances when euphemisms are useful? Explain your answer.

4. Lutz says that "inflated language" is designed to make the ordinary seem extra-ordinary, as with elevated job titles. In your opinion, is there anything wrong with elevating job titles in this way? Why or why not?

5. In your opinion, is doublespeak as widespread as Lutz claims? Are its effects as serious as he perceives them to be?

6. Examine Lutz's introductory paragraph. How does this paragraph set the tone for the piece? Is it effective?

7. What is the opposing view in this piece? How does Lutz handle it in his argument? Are there counterarguments that Lutz has missed in his essay?

8. Are there any places in the essay where Lutz employs doublespeak in his own writing? If so, what effect does this have on your reading?

9. Consider Lutz's voice in this article. Is he a reliable narrator? Does he provide adequate documentation for his assertions? Cite specific examples from the text to support your answers.

WRITING ASSIGNMENTS

1. Write an essay in which you examine instances of doublespeak in the media, a particular profession, or among your acquaintances. Make a case either for or against its usage.

2. Was there ever a time when doublespeak had an impact on your life? Write a personal narrative reflecting on the effect, positive or negative, that double-speak has had on your experience. You might consider having been swayed by advertising or political jargon.

3. Lutz defines doublespeak as "language which conceals or prevents thought" and "language which pretends to communicate but doesn't." Write an essay describing an experience wherein you used doublespeak. What was your goal in communicating as such? How was doublespeak useful to you in this situation?

4. Over the course of one day, record all the instances of doublespeak you encounter—from ads, TV shows, news articles, films, menus, and so on. (Whenever possible, photocopy or tape these instances.) In a paper, try to classify the different kinds of doublespeak you found. Analyze the different functions of doublespeak and try to determine its effects on the intended audience.

5. Look through a newspaper or magazine for a short and clear discussion of an interesting topic. Then have some fun rewriting the piece entirely in doublespeak.

Answer the &$%#* Question!

Trudy Lieberman

In the previous article, William Lutz describes some of the ways politicians use doublespeak to cloud an issue. But what happens when politicians simply refuse to answer the questions asked of them? As Trudy Lieberman explains, the political interview has become an ineffective exchange in which the politician forces his or her agenda while journalists sit helplessly asking questions that are dodged, redirected, or simply ignored. Trained by professional media-coaches, politicians know how to control an interview to their advantage. And the public, explains Lieberman, is losing out.

Journalist Trudy Lieberman is the director of the Center for Consumer Health Choices at Consumers Union, writing about health policy for *Consumer Reports*. Her writing has appeared regularly in *The Nation* and she writes a health column for the *Los Angeles Times*. She is the author of several books including *Slanting the Story: The Forces That Shape the News* (2000). Lieberman is a contributing editor to the *Columbia Journalism Review*, in which this essay was published in January 2004.

1 Last July, just as the weapons inspector David Kay was about to brief a congressional committee on what he had found in Iraq, National Security Adviser Condoleezza Rice appeared on *Jim Lehrer's NewsHour*.

2 The host, Gwen Ifill, asked whether Kay had given the president new information. Rice said the president told Kay to take his time, search in a comprehensive way, in a way that makes the case and looks at all the evidence and tells us the truth. She added that the president wanted Kay to know that we are patient in finding out. She did not answer the question.

3 Ifill tried again. "So David Kay did not bring the president new information about new discoveries at that meeting yesterday?" Ifill asked. Rice wouldn't budge. "I think that there is a danger in taking a little piece of evidence here, a little piece of evidence there. He is a very respected and capable weapons inspector. He knows how to read the Iraqi programs." Although Rice had avoided the follow-up, Ifill let her continue with the administration's pitch for war, laced with such phrases as "brutal dictator" and "ideologies of hatred."

4 The interview served up no new evidence of weapons of mass destruction, and the exchange between Ifill and Rice illustrated what a CBS correspondent, Steve Hartman, calls the "orchestrated dance where nobody gets at the truth." It's a dance choreographed by media trainers on the one hand and by unwritten and unspoken rules of acceptable journalistic behavior on the other. Television guests tiptoe around the questions while interviewers either lose control or throw out softballs aimed at making sure their subjects will want to come back. Media training, a competitive and growing industry, teaches people all the fancy steps they need to answer the questions they want to answer, not those of an inquisitive reporter. The result: in too many cases, interviews become excuses to practice public relations, and instead of shedding light, they cloud public discourse. The captive public sits and watches the waltz glide by.

5 "About all we interview any more are professional talkers," says Bob Schieffer, who tries to squeeze informational tidbits from those talkers every Sunday on CBS's *Face the Nation*. The professional part, of course, stems from who his guests are, mainly public officials. But it also flows from the teachings of media trainers, a branch of public relations that originated at J. Walter Thompson in the mid-1970s. Media training was largely a dual response to the tough questioning of Mike Wallace and others on *60 Minutes* and the needs of the new business-media outlets that called for a constant stream of corporate executives to chat on the air. Soon other PR firms established media training practices, sensing a lucrative sideline in coaching people to handle tough questions.

6 For $4,000 to $10,000 a day, trainers who are as ethically and intellectually diverse as journalists themselves teach the art of performing for the press. Thirty years ago many members of Congress did not have press secretaries, let alone

coaches to show them how to behave in front of a camera. Today it's a rare public soul who has not been media trained. The risks are higher for the untrained person, says Joyce Newman, who heads The Newman Group, a New York training firm: "Anything seen or said tracks you forever, and can come back to smack you in the face." So politicians, government bureaucrats, and as many as 70 percent of corporate CEOs are taught how to parry reporters' questions and deliver predetermined messages.

7   As journalism has morphed into a cog in a great public relations machine, the fundamental relationship between journalists and their subjects has changed, turning the craft of the interview on its head. Where once journalists took the lead, prepared in depth for interviews, zeroed in on specifics, and connected the dots for their audience, those being questioned now lead the way, coached precisely on how to wrest control. Never assume knowledge on the part of the reporter, trainers counsel, and think of the interview as a collaboration, not a confrontation. To that end, The CommCore Observer, a monthly e-mail sent to clients by The CommCore Consulting Group, one of the country's largest media training firms, advises clients "to prepare for media interviews as if they are educating the reporter. Much like a teacher develops a lesson plan, the interviewee can set context, provide perspective and control the direction of the interview."

8   At a time when the audience makes decisions based on perceptions rather than facts, the goal is to create positive perceptions of companies and their products, politicians and their policies. The techniques, however, are the same, and the effect on the audience is the same as well: the control of information. Journalists are losing that control, says James Carey, a journalism professor at Columbia. "The upper hand has shifted to the public relations apparatus and other groups. People show up on news shows for an explicit avowed political or commercial purpose." They are interested in journalists, Carey maintains, only as a conduit for their own interests and outlook. How they perform that function in the stream of mass communications gets to the nuts and bolts of media training.

Gaining the Upperhand

9   *Taking control.* One of the first rules of media training is to seize control of the interview, and skillful guests can do it from the very beginning.

10   An NPR *Talk of the Nation* program in October, which examined the regulatory efforts of the Food and Drug Administration, showed how it's done. The program host, Korva Coleman, asked Peter Van Doren, an editor at the conservative Cato Institute, whether the FDA's scientific panels ask the right questions when they review scientific data for new drugs and medical devices. "Well, I think so," he said, adding quickly: "What I'd like to talk about is just the mistaken premises that some people have, mostly the public, I think, about what science can or can't do," which launched him into his message about the costs and benefits of regulation and personal choice.

11   When interviewees twist an interview to fit their agenda, they are in effect warning the questioner what to avoid and signaling how they want to structure the questions. Senator John Warner of Virginia did it when he challenged correspondent Andrea Mitchell on NBC's *Meet the Press* last summer. When Mitchell asked him whether the president had sent Iraqis a taunting message to go after U.S.

troops, he replied that it was not a taunting message, and said: "I want to turn to this other thing"—which was a discussion of how other nations were working with the U.S. in Iraq. At another point, Mitchell tried to press him on the hunt for weapons of mass destruction. Warner said he wished his fellow Senator Mark Dayton had not said the U.S. should stop looking for weapons, then he signaled he did not want to linger on that topic, saying to Mitchell, "Let's move on to other matters. I think we've covered this." The conversation moved to security problems in Iraq. Later in the interview Warner was more explicit and asked: "Can we touch Africa?" Mitchell replied: "I want to talk about Africa, exactly," and the interview steered away from a touchy subject: the timetable for stabilizing Iraq.

12   *Dodging the question.* Some media trainers counsel clients not to answer the question that's asked, but instead to give a response that fits with the message they plan to deliver. Others insist that's deceptive and urge clients to at least acknowledge or "satisfy" the question and then steer or bridge to their messages. Being asked if the sky is blue and answering that the grass is green is out of vogue, they say.

13   "You don't have to say what you don't want to say. But you must acknowledge the question," says Davia Temin, president of Temin and Company, a strategic-marketing and crisis-management firm. Saying "no comment," though, is not advised since it's seen as an admission of guilt. Nevertheless, says the longtime New York PR executive Richard Weiner: "There are twenty-seven different ways to avoid the question and twenty-seven ways to say no comment."

14   When guests don't want to answer, they use phrases such as: That's such a complex subject . . . Your question is not relevant . . . You bring up an interesting point, but before I discuss it, I want to talk about. . . . Such dodges serve as a spring-board to the message the guest wants to send. On *Good Morning America* in November Charles Gibson asked General Richard Myers, chairman of the Joint Chiefs of Staff, if he had honestly expected so many soldiers to be in harm's way more than six months after hostilities officially ended. Myers responded not with a yes or no, but with: "You know, the Iraqi situation was complex from the start. I think we knew it was going to be very, very tough. And we've got to take the fight to them." The rest of his answer touched on Iraqis helping the U.S., intelligence, and a newly found weapons cache—a classic example of the satisfy-and-steer tech-nique drummed into every person who undergoes media training.

15   *Telling a story.* The best way to answer questions is to tell a story, says Bill McGowan, whose firm, Biomentary, of Dobbs Ferry, New York, trains business executives. Telling a story eats up time, precludes a follow-up, and supports your message.

16   Virgil Scudder, an avuncular figure who has been in the training business almost from the beginning, also believes in the tell-a-story pedagogy. "Winners come in with a story to tell and know how to tell it; losers just answer questions," he says. "Answering questions is like paying a toll on the toll road. You have to do it, but you're there to take a trip." The best trips offer anecdotes, examples, and third-party proof such as polls and words from significant historians or even *The New York Times*.

17   Once the story is told, says Jerry Doyle, CommCore's senior vice president, never "break back into jail"—that is, never repeat or return to the original question,

which may invite reporters to stay on a line of questioning you want to avoid. Instead, provide context, which can disarm the questioner.

18   *Spreading the word.* "The evidence of a good interview is not just getting out alive, it's what gets repeated," says Doyle. "Good politicians can see the headlines as they are saying them. They know what survives the editor's knife." In other words, they are trained to speak in compelling sound bites that have a chance of recirculating the next day, thus reinforcing the basic message being sold. In early November Defense Secretary Donald Rumsfeld appeared on *Fox News Sunday*. The host, Tony Snow, observed that the Iraqi people didn't like being occupied and wanted U.S. troops out sooner rather than later. Rumsfeld said he had seen polls suggesting that the Iraqis were worried the U.S. would leave too soon, and then moved into his sound bite for the next day's paper. "I agree with you, foreign troops in a country are unnatural. And the goal is not to keep them there. The goal is to keep them there only as long as they're needed and not one day longer." Sure enough, in the next day's *New York Times*, Rumsfeld's quote appeared in a page one story discussing the challenges the president faces in bringing stability to Iraq and maintaining public support.

19   *Answering the easy part.* When journalists ask a two-part question, it's a gift to the guest, who will rarely answer both parts. Coaches advise clients to tackle the easy question and go on at some length. That way the interviewer can't remind them that they didn't answer the other question, which is left hanging for the audience. Last September on CNN Paula Zahn interviewed Governor George Pataki of New York. Zahn observed that there were some strong allegations that the Bush administration through the EPA had misled New Yorkers about air quality after 9/11. "Is there anything you can say that will help make the population any more comfortable? And were New Yorkers misled?" Zahn asked. Pataki did not seem interested in challenging the EPA. He answered only the first part of Zahn's question. "We relied on the EPA's analysis," Pataki said. "And I know right now, the city and the federal government are conducting a joint investigation into the health consequences. It is something that we have to be concerned about."

20   *Pitching platitudes.* When guests send out platitudes—that is, say nice things about the people they may ultimately criticize or appear to disagree with on the air— media trainers say there's really subtle communication that's taking place. When Condoleezza Rice calls David Kay "a very respected and capable weapons inspector," when Senator John Warner refers to General Ricardo Sanchez as a "very fine and able officer"and to Senator Richard Lugar as "my distinguished friend and chairman," they are really sending a signal: don't look further for conflict between us. Such platitudes are a necessary thing in politics, says CommCore's Doyle. If they're missing from the conversation, the reporter might get suspicious and look deeper.

Journalists Play the Game

21 Increasingly, follow-up questions, which ideally should plug the gaps in an answer, are becoming casualties in the verbal joust between journalists and their well-trained guests, and too often softball questions have replaced hardball. Virgil Scudder observes what his profession has wrought: "The biggest failing of reporters today is not pinning down or following up. And they will ask a question too loosely constructed. It leaves too large a hole to go through." Sometimes the hole is so large, the

guest isn't sure how to respond. In an interview last summer with Deputy Secretary of State Richard Armitage, Fox's Greta Van Susteren said she wanted to ask him about North Korea. Her question: "All right, what about North Korea?" Armitage replied: "A bad situation. What about it?" Van Susteren answered: "Well, what are we going to do about it, if anything?"

22   While open-ended questions allow guests to start talking, they also offer them a broad platform to hawk their messages. Corporate executives can drive right through such questions as: What's your biggest challenge? How did you achieve those great earnings? Why is marketing changing? Politicians can do the same when interviewers ask: How do you explain that? Is there something to that? What about the charge that the president has politicized this whole issue? Emphasizing the point, Scudder says "most business interviews are extremely supportive and a piece of cake." Questions with obvious answers provide yet another venue for message peddling. When the *NewsHour* correspondent Jeffrey Brown asks the administrator of NASA if the culture of his agency can be fixed, is it a surprise when he replies "Oh, absolutely" and goes on with his pitch? When Paula Zahn asks Senator Joseph Lieberman to respond to Barbara Bush's comments "that you and your Democratic colleagues are a pretty sorry group," does she really expect him to say, Yes we are? Of course Lieberman said they weren't and moved to an attack on the president.

23   There are many reasons for the lack of follow-up questions. News interviews are brief and interviewers may have four or five questions the show's producer expects them to ask. Extra questions may mean the interviewer can't stick to a pre-determined script, perhaps leading to second-guessing by higher ups. With broadcast organizations now profitable members of business conglomerates, interviewers may be unsure how far they can go. One media trainer says that in the time of Edward R. Murrow and Fred Friendly, journalists could bully their guests because they knew CBS was behind them. "They can't be as abusive as they used to be," she says. So unwritten rules now dictate acceptable behavior. Ask questions too harshly, and you're outside the club. Says Columbia's Carey: "These people are not adversaries who pretend to be friends. They are friends who pretend to be adversaries." Bob Schieffer explains, "You don't want to appear rude even though the guest can be filibustering and killing time, and you can't ask what you want." Schieffer's colleague Steve Hartman says interviewers must be careful not to cut the guest off too soon or "you're going to be perceived as someone who has a bias. Everyone is concerned about how they come across in this game." They also know unhappy guests can complain. Indeed, The CommCore Observer suggests that clients meet with editors "when a reporter is not being fair or balanced." If journalists stray out of bounds, they risk embarrassment or ostracism, like one reporter at a White House press conference in early October who asked press secretary Scott McClellan five times whether the Bush administration had a double standard when it came to investigating leaks—until an exasperated McClellan cut him off, effectively signaling: I've had enough of your behavior. Says Ronald Sims, a business professor at The College of William and Mary: "The good questioners are marginalized. Everyone knows the bulldog that doesn't let go. Word gets around. Colleagues give looks. There are unwritten rules that this is not how you act so you go with the flow." Few questioners want to be known as a bulldog. The hot guests, the "big gets" as they are known in the business, will go elsewhere. Few PR executives want to book someone

on a show where the interviewer has a reputation for rough questioning. Most would rather have their clients interviewed by Larry King than by Mike Wallace.

24   Even when journalists do ask follow-ups, they rarely ask more than one. Three times is pushing it, says Schieffer. "You can't ask a question four times. It's obvious you're not going to get an answer, and it becomes boring." But is it boring, or does it cause the viewer to question the guest's credibility? Last May on *Good Morning America*, FBI director Robert Mueller refused to give any hard evidence for recommending that the U.S. go on high terror alert. Diane Sawyer tried a follow-up question suggesting that by not answering the question the agency was perhaps playing down the warning after all. Mueller shot back: "Well, I wouldn't put words in my mouth." Then in an unusual on-air admission Sawyer gave up: "I know when I've been beaten on a question and a follow-up," she said.

25   Follow-up questions do fail to draw out new information when well-trained guests dodge them as easily as the initial question, and even interviewers like Sawyer give up before eliciting a real answer. On *Saturday Today* shortly before the California recall election, host Campbell Brown asked Arnold Schwarzenegger's spokesman Sean Walsh how he defined movie-set rowdiness—which is how Schwarzenegger had described his sexual escapades with women. Walsh didn't say, replying that his boss was putting out a "message of hope and opportunity." Brown politely said that she knew all that and asked the same question again, adding, "What is okay in his view in terms of what many women seem to have interpreted as sexual harassment?" This time Walsh said that if Schwarzenegger had been "either bawdy or inappropriate or giving people hugs, that that is not something that he is going to be doing in the future," and eased into his message: "The bottom line here, from this perspective is, what are we going to do for California's future?" Brown did not ask the obvious follow-up: Is groping women the same as giving people hugs?'

26   Reporters at times do follow up with pointed questions that clarify an issue, especially when the guest answers them forthrightly. When General Wesley Clark told Aaron Brown on *CNN's News Night* in August that the U.S. entry into Iraq involved a "classic presidential-level misjudgment," Brown quickly followed up. "What was the misjudgment?" Clark told him that the president had misjudged that going to war in Iraq would solve the war on terror, adding, "Seems to me that the only terrorists we're finding there are the ones who have come back in to attack us since we arrived."

27   Certainly, there are some strong interviewers in the business. On a *60 Minutes* segment in October, Lesley Stahl noted that the government's policy of giving tax breaks for buying SUVs for work purposes was encouraging people to buy the big, gas-guzzling vehicles. When Stahl said you could almost buy the whole car for the amount of the tax break, Secretary of Energy Spencer Abraham said he would not concede that was the case. That's when Stahl said there was evidence to show that's how the tax credit was being used. Abraham admitted: "Well, I don't know. We'll have to wait and see what happens." Stahl's pursuit revealed to viewers the administration's policy of supporting tax breaks for gas-guzzlers while doing little to pressure carmakers to build more fuel-efficient SUVs.

28   But in my examination of some fifty news transcripts, sharp questioning is unusual, raising the larger question of what the audience takes away when journalism

appears to be little more than disguised public relations. Does the audience see through the culture of caution and obfuscation that permeates the news business? When TV guests practice question evasion, does the audience think twice about their credibility? Does the public see through polished answers and the platitudinous comments? Does it ask where the real meat and potatoes are?

29   Such questions bring up others: What are journalists for? Are they to analyze and interpret the news and arbitrate conflicting opinion for the public, or are they to act as mere carriers of other people's messages?

30   It's no secret that journalism has a credibility gap. Maybe it has always and by journalists who try less and less to close it.

THINKING CRITICALLY

1. Lieberman outlines the tactics that politicians use to "seize control" of an interview. What are they? After thoughtfully considering each tactic rank them according to which ones pose the greatest threat to the public.

2. According to Lieberman, why are interviews with politicians merely "excuses to practice public relations"? How have journalists lost control? What are the long-term ramifications of this shift in the balance of power between interviewer and interviewee? Explain.

3. How do you think one of the media coaches described in this essay would respond to Lieberman's points? What arguments might they present?

4. Lieberman ends her essay with two questions: What are journalists for? Are they to analyze and interpret the news and arbitrate conflicting opinion for the public, or are they to act as mere carriers of other people's messages? Answer her questions with your own viewpoint.

5. Who do you think the audience for this essay was? Who was it written for— journalists? propagandists? politicians? the general public? What did the author assume about her readers' viewpoints, media experiences, and social/political backgrounds?

6. Why do journalists "back off" instead of asking tough questions or repeating a question dodged by a politician during an interview. If you were a journalist with an important question you felt deserved an answer, what would you do if the subject of your interview avoided your question? Explain.

WRITING ASSIGNMENTS

1. In this essay, Lieberman points out that most politicians prefer to be interviewed by Larry King rather than by Mike Wallace. Watch several interviews conducted by a journalist with a local or national politician and evaluate the speech dynamic in each interview, noting the journalists' interview style, the subject matter under discussion, and the politician's willingness to answer questions. How do your observations compare to the claims Lieberman makes in her essay regarding the decline of the political interview?

2. Some of the most interesting examples of political language come from campaign debates. Find a campaign speech from either a local or national figure and evaluate it for the political double-talk and avoidance tactics described by some of the authors in this section. You can find transcripts of presidential debates at www.debates.org/pages/debtrans.html. Discuss your research in an essay.

Exploring the Language of **V I S U A L S**

Presidential Television Ads

Featured here are two campaign ads for the 2004 presidential race. While both feature John Kerry, one is approved by the John Kerry for President effort, the other by the Bush-Cheney campaign. After reviewing the ads, consider the questions that follow.

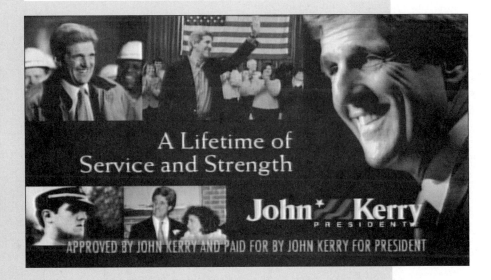

The Record

98 votes for
tax increases

APPROVED BY PRESIDENT BUSH AND PAID FOR BY BUSH-CHENEY '04, INC.

THINKING CRITICALLY

1. Who is the target audience for each ad? How does each ad appeal to the viewer?

2. Both ads feature the image of John Kerry, although one ad is for the Bush-Cheney campaign. In your opinion, is there any risk in featuring John Kerry in a Bush-Cheney campaign ad? Why or why not? Consider the image and language the ad uses in your response.

3. If you were an undecided voter and saw both of these ads, would either one influence your vote? Encourage you to seek more information? Explain.

4. What images does the John Kerry ad include, and how do these images convey a message? What is that message? Explain.

> **MAKING CONNECTIONS**
>
> 1. Locate a political speech from a gubernatorial or presidential candidate. After carefully reading the speech, try to summarize what the candidate is promising the public if he or she is elected to office. In what ways does the politician tap into common ideology to connect with voters? Is any doublespeak used in the speech? Explain.
>
> 2. Compare some of the points made in "How to Detect Propaganda" with William Lutz's article, "With These Words, I Can Sell You Anything," and Charles O'Neill's article, "The Language of Advertising," both in Chapter 6. How are Lutz's "weasel words" similar to the propagandist's attempts to appeal to emotion that the Institute's authors identify? Do you think the Institute's authors would agree with O'Neill that the propaganda of advertising uses language in a way that is special or different from everyday use?
>
> 3. Try creating some political language of your own. Imagine you are running for office—president, senator, mayor, or school committee. Using some of the features and tricks of political language discussed in this section, write a campaign speech outlining why you, and not your opponent, should be elected. Have the class critique your speech.
>
> 4. Find political speeches from a recent campaign, either local or national. Try the CNN's political pages at www.allpolitics.com or do a Google search for recent political speeches. Select one and try to identify the ways it manipulates language to sway the public.

CASE STYDY: WARSPEAK–LANGUAGE AND CONFLICT

Fighting Words: The War over Language

Jon Hooten

Our everyday language is liberally sprinkled with the language of war—we "defend" our positions, "wage price wars" at discount stores, and "battle" termite "invasions." We get "bombed" or "blitzed" at parties. Perhaps we are so free with war language because over half the population has yet to experience a true war firsthand. But as we become more removed from the original meanings of the language of war, are we in danger of blurring metaphorical issues with ones of great consequence for humanity?

Jon Hooten is an educational administrator in the School of Communication at the University of Denver. He frequently writes on culture, religion, and environmental issues. This essay first appeared in the September 2002 issue of the online magazine *PopPolitics*.

1 Mine—perhaps, ours—is the first American generation that has yet to experience a full-blown, machine-gun shooting, prisoner-taking, horror-story war.

2 We youngsters sit wide-eyed while our shaky grandfathers and crusty uncles tell tales of enemy occupation, dead buddies, pretty gals and the joy of a fresh Lucky Strike on a rainy afternoon. To those born in the late 1960s and beyond, Nazis are nothing but cultural extremists (of the "femi-" or "soup" varieties), Vietnam makes a good setting for a summer blockbuster, and the Battle of the Bulge is a corny baby boomer punch line. Simply, the realities of the nation's major wars have been lost on one—going on two and three—generations of Americans.

3 That's not to say that my generation has not lived through skirmishes, conflicts and appalling battles. Those of us sitting in high school during the winter of 1991 watched the air strikes on Baghdad through the glassy eyes of CNN, with Peter Arnett and Wolf Blitzer calling the play-by-play. As Desert Storm eventually became known as the "Gulf War," many of us wondered if this was the future of the genre that we had read about in 11th grade-history class.

4 From now on, it seemed, war would be a few nights of superpower smart-bombing and long-range tanks lobbing shells into ragtag militias commanded by egomaniacal dictators. It hardly seemed worthy of the designation "war."

5 Those of us who grew up after Vietnam simply cannot comprehend the dread that shaped older generations of Americans. Our experience of the Gulf War was an acutely sterile encounter. We watched replays of laser-guided missiles entering bunker windows, but seldom were we exposed to the sights of actual human collateral. Though tens—hundreds—of thousands of Iraqi casualties resulted, the televised images of precision war games grossly outnumbered the news clips of war's grisly human cost. Since many of us have not experienced the sights and sounds of war firsthand, we think about war rather thoughtlessly.

6 In our lack of true wartime experience, American culture has learned to deploy the images of war rather casually. The words of war were once the moral and emotional defense of the nation, corresponding with the real memories and motivations of an embattled citizenry. As war became less messy and more distant, the language of war invaded the common lexicon of America. Though you may have never noticed it, the extraordinary metaphor of war has infiltrated our quotidian use of language. (Can you count how many times "war words" are fired at you in this very paragraph?)

7 Our popular culture thinks nothing of invoking the language of conflict to describe most any topic. Pick up the morning's paper and browse through the headlines: "Mayor Defends New Budget." "Media *Blitz* Saves Kidnapped Girl." "Farmers *Battle* Summer Drought." "Browser *War* Heats Up." "Champ's Left Hook Right *on Target*."

8 Consider, for instance, the numerous ways in which the word 'bomb' is used: "Frat brothers get bombed on a Saturday night." "Your new car is 'the bomb.'" "Did you see that comedian bomb on Letterman last night?" "The quarterback threw a long bomb to win the game."

9 While we have haphazardly sprinkled our language with war's metaphors, is it possible that we have collectively forgotten how to think clearly about the literal

phenomenon? Can the collective linguistic turn from the literal to the metaphorical be without consequence?

10   Throughout history, wars have usually followed a certain pattern: They have generally involved elaborate, enduring campaigns between at least two somewhat equal forces; they have resulted in mass casualties; and—this is the most important part—they have some sort of *conclusion*. Common sense would agree with this characterization, at least in the conventional sense of the phenomenon.

11   With this definition in mind, the latter half of the twentieth century has seen a proliferation of non-war-like wars. The war on poverty that Lyndon Johnson waged in the 1960s was an elaborate public policy initiative. The war on drugs that swelled in the 1970s and 1980s became a tsunami of agencies, non-profit organizations, police action and international diplomacy. The Cold War, fought with national ideologies, economic posturing and infinite defense budgets, festered without any combat or mass casualties (at least among the superpowers) throughout the latter half of the twentieth century before finally coming to a head in the mid-1980s.

12   Now, after a decade's respite of new wars, we have another one on our hands: the war on terrorism.

13   After that inconceivable morning in September 2001, our media-sated political culture was quick to place the blame on those radicals who have become known as "the terrorists." Soon after, the "war on terror" was a go. President Bush promptly assembled his posse to round up the scoundrels who had done this—"Wanted," we were told by the president, "dead or alive." The weeks and months following that day were a slow and deliberate escalation of the war on terrorism, beginning internally with beefed up airports and FBI round-ups, then spreading—in a violent and explicit way—abroad in Afghanistan.

14   For several weeks, while the United States bombed that impoverished nation, the "war on terrorism" became known as the "war on Afghanistan." Quickly, this new war began to look like a war that the president's father fought ten years earlier. Though similar to the Gulf War in many ways, the mission in Afghanistan was very different. While Bush the Elder relied heavily on turkey-shoot combat fought from above, George W. sent in massive numbers of ground troops to hunt down "the evil ones."

15   A wobbly alliance with the locals in Afghanistan was also formed, so that fewer body bags would be sent back to the States full of our brothers and sisters. (Who knows how many Northern Alliance fighters were buried in their native soil.) And while his father had the modest goal of expelling Iraqi forces from Kuwait, Bush the Younger had grander plans of rounding up all the Al Qaeda and Taliban evil-doers he could find.

16   After the fighting in Afghanistan simmered down, and the immediate goal of capturing top terrorists was not met, the popular rhetoric of national affairs shifted away from geographic specifics to the more general "war on terrorism." No longer involving specific battles or well-defined goals, this war quickly began to look similar to other drawn-out wars with which my generation *is* familiar.

17   In 1981, first lady Nancy Reagan boldly advised us first-graders to "Just Say No to Drugs." (Abbie Hoffman is widely reported to have said, "To tell a drug addict to 'just say no' is like telling a manic depressive to 'just cheer up.'") Soon after, President Reagan instigated the all-out war on druggies. By 1988, the Anti-Drug Abuse

Act had set its national sights on both the supply and demand of illegal substances in the United States. Though the DEA had been on the scene since 1973, the Reagans took seriously the evil scourge that they saw infecting America's children. The war on drugs was born, has thrived for more than 15 years, and continues in 2002 with an overall federal budget of $19.2 billion.

18   Last time I checked, however, people still buy and use drugs with relative ease. Though the statistics of drug use wax and wane like a Santa Cruz tide, it is safe to say that the war on drugs has not been won. What's more, the war is not a winnable affair. The war on drugs is a war on a perpetual opponent. Unlike a conventional war, there will be no Normandy or Hiroshima, no crucial turning point or day of victory when all the pot heads and speed freaks will finally surrender.

19   Returning to our definition above, there is no doubt that the war on drugs largely fits the characterization of conventional war. The national strategy has certainly been a strategic battle of wits between two equally matched opponents (as the drug complex still manages to outfox the government with regularity and sophistication). This war has also lasted for more than two decades, and nobody doubts that real casualties have ensued, both domestically and abroad. The question remains, however, if this war will in fact ever come to completion. Can it be won?

20   If we put our heads to it, we will quickly recognize that a "war" of this type is nothing but a grand metaphor, a riding crop with which to whip patriotic Americans into action. In the case of the drug war, the United States has moved from metaphor to militarized efforts in the attempt to alter human habits. While these symbolic, rhetorical wars may seem to have few negative consequences, the conjuring of war's images, passions and emotions has real damaging effects. We are racing toward a finish line that doesn't exist.

21   The language of war, in all its urgency and obligation, will always motivate the patriotic and righteous. The metaphor necessarily creates an enemy, which, when characterized as such, becomes equally entrenched in the language of offense and defense. At its dark heart, a war demands division and opposition. Right vs. wrong. Good vs. evil.

22   Like the war on drugs, the war on terrorism is another overarching metaphor. Terrorism, like drug use, is an act unique to humanity, an action which will be with us for a long time. To war against terrorism is to war against an enemy that does not exist in only one place, that cannot be controlled by laws, that will perpetually be reborn in creative and cunning ways. Terrorism grows out of the fecund social and cultural and economic and religious and psychological slough that is civilization. Like the drug war, the war on terrorism can never be won.

23   By definition, terrorism is a concept or category that describes human actions. In most any dictionary, you will find no examples of what terrorism must be in order to be considered as such. In the dictionary, you will not find "hostage-taking," "suicide-bombing" and "the throwing of Molotov cocktails" under the definition of terrorism. Rather, you will find it described as systematic and violent acts to advance political ends. To war against terrorism, therefore, is to war against a classification, a description, in essence, a word.

24   How can bombs be dropped on a word?

25   At this point, you may be wondering, Doesn't this guy know that the war on terrorism is actually a war on *terrorists?* That it is a war on their weapons supply, their finances, their training camps and the axis of evil that harbors them? Doesn't he realize that this exercise in logic has nothing to do with the reality of reality?

26   Well, yes. And no. I am well aware that acts of terrorism do not commit themselves. Of course, terrorism requires the personnel, training and weapons that make violence possible; limiting all of that should therefore logically decrease the instances of terrorist acts. However, the United States must realize that this war— while focused against terrorists, their weapons, etc.—is shaped and fought through the way we speak and write about it.

27   Fighting terrorism is different than fighting cavities. It is not a localized menace that can be brushed away, drilled or filled. On Sept. 9, 2001—two days before the events that sparked the Bush's new war—Alan Block wrote in *Pravda,* "When the metaphorical use of the term [war] is common and seldom challenged, resistance to actual war becomes more difficult and uncommon." Eventually, the verbal sparring becomes literal bombing.

28   When we generalize about the evils of terrorism, we shroud the faces, politics and religion behind the acts. That which motivates the militants has become opaqued by the wordiness of bumper sticker aphorisms and campaign stump speeches. While the war on terrorism has set its sights on the perpetrators and mechanisms therein, it has ignored that which initially provokes the violence. As a damning result, the evil, as it were, will always be with us. As long as the seeds of terrorism—ignorance, injustice, exploitation—are perpetually planted by the careless hand of the superpowers, the weeds of violence will continue to steal nutrients from the fruits of civilization.

29   Politicians, prosecutors and preachers alike invoke moving imagery of cosmic battles of good and evil. Yet, many public figures use this language in knowingly figurative ways. I get the sense, though, that President Bush takes seriously his war on evil, that with enough bombs, with plenty of firepower, and if the right people can be killed, then the axis of evil will fall. He does not seem to realize that evil is perennial, that the death of one season's crops will only fertilize the next season's seedlings. By creating martyrs of the evil-doers, he is signing the marching orders of their followers and inspiring a new impassioned generation of freedom fighters.

30   I would like nothing more than to eradicate the horror that is terrorism . . . along with poverty, hunger, ecocide and oppression. But invoking the language of war does more damage than it prevents. To war against anything will eventually allow the metaphors to become realities. If the twentieth century has taught us anything, it is that words have consequences. Words persuade, encourage and tyrannize. They convey power, passion and persecution. When we invoke the language of war, figurative battles against finances become literal battles against financiers. Symbolic warfare against weapons supplies becomes bloody warfare against weapons suppliers. While we arm ourselves for war, the roots of the violence go ignored, growing deeper into the fertile soils of culture and power.

31   In a famous article that was widely distributed on the Internet just before the first Gulf War, linguist George Lakoff wrote, "It is important to distinguish what is

metaphorical from what is not. Pain, dismemberment, death, starvation, and the death and injury of loved ones are not metaphorical." Lakoff would agree that acts based on a metaphor will mirror the metaphor. Warring words will become warring deeds. Clearly, the metaphorical war on terrorism might just become a very real attack on Iraq, with real casualties and consequences.

32   When war is accepted in any form, it can be accepted in all forms. Oscar Wilde wrote in 1891, "As long as war is regarded as wicked, it will always have its fascination. When it is looked upon as vulgar, it will cease to be popular." Only when we choose to not invoke the words of war to address social ills will we begin to solve the problems that lead to violence. More often than not, we are our own worst enemy.

THINKING CRITICALLY

1. How does the fact that generations born after 1970 have not experienced a "full-blown" war influence their use of the "language of war"?

2. At the end of paragraph 6, Hooten asks his readers to count how many "war words" he has used. Identify these words, and discuss how these words have become mainstream in our regular speech.

3. In what ways, according to Hooten, has the pop-culture use of war words influenced our thinking about the "war on terrorism"? Explain.

4. What is the author's tone in this piece? What is he trying to achieve by writing this essay? Explain.

5. According to Hooten, how have the wars of the last twenty years been "nothing but grand metaphors"? Do you agree with his assertions? Explain.

6. In paragraph 23, Hooten states, "By definition, terrorism is a concept or category that describes human actions. . . . To war against terrorism, therefore, is to war against a classification, a description, a word." What does Hooten mean by this statement? How does he qualify his claim in the paragraphs that follow?

7. In paragraph 9, Hooten asks, "is it possible that we have collectively forgotten how to think clearly about the literal phenomenon [of war]?" Write a response to his question, presenting your own perspective, while addressing some of the points Hooten raises in his essay.

Terrorism and the English Language
Deroy Murdoch

How does language affect how we interpret, react to, and even remember acts of terrorism? In the next essay, writer Deroy Murdoch challenges that when we use "detached language" to describe acts of terrorism and murder, we make it easier to forget that America is at war with people who want to kill us. We also dilute the impact of the loss of life on September 11, 2001, and the true issues we face when dealing with terrorism.

Deroy Murdock is a nationally syndicated columnist. His column, "This Opinion Just In . . .," appears in newspapers nationally, including the *Washington Times*, the *New York Post*, and the *Orange County Register*. He also is a contributing editor with *National Review Online* and has appeared on ABC's *Nightline*, *NBC Nightly News*, CNN, Fox News Channel, and C-SPAN. Murdock, a member of the Council on Foreign Relations, presented this lecture as part of the Heritage Foundations program on Homeland Security on March 9, 2005. The Heritage Foundation is a research and educational institute whose mission is to "formulate and promote conservative public policies based on the principles of free enterprise, limited government, individual freedom, traditional American values, and a strong national defense."

1 I live on Manhattan Island and vividly recall watching Mohamed Atta fly American Airlines Flight 11 right over my apartment balcony in the East Village on the morning of September 11, 2001. The horror, sadness, and fear of that rotten day quickly unfolded and remain palpable even now.

2 Yet within a week, some incredibly detached language emerged to describe what happened on 9/11. Consider this message that Verizon left in my voice mail box on September 19: "During this time of crisis, we are asking all customers to review and delete all current and saved messages that are not essential," a nameless female announcer stated. "This request is necessary due to extensive damage that was recently sustained in the World Trade Center district."

3 Time of crisis? Did a tidal wave cause the "recently sustained" wreckage in Manhattan? Similarly, a company called Tullet & Tokyo Liberty referred to "the disaster that has hit New York and Washington."

4 The use of the passive voice in these and similar instances suggested that the World Trade Center and Pentagon were smashed by unguided, perhaps natural, forces.

5 Kinko's was even more elliptical. Shortly after the massacre, the photocopying company placed in its stores some very colorful posters with the Stars and Stripes superimposed upon an outline of the lower 48 states. The graphic also included this regrettable caption: "The Kinko's family extends our condolences and sympathies to all Americans who have been affected by the circumstances in New York City, Washington, D.C., and Pennsylvania."

6 Circumstances? That word describes an electrical blackout, not terrorist bloodshed.

7 Likewise, I kept hearing that people "died" in the Twin Towers or at the Pentagon. No, people "die" in hospitals, often surrounded by their loved ones while doctors and nurses offer aid and comfort. The innocent people at the World Trade Center, the Defense Department, and that field in Shanksville, Pennsylvania, were killed in a carefully choreographed act of mass murder.

A Terrorist by Any Other Name

8 The more this passive, weak, euphemistic language appeared as the war on terrorism began, the more I thought it was vital to pay close attention to the words, symbols, and images that govern this new and urgent conflict.

9 The civilized world today faces the most anti-Semitic enemy since Adolf Hitler and Josef Goebbels committed suicide in Berlin nearly 60 years ago. Militant Islam is the most bloodthirsty ideology since the Khmer Rouge eliminated one-third of

Cambodia's people. The big difference, of course, is that Pol Pot had the good manners to keep his killing fields within his own borders, as awful as that was.

10   Islamo-fascism is a worldwide phenomenon that already has touched this country and many of our allies. Yet Muslim extremists rarely have armies we can see, fighter jets we can knock from the sky, or an easily identifiable headquarters, such as the Reichs Chancellery of the 1940s or the Kremlin of the Cold War.

11   While basketball players and their fans battle each other on TV, actresses suffer wardrobe malfunctions, and rap singers scream sweet nothings in our ears, it is very easy to forget that Islamic extremists plot daily to end all of that and more by killing as many of us as possible.

12   Language can lull Americans to sleep in this new war, or it can keep us on the offensive and our enemies off balance. Here are a few suggestions to keep Americans alert to the dangers Islamic terrorism poses to this country:

13   September 11 was an attack—not just a series of coincidental strokes and heart failures that wiped out so many victims at once.

14   Victims of terrorism do not "die," nor are they "lost." They are killed, murdered, or slaughtered. We should be specific about the number of people terrorists kill. "Three thousand" killed on 9/11 sounds like an amorphous blob. The actual number—2,977—forces us to look at these people as individuals with faces, stories, and loved ones who miss them very much.

15   The precise figures are: 2,749 killed at the World Trade Center, 184 at the Pentagon, and 44 in Shanksville, Pennsylvania. Likewise, the Bali disco bombings killed 202 people, mainly Australians. The Madrid train bombings killed 191 men, women, and children.

16   Somehow, a total of 191 people killed by al-Qaeda's pals seems more ominous and concrete than a smoothly rounded 200.

17   Terrorists do not simply "threaten" us, nor is homeland security supposed to shield Americans from "future attacks." All of this is true, but it is more persuasive if we acknowledge what these people have done and hope to do once more—wipe us out.

18   Representative James Sensenbrenner (R-WI), chairman of the House Judiciary Committee, said this on *NBC Nightly News* last Sunday: "We need to tighten up our drivers' license provisions and our immigration laws so that terrorists cannot take advantage of the present system to kill thousands of Americans again." That is a perfect sound bite. There is no vague talk about "the terrorist threat" or "stopping further attacks." Sensenbrenner concisely explained exactly what is at risk, and what needs to be thwarted—no more killing of Americans by the thousands again.

19   Quote Islamo-fascist leaders to remind people of their true intentions. President George W. Bush, Heritage Foundation President Ed Feulner, or Deroy Murdock can talk about how deadly militant Islam is and how seriously we should take this gravely dangerous ideology. Far more persuasive, however, is to let these extremists do the talking.

20   However, their words are nowhere as commonly known as they should be. For instance, Osama bin Laden and Ayman al-Zawahiri said in their 1998 declaration of war on the United States: "The ruling to kill all Americans and their

allies—civilian and military—is an individual duty for every Muslim who can do it in any country in which it is possible to do it."

21   The late Iranian dictator, Ayatollah Ruhollah Khomeini, put it this way in 1980: "Our struggle is not about land or water . . . . It is about bringing, by force if necessary, the whole of mankind onto the right path." Ever the comedian, he said this in 1986: "Allah did not create man so that he could have fun. The aim of creation was for mankind to be put to the test through hardship and prayer. An Islamic regime must be serious in every field. There are no jokes in Islam. There is no humor in Islam. There is no fun in Islam. There can be no fun and joy in whatever is serious."

22   Asked what he would say to the loved ones of the 202 people killed in the October 2002 Bali nightclub bombings, Abu Bakar Bashir, leader of Indonesia's radical Jemaah Islamiyah, replied, "My message to the families is, please convert to Islam as soon as possible."

23   The phrase "weapons of mass destruction" (WMD) has been pounded into meaninglessness. It has been repeated ad infinitum. Fairly or unfairly, the absence of warehouses full of anthrax and nerve gas in Iraq has made the whole idea of "WMD" sound synonymous with "L-I-E."

24   America's enemies do not plot the "mass destruction" of empty office buildings or abandoned parking structures. Conversely, they want to see packed office buildings ablaze as their inhabitants scream for mercy. That is why I use the terms "weapons of mass death" and "weapons of mass murder."

25   When speaking about those who are killed by terrorists, be specific, name them, and tell us about them. Humanize these individuals. They are more than just statistics or stick figures.

26   I have written 18 articles and produced a Web page, HUSSEINand TERROR.com, to demonstrate that Saddam Hussein did have ties to terrorism. (By the way, I call him "Saddam Hussein" or "Hussein." I never call him "Saddam" any more than I call Joseph Stalin "Joseph" or Adolf Hitler "Adolf." "Saddam" has a cute, one-name ring to it, like Cher, Gallagher, Liberace, or Sting. Saddam Hussein does not deserve such a term of endearment.)

27   To show that Saddam Hussein's support of terrorism cost American lives, I remind people about the aid and comfort he gave to terrorism master Abu Nidal. Among Abu Nidal's victims in the 1985 bombing of Rome's airport was John Buonocore, a 20-year-old exchange student from Delaware. Palestinian terrorists fatally shot Buonocore in the back as he checked in for his flight. He was heading home after Christmas to celebrate his father's 50th birthday.

28   In another example, those killed by Palestinian homicide bombers subsidized by Saddam Hussein were not all Israeli, which would have been unacceptable enough. Among the 12 or more Americans killed by those Baathist-funded murderers was Abigail Litle, the 14-year-old daughter of a Baptist minister. She was blown away aboard a bus in Haifa on March 5, 2003. Her killer's family got a check for $25,000 courtesy of Saddam Hussein as a bonus for their son's "martyrdom."

29   Is all of this designed to press emotional buttons? You bet it is. Americans must remain committed—intellectually and emotionally—to this struggle. There are many ways to engage the American people. No one should hesitate to remind Americans that terrorism kills our countrymen—at home and abroad—and that those

whom militant Islam demolishes include promising young people with bright futures, big smiles, and, now, six feet of soil between them and their dreams.

Who Are We Fighting? Militants? Martyrs? Insurgents?

30 Melinda Bowman of Brief Hill, Pennsylvania, wrote this in a November 24 letter to the editor of the *Wall Street Journal*: "And, by the way, what is all this 'insurgent' nonsense? These people kidnap, behead, dismember and disembowel. They are terrorists." Nicely and accurately put, Ms. Bowman.

31   Is this a war on terror, per se? A war on terrorism? Or is it really a war on Islamo-fascism? It is really the latter, and we should say so.

32   Jim Guirard runs the TrueSpeak Institute in Washington, D.C. He has thought long and hard about terrorism and the English language. He informed me Tuesday—to my horror—that three years into the war on terrorism, the State Department and the CIA have yet to produce a glossary of the Arabic-language words that Middle Eastern terrorists use, as well as the antonyms for those words. Such a "Thesaurus of Terrorism" would help us linguistically to turn the war on terrorism upside down.

33   Why, for instance, do we inadvertently praise our enemies by agreeing that they fight a jihad or "holy war"? Why not correctly describe them as soldiers in a hirabah or "unholy war"?

A Weapon at the Ready

34 In closing, I would say that America and the rest of civilization can and must win this new twilight struggle against these bloodthirsty cavemen. We can and we will crush them through espionage, high-tech force, statecraft, and public diplomacy overseas.

35   Here at home, we can and will vanquish them through eternal vigilance. One of our chief weapons should be something readily available to each and every one of us—the English language.

THINKING CRITICALLY

1. Murdoch recalls his reaction to the terrorist attack on New York on September 11. To what words and phrases later used to describe the event does he object and why?

2. What words does Murdoch use to describe the terrorist attacks on 9/11 and the "dangers Islamic terrorism posses to this country"?

3. In paragraph 14, Murdoch explains the importance of numerical accuracy when describing the lives lost due to terrorism. Do you agree with his position? Why or why not?

4. What is Murdoch's objective in this essay? What does he hope to persuade his audience to do as a result of his argument?

5. Murdoch offers several suggestions on how we should use language to describe acts of terrorism and terrorists. Identify these suggestions and express your opinion about them.

6. In paragraph 26, why does Murdoch refuse to call Saddam Hussein "Saddam"? Do you agree with his logic? Explain.

The Semantics of Murder

Amir Taheri

> We would like to think that words have ascribable definitions and meanings. Language and meaning, while organic, should still have stability. However, as Amir Taheri explains, the interpretation of a single word can mean the difference between "unpardonable sin" and "heroic martyr." In this editorial, Taheri questions the way some Muslims are "playing games with words" to justify suicide attacks. Jim Guirard responds to Taheri's points in a follow up editorial on page 250.
>
> Amir Taheri is the author of *The Cauldron: Middle East Behind the Headlines* (1988). This editorial was published in the May 8, 2002, edition of the *Wall Street Journal.*

1 As President Bush and Israel's prime minister, Ariel Sharon, met in Washington on May 7, 2002, the latest mass murder rocked Tel Aviv. A blast in a pool hall killed at least 16 people and wounded at least 57 others. So, will the Palestinian who here turned himself into a walking agent of destruction be regarded by his people as a "suicide bomber," a "terrorist" or a "martyr"?

2 Many in the West assume that the Muslim world has already answered by honoring the human bombs as "martyrs." And the chorus of voices from the Muslim world does support that assumption. Foreign ministers from 57 Muslim countries met in Kuala Lumpur, Malaysia, this month with the stated intention of defining terrorism and distancing Islam from terror. Instead, they ended up endorsing the suicide bombers.

3 Iran's former president, Hashemi Rafsanjani, says he would accept the suicide of even 10% of Muslims in a nuclear war to wipe Israel off the map. Algeria's president, Abdelaziz Bouteflika, has described the bombers as "innocent blossoms of martyrdom." Ghazi Algosaibi, Saudi Arabia's ambassador in London and also a poet, has praised the human bombs as a model for Muslim youth in an ode. Ismail Abushanab, the Hamas leader in Gaza, says that 10,000 Palestinians should die while killing 100,000 Israelis as part of a strategy to "put the Jews on the run." And Saddam Hussein says the suicide bombers are "reviving Islam."

4 Many Arab television channels have enlisted their resources in the battle for the hearts and minds of the Arab world, presenting self-styled sheikhs who use sophistry to bestow religious authority on a cynical political strategy. But even these apologists of terror find it difficult to justify the bombers in terms of Islamic ethics.

5 The first difficulty they face is that Islam expressly forbids suicide. Islamic ethics underlines five "unpardonable sins": cannibalism, murder, incest, rape and suicide. The rationale is that these are evil deeds that cannot be undone. To avoid such awkwardness, the apologists of terror recently abandoned the term *entehari* ("suicidal") which was coined for human bombs when they first appeared in Lebanon in 1983.

6 The apologists also know that they cannot use the term *shahid* for the men who self-detonate in civilian areas. This is a complex term. Although it also means

"martyr," it must not be confused with the Christian concept of martyrdom. In Islam, Allah himself is the first shahid, meaning "witness" to the unity of creation. The word indicates that individuals cannot decide to become martyrs—that choice belongs only to God.

7   But this is a lofty honor. There are no more than a dozen or so "shahids" in the history of Islam—people who fell in loyal battle in defense of the faith, not in pursuit of political goals. By becoming shahid they bore testimony to the truth of God's message. The Palestinian teenager who says in video-recorded testament that he or she has decided to become a martyr is, in fact, challenging one of Allah's prerogatives.

8   To get around the semantics, terror's apologists now use the word *etsesh'had*, which literally means "affidavit." As a neologism, it means conducting "martyr-like" operations. Thus "martyr-like," the ersatz in place of the real, is used to circumvent the impossibility of regarding suicide bombers as martyrs in Islam.

9   Muslims who implicitly condone terror know they cannot smuggle a new concept into Islamic ethics, where human activities are divided into six categories along a spectrum of good and evil. Most activities fall into a gray area, half of which is described as *mobah* (acceptable though not praiseworthy), the other half as *makruh* (acceptable though best avoided).

10   Suicide bombing falls within the category that is forbidden *(haram)*. To change its status as a concept, its supporters must give a definition *(ta'rif)*, spell out its rules *(ahkam)*, fix its limits *(hodoud)*, find its place in jurisprudence *(shar'e)* and common law *(urf)*. Such an undertaking would require a large measure of consensus *(ijma'a)* among the believers, something the prophets of terror will never secure. And not a single reputable theologian anywhere has endorsed the new trick word *estesh'had*, though some have spoken with forked tongues. The reason is not hard to see.

11   Islam forbids human sacrifice. The greatest Islamic festival is the Eid al-Adha which marks the day God refused Abraham's offer to sacrifice his firstborn and, instead, substituted a lamb. A god who refuses human sacrifice for his cause can hardly sanction the same to promote the strategies of Mr. Abushanab, or Yasser Arafat. Islam also rejects the crucifixion of Christ because it cannot accept that God would claim human sacrifice in atonement of men's sins.

12   Some, like Iran's President Mohammad Khatami, present suicide bombings as acts of individual desperation. This is disingenuous. One of the girls who blew herself up, murdering almost a dozen Israelis, had been recruited at 14 and brainwashed for two years. Mounting a suicide operation needs planning, logistics, surveillance, equipment, money and postoperation publicity—in short, an organization.

13   But then, the recruiters never use their own children. No one related by blood to the leaders of Hamas or Islamic Jihad has died in suicide bombings.

14   Arafat's wife, Suha, says she would offer her son for suicide attacks. Mrs. Arafat, however, has no son, only a daughter, living with her in Paris. It is always someone else's child who must die.

A True Jihad or a Sinful War Against Innocents?
Jim Guirard

> Jim Guirard wrote this viewpoint in response to Amir Taheri's editorial. Building upon the ideas expressed in Taheri's essay, Guirard attempts to bring the former's "truth-in-language thesis even further." Guirard calls for a "heightened focus" on this war of words—a war for "the minds, hearts and souls of hundreds of millions of Muslims."
>
> Jim Guirard is an attorney, government affairs consultant, and lecturer. He served as national affairs director of the American Security Council Foundation. He has written many articles on the language of politics, and currently is president of the TrueSpeak Institute in Washington, D.C. This editorial appeared in the *Wall Street Journal* on May 27, 2002, a few weeks after Taheri's piece was published.

1 Amir Taheri's May 8 editorial-page essay "Semantics of Murder" calls for a heightened focus on the war of words between us and the terrorists—a war for the minds, hearts and souls of hundreds of millions of Muslims and of all too many Westerners as well.

2 Without repeating Mr. Taheri's expert observations about traditional Islam's sharp condemnation of suicide and of the wanton killing of innocents, as well as its highly restrictive definition of "martyrdom," here is a question-and-answer exercise designed to carry his truth-in-language thesis even further.

3 Its purpose is to draw a no-nonsense, bright-line distinction between those who support and rationalize and those who condemn and oppose genocidal terrorism of the al Qaeda, Hamas, Hezbollah, al Fatah and Islamic Jihad varieties.

4 **Question:** Do al Qaeda's actions constitute an authentic, Qur'an-approved *Jihad* (a truly holy war), or do they constitute a Qur'an-prohibited *Hirabah* (a forbidden killing of innocents and a mortally sinful "war against society") instead?

5 **Question:** Are those who conduct such a war the blessed *mujaheddin* (holy warriors) and the "martyrs for Allah" they claim to be, or are they what the Qur'an severely condemns as *mufsidoon* (evildoers) for conducting an unholy Hirabah?

6 **Question:** Are those conducting this suicidal, al Qaeda-type of warfare destined for a maiden-filled Paradise, or are they headed—unless they immediately cease and sincerely repent their evildoing—straight for *jahannam* (eternal hellfire) instead?

7 **Question:** Is this war in full accord with the *Shari'ah* (the traditional Islamic Law), or does it constitute a multi-part *tajdeef* (a gigantic blasphemy) against the peaceful and compassionate Allah, who is clearly portrayed by the Qur'an?

8 **Question:** Is the nature of the war being waged by al Qaeda and its clones a truly godly mission in the name of Allah, or is it a patently evil, destructive and *shaitaniyah* (satanic) enterprise fomented by Satan himself?

9 The five-word answer is quite plain. It is *Hirabah* conducted by *mufsidoon* destined for *jahannam* because of the *tajdeef shaitaniyah*—the satanic blasphemy— they are waging against peaceful Allah and authentic Islam.

THINKING CRITICALLY

1. What is the difference between most of the Western world's interpretation of the word *martyr* and the Islamic world's interpretation? Explain.

2. What does *shahid* mean? Why can't this word be used to describe suicide bombers? In what ways is this word in conflict with how suicide bombers view their mission and Islamic ethics?

3. What is Taheri's opinion of the suicide bombings? On what they mean to the West's impression of Islam? Explain.

4. What does *estesh'had* mean? Why are "terror's apologists" using the word to describe the actions of suicide bombers?

5. How does the deliberate use of Arabic words contribute to the message, meaning, and impact of these editorials? Explain.

6. What is the effect of Guirard's use of citing a list of questions? Do they make an effective point? Why or why not?

7. Taheri's editorial is titled "The Semantics of Murder." What does *semantics* mean? How does it apply to interpretations of crucial words such as *terrorism, suicide,* and *murder?* Can you think of other examples in which semantics plays a role in our understanding of critical events or actions?

Selling America
Sandra Silberstein

When we think of advertising, we tend to think of marketers trying to sell us something. But it isn't only products that advertising aims to promote. Sometimes ads and commercials pitch ideas and concepts, such as quitting smoking or the merits of volunteering. In the aftermath of the September 11 tragedy, the Ad Council produced an ad campaign that promoted messages of tolerance, patriotism, and diversity. The "selling of America" is the subject of this essay.

Sandra Silberstein is a linguist and professor of English at the University of Washington in Seattle. She focuses on the role of language in creating national identity and public consciousness. This piece is an excerpt from her book, *War of Words: Language, Politics and 9/11* (2002).

Make Alan Greenspan proud; buy something.
            —Dallas billboard selling classified ads

1 The Ad Council of America was founded as the War Advertising Council in 1942, in the wake of the attack on Pearl Harbor.[1] It is the group that has brought America some of its most powerful slogans, from the World War II "Loose Lips Sink Ships"[2] to Smokey the Bear's "Only You Can Prevent Forest Fires," to "Friends Don't Let Friends Drive Drunk.[3] The council is a private, nonprofit agency whose mission remains today as it was articulated in 1942:

> To identify a select number of significant public issues and to stimulate action on those issues through communications programs which make a measurable difference in society.[4]

2   After the attacks of 9/11, the Ad Council undertook to provide messages of tolerance and patriotism. The Ad Council's campaign was a manifestation of nation building as it sold America on itself, building loyalty to values of tolerance and diversity.

America Responds to the Crisis

3 In the aftermath of September 11, the Ad Council developed an extensive media campaign titled, "America Responds to the Crisis: Messages That Can Help and Heal."

4 In its government partnerships and access to the American people, the Ad Council is as close as the U.S. comes to having a national propaganda organ; it is responsible for many of the public service announcements Americans encounter on television and radio, in print, and now on the Internet. The messages of the "Crisis" campaign stressed the civic virtues of tolerance and social responsibility. But what can be seen by many as ideologically neutral public service announcements can be read quite differently by others, depending on the worldview they bring to the task.

5 Like all texts, these ads allowed for a range of readings, as recipients were able to project their own perspectives onto them. A few preliminary examples below will quickly underscore the complex task facing the Ad Council as it launched its most famous PSA, "I am an American." This potential for diverse readings can be seen first in brief examples from the Web. Ad Council Internet campaigns urge Web masters to add council banners to their sites. Examples include two reproduced below. While on the screen, each line flashes, then is replaced, in a continual loop, by the next.

> Whatver race
> Whatever country
> Whatever religion
> All families worry about the same thing
>
> Talk to your children about terrorism
> Talk to your children about tolerance

6 Turning to the last message first, we see that these very abbreviated banners require a great deal of "filling in." This is an ad campaign that asks viewers to supply familiar cultural themes and common-sense reactions to potent terms. What is the connection between talking about terrorism and talking about tolerance? Is it causal? If so, in which direction? To demonstrate the multiple possibilities, here are a few possible interpretations, together with a pair of contrasting glosses for the banner. Readers will no doubt be able to generate many others.

- *Terrorism is caused by a lack of tolerance. Inoculate your children against terrorism; teach tolerance.* As a native speaker of "Americanese," I rather think that this is at least close to an intended, first-order message. But other possibilities abound.
- *Terrorism is caused by a lack of tolerance. If we don't teach tolerance we would become vulnerable to recruitment by terrorists.* This meaning is slightly different from the first, but plausible. It works particularly if one enters the loop seeing *tolerance* first, then *terrorism*.

7 Here are quite different possibilities:

- *Tolerance is a liberal term that doesn't address the underlying roots of terrorism. Explain to your children why people turn to terrorism when despair overtakes hope.*

- *Tolerance is a liberal term that doesn't address the underlying roots of terrorism. It asks the victim to embrace tolerance while being savaged. Talk to your children about the necessity of terrorism now that despair has overtaken hope.*

8 Finally, here are two alternative glosses:

- *This is a message that Americans write to assume moral superiority over the world's desperate and poor.*
- *This is the kind of message that would save the world if everyone could see it and be schooled in it.*

9 As we can see, ad campaigns cannot guarantee a single response from a diverse audience. There is presumably an infinite number of "readings" of, and reactions to, this banner. The job of advertisers is to position targeted readers as closely as possible to at least a range of desired reactions. Those sympathetic to terrorism were presumably not the targeted audience. Predicting viewer response is a challenge, but it is also the special task of advertising. A similar set of readings could arise from the first banner:

> Whatever race
> Whatever country
> Whatever religion
> All families worry about the same thing

10 The most obvious reading in the U.S. is the universalist one: Don't lose sight of the commonalities of being human. But this is not the only reaction. There is also the racist one: *This sentiment is the luxury of those who are relatively safe; "those people" don't care about their families or they wouldn't send them off to kill us and die.* And there is the reading of the desperate: *We don't have the luxury of worrying about the physical safety of a single person; we are fighting for the survival of our people* or *homeland* or *culture*.

11 The common-sense civic virtues that the Ad Council propounds will not resonate universally. But they do appeal to a range of readers in the U.S. Within the complex and contradictory rhetoric of the nation, these ads draw on an internal discourse of what is considered the best of America. They sell the nation to itself. They remind America of its multicultural identity at a time when that could be threatened.

12 One of the print ads was particularly powerful. On the skyline of New York, where the Twin Towers had been, two long columns read as follows:

> Will hate bring it all back? Will it bring back the innocence? The sense of security? Will it bring back the husbands and wives and sons and daughters? Will hate make us better than those who hate us? Or merely bring us closer to them? Will hate help us destroy our enemies? Or will it laugh as we destroy ourselves? There are those who say we don't know who our enemy is, but we do. Our enemy is a neighborhood mosque defaced by vandals. An Arab-American storekeeper in fear of reprisal. A scared Muslim child bullied because she is different. Hate is our enemy. And when we start to hate other Americans, we have lost everything. Hate has taken enough from us already. Don't let it take you.

13   The ad identifies an enemy worse than the terrorists of 9/11, that is, the scourge of hate. But what does the slogan, "Americans Stand United" mean? On the one hand, it means that Americans are united against an internal enemy, in this case, hate. On the other hand, calls to stand united are a fairly standard wartime exhortation, and the U.S. was at war. Another possible reading of the full ad focuses on an external enemy: America will not be able to fully unite in the War on Terrorism if it is internally fractured by divisive hate. And at a distance, the ad scans like typical patriotism, urging unity in support of the current war. This combination of themes, inclusion, unity and traditional patriotism (along with the diverse readings they allow), became the Ad Council signature in several ads.

14   The[se] complex decisions of how to best unify a diverse nation (of viewers) within secular virtues are best exemplified in one of the council's TV spots.

I Am an American

15   Perhaps the most widely circulated ad was the television spot, "I am an American," which seemed to appear almost immediately after 9/11. It was created by staffers of an Austin-based ad agency who'd been in Washington, DC, on September 11. On the long drive home, they hatched the plan for the PSA, which they donated to the Ad Council. The council was able to distribute it to 3,000 media outlets nationwide.[5]

16   Americans found the PSA very powerful, and beautifully produced. A concise description came from the *Houston Chronicle*:

> The commercial shows people from the melting pot—including a firefighter, children and adults of many ethnicities—facing the camera and saying simply, "I am an American." The screen then flashes the nation's venerable motto, e *pluribus unum,* a Latin phrase that means "out of many, one."[6]

17   In fact, the ad showed more than 40 individuals—from a nun, to a police officer, to firefighters—with fully diverse skin tones and accents. Some were native speakers of a variety of English dialects, others clearly had first languages other than English. One speaker was in a wheelchair, another used sign language. Speakers stood in urban areas, including New York and San Francisco, as well as in gardens and fields. Each delivery of "I am an American" was a bit different, as the ad captured the variety of individual cadences.

18   The reaction to the ad was so rich that the Ad Council developed a Web page titled, "What people are saying about 'I am an American'." It is here that we can gain some insight into the varied receptions of this most widely distributed selling of America. We know from media coverage the intent of the ad's makers. It was designed as "a gift to the American people from the advertising industry."[7] Ad agency president, Roy Spence, reported: "We wanted to make sure that when we strike back, we don't strike back at one of our own."[8]

19   Many of the responses on the "What People are Saying" Web page were laudatory. Here are typical sentiments:

> Just thought you'd like to hear about this. I was flying out of Atlanta on Friday, September 28th. Your "I am an American" PSA came on the television monitors

as I was passing through a terminal. What followed was something I've never seen in an airport before. I stopped to watch the PSA, and like others was very moved by it. As the PSA played, more and more people stopped to watch. By the time the PSA was over, there were at least 40 people gathered around just the one monitor. With smiles on our faces, we broke up and went about our business. I just want to congratulate you on such a successful campaign and thank you for helping make the day a little bit brighter. (Chris)

Kudos. This ad captures precisely what America should be. I hope it becomes etched in every American's brain. (Robert)

Your "I am an American" television ad stirs the deepest emotions of my American soul. When I see your ad at my age of 40 years it brings tears of sadness and joy to my eyes. Sadness that an unparalleled tragedy had to occur for such an ad to have meaning in our country, but joy in that I think the time may have finally arrived when not just whites and blacks can come together but—all Americans. If I had a million dollars, I'd buy as much ad time as I could for the ad. (Norm)

Thank you for your campaign. The most destructive impact of 9/11 could well be what it turns us into. I believe your campaign will play a part in assuring that we turn into a better nation. Thanks. (Petrops)

Thanks for your ad. Very little air time in the last two weeks has been more valuable. God bless us all. (Franca, Baltimore, MD.)

20   There is, even in this ad, however, an ambiguity. Does the ad celebrate the achievement of a diverse unity of Americans or is it trying to create this? Put more starkly: Is the ad meant to celebrate or protect nonwhite Americans; does the majority need to be reminded that minorities are members of the community when the wagons are circled? The stated goals of the campaign actually lean toward the latter interpretation—"to assure that we don't strike out at one of our own."

21   The statements above respond to a rather romanticized viewing. People saw the ad as a reaffirmation of, perhaps a tutorial on, what America could be. But there was a spectrum of responses when viewers rated the ad in its portrayal of diversity. This range of responses indicates that viewers bring with them divergent ingredients from the narrative stew that is public discourse. At the risk of getting carried away with a metaphor: you are what you eat. Many people saw a refreshing range of people on the screen (perhaps because their world is not so diverse?). Within that group, Bob wrote, "It is clear that you intended everyone to be included." Margaret wrote, "the commercial . . . represents all countries and all types, shapes and colors of faces." Several writers, however, noted limitations on that diversity (perhaps because they are closer to issues of exclusion):

Your PSA is quite powerful and very useful. However, it does not include any Muslim man in Islamic Dress and any Muslim woman in Islamic Dress with the head hijab. Diversification without Muslims is indeed incomplete; Muslims are also American. (Ilyas)

With the recent aftermath of the NY and Washington bombings, male Sikhs in particular and Muslim women have faced the brunt of the backlash. I was hoping that a male Sikh with a turban and beard could be added to this ad. This would speed up the rebuilding process of our great nation and help people understand the differences between various religions and races. (Manny)

I am American and I have been watching your latest campaign on TV with a feeling of admiration, but also a profound feeling of being insulted. You failed to show a single member of the Armed Forces. How utterly thoughtless of you at a time when brave noble brothers and sisters are putting their lives at risk for all of the freedom loving people of this earth. (William)

I love ur ad . . . it is wonderful . . . but being an American citizen and wearing a headscarf i don't see myself there pleez have somebody like me too in the ad or if u need assistance i know many people who would be willing to be in it . . . hope to hear from u sooooon. (Saniya)

22   These diverse responses confirm that public service announcements, like all texts, are interpreted through a complex interaction of their content and the preexisting perspective of the viewer. Several final responses make this abundantly clear.

I just saw your "I am An American" ad, and while I can appreciate the sentiment, I found it deeply distressing and highly offensive that no European Americans were included in the segment. (Joe)

It is fascinating that fully half the faces (approximately 20) are likely European American. Clearly for viewers who are either unaccustomed to faces of color and/or uncomfortable with these images, it is possible for an equal representation to be completely misperceived. For this viewer, past some threshold, every face became one of color. This is perhaps an extreme example of what is surely universal—seeing ads through the lens of one's particular concerns. One viewer noticed in the ads her "pet peeve":

I really liked your diversity PSA. It addresses a pet peeve of mine. As an Asian American, I find myself constantly correcting my less enlightened Asian friends when they talk about so-and-so's "American" spouse. What do you mean by "American"? Aren't YOU American too? Maybe I can get off the soap box now . . . thanks. (R. Louie)

23   The last segments discussed here address assimilation. Randy, of Pennsylvania, wrote of the ads:

They Are The Best!!! Finally, people are standing up and saying that they are Americans, period. Thank you for taking the "hyphen" out of being an American. I never thought it should have been there in the first place. . . .

24   It's not the least bit clear that the folks in these ads do not think of themselves as hyphenated Americans, or that they do not take great pride in their ethnic or cultural origins. Nor is it clear that the ad makers intended a message along the lines that to be American, one has to give up hyphenated identities. But for Randy, who was presumably moved by the ad, to assert Americanism is to forego a hyphen.

25   Earl, from Pennsylvania, saw a distancing from "political correctness" in the ad:

I want to compliment you on your TV ad: "I am an American." After years of insane political correctness it is uplifting to me to see people of different ethnic backgrounds unite as one instead of using hyphens and asking for victim group hand outs. Thankfully, Clinton's "Our strength is our diversity" defiance of common sense did not affect everyone. We do have an American culture, and the nation is strong because the immigrants that came here united in to one people. Your ad reflects my beliefs and I want to thank you for placing it on TV.

26   Like all viewers, Earl read the ad through the lens of his experience and concerns. While the ad makers might well see "our strength is our diversity" as the perfect gloss for this spot, for Earl the PSA was a corrective to that sentiment. It also appears to Earl to be a denunciation of affirmative action ("victim group hand outs") and an endorsement of assimilation. For other viewers (I daresay most), the ad embraced diversity. Judy wrote from Houston, "Thanks for making Americans aware that 'we' are made up of many nationalities. That's what 'America' is," David, writing from South Carolina, spoke of the "collaboration of our nation's diversity and its unity."

27   But perhaps the single most important endorsement the Ad Council could have received was Earl's final testimonial, "Your ad reflects my beliefs." In a sense the ad did. It allowed a range of viewers to position themselves as appreciative participants in a racially diverse America. For some viewers that diversity was only visual; they read the ad with an assimilationist tinge. For many others, the ad ratified a society united in its appreciation of diversity. In its ability to allow for both of those readings, "I am an American" became a vehicle for all stripes of patriotism.

28   David, in Washington, wrote to say that he had responded as "a quiet and grateful patriot." Chris in Canada wrote to say "I haven't seen anything come close, since the tragedy, to expressing so clearly and poignantly what it is we are trying to defend. This ad will cause our enemies consternation." And David, from Pennsylvania, wrote:

> I am a navy veteran of WWII and I still remember the poster with "Loose Lips Sink Ships" on them. I am still impressed with that phrase and happy to learn that you will be adding your know-how to the upcoming struggle. That should help the American people maintain their resolve during the years to come.

29   While a good deal more complex than "Loose Lips Sink Ships," "I am an American" nonetheless worked the same side of the street: to unite a diverse country in common cause at a time of war.

Notes

1. Ad Council of America, "Message From the President of the Ad Council of America," www.adcouncil.org/crisis/index.htm.
2. Claire Cozens, "American Ad Body in Call to Arms," *Guardian Unlimited*, October 2, 2001.
3. Greg Hassell, "Altruistic Ads Try to Unite Americans," *Houston Chronicle*, September 25, 2001.
4. Ad Council.
5. Hassell
6. Ibid.
7. Ibid.
8. Ibid.

THINKING CRITICALLY

1. What was the motivation behind the Ad Council's advertising campaign "I am an American"?

2. What is the author's personal opinion of the "I am an American" campaign? Is she admiring? Critical? Concerned? Supportive? Explain.

3. How did the Ad Council use the Internet as part of the "I am an American" campaign? What opportunities does the Web provide advertisers in promoting messages? What made this campaign suitable for the Internet? Explain.

4. Silberstein explains that the television commercial for "I am an American" elicited a wide scope of "readings." That is, different people had different reactions to the ad. What were these readings and what accounted for the broad responses?

5. The author provides several interpretations of the Internet ad promoting tolerance. Respond to her analysis in your own words. Specifically, which interpretations seem to make sense to you, and which seem off target, and why? Are there any other obvious interpretations that the author missed?

6. How did the Ad Council "sell" America in the "I am an American" campaign? In your opinion, was the campaign a success? Explain.

Exploring the Language of **VISUALS**

Americans Stand United

In the preceding essay, Sandra Silberstein described this ad sponsored by the Arab American Institute and the Ad Council and designed by the Brokaw Agency to encourage tolerance during the aftermath of September 11. As you view the ad below, consider how the ad uses symbolism, language, and emotion to reach its audience and promote its message.

WILL HATE BRING IT ALL BACK? WILL IT BRING BACK THE INNOCENCE? THE SENSE OF SECURITY? WILL IT BRING BACK THE HUSBANDS AND WIVES AND SONS AND DAUGHTERS? WILL HATE MAKE US BETTER THAN THOSE WHO HATE US? OR MERELY BRING US CLOSER TO THEM? WILL HATE HELP US DESTROY OUR ENEMIES? OR WILL IT LAUGH AS WE DESTROY OURSELVES? THERE ARE THOSE WHO SAY WE DON'T KNOW WHO OUR ENEMY IS. BUT WE DO. OUR ENEMY IS A NEIGHBORHOOD MOSQUE DEFACED BY VANDALS. AN ARAB-AMERICAN STOREKEEPER IN FEAR OF REPRISAL. A SCARED MUSLIM CHILD BULLIED BECAUSE SHE IS DIFFERENT. HATE IS OUR ENEMY. AND WHEN WE START TO HATE OTHER AMERICANS, WE HAVE LOST EVERYTHING. HATE HAS TAKEN ENOUGH FROM US ALREADY. DON'T LET IT TAKE YOU.

AMERICANS STAND UNITED

Arab American Institute   (202)429-9210   www.aaiusa.org

Ad Council

THINKING CRITICALLY

1. If you were leafing through a magazine and saw this ad, would you stop to read it? Would you read the entire message? Why or why not?

2. How does this ad use symbolism to promote its message? Is it an appropriate use of symbolism? Explain.

3. What time of day is it? Is there any significance to the time of day featured in the ad? Would this ad be more effective if it pictured the New York skyline at a different time of day?

4. Consider the final line floating in the water, "Americans Stand United." What do these words mean to you? Are there other meanings in addition to your first impression?

5. What trademark logos are included in the ad? Where are they placed? Why are they there?

6. Analyze the language that makes up the Twin Towers. How accessible is it? Does it engage the audience? Explain.

MAKING CONNECTIONS

1. Try to identify as many war words as possible and their pop culture uses in to-day's lexicon. Then, discuss whether the use of these words in common speech has diluted or influenced our view of war itself.

2. Find out more information about some of the words Taheri and Guirard use in their editorials: *shahid, entehari, haram, ta'rif, ahkam, hodoud, mujaheddin, jahannam*, etc. If possible, ask a student who speaks Arabic to help you understand what these words mean. Try to make connections between the words and meanings with Western equivalents. Are some words simply untranslatable? Do the semantics of these words change how different cultures understand terrorism, war, and faith? Explain.

3. Write an essay in which you discuss your personal view of the "war on terrorism" as a label and a policy. Consider what the term means to you. What does it mean to the general population? To people from outside of the United States? Interview a spectrum of people for their viewpoint on what the phrase means, and what their interpretations might mean.

4. Several of the authors in this section, including Taheri, Guirard, and Murdoch, touch on the issue of what Islam professes, and what its followers seem to believe and support. Research this issue in greater depth in an exploratory essay. In addition to online research, try to interview some students who practice Islam for their perspective on this issue.

5. Write an essay exploring the ways the language of war has affected international relationships over the last ten years. Does it make America weaker or stronger—or does it have any impact at all? Has it improved international views of America? Is such linguistic sensitivity reciprocated? Explain.

6. In his article on the language of war, Jon Hooten quotes linguist George Lakoff (paragraph 31), "It is important to distinguish what is metaphorical from what is not." Read the article Lakoff wrote ("Gulf War Metaphor") before the Gulf War in 1991 at http://philosophy.uoregon.edu/metaphor/lakoff-l.htm and write an essay in which you explore this idea. Why is it important to make such distinctions? What are the implications of the linguistic blurring of real versus metaphorical acts of war?

7. Write a poem on a political event about which you feel strongly. After you have written your poem, consider the ways poetic expression allows you to creatively articulate and convey your feelings.

8. Inflammatory, political language carries tremendous power to influence national policy, laws, and social mores. What are our expectations of political language? How do we filter the fluff from the substance? Write an essay exploring the power of language to influence our feelings regarding the "war on terror" and the American military actions in the Middle East. You may also explore opposing viewpoints on how language is used—both nationally and internationally—to criticize the war and U.S. military activities abroad.

9. Visit the Ad Council's Web site at www.adcouncil.org, and evaluate another public service announcement (PSA) campaign. Analyze the campaign's message, audience, and slogans. What is the campaign trying to "sell"? How does it appeal to its audience? Does it allow for multiple readings? Does it reach its intended public? Explain.

LANGUAGE AND THE PRESIDENCY

The Rhetorical Presidency
Robert E. Denton, Jr. and Dan F. Hahn

In the next essay, political communication analysts Robert Denton, Jr. and Dan Hahn assert that the presidency is primarily a rhetorical institution. The president's primary function is that of a great communicator. The president is, they explain, "the one man distillation of the American people: their hopes, desires, and majesty." Everything the president says is recorded. Everything he communicates—from phone calls to addresses to Congress—carries meaning and significance.

Robert E. Denton, Jr. is head of the Department of Communications Studies at Virginia Polytechnic Institute and State University. He is the author of many books on political communication, including *Political Communications in America* (with Gary C. Woodward) and *Presidential Communication Ethics, An Oxymoron?* (ed., 2002). The following piece is an excerpt from a book he co-authored with Dan F. Hahn, *Presidential Communication* (1987).

Dan F. Hahn is a visiting professor in the Department of Culture and Communications at New York University. He is the author of many articles and convention papers exploring aspects of political communication. In addition to the book he co-authored with Robert Denton Jr., Hahn is co-author of *Listening for a President: A Citizen's Campaign Methodology* (1990), written with Ruth Gonchar Brennan.

Public sentiment is everything. With public sentiment nothing can fail, without it nothing can succeed.

—Abraham Lincoln

1 Presidents are special beings. When they talk, we listen. We want to know where they are, what they are doing, and how they are doing it. Why are they so special? They are not special physically—we have had fat ones, thin ones, tall ones, short ones, some ugly, some handsome. They are not special intellectually—they have ranged through the many gradations from smart to dumb. They are not special emotionally—some have been strengthened by the pressure, others have cracked under the strain. What makes each and every one special, however, is that they lead us, define us, protect us, and embody us. And they do so, implicitly and explicitly, through communication.

2 If you doubt the significance and importance of presidential public communication, consider the following two examples. The presidential debates of 1960 demonstrated how important public speech can be in influencing the very nature of our society. The debates were heard and watched by over 101 million Americans.[1] The election was decided by a mere 118,550 votes—votes that may well have been determined by the public debate performances of the candidates. Scholars have concluded that those viewing the debates shifted their opinion toward Kennedy and most of his last minute support came from the "undecided" voter. In fact, Kennedy's support gained about 4 percent with each debate.[2]

3   By 1979 Carter's public popularity was at an all time low. He decided to retreat with his advisors to Camp David to review his presidency. Upon reflection, Carter believed that his presidential leadership had missed its mark. He had acted, as he told David Broder, as "the head of the government" rather than as the "leader of the people."[3] He also believed that the nation was experiencing a crisis of spirit or "malaise." The answer—a campaign to wake up the American people. The *Washington Post* announced the campaign with the headline that read "Carter Seeking Oratory to Move an Entire Nation."[4]

4   President Reagan, "the great communicator," has clearly demonstrated that how a president communicates with the public is an important element in governing the nation. The rhetoric of presidents is important on several dimensions. Linguistically, their words shape ideas and stimulate action. Intellectually, their words provide rationales for action and justifications for decisions. Psychologically, their words can inspire, comfort, and motivate the nation. Socially, their words connect us as a social entity, providing the feeling of a human relationship with our leader. Ethically, their words can do good or evil, encourage justice or injustice, selfishness or selflessness. Aesthetically, their words have encompassed our grief (Lincoln's Gettysburg Address), given us hope (Franklin Roosevelt's first inaugural address), and challenged us to address the task at hand (Kennedy's inaugural address).

5   In this essay we consider the importance of the "rhetorical presidency." More specifically, we explore the dependency of modern presidents upon public communication activities and provide a basis for citizen analysis of presidential rhetoric.

Politics and Communication

6 Humans are, according to Aristotle's *Politics*, "political beings" and "he who is without a polis, by reason of his own nature and not of some accident, is either a poor sort of being [a beast] or a being higher than man [a god]."[5] And because nature makes nothing in vain, Aristotle continues, humans "alone of the animals are furnished with the faculty of language."[6] Thus, it was recognized over 2,000 years ago that politics and communication go hand in hand because they are essential parts of human nature. Public communication allows us to deal with our social environment. "There are few tools," according to Roderick Hart and his colleagues, "other than public talk with which to maintain the delicate balance between community and jungle."[7]

7   Indeed, through public speaking by our national, state, and local officials, our values and goals are defined, refined, and articulated. Their words can inspire, move, and articulate but also deceive, destroy, and exploit. Public communication, or rhetoric, serves many purposes. Karlyn Campbell recognizes several general rhetorical purposes that represent an orderly progression in terms of complexity and political utility.[8] First, rhetoric serves to create a "virtual experience." Through rhetoric we experience a range of emotions leading to corresponding behavior. In the process, rhetoric functions to alter perceptions and assist in formulating beliefs. Verbal descriptions by our leaders often serve as rationales, justifications, or motivations for collective action. Finally, much public rhetoric by officials is aimed at maintaining support, action, or the status quo.

8   According to Doris Graber, "politics is largely a word game. Politicians rise to power because they can talk persuasively to voters and political elites. Once in power, their daily activities are largely verbal."[9] Dan Nimmo concurs and argues that the purpose of political talk is to "preserve other talk." In fact, politics and communication are inseparable. "Politics, like communication, is a process, and like communication, politics involves talk. This is not talk in the narrow sense of the spoken word but talk in the more inclusive sense, meaning all the ways people exchange symbols—written and spoken words, pictures, movements, gestures, mannerisms, and dress."[10] From this perspective we may view politics as an activity of communication between persons.

Political Language

9   Political consciousness is dependent upon language, for language can determine the way in which people relate to their environment.[11] At the very least, language should be viewed as the medium for the generation and perpetuation of politically significant symbols. Political consciousness, therefore, results from a largely symbolic interpretation of sociopolitical experience. To control, manipulate, or structure the "interpretation" is a primary goal of politics in general. The language of government, in many ways, is the dissemination of illusion and ambiguity.[12] A successful politician will use rather specific linguistic devices that reinforce popular beliefs, attitudes, and values. Politically manipulated language can, therefore, promote and reinforce the existing political regime or order.

10   From this brief discussion, it is clear that what makes language political is not the particular vocabulary or linguistic form but the *substance* of the information the language conveys, the *setting* in which the interaction occurs, and the explicit or implicit *functions* the language performs. As Doris Graber observes, "When political actors, in and out of government communicate about political matters, for political purposes, they are using political languages."[13]

Functions of Political Language

11   Graber identifies five major functions of political language: information dissemination, agenda-setting, interpretation and linkage, projection for the future and the past, and action stimulation.[14] It is useful to discuss briefly each of these functions.

12   There are many ways information is shared with the public in political messages. The most obvious, of course, is the sharing of explicit information about the state of the polity. Such dissemination of information is vital to the public's understanding and support of the political system. This is especially true in democratic nations where the public expects open access to the instruments and decision-making of government officials. But the public, being sensitized to uses of language, can obtain "information" by what *is not* stated, *how* something is stated, or *when* something is stated. Often times, especially in messages between nations, the public must "read between the lines" of official statements to ascertain proper meanings and significance of statements. Such inferences are useful in gauging security, flexibility, and sincerity. Sometimes the connotations of the words used

communicate more truth than the actual statements. Are our relations with the Soviet Union "open," "guarded," or "friendly?" There are times, especially in tragedy, that the very act of speaking by an official can communicate support, sympathy, or strength. Thus, the act of speaking rather than the words spoken sometimes conveys the meaning of the rhetorical event.

13   The very topics chosen by politicians to discuss channel the public's attention and focus issues to be discussed. The agenda-setting function of political language primarily occurs in two ways. First, before "something" can become an issue, some prominent politician must articulate a problem and hence bring the issue to public attention. The issue can be rather obvious (poverty), in need of highlighting (status of American education), or created (the "Great Society"). A major way political language establishes the national agenda is by controlling the information disseminated to the general public. Within this realm there is always a great deal of competition. There are a limited number of issues that can effectively maintain public interest and attention. While certain "self-serving" topics are favored by one person, party, faction, or group, the same topics may be perceived as meaningless or even harmful to other factions, persons, or groups. While President Nixon wanted to limit discussion and public attention regarding the Watergate break-ins and tapes, rival groups wanted public debates and revelations to continue.

14   The very act of calling the public's attention to a certain issue defines, interprets, and manipulates the public's perception of that issue. Causal explanations are often freely given. Such explanations may be suspect. Control over the definitions of a situation is essential in creating and preserving political realities. Participants in election primaries, for example, all proclaim victory regardless of the number of votes received. The top vote-getter becomes the "front runner." The second place winner becomes "the underdog" candidate in an "up-hill battle." The third place candidate becomes a "credible" candidate and alternative for those "frustrated" or "dissatisfied" with the "same old party favorites." Political language defines and interprets reality as well as provides a rationale for future collective action.

15   A great deal of political rhetoric and language deals with predicting the future and reflecting upon the past. Candidates present idealized futures under their leadership and predictions of success if their policies are followed. Some predictions and projections are formalized as party platforms or major addresses as inaugurals or state of the union addresses. Nearly all such statements involve promises—promises of a brighter future if followed or Armageddon if rejected. Past memories and associations are evoked to stimulate a sense of security, better times, and romantic longings. An important function of political language, therefore, is to link us to past glories and reveal the future in order to reduce uncertainty in a world of ever increasing complexity and doubt.

16   Finally, and perhaps most importantly, political language must function to mobilize society and stimulate social action. Language serves as the stimulus, means, or rationale for social action. Words can evoke, persuade, implore, command, label, praise, and condemn. Political language is similar to other uses of language. But it also articulates, shapes, and stimulates public discussion and behavior about the allocation of public resources, authority, and sanctions.

The Rhetorical Nature of the Presidency

17 George Edwards argues that "the greatest source of influence for the president is public approval."[15] Today, as never before, presidents want not only to please the public and avoid irritating them, but also want to formulate and lead public opinion. In fact, research has shown that the higher the president's approval rating by the public the more Congress supports presidential policy decisions.[16]

18   The study of presidential rhetoric is the investigation of how presidents gain, maintain, or lose public support. For Theodore Windt, it is "a study of power, of the fundamental power in a democracy: public opinion and public support."[17] At the very least, the words of a president establish the public record of the administration, reflect the values and goals of the public, and in essence, the vocabulary becomes the favored policy (that is, New Frontier, Great Society, Star Wars, etc.). It is not surprising, therefore, that James Ceaser and his colleagues argue that "the rhetorical presidency is based on words, not power."[18] As Hart observes, the "American citizenry nevertheless require the federal archivists to scurry around behind modern chief executives and record their remarks for posterity, sparing no expense or tree for the sake of president's speeches perhaps because they have become convinced in a media-saturated age that a president is earning his keep only when he stands in public and talks."[19]

19   The speeches of presidents, indeed, differ from those of ordinary citizens or even celebrities in terms of frequency and how they must communicate.[20] In addition, presidents seldom face their entire audience and must always keep in mind the impact of their remarks on various constituencies. Presidents must be able to speak on a wide range of topics with great detail, knowing that their words are recorded and "live forever."

20   Despite the notion of the "grand oratory" of the nineteenth century, our early presidents seldom relied upon public address to win public support. George Washington usually gave only one speech a year—the one mandated in the Constitution to address Congress. Prior to 1912, the political parties conducted the presidential campaigns. Woodrow Wilson was the first presidential candidate to engage in active public campaigning.[21] In fact, an argument can be made that the framers of the Constitution did not favor "mass oratory" because it could counter "rational" and "enlightened self-interest" concerns of the citizenry.[22] The government was designed to minimize reliance upon the passions of the people and establish institutions that would be stable, efficient, and effective.

21   Between 1945 and 1975, public speeches by presidents increased 500 percent. President Gerald Ford, not a particularly effective speaker, delivered 682 public speeches in 1976 and President Jimmy Carter, also not a particularly effective speaker, averaged one speech a day during his entire term of office.[23] The reasons for the rise of the "rhetorical presidency" have already been identified in the preface of this book. But the importance and impact of modern electoral campaign politics plus the role of the mass media cannot be overemphasized. In addition, Gary Woodward argues that today's presidency is a collection of traditions and rhetorical expectations that each new president inherits. The legacies of past presidencies cannot be ignored. Presidents and their public relations staffs "are sensitive to the rhetorical precedents they have inherited. By the time a leader reaches the oval

office he has usually spent the better part of an adult lifetime soaking up its unwritten rules and potent traditions. Most presidents come to power as well-versed students of the institutional presidency."[24]

22   James Barber recognizes the importance and impact of presidential rhetoric upon their administration. In his classic, *The Presidential Character*, Barber searches for patterns in behavior of past presidents and, based upon these patterns, classifies presidents into "character types."[25] He believes there are three major influences upon a person that will shape the presidential performance: style, world view, and character. For our purposes the variable "style" is especially relevant. He defines it as "the president's habitual way of performing his three political roles: rhetoric, personal relations, and homework."[26] This means communication—public, small group, and face-to-face—to write, think, record, and articulate thoughts.

23   Although it is clear that presidential speechmaking has increased drastically, the question remains, how does it differ significantly from the speechmaking of other public figures? Hart, in his impressive work entitled *Verbal Style and the Presidency*, provides insight into the question.[27] In comparison to corporate leaders, religious leaders, political candidates, and social activists, presidents mention themselves and their actions with great frequency. In addition, presidential speechmaking tends to be more optimistic, practical, "real," and less complex than addresses by other leaders. "Humanity, practicality, and caution are the special sound of presidential discourse."[28]

24   To talk of the "rhetorical presidency" is to recognize more than the increase of and impact of presidential discourse. It is to identify a way of viewing and analyzing the office.[29] The institution of the American presidency is greater than any individual. The office greatly influences the officeholder, who must confront already established expectations of presidential performance and behavior. The set of expected presidential roles results from the interaction of the office with the public. The role sets are created, sustained, and permeated through interaction comprised of campaigns, socialization, history, and myth. There is a clear, rather systematic process of transformation from candidate to president where the candidate must confront the "political self" and the public definition of the presidential role. Thus, as a result of interacting with the public, historical expectations, and individual views of the office, the person "becomes" president. The office of the presidency, then, dictates the nature and relationship of the president with the public. Rhetoric, broadly defined, is the means of confirming or denying the public's expectations of acceptable role behavior.

25   The presidency is simply a rhetorical institution. For the public, the office is comprised of a "string of public conversations" rather than a "series of private decisions." Presidents, although they have names, are corporate models of historical images and personae created in the public's collective consciousness. Their messages are persuasive in nature and are carefully constructed for a purpose. Thus, how a policy is defined, articulated, and sold may be more important than the policy itself. For presidential rhetoric constitutes social action, provides a context for collective action, and contributes to the oral history and definition of the nation.

26   Recognition of the rhetorical presidency is also recognition of potential abuses and concerns. Presidential rhetoric may emphasize style over substance with the belief that

"words presented in stylistic finesse can solve real, difficult, even paradoxical problems."[30] There is the danger that symbols and slogans may replace policy discussions. Presidential rhetoric, although increasing, is becoming more one-way communication than two-way interaction. Thus, increased quantity of addresses in no way insures quality of interaction. Finally, too much time spent speaking, Hart observes, leaves too little time for presidential thinking in private to insure "good" policies and decisions. Speechmaking is both an art and a science, a tool for both good and evil uses.

Notes

1. Frank Stanton, "A CBS View," in *The Great Debates*, ed. Sidney Krans (Bloomington, IN: Indiana University Press, 1962), p. 66.
2. Saul Ben Zeev and Irving White, "Effects and Implications," in *The Great Debates,* ed. Sidney Kraus (Bloomington, IN: Indiana University Press, 1962), p. 334.
3. As quoted in James Ceaser et al., "The Rise of the Rhetorical Presidency," in *Essays in Presidential Rhetoric*, ed. Theodore Windt (Dubuque, IA: Kendall/Hunt, 1983), p. 3.
4. "Carter Seeking Oratory to Move an Entire Nation," *Washington Post,* July 14, 1979, pp. 15–16.
5. Aristotle, *The Politics of Aristotle*, trans. Ernest Barker (New York: Oxford University Press, 1970), p. 5.
6. Ibid., p. 6.
7. Roderick Hart, Gustav Friedrich, and William Brooks, *Public Communication* (New York: Harper & Row, 1975), p. 12.
8. Karlyn Kohrs Campbell, *The Rhetorical Act* (Belmont, CA: Wadsworth, 1982), pp. 8–14.
9. Doris Graber, "Political Language," in *Handbook of Political Communication,* ed. Dan Nimmo and Keith Sanders (Beverly Hills, CA: Sage Publications, 1981), p. 195.
10. Dan Nimmo, *Political Communication and Public Opinion in America* (Santa Monica, CA: Goodyear Publishing, 1978), p. 7.
11. The strongest statement of this notion is provided by Benjamin Lee Whorf. For him, "If a man thinks in one language, he thinks one way; in another language, another way." The structure of language "is itself the shaper of ideas, the program and guide for the individual's mental activity, for his analysis of impressions, for his synthesis of his mental stock in trade." See John Carroll, ed., *Language, Thought, and Reality: Selected Writings of Benjamin Whorf* (New York: John Wiley & Sons, 1956).
12. Murray Edelman, *Politics as Symbolic Action* (Chicago: Markham Publishing, 1971), p. 83.
13. Graber, "Political Language," p. 196.
14. Ibid., pp. 195–224.
15. George C. Edwards, *The Public Presidency* (New York: St. Martin's Press, 1983), p. 1.
16. George C. Edwards, *Presidential Influence in Congress* (San Francisco, CA: W.H. Freeman, 1980), pp. 86–100.
17. Theodore Windt, *Presidential Rhetoric (1961–1980)* (Dubuque, IA: Kendall/Hunt, 1980), p. 2.
18. Ceasar et al., "The Rise of the Rhetorical Presidency," p. 17.
19. Roderick Hart, *Verbal Style and the Presidency* (Orlando, FL: Academic Press, 1984), p. 2.
20. Ibid., p. 8.
21. Ceaser et al., "The Rise of the Rhetorical Presidency," p. 14.
22. Ibid., p. 8.
23. Hart, *Verbal Style and the Presidency*, p. 2.

24. Gary Woodward, "The Presidency: Focusing on the Role of Rhetorical Antecedents" (Paper presented at the Annual Convention of the Eastern Communication Association, Providence, Rhode Island, May 2, 1985), 1–2.

25. See James David Barber, *The Presidential Character*, 2nd ed. (Englewood Cliffs, NJ: Prentice-Hall, 1977).

26. Ibid., p. 7.

27. See Hart, *Verbal Style and the Presidency*, especially pp. 32–42.

28. Ibid., p. 41.

29. See Robert E. Denton, Jr., *The Symbolic Dimensions of the American Presidency* (Prospect Heights, IL: Waveland Press, 1982); Hart, *Verbal Style and the Presidency*, especially pp. 5–7; Theodore Windt, *Essays in Presidential Rhetoric;* and Robert E. Denton, Jr. and Gary Woodward, *Political Communication in America* (New York: Praeger, 1985).

30. Hart, *Verbal Style and the Presidency*, p. 231.

THINKING CRITICALLY

1. What, according to Denton and Hahn, makes presidential communication particularly significant and unique? What separates it from the speech of the ordinary citizen, and why?

2. Denton and Hahn note "it was recognized over 2000 years ago that politics and communication go hand in hand because they are essential parts of human nature." What do they mean? Explore the implications of this statement in your own words.

3. In what ways does the public speech of the president guide national and social values? Explain.

4. What are the general rhetorical purposes of presidential communication? Does the fact that the president's language is so publicly owned preclude the person holding office from ever having a personal or a private voice? Explain.

5. What are the five major functions of political language as outlined by Doris Graber? Explain.

6. What does George Edwards mean by the statement, "the greatest source of influence of the president is public approval"? Do you agree? Explain.

7. In your opinion, what is more critical for effective presidential communication: style or substance? Explain.

WRITING ASSIGNMENTS

1. In paragraph 8, Doris Graber states, "Politics is largely a word game." What makes language political? How is it a "word game"? Expand on these ideas based on information provided in this essay as well as from your own knowledge of politics and government.

2. Is it important that the president be a good speaker? In an essay, define the language skills necessary to be an effective leader, and explain why you think these elements are important. Use examples to support your discussion.

3. Write an essay exploring how presidential communication has changed over the last 100 years. What influence has the media, including television and radio, had on the president's use of language? Do you think the Internet will influence the role of language and the presidency? Explain.

A Nation of Victims

Renana Brooks

> President George W. Bush has been criticized for his many verbal blunders and linguistic stumbles. But what about his more deliberate use of language, especially in speeches and official addresses to the American people? Renana Brooks argues that despite the mistakes Bush makes during unscripted exchanges, his speeches contain emotionally charged, "dependency-creating" language. His words, she challenges, are deliberately chosen to cloud issues, negatively frame opposing viewpoints, and engender feelings of fear and dependency among his listeners.
>
> Renana Brooks is a clinical psychologist in Washington, D.C. She heads the Sommet Institute for the Study of Power and Persuasion. She served as expert commentator on many network programs including NBC, CBS, ABC, Fox News, CNN, and C-SPAN. This essay appeared in the June 30, 2003, issue of *The Nation*.

1 George W. Bush is generally regarded as a mangler of the English language. What is overlooked is his mastery of emotional language—especially negatively charged emotional language—as a political tool. Take a closer look at his speeches and public utterances, and his political success turns out to be no surprise. It is the predictable result of the intentional use of language to dominate others.

2 President Bush, like many dominant personality types, uses dependency-creating language. He employs language of contempt and intimidation to shame others into submission and desperate admiration. While we tend to think of the dominator as using physical force, in fact most dominators use verbal abuse to control others. Abusive language has been a major theme of psychological researchers on marital problems, such as John Gottman, and of philosophers and theologians, such as Josef Pieper. But little has been said about the key role it has come to play in political discourse, and in such "hot media" as talk radio and television.

3 Bush uses several dominating linguistic techniques to induce surrender to his will. The first is empty language. This term refers to broad statements that are so abstract and mean so little that they are virtually impossible to oppose. Empty language is the emotional equivalent of empty calories. Just as we seldom question the content of potato chips while enjoying their pleasurable taste, recipients of empty language are usually distracted from examining the content of what they are hearing. Dominators use empty language to conceal faulty generalizations; to ridicule viable alternatives; to attribute negative motivations to others, thus making them appear contemptible; and to rename and "reframe" opposing viewpoints.

4 Bush's 2003 State of the Union speech contained thirty-nine examples of empty language. He used it to reduce complex problems to images that left the listener relieved that George W. Bush was in charge. Rather than explaining the relationship between malpractice insurance and skyrocketing healthcare costs, Bush summed up: "No one has ever been healed by a frivolous lawsuit." The multiple fiscal and monetary policy tools that can be used to stimulate an economy were downsized to: "The best and fairest way to make sure Americans have that money is not to tax it away in the first place." The controversial plan to wage another war

on Iraq was simplified to: "We will answer every danger and every enemy that threatens the American people." In an earlier study, I found that in the 2000 presidential debates Bush used at least four times as many phrases containing empty language as Carter, Reagan, Clinton, Bush Senior or Gore had used in their debates.

5   Another of Bush's dominant-language techniques is personalization. By personalization I mean localizing the attention of the listener on the speaker's personality. Bush projects himself as the only person capable of producing results. In his post-9/11 speech to Congress he said, "I will not forget this wound to our country or those who inflicted it. I will not yield; I will not rest; I will not relent in waging this struggle for freedom and security for the American people." He substitutes his determination for that of the nation's. In the 2003 State of the Union speech he vowed, "I will defend the freedom and security of the American people." Contrast Bush's "I will not yield" etc. with John F. Kennedy's "Ask not what your country can do for you, ask what you can do for your country."

6   The word "you" rarely appears in Bush's speeches. Instead, there are numerous statements referring to himself or his personal characteristics—folksiness, confidence, righteous anger or determination—as the answer to the problems of the country. Even when Bush uses "we," as he did many times in the State of the Union speech, he does it in a way that focuses attention on himself. For example, he stated: "Once again, we are called to defend the safety of our people, and the hopes of all mankind. And we accept this responsibility."

7   In an article in the January 16 *New York Review of Books*, Joan Didion highlighted Bush's high degree of personalization and contempt for argumentation in presenting his case for going to war in Iraq. As Didion writes: "'I made up my mind,' he had said in April, 'that Saddam needs to go.' This was one of many curious, almost petulant statements offered in lieu of actually presenting a case. I've made up my mind, I've said in speech after speech, I've made myself clear. The repeated statements became their own reason."

8   Poll after poll demonstrates that Bush's political agenda is out of step with most Americans' core beliefs. Yet the public, their electoral resistance broken down by empty language and persuaded by personalization, is susceptible to Bush's most frequently used linguistic technique: negative framework. A negative framework is a pessimistic image of the world. Bush creates and maintains negative frameworks in his listeners' minds with a number of linguistic techniques borrowed from advertising and hypnosis to instill the image of a dark and evil world around us. Catastrophic words and phrases are repeatedly drilled into the listener's head until the opposition feels such a high level of anxiety that it appears pointless to do anything other than cower.

9   Psychologist Martin Seligman, in his extensive studies of "learned helplessness," showed that people's motivation to respond to outside threats and problems is undermined by a belief that they have no control over their environment. Learned helplessness is exacerbated by beliefs that problems caused by negative events are permanent; and when the underlying causes are perceived to apply to many other events, the condition becomes pervasive and paralyzing.

10   Bush is a master at inducing learned helplessness in the electorate. He uses pessimistic language that creates fear and disables people from feeling they can solve their problems. In his September 20, 2001, speech to Congress on the 9/11 attacks, he chose to increase people's sense of vulnerability: "Americans should not

expect one battle, but a lengthy campaign, unlike any other we have ever seen. . . . I ask you to live your lives, and hug your children. I know many citizens have fears tonight. . . . Be calm and resolute, even in the face of a continuing threat." (Subsequent terror alerts by the FBI, CIA and Department of Homeland Security have maintained and expanded this fear of unknown, sinister enemies.)

11   Contrast this rhetoric with Franklin Roosevelt's speech delivered the day after the Japanese attack on Pearl Harbor. He said: "No matter how long it may take us to overcome this premeditated invasion, the American people in their righteous might will win through to absolute victory. . . . There is no blinking at the fact that our people, our territory and our interests are in grave danger. With confidence in our armed forces—with the unbounding determination of our people—we will gain the inevitable triumph—so help us God." Roosevelt focuses on an optimistic future rather than an ongoing threat to Americans' personal survival.

12   All political leaders must define the present threats and problems faced by the country before describing their approach to a solution, but the ratio of negative to optimistic statements in Bush's speeches and policy declarations is much higher, more pervasive and more long-lasting than that of any other President. Let's compare "crisis" speeches by Bush and Ronald Reagan, the President with whom he most identifies himself. In Reagan's October 27, 1983, televised address to the nation on the bombing of the US Marine barracks in Beirut, he used nineteen images of crisis and twenty-one images of optimism, evenly balancing optimistic and negative depictions. He limited his evaluation of the problems to the past and present tense, saying only that "with patience and firmness we can bring peace to that strife-torn region—and make our own lives more secure." George W. Bush's October 7, 2002, major policy speech on Iraq, on the other hand, began with forty-four consecutive statements referring to the crisis and citing a multitude of possible catastrophic repercussions. The vast majority of these statements (for example: "Some ask how urgent this danger is to America and the world. The danger is already significant, and it only grows worse with time"; "Iraq could decide on any given day to provide a biological or chemical weapon to a terrorist group or individual terrorists") imply that the crisis will last into the indeterminate future. There is also no specific plan of action. The absence of plans is typical of a negative framework, and leaves the listener without hope that the crisis will ever end. Contrast this with Reagan, who, a third of the way into his explanation of the crisis in Lebanon, asked the following: "Where do we go from here? What can we do now to help Lebanon gain greater stability so that our Marines can come home? Well, I believe we can take three steps now that will make a difference."

13   To create a dependency dynamic between him and the electorate, Bush describes the nation as being in a perpetual state of crisis and then attempts to convince the electorate that it is powerless and that he is the only one with the strength to deal with it. He attempts to persuade people they must transfer power to him, thus crushing the power of the citizen, the Congress, the Democratic Party, even constitutional liberties, to concentrate all power in the imperial presidency and the Republican Party.

14   Bush's political opponents are caught in a fantasy that they can win against him simply by proving the superiority of their ideas. However, people do not support Bush for the power of his ideas, but out of the despair and desperation in their hearts. Whenever people are in the grip of a desperate dependency, they won't respond to

rational criticisms of the people they are dependent on. They will respond to plausible and forceful statements and alternatives that put the American electorate back in touch with their core optimism. Bush's opponents must combat his dark imagery with hope and restore American vigor and optimism in the coming years. They should heed the example of Reagan, who used optimism against Carter and the "national malaise"; Franklin Roosevelt, who used it against Hoover and the pessimism induced by the Depression ("the only thing we have to fear is fear itself"); and Clinton (the "Man from Hope"), who used positive language against the senior Bush's lack of vision. This is the linguistic prescription for those who wish to [challenge Bush's emotional language for the remainder of his presidency].

THINKING CRITICALLY

1. What is "dependency-creating" language? According to Brooks, how and why does President Bush use this type of language in his addresses to the American people?

2. What is Brooks's opinion of President Bush? Identify parts of her essay in which she reveals her personal point of view.

3. Brooks notes Bush's use of pronouns. What does she think his pronoun use reveals about his relationship with the American people and his role as president?

4. What effect do the "catastrophic words and phrases" that Bush uses have on his listeners? How does Brooks support her argument that this language is particularly damaging to the president's audience?

5. Brooks offers examples of language used by other presidents. Contrast the language used by these other leaders and analyze what it reveals about their relationship with the American public.

6. Evaluate Brooks's use of examples to support her argument. Are her examples fair and balanced? Do they support her points? Explain.

WRITING ASSIGNMENTS

1. In paragraph 4, Brooks claims to find thirty-nine examples of empty language used by President Bush in his 2003 State of the Union speech. Review this speech at www.whitehouse.gov (search for "state of union 2003") and try to identify as many instances of empty language as you can. What does a close reading of Bush's language reveal about his position on important issues? Alternatively, you may choose to argue against Brooks's position and explain why Bush's use of language is effective and purposeful.

2. Brooks asserts in this essay that President Bush uses language to create a culture of dependency in which Americans are made to feel helpless. Review the last State of the Union speech made by President George W. Bush and evaluate his use of this type of language. Write an essay in which you agree or disagree, either in whole or in part, with Brooks's assertion that Bush uses language to engender feelings of helplessness and dependency, especially as it relates to war in the Middle East.

3. Research online the psychology of "dependency-creating" and emotional language as a form of verbal abuse used to control others. Based on your research, is President Bush intentionally using such linguistic techniques to dominate others?

The Making of the Speech

D. T. Max

In the previous essay, Renana Brooks discussed the nuances of George W. Bush's language. In this article, D. T. Max describes the process of preparing a presidential speech, in this case, the president's formal oration before Congress addressing the attacks of September 11. As you read the details of how a speech is prepared for the president, consider the many stages of writing; the audience; sources of information; and details such as setting, tone, and style, that factor into the finished product.

D. T. Max is a writer and a contributing editor of the *Paris Review*. He is the author of *The Family That Couldn't Sleep* (2006). Max's articles have appeared in many journals and newspapers, including *The LA Times Sunday Book Review*, *Salon* magazine, the *Boston Phoenix*, and the *New York Times*. Max is a frequent contributor to *The New York Times Magazine*, in which this article first appeared in October 2001.

1 The president could not find the right words. Soon after the World Trade Center and the Pentagon were attacked on Sept. 11, he tried to articulate his response. In one week he gave more than a dozen speeches and remarks to comfort, rally and then— when he'd rallied too much—calm the country. To some, his language seemed undisciplined. He called the terrorists "folks" and referred to the coming battle as a "crusade." He called for "revenge," called Osama bin Laden the "prime suspect" and asked for him "dead or alive." He said "make no mistake" at least eight times in public remarks. When Bush didn't seem lost, he often seemed scared. When he didn't seem scared, he often seemed angry. None of this soothed the public. "It was beginning to look like 'Bring Me the Head of Osama bin Laden,' starring Ronald Colman," one White House official remembered.

2 In a time of national crisis, words are key to the presidency. Too many and people tune out; too few and they think he is hiding. The president knew he had not yet said the right things. He returned from Camp David the weekend after the attacks with an intense desire to make a major speech. His aides agreed. The president needed to reassure Americans while conveying a message of resolve to the world. Shaping a successful speech wouldn't be easy. Karen P. Hughes, the counselor to the president, helped write the straightforward statement the president gave on the night of the attack. The speech, delivered from the Oval Office, was poorly received; it felt too slight, too brief for the great events. Three days later, the president's speechwriting team, led by Michael Gerson, came up with an eloquent meditation on grief and resolution, which the president read at the National Cathedral. "We are in the middle hour of our grief," it began. But the beautiful speech sounded borrowed coming from Bush's mouth. The tone was too literary. The president's next speech had to be grand—but it also had to sound more like him.

3 The White House also had to decide where to give it. Among the choices the president and his advisers had was an address to Congress, which had invited him to speak before a joint session. There is no greater backdrop for a president. But some advisers were reluctant. The president couldn't march up Pennsylvania Avenue without something new to say. And according to his advisers, Bush wasn't sure yet what the administration's response to the attack would be. Some advisers

suggested a second Oval Office speech, which would be more intimate and controlled than an address to Congress. Others suggested speaking at a war college. He would look strong there.

4   Karl Rove, the president's chief political adviser, felt strongly that the president did better with a big audience. Applause revved him up. Congress, he thought, was ideal: it would build a sense of national unity. That was important. The speech was a huge political opportunity for Bush. War had given the president a second chance to define himself, an accidental shot at rebirth. Bush's first eight months had been middling. To many, he seemed a little slight for the job. His tax cut had gone through, but the education initiative, the defense transformation and the faith-based initiative were not moving forward well. Americans had still not embraced him as a leader. A strong speech could revive Bush's presidency.

5   The president decided to speak to Congress. But he wasn't sure yet what to say. The main focus of the speech was tricky to define. "He had to speak to multiple audiences," his national security adviser, Condoleezza Rice, later told me. "He was speaking to the American people, foreign leaders, to the Congress and to the Taliban."

6   Karen Hughes met Bush at the White House residence Sunday afternoon to discuss what ground the speech might cover. She jotted down notes: Who are they? Why they hate us? What victory means? How will it be won? On Monday morning, Bush talked to Hughes again. According to Hughes, he told her how to deal with the fact that military action might come anytime. "If we've done something, discuss what we have done," he told Hughes. "If not, tell people to get ready." He told her he wanted a draft quickly. Hughes called Michael Gerson and told him that he had until 7 P.M. to come up with something.

7   Gerson does not write alone. He has five other writers, two of whom he works closely with, Matt Scully and John McConnell. Scully is wiry and ironic, like a comedy writer. McConnell is more earnest. They help bring Gerson down to earth. Gerson, 37, is an owlish man who fills yellow pads with doodles when you ask him a question. He says he believes that social justice must be central in Republican thought. "The great stories of our time," he told me, "are moral stories and moral commitments: the civil rights movement, the War on Poverty." He and the president get along well. The president calls Gerson "the scribe." They share an intensely felt Christianity.

8   Gerson had written speeches with Scully and McConnell during the campaign. They worked well together. Since then, Gerson has moved up a notch: he now has an office in the basement of the West Wing. The office is prestigious but not great for writing. It is claustrophobic and illuminated by artificial light. McConnell and Scully were in the Old Executive Office Building. If the West Wing, with its plush carpeting and secretaries in heels, resembles a Sun Belt office suite, the O.E.O.B. is by comparison a funky hotel. Every office, no matter how small, had its own couch, yet no office had a matching set of chairs. It was a good place to brainstorm.

9   So Gerson crossed West Executive Avenue to see McConnell and Scully. The three writers sat around the computer in McConnell's office, Gerson in one of the gray suits he wears, bouncing nervously, Scully's feet up on the couch. They began to write, adopting the magisterial tone of presidential speechwriting. These were great events. They deserved great sentiments, a lofty style that Don Baer, a communications director in the Clinton administration, called "reaching for the marble."

The three wrote as a team, trying out sentences on each other: "Tonight we are a country awakened to danger. . . ." They went quickly. They knew there would be time to change things and plenty of hands to do it. They assumed that one of the widows of the heroes of United Airlines Flight 93 would be there, so they put in Lyzbeth Glick, the widow of Jeremy Glick, one of the men who apparently fought with the hijackers. (In fact it would be Lisa Beamer, whose husband, Todd, had also been on the plane.) They knew little for certain, and knowing little increased their natural tendency to sound like Churchill, whose writing they all liked. Gerson tried out: "In the long term, terrorism is not answered by higher walls and deeper bunkers." The team kept going: "Whether we bring our enemies to justice or bring justice to our enemies, justice will be done." The computer screen filled with rolling triads. "This is the world's fight; this is civilization's fight; this is the fight of all who believe in progress and pluralism, tolerance and freedom." Words tumbled out.

10   The patriotic riffs were falling in place. But what, and how much, could they tell the country about the administration's plans for bin Laden and Afghanistan? They received some help from John Gibson, another speechwriter. Gibson writes foreign-policy speeches for the president and the National Security Council and regularly attends meetings with Condoleezza Rice, the national security adviser, and Stephen Hadley, her deputy. Gibson has the odd job of writing public words about the government's most private decisions. He has top-secret security clearance; his hard drive is stored in a safe.

11   Gibson made contact with Richard A. Clarke, the counterterrorism director for the N.S.C. Clarke is a white-haired, stocky man who has been in the job for nearly a decade. He speaks very loudly. "Even his e-mails are blustery," one White House employee told me. Whatever the meetings were, he was still going to them. Gibson e-mailed Clarke questions that unintentionally echoed Hughes's original discussion with Bush: Who is our enemy? What do they want?

12   The e-mailed answer came in a bulleted memo. Who is our enemy? "Al Qaeda." What do they want? "That all Christians and Jews must be driven out of a vast area of the world," and "that existing governments in Islamic countries like Egypt and Saudi Arabia should be toppled. They have issued phony religious rulings calling for the deaths of all Americans, including women and children." Gibson liked the tone and authority of the response. He handed over an edited version to Gerson.

13   Using Gibson's edit, Gerson, Scully and McConnell began on the Taliban. Scully started: "We're not deceived by their pretenses to piety." Gerson wrote: "They're the heirs of all the murderous ideologies of the 20th century. By sacrificing human life to serve their radical visions, by abandoning every value except the will to power, they follow in the path of Fascism and Nazism and imperial Communism." Scully added, "And they will follow that path all the way to where it ends." They paused. Where would it end? They didn't know. But there were plenty of ready-made phrases around. McConnell threw out five or six, like crumbs from his pocket. They liked the idea of predicting the end of the Taliban's reign of terror. "You know, history's unmarked grave," McConnell said. The group bounced the phrase around until McConnell came up with: "It will end in discarded lies." Gerson liked that, too. So the line read, "history's unmarked grave of discarded lies."

14   But if the Taliban were going to wind up on the ash heap of history, then someone had to suggest how this would be accomplished. Would we attack tomorrow?
Would we mount a land invasion of Afghanistan? Would we take on Iraq as well?
No one knew. Policy and prose work their way on separate tracks at the White
House, only meeting at higher levels. Speechwriters sometimes sit around with finished speeches, waiting for the policy person to call and let them know what the
whole thing is for. Not knowing what the president was going to announce, Gerson
and his team couldn't come up with the right tone for an ending. But they had done
what they could, written a joint-session speech in a day. They sent it off to Hughes.

15   Under Secretary of State Colin Powell's guidance, the State Department drafted
the language of the goals. Condoleezza Rice walked them into the Oval Office.
There, Bush was saying that he liked the speech but the ending wasn't right; the
speechwriters and Hughes scribbled notes as he spoke. Bush was enormously
excited, Hughes recalled. The speech shouldn't end reflectively, he said. It should
end with him leading. Rice then read aloud the demands Powell sent over: deliver
the leaders of Al Qaeda to the United States; release detained foreign nationals and
protect those in Afghanistan; close the terrorist camps. Give the United States full
inspection access. Bush liked the points. Calling on the Taliban to give up bin Laden
in front of Congress would be a moment of some power. He told the speechwriters
to translate them from bureaucratese. Rice left her notes with the speechwriters.

16   The speechwriters went back to work. They laid more marble: "This is not,
however, just America's fight. And what is at stake is not just America's freedom.
This is the world's fight. This is civilization's fight."

17   Hughes took notes and put them into her copy of the speech. She was thinking
domestically: these were wrongs Americans could understand. Hughes also
amplified language that Gerson's team had written expressing compassion for the
Afghan people. What had helped Bush become president were the overtures of
compassion in his conservatism. In the days after the attack, he'd been so bellicose
that his father called to tell him to tone it down. It was time to bring back the
candidate.

18   Gerson, Scully, McConnell and Hughes sat down in Hughes's office on
Wednesday at 11 A.M. They grouped around Hughes's computer. In front of her was
a little plaque quoting Churchill: "I was not the lion, but it fell to me to give the
lion's roar." New material kept coming in. Vice President Dick Cheney sent up a
short text with McConnell defining the new cabinet position, director of homeland
security. Hughes felt that the speech didn't make the point clearly enough about
America's respect for Muslim Americans. The president's rush visit to a mosque
had gotten a good response on Monday; it was important to highlight that theme.
Hughes changed the phrase "Tonight I also have a message for Muslims in
America" to "I also want to speak tonight directly to Muslims throughout the
world. We respect your faith." She helped write the sentence "The United States respects the people of Afghanistan." Hughes was taking the speech out of marble and
making it concrete. She added "I ask you to live your lives and hug your children."
Rove stopped by; as a result of his input, the speechwriters added the line "I know
many citizens have fears tonight, and I ask you to be calm and resolute."
Rice's deputy, Stephen Hadley, who had to worry about more terrorism, suggested

reminding people that there might be more terrorism to come. "Even in the face of a continuing threat" was added to the sentence.

19   All week, the president worked on the speech at night in the residence. He likes his speeches to make a point and for the point to be clear. He hates redundancies. He took a course in American oratory at Yale and remembers how a speech divides into an introduction, main body, peroration. (He once annotated a speech with phrases like "tugs at heartstrings" and "emotional call to arms.") Bush writes his notes with a black Sharpie pen. His edits tend to simplify. He is a parer. "Bush favors active verbs and short sentences," Rove said.

20   The president had strong feelings about the speech's ending. Although they had not yet found a place for it, the writers had suggested including a quote from Franklin Delano Roosevelt in the speech's conclusion: "We defend and we build a way of life, not for America alone, but for all mankind." The president didn't want to quote anyone else. He'd said this to them in emphatic terms at a meeting the day before, explaining that he saw this as a chance to lead. "I was scribbling notes as fast as I could," Gerson said.

21   The team worked on an ending that would be all Bush. They revisited the phrase "freedom and fear are at war" and gave it a providential spin: "We know that God is not neutral between them." Without hitting it too hard, a religious note would be sounded.

22   At 1 P.M., Gerson's team met with Bush and Hughes. They pulled up their chairs around the desk in the Oval Office. "You all have smiles on your faces; that's good," Bush said. Then, wearing his glasses, he began reading the speech aloud, stopping only for a few edits. He read the new ending aloud. "It is my hope that in the months and years ahead, life will return almost to normal," it said. "Even grief recedes with time and grace." But these comforting words were not all. "I will not forget the wound to our country and those who inflicted it," the speech went on. "I will not yield. I will not rest. I will not relent in waging this struggle for freedom and security for the American people." It echoed William Lloyd Garrison ("And I will be heard!"), but it was his own. Here was his peroration, and it tugged on your heartstrings and called you to arms. The final "freedom and fear" image worked, too. The president said: "Great speech, team. Let's call the Congress." He would give the speech the next night, on Thursday the 20th.

23   The president had to rehearse. It was the first thing he'd thought of after deciding to do the speech. The more time he practices, the better his speeches come off. The downward furl of his mouth relaxes. His tendency to end every phrase with an upward cadence diminishes. The first teleprompter rehearsal was at 6:30 Wednesday night. The president came out in his blue track suit with his baseball cap on. His dog, Spot, ran around the room, nuzzling the writers as they sat listening. The president weighed the sounds in his mouth. He came to lines about the administration's domestic legislative agenda, lines that had been slowly piling up—the energy plan, the faith-based initiative, the patients' bill of rights. "This isn't the time," he said and cut them. Hughes agreed. This was the time for Bush to assert his credentials on foreign policy and not retreat into the domestic sphere.

24   Thursday morning, the day of the speech, Bush rehearsed again. He didn't like the clunky paragraph that contained the list of our allies: the Organization of

American States and the European Union, among others. It was too much of a mouthful. They would no longer hear their names spoken. State lost that round.

25   The president took a nap at 4:30, was awakened by an aide and rehearsed one more time. At 5:15 Hughes told Gerson the name of the new director of homeland security. It was Bush's old friend, the governor of Pennsylvania, Tom Ridge. The news had been held back so it wouldn't leak. Tony Blair, the British prime minister, was late arriving for dinner, and the president was offered a chance to rehearse again but said he was ready. The communications office prepared a list of sound bites and distributed them to the press: "The enemy of America is not our many Muslim friends." "Be ready." "Freedom and fear are at war."

26   The president got into his motorcade and went to the Capitol. The vice president stayed behind so they would not be in the Capitol together. It was an unprecedented security move. It meant that every time the camera showed Bush, you would think about the meaning of Cheney's absence. You would remember the crisis. Bush walked into the Capitol, a president in wartime. He wore a pale blue tie. He began: "Mr. Speaker, Mr. President pro tempore, members of Congress and fellow Americans." He was interrupted for applause 31 times.

27   A week after the speech, the flag at the White House was back at full mast, waving in the wind. Karen Hughes wore a metal American flag on her lapel, upward streaming too. Was the speech a success? For the president, yes. "He told me he felt very comfortable," Hughes said. "I told him he was phenomenal." Bush had wanted to steady the boat, and he had done it. He had shown leadership. The Congress felt included. "The president's speech was exactly what the nation needed—a message of determination and hope, strength and compassion," Ted Kennedy said. For the writers, there was catharsis: Gerson felt that by working on the speech, he had become connected to "the men digging with shovels in New York." Pundits wrote that the president had said just the right thing in a time of crisis. The Uzbeks were pleased. The Syrians were not enraged. Only the Canadians, of all people, were piqued: their mention, as part of O.A.S., had been cut so the speech wouldn't sag. Even professional speechwriters, tough critics of one another, were impressed. "It was a good, strong speech," said Ted Sorensen, who wrote speeches for John F. Kennedy. "I'm not sure 'freedom versus fear' means much. But it had a nice ring to it, and you can be sure we're on the side of freedom."

28   The very act of the speech suggested that civilized life would continue. The president had just sat around a big war map at Camp David—but instead of first doing something violent, he turned to words. Some of those words were bland. Many were vague. Other than the demands to the Taliban, there was little policy in it. "This was a strategic speech, not tactical," admitted a senior White House official.

29   This wasn't a State of the Union address. It wasn't a moment to look ahead. Bad news could wait. New presidents are terrified of looking indecisive, but this one realized it would be worse to be rash. Who are they? Where are they? How can we strike back? The coming challenge is enormous. By delivering a speech that emphasized reason over wrath, Bush bought himself some time until someone could draw a real map for the first war of the 21st century.

THINKING CRITICALLY

1. In his introduction, Max identifies several unscripted words and phrases Bush used in response to September 11. What was objectionable about these words? Explain.

2. What does Max mean when he says "words are the key to the presidency"? Do you agree? Why or why not?

3. In your opinion, is it expected and acceptable that presidents have speech writing teams? Is there a fine line between being scripted and being assisted? What is your position on presidential speech writing?

4. Describe in brief the multifaceted aspects of creating a presidential speech.

5. What is Karen P. Hughes's role in creating the presidential "voice"? How does the president's voice differ from what his speech writers create? Explain.

6. What is the importance of style in the creation and delivery of a presidential speech? What is the president's style? How does setting factor into the delivery and ultimate reception of his speech? Explain.

7. What is "bureaucratese"? Why does Bush object to it?

8. After reading this description of the etymology of a presidential speech, do you feel more or less respect for the president? Explain your point of view.

WRITING ASSIGNMENTS

1. Max explains that this speech is the one that "changed a presidency." Read about issues connected to the speech at www.whitehouse.gov/news/releases/2001/09/20010920-8.html. Read the entire speech that follows, and analyze its language, style, tone, and construction. What makes this particular speech so significant? What factors before and after its delivery contribute to its success in changing the public's perception of George W. Bush? Explain.

2. Write an essay exploring the connection between the president, his language, and public perception of his leadership. Use examples from at least three different presidents from the twentieth century as you formulate your essay.

President George W. Bush Discusses Global War on Terror

Kansas State University

January 23, 2006

1 THE PRESIDENT: Thanks for the warm welcome. Thanks for inviting me here to give the Landon Lecture. For those students who are here, I want you to know I can remember what it was like to sit through lectures. I didn't particularly like it then. Some will take a little different approach. I'm here to tell you how I see the world and how I've made some of the decisions I've made and why I made them. . . .

2   Before I get there, I do want to pay tribute to our wonderful men and women in uniform. Thank you for serving our country.

3   You know, really one of the interesting things about being the President is to invite my guys, buddies I grew up with from Texas, to the White House. It's really neat to see how they react to the majesty of the White House and the Oval Office and the South Lawn, and just the beauty of Washington. And most of them, after they get over the initial shock of seeing the White House, then come to the shock wondering how in the heck I got there.

4   But they, oftentimes, they ask me, they say, what's it like, being the President of the United States? And my answer to them is, first, it's a huge honor. But, secondly, if I had to give you a job description, it would be a decision-maker. I make a lot of decisions. I make some that you see that obviously affect people's lives, not only here, but around the world. I make a lot of small ones you never see, but have got consequence. Decision-maker is the job description.

5   First of all, when you make decisions, you've got to stand on principle. If you're going to make decisions, you've got to know what you believe. I guess the best way to summarize me is I came from Texas and I'm going back to Texas with the exact same values I had when I arrived in Washington, D.C. (Applause.)

6   In order to make good decisions, you've got to rely upon the judgment of people you trust. I'll never forget the first decision I had to make as the President. I wasn't even sworn in yet, and a fellow called me on the phone and he said, what color rug do you want to have in the Oval Office? You've got to be kidding me, man. He said, no, what color rug would you like to have in the Oval Office? I said, I don't know. He said, well, it turns out that Presidents—you've just got to know Presidents design their rugs. I said, well, to be honest with you, I don't know much about designing rugs.

7   So I called, I delegated—that's one of the things you do in decision-making. I said, Laura, how about helping design the rug? Part of being a decision-maker, though, is you've got to help—you've got to think strategically. And so I said to her—she said, what color do you want? I said, make it say this: optimistic person comes here to work every single day. You can't lead the nation, you can't make good decisions unless you're optimistic about the future.

8   So for the students here, as you take over organizations or head out of college and become involved in your life, you've got to be optimistic about—if you're going to lead somebody. Imagine somebody saying, follow me, the world is going to be worse. That's not a very good organizing principle about which to lead people. I'm optimistic about our future, and the reason I am is because I believe so strongly in what America stands for: liberty and freedom and human rights, and the human dignity of every single person. (Applause.)

9   Sometimes decisions come to your desk unexpectedly. Part of the job of a President is to be able to plan for the worst and hope for the best; and if the worst comes, be able to react to it. On September the 11th, the worst came. We got attacked. We didn't ask for the attack, but it came. I resolved on that day to do everything I can to protect the American people.

10   You know, a lot of us grew up thinking that oceans would protect us; that if there was a threat overseas, it really didn't concern us because we were safe. That's what history had basically told us—yes, there was an attack on Pearl Harbor, obviously, but it was a kind of hit-and-run and then we pursued the enemy. A lot of folks—at least, my age, when I was going to college, I never dreamed that the

United States of America could be attacked. And in that we got attacked, I vowed then, like I'm vowing to you today, that I understand my most important priority. My most important job is to protect the security of the American people.

11   I knew right after September the 11th, though, that the attacks would begin to fade in people's memory. I mean, who wants to constantly go through life thinking that you're going to get hit again? Who wants to kind of re-live those days in your memory? As a matter of fact, I asked the American people to go on about your life. But given the fact that it's human nature to forget, or try to put in the past, put the pain in the past, I want to assure you and our fellow Americans I'm not going to put it in the past. The threat to the United States is forefront in my mind. I knew that at times people would say, you know, it may be an isolated incident, let's just don't worry about it. Well, for me it's not an isolated incident. I understand there is still an enemy which lurks out there.

12   And so part of my decision-making process, part of it as you see when I begin to protect you, to do my number one priority, rests upon this fact: that there is an enemy which is relentless and desirous to bring harm to the American people, because of what we believe in. See, we're in an ideological struggle. It's very important for the students here to understand that there is an enemy which has an ideology, and they're driven by an ideology. They make decisions based upon their view of the world, which is the exact opposite of our view of the world.

13   Perhaps the best way to describe their political vision is to remind you what life was like for people living in Afghanistan when the Taliban was running that country with al Qaeda as the parasite. If you were a young girl in that society, you had no chance to get educated. If you spoke out against the view of these folks, their religious view, you could be taken to the public square and whipped. In other words, there was not freedom. There wasn't freedom to worship the way you want to, just like we believe here in the United States of America. You can worship, you can not worship in our country, and you're equally American. You can be a Christian, Jew or Muslim, and you're equally American. It's the greatness of the United States of America which—(applause)—which stands in stark contrast to what these ideologues believe.

14   Their vision of the world is dark and dim. They have got desires to spread a totalitarian empire. How do we know? Because they told us. Mr. Zawahiri, the number two in the al Qaeda network, told the world such. He might not have wanted us to read that particular thing he was sending, but nevertheless we did. And he said that, here's our designs and our desires. In other words, these people have got an ideology, and strategy to implement the ideology. They've got a—they have no heart, no conscience. They kill innocent men, women and children to achieve their objective. These folks cannot be appeased. We can't hope that nice words will change their point of view.

15   And so the decision I made right off the bat is we will find them, and we will hunt them down, and we will bring them to justice before they hurt America again. (Applause.)

16   But that requires a different kind of response than the old days of nations fighting nations. First of all, I want to step back and just tell you—I probably—I hope I say this more than once, but committing U.S. troops into harm's way is the last

option of the President. It's the hardest decision a President can make. And so when I'm telling you I made the decision, you all have got to understand, I did not take that decision lightly. I knew the consequences, but I also believed that the consequences of not acting against this enemy would mean I wasn't doing my job of working with others to protect the United States of America. (Applause.)

17   So we sent our men and women into harm's way—all volunteers. It is really important for the United States of America to have an all-volunteer Army. The best way to keep people volunteering in the Army is to make sure they got good pay, good training, good equipment and good housing for their loved ones. (Applause.)

18   But since we're not able to track vast battalions or armadas, we've got to have intelligence, good intelligence, to help us locate the dark corners of the world where these people hide. A lot of the decisions I make, and decisions future Presidents make, will be based upon the capacity of our intelligence services to find the enemy and to understand the intentions of the enemy and to share information with our allies. This is a different kind of struggle and requires the best intelligence possible. That's why we're reevaluating, constantly reevaluating, how best to use our intelligence services to be able to protect the American people.

19   We've got to be strong in diplomacy. Secretary Rice, who is a great diplomat, she followed another great—she followed another great diplomat in Colin Powell—they're constantly working to remind people about the stakes. Just like part of my job is to educate the American people about the threats we face, at a lecture series such as this, our government must constantly remind our friends and allies the nature of the enemy and the stakes that all free countries face. There's a diplomatic effort that's constantly going on.

20   You can't run your network without money, and so we're working with our friends and allies to seize terrorist assets and choke off their funding sources. In other words, what I'm telling you is, we're using all assets at our disposal to protect you in a different kind of war. In order to make the right decision about how to win this war, it's important to understand the nature of the enemy and to take the enemy's word seriously and to understand their lethality and not let the kind of lull in the action lull us to sleep.

21   Secondly, right after they attacked us, I laid out a doctrine, and it said, if you harbor a terrorist, you're equally as guilty as the terrorists. The reason I said that is because I understand that a terrorist network can sometimes burrow in society and can sometimes find safe haven from which to plot and plan. The perfect example of that was Afghanistan. For those of you who didn't pay much attention to the initial stages of this war, it became apparent to the world that Afghanistan became a safe haven. You'll hear stories about people that went into Afghanistan to be trained— trained as to how to brutally kill people, trained in different methodologies, trained in how to communicate.

22   So in other words, the enemy was able to burrow in, and felt safe and confident and secure. And I understood in this different kind of war that we had to make it clear to any country that if they harbored a terrorist, they would be held to account. And when the American President speaks, it's really important for those words to mean something. And so when I said to the Taliban, get rid of al Qaeda, and they

didn't, I made the difficult decision to commit our troops, to uphold the doctrine that if you harbor a terrorist, you're equally as guilty as the terrorist. And our kids went in, men and women alike, and liberated a country from the clutches of the barbaric regime, the Taliban.

23   And today, today in Afghanistan, think about what has happened in a brief period of time—today in Afghanistan there is a fledgling democracy. Al Qaeda no longer has run of the country; the Taliban is routed; there's an elected parliament and a president dedicated to democratic institutions. (Applause.)

24   The doctrine still stands: If you harbor a terrorist, you're equally as guilty as the terrorists who commit murder.

25   Thirdly—and this is very important for the students to understand, and others—because oceans no longer protect us, the United States of America must confront threats before they cause us harm. In other words, in the old days we could see a threat and say, well, maybe it will cause harm, maybe it won't. Those days changed, as far as I'm concerned. Threats must be taken seriously now, because geography doesn't protect us and there's an enemy that still lurks. And so early in my first term, I looked at the world and saw a threat in Saddam Hussein. And let me tell you why I saw the threat.

26   First of all, there was an immediate threat because he was shooting at our airplanes. There was what's called no-fly zones; that meant the Iraqis couldn't fly in the zones, and we were patrolling with British pilots. And he was firing at us, which was a threat—a threat to the life and limb of the troops to whom I'm the Commander-in-Chief. He was a state sponsor of terror. In other words, the government had declared, you are a state sponsor of terror. And, remember, we're dealing with terrorist networks that would like to do us harm.

27   There's a reason why he was declared a state sponsor of terror—because he was sponsoring terror. He had used weapons of mass destruction. And the biggest threat that this President, and future Presidents, must worry about is weapons of mass destruction getting in the hands of a terrorist network that would like to do us harm. That is the biggest threat we face. Airplanes were horrible; the attacks of aircraft were horrible. But the damage done could be multiplied if weapons of mass destruction were in the hands of these people.

28   The world thought Saddam Hussein had weapons of mass destruction. It wasn't just me or my administration. Our predecessor thought he had weapons of mass destruction. And there's a logical reason why—the data showed that he likely had weapons of mass destruction, and he'd use them. I told you, the last option for a President is to send troops into combat, and I was hoping that we could solve the issue, the threat, the threat to the United States by diplomatic means.

29   So I went to the United Nations. Secretary Powell carried our message to the United Nations. It said—see, now, I actually gave a speech to the United Nations, you might remember, and I said to them, basically, how many resolutions is it going to take before this threat will take us seriously? I mean, we passed, I don't know, 14, 15 different resolutions. That's a lot of resolutions. Pretty soon, if you pass that many resolutions, somebody is going to say, well, they may not mean anything. I want this body to be effective. It's important for the world, when it speaks, that people listen.

30   And so we passed another resolution that said that Saddam is in—and it unanimously passed, and the reason why is because the world thought he was a danger. It said: disarm, disclose, or face serious consequences. I'm the kind of fellow, when I—when we say something, I mean it, like I told you before. And I meant it.

31   And so Saddam Hussein was given a choice. He chose war. And so we moved and he was removed from power. And there is absolutely no doubt in my mind, America is safer for it, and the world is better off without Saddam Hussein. (Applause.)

32   A lot of people, I understand, disagreed with that decision, and that's what democracy is all about, that's what we believe in. We believe you can disagree. There's a custom in our country for people to express themselves, and it's good. It's what makes us a great country, that people can stand up and tell people what's on their mind. And we're going to keep it that way. It's very important for those who didn't agree with the decision, though, to understand the consequences of success in Iraq. It's really important we succeed, for a lot of reasons.

33   And the definition of success, by the way, is for there to be a country where the terrorists and Saddamists can no longer threaten the democracy, and where Iraqi security forces can provide for the security of their people, and where Iraq is not a safe haven from which the terrorists—al Qaeda and its affiliates—can plot attacks against America.

34   We got a strategy, and I'm going to keep talking about the strategy—it will yield a victory. And the strategy is political security and economic in nature. In economic, we're going to help them rebuild their country, help secure their oil supply so they'll have cash flow in order to invest in their people.

35   On the political front, you've seen it—you've seen what happened in one year's time. It's just amazing, I think. I guess, we take it for granted—some of us do. I don't. The fact that people have gone from living under the clutches of a tyrant who ordered the murder of thousands of his own citizens, to a society in which people last year started voting—(applause)—voting for an interim government, voting for a constitution, and then voting for a permanent government under the new constitution. The government is now—they're beginning to form.

36   In other words, you're seeing a lot of sharp elbows, probably kind of like American politics seem to some people, a lot of throwing of sharp elbows. You didn't see a lot of elbows, political elbows being thrown under the tyrant, did you? That's because tyrants don't allow for the political process to evolve. But we're watching the political process evolve, made complicated by the fact that the terrorists still want to cause destruction and death as this government is forming to try to stop it.

37   We got to step back and ask why. Why would they want to stop democracy? And the answer, because democracy stands for the exact opposite of their vision. Liberty is not their credo. And they understand a defeat to their ideology by the establishment of a free Iraq will be a devastating blow for their vision.

38   And so the Iraqis are showing incredible courage. When somebody says, if you vote, I'm going to get you, sometimes people maybe say, well, maybe I don't want to vote. Eleven million or so Iraqis went to the polls in defiance of these killers. (Applause.) It's a magical moment in the history of liberty.

39 And then on the security front, our strategy can be summed up this way: As the Iraqis stand up, we'll stand down. Look, we want the Iraqis to be prepared to take the fight to the enemy. Let me talk about the enemy real quick in Iraq. There are what we call "rejectionists." These are Sunnis that kind of like the fact that they— even though a minority inside the country—had the upper hand for a long period of time with Saddam. And they're worried about whether or not a constitution that says it will protect minority rights actually will protect minority rights. But the good news is, more and more Sunnis started to vote. And if you watch the news, they're beginning to negotiate, they're beginning to see a better way. In other words, the political process is beginning to marginalize the remaining elements of those who are trying to stop the progress.

40 One of those elements is Saddamists. These are the thugs that kind of control the country. They loved power; they don't want to give it up. And they'd like to return to the good old days, which isn't going to happen.

41 And the other group of course, is the al Qaeda types, Mr. Zarqawi, who wants us to leave Iraq. They want us to get out of Iraq so Iraq can be a safe haven. It is their stated objective: Don't worry, take your time, keep killing the innocent because America will lose its will. That's what the enemy has said. That's their words.

42 The way to defeat the enemy is for the political process to marginalize the rejectionists, and for us to train the Iraqi forces so they can find the few that want to dash the hopes of the many, and that's what we're doing.

43 Our strategy is twofold: We're on the hunt for the terrorists, and we're training Iraqis. And we're making decent progress. There are more and more Iraqi units in the fight. There's more and more country being turned over to the Iraqis. We got a lot of bases around Iraq, and more of those bases are being given to the Iraqi troops.

44 This is the year that we'll not only continue to focus on the troops, we'll continue to train Iraqi police. We've seen some problems about what it means to have lived in a society where people want to seek revenge. In other words, they use their police—status as a police person to take it out on others because of past grievances. That's not acceptable to the United States of America. And it's not acceptable to most Iraqis, either.

45 And so part of the training for police is not only to give them the capacity to handle the enemy, but to make sure they understand human rights and ethics involved with police work. And so that's what you'll be seeing. You're going to see more Iraqi troops in the fight, and more police providing security. And as a result, our commanders on the ground informed me that they thought we could reduce our troop level from the 168,000 that were there—165,000, more or less, that were there for the election—below 138,000.

46 Now, I want to emphasize something to you, you heard me say, "our commanders on the ground said," you see, sometimes in the political process people feel beholden to polls and focus groups. You don't have to worry about me. I'm going to be listening to the people that know what they're talking about, and that's the commanders on the ground in Iraq. (Applause.) They'll make the decisions. They will give the advice. Conditions on the ground will dictate our force levels over the next year, but the strategy is what I said it is: We'll stay on the offense, and we'll

give these brave Iraqis the skills and training necessary to defend their own democracy.

47   Look, this enemy cannot beat us. They cannot defeat us militarily. There's no chance. The one weapon they have, which is a lethal weapon, is the willingness to kill people. I remember the story—and it just broke my heart to think about the young soldier that was giving candy to a kid, and they set off the car bomb next to the kids. I mean, it's just—I cannot describe to you how brutal these people are. And they understand that their scenes will get on TV. And I don't know if they can adequately understand the compassion of the American people. But we're compassionate.

48   I told you one of the great beliefs of our country is every life matters, every person counts—whether it be a child here in America, or a child in Iraq. And they understand. And so part of my decision-making process is to understand the strength of the enemy—the only strength they have—and continue to remind the people that is their only strength, and the only way we can lose is if we lose our nerve and our will. The American people are resolute. They are strong. And we're not going to lose our will to these thugs and murderers. (Applause.)

49   In there long-term—in the short-term, we'll stay on the offense; in the long-term, the way to defeat these people is to spread liberty. As you study history, I want you to watch the effects of freedom around the world. One of my favorite ways to describe my belief in the capacity of freedom to help achieve peace—not only security for the American people, but peace—is to give people the example of my dad and me, in terms of Japan.

50   My dad was an 18-year-old kid and went to fight the Japanese. I promise you, a lot of folks here, relatives, did the same thing. They were called into action because the enemy had attacked us. They were the sworn enemy of the United States of America. It was a brutal war against the Japanese. Took a lot of lives—Japanese lives and American lives—to win that war. And, today, like my recent trip to the Far East, I sit down with Prime Minister Koizumi, who is the Japanese Prime Minister, and talk about the peace. Now, think about that. I particularly want the students to think about what took place when 18-year-old President 41 was fighting the Japanese, and 59-year-old 43—that would be me—is talking to the Prime Minister of the former enemy about peace. And you know what took place? A Japanese-style democracy came to be.

51   History has shown that democracies yield the peace. Europe is free, whole, and at peace because the nations are democratic. That wasn't always the case, obviously, in the 1900s. Two major wars were fought where a lot of Americans died, and yet systems and forms of government changed. And now Europe is completely different, in terms of security and peace. The Far East—I just mentioned the Japanese example. And that's what the enemy understands, and that's why they're so brutal and relentless. They understand the march of peace will be contagious. Part of my decision-making process is my firm belief in the natural rights of men and women; my belief that deep in everybody's soul is the desire to live free. I believe there's an Almighty, and I believe the Almighty's great gift to each man and woman in this world is the desire to be free. This isn't America's gift to the world, it is a universal gift to the world, and people want to be free. (Applause.)

52   And if you believe that, and if you believe freedom yields the peace, it's important for the United States of America, with friends, to lead the cause of liberty. I'm not saying to any country, you must have a democracy that looks like America. I am saying, free your people, understand that liberty is universal, and help lay that foundation of peace for generations to come. Some day an American President will be sitting down with elected leaders from a country like Iraq talking about how to keep the peace. This generation is rising to the challenge. We're looking at history, we understand our values, and we're laying that foundation of peace for generations to come. (Applause.)

53   We've also got to be diligent here at home. I'm getting ready to answer some questions. Laura said, whatever you do, don't get too windy.

54   We've created the Department of Homeland Security. We reorganized our intelligence services. I want you to know that every morning, I meet with the Director of National Intelligence or his Deputy, sometimes with the head of the CIA, and always with a briefer, CIA briefer that comes and gives me the latest intelligence and the analysis of intelligence. That's every morning in the White House, except for Sunday.

55   And the reason I do is because I told you early that my job is not to be complacent, my job is to be on the lookout—along with a lot of other people, I want you to know. We've got 800,000 state and first responders that have been trained; security is strong at the airports. I hope they stop taking off the shoes of the elderly. I must confess, they haven't taken off my shoes lately at the airport.

56   We're doing a lot of stuff, but I want to talk about two tools necessary to protect you. First, before September the 11th, our law enforcement and intelligence services weren't able to share information. For example, within the FBI, you had your law enforcement division and your intelligence division—and for a lot of reasons, if they had information about a potential terrorist, they couldn't share it. That's hard to fathom, but it's the truth. There was a wall built up, and there's a lot of reasons why the wall was built up—some of it historical, obviously, legal ramifications.

57   And I didn't think you could ask our front-line officers to defend us if they didn't have all the tools necessary to share intelligence, and to share information— by the way, tools which have been granted to use in tracking down drug dealers, for example. My attitude was, if it's good enough—these tools are good enough to find a drug dealer, then they ought to be good enough to protect us from the new threats of the 21st century.

58   And so the Congress passed what's called the Patriot Act by a huge majority. They saw the threat, and they said, wait a minute, let's make sure that if we ask the administration, and, more importantly, people in the administration to defend us, let's give them the tools necessary to defend us. Interestingly enough, the Patriot Act, some of its provisions are set to expire. I like to remind people the Patriot Act may be set to expire, but the threats to the United States haven't expired. And exactly what has changed, I asked out loud, after the attack of September the 11th and today? Those tools are still needed for our law enforcement officers. I want you to know that this Patriot Act is under constant review, and there has been no documented abuses under the Patriot Act.

59   In other words, Congress, in its wisdom, when it passed the Act, said, we'll make sure that the civil liberties of the United States are protected as we give the tools to those who are asked to take the fight to the enemy, to protect us. Congress extended this Patriot Act to February 3rd. That's not good enough for the American people, it seems like to me. When they get back there, they need to make sure they extend all aspects of the Patriot Act to protect the American people.

60   The threat still exists, is my message to members of both political parties. The tools—if they were important right after September the 11th, they're still important in 2006. The enemy has not gone away. (Applause.)

61   Let me talk about one other program—and then I promise to answer questions—something that you've been reading about in the news lately. It's what I would call a terrorist surveillance program. After the enemy attacked us, and after I realized that we were not protected by oceans, I asked people that work for you— work for me, how best can we use information to protect the American people? You might remember there was hijackers here that had made calls outside the country to somebody else, prior to the September the 11th attacks. And I said, is there anything more we can do within the law, within the Constitution, to protect the American people. And they came back with a program, designed a program that I want to describe to you. And I want people here to clearly understand why I made the decision I made.

62   First, I made the decision to do the following things because there's an enemy that still wants to harm the American people. What I'm talking about is the inter-cept of certain communications emanating between somebody inside the United States and outside the United States; and one of the numbers would be reasonably suspected to be an al Qaeda link or affiliate. In other words, we have ways to determine whether or not someone can be an al Qaeda affiliate or al Qaeda. And if they're making a phone call in the United States, it seems like to me we want to know why.

63   This is a—I repeat to you, even though you hear words, "domestic spying," these are not phone calls within the United States. It's a phone call of an al Qaeda, known al Qaeda suspect, making a phone call into the United States. I'm mindful of your civil liberties, and so I had all kinds of lawyers review the process. We briefed members of the United States Congress, one of whom was Senator Pat Roberts, about this program. You know, it's amazing, when people say to me, well, he was just breaking the law—if I wanted to break the law, why was I briefing Congress? (Laughter and applause.)

64   Federal courts have consistently ruled that a President has authority under the Constitution to conduct foreign intelligence surveillance against our enemies. Pre-decessors of mine have used that same constitutional authority. Recently there was a Supreme Court case called the Hamdi case. It ruled the authorization for the use of military force passed by the Congress in 2001—in other words, Congress passed this piece of legislation. And the Court ruled, the Supreme Court ruled that it gave the President additional authority to use what it called "the fundamental incidents of waging war" against al Qaeda.

65   I'm not a lawyer, but I can tell you what it means. It means Congress gave me the authority to use necessary force to protect the American people, but it didn't prescribe the tactics. It's an—you've got the power to protect us, but we're not

going to tell you how. And one of the ways to protect the American people is to understand the intentions of the enemy. I told you it's a different kind of war with a different kind of enemy. If they're making phone calls into the United States, we need to know why—to protect you. (Applause.)

66   And that's the world in which you live. I view it as a chance for an historic opportunity to make this place better for your children and your grandchildren— "this place" being the world. I'm just confident that if we don't lose our will, and stay strong, and that as that liberty advances, people may look back at this lecture and other speeches by people who profess the same devotion to freedom that I've had, and say, you know, maybe they're just right. Maybe America, that was founded on natural rights of men and women is a ticket for peace. Maybe that kind of view— that every person matters, that there are such things as human dignity and the basic freedoms that we feel, that becomes a huge catalyst for change for the better.

67   These troops are defending you with all their might, but at the same time, they're beginning to help change that world by spreading liberty and freedom.

68   It's such an honor to be the President of the great country that we are during such historic times, and I want to thank you for giving me a chance to describe to you some of the decision-making processes I've used to do my duty to defend the American people. God bless.

THINKING CRITICALLY

1. In the preceding essay, D. T. Max made observations regarding George W. Bush's personal use of language. Analyze the language of this speech—mindful of Max's remarks—such as the president's use of adjectives and grammar.

2. Are there any phrases in this speech that fit into William Lutz's definition of "doublespeak" (see page 225)? If so, identify them and explain why you think they are examples of doublespeak.

3. Is there any language in this speech that supports Renana Brooks's claim that Bush riddles his discourse with "empty language" and emotionally charged words designed to cloud issues or inspire feelings of fear or helplessness? If so, identify them.

4. Consider how Bush describes the fight against terrorism and the war in Iraq in this speech. Do you think he is forceful enough? Is he slanted or cautious? Is he diplomatic? Explain.

5. The White House Web site, where this speech is posted, chose to include areas where this speech was met with applause. Does such inclusion influence your reception and interpretation of the speech? Should such annotations be included? Explain.

6. The audience of this speech was a group of college students at Kansas State University. Identify areas of the speech where Bush attempts to reach out to his audience based on his words, tone, and delivery. If you were a student in the audience the day he delivered this speech, what would be your initial reaction to it, and why?

WRITING ASSIGNMENTS

1. Compare this speech to others given before and after September 11 by Bush. An archive of presidential addresses can be found at www.whitehouse.gov. After this address, did the president's use of language change? Did he seem

more confident in his messages? Explain and cite specific examples gathered from your research.

2. Review the first section of this chapter and compare the points made by the authors in that section to this speech. How would Orwell respond to this speech? Rank? Lutz? Explain.

Why JFK's Inaugural Succeeded
Thurston Clarke

> There are several presidential speeches that remain in American memory as truly great. Abraham Lincoln's Gettysburg Address is one, and John F. Kennedy's inaugural address in which he challenged, "Ask not what your country can do for you. . . ." is another. Here, Thurston Clarke provides some of the history behind this famous speech. The speech itself follows.
>
> Thurston Clarke is the author of *Ask Not: The Inauguration of John F. Kennedy and the Speech That Changed America* (2005). This editorial appeared in the *New York Times* on January 15, 2005.

1 Americans watching John F. Kennedy's 1961 inauguration on television saw a scene worthy of Currier & Ives. The marble façade of the Capitol gleamed in the sun, dignitaries wore top hats and dark overcoats and the cold air turned Kennedy's breath into white clouds. When he said, "Let the word go forth from this time and place, to friend and foe alike, that the torch has been passed to a new generation," his words actually appeared to be going forth into the exhilarating air.

2   No one knew that Kennedy was wearing long underwear so he could remove his topcoat and appear youthful and energetic, or that he had received months of tutoring from a speech coach, or that there was so much animosity among the platform's dignitaries that if grudges had weight, the entire contraption would have collapsed. No one suspected that Cardinal Richard Cushing had slowed his invocation because he believed that smoke wafting from beneath the podium came from a smoldering bomb meant for Kennedy, and he wanted to absorb the blast himself. (It was actually a short circuit.) No one knew that as Cushing droned on, Kennedy was probably improving his address in his mind. (He would make 32 alterations to the reading copy of his inaugural address as he spoke.)

3   Praise for his inaugural address came from across the political spectrum—Barry Goldwater said, "God, I'd like to be able to do what that boy did there"—and was so extravagant it seems hard to believe the nation was even more divided than it is today. Kennedy had won the 1960 election with only 49.7 percent of the popular vote, yet a Gallup poll taken soon after his inauguration showed him with an approval rating of 72 percent. His own pollster, Lou Harris, put it at an astounding 92 percent. Richard Nixon, Ronald Reagan and Bill Clinton, perhaps hoping for similar ratings, have paraphrased lines from Kennedy's speech in their own inaugural addresses.

4   The most recent offender was George W. Bush, who in 2001 translated "Ask not what your country can do for you—ask what you can do for your country" into "What you do is as important as anything government does. I ask you to seek a common good beyond your comfort; to defend needed reforms against easy attacks; to serve your nation, beginning with your neighbor."

5   Kennedy's imitators have failed to appreciate that the words in his address were only part of its magic. There was also the brilliant weather, Jackie Kennedy's wardrobe, Robert Frost's poem and a president-elect who had devoted almost as much attention to his appearance as his words—darkening his tan in Palm Beach, and fussing over the cut of his suit and the arrangement of dignitaries on the platform.

6   They have failed to appreciate something else, something that is nearly impossible to replicate. It was Kennedy's life—and his close calls with death—that gave the speech its power and urgency. Those who study the speech would do well to pay less attention to the words and more attention to how he wrote the speech and to the relationship between its words and Kennedy's character and experience.

7   Kennedy composed the most memorable and poetic lines of his inaugural during a flight from Washington to Palm Beach 10 days before his inauguration. He summoned his secretary Evelyn Lincoln into his private compartment on his plane, the *Caroline,* and told her that he wanted to dictate some "ideas" for his inaugural.

8   He had in hand a draft written by his principal speechwriter, Ted Sorensen. Throughout his campaign, Kennedy had often carried a Sorensen speech to the stage only to abandon much of it in favor of his own off-the-cuff remarks. He did this again during the Palm Beach flight, and dictated several pages of his own material. It is in Evelyn Lincoln's shorthand loops and squiggles, then, that one first reads versions of "Let every nation know, whether it wishes us well or ill, that we

shall pay any price, bear any burden, meet any hardship," and "Let the word go forth from this time and place, to friend and foe alike, that the torch has been passed to a new generation of Americans—born in this century, tempered by war, disciplined by a hard and bitter peace proud of our ancient heritage."

9   Kennedy revised his inaugural in Palm Beach, without the assistance of the focus groups or speechwriting teams that have become de rigueur. He read it aloud to his wife, rewrote some passages on sheets of yellow legal paper and consulted with Ted Sorensen. He did not need much help revising his dictation because it was essentially autobiographical. It told his story, and that of his generation: "born in this century," "tempered by war," "disciplined by a hard and bitter peace."

10   Behind this structure lay five pivotal moments in his life: his travels through Europe on the eve of World War II, his experiences in the Pacific in 1943, his visit to a devastated postwar Berlin in 1945, his tour through Asia as a young congressman in 1951, and his encounter with the abject poor during the 1960 West Virginia primary. All but one of these had occurred overseas, a reminder that he was not only the most widely traveled man ever to become president, but Kennedy had a strong emotional connection with the passages inspired by his own experiences. Throughout his political career he had sometimes choked up at Memorial Day and Veterans Day ceremonies when speaking about those who had lost their lives in World War II. Among the passages he had dictated on the flight was this one: "Since this country was founded, each generation of Americans has been summoned to give testimony to its national loyalty. The graves of young Americans who answered the call to service surround the globe."

11   Numbered among these young Americans, of course, were his brother Joseph Kennedy Jr., his brother-in-law Billy Hartington, and his PT-109 crewmen Andrew Kirksey and Harold Marney. These two sentences, a tribute to their sacrifices, would prove to be the emotional turning point of his inaugural, the moment when his voice assumed a passion he seldom revealed, inspiring the audience at the Capitol, touching even the hearts of his opponents, and, according to accounts from the time, sending half-frozen tears rolling down cheeks.

12   It is possible that a future president will evoke a similar reaction with an inaugural address, uniting Americans in a common purpose, and opening a new era of idealism, optimism and national happiness. But to accomplish this, he must do more than others have done: simply paraphrase or echo Kennedy. Instead, he will have to deliver an inaugural that so clearly engages his emotions, and so convincingly represents a distillation of the spiritual and philosophical principles guiding his life, that it will, in the end, awaken a deep emotional response from the American people, too.

President John F. Kennedy's Inaugural Address (January 20, 1961)

1   Vice President Johnson, Mr. Speaker, Mr. Chief Justice, President Eisenhower, Vice President Nixon, President Truman, Reverend Clergy, fellow citizens:

2   We observe today not a victory of party but a celebration of freedom— symbolizing an end as well as a beginning—signifying renewal as well as change.

For I have sworn before you and Almighty God the same solemn oath our forbears prescribed nearly a century and three-quarters ago.

3　The world is very different now. For man holds in his mortal hands the power to abolish all forms of human poverty and all forms of human life. And yet the same revolutionary beliefs for which our forebears fought are still at issue around the globe—the belief that the rights of man come not from the generosity of the state but from the hand of God.

4　We dare not forget today that we are the heirs of that first revolution. Let the word go forth from this time and place, to friend and foe alike, that the torch has been passed to a new generation of Americans—born in this century, tempered by war, disciplined by a hard and bitter peace, proud of our ancient heritage—and unwilling to witness or permit the slow undoing of those human rights to which this nation has always been committed, and to which we are committed today at home and around the world.

5　Let every nation know, whether it wishes us well or ill, that we shall pay any price, bear any burden, meet any hardship, support any friend, oppose any foe to assure the survival and the success of liberty. This much we pledge—and more.

6　To those old allies whose cultural and spiritual origins we share, we pledge the loyalty of faithful friends. United there is little we cannot do in a host of cooperative ventures. Divided there is little we can do—for we dare not meet a powerful challenge at odds and split asunder.

7　To those new states whom we welcome to the ranks of the free, we pledge our word that one form of colonial control shall not have passed away merely to be replaced by a far more iron tyranny. We shall not always expect to find them supporting our view. But we shall always hope to find them strongly supporting their own freedom—and to remember that, in the past, those who foolishly sought power by riding the back of the tiger ended up inside.

8　To those people in the huts and villages of half the globe struggling to break the bonds of mass misery, we pledge our best efforts to help them help themselves, for whatever period is required—not because the communists may be doing it, not because we seek their votes, but because it is right. If a free society cannot help the many who are poor, it cannot save the few who are rich.

9　To our sister republics south of our border, we offer a special pledge— to convert our good words into good deeds—in a new alliance for progress—to assist free men and free governments in casting off the chains of poverty. But this peaceful revolution of hope cannot become the prey of hostile powers. Let all our neighbors know that we shall join with them to oppose aggression or subversion anywhere in the Americas. And let every other power know that this Hemisphere intends to remain the master of its own house.

10　To that world assembly of sovereign states, the United Nations, our last best hope in an age where the instruments of war have far outpaced the instruments of peace, we renew our pledge of support—to prevent it from becoming merely a forum for invective—to strengthen its shield of the new and the weak—and to enlarge the area in which its writ may run.

11　Finally, to those nations who would make themselves our adversary, we offer not a pledge but a request: that both sides begin anew the quest for peace, before the dark powers of destruction unleashed by science engulf all humanity in planned or accidental self-destruction.

12 We dare not tempt them with weakness. For only when our arms are sufficient beyond doubt can we be certain beyond doubt that they will never be employed.

13 But neither can two great and powerful groups of nations take comfort from our present course—both sides overburdened by the cost of modern weapons, both rightly alarmed by the steady spread of the deadly atom, yet both racing to alter that uncertain balance of terror that stays the hand of mankind's final war.

14 So let us begin anew—remembering on both sides that civility is not a sign of weakness, and sincerity is always subject to proof. Let us never negotiate out of fear. But let us never fear to negotiate.

15 Let both sides explore what problems unite us instead of belaboring those problems which divide us.

16 Let both sides, for the first time, formulate serious and precise proposals for the inspection and control of arms—and bring the absolute power to destroy other nations under the absolute control of all nations.

17 Let both sides seek to invoke the wonders of science instead of its terrors. Together let us explore the stars, conquer the deserts, eradicate disease, tap the ocean depths and encourage the arts and commerce.

18 Let both sides unite to heed in all corners of the earth the command of Isaiah— to "undo the heavy burdens . . . (and) let the oppressed go free."

19 And if a beachhead of cooperation may push back the jungle of suspicion, let both sides join in creating a new endeavor, not a new balance of power, but a new world of law, where the strong are just and the weak secure and the peace preserved.

20 All this will not be finished in the first one hundred days. Nor will it be finished in the first one thousand days, nor in the life of this Administration, nor even perhaps in our lifetime on this planet. But let us begin.

21 In your hands, my fellow citizens, more than mine, will rest the final success or failure of our course. Since this country was founded, each generation of Americans has been summoned to give testimony to its national loyalty. The graves of young Americans who answered the call to service surround the globe.

22 Now the trumpet summons us again—not as a call to bear arms, though arms we need—not as a call to battle, though embattled we are—but a call to bear the burden of a long twilight struggle, year in and year out, "rejoicing in hope, patient in tribulation"—a struggle against the common enemies of man: tyranny, poverty, disease and war itself.

23 Can we forge against these enemies a grand and global alliance, North and South, East and West, that can assure a more fruitful life for all mankind? Will you join in that historic effort?

24 In the long history of the world, only a few generations have been granted the role of defending freedom in its hour of maximum danger. I do not shrink from this responsibility—I welcome it. I do not believe that any of us would exchange places with any other people or any other generation. The energy, the faith, the devotion which we bring to this endeavor will light our country and all who serve it—and the glow from that fire can truly light the world.

25   And so, my fellow Americans: ask not what your country can do for you—ask what you can do for your country.

26   My fellow citizens of the world: ask not what America will do for you, but what together we can do for the freedom of man.

27   Finally, whether you are citizens of America or citizens of the world, ask of us here the same high standards of strength and sacrifice which we ask of you. With a good conscience our only sure reward, with history the final judge of our deeds, let us go forth to lead the land we love, asking His blessing and His help, but knowing that here on earth God's work must truly be our own."

Transcription courtesy of the John F. Kennedy Presidential Library and Museum.
01/20/1961.

THINKING CRITICALLY

1. According to Thurston Clarke, what elements made John F. Kennedy's inaugural speech "great"? What factors, besides the words themselves, contributed to its success? Explain.

2. Clarke notes that at the time of Kennedy's election, the country was "even more divided than it is today." Review the language in Kennedy's speech. How does Kennedy try to inspire collaboration through language? Do you think he is successful? Explain.

3. Kennedy's approval rating jumped almost 25 percent after giving this speech, despite a controversial election and politically divided parties. Based on what you have learned from Clarke's article, and Kennedy's speech itself, explain why you think the president's rating jumped so significantly as the result of a single speech.

4. Clarke observes that many other presidents have sought to imitate Kennedy's words, including George W. Bush in 2001 (paragraph 4). How does Bush's paraphrasing of Kennedy's "ask not" statement compare to the original?

5. Would Kennedy be able to deliver this speech as effectively today as he did over 40 years ago? Why or why not?

6. How was Kennedy able to use his life experience in his speech? Do you think adding his personal experience made his speech more compelling? Explain.

7. Examine the photograph of Kennedy's inauguration that accompanies this article. How did Kennedy "set the stage" to send a visual message to the American people? Explain.

WRITING ASSIGNMENTS

1. Imagine you are a young American in 1961 hearing Kennedy's address for the first time. View Kennedy's speech at www.americanrhetoric.com/speeches/johnfkennedyinaugural.htm. Write an essay recording your impressions of the speech, how it made you feel, and your emotional reactions, if any. Include in your evaluation elements Clarke notes in his essay—how Kennedy was dressed, the placement of people on the podium, and moments of emotion that revealed his personal connection to his words.

2. Clarke wrote this editorial five days before Bush delivered his second inaugural address on January 20, 2005. Review Bush's 2005 address at www. whitehouse.gov/inaugural/index.html. Write a short essay evaluating the effectiveness of Bush's speech. What does he chose to highlight? Does his language unify or emphasize differences? Does it inspire confidence? Explain.

MAKING CONNECTIONS

1. Is presidential discourse too influential? Does everything the president says or does indeed carry particular significance or meaning to the general public? If so, what does that mean about who we want to be president, and why?

2. President Harry S. Truman once said, "the principle power that the president has is to bring people in and try to persuade them to do what they ought to do without persuasion." What did Truman mean? Write an essay exploring this statement and your opinion of Truman's assessment of the presidency.

3. Denton and Hahn explain that the president's language serves to motivate, rally, and persuade. Have you ever found yourself influenced by a particular speech made by the president? What was particularly compelling and why? Reflect on the speech and how the language the president used influenced your emotions and opinions.

4. Locate several speeches made by different presidents and compare their style, content, delivery, and message. Using information presented in this section, write an essay exploring the connection between what the president says, and how we perceive his leadership ability.

Do You Know What I'm Saying?

■ Our ability to communicate separates us from other animals and forms the foundation of our social interactions. What aspects of communication can bring us together and what can push us apart?

Although language may be what separates us from other animals, it is conversation—the ability to communicate and interact with each other—that is at the heart of our humanity. As social animals, conversation forms the foundation of our daily interactions. But conversation is more than simply speaking; it is a collaborative exercise. How we interact with each other, in social groups, with our families, among friends and acquaintances, in work situations, and with our significant others, is a critical factor in our success as human beings. This chapter explores the social dynamics of conversation, differences between male and female communication styles, and new trends in communication as we increasingly become part of the fabric of an online and wired world.

He Says, She Says: Gender Differences in Discourse

Some sociologists and psychologists claim that men and women talk differently—either due to social conditioning or basic physiology—and that the "male" form of discourse is the preferred form of communication. With the great interest in communication, a growing number of scholars are attempting to prove that important differences distinguish the way men and women use language. Most researchers present theories that such differences are the results of either discriminatory socialization or genetic disposition. The first two essays in this cluster face off as they address the assumption that woman speak more than men. In "Women Talk Too Much," Janet Holmes explains that the stereotype that women speak more than men is rooted in how our society values speech and claims this stereotype simply isn't true. Tony Kornheiser, however, comparing conversations between himself and his daughter and son, asserts, "No Detail Is Too Small for Girls Answering a Simple Question."

In "Sex Differences," linguist Ronald Macaulay says that although some differences in expression reflect social and cultural conditioning, much of the controversy regarding gender-based linguistic differences are based on myths and age-old stereotypes. Then, Clive Thompson describes how computer software can accurately determine the gender of the author of a piece of writing. While such findings may be interesting, Thompson questions the meaning of the data in "He and She: What's the Real Difference?" Rachel Rafelman explores the communication differences between men and women in social situations in "The Party Line." Finally, best-selling author and sociolinguist Deborah Tannen demonstrates how social and cultural conditioning often creates inequalities in conversations, where men dominate discourse and women let them—causing tension and resentment in "I'll Explain It to You: Lecturing and Listening."

Let's Talk About It: Conversation in Action

Conversation forms the foundation of our social interactions. This section discusses the social elements of conversation, its importance to our very existence, and its role in our culture. Ronald Wardhaugh describes the unspoken, and often unconscious, expectations we bring to everyday conversation. In "The Social Basis of

Talk," Wardhaugh explains that trust, shared experience, and expectations of universal truths play a vital role in the success of social conversation. Margaret Wheatley discusses how conversation has the power to effect social change in "Some Friends and I Started Talking." David Grambs explains why he feels defeated by "uptalk" and misuse of the word *like*, which seems to have permeated the speech of the younger generation. After years of trying to fight this insidious invader, Grambs reveals his fear that "like" is here to stay in "The Like Virus." And Robert Kuttner discusses what he feels are the detrimental effects of the instant nature of e-mail in "The Other Side of E-Mail." The section closes with a review of some common IM and text messaging terms and slang in "r u online?" by Kris Axtman.

HE SAYS, SHE SAYS: GENDER DIFFERENCES IN DISCOURSE

Women Talk Too Much
Janet Holmes

Do women really talk more than men? Many people seem to think so, but is this assumption based on stereotypes or facts? And who determines how much talk is "too much"? In this essay, linguist Janet Holmes sets out to debunk the "language myth" that women talk too much. In fact, explains Holmes, women speak less than men do in situations where their talk is most "valued." She also asserts that the claim that "women talk too much" is inherently biased because it is men, who tend to hold positions of power, who determine when there is too much talk (such as women speaking in informal settings) and when it is appropriate (men speaking in public forums).

Janet Holmes is a professor of sociolinguistics at the Victoria University of Wellington, New Zealand. Her publications include *An Introduction to Sociolinguistics* (2001) and *Women, Men and Politeness* (1995). She has published many articles on numerous sociolinguistic topics, including spoken New Zealand English, sexist language, humor, and workplace discourse.

1 Do women talk more than men? Proverbs and sayings in many languages express the view that women are always talking:

> *Women's tongues are like lambs' tails—they are never still. —English*

> *The North Sea will sooner be found wanting in water than a woman at a loss for words. —Jutlandic*

> *The woman with active hands and feet, marry her, but the woman with overactive mouth, leave well alone. —Maori*

Some suggest that while women talk, men are silent patient listeners.

> *When both husband and wife wear pants it is not difficult to tell them apart—*
> *he is the one who is listening. —American*

> *Nothing is so unnatural as a talkative man or a quiet woman. —Scottish*

Others indicate that women's talk is not valued but is rather considered noisy, irritating prattle:

> *Where there are women and geese there's noise. —Japanese*

Indeed, there is a Japanese character which consists of three instances of the character for the concept "woman" and which translates as "noisy"! My favorite proverb, because it attributes not noise but rather power to the woman speaker is this Chinese one:

> *The tongue is the sword of a woman and she never lets it become rusty.*

So what are the facts? Do women dominate the talking time? Do men struggle to get a word in edgewise, as the stereotype suggests?

The Evidence

2 Despite the widespread belief that women talk more than men, most of the available evidence suggests just the opposite. When women and men are together, it is the men who talk most. Two Canadian researchers, Deborah James and Janice Drakich, reviewed sixty-three studies which examined the amount of talk used by American women and men in different contexts. Women talked more than men in only two studies.

3   In New Zealand, too, research suggests that men generally dominate the talking time. Margaret Franken compared the amount of talk used by female and male "experts" assisting a female TV host to interview well-known public figures. In a situation where each of three interviewers was entitled to a third of the interviewers' talking time, the men took more than half on every occasion.

4   I found the same pattern analyzing the number of questions asked by participants in one hundred public seminars. In all but seven, men dominated the discussion time. Where the numbers of women and men present were about the same, men asked almost two-thirds of the questions during the discussion. Clearly women were not talking more than men in these contexts.

5   Even when they hold influential positions, women sometimes find it hard to contribute as much as men to a discussion. A British company appointed four women and four men to the eight most highly paid management positions. The managing director commented that the men often patronized the women and tended to dominate meetings:

> *I had a meeting with a [female] sales manager and three of my [male] directors*
> *once . . . It took about two hours. She only spoke once and one of my fellow di-*
> *rectors cut across her and said 'What Anne is trying to say Roger is . . .' and I*
> *think that about sums it up. He knew better than Anne what she was trying to*
> *say, and she never got anything said.*

6 There is abundant evidence that this pattern starts early. Many researchers have compared the relative amounts that girls and boys contribute to classroom talk. In a wide range of communities, from kindergarten through primary, secondary and tertiary education, the same pattern recurs—males dominate classroom talk. So on this evidence we must conclude that the stereotype of the garrulous woman reflects sexist prejudice rather than objective reality.

Looking for an Explanation

7 Why is the reality so different from the myth? To answer this question, we need to go beyond broad generalizations and look more carefully at the patterns identified. Although some teachers claim that boys are "by nature more spirited and less disciplined," there is no evidence to suggest that males are biologically programmed to talk more than females. It is much more likely that the explanation involves social factors.

What Is the Purpose of the Talk?

8 One relevant clue is the fact that talk serves different functions in different contexts. Formal public talk is often aimed at informing people or persuading them to agree to a particular point of view (e.g., political speeches, television debates, radio interviews, public lectures, etc.). Public talk is often undertaken by people who wish to claim or confirm some degree of public status. Effective talk in public and in the media can enhance your social status—as politicians and other public performers know well. Getting and holding the floor is regarded as desirable, and competition for the floor in such contexts is common. (There is also some risk, of course, since a poor performance can be damaging.)

9 Classroom research suggests that more talk is associated with higher social status or power. Many studies have shown that teachers (regardless of their gender) tend to talk for about two-thirds of the available time. But the boys dominate the relatively small share of the talking time that remains for pupils. In this context, where talk is clearly valued, it appears that the person with most status has the right to talk most. The boys may therefore be asserting a claim to higher status than the girls by appropriating the majority of the time left for pupil talk.

10 The way women and men behave in formal meetings and seminars provides further support for this explanation. Evidence collected by American, British and New Zealand researchers shows that men dominate the talking time in committee meetings, staff meetings, seminars and task-oriented decision-making groups. If you are sceptical, use a stopwatch to time the amount of talk contributed by women and men at political and community meetings you attend. This explanation proposes that men talk more than women in public, formal contexts because they perceive participating and verbally contributing in such contexts as an activity which enhances their status, and men seem to be more concerned with asserting status and power than women are.

11 By contrast, in more private contexts, talk usually serves interpersonal functions. The purpose of informal or intimate talk is not so much status enhancement

as establishing or maintaining social contact with others, making social connections, developing and reinforcing friendships and intimate relationships. Interestingly, the few studies which have investigated informal talk have found that there are fewer differences in the amount contributed by women and men in these contexts (though men still talked more in nearly a third of the informal studies reviewed by Deborah James and Janice Drakich). Women, it seems, are willing to talk more in relaxed social contexts, especially where the talk functions to develop and maintain social relationships.

12   Another piece of evidence that supports this interpretation is the *kind* of talk women and men contribute in mixed-sex discussions. Researchers analyzing the functions of different utterances have found that men tend to contribute more information and opinions, while women contribute more agreeing, supportive talk, more of the kind of talk that encourages others to contribute. So men's talk tends to be more referential or informative, while women's talk is more supportive and facilitative.

13   Overall, then, women seem to use talk to develop personal relationships and maintain family connections and friendships more often than to make claims to status or to directly influence others in public contexts. Of course, there are exceptions, as Margaret Thatcher, Benazir Bhutto and Jenny Shipley demonstrate. But, until recently, many women seem not to have perceived themselves as appropriate contributors to public, formal talk.

14   In New Zealand we identified another context where women contributed more talk than men. Interviewing people to collect samples of talk for linguistic analysis, we found that women were much more likely than men (especially young men) to be willing to talk to us at length. For example, Miriam Meyerhoff asked a group of ten young people to describe a picture to a female and to a male interviewer. It was made quite clear to the interviewees that the more speech they produced the better. In this situation, the women contributed significantly more speech than the men, both to the male and to the female interviewer.

15   In the private but semi-formal context of an interview, then, women contributed more talk than men. Talk in this context could not be seen as enhancing the status of the people interviewed. The interviewers were young people with no influence over the interviewees. The explanation for the results seems to be that the women were being more cooperative than the men in a context where more talk was explicitly sought by the interviewer.

Social Confidence

16 If you know a lot about a particular topic, you are generally more likely to be willing to contribute to a discussion about it. So familiarity or expertise can also affect the amount a person contributes to a particular discussion. In one interesting study the researcher supplied particular people with extra information, making them the "experts" on the topic to be discussed. Regardless of gender, these "experts" talked more in the subsequent discussions than their uninformed conversational partners (though male "experts" still used more talking time in conversation with uninformed women than female "experts" did with uninformed men).

17   Looking at people's contributions to the discussion section of seminars, I found a similar effect from expertise or topic familiarity. Women were more likely to ask questions and make comments when the topic was one they could claim expert knowledge about. In a small seminar on the current state of the economy, for instance, several women economists who had been invited to attend contributed to the discussion, making this one of the very few seminars where women's contributions exceeded men's.

18   Another study compared the relative amount of talk of spouses. Men dominated the conversations between couples with traditional gender roles and expectations, but when the women were associated with a feminist organization they tended to talk more than their husbands. So feminist women were more likely to challenge traditional gender roles in interaction.

19   It seems possible that both these factors—expert status and feminist philosophy—have the effect of developing women's social confidence. This explanation also fits with the fact that women tend to talk more with close friends and family, when women are in the majority, and also when they are explicitly invited to talk (in an interview, for example).

Perceptions and Implications

20 If social confidence explains the greater contributions of women in some social contexts, it is worth asking why girls in school tend to contribute less than boys. Why should they feel unconfident in the classroom? Here is the answer which one sixteen-year-old gave:

> *Sometimes I feel like saying that I disagree, that there are other ways of looking at it, but where would that get me? My teacher thinks I'm showing off, and the boys jeer. But if I pretend I don't understand, it's very different. The teacher is sympathetic and the boys are helpful. They really respond if they can show YOU how it is done, but there's nothing but "aggro" if you give any signs of showing THEM how it is done.*

Talking in class is often perceived as "showing off," especially if it is girl-talk. Until recently, girls have preferred to keep a low profile rather than attract negative attention.

21   Teachers are often unaware of the gender distribution of talk in their classrooms. They usually consider that they give equal amounts of attention to girls and boys, and it is only when they make a tape recording that they realize that boys are dominating the interactions. Dale Spender, an Australian feminist who has been a strong advocate of female rights in this area, noted that teachers who tried to restore the balance by deliberately "favoring" the girls were astounded to find that despite their efforts they continued to devote more time to the boys in their classrooms. Another study reported that a male science teacher who managed to create an atmosphere in which girls and boys contributed more equally to discussion felt that he was devoting 90 per cent of his attention to the girls. And so did his male pupils. They complained vociferously that the girls were getting too much talking time.

22   In other public contexts, too, such as seminars and debates, when women and men are deliberately given an equal amount of the highly valued talking time, there is often a perception that they are getting more than their fair share. Dale Spender explains this as follows:

> *The talkativeness of women has been gauged in comparison not with men but with silence. Women have not been judged on the grounds of whether they talk more than men, but of whether they talk more than silent women.*

In other words, if women talk at all, this may be perceived as "too much" by men who expect them to provide a silent, decorative background in many social contexts. This may sound outrageous, but think about how you react when precocious children dominate the talk at an adult party. As women begin to make inroads into formerly "male" domains such as business and professional contexts, we should not be surprised to find that their contributions are not always perceived positively or even accurately.

Conclusion

23 We have now reached the conclusion that the question "Do women talk more than men?" can't be answered with a straight "yes" or "no." The answer is rather, "It all depends." It depends on many different factors, including the social context in which the talk is taking place, the kind of talk involved and the relative social confidence of the speakers, which is affected by such things as their social roles (e.g., teacher, host, interviewee, wife) and their familiarity with the topic.

24   It appears that men generally talk more in formal, public contexts where informative and persuasive talk is highly valued, and where talk is generally the prerogative of those with some societal status and has the potential for increasing that status. Women, on the other hand, are more likely to contribute in private, informal interactions, where talk more often functions to maintain relationships, and in other situations where for various reasons they feel socially confident.

25   Finally, and most radically, we might question the assumption that more talk is always a good thing. "Silence is golden," says the proverb, and there are certainly contexts in all cultures where silence is more appropriate than talk, where words are regarded as inadequate vehicles for feelings, or where keeping silent is an expression of appreciation or respect. Sometimes it is the silent participants who are the powerful players. In some contexts the strong silent male is an admired stereotype. However, while this is true, it must be recognized that talk is very highly valued in western culture. It seems likely, then, that as long as holding the floor is equated with influence, the complexities of whether women or men talk most will continue to be a matter for debate.

THINKING CRITICALLY

1. How do the proverbs at the beginning of Holmes's essay set the tone? What is remarkable about these proverbs? Have you heard any of them? Which one do you like or dislike the most, and why?

2. In what ways does the context and setting of the conversation influence men's and women's talking patterns? Explain.

3. Holmes explains that in situations where talk is valued—in the classroom or boardroom for instance—males are likely to speak more than females. If this is true, what accounts for the excess of proverbs and sayings regarding women's talk? Explain.

4. In paragraph 20, Holmes cites a 16-year-old girl who explains why she doesn't speak more in class. Evaluate this girl's response in the context of your own social and classroom experiences in high school.

5. What, according to Holmes, are the differences between men's and women's use of talk? Do you agree or disagree with her conclusions? Explain.

WRITING ASSIGNMENTS

1. Ben Jonson, a seventeenth-century writer and playwright, wrote a popular play called *Epicene*, or, *The Silent Woman*. Locate a copy of this play and write an essay in which you make connections between attitudes toward women's talk three hundred years ago and today. How have things changed, and how are they similar?

2. Do you think that understanding gender patterns in conversation will change the way men and women speak to each other? Do you think that such changes are necessary and healthy? Alternatively, do you think that some men and women have a need for the established patterns? Explain.

No Detail Is Too Small for Girls Answering a Simple Question

Tony Kornheiser

A common complaint between the sexes is that men and women just don't speak the same language. In the next piece, sports columnist and humorist Tony Kornheiser observes the differences in the communication style of his daughter and son, and by extension, women and men. His conclusion is that "women have more to say on everything."

Tony Kornheiser writes for the *Washington Post*, hosts *The Tony Kornheiser Show* on ESPN radio, and co-hosts *Pardon the Interruption* with fellow *Post* sports columnist Mike Wilbon on ESPN2. He is the author of several books, including *Pumping Irony* (1995) and *Bald as I Want to Be* (1997).

1 The last time I ventured into my favorite column area—differences between men and women—was when the infamous Teen Talk Barbie doll came out. Barbie was given 270 things to say, and one of them was "Math class is tough!" This, of course, is infuriating, because it plays into the damaging sexual stereotype that girls are stupid in math.

2 Well, I got cute and wrote how everyone knows girls are stupid in math. I gave an example of my own daughter, whom I love dearly, and who is a sensitive and caring soul, and how when I ask her, "If a bus leaves Cleveland at 7 p.m. heading for Pittsburgh, 200 miles away, and traveling 50 miles per hour, when will it arrive?" she answers, "Do all the children have seat belts, Daddy?" I thought it was a pretty good line. But I received all kinds of nasty mail, much of it—so help me—from female mathematicians, and female actuaries and female physicists specializing in subatomic

particle acceleration. In that same column, I wrote that boys are stupid in English, yet I didn't get a single letter of protest from boys. Obviously, they couldn't read the column.

3   Anyway . . . here we go again.

4   My daughter recently came home from sleep-away camp, where she'd spent five weeks. She looked great. And I was so proud of her, going away by herself.

5   The first question I asked her was "How was camp?"

6   She began by saying, "Well, the day I left, I got on the bus, and I sat next to Ashley, and she brought Goldfish, which was good because I forgot my Now and Laters, and then Shannon came over, and she's from Baltimore, and she gets her clothes at the Gap, and she had a Game Boy, but all she had was Tetris, which I have, so we asked Jenny, who was the counselor, if anybody had Sonic the Hedgehog, but . . ."

7   She went on like this for a few minutes, still talking about the bus ride up to camp five weeks ago, and I came to the horrifying realization that she was actually going to tell me how camp was, minute by minute. Because this is what girls do (and when they grow up and become women, they do it, too, as any man can vouch for). They gather information and dispense it without discrimination. Everything counts the same! It is not that women lack the ability to prioritize information, it is that they don't think life is as simple as men do, and so they are fascinated by the multiplicity of choices that they see.

8   This is why you have to be very specific with what you ask women. If, for example, you missed a Rams game, and you know a woman who saw it, never, ever ask, "What happened?" Unless you have nowhere to go until Thursday.

9   Ask:

1. Who won?

2. What was the score?

3. Was anyone carried out on a stretcher?

10   You must get them to fast-forward.

11   Left to their own devices, girls go through life volubly answering essay questions. And boys? Multiple choice is way too complicated. Boys restrict themselves to true/false.

12   Boys do not gather and retain information, they focus on results.

13   My son went to camp for six weeks—one week longer than my daughter. As I had with my daughter, I asked him, "How was camp?"

14   He said, "Good. I busted Jason's nose." Short and to the point.

15   This was followed by, "Can we go to McDonald's?"

16   Did I mention the cheers? My daughter came back with cheers. About 187,640 musical cheers, all of which are accompanied by an intricate series of hand, feet and hip movements. She went to camp a 10-year-old, she came back a Vandella.

17   It's amazing, the affinity of girls and cheers. If you've ever been to camp, you know that girls have a special gene for cheers and that even girls who have never been to camp before—or, for that matter, been to America or spoken English before—automatically know all the cheers the moment they step off the bus. As a

boy at camp, I used to look at girls in amazement, wondering why they would waste their time like that, when they could be doing useful things like me—memorizing Willie Mays' doubles and sacrifice flies during an entire decade.

18   Boys don't do musical cheers.

19   Even during "color war," that traditional camp competition when cheering is supposed to result in points, here's how boys cheer on the way to the dining hall: They look at the other team and say, "Yo, Green Team, drop dead."

THINKING CRITICALLY

1. Kornheiser, in the context of his daughter's communication style, states that women "gather information and dispense it without discrimination." Respond to Kornheiser's assertion. Is there truth to his stereotypical description of the way men and women relay information? Explain.

2. In his introduction, Kornheiser relates how his joking about girls and math resulted in angry letters from many women, yet his comments about boys and English received no such response. What accounts for this difference? Is it more important to dispel one stereotype than it is the other? Why or why not?

3. Based on his essay, can you determine which communication style Kornheiser prefers? As a writer and columnist, is Kornheiser more "male" or "female" in his communication style? Explain.

4. How would you characterize Kornheiser's tone and style? What assumptions does he make about his audience? Does his article appeal to both sexes? Why or why not?

WRITING ASSIGNMENTS

1. Many of the authors in this section seem to defend their own gender's communication style. Write an essay in which you support your gender's communication style, or defend or analyze the style of the opposite sex. Is one better than the other? Why or why not? Remember to support your perspective with examples.

2. In his essay, Tony Kornheiser describes the differences between the way his children, one boy and one girl, communicate. How do his observations connect to stereotypes about how men and women communicate? Are these communication styles simply a fact of gender? Explain, using examples from Kornheiser's essay and from other authors in this section, such as Deborah Tannen and Janet Holmes.

Sex Differences
Ronald Macaulay

Contrary to popular belief, men and women do not speak different forms of English. Nor are there innate or genetic differences in the way males and females acquire or use language. So argues Ronald Macaulay, a professor of linguistics and an expert on language acquisition. Although social background can generate some differences in the way the sexes speak, it is pure myth and stereotyping that sex differences show up in language patterns. Males do not, for instance, instinctively gravitate to coarse language, and females are not preternaturally drawn to the language of nurturing.

Ronald Macaulay is professor of linguistics at Pitzer College in Claremont, CA. He is the author of *Generally Speaking: How Children Learn Language* (1980), *Locating Dialect in Discourse: The Language of Honest Men and Bonnie Lasses in Ayr* (1991), and *The Social Art: Language and Its Uses* (1996), from which this essay is taken.

> *I think the English women speak awfy nice. The little girls are very feminine just because they've a nice voice. But the same voice in an Englishman— nae really. I think the voice lets the men down but it flatters the girls.*
> —*Aberdeen housewife*

1   More nonsense has been produced on the subject of sex differences than on any linguistic topic, with the possible exception of spelling. Perhaps this is appropriate. The relations between the sexes have generally been considered a fit topic for comedy. In his book *Language: Its Nature, Development and Origin*, Otto Jespersen has a chapter entitled "The Woman" in which he manages to include every stereotype about women that was current at the time. It is almost unfair to quote directly but even in the 1920s Jespersen should have known better, particularly since he lived in Denmark where women have traditionally shown an independent spirit. Here are a few examples:

> There can be no doubt that women exercise a great and universal influence on linguistic development through their instinctive shrinking from coarse and gross expressions and their preference for refined and (in certain spheres) veiled and indirect expressions.
>
> Men will certainly with great justice object that there is a danger of the language becoming languid and insipid if we are always to content ourselves with women's expressions.
>
> Women move preferably in the central field of language, avoiding everything that is out of the way or bizarre, while men will often either coin new words or expressions or take up old-fashioned ones, if by that means they are enabled, or think they are enabled, to find a more adequate or precise expression for their thoughts. Woman as a rule follows the main road of language, where man is often inclined to turn aside into a narrow footpath or even to strike out a new path for himself. . . .
>
> Those who want to learn a foreign language will therefore always do well at the first stage to read many ladies' novels, because they will there continually meet with just those everyday words and combinations which the foreigner is above all in need of, what may be termed the indispensable small-change of a language.
>
> Woman is linguistically quicker than man: quicker to learn, quicker to hear, and quicker to answer. A man is slower: he hesitates, he chews the cud to make sure of the taste of words, and thereby comes to discover similarities with and differences from other words, both in sound and in sense, thus preparing himself for the appropriate use of the fittest noun or adjective.

> The superior readiness of speech of women is a concomitant of the fact that their vocabulary is smaller and more central than that of men.

2   Such stereotypes are often reinforced by works of fiction. Since little information about prosodic features or paralinguistic features is contained in the normal writing system, novelists frequently try to indicate the tone of voice by descriptive verbs and adjectives to introduce dialogue. An examination of several novels revealed an interesting difference between the expression used to introduce men's or women's speech:

MEN	WOMEN
said firmly	said quietly
said bluntly	asked innocently
said coldly	echoed obediently
said smugly	said loyally
urged	offered humbly
burst forth	whispered
demanded aggressively	asked mildly
said challengingly	agreed placidly
cried furiously	smiled complacently
exclaimed contemptuously	fumbled on
cried portentously	implored
grumbled	pleaded

The surprising part is that the two lists are totally distinct. No doubt the novelists intended to be realistic in describing two very different styles of speech but, in doing so, they also reinforce the stereotypes of men and women.

3   In the past twenty years the question of sex differences in language has been a growth industry as scholars have attempted to claim and to counter claims that there are or are not important differences in the ways in which males and females use language. It would, of course, be surprising if there were not. Both men and women will use the forms of language, registers, and styles appropriate to the activities in which they are engaged. To the extent that these activities differ between males and females, it is to be expected that their language will differ. This much is obvious. There is no need to look for a genetic basis for such differences. It is also obvious that those in a position of power often expect to be treated with deference by those over whom they have power. To the extent that in Western industrialized societies men have more often been in positions of power over women rather than the reverse, it is hardly surprising if women are sometimes found to have used deferential language. There have also been certain violent activities, such as fighting or contact sports, that until recently have been exclusively a male province, and there are forms of language appropriate to them that may have been less common among women.

4   Even in making such banal statements, one must qualify them by reference to "Western industrialized societies" or by limiting them to a single section of the community. For example, it is probably true that in Britain until World War I middle-class women were less likely to swear in public than middle-class men, but working-class women were less inhibited. (G. K. Chesterton reported that in an

argument with a fishwife he could not compete in obscenities with her but triumphed in the end by calling her "An adverb! A preposition! A pronoun!")

5   In sociolinguistic studies of complex communities such as Glasgow, New York, and Norwich, it has been shown that women in the lower middle class are likely to be closer in their speech to the women in the class immediately above them than are the men, who are likely to be closer to the men in the class immediately below them. It has been suggested that this is because lower-class speech is associated with toughness and virility and the men in the lower middle class choose to identify with this image rather than with the less "masculine" speech of the upper-class men. It may not be unimportant that in these studies the interviewers were all men.

6   There seems, however, to be a deep-seated desire to find essential differences between the speech of men and women that can either be attributed to some discriminatory kind of socialization or, even better, to genetic disposition. This can be seen in many references to sex differences in language development. Popular belief and scholarly opinion has generally maintained that girls are more advanced in language development than boys at the same age. Jespersen, for example, claimed that girls learned to talk earlier and more quickly than boys, and that the speech of girls is more correct than that of boys.

7   For about fifty years after Jespersen this view was maintained in the scholarly literature on children's development. In 1954 Professor Dorothea McCarthy published an article summarizing what was known about children's language development at that time. Her conclusion about sex differences is:

> One of the most consistent findings to emerge from the mass of data accumulated on language development in American white children seems to be a slight difference in favor of girls in nearly all aspects of language that have been studied.

8   What McCarthy actually found, however, was that the differences were not large enough to be statistically significant. Although psychologists are normally very careful not to make claims about differences that could be the result of chance (that is, are not statistically significant), McCarthy was so convinced that girls were more advanced in their speech that she chose to interpret the evidence the way she did. In a survey of the literature up till 1975, I found that none of the studies provided convincing evidence of consistent sex differences in language development. I concluded that the burden of proof remained with those who wished to claim otherwise. To the best of my knowledge, the situation has not changed since then.

9   What I did find were many examples of preconceived notions of sex differences from the assertion that girls have an innate tendency toward sedentary pursuits to claims that it is easier and more satisfying for the girl baby to imitate the mother's speech than it is for the boy baby to imitate the father's. One example will illustrate the kind of attitude:

> The little girl, showing in her domestic play the over-riding absorption in personal relationships through which she will later fulfill her role of wife, mother and "expressive" leader of the family . . . learns language early in order to communicate. The kind of communication in which she is chiefly interested at this

stage concerns the nurturant routines which are the stuff of family life. Sharing and talking about them as she copies and "helps" her mother about the house must enhance the mutual identification of mother and child, which in turn . . . will reinforce imitation of the mother's speech and promote further acquisition of language, at first oriented toward domestic and interpersonal affairs but later adapted to other uses as well. Her intellectual performance is relatively predictable because it is rooted in this early communication, which enables her (environment permitting) to display her inherited potential at an early age.

This is contrasted with the interests of boys:

Their preoccupation with the working of mechanical things is less interesting to most mothers and fathers are much less available.

As a result the boy's language development is slower:

His language, less fluent and personal and later to appear than the girl's, develops along more analytic lines and may, in favourable circumstances, provide the groundwork for later intellectual achievement which could not have been foreseen in his first few years.

Girls, of course, are more predictable:

The girl, meanwhile, is acquiring the intimate knowledge of human reactions which we call feminine intuition. Perhaps because human reactions are less regular than those of inanimate objects, however, she is less likely to develop the strictly logical habits of thought that intelligent boys acquire, and if gifted may well come to prefer the subtler disciplines of the humanities to the intellectual rigor of science.

I am not sure whether the writer considered himself a scientist, but if his writing is an example of intellectual rigor, then give me the subtlety of the humanities any day. What makes his statement all the more incredible is that it comes after describing a longitudinal study of children that showed no important sex differences in language development.

10   One of the problems with attempting to demonstrate differences in language development is that measures of linguistic proficiency, particularly for young children, are extremely crude instruments. Thus it is not surprising that samples of linguistic behavior will reveal occasional differences between subgroups of the sample. Such sex differences that have shown up on tests are much smaller than those that have been shown to relate to social background. The fact that most studies show no sex differences and that many of the findings of small differences have been contradicted in other studies should be sufficient warning against drawing conclusions about the linguistic superiority of either sex.

11   There are some differences between males and females that do not depend upon unreliable tests of language development. Boys are much more likely to suffer from speech disorders, such as stuttering, than girls. Adult males on average have deeper voices than adult females because the vibrating part of the vocal cords is about a third longer in men. However, there may be social influences on this

physiological difference. It has been claimed that in the United States women may speak as if they were smaller than they are (that is, with higher-pitched voices) and men as if they were bigger than they are (that is, with lower-pitched voices). The "Oxford voice" common among Oxford fellows (all male) at one time was remarkably high pitched, and other social groups have adopted characteristic pitch levels that are not totally "natural."

12   It was reported that once during a debate in the French parliament when a delegate pointed out that there were differences between men and women, another delegate shouted out *Vive la difference!* It is not necessary to believe that men and women are the same to be skeptical about claims as to the differences in the way men and women speak. The desire to emphasize the differences seems to be widespread. Jespersen's chapter remains as a warning signal to all who venture into this murky area that one's prejudices may show through. Jesperson obviously believed (and no doubt so did many of his readers) that what he was saying was self-evident. However, he ends the chapter by observing that "great social changes are going on in our times which may eventually modify even the linguistic relations of the two sexes." Eventually, even scholars following in Jespersen's footsteps may come to see that men and women are simply people and that what they have in common is more important than *la difference,* at least as far as their use of language is concerned.

13   It is, however, disturbing to find in a work published in 1991 the following passage by a distinguished and respected scholar:

> [I]t is clear why, as sociolinguists have often observed, women are more disposed to adopt the legitimate language (or the legitimate pronunciation): since they are both inclined towards docility with regard to the dominant usages both by the sexual division of labor, which makes them specialize in the sphere of consumption, and by the logic of marriage, which is their main if not their only avenue of social advancement and through which they circulate upwards, women are predisposed to accept, from school onwards, the new demands of the market in symbolic goods.

14 It is a salutary reminder that progress is often an illusion.

THINKING CRITICALLY

1. Why does Macaulay refer to much of the work done on sex differences as "nonsense"?

2. Macaulay charges that fiction often reinforces sexual stereotypes, as novelists attempt to introduce men's or women's speech. Are there any problems with the examples he cites? Support your answer.

3. What examples does Macaulay give to indicate how society influences male or female speech patterns?

4. Because Macaulay sees so many flaws in Jespersen's findings, why does he devote such a large portion of his article to discussing and even quoting Jespersen?

5. Does Macaulay feel that a lessening of sexist language indicates that society has made significant progress in the way it views the sexes?

6. Macaulay wrote his essay for a scholarly audience. In your opinion, is the language used in the essay more like that of a class lecture, a textbook, a radio talkshow, a professional journal, or a conference presentation? Why?

WRITING ASSIGNMENTS

1. Keep a journal of the expressions writers you encounter use to introduce male and female characters' speech. What conclusions can you draw?

2. Watch a television program with a story line (e.g., a situation comedy, a drama, or a full-length movie). Write a brief critique of the program, based on its presentation of linguistic sex differences.

He and She: What's the Real Difference?

Clive Thompson

According to a team of computer scientists, writing style can reveal gender. A computer program developed by a team at an Israeli university can identify the gender of an author with an accuracy of almost 80 percent. The program tracks different key words that each gender uses more frequently than the other. For example, women are more likely to use the words *not, wouldn't, couldn't,* and *shouldn't,* and men are more likely to use *the* and *and* more often. While the results are interesting—do they actually mean anything?

Clive Thompson is a contributing writer for *The New York Times Magazine.* His articles have also appeared in the *Washington Post, Wired* magazine, and *New York* magazine. This article was first published in the July 6, 2003, edition of the *Boston Globe.*

1 Imagine, for a second, that no byline is attached to this article. Judging by the words alone, can you figure out if I am a man or a woman?

2 Moshe Koppel can. This summer, a group of computer scientists—including Koppel, a professor at Israeli's Bar-Ilan University—are publishing two papers in which they describe the successful results of a gender-detection experiment. The scholars have developed a computer algorithm that can examine an anonymous text and determine, with accuracy rates of better than 80 percent, whether the author is male or female. For centuries, linguists and cultural pundits have argued heatedly about whether men and women communicate differently. But Koppel's group is the first to create an actual prediction machine.

3 A rather controversial one, too. When the group submitted its first paper to the prestigious journal *Proceedings of the National Academy of Sciences,* the referees rejected it "on ideological grounds," Koppel maintains. "They said, 'Hey, what do you mean? You're trying to make some claim about men and women being different, and we don't know if that's true. That's just the kind of thing that people are saying in order to oppress women!' And I said 'Hey—I'm just reporting the numbers.' "

4 When they submitted their papers to other journals, the group made a significant tweak. One of the coauthors, Anat Shimoni, added her middle name "Rachel" to her byline, to make sure reviewers knew one member of the group was female.

(The third scientist is a man, Shlomo Argamon.) The papers were accepted by the journals *Literary and Linguistic Computing* and *Text*, and are appearing over the next few months. Koppel says they haven't faced any further accusations of antifeminism.

5   The odd thing is that the language differences the researchers discovered would seem, at first blush, to be rather benign. They pertain not to complex, "important" words, but to the seemingly quotidian parts of speech: the ifs, ands, and buts.

6   For example, Koppel's group found that the single biggest difference is that women are far more likely than men to use personal pronouns—"I", "you," "she," "myself," or "yourself" and the like. Men, in contrast, are more likely to use determiners—"a," "the," "that," and "these"—as well as cardinal numbers and quantifiers like "more" or "some." As one of the papers published by Koppel's group notes, men are also more likely to use "post-head noun modification with an *of* phrase"—phrases like "garden of roses."

7   It seems surreal, even spooky, that such seemingly throwaway words would be so revealing of our identity. But text-analysis experts have long relied on these little parts of speech. When you or I write a text, we pay close attention to how we use the main topic-specific words—such as, in this article, the words "computer" and "program" and "gender."

8   But we don't pay much attention to how we employ basic parts of speech, which means we're far more likely to use them in unconscious but revealing patterns. Years ago, Donald Foster, a professor of English at Vassar College, unmasked Joe Klein as the author of the anonymous book *Primary Colors*, partly by paying attention to words like "the" and "and," and to quirks in the use of punctuation. "They're like fingerprints," says Foster.

9   To divine these subtle patterns, Koppel's team crunched 604 texts taken from the British National Corpus, a collection of 4,124 documents assembled by academics to help study modern language use. Half of the chosen texts were written by men and half by women; they ranged from novels such as Julian Barnes's *Talking It Over* to works of nonfiction (including even some pop ephemera, such as an instant-biography of the singer Kylie Minogue). The scientists removed all the topic-specific words, leaving the non-topic-specific ones behind.

10   Then they fed the remaining text into an artificial-intelligence sorting algorithm and programmed it to look for elements that were relatively unique to the women's set and the men's set. "The more frequently a word got used in one set, the more weight it got. If the word 'you' got used in the female set very often and not in the male set, you give it a stronger female weighting," Koppel explains.

11   When the dust settled, the researchers wound up zeroing in on barely 50 features that had the most "weight," either male or female. Not a big group, but one with ferocious predictive power: When the scientists ran their test on new documents culled from the British National Corpus, they could predict the gender of the author with over 80-percent accuracy.

12   It may be unnerving to think that your gender is so obvious, and so dominates your behavior, that others can discover it by doing a simple word-count. But Koppel says the results actually make a sort of intuitive sense. As he points out, if women use personal pronouns more than men, it may be because of the old sociological saw: Women talk about people, men talk about things. Many scholars of gender and language have argued this for years.

13   "It's not too surprising," agrees Deborah Tannen, a linguist and author of best-sellers such as *You Just Don't Understand: Women and Men in Conversation.* "Because what are [personal] pronouns? They're talking about people. And we know that women write more about people." Also, she notes, women typically write in an "involved" style, trying to forge a more intimate connection with the reader, which leads to even heavier pronoun use. Meanwhile, if men are writing more frequently about things, that would explain why they're prone to using quantity words like "some" or "many." These differences are significant enough that even when Koppel's team analyzed scientific papers—which would seem to be as content-neutral as you can get—they could still spot male and female authors. "It blew my mind," he says.

14   But this gender-spotting eventually runs into a $64,000 conceptual question: What the heck is gender, anyway? At a basic level, Koppel's group assumes that there are only two different states—you're either male or female. ("Computer scientists love a binary problem," as Koppel jokes.) But some theorists of gender, such as Berkeley's Judith Butler, have argued that this is a false duality. Gender isn't simply innate or biological, the argument goes; it's as much about how you act as what you are.

15   Tannen once had a group of students analyze articles from men's and women's magazines, trying to see if they could guess which articles had appeared in which class of publication. It wasn't hard. In men's magazines, the sentences were always shorter, and the sentences in women's magazines had more "feeling verbs," which would seem to bolster Koppel's findings. But here's the catch: The actual identity of the author didn't matter. When women wrote for men's magazines, they wrote in the "male" style. "It clearly was performance," Tannen notes. "It didn't matter whether the author was male or female. What mattered was whether the intended audience was male or female."

16   Critics charge that experiments in gender-prediction don't discover inalienable male/female differences; rather, they help to create and exaggerate such differences. "You find what you're looking for. And that leads to this sneaking suspicion that it's all hardwired, instead of cultural," argues Janet Bing, a linguist at Old Dominion University in Norfolk, Va. She adds: "This whole rush to categorization usually works against women." Bing further notes that gays, lesbians, or transgendered people don't fit neatly into simple social definitions of male or female gender. Would Koppel's algorithm work as well if it analyzed a collection of books written mainly by them?

17   Koppel enthusiastically agrees it's an interesting question—but "we haven't run that experiment, so we don't know." In the end, he's hoping his group's data will keep critics at bay. "I'm just reporting the numbers," he adds, "but you can't be careful enough."

THINKING CRITICALLY

1. Why is the idea that men and women communicate differently so controversial?

2. How did the computer science team from Bar-Ilan University create a program that could distinguish male and female writing with high accuracy? What words did they find were particularly important in determining gender patterns?

3. What reasons do linguists give for why women use more personal pronouns than men? Do you agree with their reasoning?

4. In paragraph 14, Thompson asks "what the heck is gender anyway?" Answer this question with your own point of view. Beyond biology, is gender innate or is it a cultural construction?

5. Some critics of gender linguistics fear that the information we accumulate regarding communication differences could be used to "oppress women." Do you think such fears are valid? Why or why not?

WRITING ASSIGNMENTS

1. Read more about gender detection computer programs at www.universalteacher.org.uk/lang/herring.txt. While programs that are able to detect gender based on writing styles are interesting, does the fact that women and men seem to write differently matter? Can this information be useful? Write a short essay explaining why you feel that gender difference in writing (a) doesn't matter at all, (b) matters a little depending on the circumstances, or (c) matters a lot. Support your viewpoint with examples where appropriate.

2. This article describes how some computer scientists developed a program that could detect the gender of an author with high accuracy. Can we detect gender using our intuition? Many people think so. As part of a class writing assignment, each student should write a one-page description of a recent event leaving out any references to their own gender that could "give away" their sex. Your instructor should either post the samples online or provide copies of each student's writing, giving each sample a number. Try to "guess" the gender of the writer of each sample, citing words or phrases that you think are more male or female. After everyone has reviewed the samples, check and see how accurate your guesses were.

The Party Line
Rachel Rafelman

When it comes to social conversation, are women more interesting than men? Do men tend to monopolize conversations? Are women more likely to depreciate their own viewpoints? In this essay, Rachel Rafelman explores the social dynamics of men and women in conversation.

Rachel Rafelman is a Canadian journalist. Her articles have appeared in several newspapers and magazines including the *National Post* and the *Globe and Mail*. She has also co-produced several programs, including *Plague City: SARS in Toronto*, and most recently, *Alice, I Think*. This article appeared in the November 1997 edition of *Toronto Life Magazine*.

1 "Everyone" was there—the media moguls, the so-called glitterati, the captains of industry, and, less importantly, the captains' wives—all elbow-to-elbow at a gala reception for the opening of a new arts centre. Flotillas of martinis on silver trays floated through the crush and were duly consumed, as gradually the crowd began to split up into discreet groups, each defined exclusively by gender: tipsy women talking "girl talk"; even tipsier men discussing business, sports, and politics.

2   The time could have been 1956, but it was, in fact, last winter (the martinis were a nice retro touch). I was there, and not being accustomed to such gatherings, I was astonished. It wasn't supposed to be like this, the guys with the guys and the girls with the girls. That was what we did in junior high. Didn't gender splits like this disappear with whitewall tires? Apparently three decades of feminism and at least one of public programs like affirmative action and gender-sensitivity training had no impact, once a certain quantity of gin and vermouth had been imbibed.

3   "The gender split at parties happens, but it isn't planned," says writer and columnist Robert Fulford. "Suddenly you see six women in one group and another group of men standing in the opposite corner and this is among people who are often 30 years younger than I am! I have to say this tendency hasn't declined the way I would have predicted 15 years ago, and I don't see a big decline in the foreseeable future, either."

4   "What can I tell you?" says Sondra Gotlieb, writer and wife of Allan Gotlieb, former Canadian ambassador to the United States, with what I interpret as being a sigh of deep resignation. "It's the same old story. The women gravitate to each other and talk about their personal lives. The men talk business."

5   Not much new here. Victorian men sent their women off to the "sitting room" while they smoked cigars, drank port and talked about . . . well, we'll never really know what they talked about. True, this practice has largely disappeared (though Sondra Gotlieb reports it is still standard dinner party protocol in Eastern Europe). Men no longer banish us. They don't have to. We do it all on our own. What's more, it seems we prefer it that way.

6   Here is a truly interesting fact: When you start canvassing men and women on the subject of their social conversational preferences, you find a great deal of agreement. Ten successful, self-confident men and women ranging in age from mid-twenties to 60-something concurred on two key points. The first, and perhaps most surprising, is that, in mixed company, men are boring. The second: Under similar conditions, women are not. The second point is kind of a corollary to the first. Given a choice, everyone prefers talking to women.

7   Of course there are boring women and interesting men. What we're dealing with here are broad strokes, generalities, even stereotypes. Okay? So now we can ask the following: Why are men boring? At least why are they so much more boring than women? The consistent answer from my interviewees is that women get involved in conversation. They get personal. Men do not.

8   "Men only want to talk about business. They don't want to get into personal stuff," says Bob Ramsay of Ramsay Writes, a Toronto communications firm. "I mean, God only knows what we would get into there!" For many men, a party is just a business meeting with food and drink, an occasion to trot their high-level contacts, deals and even resumes around the table with impunity (unless, of course, being deemed a dullard is an undesirable consequence). But for a woman to do the same would be breathtakingly inappropriate, even if she were the CEO of General Motors. Women downplay their accomplishments as a rule. "This is a good thing. It makes them more approachable. It's socially graceful," comments Margaret Wente, the editor of the *Globe and Mail's* "Report on Business." "Women are looking for a way to connect and that, in my opinion, is a strength." Wente, who's in the unusual position of being regularly chatted up by men who believe she has inside

information, doesn't necessarily regard this as a perk. "I have to tell you, these business conversations are usually as boring as bad jokes."

9   Business, although it does literally make the world go round, just doesn't make for good party talk, unless of course it is approached in a personal way. For example: "I invested heavily in Bre-X and now I can't afford to ship Reginald Jr. off to boarding school next semester." A woman might say this; a man never would. Money, as one male wag once observed, is life's report card. For women, money's a grade, but only in one subject—and something second-tier like phy ed at that. Intriguingly, Wente, insists that at her own parties the women often chat about mutual funds while the men discuss gardening. (I can hear it now: "My clematis is bigger than yours.")

10   No matter what the topic, girl talk entails the rapid disclosure of details, with the expectation of immediate and enthusiastic reciprocation. The male verbal strategy is to divulge as few personal details as possible, while assiduously avoiding all expressions of emotion that could be interpreted as weakness. "Loose lips sink ships," a popular Second World War motto, seems to rule male social discourse even 50 years later.

11   According to Geoff Pevere, a broadcaster and critic, "This personal/private thing is one of the last frontiers of gender distinction." The recent discovery of his own conflict in this realm took him aback: "I came home after spending an evening with an old [male] friend and my [female] partner asked about his partner and their baby. I couldn't answer. Those things just hadn't come up." This is the kind of omission few women comprehend since asking after spouses and offspring is nearly axiomatic in their social discourse.

12   A short time later, at a dinner party with friends, the women began to discuss an absent couple who were having marital problems. As Pevere remembers it, he and the men fell silent. "I felt it was inappropriate and yet I imagine the women felt they were sharing their concern for friends, and that the couple themselves—at least, the woman—might have interpreted it similarly."

13   Despite this, Pevere, who confesses to having been born "without the sports gene," prefers the conversation of women. Robert Fulford also finds the traditional male topics of little interest. "Most things are more interesting than business," he says. "And absolutely everything is more interesting than sports."

14   In fact, the increasing number of women now interested in competitive sports is one interlocutory development that neither welcomes. According to Pevere, it has "taken its toll on the quality of contemporary conversation." Fulford longs for the old days when "by God, at parties, you could rely on the fact that the women wouldn't know about the infield fly rule and all that stuff."

15   Kate Fillion, author of *How to Dump a Guy: A Coward's Manual* (HarperCollins), doesn't feel it matters what a man is talking about. "In my experience, men are usually monologuing at each other and at women. It's not an exchange of ideas; it's a competition." Writer Allan Fotheringham, who claims Canadian men are especially dull, agrees. He refers to male competitive chat, which politicians are particularly prone to, as "pecker stretching."

16   Fillion reports having attended many dinner parties where the men "hold forth and the women tune out," or else the women have a conversation among themselves.

And if a woman declines to conform with the gender split, or genuinely finds herself interested in their topic and aligns herself conversationally with the men, Fillion says, a price is paid. "It can be seen as flirtatious or showing off. I've also seen the other women become annoyed because she is prolonging a very boring conversation."

17 Keeping a conversation going is one of the traditional female social functions. "It's part of what we do," observes Wente. "We are the social grease people." Indeed, for centuries women have been trained to draw people out, to get others talking about themselves, and to smooth over any alarming lulls in the conversation.

18 At the same time, the verbal capabilities of women have been undermined in almost every age and culture. This is probably the reason there are no celebrated female raconteurs. Speaking, especially in a social setting, is a method of asserting oneself, something women have rarely been taught (at least by example) to allow males to dominate in conversation and they, for their part, will do so—often without being conscious of it.

19 Moreover, from early childhood, females are spoken to differently than males. The content of their speech is correspondingly soft; declarative sentences are stylistically "unfeminine" and opinions are to be expressed obliquely, with an unflagging awareness of the feelings and sensitivities of others. It's amazing how tenacious this early training can be.

20 Even highly confident, accomplished women temper their speech (often by adding a qualifier to take the edge off an expression of power) and defer, often without being aware of it, to men. Women who are otherwise liberated and articulate can be heard uttering inanities like "Oh, really" and "How fascinating" in support of a male in mid-narrative. They will nod their heads, smile a lot, assume sympathtic expressions and, most important, keep their gaze fixed unwaveringly on the speaker's face.

21 "This has always worked well. It still does," says Gotlieb, who has seen many succeed against heavy odds in the corridors of power through their so-called conversational skills. "They absolutely hang on a man's every word and make him feel as if he's the center of the universe." The man, almost invariably, walks away muttering something like, "Brilliant woman . . . great conversationalist."

22 Many of us find this very aggravating. I myself, who in the paraphrased words of Erica Jong, "can scarcely think of anything not to say," have witnessed similar scenes and been bewildered by them. How can a grown man not realize that while he's been talking nonstop for 20 minutes, his female audience has said virtually nothing? The men I polled were as perplexed as I. "Maybe it has something to do with conversation as performance, which it is for most men," says Geoff Pevere. "If you've made such a rapt audience of one woman, then you walk away feeling you've succeeded." I wasn't entirely convinced, and neither, I suspect, was he.

23 Evan Soloman, editor of *Shift* magazine, talks about the different male and female "social vocabularies." "Men talk loudly and opine with great certainty on issues they haven't got a clue about," he explains. "This is genetic stuff, developed over centuries of bragging and eating hors d'oeuvres." Women, who've presumably eaten fewer hors d'oeuvres and bragged less, have a different catalogue of social behavior. There is no gene for pontificating on their double helix. "Women ask a

question and actually listen to the answer, which is something men do not love to do," Solomon observes. "That is why, I think, we sometimes miss the point."

24   Listening is an important aspect of girl talk since it is at the very center of reciprocal communication. Women require it of each other. "I'll converse on almost any subject, but I will no longer, not ever, participate in one-sided conversations," says writer Katherine Govier. If this means chatting with women only, during the course of a four-hour cocktail party, well, so be it. "I finally feel comfortable moving away from an arrogant person who talks only about himself or herself. I don't encounter the situation as often as I used to , but I honestly have to say that lately, I've voted with my feet."

25   Not listening to women is embedded in our culture. Probably because historically, they haven't been credited with enough intellect to say anything worth hearing. And even current studies show conclusively that women talk less frequently than men, that they tell fewer narratives (especially lengthy ones) and that they are routinely interrupted by men—who just as routinely get away with it. Women who may no longer consciously believe that their silence is golden, will still instinctively endure almost any degree of conversational tedium if the speaker is male. What's more, in the very popular and egregious 1995 book *The Rules: Time-Tested Secrets for Capturing the Heart of Mr. Right*, authors Ellen Fien and Sherrie Schneider unabashedly advise single women to "follow [the man's] lead . . . be quiet and reserved . . ." Female loquacity, they warn, has dire consequences: "We know one man who stopped calling a woman he was physically attracted to because she simply didn't stop talking."

26   There is also still little gender parity in the realm of humor. Publicist Liza Herz finds herself reining in her slightly offbeat sense of humor when men are around. "I don't really want to do it, but witty women do make men nervous, and then things feel awkward. To them," Herz says, "a woman with a good sense of humour is one who laughs at their jokes." At a recent party, Herz, while talking to a man, made a quip that connected their current topic with an earlier one. "My remark wasn't even all that clever, but his reaction was 'Yeah. I get it. Oh, you're good!' as if I was trying to trip him up."

27   If clever women are resented, women without obvious professional status are baldly ignored. The simple statement "I'm an at-home mother with two kids" can clear a space faster than a backhoe, and here, women are just as guilty as men. Professional women can be quick to judge and dismiss another less career-oriented female. Full-time parenthood certainly isn't valued as highly as it should be, but this phenomenon is more complicated than that. It's that pesky early training persisting again. Women aren't taught to blow their own horns. In fact, they're not even supposed to admit to owning any instrument of that nature.

28   Some women actually go as far as to say deeply self-deprecating things like, "I'm just a housewife," accompanying the apology (and that's what it is) with a look of acute embarrasment.

29   And this knee-jerk humility can intensify when there are rampant careerists in the room. Once subjected to a barrage of dinner party introductions like "Mary Black, Merrill Lyinch" and "Frances Hill, Union Carbide," a woman I know responded anxiously, "Janice Freeman, nowhere." Not only was she putting herself

down, but she wasn't even being truthful in doing so. Janice was on sabbatical from her full-time professorship in medieval studies—a fact, needless to say, few people attending that evening ever found out.

30   Katherine Govier recalls attending a dinner party which dissolved almost at the outset into gender camps, with the women inside and the men outside, drinking beer around the barbecue. "I remember one man came in and wanted to talk to us. He hung around for awhile, clearly intimidated, and eventually wandered away." There is more energy in female conversation she feels, "and there are men who want to interact that way, too."

31   Gender issues usually come down to a matter of perception, Evan Solomon feels. He considers his female co-workers to be strong and feisty; they tell him he dominates. "There's no way I can get it right because I'm a man, not a woman. The best men can do is ensure equality in areas like education and job opportunity and then if the men still talk more than the women, well, that's just the way it is. We can't tinker on that level."

32   So where do we go from here? It may be that John Gray was right and women are from Venus while men are from Mars. But maybe that's not so bad. It does give us a whole solar system to party in.

THINKING CRITICALLY

1. According to Rafelman, what accounts for the separation of men and women in social situations? What role does communication style play in this separation?

2. Rafelman cites the different topics men and women discuss in social situations. In your opinion, is she stereotyping or is there merit to her observations? Explain.

3. If you did not know the author's gender, what conversation style does she seem to support based on her opinions in this article?

4. What cultural forces act on male and female communication? How, according to the author, can communication socialization hurt women in the business world?

5. Compare the observations Rafelman makes in her article to your own communication experience both socially and professionally. For example, at parties do the men and women tend to separate? Do they favor certain subjects? At work, are male communication styles favored? Support your answer with examples.

6. Rafelman implies that, at least in a party situation, female communication styles are preferable to male discourse. How does she support her viewpoint? Do you agree with her assertion? Explain.

WRITING ASSIGNMENTS

1. Try to identify some of the differences between the way men and women use language through cues that are connected with language but not necessarily actual words—such as pitch, tone, volume, facial expression, and touch. Write an essay from your own personal perspective analyzing the nonverbal as well as the verbal communication of men and women. Are they indeed speaking the same language?

2. The author states that both men and women think that women are better conversationalists. Why do you think she makes this judgment? Do you agree? Is this a gender stereotype, as the author admits, or is there some basis for the

observation? Do we tend to project our expectations of gender into social situations? Write an essay exploring the connection between our perception of gender and the communication style of men and women.

3. The author notes that in business, some communication styles get women more respect from men than others. Present your own viewpoint on this issue based on personal experience as well as outside research in business communication. In your opinion, is communication style in the business world an important issue? In what ways do women communicate differently from men in the business world? What styles are preferred, and why? What recommendations do communications experts recommend women employ, and do these specialists also offer advice to men?

4. Record a social conversation in which a group of men and women talk. You could videotape conversations at a party, or record a conversation in a dining hall in which both men and women are present. Write a paper analyzing the conversational patterns that emerge. Remember to include volume, tone, and rate of interruption in your analysis as well as the various subject matter discussed.

"I'll Explain It to You": Lecturing and Listening
Deborah Tannen

It is easy to assume that because English belongs to those who use it, men and women speak the same language. That may not be the case. There is strong evidence that male and female conversational patterns differ significantly. In fact, using fascinating examples from her own studies, sociolinguist Deborah Tannen shows that men and women use language in essentially different ways based on gender and cultural conditioning. From early childhood, girls use speech to seek confirmation and reinforce intimacy, whereas boys use it to protect their independence and negotiate group status. Carrying these styles into adulthood, men end up lecturing while women nod warmly and are bored. Is there hope for the sexes? Yes, says the author: by understanding each other's gender style, and by learning to use it on occasion to find a common language.

Deborah Tannen is professor of linguistics at Georgetown University. She is the author of many best-selling books on linguistics and social discourse, including *I Only Say This Because I Love You* (2001), *The Argument Culture* (1999), and *You Just Don't Understand* (1997), from which this essay is excerpted. She has been a featured guest on many news programs, including *20/20, 48 Hours*, and the *News Hour with Jim Lehrer*.

1 At a reception following the publication of one of my books, I noticed a publicist listening attentively to the producer of a popular radio show. He was telling her how the studio had come to be built where it was, and why he would have preferred another site. What caught my attention was the length of time he was speaking while she was listening. He was delivering a monologue that could only be called a lecture, giving her detailed information about the radio reception at the two sites, the architecture of the station, and so on. I later asked the publicist if she had been interested in the information the producer had given her. "Oh, yes," she answered.

But then she thought a moment and said, "Well, maybe he did go on a bit." The next day she told me, "I was thinking about what you asked. I couldn't have cared less about what he was saying. It's just that I'm so used to listening to men go on about things I don't care about, I didn't even realize how bored I was until you made me think about it."

2   I was chatting with a man I had just met at a party. In our conversation, it emerged that he had been posted in Greece with the RAF during 1944 and 1945. Since I had lived in Greece for several years, I asked him about his experiences: What had Greece been like then? How had the Greek villagers treated the British soldiers? What had it been *like* to be a British soldier in wartime Greece? I also offered information about how Greece had changed, what it is like now. He did not pick up on my remarks about contemporary Greece, and his replies to my questions quickly changed from accounts of his own experiences, which I found riveting, to facts about Greek history, which interested me in principle but in the actual telling left me profoundly bored. The more impersonal his talk became, the more I felt oppressed by it, pinned involuntarily in the listener position.

3   At a showing of Judy Chicago's jointly created art work *The Dinner Party*, I was struck by a couple standing in front of one of the displays: The man was earnestly explaining to the woman the meaning of symbols in the tapestry before them, pointing as he spoke. I might not have noticed this unremarkable scene, except that *The Dinner Party* was radically feminist in conception, intended to reflect women's experiences and sensibilities.

4   While taking a walk in my neighborhood on an early summer evening at twilight, I stopped to chat with a neighbor who was walking his dogs. As we stood, I noticed that the large expanse of yard in front of which we were standing was aglitter with the intermittent flickering of fireflies. I called attention to the sight, remarking on how magical it looked. "It's like the Fourth of July," I said. He agreed, and then told me he had read that the lights of fireflies are mating signals. He then explained to me details of how these signals work—for example, groups of fireflies fly at different elevations and could be seen to cluster in different parts of the yard.

5   In all these examples, the men had information to impart and they were imparting it. On the surface, there is nothing surprising or strange about that. What is strange is that there are so many situations in which men have factual information requiring lengthy explanations to impart to women, and so few in which women have comparable information to impart to men.

6   The changing times have altered many aspects of relations between women and men. Now it is unlikely, at least in many circles, for a man to say, "I am better than you because I am a man and you are a woman." But women who do not find men making such statements are nonetheless often frustrated in their dealings with them. One situation that frustrates many women is a conversation that has mysteriously turned into a lecture, with the man delivering the lecture to the woman, who has become an appreciative audience.

7   Once again, the alignment in which women and men find themselves arrayed is asymmetrical. The lecturer is framed as superior in status and expertise, cast in the role of teacher, and the listener is cast in the role of student. If women and men took turns giving and receiving lectures, there would be nothing disturbing about it.

What is disturbing is the imbalance. Women and men fall into this unequal pattern so often because of the differences in their interactional habits. Since women seek to build rapport, they are inclined to play down their expertise rather than display it. Since men value the position of center stage and the feeling of knowing more, they seek opportunities to gather and disseminate factual information.

8   If men often seem to hold forth because they have the expertise, women are often frustrated and surprised to find that when they have the expertise, they don't necessarily get the floor.

First Me, Then Me

9 I was at a dinner with faculty members from other departments in my university. To my right was a woman. As the dinner began, we introduced ourselves. After we told each other what departments we were in and what subjects we taught, she asked what my research was about. We talked about my research for a little while. Then I asked her about her research and she told me about it. Finally, we discussed the ways that our research overlapped. Later, as tends to happen at dinners, we branched out to others at the table. I asked a man across the table from me what department he was in and what he did. During the next half hour, I learned a lot about his job, his research, and his background. Shortly before the dinner ended there was a lull, and he asked me what I did. When I said I was a linguist, he became excited and told me about a research project he had conducted that was related to neurolinguistics. He was still telling me about his research when we all got up to leave the table.

10   This man and woman were my colleagues in academia. What happens when I talk to people at parties and social events, not fellow researchers? My experience is that if I mention the kind of work I do to women, they usually ask me about it. When I tell them about conversational style or gender differences, they offer their own experiences to support the patterns I describe. This is very pleasant for me. It puts me at center stage without my having to grab the spotlight myself, and I frequently gather anecdotes I can use in the future. But when I announce my line of work to men, many give me a lecture on language—for example, about how people, especially teenagers, misuse language nowadays. Others challenge me, for example questioning me about my research methods. Many others change the subject to something they know more about.

11   Of course not all men respond in this way, but over the years I have encountered many men, and very few women, who do. It is not that speaking in this way is *the* male way of dong things, but that it is *a* male way. There are women who adopt such styles, but they are perceived as speaking like men.

If You've Got It, Flaunt It—or Hide It

12 I have been observing this constellation in interaction for more than a dozen years. I did not, however, have any understanding of *why* this happens until fairly recently, when I developed the framework of status and connection. An experimental study that was pivotal in my thinking shows that expertise does not ensure women a place at center stage in conversation with men.

13   Psychologist H. M. Leet-Pellegrini set out to discover whether gender or expertise determined who would behave in what she terms a "dominant" way—for example, by talking more, interrupting, and controlling the topic. She set up pairs of women, pairs of men, and mixed pairs, and asked them to discuss the effects of television violence on children. In some cases, she made one of the partners an expert by providing relevant factual information and time to read and assimilate it before the videotaped discussion. One might expect that the conversationalist who was the expert would talk more, interrupt more, and spend less time supporting the conversational partner who knew less about the subject. But it wasn't so simple. On the average, those who had expertise did talk more, but men experts talked more than women experts.

14   Expertise also had a different effect on women and men with regard to supportive behavior. Leet-Pellegrini expected that the one who did not have expertise would spend more time offering agreement and support to the one who did. This turned out to be true—*except* in cases where a woman was the expert and her nonexpert partner was a man. In this situation, the women experts showed support—saying things like "Yeah" and "That's right"—far *more* than the nonexpert men they were talking to. Observers often rated the male nonexpert as more dominant than the female expert. In other words, the women in this experiment not only didn't wield their expertise as power, but tried to play it down and make up for it through extra assenting behavior. They acted as if their expertise were something to hide.

15   And perhaps it was. When the word *expert* was spoken in these experimental conversations, in all cases but one it was the man in the conversation who used it, saying something like "So, you're the expert." Evidence of the woman's superior knowledge sparked resentment, not respect.

16   Furthermore, when an expert man talked to an uninformed woman, he took a controlling role in structuring the conversation in the beginning *and* the end. But when an expert man talked to an uninformed man, he dominated in the beginning but not always in the end. In other words, having expertise was enough to keep a man in the controlling position if he was talking to a woman, but not if he was talking to a man. Apparently, when a woman surmised that the man she was talking to had more information on the subject than she did, she simply accepted the reactive role. But another man, despite a lack of information, might still give the expert a run for his money and possibly gain the upper hand by the end.

17   Reading these results, I suddenly understood what happens to me when I talk to women and men about language. I am assuming that my acknowledged expertise will mean I am automatically accorded authority in the conversation, and with women that is generally the case. But when I talk to men, revealing that I have acknowledged expertise in this area often invites challenges. I *might* maintain my position if I defend myself successfully against the challenges, but if I don't, I may lose ground.

18   One interpretation of the Leet-Pellegrini study is that women are getting a bum deal. They don't get credit when it's due. And in a way, this is true. But the reason is not—as it seems to many women—that men are bums who seek to deny women authority. The Leet-Pellegrini study shows that many men are inclined to jockey for status, and challenge the authority of others, when they are talking to men too.

If this is so, then challenging a woman's authority as they would challenge a man's could be a sign of respect and equal treatment, rather than lack of respect and discrimination. In cases where this is so, the inequality of the treatment results not simply from the men's behavior alone but from the differences in men's and women's styles: Most women lack experience in defending themselves against challenges, which they misinterpret as personal attacks on their credibility.

19   Even when talking to men who are happy to see them in positions of status, women may have a hard time getting their due because of differences in men's and women's interactional goals. Just as boys in high school are not inclined to repeat information about popular girls because it doesn't get them what they want, women in conversation are not inclined to display their knowledge because it doesn't get them what they are after. Leet-Pellegrini suggests that the men in this study were playing a game of "Have I won?" while the women were playing a game of "Have I been sufficiently helpful?" I am inclined to put this another way: The game women play is "Do you like me?" whereas the men play "Do you respect me?" If men, in seeking respect, are less liked by women, this is an unsought side effect, as is the effect that women, in seeking to be liked, may lose respect. When a woman has a conversation with a man, her efforts to emphasize their similarities and avoid showing off can easily be interpreted, through the lens of status, as relegating her to a one-down position, making her appear either incompetent or insecure.

A Subtle Deference

20 Elizabeth Aries, a professor of psychology at Amherst College, set out to show that highly intelligent, highly educated young women are no longer submissive in conversations with male peers. And indeed she found that the college women did talk more than the college men in small groups she set up. But what they said was different. The men tended to set the agenda by offering opinions, suggestions, and information. The women tended to react, offering agreement or disagreement. Furthermore, she found that body language was as different as ever: The men sat with their legs stretched out, while the women gathered themselves in. Noting that research has found that speakers using the open-bodied position are more likely to persuade their listeners, Aries points out that talking more may not ensure that women will be heard.

21   In another study, Aries found that men in all-male discussion groups spent a lot of time at the beginning finding out "who was best informed about movies, books, current events, politics, and travel" as a means of "sizing up the competition" and negotiating "where they stood in relation to each other." This glimpse of how men talk when there are no women present gives an inkling of why displaying knowledge and expertise is something that men find more worth doing than women. What the women in Aries's study spent time doing was "gaining a closeness through more intimate self-revelation."

22   It is crucial to bear in mind that both the women and the men in these studies were establishing camaraderie, and both were concerned with their relationships to each other. But different aspects of their relationships were of primary concern: their place in a hierarchical order for the men, and their place in a network of intimate connections for the women. The consequence of these disparate concerns was very different ways of speaking.

23   Thomas Fox is an English professor who was intrigued by the differences between women and men in his freshman writing classes. What he observed corresponds almost precisely to the experimental findings of Aries and Leet-Pellegrini. Fox's method of teaching writing included having all the students read their essays to each other in class and talk to each other in small groups. He also had them write papers reflecting on the essays and the discussion groups. He alone, as the teacher, read these analytical papers.

24   To exemplify the two styles he found typical of women and men, Fox chose a woman, Ms. M, and a man, Mr. H. In her speaking as well as her writing, Ms. M held back what she knew, appearing uninformed and uninterested, because she feared offending her classmates. Mr. H spoke and wrote with authority and apparent confidence because he was eager to persuade his peers. She did not worry about persuading; he did not worry about offending.

25   In his analytical paper, the young man described his own behavior in the mixed-gender group discussions as if he were describing the young men in Leet-Pellegrini's and Aries's studies:

> In my sub-group I am the leader. I begin every discussion by stating my opinions as facts. The other two members of the sub-group tend to sit back and agree with me. . . . I need people to agree with me.

Fox comments that Mr. H reveals "a sense of self, one that acts to change himself and other people, that seems entirely distinct from Ms. M's sense of self, dependent on and related to others."

26   Calling Ms. M's sense of self "dependent" suggests a negative view of her way of being in the world—and, I think, a view more typical of men. This view reflects the assumption that the alternative to independence is dependence. If this is indeed a male view, it may explain why so many men are cautious about becoming intimately involved with others: It makes sense to avoid humiliating dependence by insisting on independence. But there is another alternative: *inter*dependence.

27   The main difference between these alternatives is symmetry. Dependence is an asymmetrical involvement: One person needs the other, but not vice versa, so the needy person is one-down. Interdependence is symmetrical: Both parties rely on each other, so neither is one-up or one-down. Moreover, Mr. H's sense of self is also dependent on others. He requires others to listen, agree, and allow him to take the lead by stating his opinions first.

28   Looked at this way, the woman and man in this group are both dependent on each other. Their differing goals are complementary, although neither understands the reasons for the other's behavior. This would be a fine arrangement, except that their differing goals result in alignments that enhance his authority and undercut hers.

Different Interpretations—and Misinterpretations

29 Fox also describes differences in the way male and female students in his classes interpreted a story they read. These differences also reflect assumptions about the interdependence or independence of individuals. Fox's students wrote their responses to "The Birthmark" by Nathaniel Hawthorne. In the story, a woman's husband becomes obsessed with a birthmark on her face. Suffering from her husband's

revulsion at the sight of her, the wife becomes obsessed with it too and, in a reversal of her initial impulse, agrees to undergo a treatment he has devised to remove the birthmark—a treatment that succeeds in removing the mark, but kills her in the process.

30   Ms. M interpreted the wife's complicity as a natural response to the demand of a loved one: The woman went along with her husband's lethal schemes to remove the birthmark because she wanted to please and be appealing to him. Mr. H blamed the woman's insecurity and vanity for her fate, and he blamed her for voluntarily submitting to her husband's authority. Fox points out that he saw her as individually responsible for her actions, just as he saw himself as individually responsible for his own actions. To him, the issue was independence: The weak wife voluntarily took a submissive role. To Ms. M, the issue was interdependence: The woman was inextricably bound up with her husband, so her behavior could not be separated from his.

31   Fox observes that Mr. H saw the writing of the women in the class as spontaneous—they wrote whatever popped into their heads. Nothing could be farther from Ms. M's experience as she described it: When she knew her peers would see her writing, she censored everything that popped into her head. In contrast, when she was writing something that only her professor would read, she expressed firm and articulate opinions.

32   There is a striking but paradoxical complementarity to Ms. M's and Mr. H's styles, when they are taken together. He needs someone to listen and agree. She listens and agrees. But in another sense, their dovetailing purposes are at cross-purposes. He misinterprets her agreement, intended in a spirit of connection, as a reflection of status and power: He thinks she is "indecisive" and "insecure." Her reasons for refraining from behaving as he does—firmly stating opinions as facts—have nothing to do with her attitudes toward her knowledge, as he thinks they do, but rather result from her attitudes toward her relationships with her peers.

33   These experimental studies by Leet-Pellegrini and Aries, and the observations by Fox, all indicate that, typically, men are more comfortable than women in giving information and opinions and speaking in an authoritative way to a group, whereas women are more comfortable than men in supporting others. . . .

Listener as Underling

34 Clearly men are not always talking and women are not always listening. I have asked men whether they ever find themselves in the position of listening to another man giving them a lecture, and how they feel about it. They tell me that this does happen. They may find themselves talking to someone who presses information on them so insistently that they give in and listen. They say they don't mind too much, however, if the information is interesting. They can store it away for future use, like remembering a joke to tell others later. Factual information is of less interest to women because it is of less use to them. They are unlikely to try to pass on the gift of information, more likely to give the gift of being a good audience.

35   Men as well as women sometimes find themselves on the receiving end of a lecture they would just as soon not hear. But men tell me that it is most likely to

happen if the other man is in a position of higher status. They know they have to listen to lectures from fathers and bosses.

36   That men can find themselves in the position of unwilling listener is attested to by a short opinion piece in which A. R. Gurney bemoans being frequently "cornered by some self-styled expert who harangues me with his considered opinion on an interminable agenda of topics." He claims that this tendency bespeaks a peculiarly American inability to "converse"—that is, engage in a balanced give-and-take—and cites as support the French observer of American customs Alexis de Tocqueville, who wrote, "An American . . . speaks to you as if he was addressing a meeting." Gurney credits his own appreciation of conversing to his father, who "was a master at eliciting and responding enthusiastically to the views of others, though this resiliency didn't always extend to his children. Indeed, now I think about it, he spoke to us many times as if he were addressing a meeting."

37   It is not surprising that Gurney's father lectured his children. The act of giving information by definition frames one in a position of higher status, while the act of listening frames one as lower. Children instinctively sense this—as do most men. But when women listen to men, they are not thinking in terms of status. Unfortunately, their attempts to reinforce connections and establish rapport, when interpreted through the lens of status, can be misinterpreted as casting them in a subordinate position—and are likely to be taken that way by many men.

What's So Funny?

38 The economy of exchanging jokes for laughter is a parallel one. In her study of college students' discussion groups, Aries found that the students in all-male groups spent a lot of time telling about times they had played jokes on others, and laughing about it. She refers to a study in which Barbara Miller Newman found that high school boys who were not "quick and clever" became the targets of jokes. Practical joking—playing a joke *on* someone—is clearly a matter of being one-up: in the know and in control. It is less obvious, but no less true, that *telling* jokes can also be a way of negotiating status.

39   Many women (certainly not all) laugh at jokes but do not later remember them. Since they are not driven to seek and hold center stage in a group, they do not need a store of jokes to whip out for this purpose. A woman I will call Bernice prided herself on her sense of humor. At a cocktail party, she met a man to whom she was drawn because he seemed at first to share this trait. He made many funny remarks, which she spontaneously laughed at. But when she made funny remarks, he seemed not to hear. What had happened to his sense of humor? Though telling jokes and laughing at them are both reflections of a sense of humor, they are very different social activities. Making others laugh gives you a fleeting power over them: As linguist Wallace Chafe points out, at the moment of laughter, a person is temporarily disabled. The man Bernice met was comfortable only when he was making her laugh, not the other way around. When Bernice laughed at his jokes, she thought she was engaging in a symmetrical activity. But he was engaging in an asymmetrical one.

40   A man told me that sometime around tenth grade he realized that he preferred the company of women to the company of men. He found that his female friends

were more supportive and less competitive, whereas his male friends seemed to spend all their time joking. Considering joking an asymmetrical activity makes it clearer why it would fit in with a style he perceived as competitive. . . .

Mutual Accusations

41 Considering these dynamics, it is not surprising that many women complain that their partners don't listen to them. But men make the same complaint about women, although less frequently. The accusation "You're not listening" often really means "You don't understand what I said in the way that I meant it," or "I'm not getting the response I wanted." Being listened to can become a metaphor for being understood and being valued.

42   In my earlier work I emphasized that women may get the impression men aren't listening to them even when the men really are. This happens because men have different habitual ways of showing they're listening. As anthropologists Maltz and Borker explain, women are more inclined to ask questions. They also give more listening responses—little words like *mhm, uh-uh,* and *yeah*—sprinkled throughout someone else's talk, providing a running feedback loop. And they respond more positively and enthusiastically, for example by agreeing and laughing.

43   All this behavior is doing the work of listening. It also creates rapport-talk by emphasizing connection and encouraging more talk. The corresponding strategies of men—giving fewer listener responses, making statements rather than asking questions, and challenging rather than agreeing—can be understood as moves in a contest by incipient speakers rather than audience members.

44   Not only do women give more listening signals, according to Maltz and Borker, but the signals they give have different meanings for men and women, consistent with the speaker/audience alignment. Women use "yeah" to mean "I'm with you, I follow," whereas men tend to say "yeah" only when they agree. The opportunity for misunderstanding is clear. When a man is confronted with a woman who has been saying "yeah," "yeah," "yeah," and then turns out not to agree, he may conclude that she has been insincere, or that she was agreeing without really listening. When a woman is confronted with a man who does *not* say "yeah"—or much of anything else—she may conclude that *he* hasn't been listening. The men's style is more literally focused on the message level of talk, while the women's is focused on the relationship or metamessage level.

45   To a man who expects a listener to be quietly attentive, a woman giving a stream of feedback and support will seem to be talking too much for a listener. To a woman who expects a listener to be active and enthusiastic in showing interest, attention, and support, a man who listens silently will seem not to be listening at all, but rather to have checked out of the conversation, taken his listening marbles, and gone mentally home.

46   Because of these patterns, women may get the impression that men aren't listening when they really are. But I have come to understand, more recently, that it is also true that men listen to women less frequently than women listen to men, because the act of listening has different meanings for them. Some men really *don't*

want to listen at length because they feel it frames them as subordinate. Many women do want to listen, but they expect it to be reciprocal—I listen to you now; you listen to me later. They become frustrated when they do the listening now and now and now, and later never comes.

Mutual Dissatisfaction

47   If women are dissatisfied with always being in the listening position, the dissatisfaction may be mutual. That a woman feels she has been assigned the role of silently listening audience does not mean that a man feels he has consigned her to that role—or that he necessarily likes the rigid alignment either.

48   During the time I was working on this book, I found myself at a book party filled with people I hardly knew. I struck up a conversation with a charming young man who turned out to be a painter. I asked him about his work and, in response to his answer, asked whether there has been a return in contemporary art to figurative painting. In response to my question, he told me a lot about the history of art—so much that when he finished and said, "That was a long answer to your question," I had long since forgotten that I had asked a question, let alone what it was. I had not minded this monologue—I had been interested in it—but I realized, with something of a jolt, that I had just experienced the dynamic that I had been writing about.

49   I decided to risk offending my congenial new acquaintance in order to learn something about his point of view. This was, after all, a book party, so I might rely on his indulgence if I broke the rules of decorum in the interest of writing a book. I asked whether he often found himself talking at length while someone else listened. He thought for a moment and said yes, he did, because he liked to explore ideas in detail. I asked if it happened equally with women and men. He thought again and said, "No, I have more trouble with men." I asked what he meant by trouble. He said, "Men interrupt. *They* want to explain to *me*."

50   Finally, having found this young man disarmingly willing to talk about the conversation we had just had and his own style, I asked which he preferred: that a woman listen silently and supportively, or that she offer opinions and ideas of her own. He said he thought he liked it better if she volunteered information, making the interchange more interesting.

51   When men begin to lecture other men, the listeners are experienced at trying to sidetrack the lecture, or match it, or derail it. In this system, making authoritative pronouncements may be a way to begin an *exchange* of information. But women are not used to responding in that way. They see little choice but to listen attentively and wait for their turn to be allotted to them rather than seizing it for themselves. If this is the case, the man may be as bored and frustrated as the woman when his attempt to begin an exchange of information ends in his giving a lecture. From his point of view, she is passively soaking up information, so she must not have any to speak of. One of the reasons men's talk to women frequently turns into lecturing is *because* women listen attentively and do not interrupt with challenges, sidetracks, or matching information.

52   In the conversations with male and female colleagues that I recounted at the outset of this chapter, this difference may have been crucial. When I talked to the woman, we each told about our own research in response to the other's encouragement. When I talked to the man, I encouraged him to talk about his work, and he obliged, but he did not encourage me to talk about mine. This may mean that he did not want to hear about it—but it also may not. In her study of college students' discussion groups, Aries found that women who did a lot of talking began to feel uncomfortable; they backed off and frequently drew out quieter members of the group. This is perfectly in keeping with women's desire to keep things balanced, so everyone is on an equal footing. Women expect their conversational partners to encourage them to hold forth. Men who do not typically encourage quieter members to speak up, assume that anyone who has something to say will volunteer it. The men may be equally disappointed in a conversational partner who turns out to have nothing to say.

53   Similarly, men can be as bored by women's topics as women can be by men's. While I was wishing the former RAFer would tell me about his personal experiences in Greece, he was probably wondering why I was boring him with mine and marveling at my ignorance of the history of a country I had lived in. Perhaps he would have considered our conversation a success if I had challenged or topped his interpretation of Greek history rather than listening dumbly to it. When men, upon hearing the kind of work I do, challenge me about my research method, they are inviting me to give them information and show them my expertise—something I don't like to do outside of the classroom or lecture hall, but something they themselves would likely be pleased to be provoked to do.

54   The publicist who listened attentively to information about a radio station explained to me that she wanted to be nice to the manager, to smooth the way for placing her clients on his station. But men who want to ingratiate themselves with women are more likely to try to charm them by offering interesting information than by listening attentively to whatever information the women have to impart. I recall a luncheon preceding a talk I delivered to a college alumni association. My gracious host kept me entertained before my speech by regaling me with information about computers, which I politely showed interest in, while inwardly screaming from boredom and a sense of being weighed down by irrelevant information that I knew I would never remember. Yet I am sure he thought he was being interesting, and it is likely that at least some male guests would have thought that he was. I do not wish to imply that all women hosts have entertained me in the perfect way. I recall a speaking engagement before which I was taken to lunch by a group of women. They were so attentive to my expertise that they plied me with questions, prompting me to exhaust myself by giving my lecture over lunch before the formal lecture began. In comparison to this, perhaps the man who lectured to me about computers was trying to give me a rest.

55   The imbalance by which men often find themselves in the role of lecturer, and women often find themselves in the role of audience, is not the creation of only one member of an interaction. It is not something that men do to women. Neither is it something that women culpably "allow" or "ask for." The imbalance is created by the difference between women's and men's habitual styles. . . .

Hope for the Future

56 What is the hope for the future? Must we play out our assigned parts to the closing act? Although we tend to fall back on habitual ways of talking, repeating old refrains and familiar lines, habits can be broken. Women and men both can gain by understanding the other gender's style, and by learning to use it on occasion.

57 Women who find themselves unwillingly cast as the listener should practice propelling themselves out of that position rather than waiting patiently for the lecture to end. Perhaps they need to give up the belief that they must wait for the floor to be handed to them. If they have something to say on a subject, they might push themselves to volunteer it. If they are bored with a subject, they can exercise some influence on the conversation and change the topic to something they would rather discuss.

58 If women are relieved to learn that they don't always have to listen, there may be some relief for men in learning that they don't always have to have interesting information on the tips of their tongues if they want to impress a woman or entertain her. A journalist once interviewed me for an article about how to strike up conversations. She told me that another expert she had interviewed, a man, had suggested that one should come up with an interesting piece of information. I found this amusing, as it seemed to typify a man's idea of a good conversationalist, but not a woman's. How much easier men might find the task of conversation if they realized that all they have to do is listen. As a woman who wrote a letter to the editor of *Psychology Today* put it, "When I find a guy who asks, 'How was your day?' and really wants to know, I'm in heaven."

THINKING CRITICALLY

1. Explain the lecturer-listener relationship described in the opening paragraphs. How does Tannen explain this asymmetry in conversations? Is this pattern typical of male-female conversations in your experience—or of your family, or your peers?

2. According to the Leet-Pellegrini study, what typical role patterns evolve in conversations when women are the experts and men the nonexperts? And when men are the experts and women the nonexperts? How does Tannen explain these different reactions?

3. Does Tannen's explanation of why men challenge women's authority (paragraphs 18 and 19) seem valid to you? Or, do you think Tannen lets men off the hook too easily? Imagine you are Ms. M's academic adviser. Would you advise her to maintain or to change her current style of speaking and writing in class? What about Mr. H.?

4. According to the author, what happens when men find themselves being lectured to in a conversation with another man? Does Tannen's analysis ring true to your experience? Explain.

5. Why are men more interested in telling jokes, according to this article? In playing practical jokes? Do you agree? Can you give some exceptions?

6. Tannen closes her piece with advice on how to break old conversational habits: How to talk more if you are a listener, and how to listen more if you are a talker. Do you find her advice helpful? Oversimplified? Too optimistic? Too unrealistic? What obstacles might someone encounter in trying to break old conversational habits?

7. This piece opens with four anecdotes. What points are they making? Are the anecdotes effective? Are there subtle differences, or did you find them repetitious?

WRITING ASSIGNMENTS

1. Try a class experiment. Break into two groups: one half will hold a discussion about a topic of interest, the other half will observe the discussion group to see if the lecturer-listener patterns that Tannen describes emerge or not. What do you make of the results? Discuss your observations in a short essay, citing examples from the class discussion.

2. Many people interested in gender and language complain that communication breaks down because men attempt to dominate women. Tannen maintains that the effect of dominance ". . . is not always the result of an intention to dominate" but the result of the fact that males and females have distinctly different conversational styles based on gender and cultural conditioning. She says that as early as childhood boys learn to use speech as a way of getting attention and establishing status in a group; girls, to the contrary, use speech to confirm and maintain intimacy. Write a paper in which you support or refute Tannen's stand.

3. If you tend to be a lecturer, take the role of listener in a conversation. Or, if you tend to be a listener, experiment by being more outgoing and forceful in a conversation. Did you have difficulties adapting to a different role? Were you able to maintain it? Did you like the change, or were you uncomfortable? Did anybody notice the difference in you? Write a paper describing your experience. As Tannen does, use the summary-and-analysis approach in your discussion.

4. Write a paper explaining why you do or do not think the conversational patterns described by Tannen apply to you. Use some specific details to support your position.

Exploring the Language of **V I S U A L S**

Men Are from Belgium, Women Are from New Brunswick

Roz Chast

About a decade ago, marriage counselor John Gray published a controversial but best-selling book, *Men Are from Mars, Women Are from Venus: A Guide to Getting What You Want in Your Relationships*. Humorously explaining that men and women come from different planets (Mars and Venus), Gray postulated that the genders must respect their differences to achieve harmony. Although men and women speak a common tongue, their construction of meaning differs. For example, Gray proposed that when a woman suggests to a man that they stop and ask for directions, what he actually hears is her not trusting him to find his way without help. The cartoon by Roz Chast plays with some of Gray's concepts of male/female interpretations of language meaning. Chast's cartoons appear regularly in the *New Yorker* and the *Harvard Review*. She has illustrated several children's books and is the author of a number of cartoon collections, including *Childproof: Cartoons about Parents and Children* (1997).

THINKING CRITICALLY

1. What is Chast trying to convey in this cartoon? Does it operate on several levels? Explain.

2. Do you find this cartoon funny? Do you think that it may be more humorous to one gender than another? If so, which gender would find it funnier, and why?

3. Why does Chast claim men are from Belgium and women are from New Brunswick? Why do you think she chose these locations?

4. If you did not know the gender of the author of this cartoon, could you guess? Why or why not? Does gender matter to the success of the cartoon and the points it is trying to make? Explain.

MAKING CONNECTIONS

1. Do you think language itself can be "gendered"? For example, are there certain words that seem "male" and others that seem "female"? Review the essays by Kornheiser and Holmes and evaluate the words they use to convey their ideas. Write an essay that considers the idea of "gendered" language.

2. Have you ever found yourself at an impasse with a member of the opposite sex because your communication styles were different? For example, did you think the person you were arguing with "just didn't get it" solely because of his or her sex? Explain what accounted for the miscommunication and how you solved it.

3. Many of the authors in this section explain that men and women use language differently. Develop a list of the ways you think men and women use language differently and then develop your own theory, or expound on an existing one, to explain the communication differences. Think about the adjectives they use, their body language, why they speak, and how they present their information. If you wish, you may write about why you feel there is no difference between the ways men and women use language.

4. Record the conversations of some family members or friends as part of an experiment. Explain to the subjects that you are doing a study on language, but do not explain the details of your experiment. Try to record a conversation between two men, two women, and of a mixed group of both genders. Do you notice any differences in the ways men and women converse and use language? Evaluate your results and discuss your findings in class.

5. Nonverbal behavior can be influenced by gender, culture, and media cues that may cause people to misunderstand each other. Explore the ways you rely on nonverbal cues when communicating with others. How much do you depend on the actual words used in a conversation versus the tone, facial expressions, gestures, and mannerisms of the conversationalists? Do you think your nonverbal behavior is influence by your gender? Explain.

6. Much of this section focuses on communication differences between men and women. Do you think language itself can be "gendered"? For example, are there certain words that seem "male" and others that seem to be "female"? Review an essay by a male author and a female author in another chapter of this book and evaluate the words they use to convey their ideas. Do they indeed use language differently to convey their ideas?

LET'S TALK ABOUT IT: CONVERSATION IN ACTION

The Social Basis of Talk

Ronald Wardhaugh

Conversation is often naturally spontaneous and informal. But despite its seeming effortlessness, it is still governed by conscious and unconscious rules and principles of language, grammar, and behavior. What we say, how we say it, and to whom is much more complicated than we might think. A great deal depends on our personal expectations, opinions of the people with whom we speak, and our comfort level with the people and subject matter. In the next essay, Ronald Wardhaugh explores the characteristics of talk and the requirements of successful conversations.

Ronald Wardhaugh is a professor of linguistics and director of the Center for Language and Language Behavior at the University of Toronto. He is the author of many books on language, including *Introduction to Sociolinguistics* (1992), *Investigating Language* (1993), *Proper English: Myths and Misunderstandings About Language* (1999), and *How Conversation Works* (1985), from which the following essay is excerpted.

1 Our concern is with talk and the types of language used in talk. The major emphasis will be on conversation, the most generalized form of talk. We will also be concerned with both speakers and listeners, since talk is, as we shall see, essentially a cooperative undertaking. . . . The focus of our concern will be what happens when two or more people exchange words for some reason. Why does one person say one thing and the other reply as he or she does?

2 Talk is usually a social activity and therefore a public activity. It involves you with others, and each time you are involved with another person you must consider him or her. You must be aware of that person's feelings about what is happening, and you have some right to require him or her to do the same for you, to be aware of you and your feelings. In this sense talk is a reciprocal undertaking. Involvement in conversation therefore requires the two (or various) parties to be conscious of each other's needs, particularly the need not to be offended. Public life is possible only when the opportunities for being seriously offended are reduced to near zero. If the risks in an activity are great, you may be wise to refrain from that activity unless the potential gains are correspondingly great or you have no alternative. As we shall see, conversation is an activity which makes use of many devices in order to reduce the risks to participants. Consequently, skilled conversationalists rarely get "hurt."

3 There remains for most of us, however, a certain element of risk in any conversation. You may be hurt or you may inflict hurt in that one of the participants can emerge from the conversation diminished in some way. While it is unlikely that you insulted someone or you yourself were insulted, many lesser hurts are possible. You may have criticized another or have been criticized yourself; you may have incurred

an obligation that you did not seek or made a suggestion that another could not refuse; someone may have complimented you, thereby requiring you not only to acknowledge acceptance of that compliment but to live up to it; you may have skirted a topic which others expected you to confront, you may have offered an excuse or an apology but be left with the feeling that it was not necessarily accepted completely—someone's sincerity may therefore be suspect. During a conversation some subtle change in relationships between the parties is likely to have occurred; many conversations result in the participants having definite, residual feelings about them: of pleasure, displeasure, ease, frustration, anger, alarm, satisfaction, and so on. We are not loath to judge conversations in such terms. When we do so, we are in an important sense evaluating the risks we took, counting our gains and losses as a result of taking them, and adding everything up on our mental score cards. That we do such things is apparent from the comments we sometimes make following conversations or reporting on them to others, comments such as *He was pretty short with her, You should have heard her go on about it. Why didn't you speak up?, She shouldn't have spoken to me like that, He just grunted, never said a word*, or that sure sign that a relationship is in trouble: *You're not listening; you never listen!*

4   Indeed, if all participants in a conversation are to feel happy with it, each must feel that he or she got out of it what was sought. If you wish to appear as a "sensitive" participant in a conversation, you will therefore try to make sure that all the participants get to share in the various aspects of the conversation that will make it "successful": in selecting the topics that will be talked about; in having adequate and timely opportunities to speak; in feeling at ease in saying what needs to be said; in achieving a sense of orderliness and adequacy about what is going on and doing this as one of a group of two or more; and so on. None of these characteristics can be prescribed in advance—unless the conversation is a very formal one, for example, a meeting of some kind—so it is necessary for you at all times to be aware of just what exactly is happening in any conversation in which you participate. You must be aware of both what has gone before and what may come next, as well as where you seem to be at the moment. You must be aware that a complicated array of possibilities exists and that each choice must necessarily preclude others. You must exhibit a certain sensitivity if you are to avoid some choices so that no one may feel arbitrarily cut off either from the topic or from other participants. Your goal must be to see that everyone leaves the conversation satisfied.

5   What we can infer from all this is that if you want to be a successful conversationalist you must command a wide variety of skills. You must have a well developed feeling about what you can (or cannot) say and when you can (or cannot) speak. You must know how to use words to do things and also exactly what words you can use in certain circumstances. And you must be able to supplement and reinforce what you choose to say with other appropriate behaviors: your movements, gestures, posture, gaze, and so on. You must also attune yourself to how others employ these same skills. This is a considerable task for anyone—or *everyone*, as it turns out—to perform, so it is not surprising that individuals vary widely in their ability to be successful in conversation. You can bungle your way through or you can be witty, urbane, and always sure to say the right thing. And some can even exploit the ability they have for ends that are entirely selfish.

6   The actual requirements will vary from group to group and culture to culture. Some situations may require considerable amounts of silence and others considerable amounts of talk. Others may be partly defined by who gets to talk and in what order, for not everyone necessarily has a right to speak: contrast a state ceremonial with a Quaker meeting. And once speaking has begun, it has to stay within the bounds of the occasion: you do not deliver a lecture at a cocktail party; you do not tell a dirty joke while conveying bad news; and you do not (any longer in many places now) make sexist or racist remarks in public and hope to win or keep public office. In this broad sense linguistic behavior may be described as appropriate or not, and it is this sense of appropriateness that is the subject of studies by those who work in a discipline known as the ethnography of speaking; the study of who speaks to whom, when, how, and to what ends.

7   Certain basic conditions seem to prevail in all conversation, and many of the details of individual conversations arc best understood as attempts that speakers (and listeners) make to meet these conditions. Above all, conversation is a social activity and, as such, it shares characteristics of all social activities. These characteristics we usually take for granted so that it is only their absence we notice. When there is some kind of breakdown in society, we notice the absence of principles, conventions, laws, rules, and so on, which guided or controlled behavior in better times. Or, alternatively, we become aware of these same principles only when we have too readily accepted certain things as "normal" and then find out that we have been deceived, as when someone has tricked or "conned" us by pretending to do one thing (apparently quite normal) but actually doing another.

8   Conversation, like daily living, requires you to exhibit a considerable trust in others. Life would be extremely difficult, perhaps even impossible, without such trust. It is this trust that allows you to put money in a bank in the expectation that you will get it back on demand, to cross the street at a busy intersection controlled by either lights or a policeman, to eat food prepared by others, to plan for the future, and so on. But there is also the more general trust we have in the evidence of our senses, in the recurrence of both natural and other events, and in the essential unchanging and possibly unchangeable nature of the world and of the majority of its inhabitants. Trust in other people is the cornerstone of social living: to survive we must believe that people do not change much, if at all, from day to day and from encounter to encounter, and also that the vast majority do not set out deliberately to deceive or harm us. Indeed, we must believe them to be benevolent rather than malevolent. Without such trust in others and in what they do and say we could not get very far in coping with the world in which we find ourselves. So far as conversation is concerned, we would have little or no shared ground on which to build, and communication would become next to impossible. States of enmity and war or "not speaking" are good examples of the kinds of conditions that exist when trust is broken. However, it is important to realize that even in such cases there is almost never a complete breakdown, since the antagonists usually continue to observe certain rules and decencies. Not everything becomes "fair," which in such a case could mean only that absolutely anything might be possible, a situation therefore in which no rules of any kind would apply, an example of "savagery" in its mythical, pathological form.

9   We cannot survive without putting trust in others, but it must be a trust tempered with a certain amount of caution. We cannot insist on viewing the world with wide-eyed innocence and hope we will never be disappointed. If you want to survive and minimize the hurts you will experience, you must employ a little bit of common sense too. You must exercise certain powers of judgement and you must make sound decisions constantly. For example, in any encounter with another person, you must try to work out exactly what is going on. That requires you to exhibit characteristics for which terms like "intelligence" and "sensitivity" are often used: you must judge the actual words you hear in relation to the possible intentions of the speaker, in order to come up with a decision as to what the speaker really means. In abstract, theoretical terms, the possible permutations of meaning are immense. Fortunately, in reality, most of those possibilities are extremely unlikely. You can rule them out, and you must do so—otherwise you could never decide anything at all: you could never be in any way sure about anything anyone said to you. But that ruling-out is not done haphazardly. Certain basic principles that prevail in most conversations help you to narrow down the possibilities to a manageable set: mutual trust, the sincerity of participants, the validity of everyday appearances, and "common sense." A certain scepticism may obtain in our views of life and of human motivation, but it must have "healthy" limits. We cannot question and doubt everything or suspect every motive and still insist that we be regarded as normal people. We must seriously restrict such questioning, doubt, and suspicion; they are indicators, or markers, of very special kinds of conversation—interviews, psychiatric consultations, seminars, investigations—and such special activities must be clearly "framed" in some way to indicate their special character. In order to participate in a conversation, you must be a willing party to a certain worldview. In that respect conversation is a collusive activity. You may have reservations about certain matters, but unless you are prepared to meet others on common ground and ignore differences which can only be divisive there is little hope that any kind of meaningful communication will occur.

10   Ethnomethodologists—those who study common-sense knowledge and reasoning as they pertain to social organization—tell us that we are all parties to an agreement to inhabit a world in which things are what they appear to be and people do not in general go scratching beneath the surface of appearances. Living is largely a collusive activity, one in which you find yourself united with me because we both use our common sense and our goodwill to blind ourselves to things that do not seem to be important: we do not ask tough questions of each other; we do not seek rigid proofs; we do accept contradictions and uncertainty; and we do prefer to go along with others in most circumstances. That is how ordinary life is lived and must be lived.

11   Because conversation necessarily has a social basis, we must try to meet each other on common ground. For example, there is a general unspoken agreement among people that what we actually inhabit is a consistent, even mundane, world. It is essentially a world of the commonplace and the things in it do not change much, if at all. These "things" are also what they appear to be; they are not something else. Consequently, we tend to be amused when a "petrol station" really turns out to be a fast-food restaurant or one of James Bond's cars turns into a submarine and another into an aeroplane. Magicians exploit this kind of amusement. But if

such situations and such trickery happened continually we would undoubtedly find them stressful, or, alternatively, we would be forced to recast our image of fast-food outlets, automobiles, and trickery. That world too is one of simple causation: it is a recurrent world in which day follows night and night follows day, and so on. We see ourselves and others as consistent objects within that world; we believe we behave consistently and we tend to grant the same consistency to others.

12   We also tend to accept what we are told, taking any words spoken to us at close to face value unless we appear to have some very good reason for doing otherwise. For example, we seek only occasional clarification of remarks made to us. We are prepared to tolerate a remarkable amount of unclarity and imprecision in what we are told. We hold our peace and trust that everything will eventually work itself out to our satisfaction. So when we listen to interchanges that do involve considerable questioning and commenting, we know we are observing conversations of a special kind: for example, interrogations, psychiatric interviews, exchanges between teachers and students, and so on. If you suddenly let flow a stream of questions during what is otherwise just an ordinary conversation, you may effectively stop, or at least change, what is happening. You may well be perceived to be trying to turn something commonplace into an investigation and to be violating the basic condition of trust between participants. If I do not believe what you are telling me, I can challenge your truthfulness or I can start probing your account with questions. In either case you are likely to react in much the same way. You will become "defensive," for your trust in what we were doing together will be weakened as you find yourself under attack. I will have violated the normal unspoken agreement that I will believe what you say because in return you will believe what I say. For, after all, are not both of us reasonable, sincere, and honest individuals? Some people regard defensive behavior as "bad" behavior or evidence of some kind of guilt; it need be neither, being just a normal reaction to unwarranted offensive behavior from others.

13   Each party in a social encounter has a certain amount of "face" to maintain; many of the things that happen are concerned with maintaining appearances. I do not want to attack you in any way nor do I want you to attack me. We are, in a sense, parties to an agreement each to accept the other as the other wishes to appear. We may even go further and try to support a particular appearance the other proposes for himself or herself. If you want to act in a manner which I find somewhat peculiar, I may have very great difficulty in "calling" you on what you are doing. It is much more likely that I will go along with your performance and keep my doubts to myself. After all, you may have a good motive unknown to me for your behavior, so my initial reaction is likely to be to go along with what you are doing, to help you maintain the "face" you are presenting, rather than to propose some kind of change in your behavior. Those individuals who go around trying to "un-face" others, as it were, may find themselves unwelcome, even to each other, being constantly in violation of this norm that 'good' social behavior is based on mutual trust in appearances.

14   Conversation proceeds on the basis that the participants are reasonable people who can be expected to deal decently with one another. There must be a kind of reasonableness, a sort of "commonsenseness," in the actual choice of the words and expressions we employ. There must also be a certain rightness in the quantity as well as the quality of those words. You have to say enough to do the job that must

be done: not too little must be said nor, on the other hand, too much. Too little and someone will feel deprived of information; too much and someone will feel either imposed upon or the unwilling beneficiary of a performance rather than of a genuine instance of communication. Unreasonable language may also produce obscurity or even rouse someone to challenge what has been said. It may create problems which the participants can solve only when they have re-established the basic preconditions of trust that are necessary if anything positive is to be accomplished.

15   You must assume, too, that most others with whom you come into contact can deal adequately with the world, just as adequately as you believe you yourself deal with it. You do not readily question another's ability to state simple facts, or to ask and give directions, or to add new information to old. When you ask another person for directions, you expect that he or she will employ a scheme for giving the directions that will be adequate for the occasion. For example, if you have asked for a description of the interior of a house, you expect to get that description according to an acceptable pattern of spatial organization. You also expect certain kinds of information and not other kinds and to get information that is adequate for the purpose you have in mind, if you have made that purpose clear in some way. And that expectation is generally fulfilled. "Basic" information is fairly easily accessible, but we should notice how difficult it is quite often to gain certain further kinds of information—or to supply that information if we are asked for it. A lot of "information" that we actually have access to never becomes part of that body of information we rely on for ordinary living and routine communication with others. Police officers, for example, have to be specially trained to observe certain kinds of details that are, indeed, accessible to the general public. But what they observe and report is very different from what we, commonplace actors in a commonplace world, observe and are therefore able to report. We actually see the same things but we do not observe and record them in the same way; there is really no need to do so, for we know that everyday life does not usually require that intensity of observation. The events in our everyday world are necessarily mundane: life would quickly become unbearable if it were not so ordered and predictable and consequently so unworthy of close and continuing attention.

16   The kind of world in which we see ourselves and others existing is also one in which personal behavior is consistent—or should be. When we meet another person repeatedly, we assume that that person's behavior is consistent. The other is the "same" person from encounter to encounter and there is little, if any, fluctuation in behavior. When a person is consistently inconsistent, which is therefore a consistent fact in itself, we assume that he will continue to be inconsistent. Indeed, if you notice a change in consistency when you meet someone, you are likely to make a comment to that effect or express some concern, possibly to others rather than to the person himself. You may quietly ask yourself *What is up with him?* or *What have I done to make Sally say that?* Or, having noticed John's "peculiar" behavior, you may ask Bill *Why is John behaving the way he is these days?* The relative infrequency of such expressions of concern indicates how "normal" most continuing encounters are; the everyday sameness of behavior and routine does not require notice or comment, except perhaps about that very sameness: *What's new? Nothing!*

17   Just as we expect the behavior of others to be consistent, so we also view the world consistently; our beliefs about it and about how its various bits and pieces relate to one another change slowly, if at all. We tend to have rather fixed ideas about our place within that world, of who we are and how we relate to others, and this observation is true even of those whose world is partly a world of fantasy. Only schizophrenics inhabit more than one world, thereby appearing to inhabit one world inconsistently. Each of us has a picture or self-image of himself or herself and of the various others in our environment, and we seek to keep these pictures consistent. A particular picture may also have more than a single dimension to it: for example, we may have both a public image and a very different private one. If we do, we must try to keep the two apart. The private lives of public figures are of interest to us not only because they show us quite different aspects of character, but also because we can try to judge how successful the individuals are in separating the two existences. We may also be tempted to evaluate one existence, particularly the public one, against what we come to know of the other. Much of the appeal of biographies lies in attempts to reconcile the various images of the subjects.

18   We function in a world of normal appearances and usually do not probe beneath the surface of events, and in general, we believe that everybody else behaves in that respect much as we do, sharing with us a similar approach to daily existence. Those who probe are people like scientists and psychiatrists, but even their probing is restricted to a very narrow range of activities. Indeed, we go further and assume that those with whom we deal share much specific information about the world. One simple way of convincing yourself that this is so, that there is considerable shared background knowledge in any conversation, is to insist that each party make everything quite explicit in the very next conversation you have. That conversation will quickly degenerate: you may find yourself accused of being crazy, pedantic, or disruptive, or you may be assigned some other clearly antisocial label. Tempers are also likely to become frayed. Another way is to attempt to find out from newspapers, magazines, or radio and TV reports what is happening on some issue by using only the actual words you read or hear on a single specific occasion, completely disregarding any previous knowledge you might have of the topic. You will probably not be able to make much sense of what you either read or hear. One of the great difficulties you encounter in reading a local newspaper in a place you happen to be visiting is your lack of the background knowledge necessary to interpret what you are reading. This lack makes many items of local news either obscure or elusive: you lack knowledge of the people, the events, and the issues and have little or nothing on which to hang any details you are presented with. But the locals do not experience this difficulty.

19   Common knowledge, then—that is, "what everyone knows"—is necessarily something that is culture-loaded and varies from group to group. Much of what everyone knows is also either scientifically unwarranted or very superficial. For example, there are numerous stereotypes in this kind of knowledge—ideas we have about the "typical" behavior and characteristics of people or objects. But that should not surprise us, because, after all, that is essentially what norms themselves are in one sense—abstractions based on certain kinds of experiences which apparently typify some kind of general behavior. Many people go through life holding the view that common knowledge and stereotypes characterize a sort of truth about

the world; others are somewhat more critical and conscious of the complexities that lie behind such a simple belief. What we must not assume, however, is that common knowledge is always false and stereotyping is always bad; social harmony is possible only if there are things we can agree on, and there are measures of agreement. What may be important is how fixed are the measures any society uses, not the existence of the measures themselves.

20   For any particular conversation it is also possible to show that there are differences between the parties in the specific things that they know in contrast to the kinds of background knowledge that they share. No two people have identical backgrounds, so in any conversation the participants will have different kinds of knowledge about almost any topic that is likely to be mentioned. If only two people, Fred and Sally, are involved, there will be certain matters known to both, some because "everybody knows such things" and others because both Fred and Sally happen to know them. Then there will be matters known to only one of the speakers, so that Fred will know something that Sally does not know, or Sally something that Fred does not know. In addition, there will be partly known information: Fred or Sally, or both, may partly know something or know parts of something, but not necessarily the same parts. And Fred or Sally, or both again, may believe that the other knows something that the other actually does not know. As we can see, there are numerous possible permutations in who knows what, who believes who knows what, and so on.—Again, there are predictable consequences: conversation can proceed only on the basis that the participants share a set of beliefs, that is, certain things must be known to all parties; others may be known; some will have to be explained; questions may be asked for clarification; difficulties will be negotiated or cleared up somehow; people will be understanding and tolerant; and the various processes that are involved will be conducted decently. If only one participant in a conversation refuses to subscribe to these beliefs and to conduct himself or herself accordingly, the others will become irritated, confused, or frustrated, and may well abandon any attempt to continue what they have begun.

21   Since most participants in a conversation usually do share a certain amount of background knowledge about "proper" behavior and the "right" way to do things, much of what they say can be understood if we, too, are familiar with the knowledge they share. Their references to places, times, and events, and their accounts and descriptions are related to what they know and what they believe the others know. A participant in a conversation must believe that he or she has access to the same set of reference points that all the other participants have access to; all he or she needs do in conversing is use those points for orientation, and listeners will comprehend. And such a belief is largely justified. What is hardly ever necessary in a conversation is to begin at the very beginning of anything and to treat everyone and everything as unique and somehow without antecedents. In a trivial sense every occasion is unique, but procedures exist which minimize novelty and maximize normality—accepted ways of asking and giving directions, rules for regulating who speaks to whom and about what, and basic principles for conducting yourself, for example, with complete strangers.

22   A conversation between familiars offers a very special mix of knowledge. There are matters in it which the parties know but are reluctant to refer to directly, although they may allude to them if necessary. There are matters which are in the

conversation by reason of the fact that they are deliberately avoided—their absence is conspicuous. And then there are the actual topics of the conversation. However, these topics are not introduced logically, as it were, but rather in a variety of ways according to the needs of the individuals and of the occasion, with each participant willing to let a topic emerge as seems natural at the time in the expectation that its various bits and pieces will hold together.

23   In general conversation with others it is ordinary, everyday, "commonsense" knowledge that we assume they share with us. In certain circumstances, as between professionals, we can also assume a sharing of specialized knowledge. We must always take great care when we refer to items outside these shared areas. We cannot rely on others knowing what we know. They may not even share the same assumptions about what it means to "know" something. A physicist's knowledge of matter is different from a lay person's, and an actor's view of character is unlikely to be the same as that of a psychiatrist. Explanations may well become necessary, and they may not be easily provided. Briefing is one kind of explaining behavior in such circumstances. But a recurrent difficulty is knowing just how much to say on a particular occasion and then judging how successful we have been in saying it. This is particularly crucial if we then proceed to treat this "new" information we supply henceforth as part of our listeners' everyday knowledge. It may not be easily incorporated into existing knowledge, as anyone who has ever taught well knows, for it is one thing to teach something and quite another to learn it.

24   Repetition and checking up therefore become a very necessary part of conversation. They are demanded by the general requirement of language and communication that you must always say more than you minimally need to say so that you will not be misunderstood. The person you are talking to also must have checking devices to indicate whether you are being understood: for example, certain kinds of gestures or glances, which, because of the puzzlement they show, require you to offer some further explanation; outright questions; some kinds of denial behavior; and so on. In other words, as a speaker you are not free to indulge in a monologue, disregard those who are listening to you, and assume you are being understood. You must work to be understood and you must be sensitive to your audience. One consequence is that sophisticated public communicators are much more likely to seek other ways than formal speeches in order to get their views across to an audience which, by its nature, cannot ask for clarifications—a president's "fireside chats," press conferences, staged interviews, and appearances before favorable groups or friendly committees.

25   What should be apparent from what we have said is that successful conversations exploit many of the same principles that underlie all forms of social existence. There is really nothing "special" or unique about conversation in that sense. To get through a week in your life, you must be prepared to accept things for what they appear to be and put your trust in that appearance. You must also assume a certain regularity and continuity of existence. To do otherwise is to be paranoid or act antisocially. When disaster strikes and the "normal," consistent world vanishes, people often find themselves unable to cope with the changed circumstances of their lives. They no longer have the necessary reference points on which to pin their existence. Conversation is a form of 'coping' behavior which relies heavily on just those same sets of assumptions that allow us to drive to work safely, drink water in a restaurant,

cash a government cheque, and even go to sleep at night. Saying *Hi* to Sally and expecting Sally to say *Hi* in return is much the same kind of thing, or asking a stranger *Excuse me, do you have the time?* and getting the reply *Yes, it's ten to four.*

26   Without routine ways of doing things and in the absence of norms of behavior, life would be too difficult, too uncertain for most of us. The routines, patterns, rituals, stereotypes even of everyday existence provide us with many of the means for coping with that existence, for reducing uncertainty and anxiety, and for providing us with the appearance of stability and continuity in the outside world. They let us get on with the actual business of living. However, many are beneath our conscious awareness; what, therefore, is of particular interest is bringing to awareness just those aspects of our lives that make living endurable (and even enjoyable) just because they are so commonly taken for granted.

THINKING CRITICALLY

1. What are our unconscious expectations in social conversation? How do social dimensions of language impact the quality and substance of everyday discourse? Explain.

2. In what ways must we consider the person with whom we converse? What factors do we consciously and unconsciously process as we engage in conversation with another person?

3. How can we hurt others or hurt ourselves during conversation? Describe a situation in which you unintentionally hurt someone or yourself during a conversation.

4. What is the role of trust in everyday conversation? Consider the role of trust in your own conversations. How does the element of trust influence what you say and to whom? Explain.

5. What skills, according to the author, must a successful conversationalist possess?

6. What are the basic conditions that the author identifies as necessary for all conversations to take place? Explain.

7. What is the author's thesis and how does he support it? How effective are his examples in supporting his claims? Can you think of other areas in the essay where examples would be useful? Explain.

8. In what ways does effective conversational discourse depend on our shared sense of a "mundane" existence?

WRITING ASSIGNMENTS

1. Tape a conversation between two people discussing an everyday topic such as their weekend activities or a current event. Analyze their discussion, applying some of the conversational elements Wardhaugh describes. For example, what assumptions do the conversationalists hold in common? How do they exhibit trust? Do they risk hurting one another by making a conversational blunder? Explain.

2. Write an essay exploring the concept of trust in conversation. Why is trust so important to the success of social conversation? Describe situations from your own experience in which trust played an important role in the success or failure of a conversation.

Some Friends and I Started Talking:
Conversation and Social Change

Margaret J. Wheatley

We spend our lives having conversations. The huge explosion of cell phone use in the last five years is testimony to how much time and money we are willing to expend in search of conversation. Communication is fundamental to our survival. It not only is used to articulate needs and wants, but also our dreams, desires, fears, and goals. We use conversation to argue, console, share beliefs, develop thoughts, and discover more about each other. And it is from discussion and the exchange of ideas that great social movements are born. In the next essay, Margaret Wheatley explains why conversation can be a compelling tool for change. As Wheatley explains, "all social change begins with a conversation."

Margaret Wheatley is a well-known authority on organizational develop-ment. She is president of the Berkana Institute in Provo, Utah. She is the author of several books, including *Leadership and the New Science* (1992, co-authored with Myron Kellner-Rogers) and *A Simpler Way* (1996). The following essay first appeared in the *UTNE Reader* and is excerpted from her book, *Turning to One Another* (2002).

1   A Canadian woman told me this story. She was returning to Vietnam to pick up her second child, adopted from the same orphanage as her first child. On her visit two years earlier she had seen challenging conditions at the orphanage and had vowed this time to take medical supplies. "They needed Tylenol, not T-shirts or trinkets," she said to a friend one day. The friend suggested that the most useful thing to take would be an incubator. The woman was surprised (she'd been thinking bandages and pills), but she started making calls, looking for an incubator. Weeks later, she had been offered enough pediatric medical supplies to fill four 40-foot shipping containers! And 12 incubators. From a casual conversation between two friends, a medical relief effort for Vietnamese children emerged. And it all began when "some friends and I started talking."

2   Stories like this are plentiful. Nothing has given me more hope recently than to observe how simple conversations give birth to actions that can change lives and re-store our faith in the future. There is no more powerful way to initiate significant social change than to start a conversation. When a group of people discover that they share a common concern, that's when the process of change begins.

3   Yet it's not easy to begin talking to one another. We stay silent and apart from one another for many reasons. Some of us never have been invited to share our ideas and opinions. From early school days we've been instructed to be quiet so others can tell us what to think. Others have soured on conversation, having sat through too many meetings that degenerated into people shouting, or stomping out angrily, or taking control of the agenda.

4   But true conversation is very different from those sorts of experiences. It is a timeless and reliable way for humans to think together. Before there were class-rooms, meetings, or group facilitators, there were people sitting around talking. When we think about beginning a conversation, we can take courage from the fact

that this is a process we all know how to do. We are reawakening an ancient practice, a way of being together that all humans intimately understand.

5   We also can take courage in the fact that many people are longing to converse again. We are hungry for a chance to talk. People want to tell their stories, and are willing to listen to yours. I find that it takes just one person to start a conversation, because everyone else is eager to talk once it has begun. "Some friends and I started talking. . . ." Change doesn't happen from a leader announcing the plan. Change begins from deep inside a system, when a few people notice something they will no longer tolerate, or when they respond to someone's dream of what's possible.

6   It's easy to observe this in recent history. The Solidarity trade union movement in Poland began with conversation—less than a dozen workers in a Gdansk shipyard in 1980 speaking to each other about despair, their need for change, their need for freedom. Within months, Solidarity grew to 9.5 million workers. There was no e-mail then, just people talking to each other about their own needs, and finding that millions of fellow citizens shared their feelings. In a short time, they shut down the country, and changed the course of history.

7   To make important changes in our communities, our society, our lives, we just have to find a few others who care about the same thing we do. Together we can figure out the first step, then the second, then the next. Gradually, we grow powerful. But we don't have to start with power, only with passion.

8   Even among friends, starting a conversation can take courage. But conversation also *gives* us courage. Thinking together, deciding what actions to take, more of us become bold. As we learn from each other's experiences and interpretations, we see issues in richer detail. This clarity can help us see both when to act and when not to. In some cases, the right timing means doing nothing right now. Talking can be enough for the time being.

9   If conversation is the natural way that humans think together, what gets lost when we stop talking? Paulo Freire, the influential Brazilian educator who used education to support poor people in transforming their lives, said that we "cannot be truly human apart from communication. . . . To impede communication is to reduce people to the status of things."

10   When we don't talk to one another in a meaningful way, Freire believes, we never act to change things. We become passive and allow others to tell us what to do. Freire had a deep faith in every person's ability to be a clear thinker and a courageous actor. Not all of us share this faith, but it is necessary if we are to invite colleagues into conversation. Sometimes it is hard to believe that others have as much to offer as we do in the way of concern and skill. But I have found that when the issue is important to others, they will not disappoint us. If you start a conversation, others will surprise you.

11   Near my home in Utah, I watched a small group of mothers cautiously begin meeting about a problem in the community: They wanted their children to be able to walk to school safely. They were shocked when the city council granted their request for a pedestrian traffic light. Encouraged by this victory, they started other projects, each more ambitious than the last. After a few years, they participated in securing a federal grant for neighborhood development worth tens of millions of dollars. Today, one of those mothers has become an expert on city housing, won a

seat on the city council, and completed a term as council chair. When she tells her story, it begins like so many others: "Some friends and I started talking. . . ."

12   For conversation to become a powerful tool in society, we must take it seriously and examine our own role in making it successful. Here are some basic principles I've learned over years of hosting formal conversations around the country.

13   We acknowledge one another as equals. One thing that makes us equal is that we need each other. Whatever any one of us knows alone, it is not enough to change things. Someone else is bound to see things that we need to know.

14   We try to stay curious about each other. I maintain my curiosity by reminding myself that everyone has something to teach me. When others are saying things I disagree with, or have never thought about, or that I consider foolish or wrong, I remind myself that I really can learn from them—if I stay open and do not shut them out.

15   We recognize that we need each other's help to become better listeners. The greatest barrier to good conversation is that as a culture we're losing the capacity to listen. We're too busy. We're too certain of our own views. We just keep rushing past each other. At the beginning of any conversation I host, I make a point of asking everyone to help each other listen. This is hard work for almost everyone, but if we talk about listening at the start of a conversation, it makes things easier. If someone hasn't been listening to us, or misinterprets what we say, we're less likely to blame that person. We can be a little gentler with the difficulties we experience in a group if we make a commitment at the start to help each other listen.

16   We slow down so we have time to think and reflect. Most of us work in places where we rarely have time to sit together and think. We dash in and out of meetings where we make hurried, not thoughtful, decisions. Working to create conditions for a true spirit of conversation helps rediscover the joy of thinking together.

17   We remember that conversation is the natural way humans think together. Conversation is not a new invention for the 21st century; we're restoring a tradition from earlier human experience. It does, however, take time to let go of our modern ways of being in meetings, to get past the habits that keep us apart—speaking too fast, interrupting others, monopolizing the time, giving speeches or making pronouncements. Many of us have been rewarded for these behaviors, becoming more powerful by using them. But the blunt truth is that they don't lead to wise thinking or healthy relationships.

18   We expect it to be messy at times. Life doesn't move in straight lines; and neither does a good conversation. When a conversation begins, people always say things that don't connect. What's important at the start is that everyone's voice gets heard, that everyone feels invited into the conversation. If you're hosting the conversation, you may feel responsible for pointing out connections between these diverse contributions, but it's important to let go of that impulse and just sit with the messiness. The messy stage doesn't last forever. If we suppress the messiness at the beginning, it will find us later on and be more disruptive. The first stage is to listen well to whatever is being said, forgetting about neat thoughts and categories, knowing that all contributions add crucial elements to the whole. Eventually, we will be surprised by how much we share.

19   The practice of true talking takes courage, faith, and time. We don't always get it right the first time, and we don't have to. We need to settle into conversation: we

don't just do it automatically. As we risk talking to each other about things we care about, as we become curious about each other, as we slow things down, gradually we remember this timeless way of being together. Our rushed and thoughtless behaviors fade away, and we sit quietly in the gift of being together, just as humans have always done.

20   Another surprising but important element of conversation is a willingness to be disturbed, to allow our beliefs and ideas to be challenged by what others think. No one person or perspective can solve our problems. We have to be willing to let go of our certainty and be confused for a time.

21   Most of us weren't trained to admit what we don't know. We haven't been rewarded for being confused, or for asking questions rather than giving quick answers. We were taught to sound certain and confident. But the only way to understand the world in its complexity is to spend more time in the state of *not* knowing. It is very difficult to give up our certainties—the positions, beliefs, and explanations that lie at the heart of our personal identities. And I am not saying that we have to give up what we believe. We only need to be curious about what others believe, and to acknowledge that their way of interpreting the world might be essential to us.

22   I think it's important to begin a conversation by listening as best you can for what's different, for what surprises you. We have many opportunities every day to be the one who listens, curious rather than certain. If you try this with several people, you might find yourself laughing in delight as you realize how many unique ways there are to be human. But the greatest benefit of all is that listening moves us closer. When we listen with as little judgment as possible, we develop better relationships with each other.

23   Sometimes we hesitate to listen for what's different because we don't want to change. We're comfortable with our lives, and if we listened to anyone who raised questions, we might feel compelled to engage in new activities and ways of thinking. But most of us do see things in our lives or in the world that we would like to be different. If that's true, it means we listen more, not less. And we have to be willing to move into the very uncomfortable place of uncertainty.

24   We may simply fear the confusion that comes with new ideas in unsettled forms. But we can't be creative if we refuse to be confused. Change always starts with confusion; cherished interpretations must dissolve to make way for what's new. Great ideas and inventions miraculously appear in the space of not knowing. If we can move through the fear and enter the abyss we are rewarded greatly. We rediscover we're creative.

25   As the world grows more puzzling and difficult, most of us don't want to keep struggling through it alone. I can't know what to do from my own narrow perspective. I need a better understanding of what's going on. I want to sit down with you and talk about all the frightening and hopeful things I observe, and listen to what frightens you and gives you hope. I need new ideas and solutions for the problems I care about. And I know I need to talk to you to discover them. I need to learn to value your perspective, and I want you to value mine. I expect to be disturbed by what I hear from you. I know we don't have to agree with each other in order to think well together. There is no need for us to be joined at the head. We are joined by our human hearts.

THINKING CRITICALLY

1. How does Wheatley's introductory story about the Canadian woman set the tone and theme for the rest of her essay? Explain.

2. Did this essay change the way you think about the power of conversation? About how you listen and how you converse? Explain.

3. Why do we "stay silent and apart from one another" in today's society? What reasons does Wheatley give? Can you think of additional reasons for people's reluctance to engage in conversation?

4. What, according to the author, is "true conversation"? Identify the elements of true conversation. How do your own everyday conversations compare to her definition? Explain.

5. Compare the points Wheatley makes about speaking and listening to the points Deborah Tannen makes about "lecturing and listening" in her essay in the preceding section of this chapter. On what points do they agree? Do you think Tannen would disagree with any of Wheatley's suggestions? Why or why not?

6. What happens when people stop talking? Explain.

WRITING ASSIGNMENTS

1. Wheatley provides several examples of conversations that changed society. Can you think of other examples that would support her thesis? Identify at least two other examples and discuss how conversation and discussion led to change.

2. In making suggestions for productive conversation, Wheatley states that we also enter conversation with a "willingness to be disturbed," and to have our beliefs challenged. Write about a conversation from your personal experience in which your beliefs were challenged. Did you try to see the other viewpoint? Did you focus on defending your beliefs? After reading this essay, would you try to conduct the conversation differently? Explain.

3. Among the aristocracy of the eighteenth century, salons became the rage. Salons were rooms in which people of social or intellectual distinction would gather to discuss topics and exchange ideas. (Salons later gave way to the parlors of the nineteenth century. The root word of *parlor* is *parler*, which is old French for "talk.") Many Internet salons have emerged online, reviving this tradition. Visit an Internet salon and read some of the exchanges http://café.utne.com or http://theworldcafe.org. Write an essay comparing some of the points Wheatley makes in this essay regarding the power of conversation and the dialogues you read online. In what ways are people using Internet cafés to promote social change? Explain.

The Like Virus
David Grambs

For at least 20 years, the conversational filler "like" has permeated American dialogue to become part of the mainstream lexicon. "Like" is usually accompanied by "uptalk," in which statements sound like questions through a rising inflection of pitch at the end of the sentence or comment. From the language of teens and twenty-somethings, "like" has infected our conversational patterns, overrun our malls, and even invaded the workplace. In the next piece, David Grambs offers some insights on the phenomenon of "like," now that it appears to be here to stay, at least, like for a while?

David Grambs is a writer and editor and served as a staff member of the first edition of the *American Heritage Dictionary* (1969). He is the author of several books on words, including *The Random House Dictionary for Writers and Readers* (1990), *Death by Spelling* (1989), and *The Endangered English Dictionary* (1997). This essay appeared in the August 2001 issue of *The Vocabula Review*.

1   And like I'm, like, really grossed out, like . . .

2   The L-word. A kind of weightless backpack word that's more and more giving us humpbacked spoken English, the lite like has been airily clogging American sentences for years now. The war against the usage—well, it wasn't much of a war, alas—has been lost for some time, and we language-conscious losers are all trying to learn to live with the new, disjunctive babble.

3   Still, I believe the phenomenon is worth standing back from and taking a look at, as opposed to shrugging or winking at its growth. What does the new, gratuitous use of like really represent in our language, functionally and lexically? What do the purportedly authoritative dictionaries tell us? And, as I ask myself every time I hear it, what price is literate, listenable English paying for its increasing currency?

4   Like-speech, or like-orrhea, is a curious, self-contained medium. With its attendant (usually) limited vocabulary and all-thumbs expressiveness, it's almost a kind of verbal hand-gesturing or mimicry, if not a middle-class pidgin. The kids—and more and more adults—seem locked in a kind of cawing hyperpresent tense. Many have strangely unresonant, throat-blocked, or glottal voices and use "up-talk," the tendency to end all sentences in a rising, questioning inflection.

5   Yes, they're mostly young people (though again, increasingly, exponentially, by no means just young people). But at times I think I'm hearing the voices of Loony Tunes and Merry Melodies creatures, each lost in rote subjectivity. At my neighborhood café a few years ago, where some local prep school kids hung out, I particularly remember one tall, chain-smoking girl, always dressed in black, who couldn't go five or six words without coughing up a viral like. None of her peers batted an eye at this. She was speaking their language—a language in which the role of the indispensable L-word isn't so much to mean as it is to stylize. Or is it destylize?

6   Semantically, the viral like (in the new, ever-insertable usage) is far less a legitimate word than a form of coping punctuation, a lame, reflexive stalling tactic for the syntactically challenged. It's plainly what rigorous old teachers or editors might have called "an excrescence," and it's quickly becoming the verbal security blanket and a virtual speech impediment for an entire generation—and generations to come—of Americans, from Generation X to Generation Z and beyond. It adds as much to our fair English language as barnacles do to a wharf or calculi to a healthy kidney. Apologists for this speechway—rest assured, it has multitudes of shrugging, unblinking defenders—explain that the constantly repeated word serves as a wonderfully stylish form of ironic punctuation. And here I thought it was just a terribly bad speech habit.

7   As you well know, this linguistic fifth column has been settling in since the 1980s. Its mindless use is sadly symptomatic of our slack-tongued American zeitgeist, of what might be called our flailing, contemporary more-or-lessness or

something-like-thatness. We live, after all, in the *Age of Or Whatever*. It's not cool to be too clear, articulate, or specific about things.

8   Where did it come from? A California beach cave? Those old Valley Girls? (A Moon Unit Zappa song has been cited as seminal.) Saddam Hussein? MTV? A brain softener in our reservoirs, related to the cause of attention deficit disorder? The new like-speech has been related to the colorful old hipster use of the word, but I think it's a horse of another, colorless color. There is doubtless an interestingly complicated rationale for its origins linguistically and sociologically, but I'll settle for a bluntly simple answer. I think it comes from a peculiarly infectious strain of laziness, or mental or communicative slackness. Of course, it's hip and ironic laziness. It's, like, postmodern laziness.

9   Probably nothing has spread the L-word so quickly as American television has. Turn on your set nowadays and see how far into a talk show or celebrity interview you can go without hearing that hiccup vocable. (Most standup comedians can no more do without it than they can without their lame, stock "Thanks—you've been great!" exit escape.) It's a whiny bug in the ear to any plain-speaking person, yet the word has acquired an almost emblematic force. It has become a watchword of glibly media-driven American pop culture. Keeping it ceaselessly in play seems to be a form of bonding between those who don't want to appear to be too threateningly to the point, or is it too old?

10   One of its defenders in the *New York Times* a few years ago said the new use of like is really just a rhetorical device. Sometimes it is used as a phonic punctuation mark to signal "important information ahead." (When used two, three times in one sentence? The important information is usually, oh, a subsequent noun or an elusive adjective. It's exhausting to the rest of us to have to be so constantly alert to momentous divulgence, or completion of a sentence.) It also replaces, the writer noted, the dramatic, silent pause, which, he quickly added, is now "passé." (To which remark I can only ask for a moment of silence.) Or an interlaced like is really to provide a kind of postmodern "tempering" of any possible harshness of meaning. (It's very important today to placate repeatedly in one's conversation.) And of course it's also a pioneering "verb form," as in And I was like, "Whatever, you liar." More recently, a reputable linguistics professor said we shouldn't get all huffy about the "ironizing" usage: it now serves as a useful device to "distance" oneself from one's own words. I must confess that distancing myself more and more from what I say has never been one of my goals in life.

11   And what, pray tell, would somebody such as Jane Austen or Ernest Hemingway—or H. L. Mencken—have had to say about this delightfully ironic linguistic phenomenon? Or imagine, if you will, for a little grotesque perspective, a classic play such as Oscar Wilde's *The Importance of Being Earnest* performed in like-speak. Maybe ten years from now, an avant-garde director—who knows?

12   As cultural archcritic John Simon says in his introduction to the sobering book *Dumbing Down*:

> To a muddled mind, like may constitute a grace note, a bit of appoggiatura with which to decorate or even authenticate one's discourse. To the simple soul, those likes are so many hard, gemlike rhinestones. But, as with most nonsensical

things, opposite interpretations may apply just as well. Thus like may be a dis-avowal of responsibility: if you say "I was like minding my own business," the like may cover you if someone discovers that you weren't minding it. . . . Eventually, though, the like becomes a mere unthinking habit, a verbal rut.

13   When a usage inexorably takes root, so do its apologists, including those who work on dictionaries. Language, and especially English, constantly changes, and so it should. (I have worked on the staffs of two U.S. dictionaries.) Yet it won't do to say like-orrhea is just another passing, trendy neologism or speech habit. It won't do because it's not a mere slang or buzz word and because it's not passing. Above all, it won't do because of what all those likes replace or avoid, what, infectingly, they betoken: an increasingly lazy recourse to choppy, bland, dysfunctional English.

14   If your own speech is showing more and more lite likes, you might ask yourself why your generation is the first in more than 200 years of U.S. history to have a desperate, ongoing need for a single flavorless four-letter communicational rest stop.

15   Then there are the two million-dollar questions:

- What in fact does the lite like actually mean?
- What part of speech is it? Take the sentence (please) And she's like, "Like, it wasn't like anything I've, like, ever seen." Do the various (four) likes here all have the same part of speech?

Which is another way of inquiring, what do our contemporary lexicographers have to say about it?

16   The equivocal—downright waffling— way our current American dictionaries (hands-off descriptive, never prescriptive) handle the ever-morphing interloper is less than instructive, and somewhat depressing. Admittedly, dealing with it in definitional terms is not an enviable task. Unfortunately, the dictionaries' respective definitions of the usage are not even accurately descriptive.

17   The leading American lexicon says that the latter-day like has two parts of speech, adverb and conjunction. You will find this in the tenth edition of *Merriam Webster's Collegiate Dictionary* (1993):

> like adv. . . . 3. used interjectionally in informal speech often to emphasize a word or phrase (as in "He was, like, gorgeous") or for an apologetic, vague, or unassertive effect (as in "I need to, like, borrow some money") 4. NEARLY: APPROXIMATELY (the actual interest is more like 18 percent)—used interjectionally in informal speech with expressions of measurement (it was, like, five feet long) (goes there every day, like).

A curious definition. It doesn't so much provide a meaning for like as it does hold it at arm's length and note that it is used "interjectionally." It tells us that it is used to emphasize a word or—or?—for an apologetic, vague, or unassertive effect. A questionable, contradictory pairing of meanings to be covered under one definition. And for the dictionary to say that the word is used for an apologetic, vague, or unassertive effect suggests that it is used artfully by articulate people as some kind of intentional rhetorical device. No, not quite the truth of the matter.

18   Are these meanings, denotations? The word is "used," and it is used for an "effect." How many other adverbs used in midsentence have to be set off in print by commas (though they aren't in all cases), almost as if to say that the interruptive word has no clear purpose (or meaning) in the sentence? It's interjectional indeed.

19   Merriam Webster also parcels out an "interjectional" sense of the word under its entry for like as a conjunction. It says the viral like is used to "introduce" a quotation, paraphrase, or thought. ("And I'm like, go away!") True enough in practice, though this is an interesting, not to say inventive, notion. And why a word deemed to "introduce" an expression would be considered a conjunction, or connective, I have no idea. What the lite like primarily introduces is an implicit admission that the speaker doesn't want to bother completing an unbroken grammatical clause, or maybe can't—or just can't stop using the word. Like doesn't introduce. It supplants or forestalls, with graceless urgency.

20   The unabridged Random House dictionary (1987) also gives the more and more acceptable adverbial sense of "nearly, closely, approximately," as well as another sense:

> like interj. . . . . 28. Informal. used esp. in speech, esp. nonvolitionally or habitually, to preface a sentence, to fill a pause, to express uncertainty, or to intensify or neutralize a following adjective: Like, why didn't you write to me? The music was, like, really great, you know?

21   Here we read that the all-purpose, no-purpose like is not an adverb. It's not a conjunction. It's an interjection. Now, does like express uncertainty—or expose it? Or attempt to dress it up? Or interlard pure lard? Random House doesn't claim an "emphasizer" function for the word. Instead, it says it is used to intensify or neutralize a following adjective. Intensify or neutralize? Hmm. Another curiously contradictory pairing. Worth noting is the prefatory "used esp. in speech, esp. nonvolitionally or habitually, to preface a sentence." The most interesting, even amusingly give-away, word here is "nonvolitionally."

22   From these lexical tightrope acts, it's hard not to get the sense that assigning parts of speech to the viral like leaves one, if not between a rock and a hard place, between a slippery slope and a will-o'-the-wisp.

23   More recently, the handsome *American Heritage Dictionary* (fourth edition) has shown more common sense in its handling of the viral like and backed off a bit. Instead of trying torturously to allot the shifty, slack usage a part or parts of speech, it covers the phenomenon as an idiom:

> be like Informal To say or utter. Used chiefly in oral narration: "And he's like, 'Leave me alone!'"

24   A final "Our Living Language" note commendably points out that what follows an "I'm like . . . " expression may be an actual quotation, or a brief imitation of another person's behavior, or a summarization of a past attitude or reaction—or it might instead signify either the speaker's attitude at the time or what he "might have said." Which? Exactly—make that inexactly—the point. But the AHD has nothing to say about all the other, more gratuitous placements of like pretty much anywhere within sentences in this American day and age. But if it walks like a duck and talks like a duck . . . ?

25   If we're not going to recognize it for the duck that it is, I'd venture to say that one can, deductively, come up with quite a few more, or competing, meanings (as opposed to "uses") for the viral like, according to the context of its various encroachments in sentences.

26   It can mean "possibly" (He couldn't, like, be there). It can mean "let's say" or "say" or "for example" (If we were to, like, meet at the movie theater, there'd be no problem). It can mean "you know" (Yeah, like, the Holocaust, it was, like, a bad thing). It can mean "responding by" or "reacting by" (And then they're, like, running and hiding in the woods). It can mean "the situation is" or "at the beginning" (Like, all the people have been wiped out by this Death Planet). It can mean "dare I ask it" (Would you, like, marry me?). It can mean "or something like that" (It's a social organization, like). It can mean "get this" or "I'm not kidding" (It was, like, ten below outside). And so, like, on. Similarly, I suspect, one could make a procrustean case for the intrusive like's being just about any part of speech.

27   If these jokers-wild meanings can be said to have any legitimacy, what does that say about the dictionaries' handling of the problem? Maybe that the new L-word additive is not so much a word as it is an uttered wild card, and that we are in for a long, babbling game ahead.

28   It will certainly be interesting to see how dictionary editions ten or twenty years from now categorize and define the compulsive, drop-in like. Possibly, I fear, by noting that it is the single word—shibboleth—that most instantly identifies or characterizes an American anywhere in the world.

29   For now, what is more interesting, perhaps, is what today's dictionaries, with their carefully nonjudgmental hedging or tenuous best shot, don't tell you: that this "informal" usage is fundamentally an egregious, wildly contagious oral tic, and one quite infra dig in standard written English. Like-orrhea in current television or movie dialogue is usually somewhat satirical (but probably less and less so, sadly). A character whose speech is laced with lallygagging likes is invariably being pegged as immature, uneducated, thoroughly self-involved, or ditsy, if not a voluble airhead.

30   Except for its sense of "about" or "approximately," one could say that the new like probably, most often, has one essential meaning, and, ironically, it's a complete thought: "Uh, bear with me." Or is it: "Whoa and whew, it's kind of exhausting to get the right words together without taking a little break between them"? Or possibly: "Please, take no offense from anything that precedes or follows until my next like"?

31   By now, like-speech is indisputably becoming for millions a veritable pseudo-speech style. But what the usage really is, of course, is a hesitation form, along the lines of uh, well, I mean, or um. Hesitation forms are sentence litter, indeterminate words or word elements, basically meaningless and interruptive filler locutions. (Utterance that is filled with such paltering signposts is called embolalia.) Like-orrhea, no matter how numbly glib its ring, usually betokens the incessant need to pause and recalibrate or dumb down even the simplest thoughts. It's analogous to the midsentence constructional shift called anacoluthon, and a little like those iterated watchwords of expressional (and so expressive) insecurity: you know? right? okay? you understand what I'm saying? Actually, it's far worse because it's a microchip version: it can be tucked inside sentences wherever and whenever rather than being a mere trailing irritant. (It is indeed an "in word.")

32   The "meaningless like" is for John Simon a dreadful piece of detritus:

> The I means, you knows, kind ofs, and sort ofs are bad enough; but they at
> least form a hesitation waltz to give the speaker time to gather his next
> thought, or focus more tightly on the current one. That bit of verbal litter, like,
> however, is something else—"something else" in the slang sense as well:
> something unconscionable, weird. It must not be mistaken for a more elegant
> synonym of er, with which speakers formerly tried to carpet the interstices of
> thought. It is too frequent to be that; nobody erred that consistently—not even
> a lighter-than-airhead on Hollywood Boulevard.

33   To a nonlike-orrheac, hearing the speech of a like-ridden conversationalist is
like enduring reflexive, repetitive name-dropping by somebody who hasn't a clue
that the name being dropped, and dropped, and dropped, is known to nobody else.
But well beyond its general emptiness and annoyingness, the like virus is deplorable because of what goes along with it—what it avoids, covers up for, or ne-
cessitates. Where you find like-orrhea, you'll usually find concomitant sins:

- A knee-jerk or anxious (take your pick) "filling in" of any moment of hesitation in speech. Momentary silence—reflectiveness, that little pause for the
right word, a subtle change in speech rhythm—has never been more golden.
- An inability to articulate fundamental indirect discourse, to report simple and co-
herently what somebody else said. Like injections generally—very generally—
leave blitheringly unclear whether what follows are actual, stated words, a paraphrase of those words, or just the like user's rounded-off, subjective impression
of the other person's feelings. ("And she's like, I'm not going there!")
- An eager dependency on the present tense. There is in writing the so-called historical present, of course. Because the new penchant for framing the most banal discourse in the present tense comes out of insecurity in using—or impatience with formulating?—ordinary past tenses, one could call this the
hysterical present.
- A reluctance or inability to use basic elements of our rich English syntax—that
is, to articulate compound or complex sentences, sentences with dependent
clauses, sentences with verbs in more than one tense.
- A begging-off from the challenge to be at all interesting or persuasive to
intelligent others—to think on one's feet without that four-letter stall-mate.
The drone of verbiage clotted with little like blockages guarantees that, whatever the content, one will be irritating or stupefying. Or a less than thrilling job
applicant.
- A limited vocabulary. Like-orrhea signals flailing approximation and avoidance of any effort at being articulate, much less eloquent. Interesting or apt
words don't usually go along with it. Those happily unconscious of speaking a
kind of communicable but uncommunicative mush can't spend much time
around dictionaries or Updike novels.
- More words. One thing we definitely don't need in our talk-engulfed multime-
dia age is extra verbiage, or pandemic overuse of one word that just doesn't
pay its own way.

34   The great English writer George Orwell, still admired for his passion about clarity and truth in language, did not favor the particularly British fondness for using the "not un-" locution, with a kind of snobbish coyness, as in "It's not un-interesting," instead of, plainly, "It's interesting." Orwell proposed a remedy for the mannerism. "One can cure oneself of the not un- formation by memorizing this sentence: 'A not unblack dog was chasing a not unsmall rabbit across a not ungreen field.'"

35   If you've already caught the like virus, I suggest one of three ways to cure yourself:

- One way is to memorize (as a kind of linguistic memento mori) this sentence: "Like, like as not, to tell it like it is, like Jane has no, like, liking for the like, likes of, like Dick, like it or not."
- Or every time you catch yourself using the L-word crutch, stop—and punish yourself by repeating word for word what you just said but this time substituting for each like the word kumquat.
- Or—simplest of all—just say no. Pure abstinence. Can you do it?

36   Me, I'm willing to live with the viral like in the sense of about or approximately. Otherwise, it should be recognized for what it is. It's not an adverb. It's not a conjunction. It's not an interjection. It's not an artful piece of introductory rhetoric. It's not a valid replacement for the verb to say. It's not a compellingly hip and ironic postmodern conversational style. It's not a trendy word that will pass. It's contemporary America's favorite wad of verbal bubble gum, and it's getting stickier every day.

THINKING CRITICALLY

1. How does Grambs describe the phenomenon of "like"? Are you familiar with the usage of this word in modern speech? If so, do you or any of your friends suffer from "like-orrhea"? From your observations, would you agree with Grambs that the use of "like" is on the rise?

2. According to Grambs, what are the origins of "like"? What groups have used "like" in the past, and who uses it now? How has it expanded over the last decade?

3. Grambs notes that some defenders of "like" claim it can help speakers "distance" themselves from their words. Why would we want to "distance" ourselves from our speech? Do you agree, as Grambs asserts in paragraph 7, that "it's not cool to be too clear, articulate, or specific about things"? Explain.

4. What is Grambs's opinion of "like" and its entrenchment in American discourse? What explanations does he give for his feelings regarding the use of the word?

5. Given that the phenomenon of "like" is an oral one, how well does Grambs explore its role linguistically and socially? Are you able to "hear" what he is talking about? Do his examples serve as effective "translations"? Explain.

6. Grambs claims that "a character whose speech is laced with lallygagging likes is invariably being pegged as immature, uneducated, thoroughly self-involved, or ditsy." Do you agree with this observation? If "like" has become as mainstream as Grambs fears, why does this stereotype of its usage remain?

7. Grambs offers several suggestions at the end of his essay for eliminating "like-orreah." If you use like frequently in your own speech, would you attempt to eliminate it? Why or why not? As an exercise, test one of his suggestions—such as replacing the word "like" with "kumquat" and see how pervasive the word is in your conversation.

WRITING ASSIGNMENTS

1. Grambs identifies teenagers and young "twenty-somethings" as the most frequent users of "like," but he finds that other, older groups are using it as well. Conduct interviews with other students to determine their familiarity with and usage of "like," in their conversational style. Write a paper exploring your findings. Try to determine if different demographic groups have different responses. Also, what different theories do your respondents have as to the origins and popularity of the word "like" in conversation? Will it indeed become a mainstream part of speech?

2. Grambs wonders what *The Importance of Being Earnest* by Oscar Wilde would be like performed in like-speak. Locate a copy of the play and rewrite a portion of it, making strategic use of like-speak. What happens to the dialogue? Does it modernize it? Make it sound uneducated or ditsy? Explain.

3. Write a paper in which you question the idea of standard or proper American English. What does the definition mean? What groups or dialects fall outside the standard, and what are the consequences of this? Should there be a language standard in the United States? Explain.

The Other Side of E-Mail

Robert Kuttner

Few people would disagree that e-mail is revolutionizing how we communicate. Individuals who never wrote an ordinary letter before now spend hours online composing and sending electronic messages. We can communicate to virtually every corner of the world with the push of a button. But what is the price of this easy and efficient new mode of communication? Robert Kuttner contends that instead of freeing our time, e-mail is, in fact, a time "thief." He declares that although e-mail has many uses, there is a darker side to it that we must consider when employing this medium.

Founder and co-editor of *The American Prospect*, a bimonthly journal of policy and politics, Robert Kuttner is also one of five contributing columnists to *Business Week*'s "Economic Viewpoint." His work has appeared in many publications including the *New York Times*, the *Atlantic Monthly*, and *Harvard Business Review*. Kuttner is the author of five books, including *The End of Laissez Faire* (1991) and *Everything for Sale: The Virtues and Limits of Markets* (1997). The following editorial appeared in the April 19, 1998, issue of the *Boston Globe*.

1 A few years ago, when my daughter was a college freshman, I wrote a column singing the praises of e-mail. We were, suddenly, corresponding. It was, I decided, the revenge of print on electronics—a whole generation raised on the tube and the phone, rediscovering the lost art of writing letters. How utterly charming.

2   Now I'm not so sure. Like all new media, e-mail has a dark side. To be sure, it saves a great deal of time and paperwork and has facilitated new, unimagined forms of affinity. However, e-mail is also a thief. It steals our time and our privacy. It deceives us into thinking we have endless additional hours in the day to engage in far-flung communications that we may or may not need or want.

3   All of a sudden, on top of everything else we have to do, e-mail is one more garden demanding tending.

4   E-mail brings a kind of pseudo-urgency that demands an instant response. It creates false intimacies. Recently, I got an e-mail message from a perfect stranger, a student who had read one of my articles and wanted help on a term paper. I was touched, but alas, there aren't enough hours in the day. Yet something about the message made me feel I needed to apologize for not being able to do her homework. With e-mail, it's too easy to hit the reply key, with results you may regret. One acquaintance, thinking she was just responding to a note from a close friend, accidentally sent a highly personal message to the friend's entire mailing list.

5   I recently had a painful quarrel triggered by e-mail messages. A dear friend and I were both having a very busy week and imposing on each other's time. Without quite intending to, we ended up firing salvos of e-mail back and forth of escalating testiness until we had quite insulted each other. We apologized, in person.

6   This mishap could not have occurred either by phone or by ordinary mail. When talking to someone, you pay attention to tonality. And when you write a letter, you read it over a few times before sending it. But e-mail is tone-deaf and all too instant. It is ephemeral, yet irrevocable. Once you've banged out your message and sent it into the ether, you can't take it back.

7   E-mail is a great convenience—for the sender. The recipient is presumed to have infinite time and interest. It is the equivalent of endless Christmas letters from boring distant relatives all year long.

8   Bosses get in the habit of sending down incessant e-mail messages from on high, as if anyone cared. (Now hear this . . .) A large corporation with which I am vaguely affiliated sends me more messages than I could possibly want to have, let alone answer.

9   E-mail is also not secure. The magazine that I edit regularly gets highly personal missives, sent by mistake to the wrong e-mail address thanks to a typo. With the phone, you know as soon as you have a wrong number. And mis-addressed letters either get returned or end up in the dead letter office.

10   At one company, two people carrying on an affair were incautiously sending each other intimate e-mail, which a supervisor discovered. To make matters worse, they were making snide comments about the supervisor. Security escorted them from the premises.

11   E-mail is also easily forwarded and deliberately or mistakenly put into mass circulation. Don't e-mail anything private unless you are prepared to see it crop up all over the World Wide Web. E-mail, like talk radio, reduces inhibitions; it is democratic to the point of moronic. And I've not even gotten to mass junk e-mail, known in the trade as spam.

12   I know, I know, the Internet is a marvel. And it is. And, sure, e-mail is great for scheduling meetings, for sending and receiving research materials, for allowing people in remote locations to collaborate on projects. But novelty and low cost tend to breed excess.

13   Like every new tool, from the wheel to nuclear energy, electronic communication will take a while to find its proper etiquette and niche. In the meantime, it is an awkward adolescent that has borrowed the family car, hormones raging and radio blaring, with little regard for the rules of the road.

14   Of course, some fans of e-mail may find these words controversial or offensive. So if you have any comments on this column, my e-mail address is . . . no, actually, send me a letter.

THINKING CRITICALLY

1. According to Kuttner, how does e-mail transcend the generation gap? Can you think of other ways that e-mail bridges gaps between groups of people?

2. How is e-mail a "thief"? Do you agree with Kuttner's assessment? Describe the ways e-mail can make life more complicated, rather than simplify it. Would you have more, or less time, without e-mail access? Explain.

3. How does e-mail "reduce inhibitions" (paragraph 11)? What are the social perils of e-mail? Describe the complications of e-mail that are not found in other communication mediums such as the telephone or ordinary face-to-face conversation.

4. What function does e-mail have in today's society? How have our lives changed because of it? What influence has it had on our communication style and habits?

5. What could be the long-term effects of e-mail on social discourse? On how we converse with each other? Explain.

6. Kuttner compares the Internet to a garden that requires constant tending. How effective is this metaphor? Explain.

WRITING ASSIGNMENTS

1. A popular television commercial for an Internet employment agency features a man writing an insulting letter to his boss only to have a toy fall off his monitor and hit the "enter" key, sending his message. Have you ever had a mishap with e-mail such as the ones described by Kuttner in this article? Describe your experience. How did it influence your use of e-mail in the future?

2. How does e-mail differ from ordinary conversation? Drawing from your personal experience, write a paper in which you predict the influence of e-mail on social discourse and how we converse with each other offline.

3. Visit the chatrooms of several different groups and evaluate the communication style of the participants. Can you distinguish any trends or common behaviors in their language? For example, do teen chatrooms employ more symbolic language than ones frequented by older populations? Is this language more inclusive or exclusive to a new visitor? Write a paper evaluating the differences in Internet communication as demonstrated by various populations in specific chatrooms.

'r u online?': The Evolving Lexicon of Wired Teens

Kris Axtman

As Instant Messaging (IM) and "texting" become a preferred method of communication, the English language is being used in new and creative ways. What does this phenomenon mean for how the younger generation communicates? This article appeared in the December 12, 2002 edition of *The Christian Science Monitor*.

1 The conversation begins on the computer, nothing too atypical for a pair of teenage boys bored on a Friday night:

Garret: hey
Josh: sup
Garret: j/cu
Josh: same
Garret: wut r u doing 2nite
Josh: n2m
Garret: cool

2 Need a translation? Not if you're a 13-year-old who's been Internet-connected since birth. For the rest of us, welcome to the world of Net Lingo—the keyboard generation's gift to language and culture. "sup" is not a call to supper, but a query: "What's up?" And Josh's "n2m" reply? "Not too much."

3 As in every age, teenagers today are adapting the English language to meet their needs for self-expression. But this time, it's happening online—and at lightning speed. To some, it's a creative twist on dialogue, and a new, harmless version of teen slang. But to anxious grammarians and harried teachers, it's the linguistic ruin of Generation IM (instant messenger).

4 Whatever it is, the result fills Internet chat rooms, e-mail, and the increasingly popular instant messenger, on which correspondents fire off confessions, one-liners, and blather in real-time group chats or, more often, fleet-fingered tête-a-têtes.

5 "This is really an extension of what teenagers have always done: recreate the language in their own image. But this new lingo combines writing and speaking to a degree that we've never seen before," says Neil Randall, an English professor at the University of Waterloo and author of "Lingo Online: A Report on the Language of the Keyboard Generation."

6 The result, he says, is the use of writing to simulate speech—a skill not formally taught. In the process, typed communication has entered a new era of speed.

In a third-floor bedroom in Houston, Garret Thomas has three online conversations going at once. That's nothing, he says. Sometimes he chats with as many as 20 people at a time—chosen from his 200-plus "buddy list" that shows which of his friends are online and available. "I'm a really fast typer," says the redhead.

7 Though creating unique speech patterns is nothing new for the younger set, this generation is doing it in a novel way.

8 New acronyms, abbreviations, and emoticons—keyboard characters lined up to resemble human gestures or expressions, such as smiling :)—are coined daily.

9 Indeed, almost 60 percent of online teenagers under age 17 use IM services, offered free by Internet providers such as Yahoo and America Online, according to Nielsen/NetRatings.

10 "All of my friends are on instant messenger," says Garret, not looking up from his cryptic chat with Josh. "It's just easier to talk to them this way."

11 Not like the fate of the universe depends on what they're saying. With one friend, he's talking about his rotten Spanish teacher who actually expects the class to participate. With another, he's debating the evening's options: the mall, a movie, chillin' at his house. With a third, he's deep in a discussion about how he never gives more than one-word answers. "who cares," Garret types.

12 "hey, that's two getting better," comes the reply.

13 In between all this, there's a whole bunch of "j/j" (just joking), "lol" (laughing out loud), and brb ("be right back"). In other words, typical teen chatter.

14 "Instant messaging has just replaced the phone . . . for their generation," says Mary Anne Thomas, a Houston mother on the other side of town, with two teen boys addicted to IM. She has noticed that her oldest son, who's normally quite shy around girls, feels more comfortable talking to them online—a positive, she thinks.

15 A negative, though, is that their grammar is becoming atrocious, and Net lingo is starting to show up on school assignments: "They talk with these abbreviated words and run-on sentences with no punctuation. I call it speed talking, and it's starting to carry over into their homework," she says. That's an issue that teachers around the country have been struggling with recently as instant messaging grows in popularity.

16 Another double-edged consequence comes in a culture of multitasking. Mrs. Thomas's oldest son spends about three hours on instant messenger each night. He'll talk to friends, download music, do homework, surf the Internet—all at the same time.

17 Because of the Internet, experts say, kids today are able to multitask like no other generation. But with that frenetic multitasking, others say, comes easy distraction—and the shrinking of already-short attention spans.

18 Garret says he gets onto IM when he's doing homework, and manages about eight different tasks at one time. Showing incredible focus—or frenzy—he flips from one screen to the next, rapidly firing off messages while surfing the Net and gabbing on the phone. (No, IM hasn't replaced the phone entirely.)

19 Now a high-school freshman, he says most of his friends were on IM by junior high, and he picked up the lingo as he went along. New terms get passed between friends, and different groups and regions of the country have their own IM lexicons, with particular acronyms, abbreviations, and emoticons that mirror their inside jokes and experience. Tonight, he tells a friend that he's "j/c." She asks, "what is j/c."

20 "just chillin'," he types, certain that she will use it in the future.

Experts say the intent of lingo—in any generation—is to signify "inness" with a particular group. And while teens have long pushed the boundaries of language, they are now doing it in written form.

21 "This is a new kind of slang, a written slang. We've never had anything like it before," says Robert Beard, professor emeritus of linguistics at Bucknell University in Lewisburg, Pa., and creator of yourDictionary.com.

22   Some parents worry that teens could get into trouble by talking to so many different—and sometimes unknown—buddies. Certainly, that's happened. But Dr. Randall says he found in his study that teens are quite aware of that issue and know how to protect themselves.

23   Even with his large buddy list, Garret gets it. He begins chatting with someone he hasn't talked to in awhile, and when that person attacks him and uses profanity, he quickly ends the conversation.

24   "I'm not talking to him anymore," he says, slightly shaken, and then uses the software to block all incoming messages from that screen name.

25   "I guess it's time to clean out my buddy list."

Some Common IM Lingo
AFK: Away From Keyboard
BBL: Be Back Later
BRB: Be Right Back
IMHO: In My Humble Opinion
JK: Just Kidding
LOL: Laughing Out Loud
LYLAS: Love You Like a Sister
NP: No Problem
OMG: Oh My God
OTP: On the Phone
ROFL: Rolling on Floor Laughing
TTFN: Ta-Ta for Now
TTYL: Talk to You Later
YW: You're Welcome

THINKING CRITICALLY

1. Do you use IM and text messaging slang and shorthand to communicate with your friends? If so, do you ever use IM acronyms in spoken speech, or in note-taking or class assignments? Explain.

2. Visit Netlingo.com or stands4.com. Review the different terms used in IM and text messaging. How many terms are you familiar with? Would you use these terms in any other situation besides electronic communication? Why or why not?

3. In your opinion, should educators be concerned that the younger generation's frequent usage of IM acronyms, slang, and emoticons will affect their language use and ability to communicate offline? Should teachers allow this new form of communication to be used offline, such as in school assignments? Explain.

MAKING CONNECTIONS

1. Write a paper in which you examine the effects of certain dialects or speech patterns on the perception of those who use and/or hear it. How are stereotypes created by speech patterns? Explain.

2. Write a response to one of the authors in this section in which you explain why you agree, disagree, or partially agree with their observations on conversation.

Support your response with examples from your own experience, outside research using resources from the supplemental Web site, and other arguments presented in this section.

3. Select two issues of the same popular magazine, one from 30 years ago, and one from the last six months. *Time, Newsweek, People, Ladies Home Journal, Mademoiselle, Vogue, Maxim*, etc. Describe differences you notice in the language of the advertising and articles between the past and present. Include observations about sexist language, references to children and teenagers, social interaction, etc.

4. What effect has "political correctness" had on our everyday conversation? What issues of trust do we presume with politically correct language? Explain.

5. What nonverbal cues do you project to others? In a few paragraphs, analyze yourself and the "vibes" you give to those around you through your body language, the way you walk, your facial expressions, dress style, and mental attitude.

■ This image perfectly encapsulates the language of mass media and advertising. What you see is NBC's giant Astrovisions screen telecasting NBC's news and other programming to the crowds. No doubt you recognize Times Square from the advertising billboards that act as place markers here and around the world.

Much of what we know about the world comes from what the media tell us through television, radio, newspapers, magazines, and movies. Similarly, how we perceive that world is influenced by the media's presentation of it. Underwriting most of that media is advertising. Nearly $200 billion is spent every year on television commercials and print ads—more than the gross national product of many countries in the world—accounting for a quarter of each television hour and the bulk of most newspapers and magazines. Tremendous power lies in the hands of those who control the media and write the ads. In this chapter, we will examine the tremendous power of television media and advertising—and explore how each uses and abuses the power of words.

As Seen on TV

At the beginning of the twentieth century, the written word was the prime mover of information and mass entertainment. Books, newspapers, literary journals, and tabloids were the way people got information, shared the latest fashions, and were entertained. Now, a century later, we are a culture dependent on the spoken word—to each other face-to-face, on telephones, radio, television, and film. But what does this shift mean for language? Some critics claim that language is becoming slovenly and unimaginative as media attempt to reach mass audiences. The creative use of language is being lost in an effort to reach the "lowest common denominator."

With today's rabid competition for audience and revenue, the evening news, some say, has become just another form of entertainment—high-power visuals and low-power English. In "TV News: All the World in Pictures," Neil Postman and Steve Powers eloquently argue that TV news, with its heavy reliance on dramatic and dynamic images, has been packaged to suit the requirements of show biz rather than journalism—the result being the corruption of our knowledge and views of world affairs. But it isn't just the news that has become more graphic. Many people also complain that television language aims to shock. The next two pieces take a closer look at television's increasing level of "bad language" and how people are responding to this censorship shift. First, John H. McWhorter discusses the disparity between the language we use in real life and the language the FCC bans as inappropriate on television and in the media in "Oh, R-o-ob, The Bad Words Won't Go Away." A series of letters responding to a BBC poll on the issue follow his essay. Deborah Tannen describes how television's love affair with conflict and confrontation is filtering into everyday conversation, in "Taking TV's 'War of Words' Too Literally." The section ends with an essay by Tom Shachtman called "The Entertained Culture." He asserts television's quest to reach wide audiences means scriptwriters must tailor their language to "aim lower." The result, he fears, is that slimmer scripts and elementary-level language will have a negative impact on our linguistic future.

The Language of Advertising

Advertising is everywhere—television, newspapers, magazines, the Internet, the exterior of buses, and highway billboards; it's printed on T-shirts, hot dogs, postage stamps, and even license plates. It is the driving force of our consumer economy. It's everywhere people are, and its appeal goes right to the quick of our fantasies: happiness, material wealth, eternal youth, social acceptance, sexual fulfillment, and power. And it does so in carefully selected images and words. It is the most pervasive form of persuasion in America and, perhaps, the single manufacturer of meaning in our consumer society. Yet, most of us are so accustomed to advertising that we hear it without listening and see it without looking. But if we stopped to examine how it works, we might be amazed at just how powerful and complex a psychological force advertising is. In this section, we examine how a simple page in a magazine or a 15-second TV spot feeds our fantasies and fears with the sole intention of separating us from our money.

By its very nature the language of advertising is a very special language—one that combines words cleverly and methodically. On that point, the authors of the next two essays are in agreement. But beyond that, their views diverge widely. In the first piece, "With These Words, I Can Sell You Anything," language-watcher William Lutz argues that advertisers tyrannically twist simple English words so that they appear to promise just what the consumer desires. Taking a defensive posture in "The Language of Advertising," Charles A. O'Neill, a professional advertiser, admits that the language of ads can be very appealing. He makes a persuasive argument that no ad can force consumers to lay their money down. Marketing guru Herschell Gordon Lewis takes a closer look at some of the words and techniques described by Lutz and O'Neill in "Language Abuse." Then, Carrie McLaren explores how antismoking campaigns directed, perhaps ironically, by big tobacco companies, aim to be ineffective by deliberately missing their target audiences, teens, in "How Tobacco Company Anti-Smoking Ads Appeal to Teens." The section ends with a series of ads for discussion and review.

| AS SEEN ON TV

TV News: All the World in Pictures
Neil Postman and Steve Powers

Ideally, the news media should be concerned exclusively with facts, logic, and objective analysis. For the most part, major American newspapers and wire services strive to fulfill those ideals. But what about television news? How can a medium whose fast-paced and dynamic images are intended for viewing pleasure deliver unbiased news? According to Neil Postman and Steve Powers, it can't. In this essay, the authors argue that nightly news is a visual entertainment package that creates the illusion of keeping the public informed. They argue that broadcast news shows are, on the contrary, "re-creations" that reveal the world as a series of incoherent and meaningless fragments.

Neil Postman is a critic, writer, communication theorist, and chairman of the Department of Communication Arts at New York University. He is the author of 19 books, including *Amusing Ourselves to Death* (1985) and *Conscientious Objections* (1992). Steve Powers is an award-winning journalist with more than 30 years of experience in broadcast news, including serving as a correspondent for Fox Television News and the ABC Information Radio Network. Postman and Powers are co-authors of the book, *How to Watch TV News* (1992), from which this essay is excerpted.

1 When a television news show distorts the truth by altering or manufacturing facts (through re-creations), a television viewer is defenseless even if a re-creation is properly labeled. Viewers are still vulnerable to misinformation since they will not know (at least in the case of docudramas) what parts are fiction and what parts are not. But the problems of verisimilitude posed by re-creations pale to insignificance when compared to the problems viewers face when encountering a straight (no-monkey-business) show. All news shows, in a sense, are re-creations in that what we hear and see on them are attempts to represent actual events, and are not the events themselves. Perhaps, to avoid ambiguity, we might call all news shows "re-presentations" instead of "re-creations." These re-presentations come to us in two forms: language and pictures. The question then arises: what do viewers have to know about language and pictures in order to be properly armed to defend themselves against the seductions of eloquence (to use Bertrand Russell's apt phrase)? . . .

2 [Let us look at] the problem of pictures. It is often said that a picture is worth a thousand words. Maybe so. But it is probably equally true that one word is worth a thousand pictures, at least sometimes—for example, when it comes to understanding the world we live in. Indeed, the whole problem with news on television comes down to this: all the words uttered in an hour of news coverage could be printed on one page of a newspaper. And the world cannot be understood in one page. Of course, there is a compensation: television offers pictures, and the pictures move. Moving pictures are a kind of language in themselves, but the language of pictures differs radically from oral and written language, and the differences are crucial for understanding television news.

3 To begin with, pictures, especially single pictures, speak only in particularities. Their vocabulary is limited to concrete representation. Unlike words and sentences, a picture does not present to us an idea or concept about the world, except as we use language itself to convert the image to idea. By itself, a picture cannot deal with the unseen, the remote, the internal, the abstract. It does not speak of "man," only of *a* man; not of "tree," only of *a* tree. You cannot produce an image of "nature," any more than an image of "the sea." You can only show a particular fragment of the here-and-now—a cliff of a certain terrain, in a certain condition of light; a wave at a moment in time, from a particular point of view. And just as "nature" and "the sea" cannot be photographed, such larger abstractions as truth, honor, love, and falsehood cannot be talked about in the lexicon of individual pictures. For "showing of" and "talking about" are two very different kinds of processes: individual pictures give us the world as object; language, the world as idea. There is no such thing in nature as "man" or

"tree." The universe offers no such categories or simplifications; only flux and infinite variety. The picture documents and celebrates the particularities of the universe's infinite variety. Language makes them comprehensible.

4   Of course, moving pictures, video with sound, may bridge the gap by juxtaposing images, symbols, sound, and music. Such images can present emotions and rudimentary ideas. They can suggest the panorama of nature and the joys and miseries of humankind.

5   Picture—smoke pouring from the window, cut to people coughing, an ambulance racing to a hospital, a tombstone in a cemetery.

6   Picture—jet planes firing rockets, explosions, lines of foreign soldiers surrendering, the American flag waving in the wind.

7   Nonetheless, keep in mind that when terrorists want to prove to the world that their kidnap victims are still alive, they photograph them holding a copy of a recent newspaper. The dateline on the newspaper provides the proof that the photograph was taken on or after that date. Without the help of the written word, film and videotape cannot portray temporal dimensions with any precision. Consider a film clip showing an aircraft carrier at sea. One might be able to identify the ship as Soviet or American, but there would be no way of telling where in the world the carrier was, where it was headed, or when the pictures were taken. It is only through language—words spoken over the pictures or reproduced in them—that the image of the aircraft carrier takes on specific meaning.

8   Still, it is possible to enjoy the image of the carrier for its own sake. One might find the hugeness of the vessel interesting; it signifies military power on the move. There is a certain drama in watching the planes come in at high speeds and skid to a stop on the deck. Suppose the ship were burning: that would be even more interesting. This leads to an important point about the language of pictures. Moving pictures favor images that change. That is why violence and dynamic destruction find their way onto television so often. When something is destroyed violently it is altered in a highly visible way; hence the entrancing power of fire. Fire gives visual form to the ideas of consumption, disappearance, death—the thing that burned is actually taken away by fire. It is at this very basic level that fires make a good subject for television news. Something was here, now it's gone, and the change is recorded on film.

9   Earthquakes and typhoons have the same power. Before the viewer's eyes the world is taken apart. If a television viewer has relatives in Mexico City and an earthquake occurs there, then he or she may take a special interest in the images of destruction as a report from a specific place and time; that is, one may look at television pictures for information about an important event. But film of an earthquake can be interesting even if the viewer cares nothing about the event itself. Which is only to say, as we noted earlier, that there is another way of participating in the news—as a spectator who desires to be entertained. Actually to see buildings topple is exciting, no matter where the buildings are. The world turns to dust before our eyes.

10   Those who produce television news in America know that their medium favors images that move. That is why they are wary of "talking heads," people who simply appear in front of a camera and speak. When talking heads appear on television,

there is nothing to record or document, no change in process. In the cinema the situation is somewhat different. On a movie screen, closeups of a good actor speaking dramatically can sometimes be interesting to watch. When Clint Eastwood narrows his eyes and challenges his rival to shoot first, the spectator sees the cool rage of the Eastwood character take visual form, and the narrowing of the eyes is dramatic. But much of the effect of this small movement depends on the size of the movie screen and the darkness of the theater, which make Eastwood and his every action "larger than life."

11   The television screen is smaller than life. It occupies about 15 percent of the viewer's visual field (compared to about 70 percent for the movie screen). It is not set in a darkened theater closed off from the world but in the viewer's ordinary living space. This means that visual changes must be more extreme and more dramatic to be interesting on television. A narrowing of the eyes will not do. A car crash, an earthquake, a burning factory are much better.

12   With these principles in mind, let us examine more closely the structure of a typical newscast, and here we will include in the discussion not only the pictures but all the non-linguistic symbols that make up a television news show. For example, in America, almost all news shows begin with music, the tone of which suggests important events about to unfold. The music is very important, for it equates the news with various forms of drama and ritual—the opera, for example, or a wedding procession—in which musical themes underscore the meaning of the event. Music takes us immediately into the realm of the symbolic, a world that is not to be taken literally. After all, when events unfold in the real world, they do so without musical accompaniment. More symbolism follows. The sound of teletype machines can be heard in the studio, not because it is impossible to screen this noise out, but because the sound is a kind of music in itself. It tells us that data are pouring in from all corners of the globe, a sensation reinforced by the world map in the background (or clocks noting the time on different continents). The fact is that teletype machines are rarely used in TV news rooms, having been replaced by silent computer terminals. When seen, they have only a symbolic function.

13   Already, then, before a single news item is introduced, a great deal has been communicated. We know that we are in the presence of a symbolic event, a form of theater in which the day's events are to be dramatized. This theater takes the entire globe as its subject, although it may look at the world from the perspective of a single nation. A certain tension is present, like the atmosphere in a theater just before the curtain goes up. The tension is represented by the music, the staccato beat of the teletype machines, and often the sight of news workers scurrying around typing reports and answering phones. As a technical matter, it would be no problem to build a set in which the newsroom staff remained off camera, invisible to the viewer, but an important theatrical effect would be lost. By being busy on camera, the workers help communicate urgency about the events at hand, which suggests that situations are changing so rapidly that constant revision of the news is necessary.

14   The staff in the background also helps signal the importance of the person in the center, the anchor, "in command" of both the staff and the news. The anchor plays the role of host. He or she welcomes us to the newscast and welcomes us back from the different locations we visit during the filmed reports.

15   Many features of the newscast help the anchor to establish the impression of control. These are usually equated with production values in broadcasting. They include such things as graphics that tell the viewer what is being shown, or maps and charts that suddenly appear on the screen and disappear on cue, or the orderly progression from story to story. They also include the absence of gaps, or "dead time," during the broadcast, even the simple fact that the news starts and ends at a certain hour. These common features are thought of as purely technical matters, which a professional crew handles as a matter of course. But they are also symbols of a dominant theme of television news: the imposition of an orderly world—called "the news"—upon the disorderly flow of events.

16   While the form of a news broadcast emphasizes tidiness and control, its content can best be described as fragmented. Because time is so precious on television, because the nature of the medium favors dynamic visual images, and because the pressures of a commercial structure require the news to hold its audience above all else, there is rarely any attempt to explain issues in depth or place events in their proper context. The news moves nervously from a warehouse fire to a court decision, from a guerrilla war to a World Cup match, the quality of the film most often determining the length of the story. Certain stories show up only because they offer dramatic pictures. Bleachers collapse in South America: hundreds of people are crushed—a perfect television news story, for the cameras can record the face of disaster in all its anguish. Back in Washington, a new budget is approved by Congress. Here there is nothing to photograph because a budget is not a physical event; it is a document full of language and numbers. So the producers of the news will show a photo of the document itself, focusing on the cover where it says "Budget of the United States of America." Or sometimes they will send a camera crew to the government printing plant where copies of the budget are produced. That evening, while the contents of the budget are summarized by a voice-over, the viewer sees stacks of documents being loaded into boxes at the government printing plant. Then a few of the budget's more important provisions will be flashed on the screen in written form, but this is such a time-consuming process—using television as a printed page—that the producers keep it to a minimum. In short, the budget is not televisable, and for that reason its time on the news must be brief. The bleacher collapse will get more time that evening.

17   While appearing somewhat chaotic, these disparate stories are not just dropped in the news program helter-skelter. The appearance of a scattershot story order is really orchestrated to draw the audience from one story to the next—from one section to the next—through the commercial breaks to the end of the show. The story order is constructed to hold and build the viewership rather than place events in context or explain issues in depth.

18   Of course, it is a tendency of journalism in general to concentrate on the surface of events rather than underlying conditions; this is as true for the newspaper as it is for the newscast. But several features of television undermine whatever efforts journalists may make to give sense to the world. One is that a television broadcast is a series of events that occur in sequence, and the sequence is the same for all viewers. This is not true for a newspaper page, which displays many items simultaneously, allowing readers to choose the order in which they read them.

If newspaper readers want only a summary of the latest tax bill, they can read the headline and the first paragraph of an article, and if they want more, they can keep reading. In a sense, then, everyone reads a different newspaper, for no two readers will read (or ignore) the same items.

19   But all television viewers see the same broadcast. They have no choices. A report is either in the broadcast or out, which means that anything which is of narrow interest is unlikely to be included. As NBC News executive Reuven Frank once explained:

> A newspaper, for example, can easily afford to print an item of conceivable interest to only a fraction of its readers. A television news program must be put together with the assumption that each item will be of some interest to everyone that watches. Every time a newspaper includes a feature which will attract a specialized group. it can assume it is adding at least a little bit to its circulation. To the degree a television news program includes an item of this sort . . . it must assume that its audience will diminish.

20   The need to "include everyone," an identifying feature of commercial television in all its forms, prevents journalists from offering lengthy or complex explanations, or from tracing the sequence of events leading up to today's headlines. One of the ironies of political life in modern democracies is that many problems which concern the "general welfare" are of interest only to specialized groups. Arms control, for example, is an issue that literally concerns everyone in the world, and yet the language of arms control and the complexity of the subject are so daunting that only a minority of people can actually follow the issue from week to week and month to month. If it wants to act responsibly, a newspaper can at least make available more information about arms control than most people want. Commercial television cannot afford to do so.

21   But even if commercial television could afford to do so, it wouldn't. The fact that television news is principally made up of moving pictures prevents it from offering lengthy, coherent explanations of events. A television news show reveals the world as a series of unrelated, fragmentary moments. It does not—and cannot be expected to—offer a sense of coherence or meaning. What does this suggest to a TV viewer? That the viewer must come with a prepared mind—information, opinions, a sense of proportion, an articulate value system. To the TV viewer lacking such mental equipment, a news program is only a kind of rousing light show. Here a falling building, there a five-alarm fire, everywhere the world as an object, much without meaning, connections, or continuity.

THINKING CRITICALLY

1. According to Postman and Powers, how are still pictures like language? How are they different?

2. How do juxtapositions with other images, symbols, sound, music, or printed or verbal language help present the meaning of moving images (paragraph 4)? For each example in paragraphs 5–7, describe how these juxtapositions supply meaning to the moving images.

3. According to the authors, why are violence and destruction so often part of TV news stories? How are violence and destruction better suited for TV than other stories? How do TV screens make such stories more suited to TV than other stories?

4. Why are music, machine sounds, and news workers routinely included in TV news broadcasts? How do these nonessential cues help make news broadcasts seem interesting and important?

5. What devices do news broadcasters use to make them seem in control of "the disorderly flow of events"? Why are stories placed in a particular sequence? How might such a sequence affect audience viewing habits?

6. Why do TV news stories concentrate on "the surface of events rather than underlying conditions"? Why do broadcasters sometimes omit stories that are important but that would interest (or be understood by) only a minority of viewers?

7. What attitude do Postman and Powers convey in their first paragraph about television news shows? What kind of judgments about TV news did you expect to find throughout the rest of the article? What analogies and phrases help you identify the authors' attitude?

8. What attitude is conveyed in comparing TV news to theater? Beyond the aspect of spectacle, what additional denotations or connotations are implicit in the term *theater*? How do these suggest the authors' distrust of TV as a reliable, accurate source of news information? (See paragraph 13.)

9. What kinds of "important" news events are overwhelmed or lost by TV's visual reportage? How significant are such stories to the purpose(s) of news reporting? Do the authors convince you of the urgency of such stories? Would their point seem less urgent if they had focused on sports and weather reporting, for example?

WRITING ASSIGNMENTS

1. Using a family photograph, or a photo of friends, describe how this still picture conveys only a limited idea of what it shows. Did anything happen before or after the photo was snapped to make it especially important to you? Was anyone in the picture faking pleasure or caught in an uncharacteristic posture? In short, what might a stranger miss in this photo?

2. How do you think Postman and Powers would analyze the effect of closed captioning on television? Do you think they would include closed captioning as a visual element? Support your answer.

3. Videotape a network or local television newscast. First, watch the newscast with the sound (and/or closed captioning) turned off; then, watch the whole newscast with the sound (and/or closed captioning) turned on. Select three stories near the beginning of the broadcast and record your impressions about how important each was. Did you have different impressions when the sound (or closed captioning) accompanied the pictures? Why or why not?

4. Discuss the impact and role of TV news reporting on topics such as the war in Iraq, the civil rights movement, school shootings, the destruction of the Twin Towers of the World Trade Center, suicide bombings in Israel, or some other highly visible current event. How does television news, particularly the images it uses, help to create news rather than just retell it?

Oh, R-o-ob, The Bad Words Won't Go Away

John H. McWhorter

Language taboos usually reflect the social and cultural mores of the time. The Victorians—history's famous social conservatives—coined many words and phrases in an effort to avoid describing body parts or sexual situations. Victorian's asked for a "drumstick" rather than a chicken leg, pregnant women were said to be in "a delicate condition" and arms and legs were dubbed merely "limbs." While much has changed, the language taboos we enforce on television and the media today may seem almost Victorian. Should the language we hear in the media reflect the language used in the real world, by real people? In the next piece, John McWhorter discusses the disparity between how we speak in real life, and the language the FCC bans as unacceptable.

John McWhorter is a senior fellow at the Manhattan Institute and author of several books on language including *The Power of Babel: A Natural History of Language* (2002), *Doing Our Own Thing: The Degradation of Language and Music in America and Why We Should, Like, Care* (2003), and most recently, *Defining Creole* (2005). He has written on race and cultural issues for many publications including the *Wall Street Journal*, the *Chronicle of Higher Education*, the *National Review*, and the *New York Times*. He has also appeared on *Dateline NBC*, *Talk of the Nation*, *Today*, *Good Morning America*, and the *NewsHour with Jim Lehrer*. This article appeared in the December 28, 2003, edition of the *Washington Post*.

1 I am currently making my way through the new DVD set of the first season of "The Dick Van Dyke Show." In an episode that aired in 1962, Rob and Laura Petrie are horrified that their son has picked up a "dirty word." The viewer does not learn the word itself; Laura only whispers it into the phone, her hand cupped over her mouth, and she and Rob are incensed that their son has been exposed to "evil."

2 This was certainly a sanitized version of the linguistic reality of the day. But the distortion itself reflects an America that is anthropologically fascinating from our perspective [today]. A TV mom whispering a mild curse word into the phone rather than just saying it out loud is hopelessly implausible today, and getting ever more so.

3 This has never been more clear than it became a couple of weeks ago, when flavor-of-the-month Nicole Richie, appearing on Fox TV's "Billboard Music Awards" broadcast, casually dropped some classic four- (and more) letter words into her reminiscences of her stint on the reality show "The Simple Life." Fox's switchboard lit up with indignant callers, but the network received not even a slap on the wrist from the Federal Communications Commission, the agency that watchdogs on-air language. That's because two months before, unbeknown to many of us, the FCC had decreed a new era in American public language usage.

4 After receiving complaints that Irish rocker Bono had crowed, "This is really, really f---ing brilliant!" on the "Golden Globe Awards" broadcast in January 2003, also on Fox, the FCC's enforcement bureau ruled that this adjectival usage of the F-word does not qualify as "patently offensive as measured by contemporary community standards for the broadcast medium." Predictably, this has not gone down well with some, from the Parents Television Council (which organized most of the

Bono complaints) to congressmen to FCC Chairman Michael Powell himself, who played no part in the ruling and deemed it "reprehensible" that children might hear the F-word in any form on the air. But like it or not, we'd better get used to it. We are today a society that elevates giving the finger to "the man" to a sign of enlightenment. So there are bound to be more such rulings, and at the end of the day, we are best advised to fasten our seat belts and accept them.

5   We obsess over the encroachment of vulgar words into public spaces on pain of a stark inconsistency, one that will appear even more ridiculous to future generations than some Victorians calling trousers "nether garments" does to us. At least the Victorians' vocabulary taboos reflected mores that permeated society. Theirs was a world in which an author of a slang dictionary would have had trouble finding a publisher, people sequestered themselves under reams of fabric, illegitimate birth was a scandal, and sex was never spoken of in "polite society." Even as late as the Camelot era, Rob and Laura slept in twin beds and never went to the bathroom.

6   However we judge all this, it at least comprised a coherent worldview, of the sort that anthropologists deem a hallmark of human social organization. For generations, people were openly uptight about "those things" across the board. But we no longer are. And thus, banning the F-adjective in 2003 becomes a random, isolated gesture, displaying a studied daintiness that can only be defended with stammering vaguenesses.

7   Our America was just on the horizon when that Dick van Dyke episode I described aired. A few years later, the counterculture movement began. It arose as a rejection of the Vietnam War, segregation and political censorship, but soon broadened into an embrace of more visceral facets of the anti-establishment ideology: an embrace of the spontaneous, the "authentic," the "real." Naturally this included forms of speech once banned from public discourse.

8   Some of this was merely common speech itself. In 1848, everyday language was so rare on the stage that when the actor Frank Chanfrau ventured Bowery Boy street speech with the line "I ain't a-goin' to run wild wid dat mercheen no more," working-class Irish audiences in New York stopped the show with riotous applause for several minutes. But in the 1960s, this public airing of casual talk became ordinary. Students at Berkeley followed up the political Free Speech movement of 1964 with a "Filthy Speech movement" the next year, featuring placards emblazoned with the F-word. Over the next 20 years, "damn" and "hell" became typical on stage and screen.

9   Few of us mind this today. We giggle at the stir over Clark Gable's Rhett Butler saying—horrors!—I don't give a "damn" in the 1939 movie "Gone With the Wind." We see Puritanism in the Motion Picture Production Code banning the winkiness of Mae West's routines and sanitizing cartoon flapper Betty Boop into a high-collared hausfrau. And we see as a moral victory the recent posthumous pardoning of comedian Lenny Bruce, who was convicted in the 1960s for using obscenities in his nightclub act.

10   How overwrought, of course. But if we view as antique the Catholic matrons who banned the "authenticity" we now cherish in pre–Production Code movies, then where do we draw the line in terms of what we decree as inappropriate nowadays?

11   The Communications Act of 1934, which established the FCC, stipulated such a line. This law, penned by people born in Victorian America, decreed to be publicly inappropriate language that "describes or depicts sexual or excretory activities or organs." But this only leads to a question: If we are now so comfortable acknowledging, discussing and even displaying our most private "parts" in public, then precisely what is the logical justification for refraining from using words that connote what we do with them?

12   After all, this is an America where the actress Téa Leoni purrs in *TV Guide* about having "mated often" with an ex-lover, academics celebrate the profanity in rap music as visionary, sensitive adults are warmly fascinated by Eminem, R-rated movies are common coin among teenagers, unmarried celebrity couples casually announce the expectation of babies, young men show their underwear above their belts, and young women in "low-rider" jeans display a netherly fissure celebrated in some places as "the new cleavage."

13   In this context, to resist using a particular vulgarity on television stands not as a conviction inherent to our national fabric, but as an emotional sentiment brandished by a minority. Rob and Laura's quaintness in our eyes reveals that the counterculture has become our warp and woof. We seek as narrow a gulf as possible between public show and private reality. To us, the sentiment Bono expressed with his "f---ing brilliant" channels an individuality, humility and even warmth that no formal translation such as "truly amazing" could. It channels exactly the "get real" essence that makes it seem odd to us that when Laura is carrying Richie she must be referred to as "expecting" because of a sense that "pregnant" is too vulgar.

14   I should say, however, that though I never knew Rob and Laura's America, I am no more immune to visceral responses to profanity than anyone else. Long ago a woman with whom I had a dinner date casually let fly with a term for what Victorians might have referred to as the female pudendum. Even I had a gut-level sense that this was "a bit much."

15   But gut-level was all it was, and "a bit much" does not suffice as a basis for coherent public policy. After all, the producers of Dick Van Dyke got angry mail from viewers who thought the snug capri pants Mary Tyler Moore wore on the show were "a bit much." We chuckle now. But on what basis can we casually accept seeing ever more of the human bodies that horrified the ladies of the Junior League in 1962 and yet insist on "drawing a line" at words that connote activities connected with those bodies? If we affectionately give our children books such as "Our Bodies, Ourselves," celebrating the joys of sex, how can we defend decrying Bono's jolly exclamation for hinting that, well, people have sex?

16   Surely we fear the slippery slope. I certainly itch at the notion of sitcom characters using the word my date used. But public norms never leap far ahead of the majority's primal sense of propriety. I suspect that most of us, if we saw Kelsey Grammer's Frasier let out with "That's f--- amazing," would celebrate the character's "loosening up" a bit. The word has gotten as far as it has because it is now common enough in casual speech to qualify for most as more colorful than truly profane. It is questionable that it even connotes the sexual anymore. This is typical of how words evolve through time. Technically, for instance, "ice cream" means cream rendered through ice, or "iced cream," but few of us process it consciously

that way—in casual speech it is now a single word, "ayeskream." The F-adjective is now one of many intensifiers in English, like "extremely," with a flavor surely pungent but barely sexual. In that light, the FCC's decision was not mere hair-splitting, but linguistically honest, and reflects our "contemporary community standards."

17   Thus we are witnessing less a linguistic free-for-all than a narrowing of the gap between the formal and the informal in public discourse. Because advertisers are loath to offend any significant number of their potential customers, the few words we now process as truly beyond the pale will likely only hit the tube after having lost much of their sting through constant use.

18   The days when even mild epithets were never uttered in public language are gone for good. The exoticness of Rob and Laura's world to us demonstrates that we have transformed ourselves beyond it forever. As far as language on television goes, unless we shed our affection for "getting real"—and there are no indications that we will—we can only hold on to our hats.

19   But then we don't really wear hats anymore—and that's the point. Just like clothing, our language reflects who we are, and we are a people who can only deem most profanity "evil" if we are ready to be seen 50 years from now as being as laughable as the producers of "Gilligan's Island" who required Mary Ann to keep her navel covered.

THINKING CRITICALLY

1. What is McWhorter's opinion of banned words on television? In your opinion, should foul or offensive language on television be banned? Why or why not?

2. McWhorter notes that "We are today a society that elevates giving the finger to 'the man' to a sign of enlightenment." What does he mean? Explain.

3. What role has the popular HBO series *The Sopranos* played in the increase of coarse language on television? Explain.

4. This article was written for a newspaper, and uses a standard reporting style. Can you tell how the author feels about this issue? If so, cite examples from the article that reveal his opinion.

5. Throughout most of his article McWhorter refers to various obscenities as the "F--- word" etc. Why do you think he chose not to use the actual obscenities? What does this tell you about the role of obscenity censorship in the print media? Explain.

6. How did the Victorian's vocabulary taboos reflect social and cultural mores of their time? Do current vocabulary taboos in the media reflect similar mores today? Why or why not? Explain.

7. What language forces television censors to really draw the line? Are there degrees of offensive language? If some of it is allowed, should all of it be permissible? Why or why not?

WRITING ASSIGNMENTS

1. McWhorter cites several incidents that have tested the limits of taboo language on television. Brainstorm a list of shows that seek to "push the envelope" terms of "taboo" language. Watch one or two of these shows, and then critique of them, noting how the language contributes or detracts

program. For example, would *South Park* be funny if its characters did not use taboo language? Would *The Sopranos* or *Sex and the City* seem less edgy? Explain.

2. McWhorter points out that taboo language simply reflects our social mores. Our language values in the 1960s are not the same values we hold today. What is your opinion about this issue? Write an essay explaining why you think we should be able to use taboo language uncensored in the media. Does taboo language help television characters sound like "real people," and reflect our reality? Alternatively, you could explain why we should protect children and those easily offended from taboo language on television.

Is Bad Language Unacceptable on TV?

BBC Online

In the previous article, John H. McWhorter discussed the shifting rules of taboo language on television. This next piece takes a closer look at the subject of taboo words. Readers of the BBC Online discussion forum, "Talking Point," were asked, "Is bad language unacceptable on TV . . . or have swear words and offensive language become an accepted part of TV output?" As you read the responses posted on the discussion board, consider the different arguments posted, and how you personally feel about the subject.

1 BBC: *Is bad language unacceptable on TV?*

2 The use of racially abusive language on television and radio is an area of increasing concern among viewers and listeners, a new study has revealed. The report also suggests most adults with children want their homes to be expletive free. Stephen Whittle, Director of the Broadcasting Standards Commission in England, says there is an acceptance that swearing and offensive language is used in daily life, and may be appropriate if a program is aimed at adults.

3 But he says people "would prefer their homes to remain an expletive deleted zone for children." Is swearing still a matter of major concern to you? Or have swear words and offensive language become an accepted part of TV output? Here are some responses to this question featured on the *BBC Online*'s "Talking Point":

4 There's a simple answer to all those complaining. If you don't like it then don't watch it. There is nothing more annoying than listening to outraged people ___ ___lain about what they had to watch the night before. No one makes ___ them so if you hear bad language/see sex scenes/view violence then ___ e channels instead of watching all three hours and then complaining ___ fterwards. YOU DON'T HAVE TO WATCH IT. It's true that at times ___ rograms it seems the language is used purely to shock rather than as ___ script/plot/characters but if you sit and watch it all instead of turn- ___ witching off then you can't then blame your shock and outrage on ___ m makers.

James, UK

5   There is no justification to the use of bad language on TV. It is unacceptable. How can a parent positively correct a child who uses bad language if all they hear on TV is filthy language every minute?

Ruskin Kwofic, USA

6   Not only is swearing wrong and extremely offensive, even worse than that is the constant blasphemy on TV. This is especially hurtful to a Christian like myself when it is done to make people laugh. We should not be blaspheming or condoning this when we laugh or otherwise accept it passively or actively. It is too easy to say, ". . . use the off switch . . . ," this is not the answer. Does any parent want to encourage their child to swear and adopt negativity? Rather it would be more constructive to teach them the values of right and wrong. To sum up, all who own a television license are entitled to be informed and entertained by its purchase and that means all.

K. D., Wales

7   Protecting children is a big chunk of what responsible parenting is about, and protecting their minds and emotions is just as important as physical protection, if not more so. Of course they'll come across it elsewhere, but it's clear that the extent will be increased or decreased by the levels of exposure of their peers. As a parent I find the so-called watershed is no guarantee at all that my kids won't hear swearing on the television. Please can we have a consistently regulated watershed?

Tom Richards, UK

8   I consider the television to be a guest. I would not allow a visitor to my house to use swearing and foul language in front of me or my children. I consider the television to be a guest, and when it offends, off it goes!

J. Herbert, UK

9   It really is stupid to campaign for protecting young people against swearing on TV. By the time you reach 12 years old you've heard every word under the sun a million times in the playground. Anyone who fails to realize this is just completely ignorant.

Darren Meale, UK

10   Bad language is nothing compared to all the violent shows on so many series. I prefer to hear someone pronounce a four-letter word than to see them beaten to death or killed in a TV series. Bad language is part of the everyday life of most people. Violence is not.

Luc Masuy, Belgium

11   The use of bad language in TV or cinema is not a reflection of society, but rather an excuse by writers and actors to hide the fact that they can no longer produce real drama or real emotion. The use of swearing to emphasize a point is only there to mask the lack of understanding and talent. Media twenty years ago didn't need to use bad language—the skill in presenting drama and emotion was there anyway. Sorry, no swearing on TV or cinema at all for me.

Steve Gittins, UK

12   In writing drama one of the first rules is to make your characters believable. Censorship of bad language could lead to some of the most unbelievable characters ever portrayed on television. People swear. For instance, a prison drama in which no one ever swore would be ridiculous. What sort of programs you allow your children to watch is up to you. But they will hear swearing in the real world—you can't censor that.

Colin Wright, UK

13   Why is it necessary? Surely we can use descriptive adjectives without resorting to bad language. It is not enough to say it is a part of life. We have the power to adopt better social attitudes; instead many people seem content with debasing everything.

Jill Doe, Wales

14   All drama revolves around conflict and jeopardy so bad language in itself is not wrong, it all depends on the context it is used in. Imagine if Shakespeare or Chaucer had been prevented from writing and performing their work without the "bawdy" language, the swearing of their day. As long as it doesn't become meaninglessly used and the watershed is observed to my eyes at least, it is acceptable.

James Newman, UK

15   Please keep it off our screens. You only have to listen to children going to school to see how commonplace it has become.

Gerry, Scotland

16   It may be the duty of our media/entertainment outlets to reflect the standards and behavior of our society and culture, but they surely also have some responsibility to set the standard. By merely reflecting, because they permeate every level of society, they take the lead in the general debasement of "generally accepted standards of behavior." I am not prudish or offended by bad language/behavior on TV and radio, per se, but it often makes me wince!

Mark M. Newdick, USA

17   As a relatively liberal minded young person, I am not outraged by occasional bad language on television, but at the same time, I do not think that it is necessary. Bad language is neither amusing nor particularly effective in stressing a point. It is just fashion—and a very cheap fashion at that. It's best to leave it in the cinemas (if it is really required there) and edit the more stronger language out before it appears on television. Personally, I have never found that a movie is lacking punch just because a few profanities have been deleted. Indeed, this should be the test to see whether a film is worth its weight at all.

Robert Kidd, Australia

18   My personal experience of working in an environment where swearing was the norm was to swear more. When I changed jobs where swearing was banned I stopped. The best thing to do is to avoid swearing in the main but keep a little to be realistic, and hence cut down on the excessive use of profanities in society.

Gavin Pearson, USA

19   As adults, we can accept bad language on TV programs, as long as it relates to the program in question (i.e., drama series or films). However, children should not have to hear that sort of language. I'm not a prude by any means, but I find it really depressing when I hear children from toddler age and up using foul language. Of course, they may learn this from their parents and other family members, but let's minimize their exposure by keeping it out of children's programs.

Karen, UK

20   The simple fact of the matter is if you don't like the swearing then turn over! Anything that your children may or may not hear on TV they are certainly going to hear in the real world. People need to wake up and understand that the censorship of television is going beyond a joke. I'm all for restricting bad language before a time when children are likely to be up but can someone please explain to me the necessity to cut swear words from a film at 10:30 or 11:00. People can say they are offended as much as they like but the simple fact is that you control what you watch, if you're offended by swearing then turn it off. Welcome to the real world people, people swear!

Richard Tyacke, England

THINKING CRITICALLY

1. What is your personal opinion of bad language on television? Is it no big deal? A fact of life? Or is it unacceptable?

2. Is the reality that people swear—as one posting claims—valid support that it should be acceptable television fare? Why or why not?

3. Several respondents to this question state that if you don't like bad language on television, turn off the set. Respond to this statement in your own words.

4. Several forum participants qualify their responses with "I'm not a prude." What are the implications of the word *prude*? Is it prudish to object to bad language? Why or why not?

5. Select one or two of the postings featured in this article and write a response to it, addressing the points it raises.

WRITING ASSIGNMENTS

1. One forum participant comments that while the entertainment industry should reflect society and culture, the industry also has some responsibility to "set the standard." What should the standard be? Write an essay exploring the responsibility of the entertainment industry to the cultural standards of a society.

2. One respondent, James Newman, points out that bad language depends on the context in which it is used. "Imagine if Shakespeare or Chaucer had been prevented from writing and performing their work without 'bawdy' language, the swearing of their day." Research this assertion. What sort of bawdy language did these two writers use and how did it contribute to the flavor of their work? How would their work be different if they were restricted to neutral language? In this context, does Newman make a valid point?

Taking TV's "War of Words" Too Literally

Deborah Tannen

> In this essay, linguistic professor Deborah Tannen examines the ways in which we approach arguments and debates in our society. If ratings are any indication of American's viewing tastes, our culture prefers angry conflict to patient discussion. Tannen describes her personal experience on a television talk show, a program on which she hoped thoughtful deliberation with other participants would help promote a meaningful dialogue. Instead, she found herself the unwilling participant in an aggressive shouting match. Beyond mere entertainment, what is this style of television teaching viewers about the way we address conflict and solve problems?
>
> Deborah Tannen is a professor of linguistics at Georgetown University. She has been a featured guest on many news programs, including *20/20, 48 Hours,* and the *NewsHour with Jim Lehrer.* Tannen is the author of many best-selling books on linguistics and social discourse, including *The Argument Culture* (1999), and *I Only Say This Because I Love You* (2001). This article appeared in the weekly edition of the *Washington Post* on March 23, 1998.

1   I was waiting to go on a television talk show a few years ago for a discussion about how men and women communicate, when a man walked in wearing a shirt and tie and a floor-length skirt, the top of which was brushed by his waist-length red hair. He politely introduced himself and told me that he'd read and liked my book *You Just Don't Understand,* which had just been published. Then he added, "When I get out there, I'm going to attack you. But don't take it personally. That's why they invite me on, so that's what I'm going to do."

2   We went on the set and the show began. I had hardly managed to finish a sentence or two before the man threw his arms out in gestures of anger, and began shrieking—briefly hurling accusations at me, and then railing at length against women. The strangest thing about his hysterical outburst was how the studio audience reacted: They turned vicious—not attacking me (I hadn't said anything substantive yet) or him (who wants to tangle with someone who screams at you?) but the other guests: women who had come to talk about problems they had communicating with their spouses.

3   My antagonist was nothing more than a dependable provocateur, brought on to ensure a lively show. The incident has stayed with me not because it was typical of the talk shows I have appeared on—it wasn't, I'm happy to say—but because it exemplifies the ritual nature of much of the opposition that pervades our public dialogue.

4   Everywhere we turn, there is evidence that, in public discourse, we prize contentiousness and aggression more than cooperation and conciliation. Headlines blare about the Star Wars, the Mommy Wars, the Baby Wars, the Mammography Wars; everything is posed in terms of battles and duels, winners and losers, conflicts and disputes. Biographies have metamorphosed into demonographies whose authors don't just portray their subjects warts and all, but set out to dig up as much dirt as possible, as if the story of a person's life is contained in the warts, only the warts, and nothing but the warts.

5   It's all part of what I call the argument culture, which rests on the assumption that opposition is the best way to get anything done: The best way to discuss an idea is to set up a debate. The best way to cover news is to find people who express the most extreme views and present them as "both sides." The best way to begin an essay is to attack someone. The best way to show you're really thoughtful is to criticize. The best way to settle disputes is to litigate them.

6   It is the automatic nature of this response that I am calling into question. This is not to say that passionate opposition and strong verbal attacks are never appropriate. In the words of Yugoslavian-born poet Charles Simic, "There are moments in life when true invective is called for, when it becomes an absolute necessity, out of a deep sense of justice, to denounce, mock, vituperate, lash out, in the strongest possible language." What I'm questioning is the ubiquity, the knee-jerk nature of approaching almost any issue, problem or public person in an adversarial way.

7   Smashing heads does not open minds. In this as in so many things, results are also causes, looping back and entrapping us. The pervasiveness of warlike formats and language grows out of, but also gives rise to, an ethic of aggression: We come to value aggressive tactics for their own sake—for the sake of argument. Compromise becomes a dirty word, and we often feel guilty if we are conciliatory rather than confrontational—even if we achieve the result we're seeking.

8   Here's one example. A woman called another talk show on which I was a guest. She told the following story: "I was in a place where a man was smoking, and there was a no-smoking sign. Instead of saying 'You aren't allowed to smoke in here. Put that out!' I said, 'I'm awfully sorry, but I have asthma, so your smoking makes it hard for me to breathe. Would you mind terribly not smoking?' When I said this, the man was extremely polite and solicitous, and he put his cigarette out, and I said, 'Oh, thank you, thank you!' as if he'd done a wonderful thing for me. Why did I do that?"

9   I think the woman expected me—the communications expert—to say she needs assertiveness training to confront smokers in a more aggressive manner. Instead, I told her that her approach was just fine. If she had tried to alter his behavior by reminding him of the rules, he might well have rebelled: "Who made you the enforcer? Mind your own business!" She had given the smoker a face-saving way of doing what she wanted, one that allowed him to feel chivalrous rather than chastised. This was kinder to him, but it was also kinder to herself, since it was more likely to lead to the result she desired.

10   Another caller disagreed with me, saying the first caller's style was "self-abasing." I persisted: There was nothing necessarily destructive about the way the woman handled the smoker. The mistake the second caller was making—a mistake many of us make—was to confuse ritual self-effacement with the literal kind. All human relations require us to find ways to get what we want from others without seeming to dominate them.

11   The opinions expressed by the two callers encapsulate the ethic of aggression that has us by our throats, particularly in public arenas such as politics and law. Issues are routinely approached by having two sides stake out opposing positions and do battle. This sometimes drives people to take positions that are more adversarial than they feel—and can get in the way of reaching a possible resolution. . . .

12   The same spirit drives the public discourse of politics and the press, which are increasingly being given over to ritual attacks. On Jan. 18, 1994, retired admiral Bobby Ray Inman withdrew as nominee for Secretary of Defense after several news stories raised questions about his business dealings and his finances. Inman, who had held high public office in both Democratic and Republican administrations, explained that he did not wish to serve again because of changes in the political climate—changes that resulted in public figures being subjected to relentless attack. Inman said he was told by one editor, "Bobby, you've just got to get thicker skin. We have to write a bad story about you every day. That's our job."

13   Everyone seemed to agree that Inman would have been confirmed. The news accounts about his withdrawal used words such as "bizarre," "mystified" and "extraordinary." A *New York Times* editorial reflected the news media's befuddlement: "In fact, with the exception of a few columns, . . . a few editorials and one or two news stories, the selection of Mr. Inman had been unusually well received in Washington." This evaluation dramatizes how run-of-the-mill systematic attacks have become. With a wave of a subordinate clause ("a few editorials . . ."), attacking someone personally and (from his point of view) distorting his record are dismissed as so insignificant as to be unworthy of notice.

14   The idea that all public figures should expect to be criticized ruthlessly testifies to the ritualized nature of such attack: It is not sparked by specific wrongdoing but is triggered automatically.

15   I once asked a reporter about the common journalistic practice of challenging interviewees by repeating criticism to them. She told me it was the hardest part of her job. "It makes me uncomfortable," she said. "I tell myself I'm someone else and force myself to do it." But, she said she had no trouble being combative if she felt someone was guilty of behavior she considered wrong. And that is the crucial difference between ritual fighting and literal fighting: opposition of the heart.

16   It is easy to find examples throughout history of journalistic attacks that make today's rhetoric seem tame. But in the past such vituperation was motivated by true political passion, in contrast with today's automatic, ritualized attacks—which seem to grow out of a belief that conflict is high-minded and good, a required and superior form of discourse.

17   The roots of our love for ritualized opposition lie in the educational system that we all pass through.

18   Here's a typical scene: The teacher sits at the head of the classroom, pleased with herself and her class. The students are engaged in a heated debate. The very noise level reassures the teacher that the students are participating. Learning is going on. The class is a success.

19   But look again, cautions Patricia Rosof, a high school history teacher who admits to having experienced just such a wave of satisfaction. On closer inspection, you notice that only a few students are participating in the debate; the majority of the class is sitting silently. And the students who are arguing are not addressing subtleties, nuances or complexities of the points they are making or disputing. They don't have that luxury because they want to win the argument—so they must go for the most dramatic statements they can muster. They will not concede an opponent's point—even if they see its validity—because that would weaken their position.

20   This aggressive intellectual style is cultivated and rewarded in our colleges and universities. The standard way to write an academic paper is to position your work in opposition to someone else's. This creates a need to prove others wrong, which is quite different from reading something with an open mind and discovering that you disagree with it. Graduate students learn that they must disprove others' arguments in order to be original, make a contribution and demonstrate intellectual ability. The temptation is great to oversimplify at best, and at worst to distort or even misrepresent other positions, the better to refute them.

21   I caught a glimpse of this when I put the question to someone who I felt had misrepresented my own work: "Why do you need to make others wrong for you to be right?" Her response: "It's an argument!" Aha, I thought, that explains it. If you're having an argument, you use every tactic you can think of—including distorting what your opponent just said—in order to win.

22   Staging everything in terms of polarized opposition limits the information we get rather than broadening it.

23   For one thing, when a certain kind of interaction is the norm, those who feel comfortable with that type of interaction are drawn to participate, and those who do not feel comfortable with it recoil and go elsewhere. If public discourse included a broad range of types, we would be making room for individuals with different temperaments. But when opposition and fights overwhelmingly predominate, only those who enjoy verbal sparring are likely to take part. Those who cannot comfortably take part in oppositional discourse—or choose not to—are likely to opt out.

24   But perhaps the most dangerous harvest of the ethic of aggression and ritual fighting is—as with the audience response to the screaming man on the television talk show—an atmosphere of animosity that spreads like a fever. In extreme forms, it rears its head in road rage and workplace shooting sprees. In more common forms, it leads to what is being decried everywhere as a lack of civility. It erodes our sense of human connection to those in public life—and to the strangers who cross our paths and people our private lives.

THINKING CRITICALLY

1. Do you agree with Tannen's assertion that our public discussions about controversial issues have turned into "battles and duels" by the media? Explain why or why not. Look through several current newspapers or magazines to see if you can find evidence supporting an argument for or against this trend. Do other forms of media such as radio also encourage this approach?

2. What is Tannen's purpose in this essay? Restate her claims in your own words and explain whether you agree or disagree with her thesis and why.

3. In paragraphs 8 and 9, Tannen describes a woman who dealt with a conflict by being conciliatory and even apologetic. Although her approach worked, she and other listeners felt that she should have been more assertive and demanding in her approach. What is your own opinion of how the woman dealt with the situation, and why?

4. What impact does the popularity of "argument culture" television programming have on our language and conversation styles? Explain.

5. Tannen notes in paragraphs 18–20 that students who engage in confrontational-style discourse get more attention from teachers than students who do not. In your own experience, do you agree or disagree with this observation?

6. Is there anything wrong with "argument culture"-style communication? Is it indeed a cause for concern, or is it simply a way to solve problems and disagreements? Are arguments really based on winning or losing a position? Should they be? Explain.

WRITING ASSIGNMENTS

1. Watch several television talk-show programs and consider how the "argument culture" is affecting our ability to resolve controversial issues. How do the participants of the programs listen to the words of other people on the program? Are they responding to what is actually said on the program, or merely restating their own opinions? Do they shout, threaten, or interrupt? If so, what effect does this behavior have on the other participants, the audience, and even the host? Explain.

2. In your opinion, has the prevalence of talk shows supporting an argumentative conflict-resolution format filtered into common discourse? In other words, do these television programs influence our culture as a whole? Explain.

3. Write an essay in which you explore the role language plays in solving disagreements. Why is language important to the way our culture addresses conflict? In what ways do we fail to consider language when we argue? In what ways do we use language to our advantage? Explain.

The Entertained Culture
Tom Shachtman

"We have become a country of mass audiences," observes Tom Shachtman in the next essay. Shachtman explains that in an effort to reach as broad an audience as possible, the language used by television media is usually aimed at the lowest linguistic level. This "dumbing down" of language, fears Shachtman, ultimately erodes the grace and fluidity of our language as a whole.

Tom Shachtman teaches writing at New York University. He is the author of several books of fiction and nonfiction, including *Skyscraper Dreams: The Great Real Estate Dynasties of New York* (1991) and *Terrors and Marvels: How Science and Technology Changed the Character and Outcome of World War II* (2002). The following essay is excerpted from his 1995 book, *The Inarticulate Society: Eloquence and Culture in America*.

1   A published novelist moved to Hollywood to join her fiancé and looked for employment in the area's main industry. After she had cut her scriptwriting teeth on occasional television series episodes, she was asked to join the writing staff of a new situation comedy commissioned by a major network. She arrived at the first script meeting brimming over with innovative and quirky ideas for plots, character traits, lines of dialogue. The senior creators heard her out for a few minutes, then enjoined her to remember: "This is television—aim lower."

2   She was perturbed and a bit shocked by that directive, but she should not have been surprised, because aiming lower is what the creators have come to believe is usually required in order to reach the inordinately large audience necessary to keep a prime-time network television show on the air. And part of aiming lower has been to restrict substantially the vocabulary, sentence structure, word usage, and cultural referents in television scripts.

3   We have become a country of mass audiences. The average American spends half of his or her daily waking hours watching, reading, or listening to some product of the mass media. Most Americans watch thirty hours of television a week, or 1,550 hours a year (during which, according to one estimate, they encounter 37,822 commercials), listen to the radio 1,160 hours a year, spend 180 hours a year reading some part of a newspaper and 110 hours a year reading magazines. We each buy fifteen books a year, and although this appears to be a substantial number, most of the books purchased are considered to be in the category of trashy novels. Surveys conclude that the "most read" portion of any newspaper is Ann Landers's advice column and that the most frequently read magazine is *TV Guide*. The vocabulary and sentence-difficulty level of such readings is quite low, not much above grade-school level. In 1992 Americans spent $12 billion to buy or rent videos, a figure that translates into 49.5 rentals per family a year, about one video each week. Add in a few hours for going to the movies or listening to audio cassettes and CDs, and the total number of hours that the average American spends attending to mass media products comes to more than fifty per week, more time than the average American spends on the job or at school, more hours than he or she devotes to any single activity other than sleeping.[1]

4   A trend toward convergence of the entertainment and news/information industries has made certain that the language practices of one sector largely reproduce the practices of the other, and both aim lower, with dire consequences for articulateness. Because television has tremendous power to influence its viewers, it is legitimate to be concerned with the nature and the accuracy of the medium's representations of reality. Meticulous studies of program content and viewing habits conducted over the course of several decades by George Gerbner and his associates at the Annenberg School have reached the unsurprising conclusion that both fictional and nonfictional broadcasts give viewers inaccurate and misleading representations of reality. Among their findings: Crime is ten times more prevalent on television than it is in the FBI's annual statistics on criminal activity. More than half of television's fictional characters are involved in a violent confrontation each week. Habitual television watchers—defined as those who turn their sets on for more than four hours a day—come to believe the skewed version of reality that is broadcast and to disbelieve reality itself. Not only do such "heavy viewers" perceive crime unrealistically, with a serial killer lurking behind every tree, but they also develop other misperceptions about our society: Their sense of reality comes to reflect television's inaccurate portrayal of who we are and what we do. On prime-time television, nine out of every ten characters are middle-class, less than 1 percent are lower-class, and only one-quarter have blue-collar jobs. On television, only one out of every ten characters is married; women

age quickly—there are many youthful female characters and some recognizably older ones, but few are in their middle years. Conversely, the facts show that two out of every three jobs in this country are classified as blue collar, and most women in the country are married and middle-aged. While 80 percent of the convicted criminals in the United States are young, male and largely from a minority background, the villains seen on television are even more disproportionately young, male, lower-class, minority or foreign-born or mentally ill. "Losers" on television programs are mostly likely to be female, old, unmarried, and/or poor. Similarly, heavy viewers overestimate the number of people in this country employed as doctors, lawyers, and managers, and hold such mistaken beliefs as that the older population of the country is sick, ineffectual, and makes up less of the whole than do the young people whose counterparts fill the bulk of the roles on popular television shows.

5   What do these misrepresentations have to do with the decline in articulate speech? The answer lies in a further investigation into the nature of the misrepresentations, for they are not accidental. Rather, they are a result of marketing analysis, which consistently advises the creators of television programs to aim lower in order to reach broader audiences. That has precipitated the industry into a self-perpetuating cycle of infinite regression, a cycle in which the most effective product is always the one aimed lower than the previous one.

6   Must the need to ensure a large audience automatically mean that the makers of mass media entertainments should trim their creative sails? Clearly, the industry itself has concluded that an entertainment product cannot be both widely popular and of high quality, but there is no intrinsic reason why quality and sales appeal cannot be combined. One of the more popular programs in the early days of commercial television was *Omnibus*, a program of decidedly elite culture but aimed at a mass audience presumed to want to be led upward rather than downward. Other, occasional broadcasts also aimed higher. In a 1950s program designed for young audiences, Leonard Bernstein electrified a generation of viewers and listeners with his demonstration of why an orchestra needs a conductor. Bernstein and the producers of the program assumed that most children—indeed, most people in the viewing audience—had never been to a live concert, but that did not deter the program's creators from making an intelligent point. The composer began at the podium, started the orchestra on a familiar classical theme, and then walked away, leaving the orchestra to its own devices; within a minute, the music turned dissonant and sour, as each instrument player followed his or her own beat. When Bernstein returned to explain what precisely a conductor does, very few in the home mass audience dared turn to another channel.

7   It had been the function of entertainment producers for many centuries to adhere to elite standards and to assume that part of their task was to bring wider and wider audiences up to those standards. That task was most overtly pursued in the age of Addison, Steele, and Henry Fielding, who wrote popular plays and novels. Many of their works were transparently about the spoken word. They offered readers choice phrases to repeat as well as models of good and bad speech. Television now provides models of words to say and how to say them; however, the models are too often based on the worst uses of language. Rather than use their reserves of

ingenuity to entertain, today's producers totally abandon any adherence to high standards or to educating as well as titillating audiences and fall back on the most basic elements at their disposal—an attitude that fosters appeals to base instincts, the too ready exclusion of references to anything other than pop culture, and the endless recycling of familiar material. Circuitous marketing logic becomes self-fulfilling prophecy, and it is heresy to suggest that the intellectually more complicated products of the foreign film industry or the highbrow programs seen on public television might fare better in commercial terms if they had the same financial and promotional backing and the same wide distribution as the products of the mainstream. "Nobody ever went broke underestimating the taste of the American public" goes the phrase attributed to H. L. Mencken. He meant it as an indictment; today's pop culture purveyors treat it as a directive.

8   This directive implies a high degree of contempt for the audience. It expresses a belief that the audience is infinitely malleable and easily led, that it has no intelligence at all, or not enough to see through marketing tricks. It tries to turn audiences into mere consumers who have no more choice in how they react to a stimulus than do hungry animals confronted with food. As Theodor Adorno and the other members of the Frankfurt School pointed out fifty years ago, one of the main purposes of mass culture is to keep the consumer's responses at an infantile level, and thereby to manipulate the consumer with false promises of libidinal gratification.[2] In the ensuing half-century, the purveyors have only become more skilled at their task. The corollary of the directive about taste is that a product will make a great deal of money if it is aimed low. That belief—for it is only a guess—has become the engine of Hollywood, affecting every part of motion picture and television production, from casting to script development to the props on the set. The fact is that Hollywood producers cannot predict with any degree of certainty what will or will not make money. Out of fear of not making money, they resort to the elements that seem most likely to ensure that the product makes money. Certain stars are labeled as "bankable" because such a star's agreement to play a major role in a movie enables the producer to obtain funding for it. A star's bankability, in turn, derives from the presumed (and unproved) relationship between the degree of success of the star's most recent picture and his or her performance.

9   The marketing mentality also skews the writing process. To make a point about just this, one of the most successful American scriptwriters, William Goldman, cites in his memoir a pithy line from Joseph Mankiewicz's *The Barefoot Contessa*, which starred Humphrey Bogart and Ava Gardner: "What she's got, you couldn't spell, and what you've got, you *used* to have." In 1954, Goldman argues, that line could be put in the mouth of a minor character, Bogart's wife, but today it would have to be said by one of the stars, or it would be cut from the script: "Giving that line to the wife, in today's movie world, is not just incorrect screenwriting, it is lethal. Today, you must give the star everything."[3] Giving the star everything contributes to the downward spiral by centering movies more and more on the star's bankable presence. In similar moves based on marketing and appealing to base instincts, beautiful women and handsome men are always cast in the leading roles on the assumption that no one will want to gaze at a less than pretty face. When Farrah Fawcett was asked if it was the acting abilities of herself and the two other top

models in starring roles that ensured the success of the television series *Charlie's Angels,* she reportedly replied that it was more likely to have been the fact that none of the women wore brassieres.

10   Classic behavioral psychology experiments have repeatedly demonstrated that when image and sound are presented concurrently, a subject is better able to recall the image than the sound and retains that image in memory for a longer time. Producers seize on this, too, as rationale to get rid of words and to rely only on the visual nature of moving pictures. Where filmmakers err is in assuming that audiences always prefer the visual to the verbal or that film is only visual. There has always been tension between literacy and the visual image in films, but in the talking films of the 1930s and 1940s, dialogue was considered supremely important. The verbal byplay of Nick and Nora Charles in the *Thin Man* series of mystery films was one of its glories; by comparison, the character of the supposedly literate mystery novelist played by Angela Lansbury in *Murder, She Wrote* on television is entirely witless. The notion that a picture is worth a thousand words has wreaked insidious and far-reaching havoc in Hollywood, for now the film and television industries have embraced visual storytelling without pausing to determine which words a picture can or should replace. As most film and videotape editors will readily admit, the ultra-rapid cutting between images best exemplified by MTV videos, which has already taken over commercials and is creeping into all Hollywood feature and television production, is incapable of telling complex or subtle stories; it is most appropriately used in conveying emotional impact. The end result of choosing only pictures to tell stories is products in which rapidly changing images convey information in ways that are often deliberately illogical, disorienting, and surreal.

11   The need for writing good dialogue has been obviated by the producers' belief that audiences prefer physical action to words. Filmmakers are urged to give the audience more and more physical action, fewer and fewer words, and characters who are even less inclined to speech than the audience itself. Sylvester Stallone—more precisely, the roles in which he has achieved his greatest commercial success—is a prime example of the current generation of inarticulate screen heroes who make John Wayne's strong-and-silent cowboys and soldiers seem loquacious by comparison. Stallone's Rocky Balboa and John Rambo, and the appallingly similar characters played by Arnold Schwarzenegger, by Clint Eastwood as Dirty Harry, by Mel Gibson in the *Lethal Weapon* series, by Bruce Willis in the *Die Hard* films, and even by John Travolta in *Saturday Night Fever* or *Pulp Fiction* speak in fragments or incomplete sentences when they voice words at all, and employ a severely stunted, reflexively profane vocabulary. Equally important, they and virtually all the other characters in these films are ignorant of history and make no references to literature, art, or anything else except other recent products of popular culture, such as commercial advertisements. When they have a choice between physical and verbal solutions to a given problem, they unhesitatingly go for the blow. If they have any breath to spare, they accompany it with a wisecrack.

12   To have characters speak lines that are brief, pithy, and memorable is one of the goals of all Hollywood films and the source of the scriptwriter's imperative to

"write short." Never say in ten words what you can get across in five. Linda Seger, a script doctor, gives this advice in *Making a Good Script Great:* After a writer prunes the script so that it focuses mainly on the images and actions of the story, the writer should reexamine what has been removed. "If these sections were long speeches, see if you can reduce the pertinent information to a sentence or two. . . . If some of [the scenes] reveal character through talk, try to find an image or an action you can substitute for the dialogue."[4] The imperative has corollaries, such as never have a character who overexplains, and never continue a scene past a trenchant "button line." William Goldman, the screenwriter of *Butch Cassidy and the Sundance Kid,* a movie well regarded for its quips, quotes in his memoir the scene in which Butch walks up to a modern-looking, heavily barred bank and asks a guard, "What was the matter with the old bank this town used to have? It was beautiful." The guard says that people kept robbing it, and Butch walks off, saying, "That's a small price to pay for beauty." Seventeen years after the movie, Goldman reprints the dialogue in his memoir, and comments:

> I happen not to believe Butch's final retort—I don't think he'd say it and I think it's smart-ass. There's a lot about the screenplay I don't like, the smart-assness just being one of them. I also find that there are too many reversals and that the entire enterprise suffers, on more than one occasion, from a case of the cutes.[5]

13   The idealization of writing short and cute in movies is the logical result of competition with television and its cult of the one-liner, the quotable joke that enlivens situation comedies. Each sitcom character must respond to any comment with a single, snappy, mirth-provoking line; just in case we miss the joke, it is highlighted by a laugh track that reminds us to join in the fun. Let us cheerfully admit that the writing in sitcoms is frequently funny—I myself cannot watch a good sitcom without being often moved to laughter, and neither can you. The problem is that the producer's compulsive need to make the audience chortle at every second or third line is, for the writer, a smotherer of invention. Plot and character development, or the interplay of themes and ideas, must be forgone in the all-consuming quest for the perfect retort.

14   In the era before cable television, the prevailing theory of programming was based on the view that Americans wanted to watch something, few choices were available, and the least objectionable program, or LOP, would be the most widely watched. Now that the menu of viewing choices has been expanded, the LOP has been replaced by the LCD—the lowest common denominator. This principle operates, for example, in the decision to schedule the most sensational made-for-television and feature movies during May and November. In those "sweeps" periods, viewership is measured and ratings are established, and they become the basis for the advertising rates on which the networks' and syndicators' revenues depend. Among the principal ingredients in the offerings made especially for sweeps period are larger than usual doses of violence. Violence is hip right now, and highly commercial. For instance, violence is an accepted sales tool for the breakfast cereals and toys advertised on children's cartoon programs. A recent study by Gerbner and

associates tallied 7.8 violent acts per children's program, or 32 per hour—more such acts per hour than in any other form of programming. The National Coalition on Television Violence says that the leader in showcasing violence is the cable network MTV, with 29 instances of "violent or hostile imagery" per hour, and with one-third of its videos containing some violent elements.[6]

15   A controversy rages over whether depicted violence in entertainment has any direct relationship to the raising of the level of violence in individuals or in society as a whole. What is more relevant to this discussion is the dire effect that the producers' craving for violence has on writers and other creators of entertainment. The creative difficulty lies in the fact that violence is often so visually and emotionally compelling that it tends to overshadow any other dramatic element. When Shakespeare wrote his *Henry V,* he made sure that the battle of Agincourt took place offstage, and he invoked a "muse of fire" to help his audience properly imagine it. In Laurence Olivier's film adaptation of the play, made almost fifty years ago, the battle appears on screen but in a relatively tasteful and limited way; in Kenneth Branagh's much lauded 1992 film version, the battle takes up many minutes, during which Branagh fills the screen with slow-motion shots of swords and spears impaling bodies amid mud and flying gobs of blood and bone—so much detail that the battle sequence nearly overwhelms the original text.

16   Violence takes focus. Violence is more quickly depicted than verbal action, and in films and television, every second counts. Violence obscures plots that make no sense and characters that have no depth. Violence does not require good actors and actresses, or even performers who have good speaking voices. Two other LCD elements are on the rise in commercial broadcasting, overt sex and profanity, and the same charges can be leveled against them: They take focus, serve to obscure silly plots and weak characters, are more easily portrayed, and do not require deft performers.

17   The 1993 fall television season, according to the critic Tom Shales, reflected an "obsession" with sex that "seems to have been cranked up to a new high." Shales reprinted examples of smutty jokes and profanity from pilots he had watched, including bits from such new programs as *Family Album, It Had To Be You,* and *The Trouble With Larry* (CBS); *Daddy Dearest* and *Living Single* (Fox); *The John Larroquette Show* (NBC); and *Grace Under Fire* (ABC).[7] By common consent, the worst offender of the fall 1993 season was not a sitcom but an hour-long drama, *N.Y.P.D. Blue* (ABC), which featured nudity and language previously considered too obscene for prime-time network television. The admired producer Steven Bochco, whose company created the series, told reporters that he had deliberately incorporated those elements because he is in a struggle for viewers with cable television, which runs full-length motion pictures with "adult" content. "I don't think we can at ten o'clock with our hour dramas effectively compete any longer unless we can paint with some of the same colors that you can paint with when you make a movie," he stated.[8] The shock value of the nudity and profanity attracted some viewers and repelled others, but those "colors" were toned down after the first few episodes. Later reviews, which were quite enthusiastic, stressed the series' good stories and believable characters. Indeed, *N.Y.P.D. Blue* has gone on to become a critical and commercial success, and many critics and viewers have wondered why

the creators considered it important in the first place to pander to base instincts. It appears that nudity and profanity were deemed essential at the outset because the creators and the ABC network executives were somehow afraid not to include LCD elements, lest their enterprise fail commercially for lack of them. They were also enamored of the publicity generated by the controversy over the nudity and profanity. Heightening viewer interest through controversy is a well-known tool in the marketer's belt. With these craven (and possibly unnecessary) actions on the part of the creators and the network, the downward regressive cycle took another turn for the worse.

Notes

1. Figures from Anthony R. Pratkanis and Eliot Aronson, *Age of Propaganda*, 1992; Kathleen Hall Jamieson and Karlyn Kohrs Campbell, *The Interplay of Influence*, 1988; Peter M. Nichols, "Home Video" column, *New York Times*, July 30, 1993. *Newsweek*, August 2, 1993, reports that Nielsen Media Research estimates the average daily viewing time for television as six hours and forty-six minutes.
2. See Martin Jay, *The Dialectical Imagination: A History of the Frankfurt School and the Institute of Social Research, 1923–1950*, 1973.
3. William Goldman, *Adventures in the Screen Trade,* 1983.
4. Linda Seger, *Making a Good Script Great,* 1987.
5. Goldman, *Adventures in Screen Trade.*
6. Statistics reported in "Kiddie TV Packs the Most Punch," an Associated Press story in *New York Post*, January 28, 1993, and Don Feder, "MTV = Mindless TV," *New York Post*, April 22, 1993.
7. Tom Shales, "Saturated with Sex," *New York Post,* September 13, 1993.
8. Elizabeth Kolbert, "Not Only Bochco's Uniforms Are Blue," *New York Times;* July 26, 1993.

THINKING CRITICALLY

1. Discuss how Shachtman's opening paragraphs establish the tone and theme for his essay. Is his choice of the story of the novelist-turned-screenwriter an effective way to introduce his topic? Explain.

2. What does "aiming lower" mean for television scripts and language? Does this principle have implications for spoken language as a whole? Why or why not?

3. How does Shachtman's use of the history of television dialogue and language support his argument regarding television today? Are his comparisons relevant? Explain.

4. What is the relationship between the skewed reality depicted on television and the decline of articulate speech? Explain.

5. What is the author advocating in this essay? Who is his audience? Cite specific examples from the text that reveal his assumptions about his audience.

6. What is the connection between advertising and marketing interests and television language? How has advertising influenced scripts and television programming? In your opinion, has advertising had a detrimental influence on television language? Why or why not?

7. In several parts of this essay, the author speaks directly to his readers. Evaluate this writing technique.

WRITING ASSIGNMENTS

1. In this essay, the author explains how television presents viewers with a skewed sense of reality. Write an essay exploring this issue. Should television more accurately depict reality—the people, places, and circumstances of life? What are the possible consequences when television exaggerates reality such as crime? Support your essay with information from the essay and your personal experience.

2. Shachtman compares television dialogue from the past and present. Conduct your own analysis of television language. Watch several television programs from the 1950s or 1960s, and from current offerings. Try to watch programs that deal with similar subject matter, such as family comedies, or detective or crime programs. Has television dialogue and the general use of language changed over the last 40 years? If so, in what ways?

Two-Headed Monsters

From the Columbia Journalism Review

Words are the business of journalism, and accuracy of usage is undoubtedly the pride of any newspaper. Occasionally, however, words may turn against the meaning intended, as is the case when printer's devils plague the presses. The result is news gone askew. Such was the case in the real headlines shown here, in which unforeseen misprints, double entendres, and grammatical goofs turned into news that did not fit the print. The *Columbia Journalism Review,* a watchdog magazine of the media, has a department called "The Lower Case" that gathers such gaffes; these examples were originally reprinted there.

Chinese general donated to Clinton campaign

The Pantagraph (Bloomington-Normal, Ill.) 4/5/99

Death to be explained

Home News Tribune (East Brunswick, N.J.) 4/16/98

Litigant has no right to lay adviser in chambers

London Times 3/8/99

Judge dismisses charges against duck protecting non-hunter

The Knoxville News-Sentinel 2/24/99

Breast implants prominent

The Olathe (Kan.) *Daily News* 2/2/99

Clinton takes credit for drop in unwed birth rate

The Ashland (Ore.) *Daily Tidings* 10/5/96

Shooting witness helps build murder case

The Times (Northwest Ind.) 7/10/98

Experts suggest education standards might be to lofty
The Courier-News (N.J.) 1/25/99

Steamed pudding and crap dip
The Sacramento Beef 12/27/98

FBI adds to reward for killing suspects
The Olympian (Olympia, Wash.) 7/15/98

Socks Lower in Tokyo
The New York Times 8/17/98

Lamb Retiring From USU Animal Department
The Times (Northwest Ind.) 7/10/98

Giant women's health study short of volunteers
Aruba Today (Caribbean) 7/13/97

U.S., Brits agree to bomb trial at Hague
Jefferson City Post-Tribune (Mo.) *Daily News* 08/24/98

Call for Ban on Toys For Tots Made of Vinyl
San Francisco Chronicle 11/20/98

Toxic street residents storm out of public meeting
Daily News (Nanaimo, B.C.) 08/13/98

Doctor discusses his action with infant
Seattle Post-Intelligencer 09/07/98

School testing mushrooms
Marshfield News-Herald (Wis.) 08/25/98

Hitler used to sell potato chips
The New Mexican 6/2/98

Dog rules on agenda in Old Orchard
Portland (Maine) Press Herald 5/18/99

Pope remembers shooting victims

The New World (Chicago) 4/25/99

Mattel recalls eating dolls

The Burlington (Vt.) *Free Press* 1/7/97

UMaine women selling fast in Portland

Morning Sentinel (Waterville, Me.) 12/18/96

Banana faces sodomy charges

The Examiner (Cork, Ireland) 5/9/97

Great night for Trojans

Terra Linda girls on fire

Marin Independent Journal (Calif.) 2/22/96

Man kills himself hours before appearing in court

Richmond Hill-Bryan County News (Ga.) 8/6/97

Will women in combat stop sexual misconduct?

New Holstein (Wis.) *Reporter* 12/19/96

Police patrol vandalized site nearly 40 times

The Orlando Sentinel 4/17/99

9 hammers in home of hooker attack suspect

San Francisco Examiner 10/24/97

MAKING CONNECTIONS

1. Over the course of a week, watch several different local newscasts and consider the ways they support or refute Postman's and Powers' assertions on TV news broadcasts. How are the programs similar and different? How do the programs distinguish themselves from each other? Or do they? How are the stories they present similar or different? Explain.

2. How has bad language infiltrated the film and television industry over the last decade? Using library resources or the Internet, research what laws or codes guided the use of language in the television industry over the last 50 years. How have standards changed over time? Once you have gathered your research, write an essay about which standards or codes seem most appropriate for today's audiences.

3. You are a television news producer who must develop a local news broadcast program for a local network. Conduct a survey on what people want to watch on the television news. Consider your questions carefully. After gathering your information, design your newscast and explain in detail the rationale behind your program's design. How much does your program resemble others already on the air? What distinguishes your program? Or do you rely on popular conventions already in place? Explain.

4. The BBC's "Talking Point" forum invited readers to respond with their personal opinion of bad language on television. Take an informal poll of your own regarding foul language on television and see if your results are similar to the ones posted by the BBC Online, or quite different. Be sure to poll people of different ages, since only asking young people may skew your results. Brainstorm a list of about 10 questions to include in your poll. You may want to ask for information such as: age, sex, and how much television the respondent watches in an average week in addition to the questions about language.

5. Brainstorm a list of shows that seek to "push the envelope" in terms of foul language; watch one or two of these shows, and then write a critique of these programs asserting your personal viewpoint on this issue.

THE LANGUAGE OF ADVERTISING

With These Words, I Can Sell You Anything
William Lutz

In "Politics and the English Language," featured in Chapter 4, George Orwell writes that the "great enemy of clear language is insincerity." To fill the gap "between one's real and one's declared aims," he explains, one simply resorts to inflated language to give importance to the insignificant. Of course, Orwell is talking about the irresponsible habit of government officials who use language to exploit and manipulate. But he could just as well have been talking about the language of advertisers. At least that's the opinion of William Lutz, who assails the linguistic habits of hucksters. In this essay, he alerts readers to the special power of "weasel words"—those familiar and sneaky critters that "appear to say one thing when in fact they say the opposite, or nothing at all."

William Lutz has been called the George Orwell of the 1990s. Chair of the Committee on Public Doublespeak of the National Council of Teachers of English, Lutz edits the *Quarterly Review of Doublespeak*, a magazine dedicated to the eradication of misleading official statements. He also teaches in the English department at Rutgers University. He is the author of *Beyond Nineteen Eighty-Four* (1989), *Doublespeak* (1989), from which this essay is taken, and most recently, *Doublespeak Defined* (1999).

1 One problem advertisers have when they try to convince you that the product they are pushing is really different from other, similar products is that their claims are subject to some laws. Not a lot of laws, but there are some designed to prevent fraudulent or untruthful claims in advertising. Even during the happy years of non-regulation under President Ronald Reagan, the FTC did crack down on the more blatant abuses in advertising claims. Generally speaking, advertisers have to be careful in what they say in their ads, in the claims they make for the products they advertise. Parity claims are safe because they are legal and supported by a number of court decisions. But beyond parity claims there are weasel words.

2   Advertisers use weasel words to appear to be making a claim for a product when in fact they are making no claim at all. Weasel words get their name from the way weasels eat the eggs they find in the nests of other animals. A weasel will make a small hole in the egg, suck out the insides, then place the egg back in the nest. Only when the egg is examined closely is it found to be hollow. That's the way it is with weasel words in advertising: Examine weasel words closely and you'll find that they're as hollow as any egg sucked by a weasel. Weasel words appear to say one thing when in fact they say the opposite, or nothing at all.

"Help"—The Number One Weasel Word

3 The biggest weasel word used in advertising doublespeak is "help." Now "help" only means to aid or assist, nothing more. It does not mean to conquer, stop, eliminate, end, solve, heal, cure, or anything else. But once the ad says "help," it can say just about anything after that because "help" qualifies everything coming after it. The trick is that the claim that comes after the weasel word is usually so strong and so dramatic that you forget the word "help" and concentrate only on the dramatic claim. You read into the ad a message that the ad does not contain. More importantly, the advertiser is not responsible for the claim that you read into the ad, even though the advertiser wrote the ad so you would read that claim into it.

4   The next time you see an ad for a cold medicine that promises that it "helps relieve cold symptoms fast," don't rush out to buy it. Ask yourself what this claim is really saying. Remember, "helps" means only that the medicine will aid or assist. What will it aid or assist in doing? Why, "relieve" your cold "symptoms." "Relieve" only means to ease, alleviate, or mitigate, not to stop, end, or cure. Nor does the claim say how much relieving this medicine will do. Nowhere does this ad claim it will cure anything. In fact, the ad doesn't even claim it will do anything at all. The ad only claims that it will aid in relieving (not curing) your cold symptoms, which are probably a runny nose, watery eyes, and a headache. In other words, this medicine probably contains a standard decongestant and some aspirin. By the way, what does "fast" mean? Ten minutes, one hour, one day? What is fast to one person can be very slow to another. Fast is another weasel word.

5   Ad claims using "help" are among the most popular ads. One says, "Helps keep you young looking," but then a lot of things will help keep you young looking, including exercise, rest, good nutrition, and a facelift. More importantly, this ad doesn't say the product will keep you young, only "young *looking*." Someone may look young to one person and old to another.

6   A toothpaste ad says, "Helps prevent cavities," but it doesn't say it will actually prevent cavities. Brushing your teeth regularly, avoiding sugars in foods, and flossing daily will also help prevent cavities. A liquid cleaner ad says, "Helps keep your home germ free," but it doesn't say it actually kills germs, nor does it even specify which germs it might kill.

7   "Help" is such a useful weasel word that it is often combined with other action-verb weasel words such as "fight" and "control." Consider the claim, "Helps control dandruff symptoms with regular use." What does it really say? It will assist in controlling (not eliminating, stopping, ending, or curing) the *symptoms* of dandruff, not the cause of dandruff nor the dandruff itself. What are the symptoms of

dandruff? The ad deliberately leaves that undefined, but assume that the symptoms referred to in the ad are the flaking and itching commonly associated with dandruff. But just shampooing with *any* shampoo will temporarily eliminate these symptoms, so this shampoo isn't any different from any other. Finally, in order to benefit from this product, you must use it regularly. What is "regular use"—daily, weekly, hourly? Using another shampoo "regularly" will have the same effect. Nowhere does this advertising claim say this particular shampoo stops, eliminates, or cures dandruff. In fact, this claim says nothing at all, thanks to all the weasel words.

8   Look at ads in magazines and newspapers, listen to ads on radio and television, and you'll find the word "help" in ads for all kinds of products. How often do you read or hear such phrases as "helps stop . . . ," "helps overcome . . . ," "helps eliminate . . . ," "helps you feel . . . ," or "helps you look . . . "? If you start looking for this weasel word in advertising, you'll be amazed at how often it occurs. Analyze the claims in the ads using "help," and you will discover that these ads are really saying nothing.

9   There are plenty of other weasel words used in advertising. In fact, there are so many that to list them all would fill the rest of this book. But, in order to identify the doublespeak of advertising and understand the real meaning of an ad, you have to be aware of the most popular weasel words in advertising today.

Virtually Spotless

10 One of the most powerful weasel words is "virtually," a word so innocent that most people don't pay any attention to it when it is used in an advertising claim. But watch out. "Virtually" is used in advertising claims that appear to make specific, definite promises when there is no promise. After all, what does "virtually" mean? It means "in essence of effect, although not in fact." Look at that definition again. "Virtually" means *not in fact*. It does *not* mean "almost" or "just about the same as," or anything else. And before you dismiss all this concern over such a small word, remember that small words can have big consequences.

11   In 1971 a federal court rendered its decision on a case brought by a woman who became pregnant while taking birth control pills. She sued the manufacturer, Eli Lilly and Company, for breach of warranty. The woman lost her case. Basing its ruling on a statement in the pamphlet accompanying the pills, which stated that, "When taken as directed, the tablets offer virtually 100% protection," the court ruled that there was no warranty, expressed or implied, that the pills were absolutely effective. In its ruling, the court pointed out that, according to *Webster's Third New International Dictionary,* "virtually" means "almost entirely" and clearly does not mean "absolute" (*Whittington v. Eli Lilly and Company,* 333 F. Supp. 98). In other words, the Eli Lilly company was really saying that its birth control pill, even when taken as directed, *did not in fact* provide 100 percent protection against pregnancy. But Eli Lilly didn't want to put it that way because then many women might not have bought Lilly's birth control pills.

12   The next time you see the ad that says that this dishwasher detergent "leaves dishes virtually spotless," just remember how advertisers twist the meaning of the weasel word "virtually." You can have lots of spots on your dishes after using this detergent and the ad claim will still be true, because what this claim really means

is that this detergent does not *in fact* leave your dishes spotless. Whenever you see or hear an ad claim that uses the word "virtually," just translate that claim into its real meaning. So the television set that is "virtually trouble free" becomes the television set that is not in fact trouble free, the "virtually foolproof operation" of any appliance becomes an operation that is in fact not foolproof, and the product that "virtually never needs service" becomes the product that is not in fact service free.

New and Improved

13 If "new" is the most frequently used word on a product package, "improved" is the second most frequent. In fact, the two words are almost always used together. It seems just about everything sold these days is "new and improved." The next time you're in the supermarket, try counting the number of times you see these words on products. But you'd better do it while you're walking down just one aisle, otherwise you'll need a calculator to keep track of your counting.

14   Just what do these words mean? The use of the word "new" is restricted by regulations, so an advertiser can't just use the word on a product or in an ad without meeting certain requirements. For example, a product is considered new for about six months during a national advertising campaign. If the product is being advertised only in a limited test market area, the word can be used longer, and in some instances has been used for as long as two years.

15   What makes a product "new"? Some products have been around for a long time, yet every once in a while you discover that they are being advertised as "new." Well, an advertiser can call a product new if there has been "a material functional change" in the product. What is "a material functional change," you ask? Good question. In fact it's such a good question it's being asked all the time. It's up to the manufacturer to prove that the product has undergone such a change. And if the manufacturer isn't challenged on the claim, then there's no one to stop it. Moreover, the change does not have to be an improvement in the product. One manufacturer added an artificial lemon scent to a cleaning product and called it "new and improved," even though the product did not clean any better than without the lemon scent. The manufacturer defended the use of the word "new" on the grounds that the artificial scent changed the chemical formula of the product and therefore constituted "a material functional change."

16   Which brings up the word "improved." When used in advertising, "improved" does not mean "made better." It only means "changed" or "different from before." So, if the detergent maker puts a plastic pour spout on the box of detergent, the product has been "improved," and away we go with a whole new advertising campaign. Or, if the cereal maker adds more fruit or a different kind of fruit to the cereal, there's an improved product. Now you know why manufacturers are constantly making little changes in their products. Whole new advertising campaigns, designed to convince you that the product has been changed for the better, are based on small changes in superficial aspects of a product. The next time you see an ad for an "improved" product, ask yourself what was wrong with the old one. Ask yourself just how "improved" the product is. Finally, you might check to see whether the "improved" version costs more than the unimproved

one. After all, someone has to pay for the millions of dollars spent advertising the improved product.

17   Of course, advertisers really like to run ads that claim a product is "new and improved." While what constitutes a "new" product may be subject to some regulation, "improved" is a subjective judgment. A manufacturer changes the shape of its stick deodorant, but the shape doesn't improve the function of the deodorant. That is, changing the shape doesn't affect the deodorizing ability of the deodorant, so the manufacturer calls it "improved." Another manufacturer adds ammonia to its liquid cleaner and calls it "new and improved." Since adding ammonia does affect the cleaning ability of the product, there has been a "material functional change" in the product, and the manufacturer can now call its cleaner "new," and "improved" as well. Now the weasel words "new and improved" are plastered all over the package and are the basis for a multimillion-dollar ad campaign. But after six months the word "new" will have to go, until someone can dream up another change in the product. Perhaps it will be adding color to the liquid, or changing the shape of the package, or maybe adding a new dripless pour spout, or perhaps a ——————. The "improvements" are endless, and so are the new advertising claims and campaigns.

18   "New" is just too useful and powerful a word in advertising for advertisers to pass it up easily. So they use weasel words that say "new" without really saying it. One of their favorites is "introducing," as in, "Introducing improved Tide," or "Introducing the stain remover." The first is simply saying, here's our improved soap: the second, here's our new advertising campaign for our detergent. Another favorite is "now," as in, "Now there's Sinex," which simply means that Sinex is available. Then there are phrases like "Today's Chevrolet," "Presenting Dristan," and "A fresh way to start the day." The list is really endless because advertisers are always finding new ways to say "new" without really saying it. If there is a second edition of this book, I'll just call it the "new and improved" edition. Wouldn't you really rather have a "new and improved" edition of this book rather than a "second" edition?

Acts Fast

19   "Acts" and "works" are two popular weasel words in advertising because they bring action to the product and to the advertising claim. When you see the ad for the cough syrup that "Acts on the cough control center," ask yourself what this cough syrup is claiming to do. Well, it's just claiming to "act," to do something, to perform an action. What is it that the cough syrup does? The ad doesn't say. It only claims to perform an action or do something on your "cough control center." By the way, what and where is your "cough control center"? I don't remember learning about that part of the body in human biology class.

20   Ads that use such phrases as "acts fast," "acts against," "acts to prevent," and the like are saying essentially nothing, because "act" is a word empty of any specific meaning. The ads are always careful not to specify exactly what "act" the product performs. Just because a brand of aspirin claims to "act fast" for headache relief doesn't mean this aspirin is any better than any other aspirin. What is the "act" that this aspirin performs? You're never told. Maybe it just dissolves quickly. Since aspirin is a parity product, all aspirin is the same and therefore functions the same.

Works Like Anything Else

21 If you don't find the word "acts" in an ad, you will probably find the weasel word "works." In fact, the two words are almost interchangeable in advertising. Watch out for ads that say a product "works against," "works like," "works for," or "works longer." As with "acts," "works" is the same meaningless verb used to make you think that this product really does something, and maybe even something special or unique. But "works," like "acts," is basically a word empty of any specific meaning.

Like Magic

22 Whenever advertisers want you to stop thinking about the product and to start thinking about something bigger, better, or more attractive than the product, they use that very popular weasel word, "like." The word "like" is the advertiser's equivalent of a magician's use of misdirection. "Like" gets you to ignore the product and concentrate on the claim the advertiser is making about it. "For skin like peaches and cream" claims the ad for a skin cream. What is this ad really claiming? It doesn't say this cream will give you peaches-and-cream skin. There is no verb in this claim, so it doesn't even mention using the product. How is skin ever like "peaches and cream"? Remember, ads must be read literally and exactly, according to the dictionary definition of words. (Remember "virtually" in the Eli Lilly case.) The ad is making absolutely no promise or claim whatsoever for this skin cream. If you think this cream will give you soft, smooth, youthful-looking skin, you are the one who has read that meaning into the ad.

23   The wine that claims "It's like taking a trip to France" wants you to think about a romantic evening in Paris as you walk along the boulevard after a wonderful meal in an intimate little bistro. Of course, you don't really believe that a wine can take you to France, but the goal of the ad is to get you to think pleasant, romantic thoughts about France and not about how the wine tastes or how expensive it may be. That little word "like" has taken you away from crushed grapes into a world of your own imaginative making. Who knows, maybe the next time you buy wine, you'll think those pleasant thoughts when you see this brand of wine, and you'll buy it. Or, maybe you weren't even thinking about buying wine at all, but now you just might pick up a bottle the next time you're shopping. Ah, the power of "like" in advertising.

24   How about the most famous "like" claim of all, "Winston tastes good like a cigarette should"? Ignoring the grammatical error here, you might want to know what this claim is saying. Whether a cigarette tastes good or bad is a subjective judgment because what tastes good to one person may well taste horrible to another. Not everyone likes fried snails, even if they are called escargot. (*De gustibus non est disputandum*, which was probably the Roman rule for advertising as well as for defending the games in the Colosseum.) There are many people who say all cigarettes taste terrible, other people who say only some cigarettes taste all right, and still others who say all cigarettes taste good. Who's right? Everyone, because taste is a matter of personal judgment.

25   Moreover, note the use of the conditional, "should." The complete claim is, "Winston tastes good like a cigarette should taste." But should cigarettes taste good? Again, this is a matter of personal judgment and probably depends most on one's experiences with smoking. So, the Winston ad is simply saying that Winston cigarettes are just like any other cigarette: Some people like them and some people don't. On that statement R. J. Reynolds conducted a very successful multimillion-dollar advertising campaign that helped keep Winston the number-two-selling cigarette in the United States, close behind number one, Marlboro.

Can It Be Up to the Claim

26 Analyzing ads for doublespeak requires that you pay attention to every word in the ad and determine what each word really means. Advertisers try to wrap their claims in language that sound concrete, specific, and objective, when in fact the language of advertising is anything but. Your job is to read carefully and listen critically so that when the announcer says that "Crest can be of significant value . . ." you know immediately that this claim says absolutely nothing. Where is the doublespeak in this ad? Start with the second word.

27   Once again, you have to look at what words really mean, not what you think they mean or what the advertiser wants you to think they mean. The ad for Crest only says that using Crest "can be" of "significant value." What really throws you off in this ad is the brilliant use of "significant." It draws your attention to the word "value" and makes you forget that the ad only claims that Crest "can be." The ad doesn't say that Crest *is* of value, only that it is "able" or "possible" to be of value, because that's all that "can" means.

28   It's so easy to miss the importance of those little words, "can be." Almost as easy as missing the importance of the words "up to" in an ad. These words are very popular in sale ads. You know, the ones that say, "Up to 50% Off!" Now, what does that claim mean? Not much, because the store or manufacturer has to reduce the price of only a few items by 50 percent. Everything else can be reduced a lot less, or not even reduced. Moreover, don't you want to know 50 percent off of what? Is it 50 percent off the "manufacturer's suggested list price," which is the highest possible price? Was the price artificially inflated and then reduced? In other ads, "up to" expresses an ideal situation. The medicine that works "up to ten times faster," the battery that lasts "up to twice as long," and the soap that gets you "up to twice as clean" all are based on ideal situations for using those products, situations in which you can be sure you will never find yourself.

Unfinished Words

29 Unfinished words are a kind of "up to" claim in advertising. The claim that a battery lasts "up to twice as long" usually doesn't finish the comparison—twice as long as what? A birthday candle? A tank of gas? A cheap battery made in a country not noted for its technological achievements? The implication is that the battery lasts twice as long as batteries made by other battery makers, or twice as long as earlier model batteries made by the advertiser, but the ad doesn't really make these

claims. You read these claims into the ad, aided by the visual images the advertiser so carefully provides.

30   Unfinished words depend on you to finish them, to provide the words the advertisers so thoughtfully left out of the ad. Pall Mall cigarettes were once advertised as "A longer, finer and milder smoke." The question is, longer, finer, and milder than what? The aspirin that claims it contains "Twice as much of the pain reliever doctors recommend most" doesn't tell you what pain reliever it contains twice as much of. (By the way, it's aspirin. That's right; it just contains twice the amount of aspirin. And how much is twice the amount? Twice of what amount?) Panadol boasts that "nobody reduces fever faster," but, since Panadol is a parity product, this claim simply means that Panadol isn't any better than any other product in its parity class. "You can be sure if it's Westinghouse," you're told, but just exactly what it is you can be sure of is never mentioned. "Magnavox gives you more" doesn't tell you what you get more of. More value? More television? More than they gave you before? It sounds nice, but it means nothing, until you fill in the claim with your own words, the words the advertisers didn't use. Since each of us fills in the claim differently, the ad and the product can become all things to all people, and not promise a single thing.

31   Unfinished words abound in advertising because they appear to promise so much. More importantly, they can be joined with powerful visual images on television to appear to be making significant promises about a product's effectiveness without really making any promises. In a television ad, the aspirin product that claims fast relief can show a person with a headache taking the product and then, in what appears to be a matter of minutes, claiming complete relief. This visual image is far more powerful than any claim made in unfinished words. Indeed, the visual image completes the unfinished words for you, filling in with pictures what the words leave out. And you thought that ads didn't affect you. What brand of aspirin do you use?

32   Some years ago, Ford's advertisements proclaimed "Ford LTD—700% quieter." Now, what do you think Ford was claiming with these unfinished words? What was the Ford LTD quieter than? A Cadillac? A Mercedes Benz? A BMW? Well, when the FTC asked Ford to substantiate this unfinished claim, Ford replied that it meant that the inside of the LTD was 700% quieter than the outside. How did you finish those unfinished words when you first read them? Did you even come close to Ford's meaning?

Combining Weasel Words

33 A lot of ads don't fall neatly into one category or another because they use a variety of different devices and words. Different weasel words are often combined to make an ad claim. The claim, "Coffee-Mate gives coffee more body, more flavor," uses Unfinished Words ("more" than what?) and also uses words that have no specific meaning ("body" and "flavor"). Along with "taste" (remember the Winston ad and its claim to taste good), "body" and "flavor" mean nothing because their meaning is entirely subjective. To you, "body" in coffee might mean thick, black, almost bitter coffee, while I might take it to mean a light brown, delicate coffee. Now, if you

think you understood that last sentence, read it again, because it said nothing of objective value; it was filled with weasel words of no specific meaning: "thick," "black," "bitter," "light brown," and "delicate." Each of those words has no specific, objective meaning, because each of us can interpret them differently.

34   Try this slogan: "Looks, smells, tastes like ground-roast coffee." So, are you now going to buy Taster's Choice instant coffee because of this ad? "Looks," "smells," and "tastes" are all words with no specific meaning and depend on your interpretation of them for any meaning. Then there's that great weasel word "like," which simply suggests a comparison but does not make the actual connection between the product and the quality. Besides, do you know what "ground-roast" coffee is? I don't, but it sure sounds good. So, out of seven words in this ad, four are definite weasel words, two are quite meaningless, and only one has any clear meaning.

35   Remember the Anacin ad—"Twice as much of the pain reliever doctors recommend most"? There's a whole lot of weaseling going on in this ad. First, what's the pain reliever they're talking about in this ad? Aspirin, of course. In fact, any time you see or hear an ad using those words "pain reliever," you can automatically substitute the word "aspirin" for them. (Makers of acetaminophen and ibuprofen pain relievers are careful in their advertising to identify their products as nonaspirin products.) So, now we know that Anacin has aspirin in it. Moreover, we know that Anacin has twice as much aspirin in it, but we don't know twice as much as what. Does it have twice as much aspirin as an ordinary aspirin tablet? If so, what is an ordinary aspirin tablet, and how much aspirin does it contain? Twice as much as Excedrin or Bufferin? Twice as much as a chocolate chip cookie? Remember those Unfinished Words and how they lead you on without saying anything.

36   Finally, what about those doctors who are doing all that recommending? Who are they? How many of them are there? What kind of doctors are they? What are their qualifications? Who asked them about recommending pain relievers? What other pain relievers did they recommend? And there are a whole lot more questions about this "poll" of doctors to which I'd like to know the answers, but you get the point. Sometimes, when I call my doctor, she tells me to take two aspirin and call her office in the morning. Is that where Anacin got this ad?

Read the Label, or the Brochure

37 Weasel words aren't just found on television, on the radio, or in newspaper and magazine ads. Just about any language associated with a product will contain the doublespeak of advertising. Remember the Eli Lilly case and the doublespeak on the information sheet that came with the birth control pills. Here's another example.

38   In 1983, the Estée Lauder cosmetics company announced a new product called "Night Repair." A small brochure distributed with the product stated that "Night Repair was scientifically formulated in Estée Lauder's U.S. laboratories as part of the Swiss Age-Controlling Skincare Program. Although only nature controls the aging process, this program helps control the signs of aging and encourages skin to

look and feel younger." You might want to read these two sentences again, because they sound great but say nothing.

39   First, note that the product was "scientifically formulated" in the company's laboratories. What does that mean? What constitutes a scientific formulation? You wouldn't expect the company to say that the product was casually, mechanically, or carelessly formulated, or just thrown together one day when the people in the white coats didn't have anything better to do. But the word "scientifically" lends an air of precision and promise that just isn't there.

40   It is the second sentence, however, that's really weasely, both syntactically and semantically. The only factual part of this sentence is the introductory dependent clause—"only nature controls the aging process." Thus, the only fact in the ad is relegated to a dependent clause, a clause dependent on the main clause, which contains no factual or definite information at all and indeed purports to contradict the independent clause. The new "skincare program" (notice it's not a skin cream but a "program") does not claim to stop or even retard the aging process. What, then, does Night Repair, at a price of over $35 (in 1983 dollars) for a .87-ounce bottle do? According to this brochure, nothing. It only "helps," and the brochure does not say how much it helps. Moreover, it only "helps control," and then it only helps control the "*signs* of aging," not the aging itself. Also, it "encourages" skin not to *be* younger but only to "look and feel" younger. The brochure does not say younger than what. Of the sixteen words in the main clause of this second sentence, nine are weasel words. So, before you spend all that money for Night Repair, or any other cosmetic product, read the words carefully, and then decide if you're getting what you think you're paying for.

Other Tricks of the Trade

41 Advertisers' use of doublespeak is endless. The best way advertisers can make something out of nothing is through words. Although there are a lot of visual images used on television and in magazines and newspapers, every advertiser wants to create that memorable line that will stick in the public consciousness. I am sure pure joy reigned in one advertising agency when a study found that children who were asked to spell the word "relief" promptly and proudly responded "r-o-l-a-i-d-s."

42   The variations, combinations, and permutations of doublespeak used in advertising go on and on, running from the use of rhetorical questions ("Wouldn't you really rather have a Buick?" "If you can't trust Prestone, who can you trust?") to flattering you with compliments ("The lady has taste." "We think a cigar smoker is someone special." "You've come a long way baby."). You know, of course, how you're *supposed* to answer those questions, and you know that those compliments are just leading up to the sales pitches for the products. Before you dismiss such tricks of the trade as obvious, however, just remember that all of these statements and questions were part of very successful advertising campaigns.

43   A more subtle approach is the ad that proclaims a supposedly unique quality for a product, a quality that really isn't unique. "If it doesn't say Goodyear, it can't be polyglas." Sounds good, doesn't it? Polyglas is available only from Goodyear because Goodyear copyrighted that trade name. Any other tire manufacturer could

make exactly the same tire but could not call it "polyglas," because that would be copyright infringement. "Polyglas" is simply Goodyear's name for its fiberglass-reinforced tire.

44   Since we like to think of ourselves as living in a technologically advanced country, science and technology have a great appeal in selling products. Advertisers are quick to use scientific doublespeak to push their products. There are all kinds of elixirs, additives, scientific potions, and mysterious mixtures added to all kinds of products. Gasoline contains "HTA," "F–130," "Platformate," and other chemical-sounding additives, but nowhere does an advertisement give any real information about the additive.

45   Shampoo, deodorant, mouthwash, cold medicine, sleeping pills, and any number of other products all seem to contain some special chemical ingredient that allows them to work wonders. "Certs contains a sparkling drop of Retsyn." So what? What's "Retsyn"? What's it do? What's so special about it? When they don't have a secret ingredient in their product, advertisers still find a way to claim scientific validity. There's "Sinarest. Created by a research scientist who actually gets sinus headaches." Sounds nice, but what kind of research does this scientist do? How do you know if she is any kind of expert on sinus medicine? Besides, this ad doesn't tell you a thing about the medicine itself and what it does.

Advertising Doublespeak Quick Quiz

46 Now it's time to test your awareness of advertising doublespeak. (You didn't think I would just let you read this and forget it, did you?) The following is a list of statements from some recent ads. Your job is to figure out what each of these ads really says:

> DOMINO'S PIZZA: "Because nobody delivers better."
> TUMS: "The stronger acid neutralizer."
> LISTERMINT: "Making your mouth a cleaner place."
> CASCADE: "For virtually spotless dishes nothing beats Cascade."
> NUPRIN: "Little. Yellow. Different. Better."
> ANACIN: "Better relief."
> SUDAFED: "Fast sinus relief that won't put you fast asleep."
> ADVIL: "Advanced medicine for pain."
> PONDS COLD CREAM: "Ponds cleans like no soap can."
> MILLER LITE BEER: "Tastes great. Less filling."
> PHILIPS MILK OF MAGNESIA: "Nobody treats you better than MOM (Philips Milk of Magnesia)."
> BAYER: "The wonder drug that works wonders."
> CRACKER BARREL: "Judged to be the best."
> KNORR: "Where taste is everything."
> ANUSOL: "Anusol is the word to remember for relief."
> DIMETAPP: "It relieves kids as well as colds."
> LIQUID DRANO: "The liquid strong enough to be called Dra–no."
> JOHNSON & JOHNSON BABY POWDER: "Like magic for your skin."
> PURITAN: "Make it your oil for life."

PAM: "Pam, because how you cook is as important as what you cook."
IVORY SHAMPOO AND CONDITIONER: "Leave your hair feeling Ivory
clean."
TYLENOL: "Stop. Think. Tylenol."
ALKA-SELTZER PLUS: "Fast, effective relief for winter colds."

The World of Advertising

47 In the world of advertising, people wear "dentures," not false teeth; they suffer from "occasional irregularity," not constipation; they need deodorants for their "nervous wetness," not for sweat; they use "bathroom tissue," not toilet paper; and they don't dye their hair, they "tint" or "rinse" it. Advertisements offer "real counterfeit diamonds" without the slightest hint of embarrassment, or boast of goods made out of "genuine imitation leather" or "virgin vinyl."

48 In the world of advertising, the girdle becomes a "body shaper," "form persuader," "control garment," "controller," "outerwear enhancer," "body garment," or "anti-gravity panties," and is sold with such trade names as "The Instead," "The Free Spirit," and "The Body Briefer."

49 A study some years ago found the following words to be among the most popular used in U.S. television advertisements: "new," "improved," "better," "extra," "fresh," "clean," "beautiful," "free," "good," "great," and "light." At the same time, the following words were found to be among the most frequent on British television: "new," "good-better-best," "free," "fresh," "delicious," "full," "sure," "clean," "wonderful," and "special." While these words may occur most frequently in ads, and while ads may be filled with weasel words, you have to watch out for all the words used in advertising, not just the words mentioned here.

50 Every word in an ad is there for a reason; no word is wasted. Your job is to figure out exactly what each word is doing in an ad—what each word really means, not what the advertiser wants you to think it means. Remember, the ad is trying to get you to buy a product, so it will put the product in the best possible light, using any device, trick, or means legally allowed. Your only defense against advertising (besides taking up permanent residence on the moon) is to develop and use a strong critical reading, listening, and looking ability. Always ask yourself what the ad is really saying. When you see ads on television, don't be misled by the pictures, the visual images. What does the ad *say* about the product? What does the ad *not* say? What information is missing from the ad? Only by becoming an active, critical consumer of the doublespeak of advertising will you ever be able to cut through the doublespeak and discover what the ad is really saying.

THINKING CRITICALLY

1. How did *weasel words* get their name? Does it sound like an appropriate label? Why, according to Lutz, do advertisers use them?

2. What regulations restrict the use of the word *new*? How can these regulations be sidestepped according to the author? In your opinion, do these regulations serve the interests of the advertiser or the consumer?

3. Do you think that most people fail to comprehend how advertising works on them? When you read or watch ads, do you see through the gimmicks and weasel words?

4. Take a look at Lutz's Doublespeak Quick Quiz on pages 409–410. Select five items and write a language analysis explaining what the ad really says.

5. According to the author, how can consumers protect themselves against weasel words?

6. The author uses "you" throughout the article. Do you find the use of the second person stylistically satisfying? Do you think it is appropriate for the article?

7. What do you think of Lutz's writing style? Is it humorous? informal? academic? What strategies does he use to involve the reader in the piece?

WRITING ASSIGNMENTS

1. The essays in this section deal with advertising language and its effects on consumers and their value systems. Describe how understanding the linguistic strategies of advertisers—as exemplified here by Lutz—will or will not change your reaction to advertising.

2. As Lutz suggests, look at some ads in a magazine and newspaper (or television and radio commercials). Then make a list of all uses of "help" you find over a 24-hour period. Examine the ads to determine exactly what is said and what the unwary consumer thinks is being said. Write up your report.

3. Invent a product and have some fun writing an ad for it. Use as many weasel words as you can to make your product shine.

4. Undertake a research project on theories of advertising. Find books by professional advertisers or texts for courses in advertising and marketing. Then go through them trying to determine how they might view Lutz's interpretation of advertising techniques. How would the authors view Lutz's claim that advertising language is loaded with "weasel words"?

The Language of Advertising
Charles A. O'Neill

Taking the minority opinion is a former advertising executive Charles A. O'Neill, who disputes the criticism of advertising language by William Lutz and other critics of advertising. While admitting to some of the craftiness of his profession, O'Neill defends the huckster's language—both verbal and visual–against claims that it debases reality and the values of the consumer. Examining some familiar television commercials and recent print ads, he explains why the language may be seductive but far from brainwashing.

This essay, originally written for *Exploring Language,* has been updated for this text. Charles O'Neill is an independent marketing consultant.

1   In 1957, a short dozen years after World War II, many people had good reason to be concerned about Science. On the one hand, giant American corporations offered the promise of "Better Living Through Chemistry." Labs and factories in the U.S. and abroad turned out new "miracle" fabrics, vaccines, and building materials.

Radar and other innovative technology developed during the War had found important applications in the fast-growing, surging crest of consumer-centric, late 1950s America.

2   But World War II American Science had also yielded The Bomb. Specialists working in a secret desert laboratory had figured out how to translate the theoretical work of Dr. Einstein, and others, into weapons that did exactly what they were intended to do, incinerating hundreds of thousands of civilian Japanese men, women and children in the process. The USSR and the USA were locked in an arms race. Americans were told the Soviets held the advantage. Many families built bomb shelters in the yard, and millions of school children learned to "Duck and Cover."

3   So when Vance Packard wrote a book about a dark alliance of social scientists with product marketers and advertisers, an alliance forged in order to gain a better understanding of "people's subsurface desires, needs, and drives," to "find their points of vulnerability," he struck a resonant chord. The scientists who had brought us the weapons that helped win the war had now, apparently, turned their sights on the emerging consumer society. By applying the principles of laboratory experimentation and scientific reasoning to learn about the fears, habits and aspirations of John and Mary Public, they would help businesses create products whose sales would be fueled by ever-more powerful advertising. In the view of Virginia Postrel, (writing in the *Wall Street Journal* in August 1999), the book "envisions consumers as passive dupes who never catch on even to the most obvious manipulations." Among many examples cited, Mr. Packard noted that what he called "depth probers" had learned that "fear of stern bankers was driving borrowers to more expensive loan companies. Banks began training their employees to be nice so as to attract more business." We were led to believe the banker's smile was a form of manipulation, a contrived courtesy. The book was itself a bestseller.

4   In fairness to Mr. Packard, the decade of the 1950s did offer numerous examples of consumer excess. Cars from the era sported tail fins stretched to new extremes, for no aerodynamic or practical purpose. And it is impossible to miss the overtly sexual reference in the jutting chrome bumpers of the era's most flamboyant road machines. The story of manufactured excess could be extended through all product categories. Of course, it could also be extended through all decades, including our own. Just as Mr. Packard's book so well reflected the uncertainty and angst of the times, cars and other products reflected American popular culture—a world in which jet planes and the race to space dominated headlines. It was also a world in which Big was best, in starlets as well as the family car.

5   Mr. Packard is certainly not alone as a critic of advertising. Every decade has brought a new generation of critics. We recognize the legitimacy—even the value— of advertising, but on some level we can't quite fully embrace it as a "normal" part of our experience. At best, we view it as distracting. At worst, we view it as dangerous to our health and a pernicious threat to our social values. Also lending moral support to the debate about advertising is no less an authority than the Vatican. In 1997, the Vatican issued a document prepared by the Pontifical Council, titled "Ethics in Advertising." Along with acknowledgment of the positive contribution of advertising (e.g., provides information, supports worthy causes, encourages competition and innovation), the report states, as reported by the *Boston Globe*, "In the competition to attract ever larger audiences . . . communicators can find themselves

pressured . . . to set aside high artistic and moral standards and lapse into superficiality, tawdriness and moral squalor."

How does advertising work? Why is it so powerful? Why does it raise such concern? What case can be made for and against the advertising business? In order to understand advertising, you must accept that it is not about truth, virtue, love, or positive social values. It is about money. Ads play a role in moving customers through the sales process. This process begins with an effort to build awareness of a product, typically achieved by tactics designed to break through the clutter of competitive messages. By presenting a description of product benefits, ads convince the customer to buy the product. Once prospects have become purchasers, advertising is used to sustain brand loyalty, reminding customers of all the good reasons for their original decision to buy.

6   But this does not sufficiently explain the ultimate, unique power of advertising. Whatever the product or creative strategy, advertisements derive their power from a purposeful, directed combination of images. Images can take the form of words, sounds, or visuals, used individually or together. The combination of images is the language of advertising, a language unlike any other.

7   Everyone who grows up in the Western world soon learns that advertising language is different from other languages. We may have forgotten the sponsors, but we certainly know these popular slogans "sound like ads."

"Where's the Beef?" (Wendy's restaurants, 1984)
"Please, Don't Squeeze the Charmin." (Charmin bathroom tissue, 1964)
"I Can't Believe I Ate the Whole Thing." (Alka-Seltzer, 1977)
"M'm! M'm! Good!" (Campbell's Soup, 1950)
"I've Fallen, and I Can't Get Up!" (Lifecall, 1990)

Edited and Purposeful

8   In his book, *Future Shock,* Alvin Toffler described various types of messages we receive from the world around us each day. Much of normal, human experience is merely sensory, "not designed by anyone to communicate anything." In contrast, the language of advertising is carefully engineered, ruthlessly purposeful. Advertising messages have a clear purpose; they are intended to trigger a specific response.

9   The response may be as utterly simple as "Say, I *am* hungry. Let's pull right on up to the drive-through window and order a big, juicy Wendy's burger, fast!"

10   In the case of some advertising, our reactions may be more complex. In 1964, the Doyle Dane Bernbach agency devised an elegantly simple television ad for President Lyndon Johnson's campaign against his Republican challenger, Barry Goldwater. A pretty young girl is shown picking petals from a daisy, against the background of a countdown. The ad ends with the sound of an explosion. This ad, ranked number 20, among *TV Guide*'s assessment of the 50 greatest TV commercials of all time, was broadcast once, but it had succeeded in underscoring many voters' greatest fear: a vote for the GOP was a vote for nuclear war; a vote for Johnson was a vote for peace. The ad's overwhelming, negative message was too much even for President Johnson, who ordered it replaced.

11   This short TV spot reached well beyond hunger—"Fast food—yummy!"—into a far more sacred place: "Honey, they want to kill our kids!"

Rich and Arresting

12 Advertisements—no matter how carefully "engineered"—cannot succeed unless they capture our attention. Of the hundreds of advertising messages in store for us each day, very few will actually command our conscious attention. The rest are screened out. The people who design and write ads know about this screening process; they anticipate and accept it as a premise of their business.

13 The classic, all-time favorite device used to breach the barrier is sex. The desire to be sexually attracted to others is an ancient instinct, and few drives are more powerful. A magazine ad for Ultima II, a line of cosmetics, invites readers to "find everything you need for the sexxxxiest look around . . ." The ad goes on to offer other "Sexxxy goodies," including "Lipsexxxxy lip color, naked eye color . . . Sunsexxxy liquid bronzer." No one will accuse Ultima's marketing tacticians of subtlety. In fact, this ad is merely a current example of an approach that is as old as advertising. After countless years of using images of women in various stages of undress to sell products, ads are now displaying men's bodies as well. A magazine ad for Brut, a men's cologne, declares in bold letters, "MEN ARE BACK"; in the background, a photograph shows a muscular, shirtless young man preparing to enter the boxing ring—a "manly" image indeed; an image of man as breeding stock.

14 Every successful advertisement uses a creative strategy based on an idea that will attract and hold the attention of the targeted consumer audience. The strategy may include strong creative execution or a straightforward presentation of product features and customer benefits.

15 Even if the text contains no incongruity and does not rely on a pun for its impact, ads typically use a creative strategy based on some striking concept or idea. In fact, the concept and execution are often so good that many successful ads entertain while they sell.

16 Consider, for example, the campaigns created for Federal Express. A campaign was developed to position Federal Express as the company that would deliver packages, not just "overnight," but "by 10:30 A.M." the next day. The plight of the junior executive in "Presentation," one early TV ad in the campaign, is stretched for dramatic purposes, but it is, nonetheless, all too real: The young executive, who is presumably to try to climb his way up the corporate ladder, is shown calling another parcel delivery service and all but begging for assurance that he will have his slides in hand by 10:30 the next morning. "No slides, no presentation," he pleads. Only a viewer with a heart of stone can watch without feeling sympathetic as the next morning our junior executive struggles to make his presentation sans slides. He is so lost without them that he is reduced to using his hands to perform imitations of birds and animals in the shadows on the movie screen. What does the junior executive viewer think when he or she sees the ad?

1. Federal Express guarantees to deliver packages "absolutely, positively overnight."

2. Federal Express packages arrived early in the day.

3. What happened to that fellow in the commercial will absolutely not happen to me, now that I know what package delivery service to call.

A sound, creative strategy supporting an innovative service idea sold Federal Express.

17   Soft drink and fast-food companies often take another approach. "Slice of life" ads (so-called because they purport to show people in "real-life" situations) created to sell Coke or Pepsi have often placed their characters in Fourth of July parades or other family events. The archetypical version of this ad is filled-to-overflowing with babies frolicking with puppies in the sunlit foreground while their youthful parents play touch football. On the porch, Grandma and Pops are seen quietly smiling as they wait for all of this affection to transform itself in a climax of warmth, harmony, and joy. In part, these ads work through repetition: How-many-times-can-you-spot-the-logo-in-this-commercial?

18   These ads seduce us into feeling that if we drink the right combination of sugar, preservatives, caramel coloring, and secret ingredients, we'll join the crowd that—in the words of Coca-Cola's ad from 1971—will help "teach the world to sing . . . in perfect harmony." A masterstroke of advertising cemented the impression that Coke was hip: not only an American brand, but a product and brand for all peace-loving peoples everywhere!

19   If you don't buy this version of the American Dream, search long enough and you are sure to find an ad designed to sell you what it takes to gain prestige within whatever posse you do happen to run with. As reported by the *Boston Globe*, "the malt liquor industry relies heavily on rap stars in delivering its message to inner-city youths, while Black Death Vodka, which features a top hatted skull and a coffin on its label, has been using Guns N' Roses guitarist Slash to endorse the product in magazine advertising." A malt liquor company reportedly promotes its 40-ounce size with rapper King T singing, "I usually drink it when I'm just out clowning, me and the home boys, you know, be like downing it . . . I grab me a 40 when I want to act a fool." A recent ad for Sasson jeans is a long way from Black Death in execution, but a second cousin in spirit. A photograph of a young, blonde (they do have more fun, right?) actress appears with this text: "Baywatch actress Gene Lee Nolin Puts On Sasson. OOLA-LA. Sasson. Don't put it on unless it's Sasson."

20   Ads do not often emerge like Botticelli's Venus from the sea, flawless and fully grown. Most often, the creative strategy is developed only after extensive research. "Who will be interested in our product? How old are they? Where do they live? How much money do they earn? What problem will our product solve?" Answers to these questions provide the foundation on which the creative strategy is built.

Involving

21   We have seen that the language of advertising is carefully engineered; we have discovered a few of the devices it uses to get our attention. Coke and Pepsi have caught our eye with visions of peace and love. An actress offers a winsome smile. Now that they have our attention, advertisers present information intended to show us that their product fills a need and differs from the competition. It is the copywriter's responsibility to express, exploit, and intensify such product differences.

22   When product differences do not exist, the writer must glamorize the superficial differences—for example, differences in packaging. As long as the ad is trying to get our attention, the "action" is mostly in the ad itself, in the words and visual images. But as we read an ad or watch it on television, we become more deeply involved. The action starts to take place in us. Our imagination is set in motion, and

our individual fears and aspirations, quirks, and insecurities, superimpose themselves on that tightly engineered, attractively packaged message.

23   Consider, once again, the running battle among the low-calorie soft drinks. The
cola wars have spawned many "look-alike" advertisements, because the product
features and consumer benefits are generic, applying to all products in the category.
Substitute one cola brand name for another, and the messages are often identical,
right down to the way the cans are photographed in the closing sequence. This strategy relies upon mass saturation and exposure for impact.

24   Some companies have set themselves apart from their competitors by making
use of bold, even disturbing, themes and images. For example, it was not uncommon not long ago for advertisers in the fashion industry to make use of gaunt,
languid models—models who, in the interpretation of some observers, displayed a
certain form of "heroin chic." Something was most certainly unusual about the
models appearing in ads for Prada and Calvin Klein products. A young woman in a
Prada ad projects no emotion whatsoever; she is hunched forward, her posture suggesting that she is in a trance or drug-induced stupor. In a Calvin Klein ad, a young
man, like the woman in the Prada ad, is gaunt beyond reason. He is shirtless. As if
to draw more attention to his peculiar posture and "zero body fat" status, he is
shown pinching the skin next to his navel. One well-recognized observer of public
morality, President Clinton, commented on the increasing use of heroin on college
campuses, noting that "part of this has to do with the images that are finding their
way to our young people." One industry maven agreed, asserting that "people got
carried away by the glamour of decadence."

25   Do such advertisers as Prada and Calvin Klein bear responsibility—morally, if
not legally—for the rise of heroin use on college campuses? Does "heroin chic" and
its depiction of a decadent lifestyle exploit certain elements of our society—the
young and clueless, for example? Or did these ads, and others of their ilk, simply
reflect profound bad taste? In fact, on one level, all advertising is about exploitation: the systematic, deliberate identification of our needs and wants, followed by
the delivery of a carefully constructed promise that Brand X will satisfy them.

26   Symbols offer an important tool for involving consumers in advertisements.
Symbols have become important elements in the language of advertising, not so
much because they carry meanings of their own, but because we bring meaning to
them. One example is provided by the campaign begun in 1978 by Somerset Importers for Johnnie Walker Red Scotch. Sales of Johnnie Walker Red had been trailing sales of Johnnie Walker Black, and Somerset Importers needed to position Red
as a fine product in its own right. Their agency produced ads that made heavy use of
the color red. One magazine ad, often printed as a two-page spread, is dominated by
a close-up photo of red autumn leaves. At lower right, the copy reads, "When their
work is done, even the leaves turn to Red." Another ad—also suitably dominated by
a photograph in the appropriate color—reads: "When it's time to quiet down at the
end of the day, even a fire turns to Red." Red. Warm. Experienced. Seductive.

27   Advertisers make use of a great variety of techniques and devices to engage us in
the delivery of their messages. Some are subtle, making use of warm, entertaining, or
comforting images or symbols. Others, like Black Death Vodka and Ultima II, are
about as subtle as MTV's "Beavis and Butt-head." Another common device used
to engage our attention is old but still effective: the use of famous or notorious

personalities as product spokespeople or models. Advertising writers did not invent the human tendency to admire or otherwise identify themselves with famous people. Once we have seen a famous person in an ad, we associate the product with the person: "Britney Spears drinks milk. She's a hottie. I want to be a hottie, too. 'Hey Mom, Got Milk?'" "Guns 'N Roses rule my world, so I will definitely make the scene with a bottle of Black Death stuck into the waistband of my sweat pants." "Gena Lee Nolin is totally sexy. She wears Sasson. If I wear Sasson, I'll be sexy, too." The logic is faulty, but we fall under the spell just the same. Advertising works, not because Britney is a nutritionist, Slash has discriminating taste, or Gena knows her jeans, but because we participate in it. In fact, we charge ads with most of their power.

A Simple Language

28 Advertising language differs from other types of language in another important respect; it is a simple language. To determine how the copy of a typical advertisement rates on a "simplicity index" in comparison with text in a magazine article, for example, try this exercise: Clip a typical story from the publication you read most frequently. Calculate the number of words in an average sentence. Count the number of words of three or more syllables in a typical 100-word passage, omitting words that are capitalized, combinations of two simple words, or verb forms made into three-syllable words by the addition of *–ed* or *–es*. Add the two figures (the average number of words per sentence and the number of three-syllable words per 100 words), then multiply the result by .4. According to Robert Gunning, if the resulting number is 7, there is a good chance that you are reading *True Confessions.*(2) He developed this formula, the "Fog Index," to determine the comparative ease with which any given piece of written communication can be read.

29 Let's apply the Fog Index to the complete text of Britney Spears' 1999 ad for the National Fluid Milk Processing Board ("Got Milk?")

> Baby, one more time isn't enough.
> 9 out of 10 girls don't get enough calcium. It takes about 4 glasses of milk every day. So when I finish this glass, fill it up, baby. Three more times.

The average sentence in this ad is 7.4 words. There is only one three-syllable word, *calcium*. Counting *isn't* and *don't* as two words each, the ad is 40 words in length. The average number of three syllable words per hundred is 2.5.

7.4 words per sentence
+ 2.5 three syllable words/100
9.9
3.4
3.96

30 According to Gunning's scale, this ad is about as hard to read as a comic book. But of course the text is only part of the message. The rest is the visual; in this case, a photo of pop star Britney Spears sprawled across a couch, legs in the air, while she talks on the phone. A plate holding cookies and a glass of milk is set next to her.

31 Why do advertisers generally favor simple language? The answer lies with the consumer: The average American adult is subject to an overwhelming number of

commercial messages each day. As a practical matter, we would not notice many of these messages if length or eloquence were counted among their virtues. Today's consumer cannot take the time to focus on anything for long, much less blatant advertising messages. Every aspect of modern life runs at an accelerated pace. Overnight mail has moved in less than ten years from a novelty to a common business necessity. Voice mail, pagers, cellular phones, e-mail, the Internet—the world is always awake, always switched on, and hungry for more information, now. Time generally, and TV-commercial time in particular, is now dissected into increasingly smaller segments. Fifteen-second commercials are no longer unusual.

32   Advertising language is simple language; in the ad's engineering process, difficult words or images—which in other forms of communication may be used to lend color or fine shades of meaning—are edited out and replaced by simple words or images not open to misinterpretation. You don't have to ask whether King T likes to "grab a 40" when he wants to "act a fool," or whether Gena wears her Sassons when she wants to do whatever it is she does.

Who Is Responsible?

33 Some critics view the advertising business as a cranky, unwelcomed child of the free enterprise system—a noisy, whining, brash kid who must somehow be kept in line, but can't just yet be thrown out of the house. In reality, advertising mirrors the fears, quirks, and aspirations of the society that creates it (and is, in turn, sold by it). This factor alone exposes advertising to parody and ridicule. The overall level of acceptance and respect for advertising is also influenced by the varied quality of the ads themselves. Some ads, including a few of the examples cited here, seem deliberately designed to provoke controversy. For example, it is easy—as President Clinton and others charged—to conclude that clothing retailers deliberately glamorized the damaging effects of heroin addiction. But this is only one of the many charges frequently levied against advertising:

1. Advertising encourages unhealthy habits.

2. Advertising feeds on human weaknesses and exaggerates the importance of material things, encouraging "impure" emotions and vanities.

3. Advertising sells daydreams—distracting, purposeless visions of lifestyles beyond the reach of the majority of the people who are most exposed to advertising.

4. Advertising warps our vision of reality, implanting in us groundless fears and insecurities.

5. Advertising downgrades the intelligence of the public.

6. Advertising debases English.

7. Advertising perpetuates racial and sexual stereotypes.

34   What can be said in advertising's defense? Advertising is only a reflection of society. A case can be made for the concept that advertising language is an acceptable stimulus for the natural evolution of language. Is "proper English" the language most Americans actually speak and write, or is it the language we are told we should speak and write?

35   What about the charge that advertising debases the intelligence of the public? Those who support this particular criticism would do well to ask themselves another question: Exactly how intelligent is the public? Sadly, evidence abounds that "the public" at large is not particularly intelligent, after all. Johnny can't read. Susie can't write. And the entire family spends the night in front of the television, channel surfing for the latest scandal—hopefully, one involving a sports hero or political figure said to be a killer or a frequent participant in perverse sexual acts.

36   Ads are effective because they sell products. They would not succeed if they did not reflect the values and motivations of the real world. Advertising both reflects and shapes our perception of reality. Consider several brand names and the impressions they create: Ivory Snow is pure. Federal Express won't let you down. Absolut is cool. Sasson is sexxy. Mercedes represents quality. Our sense of what these brand names stand for may have as much to do with advertising as with the objective "truth."

37   Advertising shapes our perception of the world as surely as architecture shapes our impression of a city. Good, responsible advertising can serve as a positive influence for change, while generating profits. Of course, the problem is that the obverse is also true: Advertising, like any form of mass communication, can be a force for both "good" and "bad." It can just as readily reinforce or encourage irresponsible behavior, ageism, sexism, ethnocentrism, racism, homophobia, heterophobia—you name it—as it can encourage support for diversity and social progress. People living in society create advertising. Society isn't perfect. In the end, advertising simply attempts to change behavior. Do advertisements sell distracting, purposeless visions? Occasionally. But perhaps such visions are necessary components of the process through which our society changes and improves.

38   Perhaps, by learning how advertising works, we can become better equipped to sort out content from hype, product values from emotions, and salesmanship from propaganda.

THINKING CRITICALLY

1. O'Neill's introduction describes the "alliance" between science and consumer marketing during the 1950s, especially as it connected to the automotive industry. Evaluate the alliance he describes. Review some automobile advertisements from the 1950s and 1960s to help you formulate your response. How would you assess this relationship between science and marketing today?

2. O'Neill says that advertisers create in consumers a sense of need for products. Do you think it is ethical for advertisers to create such a sense when their products are "generic" and do not differ from those of the competition? Consider ads for gasoline, beer, and instant coffee.

3. Toward the end of the essay, O'Neill anticipates potential objections to his defense of advertising. What are some of these objections? What does he say in defense of advertising? Which set of arguments do you find stronger?

4. O'Neill describes several ways in which the language of advertising differs from other kinds of language. Briefly list the ways he mentions. Can you think of any other characteristics of advertising language that set it apart?

5. O'Neill says in paragraph 26 that "[symbols] have become important elements in the language of advertising." Can you think of some specific symbols from the

advertising world that you associate with your own life? Are they effective symbols for selling? Explain your answer.

6. In paragraph 27, O'Neill claims that celebrity endorsement of a product is "faulty" logic. Explain what he means. Why do people buy products sold by famous people?

7. William Lutz teaches English and writes books about the misuse of language. Charles O'Neill is a professional advertiser. How do their views about advertising reflect their occupations? Which side of the argument do you agree with?

8. How effective do you think O'Neill's introductory paragraphs are? How well does he hook the reader? What particular audience might he be appealing to early on? What attitude toward advertising is established in the introduction?

WRITING ASSIGNMENTS

1. Obtain a current issue of each of the following publications: the *New Yorker, Time, GQ, Vogue,* and *People.* Choose one article from each periodical and calculate its Fog Index according to the technique described in paragraphs 28 and 29. Choose one ad from each periodical and figure out its Fog Index. What different reading levels do you find among the publications? What do you know about the readers of these periodicals from your survey of the reading difficulty of the articles? Write up your findings in a paper.

2. O'Neill believes that advertising language mirrors the fears, quirks, and aspirations of the society that creates it. Do you agree or disagree with this statement? Explain in a brief essay.

3. Working with a group of classmates, develop a slogan and advertising campaign for one of the following products: sneakers, soda, a candy bar, or jeans. How would you apply the principles of advertising, as outlined in O'Neill's article, to market your product? After completing your marketing strategy, "sell" your product to the class. If time permits, explain the reasoning behind your selling technique.

Language Abuse
Herschell Gordon Lewis

The next essay, written by one of the most prolific marketing writers of the twentieth century, takes a humorous, but candid look at the marketing language used by copywriters to get us to part with our money. As Lewis explains in this piece written for an advertising audience, unimaginative language and worn-out clichés alienate consumers and dilute our language as a whole.

Herschell Gordon Lewis is the author of over 20 books on marketing and advertising, including *Herschell Gordon Lewis on the Art of Writing Copy* (1988) and *Marketing Mayhem* (2001), from which this essay is excerpted. His columns on marketing and copywriting have appeared in many advertising publications.

1   Today's marketers throw terms the way they'd throw confetti . . . and with just about as much impact.

2   Yes, yes, of course we have "Free" and "New" and "Important" used so often and so unrelated to a specific offer we have the feeling some child has hit a macro button on a computer keyboard or, worse, the computer is operating without human intervention.

3   Here's an ad in a free-standing insert in the Sunday paper: "Great news! Metab-o-lite now has a full line of products for extra energy and increased metabolism!" By golly, they're right on the money. We haven't had such great news since Gutenberg. Here's a mailing from a company selling hams by mail. It's labeled. "Urgent!" By golly, *they're* right on the money too. We'd better act now or they'll run out of hams. Then where would we be?

4   (Parenthetically, "Act now!" is another phrase that ought to be sent to that great Lexicographical Purgatory.)

5   We have offers from credit cards—dozens of credit cards, all leaning on the same everlasting arms of credit reporting bureaus—telling us we've been pre-approved . . . and then asking us for so much financial information or warning us that we may *not* be pre-approved that we wonder whether one person wrote the envelope copy, went on vacation, and was replaced by another person who wrote the deadly-warning text while unaware of the commitment the envelope made.

6   One of the most puzzling aspects of marketing mayhem is the plethora of indecipherable automobile names. Who, oh, who, decided to call the Cheap Cadillac "Catera"? The initial campaign for that status-busting car has (thankfully) been discontinued, but we should remember "The Caddy that zigs" as a no-brain totem. Denali, Escalade, Allante—who came up with these? What image is the car supposed to project?

7   And our tired old standby "Free" is reduced to limping, in The Age of Skepticism. Certainly more than half the offers that begin with a huge "Free!" are followed by an "if . . ." or "when . . ." condition. What we've done to that poor word is criminal, and what makes the criminality worse is that so many uses of free are the result of desperation. We don't have anything else to say, so we drag in "Free!" and because it doesn't fit, we have to saddle it with conditions and exclusions and exceptions.

8   The language abusers don't care. They throw terms, they invent unpronounceable product names, they assault us with cliché after cliché. Response slides. And can you believe it, they're actually surprised to see their own murder victim die.

9   What we really need is an uprising, a revolution, a mutiny in which we organize and fight the deadly marketing-murdering forces of term-throwing. We need to impose a gigantic penalty on the use of "Important" and "Free" and "0% APR" . . . until and unless those terms once again run pure.

10   With that imprecation, take a look at some case histories.

The Importance of Saying "Important"

11 I'm getting more and more steamed at hit-and-run copywriters.
Who or what are hit-and-runners? They're the ones who know a couple of action words but don't know what damage they're doing by using these words and not justifying them.

12   Some of the words:

- Important
- Urgent
- Personal
- Hurry
- Rush

I've left off the mandatory exclamation points . . . although adding one after "Personal" is an Open Sesame to anyone other than the target, to peek inside (and be the first one to be disappointed).

13   What's wrong with all these imperatives? you ask. Not a thing—IF what follows *is* important or urgent or personal or legitimizes the demand for fast action.

14   But here's an envelope—a 9" × 12" jumbo—from a publication in the meetings and conventions field. In big stencil type on the envelope is the word "URGENT."

15   Urgent, huh? Then why does the postal indicia say "Bulk Rate"? How come it's urgent for me but not for you?

16   And what's inside? No letter. You're reading right, *no letter*. Bulk rate urgency without any semi-personal communication? Gee, that'll do a lot for the credibility of everybody else's direct response.

17   What *was* enclosed was a beautifully printed brochure, on whose cover is the cryptic message:

> *Can You Imagine Having the Power*
> *To Increase the Value of Gold?*

Yeah, yeah, it's not only too prettily laid out to be "urgent"; it's also too lyrical. (The eventual reference: Gold awards for the best hotels and resorts and golf courses.)

18   Look: Stay in character. How easy all this is if you STAY IN CHARACTER.

19   Aw, but I know what happened. Some consultant told them to put "Urgent" on the envelope. He or she was hired only for the day, so there wasn't time to explain that if we cry, "Wolf!" we'd better show them a wolf.

20   "Urgent" isn't the abused word winner. By far the most abused word we have—even surpassing "Free" and "New"—is "Important."

21   Hey, guys, *Important* isn't a stand-alone. Every time you kick it in the head, you weaken it a little more for the rest of us.

Important To Whom?

22 Here's an envelope. It says, all caps: *IMPORTANT FINANCIAL DOCUMENT ENCLOSED.* Yes, it's a manila envelope with those fake "Instructions to postmaster" instructions we've all used. Yes, the window shows "Pay to the order of" next to my name. But I *know*, as I open the envelope, the importance is to the sender, not the recipient.

23   Yep. It's a standard fake check, with the words "This is not a check" printed on it. It offers me a home equity loan, if I qualify. A reply card lets me choose between bill consolidation, home improvements, major purpose, refinancing an existing loan, or other. Okay, I choose other—a not-for-profit campaign to stamp out unauthorized use of the word "Important." Where's the importance here? It's a flat, standard financial offer every homeowner gets two or three times a week. That key misused word on the envelope has no backup inside.

24   Another problem: The "Important" infection has spread so it's now an epidemic. Two competitive mailings, mailed within a week or two of this one, use the same fake check gimmick and the same claim of importance. One tells me: "IMPORTANT: Your Single Family Residence has been reviewed."

25   Gee, I guess that is important. It isn't every day that my Single Family Residence is not only given caps/l.c. treatment but is also reviewed. I qualify for $35,000 more (than what?).

26   The American Express Platinum Card is never far behind. It shucks its mantle of dignity but manages to water down the promise:

> IMPORTANT
> INFORMATION
> For Automatic Flight
> Insurance Enrollees

I hadn't known I enrolled for this, but maybe it was a negative option. Anyway, the "Important" information is that I can upgrade my coverage "to the highest level of accident protection." Now, is that elite status, or what!

27   One "Important Information Enclosed" fibber adds a deadline date and "Final Notice" in a second window. Uh-oh! (And of course it has the boiler-plate "Postmaster . . ." imperative.) Final notice? What have I done? Or not done? Aha! It's my last chance "to upgrade your present vehicle to a brand-new Honda or KIA." Hey, fellas, I hate to rain on your parade, but I'm driving a Jaguar convertible. How about having a clue about who you're selling to?

28   What's the next one? A plain white jumbo window envelope with "IMPORTANT INFORMATION ENCLOSED" in red above the window. Of course, the Bulk Rate indicia, in the same red, rides serenely above this legend.

29   Inside is one of the most impenetrable documents I've ever tried to look at. It's a prospectus for Fidelity Advisor Funds Class A, Class T, and Class B. No letter. No indication of what makes this important. Every indication of why the word "Bulk" is more apt than the word "Important."

30   And on we go, into this pseudo-psychological jungle. The Discover Card takes a stern parental position:

> *Important:*
> Please open at once.
> DO NOT DISCARD.

31   Yeah, guys, but you've joined the "Bulk rate" parade. Oh, what the heck—even though it parallels the dire warning on the tags attached to pillows and mattresses, I'll open it.

32   I wish I hadn't.

33   The message from Discover (I haven't used this card since 1992, when Costco wouldn't accept any others) tells me, "Enclosed are four Discover® Card Checks just for you. Use them to . . ." Naturally, that "®" symbol destroys any rapport, but this doesn't bother me because I've built up an immunity to ® and ™ symbols, legal necessities for immediate identification and pomposities when overused.

A Simple Little Rule

34 I have a theory: Somebody writes the envelope copy, goes on vacation, and is eaten by a shark. Somebody else rushes in to write the enclosures; in the heat of getting these out, whatever is written on the envelope is overlooked.

35   How simple it is!

36   I have a little rule I've both preached and employed ever since the Fake Importance Syndrome showed up and developed into a Nile virus-like plague:

> *If you claim importance, prove it.*

See how uncomplicated those six words are? They *force* the creative team out of the hit-and-run bunker, onto the open battlefield.

37   So when Sprint sends me a letter (presorted first class . . . I'm moving up!) with the legend "Important news about your telephone service," I first take a deep breath, hoping it won't be a stupid message tied to Candice Bergen or Sela Ward, then open it to find what I expected to find: "Now your small business can get the same quality and value you enjoy on long distance, for all your *local toll* calls, too."

38   Is a puzzlement. My business isn't that small (should I be insulted?), and Sprint isn't our long distance provider. I wouldn't expect a company with the creative depth they have to die in the heading with limp words such as *quality* and *value*. Those are peculiarities, but they aren't germane to the point here, which is: What's so important? Couldn't the creative team have adapted envelope copy to intrigue me rather than generate just another weak cliché?

39   Hey, Sprint and Discover and AmEx and all you Honda dealers out there: Want to add some octane to your messages? *If you claim importance, prove it.*

40   Remember that, will you? It's important.

"Free at Last"? Well, Sort of . . . Except . . .

41 One of the great wonders of our time is that the word "Free" survives.

42   We've kicked it in the head, stomped on it with golf shoes, strangled it with adjectival qualifiers, drowned it in a sea of asterisks, maimed it with "if" phrases, and suffocated it with cheap rhetorical varnish . . . and still it survives.

43   As any resident of the former Yugoslavia might point out: Survival isn't equivalent to thriving.

44   Today's target doesn't accept "Free!" as really free, the way his or her forebearers did a generation ago. Today's "What's the angle?" hesitation is often precursor to a consultation with one of those lawyers slathering for the typical unreasonable percentage of a class action settlement. We can be next in line for that reaction.

"It isn't 'Free,' you dummy. It's 'Complimentary.' Or it's 'No extra charge.' But it isn't 'free.' " "Oh."

45 Writing for credit card companies and financial institutions, I often encounter the warning: "We can't say it's free. We can only say it's complimentary or at no extra charge."

46   That a difference in perception between "free" and "complimentary" exists (and only the sedate marketers heed that difference in perception) is an indication of the litigious, looking-for-trouble early 21st century societal structure. That one of the mailings coming to me spelled the word *complementary*—a word that has a totally different meaning—is an indication of the borderline literacy of some of our confréres.

47   Anybody who has practiced advertising, marketing, or basic salesmanship for more than 20 minutes is aware of the idiosyncrasies surrounding the word "Free." For example, we all refer to "Free Gift." Now, come on, have we ever heard of a gift that isn't free? That isn't the point. The redundancy "Free Gift" pulls. That's what matters, because we deal in response, not logic.

48   So I suppose we'll expand to "Totally Free Gift" and then to "100% Totally Free Gift." Does that make us charlatans? Certainly not. It makes us salespeople, sensitive to what motivates our targets.

49   When I was about six years old, living near Pittsburgh, I visited relatives in Detroit. Detroit had a paper called *The Free Press*. Gee, I wondered, how could they make any money? (The last few years have proved me right. Apparently they can't.) My aunt didn't disabuse me of the notion, and I was lucky that I didn't just grab a paper off the newsstand: After all, it was free.

50   So was Radio Free Europe. The magic of the word has been inescapable. In David Ogilvy's *Confessions of an Advertising Man*, published two generations ago, he singled out *Free* as one of the powerful motivators. That power still drives the marketing engine, though it no longer purrs on all twelve cylinders.

51   Why has *free* begun to sputter, running so roughly it even backfires now and then? Because of a venerable monolith of a rule affecting all forms of force-communication:

Sameness = boredom.
Overuse = abuse.

52   We lean on "free" the way a cripple leans on a crutch. It may not save us, but it supports us. But it doesn't support us as profoundly as it supported our predecessors a generation ago.

53   A generation ago, a free offer wasn't a novelty but neither was it a daily occurrence. Today, we fish around for something in an offer, something we can isolate so we can say we're including it free.

54   The creeping cynicism among those who read, see, or hear our messages is based on two factors. They're responsible for the first one and we're the generators of the second.

Theirs:
A universal "I want mine" attitude has replaced the kinder, gentler "Gee, thanks!" of earlier times.
Ours:
To work the magical word into the mix, we hedge—"Free with your third shipment," "Free when you've collected the complete set," "Free if yours is one of the first 50 replies we receive."

55   And we have the old dependable "Buy one, get one free," which usually outpulls "Two for the price of one" or "Buy two and get 50% off." So even though the clock is ticking, even though worn spots are showing, even though the FCC occasionally growls, the Old Dependable still churns out response for us.

56   Understand, please: I keep score the same way I hope you do: by response, not by critical accolades or art directors' awards. So I'm in there, milking our favorite word just as you are. I'm not going to let pride stand in the way of response.

57   But I'm glad I'm operating during this generation. By the next one, we may have damaged our durable crutch so deeply it may not support those who follow us in our most noble profession.

New and Improved: A Good Old-fashioned Home-made Original

58 How big a house do you need to make "home-made" ice cream?

59   If you have one of those electric gadgets that can turn out a pint of mushy ice cream for about eleven dollars' worth of ingredients, you can prepare that pint in a studio apartment. But you'd need every room in a mansion to supply a chain of stores.

60   My son Bob took his two little daughters out for some ice cream. He chuckled when he told me about it:

61   "It's called 'Kemp's Home-Made ice cream,' " he said. "They sell it in a couple of hundred stores. I'd like to go to their house and watch Mrs. Kemp wrestling with half a ton of chocolate syrup."

62   The "home-made" conceit set me to thinking about all the phrases we in the force-communication universe corrupt in our mindless grappling for attention and sales.

63   One of the most obvious . . . and it also applies to ice cream . . . is "old-fashioned." Curious, isn't it, in the rocket-speed Internet era, that we venerate the past when we're describing a space-age pistachio-nut concoction. Oh, we understand the sales pitch behind the label: Contemporary products, they tell us, are loaded with ersatz ingredients such as sawdust and iron filings and camel dung; theirs come from cows whose udders are massaged with Jergen's Lotion.

64   So okay, "old-fashioned" can be a smart (if semi-subliminal) marketing ploy. But please, please, refuse to buy any item advertising itself as "old-fashion." Truncating the phrase is the work of semi-literates, and if you patronize them what does that say about *you?*

65   Two curious descriptions are "original" and "new and improved." Even more curious is the oxymoron resulting from combining them—a symbol of copywriting desperation. (My old friend Don Logay points out that the two terms are mutually exclusive—something can't be both "new" and "improved.")

66   What benefit does the word "original" transmit? In one of its purer interpretations, the word means *unchanged*. First (original) definition, *American Heritage Dictionary*: "Preceding all others in time." Would you want to be writing or handling a layout or doing a spreadsheet with your *original* computer, which in 1986 was the wonder of its time with 20 megabytes of memory and 4 megabytes of RAM? Would you want to submit yourself to the *original* treatment for many illnesses—heated cups stuck onto your back by the local barber?

67   "New and improved" is a nondescript non-description. In what way? I remember without any particular fondness reading that phrase on containers of the semi-tasteless orange drink Tang. Oh, yeah, I had to admire the honesty behind it—"The previous formulation wasn't very good but we marketed it anyway."

68   "New and improved" somehow parallels a sign on a failed business: "Under new management." So what? Those of us whose incomes depend on success in driving customers or clients through the door certainly ought to know that *benefit* outsells thin chest-thumping. In what way is it new? In what way is it improved?

Or is the claim a hope that dissatisfied buyers will ignore their previous disgruntlement?

69   Yeah, I'm being wry, but the conclusion isn't wry: Whatever use we make of "original" and "new and improved," we have better expressions at our command; or, at least, as professionals we *should* have better expressions at our command.

Adding to the List

70 Let's add two massive entries to our list: "heavy duty" and "heavyweight." I admit to being a sometime patron of "heavy duty"; but after buying some "heavy duty" AA batteries at Walgreens, I no longer can accept the term without challenging it as puffery. Wouldn't it be nice if our bureau-crazed government added one more: The Department of Heavy Duty Evaluation?

71   "Heavyweight" doesn't carry as heavy a burden as "heavy duty," so let's consider this just a preliminary warning, a caution: If you describe something as a heavyweight, meaning anything other than avoirdupois, accompany that claim with an explanation.

72   Which brings us to "discount." Living in Florida, I've become immunized to the word, which attaches itself leechlike to stores and space ads and mailings and Web offerings, often mindlessly and often duplicitously. Oh, it still works on the unaware. For those of us whose skepticism it regularly feeds, the word needs validation. Who has been responsible for the latter-day rash of unbacked claims of "discount"? Wal-Mart? No, Wal-Mart's prices actually are discounted. A simple demand: Discounted from *what*?

73   What else? "King-size." For beds and bedding, it's a measurable absolute. For a claim from the clouds, it conjures up the image of getting something bigger and/or more intense than we're paying for. We see the intensification at work in "King-size discount." The Mother of all discounts? Based on the typical shouter of the phrase, it should only be.

74   A recent addition—in fact, I'd place it from 1998 upward—is "Enterprise." Now, this isn't the original *enterprise* as we've always known it; nor is it the starship. No, no, it's the new and improved *Enterprise* with a capital "E," grasped to the bosom of electron-lovers. We see magazine columns and entire books with the "Enterprise Computing" title. What does it mean? I've asked several who inhabit that half-world to explain the term; invariably the answer is something like, "It's the whole thing . . . the entire . . . well, the entire enterprise." Oh. Thanks.

75   One more for now: "World class." I have no idea whence this phrase came; somehow I associate it with that marvel of corruption, the Olympic Games. But maybe I'm wrong. Our shrunken globe rubber-banded into a tight little ball by jet aircraft and discounted (for real) fares, has eliminated many of the peaks and valleys we used to assume were there, between Texas and Tajikistan. So "world class" already may be on the route to join "23 skiddoo" and "hooch inspector" and "cuspidor" as a once-active expression.

76   Aw, enough already. Are these the only candidates? Even as you read this, you undoubtedly have others to contribute. If you have some favorites, tell me so and we might immortalize them and you in another book of harangues. But don't give me "ultimate" or "your partner in . . ." I'm saving those.

THINKING CRITICALLY

1. Describe the voice you hear in this essay. How does Lewis balance humor and a sense of concern regarding the ineffective use of language in advertising today? Cite examples from the essay to support your conclusion.

2. What is the connection between language abuses made by advertising copywriters and consumer apathy? How do language abuses made by advertising writers "weaken" language? Explain.

3. What, according to Lewis, is the most "abused" word used in marketing today? Why does he feel that this word surpasses other overused words such as "free" and "new"? Do you agree with his assessment?

4. What advice does Lewis give marketing writers to prevent the distribution of boring or ineffectual copy? As a consumer, do you agree with his advice?

5. Does the fact that Lewis is an experienced marketing writer influence your reception of his argument? Why or why not?

6. How does Lewis use examples to support his criticisms of language abuse in advertising? Explain.

7. Is there a difference between "free" and "complimentary"? Explain. What is the legal difference? Explain.

WRITING ASSIGNMENTS

1. In this essay, Lewis highlights some marketing ploys that he finds particularly annoying and ineffective. Identify some commercials or advertisements that especially annoyed you. Why exactly did they bother you? Try to locate any cultural, linguistic, social, or intellectual reasons behind your annoyance or distaste. How do these commercials compare to the marketing criticisms expressed in Lewis's article?

2. Lewis draws several examples of language abuses from companies such as Sprint, Discover, and Wal-Mart. Examine a few of these companies' marketing campaigns in detail. Write an essay that compares the language in these ads to the language Lewis describes. Discuss whether or not you find any of the ads you have gathered effective.

How Tobacco Company "Anti-Smoking" Ads Appeal to Teens
Carrie McLaren

Cigarette companies discouraging kids from smoking? Sound too good to be true? According to designer and writer Carrie McLaren, it is. As part of the big tobacco settlement, cigarette companies must devote funds to antismoking efforts discouraging children from the habit. On the surface, it sounds like a great idea. But as McLaren explains, hokey campaigns and slogans are ineffectual, missing their target audience and possibly even encouraging kids to smoke.

Carrie McLaren is a designer and writer. She is also the editor for *Stay Free!* magazine, a nonprofit journal that explores the politics of the mass media and consumer culture. This article appeared in the Summer 2000 issue of *Stay Free!*

1 You've got to hand it to Philip Morris. The company has somehow managed to spend an estimated $100 million on a new corporate image campaign without once mentioning tobacco. Happy kids—lots of them—fill the ads, in which actors portraying blue-collar workers discuss feeding the hungry, fighting domestic violence, and protecting the world from natural disasters . . . all, as it says onscreen, based on a true story. In other words, an invisible subtitle reads, most cigarette advertising isn't.

2 As *Adweek* pointed out, Philip Morris is spending far more on advertising its charitable efforts (the $100 million) than on the charitable efforts themselves ($60 million).

3 Lorillard Tobacco, makers of Newport cigarettes, has recently launched its own campaign: *Tobacco is whacko if you're a teen.* As part of the settlement reached by Big Tobacco and state attorneys general in 1997, Lorillard et al. must spend $500 million a year on anti-tobacco advertising. The whacko campaign is presumably an attempt to speak to teens in their own language. But would anyone under eighteen take advice from someone who used the word whacko? Being out of touch with high school jargon, I searched Geocities homepages to see how common particular slang words are. I've no clue how many Geocities users are under eighteen, so the methodology needs some work. Nevertheless: stupid brought up 383,512 hits; crap 168,655; and whacko a lowly 6,568, including usages such as Mousty's Wacko Petz, Ask Wacko and Wacko's Wacky World. Unless the advertising geniuses behind the campaign are themselves whacko, surely they knew these ads wouldn't work.

4 The marketers at Lorillard are clearly less interested in curbing teen smoking than in appearing to do so. Whacko ads appear in magazines such as *Teen People* and *Seventeen* but also *Spin*, where they stand out like a sore thumb amid pierced hipsters and Diesel-inspired surrealists. As any market researcher could tell you, Spin's audience would ignore anything labeled for a teen.

5 Lorillard's strategy, which is far more subtle than Philip Morris's, is made clear in *Advertising Age*'s rave review. Columnist Bob Garfield calls it as categorical a denunciation as you could ever wish for. Sure, if you're a parent or over forty, that's the impression Lorillard is aiming for. Lorillard's true target audience is closer to Garfield's age than teenagers'.

6 Of course, tobacco is not the sole producer of dubious public service campaigns. The Ad Council was formed in 1942 to improve public opinion of advertising; to, in effect, advertise advertising. Thanks to its efforts, those of us growing up in the late '70s were raised to believe that America's environmental problems were due to litter, and the disappearance of greenlands to careless, fire-wielding picnickers. Social marketing campaigns tend to be concerned more with public relations than the purported cause.

7 Still, there's no need to throw the baby out with the bathwater—at least not yet. Bob Garfield may consider Lorillard's the most resonant anti-tobacco campaign but two state-sponsored efforts prove him wrong. Question It is the youth campaign launched by the Partership for a Healthy Mississippi; Truth (www.wholetruth.com) is the Florida equivalent. Unlike the youth campaigns produced by tobacco companies, the states don't pretend that talking down to the audience works. They recognize that smoking is an act of rebellion, and that kids are more inclined to start not in spite of anti-tobacco propaganda but because of it.

8   Question It confronts teens with their own reactionary rebellion. The underlying message of the campaign is that, far from symbolizing freedom and adulthood, tobacco use is a form of obedience—obedience to tobacco companies. This is closer to the categorical denunciation some of us would hope for, and it is carried out using the sort of edgy graphics and unscripted dialogue you might find in a Reebok commercial. Or so says the press kit. I've only seen the website but was immediately won over by its poignant animation. The front page of the site leads off with a blood-sucking mosquito, dressed in a suit, who meets his end when his host smashes the creature in a pool of blood.

9   Elsewhere on the site, *Spin Doctors: How the Tobacco Industry Worms Their Way Into Your Head* details tricks of the trade. Another section, *Beat the Odds . . . How to Make $$$ When 11,000 of Your Customers Die Everyday*, includes a game called Tease the Weasel. By answering tobacco-related trivia, players determine the fate of R.J., the resident corporate weasel. Answer wrong and R.J. gets another bag of money.

10   Both Question It and the Truth campaigns turn the tables and target tobacco marketing . . . carefully, I might add, for the tobacco settlement forbids them from attacking tobacco companies directly. Television commercials produced by Truth's Florida ad agency Crispin Porter Bogusky show teens making crank calls to ad agencies and Hollywood execs. Another commercial rather brilliantly portrays the tobacco industry's dedicated search for a scientist offering the right (i.e. pro-tobacco) evidence. Watching these spots, the viewer is easily seduced by the confident cool of the young activists, all wholly likable, believable, real people types. And there are signs the campaign works. In Florida, the number of teens who said they were smokers dropped from 23.3% to 20.9%, about 31,000 fewer smokers, a year after the campaign launched. A subsequent survey found that the number of Florida middle schoolers who said they smoke dropped almost in half in just one year; smoking by high school students dropped 17%. That makes it the second year in a row that teen smoking has dropped dramatically in Florida. According to Stanton Glantz, a professor of medicine at UC San Francisco, this makes Truth the most effective effort to reduce teen smoking in the world. It also underlines the absurdity of trusting the tobacco companies—whose campaigns pale in comparison—to police themselves.

11   Oddly, Florida governer Jeb Bush hasn't taken kindly to Truth; his administration withdrew funding for 2000. He couldn't kill it, though. Crispin Porter Bogusky was selected to launch the first national anti-youth smoking campaign. A new batch of Truth ads started appearing nationally in February. One of the ads featured hundreds of body bags piling up around the Philip Morris building; another showed teens ambushing Philip Morris personnel, Michael Moore-style, with a lie detector. Unfortunately, the tobacco industry bullied the American Legacy Foundation—the nonprofit set up with settlement money—into pulling the ads. Even if they hadn't, the chances for the ads running was unlikely: NBC, ABC and CBS had all rejected the initial storyboards submitted to the networks. Two subsequent Truth commericals were also canned and Philip Morris threatened to sue. The problem with these ads, apparently, is that they actually worked.

12   Of course, positive propaganda is still propaganda, and its limits are clearly visible with Truth. The name alone serves as its own warning: from Pravda to

Fundamentalist Christians to objectivist journalists, anyone claiming a monopoly on truth begs scrutiny. Levi's recent ad campaign was The Truth. So were last year's ex-gay testimonials, sponsored by Americans for Truth About Homosexuality and others.

13   Well positioned though they be, Question It and Truth offer the most for their cause when they go beyond the language of advertising. After all, the same advertising industry behind selling cigarettes is behind unselling them. Consciously questioning this authority will get teens farther in the long run than catchy slogans and soundbites. While it won't earn them any bonus points with the crowd at Advertising Age, the state efforts encourage students to report on tobacco marketing in their area, to write tobacco execs with complaints, and to get involved in grassroots actions . . . not bad for a public service campaign.

THINKING CRITICALLY

1. According to McLaren, why does the language used by the Lorillard antismoking campaign fail to appeal to teens? Do you agree? Explain.

2. Visit the Web site of the nonprofit antismoking organization McLaren cites: Truth (www.wholetruth.com). How does the campaign on this Web site compare to the ones created by the tobacco companies?

3. What challenges do nonprofit antismoking organizations face in airing their ads? Do the tobacco companies face similar challenges?

4. Do you think that antismoking campaigns in general could help discourage teens from smoking? Why or why not?

5. What is the position of the author on antismoking campaigns led by tobacco companies? by nonprofit organizations? Identify specific lines in her essay in which she reveals her position. Does any personal bias on the part of the author influence your opinion of her essay, or does she present the issue fairly? Explain.

WRITING ASSIGNMENTS

1. Write an essay exploring the effectiveness or ineffectiveness of the Lorillard Tobacco Company's 2000 antismoking campaign *"Tobacco is whacko if you're a teen."* Does it reach its target audience? Why or why not? On what grounds does it discourage smoking? What does the slogan imply about tobacco if you are *not* a teen?

2. Other tobacco companies have introduced antismoking campaigns. Philip Morris's prevention ad tells youth to "Think. Don't Smoke." Do you think this will discourage kids from smoking? Could it be actually using reverse-psychology to encourage kids to smoke? Why do you think teens smoke? Write an essay exploring the role of teen psychology on the desire to smoke or engage in other risk-taking behaviors.

3. Design an antismoking campaign that you feel would be effective in discouraging kids from smoking that could air on television and in print. Describe the goals of your ad campaign, your use of teen psychology and language, and why you feel your project would be effective. Share your campaign with the class as part of a larger class debate on antismoking campaigns.

Exploring the Language of V I S U A L S

Current Advertisements

Take a look at the following magazine advertisements for different products and services. The sales pitches and marketing techniques take different slants—some relying on hard-sell copy, others hoping to arrest your attention with creative visuals; some taking the informative, even chatty approach, and others making an appeal to emotions. Following each ad is a list of questions to help you analyze the individual spreads and strategies. These questions should help stimulate class discussion and provide ideas for future papers.

THINKING CRITICALLY

1. How does this ad differ from the other sneaker ad in this section for Sketchers? Include an analysis of the model, the language, and the overall impression each ad gives the viewer in your response.

2. Why are certain words in the young woman's monologue presented in capital letters? What effect does this give the ad and the message it is trying to convey?

3. Interpret the last line of the young woman's monologue, "But hey, I have a boyfriend?" What is she telling the reader? Why would she include this information as important?

4. Would this ad convey a different message if it did not include the monologue on the right? If the young woman was looking directly ahead? Explain.

5. Why does the young woman call herself a "hot chick"? Who usually uses a term like this? If you are female, would you like to be known as a "hot chick"? Why or why not?

Nike

Escort (radar detector)

THINKING CRITICALLY

1. In what ways does the man in the photograph represent the product? What sort of person is he supposed to represent? Explain.

2. What does the caption tell us about the product and the target audience for the product? Does it aim to appeal to a particular consumer, or encourage others to be like the man in the photo? Explain.

3. In what magazines would you expect to see an ad like this? How would it best reach its target audience?

4. Where is the man in the ad looking? What is his facial expression? The color of his eyes? Would this ad be more effective if he had a different expression? were clean shaven? female?

THINKING CRITICALLY

1. Would you know what this ad was selling if the logo and the copy were not provided? Would there be any ambiguity about what was being sold? How much does this ad depend on name and image recognition? Explain.

2. Where would you expect to see an ad like this and why? If you were an advertising executive, where would you place this ad? How would you target your purchasing public? Explain.

3. This ad uses the tagline "Life Takes Indulgence." What does this line imply about Visa? About the intended audience for the ad? What message does the tagline convey about the product and how you should use it? Explain.

4. This ad appeared in *Rolling Stone* magazine. How does the ad appeal to that magazine's readership? Would the ad work in another publication, such as *People* magazine, or *Good Housekeeping*? Explain.

5. Evaluate the effectiveness of the slogan "Life Takes Indulgence."

Skechers

THINKING CRITICALLY

1. Would you know what this ad was selling if the word "Skechers" was not in the ad? Would there be any ambiguity about what was being sold in the advertisement? How much does this ad depend on name and image recognition? Explain.

2. Does the woman in the picture represent the product? What consumers are likely to be swayed to purchase Skechers because this woman "wears" them?

3. Do you think this ad effectively sells the product? What words would you use, if any, to make the ad more effective?

Got Milk?

Serena Williams October 2005 www.milknewsroom.com/ads.htm

THINKING CRITICALLY

1. Review the caption featured in this ad. How does the caption connect to the person in the ad? What message does it convey? What do you need to already know to understand the caption, the message, and who the person in the ad is?

2. Who is the target audience for this ad? Where would you expect to see this ad?

3. How does this ad use Serena Williams and her expression and pose to project an image about milk? Would this ad be effective if it featured a different popular athlete, such as Alex Rodriguez or Tom Brady?

4. Who drinks milk? Do you think this ad would encourage kids to drink more mllk? Adults? Why or why not?

MAKING CONNECTIONS

1. Clip three ads for products that use sex as a selling device such as automobiles or alcohol. Explain how sex helps sell the products. Would feminists consider these ads demeaning to women?

2. Choose a brand-name product you use regularly and one of its competitors—products whose differences are negligible, if they exist at all. Examine some advertisements for each brand. Write a short paper explaining what really makes you prefer your brand.

3. Herschell Gordon Lewis complains how ads employ "in your face" tactics to sell products. Brainstorm a list of "aggressive" ads that you have seen in magazines or on TV and discuss whether or not you find their tactics effective. Be sure to refer to specific details of the ads (particularly the language used) to support your claims.

4. William Lutz characterizes the language used in ads as "weasel words"—that is, language that pretends to do one thing, while really doing another. Explore your campus for examples of weasel words. Look not only at ads, but also at material such as university brochures and pamphlets that are sent to prospective students, and/or any political contests taking place (i.e., students running for the student government or candidates for office speaking at your campus). Write down all examples of weasel words and report back to your classmates.

Censorship and Free Speech

■ We saw Margaret Sanger gagged in Chapter 2. Here, an artist uses the same gag imagery and a symbol of liberty to make a point about free speech in America. Just what are the limits of our First Amendment rights? (Rohan Van Twest, photographer)

"**C**ongress shall make no law . . . abridging the freedom of speech, or of the press." With these simple words, the writers of the Constitution created one of the pillars of our democratic system of government—the First Amendment guarantee of every American's right to the free exchange of ideas, beliefs, and political debate. Most Americans passionately support their right to express themselves without fear of government reprisal. However, over the years questions have arisen about whether limits should be imposed on our right to free expression when the exercise of that right imposes hardship or pain on others. What happens when the right of one person to state his or her beliefs conflicts with the rights of others to be free from verbal abuse? What happens when free expression runs counter to community values? At what point does the perceived degree of offensiveness warrant censorship? And at what point does censorship threaten to undermine our constitutional rights? In this chapter, we look at three particular areas that have generated debate and dialogue recently: censorship and books, biased language and hate speech, and censorship of campus speech.

Censorship and Books

The censorship of books challenges the rights guaranteed by the First Amendment on two fronts: the right to express ideas freely and the right to have access to the ideas of others. In "The Freedom to Read," the American Library Association (ALA) and the Association of American Publishers explore the effects of censorship attempts on Americans' freedom to read and affirm the importance of making all viewpoints available for public scrutiny, even when the ideas are unpopular and offensive. The next two essays present different points of view on the issue of banned books. Jeff Jacoby, in "Book-Banning, Real and Imaginary" takes the position that there is no "book banning" threat in the United States, merely a bunch of parents who want a voice in what their children read in school. Author Judy Blume, however, explains in her editorial, "Is Harry Potter Evil?" that book censorship is harmful, both to children and to our free society.

Perhaps no other piece of American literature has stirred up more debates about book banning than Mark Twain's 1885 classic, *Adventures of Huckleberry Finn*. It was immediately banned by the Concord, Massachusetts, Public Library the year it was published and, according to the ALA, it continues to be banned today in libraries throughout America—but for very different reasons. In tribute to the book's fame, we have reproduced an early cover of the classic for analysis and discussion. We conclude this section with an "afterword" of sorts by renowned science fiction author Ray Bradbury, who presents a rather lively perspective on the question of editing literary works to accommodate popular notions of political correctness.

Biased Language and Hate Speech

America is the most diverse society on earth, home to people of every race, nation, religion, and creed. Because of this diverse mix, our ability to comprehend all that "otherness" is sometimes overwhelmed, and we fall into the trap of reducing different people to handy but offensive labels. Perhaps even more damaging than stereotypes are racial epithets, in which words are used to deliberately wound. Forged by ignorance, fear, and intolerance, these words that hurt damningly reduce people to nothing more than a race, religion, gender, or body type. Such words aim to make the victim seem less than human, less worthy of respect. This section examines how biased language and hate speech is used to belittle, demean, or marginalize a person or a group of people.

The first reading takes a close look at "hate speech" and "political correctness." Linguist Robin Tomach Lakoff examines the connection between hate speech and the First Amendment, from right and left political viewpoints. Then, author of a popular "politically correct" language handbook, Rosalie Maggio describes how English subtly perpetuates prejudice and offers some simple guidelines for avoiding offensive stereotypes and exclusionary expressions. Arguing with Maggio's position is literary critic and journalist Michiko Kakutani, whose "The Word Police" vehemently condemns such "language-laundering" efforts. Ward Churchill explains why using Native American mascots for sports teams is both insulting and injurious to Native Americans in "Crimes Against Humanity." And Gloria Naylor describes how her experience with perhaps the most inflammatory racially charged word of all, *nigger*, forced her to confront ugly racial prejudice while still a child.

Case Study: Censorship and Free Speech on Campus

The free and open exchange of ideas seems critical to the goals of higher education. However, when the ideas expressed are racist, sexist, or otherwise offensive toward specific groups on campus, do universities and colleges have the right to censor and punish that form of speech? This case study takes a look at this issue in depth, presenting multiple points of view. For example, in "Regulating Racist Speech on Campus," Charles R. Lawrence, III argues that verbal harassment violates student victims' rights to an education. Colleges and universities must act to prevent such harassment from happening by restricting this form of speech, he believes. Taking the opposite side, Alan Charles Kors finds this form of censorship objectionable and dangerous, arguing that it chills freedom of expression and opinion. Alternatively, Stanley Fish argues that truly free speech doesn't really exist, on campus or anywhere else—it is merely a rhetorical construct used by those in power to forward political agendas. The section ends with a discussion on the Academic Bill of Rights proposed by attorney David Horowitz.

CENSORSHIP AND BOOKS

The Freedom to Read
American Library Association

> The American Library Association, founded in 1876, is the oldest and largest national library association in the world. Addressing the needs of state, public, school, and academic libraries, it has over 55,000 members across the country. Dedicated to preserving the freedom of information distribution and assuring the access to information for all, the ALA has even written its own "Bill of Rights." The following document was originally drafted and adopted in 1953. It was later revised in 1991, in response to increasing pressure from special interest groups to censor or limit the distribution of certain books to American libraries and schools. What follows represents the 2004 revision.

1 The freedom to read is essential to our democracy. It is continuously under attack. Private groups and public authorities in various parts of the country are working to remove or limit access to reading materials, to censor content in schools, to label "controversial" views, to distribute lists of "objectionable" books or authors, and to purge libraries. These actions apparently rise from a view that our national tradition of free expression is no longer valid; that censorship and suppression are needed to counter threats to safety or national security, as well as to avoid the subversion of politics and the corruption of morals. We, as individuals devoted to reading and as librarians and publishers responsible for disseminating ideas, wish to assert the public interest in the preservation of the freedom to read.

2 Most attempts at suppression rest on a denial of the fundamental premise of democracy: that the ordinary individual, by exercising critical judgment, will select the good and reject the bad. We trust Americans to recognize propaganda and misinformation, and to make their own decisions about what they read and believe. We do not believe they are prepared to sacrifice their heritage of a free press in order to be "protected" against what others think may be bad for them. We believe they still favor free enterprise in ideas and expression.

3 These efforts at suppression are related to a larger pattern of pressures being brought against education, the press, art and images, films, broadcast media, and the Internet. The problem is not only one of actual censorship. The shadow of fear cast by these pressures leads, we suspect, to an even larger voluntary curtailment of expression by those who seek to avoid controversy or unwelcome scrutiny by government officials.

4 Such pressure toward conformity is perhaps natural to a time of accelerated change. And yet suppression is never more dangerous than in such a time of social tension. Freedom has given the United States the elasticity to endure strain. Freedom keeps open the path of novel and creative solutions, and enables change to come by choice. Every silencing of a heresy, every enforcement of an orthodoxy,

diminishes the toughness and resilience of our society and leaves it the less able to deal with controversy and difference.

5   Now as always in our history, reading is among our greatest freedoms. The freedom to read and write is almost the only means for making generally available ideas or manners of expression that can initially command only a small audience. The written word is the natural medium for the new idea and the untried voice from which come the original contributions to social growth. It is essential to the extended discussion that serious thought requires, and to the accumulation of knowledge and ideas into organized collections.

6   We believe that free communication is essential to the preservation of a free society and a creative culture. We believe that these pressures toward conformity present the danger of limiting the range and variety of inquiry and expression on which our democracy and our culture depend. We believe that every American community must jealously guard the freedom to publish and to circulate, in order to preserve its own freedom to read. We believe that publishers and librarians have a profound responsibility to give validity to that freedom to read by making it possible for the readers to choose freely from a variety of offerings.

7   The freedom to read is guaranteed by the Constitution. Those with faith in free people will stand firm on these constitutional guarantees of essential rights and will exercise the responsibilities that accompany these rights.

8   We therefore affirm these propositions:

1. *It is in the public interest for publishers and librarians to make available the widest diversity of views and expressions, including those that are unorthodox, unpopular, or considered dangerous by the majority.*

Creative thought is by definition new, and what is new is different. The bearer of every new thought is a rebel until that idea is refined and tested. Totalitarian systems attempt to maintain themselves in power by the ruthless suppression of any concept that challenges the established orthodoxy. The power of a democratic system to adapt to change is vastly strengthened by the freedom of its citizens to choose widely from among conflicting opinions offered freely to them. To stifle every nonconformist idea at birth would mark the end of the democratic process. Furthermore, only through the constant activity of weighing and selecting can the democratic mind attain the strength demanded by times like these. We need to know not only what we believe but why we believe it.

2. *Publishers, librarians, and booksellers do not need to endorse every idea or presentation they make available. It would conflict with the public interest for them to establish their own political, moral, or aesthetic views as a standard for determining what should be published or circulated.*

Publishers and librarians serve the educational process by helping to make available knowledge and ideas required for the growth of the mind and the increase of learning. They do not foster education by imposing as mentors the patterns of their own thought. The people should have the freedom to read and consider a broader range of ideas than those that may be held by any single librarian or publisher or government or church. It is wrong that what one can read should be confined to what another thinks proper.

3. *It is contrary to the public interest for publishers or librarians to bar access to writings on the basis of the personal history or political affiliations of the author.*

No art or literature can flourish if it is to be measured by the political views or private lives of its creators. No society of free people can flourish that draws up lists of writers to whom it will not listen, whatever they may have to say.

4. *There is no place in our society for efforts to coerce the taste of others, to confine adults to the reading matter deemed suitable for adolescents, or to inhibit the efforts of writers to achieve artistic expression.*

To some, much of modern expression is shocking. But is not much of life itself shocking? We cut off literature at the source if we prevent writers from dealing with the stuff of life. Parents and teachers have a responsibility to prepare the young to meet the diversity of experiences in life to which they will be exposed, as they have a responsibility to help them learn to think critically for themselves. These are affirmative responsibilities, not to be discharged simply by preventing them from reading works for which they are not yet prepared. In these matters values differ, and values cannot be legislated; nor can machinery be devised that will suit the demands of one group without limiting the freedom of others.

5. *It is not in the public interest to force a reader to accept the prejudgment of a label characterizing any expression or its author as subversive or dangerous.*

The ideal of labeling presupposes the existence of individuals or groups with wisdom to determine by authority what is good or bad for others. It presupposes that individuals must be directed in making up their minds about the ideas they examine. But Americans do not need others to do their thinking for them.

6. *It is the responsibility of publishers and librarians, as guardians of the people's freedom to read, to contest encroachments upon that freedom by individuals or groups seeking to impose their own standards or tastes upon the community at large; and by the government whenever it seeks to reduce or deny public access to public information.*

It is inevitable in the give and take of the democratic process that the political, the moral, or the aesthetic concepts of an individual or group will occasionally collide with those of another individual or group. In a free society individuals are free to determine for themselves what they wish to read, and each group is free to determine what it will recommend to its freely associated members. But no group has the right to take the law into its own hands, and to impose its own concept of politics or morality upon other members of a democratic society. Freedom is no freedom if it is accorded only to the accepted and the inoffensive. Further, democratic societies are more safe, free, and creative when the free flow of public information is not restricted by governmental prerogative or self-censorship.

7. *It is the responsibility of publishers and librarians to give full meaning to the freedom to read by providing books that enrich the quality and diversity of thought and expression. By the exercise of this affirmative responsibility, they can demonstrate that the answer to a "bad" book is a good one, the answer to a "bad" idea is a good one.*

The freedom to read is of little consequence when the reader cannot obtain matter fit for that reader's purpose. What is needed is not only the absence of restraint, but the positive provision of opportunity for the people to read the best that has been thought and said. Books are the major channel by which the intellectual inheritance is handed down, and the principal means of its testing and growth. The defense of the freedom to read requires of all publishers and librarians the utmost of their faculties, and deserves of all Americans the fullest of their support.

9   We state these propositions neither lightly nor as easy generalizations. We here stake out a lofty claim for the value of the written word. We do so because we believe that it is possessed of enormous variety and usefulness, worthy of cherishing and keeping free. We realize that the application of these propositions may mean the dissemination of ideas and manners of expression that are repugnant to many persons. We do not state these propositions in the comfortable belief that what people read is unimportant. We believe rather that what people read is deeply important; that ideas can be dangerous; but that the suppression of ideas is fatal to a democratic society. Freedom itself is a dangerous way of life, but it is ours.

THINKING CRITICALLY

1. What attempts at suppression of information is the ALA concerned about? Do the authors provide any examples? Are examples necessary to support their argument? Explain.

2. In paragraph 4, the document states that "pressures toward conformity present the danger of limiting the range and variety of inquiry and expression on which our democracy and our culture depend." What do the authors mean by this statement? How do you think opponents to this declaration (such as those who are exerting the "pressure toward conformity") would respond?

3. Can you think of any attempts by certain groups to control the accessibility of written material (besides pornography) because it is unacceptable? Explain the circumstances and the reaction to their censorship attempt.

4. The writers mention the labeling of books (Item 5). To what is the ALA objecting? Are they against all types of labels? Explain.

5. How do the writers use the First Amendment and the Constitution to support their argument? Is this an effective means of persuasion? Explain.

WRITING ASSIGNMENTS

1. Analyze the seven "declarations" of the ALA document and formulate a response to each. What questions do you have about them? What exceptions to these "declarations" can you anticipate?

2. Can you think of any type of publication that should be suppressed? If so, write a letter to the authors of the ALA in which you explain your reasoning. In your letter, make clear the kinds of negative consequences that could result should such a publication be publicly available.

The 10 Most Frequently Challenged Books of 2005
American Library Association

This list represents the top ten books reported challenged to the American Library Association's Office for Intellectual Freedom, who compiled this list. The ALA received 405 official challenges in 2005, which is defined as a formal, written complaint filed with a library or school requesting that materials be removed due to inappropriate content. Most challenges are reported by public libraries and school libraries. According to Judith F. Krug, director of the ALA Office for Intellectual Freedom, for each reported challenge, another four or five likely remain unreported. The list is periodically updated and posted online at the American Library Association's Web site at www.ala.org. Off the list this year, but on for several years past was *Adventures of Huckleberry Finn* by Mark Twain.

1. *It's Perfectly Normal* by Robie H. Harris for homosexuality, nudity, sex education, religious viewpoint, abortion and being unsuited to age group

2. *Forever* by Judy Blume for sexual content and offensive language

3. *The Catcher in the Rye* by J. D. Salinger for sexual content, offensive language and being unsuited to age group

4. *The Chocolate War* by Robert Cormier for sexual content and offensive language

5. *Whale Talk* by Chris Crutcher for racism and offensive language

6. *Detour for Emmy* by Marilyn Reynolds for sexual content

7. *What My Mother Doesn't Know* by Sonya Sones for sexual content and being unsuited to age group

8. Captain Underpants series by Dav Pilkey for antifamily content, being unsuited to age group and violence

9. *Crazy Lady!* by Jane Leslie Conly for offensive language

10. *It's So Amazing! A Book about Eggs, Sperm, Birth, Babies and Families* by Robie H. Harris for sexual education and sexual content

Book-Banning, Real and Imaginary

Jeff Jacoby

Each year, usually during the fourth week of September, the American Library Association observes "National Banned Book Week." To promote dialogue on the issue of censorship and book banning, the ALA publishes a list of books that have been challenged. Its goal is to raise national consciousness regarding what the association perceived to be an escalating problem nationwide. This view, however, is skewed, says Jeff Jacoby. Our nation, he explains, isn't facing a book-banning crisis. Jacoby contends that the "banned books" on the ALA list are really books that have been merely considered "objectionable," usually by parents. And objecting to certain books isn't censorship.

Jeff Jacoby is often called the "conservative voice" of the *Boston Globe* where he is an editorial columnist. This editorial first appeared in the *Boston Globe* on September 21, 2001.

1 So you're proud to be an American? Glad to live in this sweet land of liberty, a country of fanatics hate because of its freedom, pluralism, and openness to new ideas? Well, just in time to pop that illusion, the American Library Association is back with Banned Books Week, its annual attempt to convince us that censorship is alive and well and eating way at our intellectual right to choose.

2 Not to worry. Your freedom to read isn't under attack. No censors are stalking you, no library is being stripped. On the contrary: Never have more books by more authors on more subjects been more readily available to more people. Americans have things to worry about these days, but book-banning isn't among them. For a "banned book," it turns out, doesn't mean a book that has been banned. It means a book about which somebody, usually a parent, has raised an objection—typically that it is too violent or sexually explicit or that it is not age-appropriate. The vast majority of these complaints deal with books assigned in school classes or found in school libraries. And as even the ALA acknowledges, the complaints usually go nowhere and the books stay where they are.

3 In short, the fanatics and book-burners against whom Banned Books Week is meant to keep us vigilant are mostly parents who raise questions about their kids' reading material. In the world according to the American Library Association, moms and dads are the enemy.

4 And the books this enemy is trying to ban? No. 1 on the ALA's current list is J. K. Rowling's *Harry Potter* series. No. 5 is John Steinbeck's *Of Mice and Men*. No. 6 is Maya Angelou's *I Know Why the Caged Bird Sings*. Those books can be found in 98 percent of the nation's bookstores and 99 percent of its libraries. They can be bought over the Web, listened to on tape, and read in a host of foreign languages. This is censorship?

5 Of course not every complaint about a book is reasonable. Parents who want to keep *Huckleberry Finn* and *Native Son* out of students' hands deserve to get short shrift. But not every complaint is unreasonable, either. Some books do contain vile language or graphic sex and violence; some books are inappropriate for younger readers. A parent who asks the local library to limit her 11-year-old's

access to *The Turner Diaries* because she doesn't want him reading neo-Nazi literature is hardly a fanatic. Yet the ALA makes no allowance for common sense. Anyone who challenges any book for any reason is "banning books."

6   Unless they work for a library or bookstore, that is. Nowhere does the ALA warn against, say, the bookstore buyer who refuses to stock a book because he doesn't like its message or the librarian who suppresses works by authors he disagrees with. "The selection criteria that librarians use may not always be what everybody wants," says spokeswoman Larra Clark. "I don't see that it's a real problem."

7   She ought to meet Tom Spence. He is the president of Spence Publishing Company, a small press dedicated to books on cultural and social issues written from a conservative outlook. Among its current offerings are A. J. Conyers's history of toleration, *The Long Truce*; *Shows About Nothing*, a study of film and TV by Boston College philosopher Thomas Hibbs; David Horowitz's bracing polemic on racial politics, *Hating Whitey*; and *Love and Economics: Why the Laissez-Faire Family Doesn't Work,* by the economist (and Forbes columnist) Jennifer Roback Morse. Serious books by serious authors, in other words, and presumably of interest to serious bookstores and libraries.

8   But consider some of the responses Spence received after mailing his Spring 2001 catalog.

9   From the director of a state university bookstore:

> *I wish to be REMOVED from your mailing list. I find some of your titles to be offensive and outright simple minded. I will not sell your titles in any of my stores so please do not promote these ridiculous books to me!*

10   From the manager at a Berkeley, Calif., bookstore:

> *Please take me off your mailing list. . . . We do NOT sell fascist publications.*

11   From the books editor at a major Midwestern daily, after receiving a review copy of *Love and Economics*.

> *Please take me off of your contact list. If you want to reach a narrow-minded audience, try the small-town rags.*

12   Then there was the public library in West Haven, Connecticut, that ordered Spence not to send any more catalogs. When the publisher called to ask why, the librarian hung up on him—four times.

13   Bookstores, libraries, and newspapers can't acquire or review every new book, of course. But should entire catalogs be blackballed or publishers insulted because of the ideological prejudice of the librarian or books editor? Isn't that a form of "book banning"? Maybe the ALA ought to take a closer look.

THINKING CRITICALLY

1. Consider the word *banned* and the word *challenged*. Do they mean the same thing? Is the American Library Association inflaming or exaggerating the issue of objectionable books by calling the week they discuss this issue "Banned Books Week"? Would the phrasing "Challenged Books Week" be more accurate? less effective? Explain.

2. What is Jacoby's argument against the ALA's Banned Books Week? Does he support his argument with reasonable evidence? Explain.

3. Jacoby comments that the books the "enemy" is trying to ban are found in 98 percent of the nation's bookstores and 99 percent of the nation's libraries. He then asks, "Is this censorship?" (paragraph 4). Answer his question.

4. According to Jacoby, what objections to books are "unreasonable"? Does the fact that he qualifies some objections as unthreatening, and others unreasonable, undermine his argument?

5. Consider Jacoby's closing comments regarding librarians and bookstore owners who refuse to stock certain titles, usually conservative ones, with which they do not agree. Is this simply another form of censorship? Explain.

WRITING ASSIGNMENTS

1. Is censorship of written materials ever permissible? If so, under what conditions? If not, why not? Write up your thoughts in an essay.

2. Have you ever encountered or heard of the banning of books in schools? If so, who proposed the censorship and why was it enforced? Write about the experience in an essay.

Exploring the Language of V I S U A L S

Banned Books Week 2006

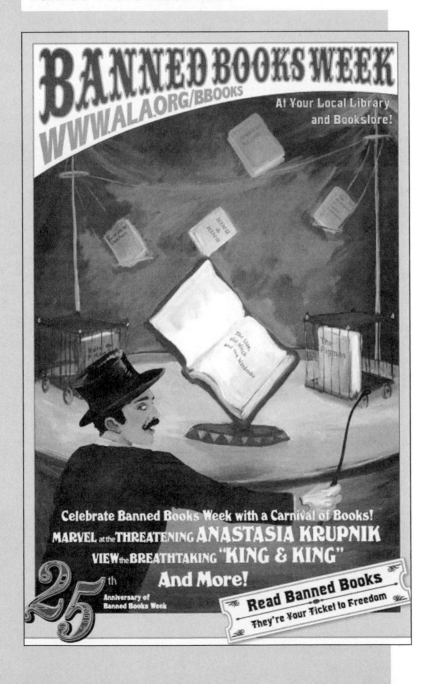

THINKING CRITICALLY

1. Who is the intended audience for this poster? What clues reveal the target audience? Explain.

2. What titles are featured in the poster? Are you familiar with any of them? Identify the ones you do know and look up the unfamiliar titles online. Explain what content might be considered objectionable, thus qualifing the books for the "Banned Books" list.

3. What does this poster encourage viewers to do, and how does it entice viewers to participate in "Banned Books Week 2006"? Explain.

4. Evaluate the "ticket stub" at the bottom of the poster. Why does the ALA claim that reading banned books is a "ticket to freedom"? Do you agree? Explain.

Is Harry Potter Evil?

Judy Blume

Editorial columnist Jeff Jacoby has noted that the most objected to books in 2001 (and 2002) were the Harry Potter series. According to the ALA, Harry Potter books were in the top 10 overall most challenged reading material from 1990 to 2000. In the next editorial, author Judy Blume (who has no less than five books on the 100 Most Challenged Books list) explains that it is dangerous to shrug off book censorship. Objecting to books such as the Harry Potter series harms not just the children who do not understand all the fuss, but also free society, which we treasure.

Judy Blume is the author of more than 20 books, including the frequently challenged *Are You There God? It's Me, Margaret; Tiger Eyes; Then Again, Maybe I Won't;* and *Blubber.* She is the editor of *Places I Never Meant to Be: Original Stories by Censored Writers.* This editorial first appeared in the *New York Times* on October 22, 1999.

1 I happened to be in London last summer on the very day *Harry Potter and the Prisoner of Azkaban,* the third book in the wildly popular series by J. K. Rowling, was published. I couldn't believe my good fortune. I rushed to the bookstore to buy a copy, knowing this simple act would put me up there with the best grandmas in the world. The book was still months away from publication in the United States, and I have an 8-year-old grandson who is a big Harry Potter fan.

2 It's a good thing when children enjoy books, isn't it? Most of us think so. But like many children's books these days, the Harry Potter series has recently come under fire. In Minnesota, Michigan, New York, California and South Carolina, parents who feel the books promote interest in the occult have called for their removal from classrooms and school libraries.

3 I knew this was coming. The only surprise is that it took so long—as long as it took for the zealots who claim they're protecting children from evil (and evil can be found lurking everywhere these days) to discover that children actually like these books. If children are excited about a book, it must be suspect.

4 I'm not exactly unfamiliar with this line of thinking, having had various books of mine banned from schools over the last 20 years. In my books, it's reality that's seen as corrupting. With Harry Potter, the perceived danger is fantasy. After all, Harry and his classmates attend the celebrated Hogwarts School of Witchcraft and Wizardry. According to certain adults, these stories teach witchcraft, sorcery and satanism. But hey, if it's not one "ism," it's another. I mean Madeleine L'Engle's *A Wrinkle in Time* has been targeted by censors for promoting New Ageism, and Mark Twain's *Adventures of Huckleberry Finn* for promoting racism. Gee, where does that leave the kids?

5 The real danger is not in the books, but in laughing off those who would ban them. The protests against Harry Potter follow a tradition that has been growing since the early 1980's and often leaves school principals trembling with fear that is then passed down to teachers and librarians.

6   What began with the religious right has spread to the politically correct. (Remember the uproar in Brooklyn last year when a teacher was criticized for reading a book entitled *Nappy Hair* to her class?) And now the gate is open so wide that some parents believe they have the right to demand immediate removal of any book for any reason from school or classroom libraries. The list of gifted teachers and librarians who find their jobs in jeopardy for defending their students' right to read, to imagine, to question, grows every year.

7   My grandson was bewildered when I tried to explain why some adults don't want their children reading about Harry Potter. "But that doesn't make any sense!" he said. J. K. Rowling is on a book tour in America right now. She's probably befuddled by the brouhaha, too. After all, she was just trying to tell a good story.

8   My husband and I like to reminisce about how, when we were 9, we read straight through L. Frank Baum's Oz series, books filled with wizards and witches. And you know what those subversive tales taught us? That we loved to read! In those days I used to dream of flying. I may have been small and powerless in real life, but in my imagination I was able to soar.

9   At the rate we're going, I can imagine next year's headline: "'Goodnight Moon' Banned for Encouraging Children to Communicate With Furniture." And we all know where that can lead, don't we?

THINKING CRITICALLY

1. How does Blume engage her audience? What techniques does she use to connect with her readers and encourage them to see her point of view? Explain.

2. What is a "zealot"? Why does Blume use this word to describe people who don't want their children to read certain books, including the Harry Potter series?

3. What is the "perceived danger" of the Harry Potter books? How does the author react to this "danger"? Do you think the fact that her own books have been banned influenced her reaction to objections to the Harry Potter books? Why or why not?

4. Consider Blume's concluding statements on book censorship. What is the tone of her hypothetical example of a headline featuring *Goodnight Moon*? Is it an effective ending to her editorial? Why or why not?

WRITING ASSIGNMENTS

1. Do parents have the right to object to certain books being used as reading material in school? Write an essay exploring the rights of parents to determine what their children read.

2. In your opinion, do you have the right to restrict the reading material of others? If there were a book to which you objected, would you attempt to have it banned from your child's school library? Why or why not?

Exploring the Language of **V I S U A L S**

Huckleberry Finn Banned!

Even when it was first published in 1885, Mark Twain's *Adventures of Huckleberry Finn* was the topic of controversy. That year, the public library in Concord, Massachusetts, banned it as "rude, coarse, and inelegant." More than one hundred years later,

with its revealing description of racism and slavery, it is still the most frequently challenged book in American schools. The classic novel describes the journey and revelations of a young man who decides to escape the rules of society by floating on a raft down the Mississippi River with an escaped slave named Jim. Although considered by many scholars to be a "staunchly anti-racist novel," African-American writer Toni Morrison conjectures that it unsettles people because it realistically depicts race relations—including the liberal use of the word *nigger*—in the pre–Civil War South to a society that is still divided along racial lines.

Nonetheless, most educators believe, as Ernest Hemingway expresses in the cover quotation, that Twain's work is a fundamental and shaping work of American literature essential to our understanding of the American experience. Attempts to ban the book raise many questions. Do we ignore the parts of American history that make us feel uncomfortable? Should books be banned if parents or teachers object to their content and if so, what content is considered "dangerous" or "harmful"? Finally, who decides what is acceptable for students to read? Although this issue raises many questions, the one thing that we do know, is that the *Huckleberry Finn* controversy will continue for many decades to come.

THINKING CRITICALLY

1. Does the cover of this edition of *Adventures of Huckleberry Finn* reveal anything about the controversy associated with it? Does the cover seem appropriate to the story and its theme? Explain.

2. Did you have to read *Adventures of Huckleberry Finn* in school? If so, what were your impressions of the story? Do you recall any objections you, your peers, your parents, or your teachers had to the novel? If the book was banned in your school, discuss the school committee's reasons for doing so and how you felt about such a measure.

3. Respond to the quote by Ernest Hemingway featured on the front jacket of this edition of *Adventures of Huckleberry Finn*. Do you agree with Hemingway's assessment? Why or why not?

4. Many of the people who call for the banning of *Adventures of Huckleberry Finn* from public libraries are concerned about the exposure of racial epithets to children. But what do you make of the fact that some of these same people were once part of the Free Speech Movement of the 1960s? Do you see this turnabout as justified or as hypocritical? Has political correctness gone too far? Or do you think that the "racial" material of the Twain classic is unsuitable for children?

5. Go to the University of Virginia's Mark Twain archives at http://etext.lib.virginia.edu/twain/huckfinn.html and examine some of the reviews and illustrations of the first edition of *Adventures of Huckleberry Finn*. Discuss these reviews and illustrations in the context of society both then and now.

Author's Afterword from *Fahrenheit 451*

Ray Bradbury

> First published in 1953, the classic science fiction novel *Fahrenheit 451* by Ray Bradbury depicts a future in which books forbidden by a totalitarian government are burned. In the novel, firemen don't put out fires—they start them, burning books in giant bonfires. By controlling information, the government creates a society in which the appearance of happiness is the highest goal—a place where trivial information is good, and knowledge and ideas are bad. The novel raises questions, including what is the price of censorship "protection" and who decides what is acceptable to read? The statement that follows is a recent response to readers and editors suggesting that Bradbury edit his stories to, ironically, make them more "acceptable" to certain audiences.
>
> Ray Bradbury is the author of more than five hundred short stories, novels, plays, and poems, including *The Martian Chronicles* (1950) and *The Illustrated Man* (1951). He has won numerous awards for his writing, including the Grand Master Award from the Science Fiction Writers of America.

1 About two years ago, a letter arrived from a solemn young Vassar lady telling me how much she enjoyed reading my experiment in space mythology, *The Martian Chronicles.*

2 But, she added, wouldn't it be a good idea, this late in time, to rewrite the book inserting more women's characters and roles?

3 A few years before that I got a certain amount of mail concerning the same Martian book complaining that the blacks in the book were Uncle Toms and why didn't I "do them over"?

4 Along about then came a note from a Southern white suggesting that I was prejudiced in favor of the blacks and the entire story should be dropped.

5 Two weeks ago my mountain of mail delivered forth a pipsqueak mouse of a letter from a well-known publishing house that wanted to reprint my story "The Fog Horn" in a high school reader.

6 In my story, I had described a lighthouse as having, late at night, an illumination coming from it that was a "God-Light." Looking up at it from the viewpoint of any sea-creature one would have felt that one was in "the Presence."

7 The editors had deleted "God-Light" and "in the Presence."

8 Some five years back, the editors of yet another anthology for school readers put together a volume with some 400 (count 'em) short stories in it. How do you cram 400 short stories by Twain, Irving, Poe, Maupassant and Bierce into one book?

9 Simplicity itself. Skin, debone, demarrow, scarify, melt, render down and destroy. Every adjective that counted, every verb that moved, every metaphor that weighed more than a mosquito—out! Every simile that would have made a sub-moron's mouth twitch—gone! Any aside that explained the two-bit philosophy of a first-rate writer—lost!

10 Every story, slenderized, starved, bluepenciled, leeched and bled white, resembled every other story. Twain read like Poe read like Shakespeare read like

Dostoevsky read like—in the finale—Edgar Guest. Every word of more than three syllables had been razored. Every image that demanded so much as one instant's attention—shot dead.

11   Do you begin to get the damned and incredible picture?

12   How did I react to all of the above?

13   By "firing" the whole lot.

14   By sending rejection slips to each and every one.

15   By ticketing the assembly of idiots to the far reaches of hell.

16   The point is obvious. There is more than one way to burn a book. And the world is full of people running about with lit matches. Every minority, be it Baptist/ Unitarian, Irish/Italian/Octogenarian/Zen Buddhist, Zionist/Seventh-day Adventist, Women's Lib/Republican, Mattachine/Four Square Gospel feels it has the will, the right, the duty to douse the kerosene, light the fuse. Every dimwit editor who sees himself as the source of all dreary blanc-mange plain porridge unleavened literature, licks his guillotine and eyes the neck of any author who dares to speak above a whisper or write above a nursery rhyme.

17   Fire-Captain Beatty, in my novel *Fahrenheit 451*, described how the books were burned first by minorities, each ripping a page or a paragraph from this book, then that, until the day came when the books were empty and the minds shut and the libraries closed forever.

18   "Shut the door, they're coming through the window, shut the window, they're coming through the door," are the words to an old song. They fit my lifestyle with newly arriving butcher/censors every month. Only six weeks ago, I discovered that, over the years, some cubby-hole editors at Ballantine Books, fearful of contaminating the young, had, bit by bit, censored some 75 separate sections from the novel. Students, reading the novel which, after all, deals with censorship and book-burning in the future, wrote to tell me of this exquisite irony. Judy-Lynn Del Rey, one of the new Ballantine editors, is having the entire book reset and republished this summer with all the damns and hells back in place.

19   A final test for old Job II here: I sent a play, *Leviathan 99*, off to a university theater a month ago. My play is based on the "Moby Dick" mythology, dedicated to Melville, and concerns a rocket crew and a blind space captain who venture forth to encounter a Great White Comet and destroy the destroyer. My drama premiers as an opera in Paris this autumn. But, for now, the university wrote back that they hardly dared do my play—it had no women in it! And the ERA ladies on campus would descend with ballbats if the drama department even tried!

20   Grinding my bicuspids into powder, I suggested that would mean, from now on, no more productions of *Boys in the Band* (no women), or *The Women* (no men). Or, counting heads, male and female, a good lot of Shakespeare that would never be seen again, especially if you count lines and find that all the good stuff went to the males!

21   I wrote back maybe they should do my play one week, and *The Women* the next. They probably thought I was joking, and I'm not sure that I wasn't.

22   For it is a mad world and it will get madder if we allow the minorities, be they dwarf or giant, orangutan or dolphin, nuclear-head or water-conversationalist,

pro-computerologist or Neo-Luddite, simpleton or sage, to interfere with aesthetics. The real world is the playing ground for each and every group, to make or unmake laws. But the tip of the nose of my book or stories or poems is where their rights end and my territorial imperatives begin, run and rule. If Mormons do not like my plays, let them write their own. If the Irish hate my Dublin stories, let them rent typewriters. If teachers and grammar school editors find my jawbreaker sentences shatter their mushmilk teeth, let them eat stale cake dunked in weak tea of their own ungodly manufacture. If the Chicano intellectuals wish to re-cut my "Wonderful Ice Cream Suit" so it shapes "Zoot," may the belt unravel and the pants fall.

23 For, let's face it, digression is the soul of wit. Take philosophic asides away from Dante, Milton or Hamlet's father's ghost and what stays is dry bones. Laurence Sterne said it once: Digressions, incontestably, are the sunshine, the life, the soul of reading! Take them out and one cold eternal winter would reign in every page. Restore them to the writer—he steps forth like a bridegroom, bids them all-hail, brings in variety and forbids the appetite to fail.

24 In sum, do not insult me with the beheadings, finger-choppings or the lung-deflations you plan for my works. I need my head to shake or nod, my hand to wave or make into a fist, my lungs to shout or whisper with. I will not go gently onto a shelf, degutted, to become a non-book.

25 All you umpires, back to the bleachers. Referees, hit the showers. It's my game. I pitch, I hit, I catch. I run the bases. At sunset I've won or lost. At sunrise, I'm out again, giving it the old try.

26 And no one can help me. Not even you.

THINKING CRITICALLY

1. According to Bradbury, what happens when books are edited to make them more "acceptable" to audiences? Do you agree with him? Explain.

2. Bradbury compares himself to the biblical figure Job. What is the effect of this comparison? Why does he use it? How might it be ironic?

3. Consider the tone Bradbury uses in this essay. Is he angry, defiant, sarcastic, or resigned? How does his tone influence the audience's reception of his points? What does he hope to impress upon his readers?

4. What is the impact of Bradbury's final statement? Explain.

WRITING ASSIGNMENT

1. In paragraph 22, Bradbury proclaims, ". . . it is a mad world and it will get madder if we allow the minorities . . . to interfere with aesthetics." Do you agree with him, or do you think he protests too much? Do you think there are works—including Bradbury's—that could, or should, be rewritten to better reflect or appeal to a more diversified audience? Write Ray Bradbury a letter explaining why you agree or disagree with his views.

MAKING CONNECTIONS

1. Is censorship of written materials ever permissible? If so, under what conditions? If not, why not? Write your thoughts in an essay.

2. Have you ever encountered or heard of the banning of books in schools? If so, who proposed the censorship and why was it enforced? Write about the experience in an essay.

3. As violence in and outside of school has escalated in recent years, complaints about reading material for children have shifted from outrage about sexual matters to concern about violence. Although recent efforts to pass legislation making it a felony to expose children to books, movies, and video games that contain explicit sex or violence have failed, the debate lingers among the book stacks of public and school libraries. Some argue that reading about violence is not the same as watching movie mayhem. Others say both have the same detrimental effects on young people. What do you think? Write an essay in which you explore the effects of graphic violence in books versus violence on the screen. The following titles have recently been singled out for criticism: *Of Mice and Men* by John Steinbeck (1937), *A Time to Kill* by John Grisham (1989), *More Scary Stories to Tell in the Dark* by Alvin Schwartz (1984), *I Know What You Did Last Summer* by Lois Duncan (1973), *The Devil's Storybook* by Natalie Babbitt (1974), and *Hannibal* by Thomas Harris (1999).

4. Was *Adventures of Huckleberry Finn* banned in your elementary or high school? Were any other books? If so, which ones and why? If you are not sure, contact your former English teachers or local school committee to find out if any books are not on the accepted reading lists. Were students aware of the forbidden books, or was the subject not an issue? Were students more eager to read the banned books?

5. Take an opinion poll on book-banning in your area. Ask individuals from different age groups for their perspective on book-banning. If a respondent is in favor of restricting book access, ask for a list of books to be banned. Can you draw any conclusions from your research?

BIASED LANGUAGE AND HATE SPEECH

Hate Speech

Robin Tolmach Lakoff

While the First Amendment protects free speech, not protected. You cannot, for example, yell "fire" in a crowded th threaten someone with bodily harm, commit perjury, or another individual. Less clear are attitudes toward "fighting are "so very bad that, upon hearing them, an ordinary pers and words that hurt such as racial epithets. This is the lang

to the "politically correct"—or p.c.—movement. In this article, linguist Robin
Tomach Lakoff takes a look at both sides of the p.c. "hate speech" debate.
Should hate speech be protected under the First Amendment? As Lakoff
explains, how we feel about this issue is closely connected to how we view the
power of language itself.

Robin Tomach Lakoff is a professor of linguistics at the University of California Berkeley. She is the author of several books on language and politics,
most recently *Talking Power: The Politics of Language in Our Lives* (1990) and
The Language War (2000), from which this essay is excerpted.

1 The jewel in the anti-p.c. crown is the First Amendment, newly claimed by the right
as its own. Historically the First Amendment was a thorn in the conservative side: it
offered protection to nonmajoritarian views, lost causes, and the disenfranchised—
not to mention, of course, Communists and worse. From the Sedition Act of the
Adams administration to continual attempts to pass a constitutional amendment
banning flag-desecration, conservatives have always tried to impose sanctions on
free expression, while liberals have tried to keep the "marketplace of ideas" open to
all traders. For most of this century it has been the liberal wing of the Supreme
Court that has struck down constraints on expression, from Nazi marches to anti-
war protests, and the conservative wing that has tried to keep them in effect. But
when the shoe is on the other foot and language control is passing from them, conservatives rethink that position. If p.c. can be framed as an attempt to wrest from *us*
our historical right to use whatever language we want, whenever we want, to
whomever we want, its proponents can be made out to be opponents of free speech
and—voilà—we are metamorphosed into all-American defenders of the First
Amendment against the infidel Hun, or the p.c. professoriate.

2 No one is expressly demanding the right to make use of hateful slurs. As Mari
Matsuda notes, those with media access, the educated upper classes, need not stoop
so low: "The various implements of racism find their way into the hands of different dominant-group members. Lower- and middle-class white men might use violence against people of color, whereas upper-class whites might resort to private
clubs or righteous indignation against 'diversity' and 'reverse discrimination'" (in
Matsuda et al. 1993, 23). So a member of a higher caste might never actually be exposed to virulent racist or sexist language among his associates, and therefore
might be able to claim that it didn't exist any more or need not be taken seriously
(because *we* don't have to encounter it in its more distasteful forms). And while
there do exist epithets to be hurled at males and whites ("phallocrat," "honky"),
they lack the sting of slurs against women, blacks, Latinos, and Asians. That is because, according to Matsuda, "racist speech proclaims racial inferiority and denies
the personhood of target-group members. All members of the target group are at
once considered alike and inferior" (36).

3 But a proclamation of inferiority is meaningful, or even possible, only if it can
piggyback on an older stereotype of one race (or gender) as inferior: the "Snark
Rule," which states that repetition makes a statement "true." Judith Butler defines
hate speech as working through the repetition of similar prior speech acts: "hate
speech is an act that recalls prior acts, requiring a future repetition to endure" (1997,
if your group, or you as an individual member of that group, have never been

subjected to epithets in the past, no words directed at you, however irritating, can have the full noxious effect of true hate speech. That is not to say that such language is benign. But if you are not a member of a historically submerged group, "you just don't get it," since you don't have a visceral understanding of the harm such speech can do. So it's relatively easy for you to see racist and sexist language and behavior as "just kidding" or "childish horseplay" and not demand a remedy for it.

4   Those who don't have personal reasons to feel that hateful epithets are damaging and who at the same time feel that any challenge to the right to use such speech is a serious threat to the First Amendment are apt to feel not only permitted but obligated, as a sacred duty, to oppose any attempts to legislate language control—at least those that come from the other side and attempt to constrain *our* preferred linguistic possibilities. Laws that might constrain *theirs* are still unproblematic. Hence the right's continuing attempts to outlaw flag-burning, and the loud ruckus on the right that followed the 1989 five-to-four Supreme Court decision (*Texas v. Johnson*) that flag-burning constituted permissible expression under the First Amendment.[1]

5   To listen to some born-again First Amendment advocates, you would believe that its guarantee of free speech is and has always been absolute. But that is far from the case. Courts have always recognized the validity of competing claims: "clear and present danger," "falsely shouting 'fire' in a crowded theater," imminent threat, "fighting words," national interest, libel, threats, subornation of perjury, perjury itself, and others. Even some speech rights we consider uncontroversial today—including the right to provide birth control information or the right to protest the government's involvement in a war—were guaranteed only after arduous struggles. Even if hate speech regulations were to be enforced, that would not be the first curtailment of the absolute right to say anything, under any circumstances. In pondering the need for legislation against hate speech, the first question to address is the validity of competing interests. Does the right to enjoy speech that is as free as possible outweigh the right to "the equal protection of the laws" guaranteed to each of us under the Fourteenth Amendment, or vice versa?

6   This argument pits supporters of the Fourteenth Amendment (Critical Race Theorists and anti-pornography feminists like Catharine MacKinnon) against the odd couple composed of card-carrying ACLU liberals and conservative First Amendment supporters. Everyone agrees that hate speech is deplorable, and no reasonable person would ever indulge in any form of it. But the sides differ on what is to be done and on the consequences of what is done. Is racism so pervasive across this country and on college campuses, and other remedies so ineffectual, that speech codes must be enforced to guarantee to all the equal protection mandated by the Fourteenth Amendment? Or is the problem exaggerated—are there other ways to combat it, and does the need for preserving the First Amendment outweigh the responsibility to enforce the Fourteenth?

7   As a card-carrying ACLU member who is also a member of a couple of historically targeted groups, and as a member of a profession that abhors an unqualified statement, I naturally straddle the line. Others are more decisive. The CRTists tend to see hate speech as deeply pervasive, an increasing "epidemic" that can only be stopped by the immunization of speech codes. In the introduction to *Words That Wound*, its four authors argue that "Incidents of hate speech and racial harassment

are reported with increasing frequency and regularity, particularly on American college campuses, where they have reached near epidemic proportions" (Matsuda et. al. 1993, 1).

8   Since no figures are given, it is difficult to assess the accuracy of the claim. Even reports of an increasing number of acts of hate speech on college campuses would not necessarily show that hate speech had reached "epidemic" proportions—and might not even be an unequivocally bad thing. First, the larger numbers might merely be the result of more such acts being reported, a sign that minorities are being listened to more and taken more seriously than they used to be and that they now feel safe enough to complain. Even if there actually are more acts committed, that might merely mean that the presence of more minorities and women in places where they previously had not had entree creates more readily available targets, and arouses more resentment. But even if the authors of *Words That Wound* have identified a real problem of endemic racism and sexism in America, the remedy is still not obvious: to some it is not even apparent that any remedy is needed, much less what remedy will work and occasion the least interference with freedom of speech.

Language: Thought or Action?

9 Once again language is the problem. We don't know how to legislate hate speech, because we don't really know how to classify any kind of speech, which we would have to do before we could safely legislate against it. We are pretty clear on other kinds of human activity. Most of us would agree that thought cannot be an object of legislation and should not become one even if science could develop ways to peer into our minds. On the other hand, overt actions are always subject to control by law, and we would agree that they have to be, if we are to live together more or less peaceably in a state of civilization. We may argue about what kinds of actions should be punishable, and how, but punished bad actions must be. Language is intermediate between thought and action: it is thought made observable. It straddles the line between the abstract and the concrete, the ethereal and the corporeal. Which of its aspects—the ethereal or the physical—should be the basis of our legal understanding of the capacity of language to do harm? Is language inconsequential and therefore immune to legislation? Or is language equivalent to action—world-changing and so capable of harm—in which case legal notice must be taken of injurious linguistic behavior?

10   We teach our children the proverb "Sticks and stones may break my bones, but words will never harm me." Do we offer this saying as truth or as wishful magic: believe it and the pain will go away? Probably we would not be so quick to teach our children these words if we did not fear that the opposite was true. In our natural desire to save our children from pain, we encourage them to deny their feelings. But denial doesn't make it so.

11   We have only recently become a psychologically conscious society. Only in the last hundred years or so have we talked about psychic *wounds* and mental *diseases*. We are never sure whether we mean those expressions as literal descriptions or metaphors. We know that an autopsy on someone suffering from psychic trauma would reveal no physical evidence of that "wound." Yet there now exist physical

interventions in the form of drugs that "cure" these traumas, and this possibility of physical "cure" argues for the physical reality of the symptoms.

12   When our legal system was established, it seemed clear that words were not deeds, so only physical misbehaviors were legally actionable. The legal systems of all societies specify punishments or remedies for physical harm. The wound is visible; witnesses may have observed exactly what occurred. There may be disagreement among the parties about the interpretation of the events: Did the victim do anything to provoke the act? Did the perpetrator perform it intentionally? Did he mean to do harm? To do as much harm as he did? Are there other extenuating circumstances? But all participants can agree that something took place that changed the physical world.

13   But what about "words that wound"? Is that expression even meaningful? Are those who feel verbally wounded describing a real interaction with real and adjudicable consequences, or are they merely oversensitive souls who should grow up and take it like a man? If outsiders can't observe the damage, how can anyone prescribe a legal remedy for it?

14   If observers can agree on the amount and kind of force employed to make a physical wound, they can agree on the amount of damage probably sustained by the victim: their conclusions are based on scientifically demonstrable physical laws. But words mean different things to different people in different contexts: a word that would shock and intimidate a woman uttered by a strange man on a dark street at night might be a delightful expression of intimacy between her and someone she loves and trusts. African Americans can call one another "nigger" with relative impunity under specific conditions, but a white person cannot do the same. Language by nature is ambiguous and sensitive to context. The law by necessity strives to be precise and decontextualized. There is a discontinuity between the two words in the expression "language crime." Yet the law recognizes several: threats, defamation, offers of bribes, and perjury, for example. To make these concepts workable, we need to reach a formal understanding of language and its relation to action.

Speech Acts: "Only Theory" or Reality?

15 Relevant here is the discussion of J. L. Austin's theory of performative speech acts. Austin concluded that language was equivalent to action, in that all utterances were performative and all performatives were world-changing—that is, actions. That theory has had important consequences for several academic fields: philosophy and linguistics (naturally), as well as literary theory, anthropology, and education. As long as it is confined safely within academia, it is mere theory that applies only to ideas, with few actual consequences. But in recent years, it has been incorporated into the discourse of the law, by both legal scholars (as in several papers of Peter Tiersma [1986, 1987]) and sociolinguists (see, for example, Shuy 1993). But nowhere does speech act theory have such concrete and far-reaching consequences as in the definitions of hate speech and its legal status.

16   Those who believe in Austin's formulation are likely to follow it to its logical conclusion: that linguistic misbehavior is a type of bad action and should be treated as such by the law, criminally and civilly. A strict Austinian is likely to support speech codes. If problems of enforceability arise based on the vagueness or ambiguity of

language, it is the job of the codifiers to rewrite their statutes clearly enough to solve the problem. Those who disagree with Austin are apt to treat words very differently from actions, beyond the reach of legal remedy in most or even all cases.

17   There are many mixed positions and evasions, depending on the ability to draw and maintain a distinction between those kinds of language that constitute action-equivalents and others that are closer to thought-equivalents. Since the 1920's First Amendment law has divided utterances along those lines: language that constitutes "expression" and receives a high degree of protection under the First Amendment, versus language that constitutes "conduct" and doesn't. A political opinion like "the Republicans deserve to win" will be counted in the first set and be protected, while a threat (even in indirect form) like, "I have a gun and I know how to use it" will under many circumstances be judged "conduct" and treated as a criminal action.

18   A crucial concept is that of "fighting words," as addressed in the 1942 Supreme Court decision *Chaplinsky v. New Hampshire*, which established the category of "fighting words" as unprotected action-equivalents. Chaplinsky, a Jehovah's Witness, got into a verbal altercation with the town marshal of Rochester, New Hampshire, in the course of which he used language considered very shocking in its time, calling the marshal a "Goddamned racketeer" and a "damned Fascist."[2] He was arrested and found guilty under the town's speech code, which prohibited "fighting words." The case was appealed up to the U.S. Supreme Court, which found for the state. In its unanimous opinion, the Court defined "fighting words"; "There are certain well-defined and narrowly limited classes of speech, the prevention and punishment of which have never been thought to raise any Constitutional problem. These include the lewd and obscene, the profane, the libelous, and the insulting or 'fighting' words—those which by their very utterance inflict injury or tend to incite an immediate breach of the peace."

19   Significantly *Chaplinsky*, as well as later decisions citing it as precedent, locate the justification for the "fighting words" exception in the government's duties to prevent injury to citizens and keep the peace. The former has been essentially negated by later opinions, while the latter has provided appellate courts with an enduring can of worms. If the danger of "fighting words" is that the addressee is apt to lose control and breach the peace (the "breach" is accomplished, in this perspective, only via actions, not via the offensive utterance itself), why not hold the breacher, not the utterer, responsible? The Court's assumption is that some words are so very bad that on hearing them, an ordinary person *must* strike out (as reflexively as, when the doctor taps your knee with a hammer, you *have* to jerk your leg). No psychological or other evidence is cited in support of this proposition.

20   *Chaplinsky* would seem to suggest that verbal aggressors should pick their targets carefully. Persons with less testosterone are known to be less likely than those with more to react physically to provocation. So, presumably, insulting women is more likely to be constitutional under *Chaplinsky* than insulting men, and it's probably better to insult someone smaller than you (who will be less likely to "breach the peace") than someone larger. Scholars who try to justify speech codes these days, like the authors of *Words That Wound,* avoid the morass by thinking in terms of psychic rather than physical trauma. But the "fighting words" exception was not meant to cover psychic wounds, and even if it were determining whether psychic

trauma has occurred is—if possible at all—not the business of a court of law and a lay jury.

21   As fond as linguists are of Austinian doctrine (if words are actions, then what we linguists do is important), we must recognize that in fact words are not the same as actions. Most people given the choice between a vile epithet and a punch in the nose would opt for the former. Arguably this is because the second has immediate and obvious painful consequences, while the effects of the first take longer to emerge and are harder to link directly to their cause. If, as the judge said in admitting *Ulysses* into the country, no woman was ever seduced by a book, so no one was ever killed by a word. If language is world-changing, the way it works is different from that of direct action, and less accessible to legal investigation.

22   Franklyn Haiman, in *"Speech Acts" and the First Amendment* (1993), proposes that language is "mediated" action. Austin is not quite right, he suggests, in equating performativity with action. When I give an order, you have to perform the mental act of *deciding* or *willing* to obey me. Even in the clearer case of excommunication, the recipient must determine that the appropriate conditions are met and decide to behave as an excommunicated person in the future, for it to succeed. The words alone, Haiman points out, are meaningless: they derive force through the agreement by all participants on the nature of the real-world circumstances in which they find themselves.

23   But Haiman is not quite right to dismiss the word-as-action theory entirely. While words are not directly as world-changing as actions are, they are indirectly or psychologically world-changing. If I make a promise to you, that utterance forever alters our relationship and the way I think about it and behave toward you, and you toward me, in the future. To say that speech is not action is to fall into the logical error of drawing a sharp distinction between mind and body.

24   How we feel about hate speech and the First Amendment reflects our view of language itself. If we believe that words are not world-changing, we are apt to be comfortable with an interpretation of the First Amendment that permits much more freedom of speech than is permitted to action. But this leeway comes at the price, ironically, of devaluing language—seeing it as non-action, essentially harmless.

Notes

1. At this writing, an anti–flag desecration law has passed the House of Representatives and is considered likely to pass the Senate.
2. Chaplinsky admitted making the basic statement, but said that as a Jehovah's Witness, he would never have uttered the d-word.

THINKING CRITICALLY

1. This article comments on "right" and "left" attitudes toward the First Amendment. To what does this refer? In what ways have the political left and right used the First Amendment to forward their own agendas? Explain.

2. In several places in this essay, Lakoff strategically puts certain words in italics, including pronouns. Why does she do this? How does her use of italics contribute to what she is trying to relay to the reader? Explain.

3. What is the author's personal position on politically correct language and hate speech codes? When does her position become clear? Does she fairly describe both sides of the issue? Explain.

4. Why does Lakoff say some racial epithets are worse than others? For example, are "phallocrat" and "honkey" parallel to other racial slurs? Why or why not?

5. What is the "Snark rule"? How does it relate to the impact of hate speech on a population?

6. In paragraph 5, Lakoff cites several examples of kinds of speech not protected by the First Amendment. How can her examples be used to support both sides of the hate speech argument? Explain.

7. In her discussion of *Chaplinksy v. New Hampshire* (paragraphs 18–20), Lakoff concludes that the ruling on the case "would seem to suggest that verbal aggressors should pick their targets carefully . . . So, presumably, insulting women is more likely to be constitutional than insulting men. . . ." Describe the case and how Lakoff draws such a conclusion. Do you agree? Why or why not?

8. In paragraph 21, Lakoff explains why she feels that words are not actions. On what does she base her assessment? Why does she feel that Austin and Haiman are incorrect in their presumption that action and speech are corollaries? Explain.

9. In her closing comments, Lakoff comments that how we feel about hate speech has a great deal to do with how we feel about language. In your own words, explain what she means by this statement.

WRITING ASSIGNMENTS

1. In your experience, has anyone called you, or a member of a group to which you belong, a name you found offensive? How did that incident make you feel? What was your response? Write a paper based on your answer.

2. In this essay, Lakoff notes that individuals or groups who do not have a history of hearing hate speech "just don't get it." It is the historical repetition and legacy of such language that give racial and sexist epithets their sting. Write an essay exploring this idea from your own viewpoint.

Bias-Free Language: Some Guidelines
Rosalie Maggio

The growing reality of America's multiculturalism has produced a heightened sensitivity to language offensive to members of minority groups. In response, a number of bias-free language guides have been written—guides that caution against terms that might offend not only racial and ethnic groups but women, gays, senior citizens, the handicapped, animal lovers, and the overweight. One of the most successful guides is Rosalie Maggio's *The Dictionary of Bias-Free Usage: A Guide to Nondiscriminatory Language* (1991). In the following excerpt from that guide's introduction, the author discusses how to evaluate and recognize language bias, and why it should be avoided.

Rosalie Maggio is also the author of *The Nonsexist Word Finder* (1987), *How to Say It: Words, Phrases, Sentences, and Paragraphs for Every Situation* (1990), and, most recently, *The Art of Talking to Anyone* (2005). She has edited many college textbooks and published hundreds of stories and articles in educational publications and children's magazines. Her work has received several literary honors and awards for children's fiction and research on women's issues.

1 Language both reflects and shapes society. The textbook on American government that consistently uses male pronouns for the president, even when not referring to a specific individual (e.g., "a president may cast his veto"), reflects the fact that all our presidents have so far been men. But it also shapes a society in which the idea of a female president somehow "doesn't sound right."

2 Culture shapes language and then language shapes culture. "Contrary to the assumption that language merely reflects social patterns such as sex-role stereotypes, research in linguistics and social psychology has shown that these are in fact facilitated and reinforced by language" (Marlis Hellinger, in *Language and Power*, ed., Cheris Kramarae et al.).

3 Biased language can also, says Sanford Berman, "powerfully harm people, as amply demonstrated by bigots' and tyrants' deliberate attempts to linguistically dehumanize and demean groups they intend to exploit, oppress, or exterminate. Calling Asians 'gooks' made it easier to kill them. Calling blacks 'niggers' made it simpler to enslave and brutalize them. Calling Native Americans 'primitives' and 'savages' made it okay to conquer and despoil them. And to talk of 'fishermen,' 'councilmen,' and 'longshoremen' is to clearly exclude and discourage women from those pursuits, to diminish and degrade them."

4 The question is asked: Isn't it silly to get upset about language when there are so many more important issues that need our attention?

5 First, it's to be hoped that there are enough of us working on issues large and small that the work will all get done—someday. Second, the interconnections between the way we think, speak, and act are beyond dispute. Language goes hand-in-hand with social change—both shaping it and reflecting it. Sexual harassment was not a term anyone used twenty years ago; today we have laws against it. How could we have the law without the language; how could we have the language without the law? In fact, the judicial system is a good argument for the importance of "mere words"; the legal profession devotes great energy to the precise interpretation of words—often with far-reaching and significant consequences.

6 On August 21, 1990, in the midst of the Iraqi offensive, front-page headlines told the big story: President Bush had used the word *hostages* for the first time. Up to that time, *detainee* had been used. The difference between two very similar words was of possible life-and-death proportions. In another situation—also said to be life-and-death by some people—the difference between *fetal tissue* and *unborn baby* (in referring to the very same thing) is arguably the most debated issue in the country. So, yes, words have power and deserve our attention.

7 Some people are like George Crabbe's friend: "Habit with him was all the test of truth, / it must be right: I've done it from my youth." They have come of age using *handicapped, black-and-white, leper, mankind,* and pseudogeneric *he*; these terms must therefore be correct. And yet if there's one thing consistent about language it is that language is constantly changing; when the *Random*

House Dictionary of the English Language: 2nd Edition was published in 1988, it contained 50,000 new entries, most of them words that had come into use since 1966. There were also 75,000 new definitions. (Incidentally, *RHD-II* asks its readers to "use gender-neutral terms wherever possible" and it never uses *mankind* in definitions where *people* is meant, nor does it ever refer to anyone of unknown gender as *he*.) However, few supporters of bias-free language are asking for changes; it is rather a matter of choice—which of the many acceptable words available to us will we use?

8   A high school student who felt that nonsexist language did demand some changes said, "But you don't understand! You're trying to change the English language, which has been around a lot longer than women have!"

9   One reviewer of the first edition commented, "There's no fun in limiting how you say a thing." Perhaps not. Yet few people complain about looking up a point of grammar or usage or checking the dictionary for a correct spelling. Most writers are very fussy about finding the precise best word, the exact rhythmic vehicle for their ideas. Whether or not these limits "spoil their fun" is an individual judgment. However, most of us accept that saying or writing the first thing that comes to mind is not often the way we want to be remembered. So if we have to think a little, if we have to search for the unbiased word, the inclusive phrase, it is not any more effort than we expend on proper grammar, spelling, and style.

10   Other people fear "losing" words, as though there weren't more where those came from. We are limited only by our imaginations; vague, inaccurate, and disrespectful words can be thrown overboard with no loss to society and no impoverishment of the language.

11   Others are tired of having to "watch what they say." But what they perhaps mean is that they're tired of being sensitive to others' requests. From childhood onward, we all learn to "watch what we say": we don't swear around our parents; we don't bring up certain topics around certain people; we speak differently to friend, boss, cleric, English teacher, lover, radio interviewer, child. Most of us are actually quite skilled at picking and choosing appropriate words; it seems odd that we are too "tired" to call people what they want to be called.

12   The greatest objection to bias-free language is that it will lead us to absurdities. Critics have posited something utterly ridiculous, cleverly demonstrated how silly it is, and then accounted themselves victorious in the battle against linguistic massacre. For example: "So I suppose now we're going to say: He/she ain't heavy, Father/Sister; he/she's my brother/sister." "I suppose next it will be 'ottoperson'." Cases have been built up against the mythic "woperson," "personipulate," and "personhole cover" (none of which has ever been advocated by any reputable sociolinguist). No grist appears too ridiculous for these mills. And, yes, they grind exceedingly small. Using a particular to condemn a universal is a fault in logic. But then ridicule, it is said, is the first and last argument of fools.

13   One of the most rewarding—and, for many people, the most unexpected—side effects of breaking away from traditional, biased language is a dramatic improvement in writing style. By replacing fuzzy, overgeneralized, cliché-ridden words with explicit, active words and by giving concrete examples and anecdotes instead

of one-word-fits-all descriptions you can express yourself more dynamically, convincingly, and memorably.

14   "If those who have studied the art of writing are in accord on any one point, it is on this: the surest way to arouse and hold the attention of the reader is by being specific, definite, and concrete" (Strunk and White, *The Elements of Style*). Writers who talk about *brotherhood* or *spinsters* or *right-hand men* miss a chance to spark their writing with fresh descriptions; they leave their readers as uninspired as they are. Unthinking writing is also less informative. Why use the unrevealing *adman* when we could choose instead a precise, descriptive, inclusive word like *advertising executive, copywriter, account executive, ad writer,* or *media buyer?*

15   The word *manmade*, which seems so indispensable to us, doesn't actually say very much. Does it mean artificial? Handmade? Synthetic? Fabricated? Machine-made? Custom-made? Simulated? Plastic? Imitation? Contrived?

16   Communication is—or ought to be—a two-way street. A speaker who uses *man* to mean *human being* while the audience hears it as *adult male* is an example of communication gone awry.

17   Bias-free language is logical, accurate, and realistic. Biased language is not. How logical is it to speak of the "discovery" of America, a land already inhabited by millions of people? Where is the accuracy in writing "Dear Sir" to a woman? Where is the realism in the full-page automobile advertisement that says in bold letters, "A good driver is a product of his environment," when more women than men influence car-buying decisions? Or how successful is the ad for a dot-matrix printer that says, "In 3,000 years, man's need to present his ideas hasn't changed. But his tools have," when many of these printers are bought and used by women, who also have ideas they need to present? And when we use stereotypes to talk about people ("isn't that just like a welfare mother/Indian/girl/old man"), our speech and writing will be inaccurate and unrealistic most of the time.

Definition of Terms

Bias/Bias-Free

18 Biased language communicates inaccurately about what it means to be male or female; black or white; young or old; straight, gay, or bi; rich or poor; from one ethnic group or another; disabled or temporarily able-bodied; or to hold a particular belief system. It reflects the same bias found in racism, sexism, ageism, handicappism, classism, ethnocentrism, anti-Semitism, homophobia, and other forms of discrimination.

19   Bias occurs in the language in several ways.

1. Leaving out individuals or groups. "Employees are welcome to bring their wives and children" leaves out those employees who might want to bring husbands, friends, or same-sex partners. "We are all immigrants in this country" leaves out Native Americans, who were here well before the first immigrants.

2. Making unwarranted assumptions. To address a sales letter about a new diaper to the mother assumes that the father won't be diapering the baby. To write

"Anyone can use this fire safety ladder" assumes that all members of the household are able-bodied.

3. Calling individuals and groups by names or labels that they do not choose for themselves (e.g., *Gypsy, office girl, Eskimo, pygmy, Bushman, the elderly, colored man*) or terms that are derogatory (*fairy, libber, savage, bum, old goat*).

4. Stereotypical treatment that implies that all lesbians/Chinese/women/people with disabilities/teenagers are alike.

5. Unequal treatment of various groups in the same material.

6. Unnecessary mention of membership in a particular group. In a land of supposedly equal opportunity, of what importance is a person's race, sex, age, sexual orientation, disability, or creed? As soon as we mention one of these characteristics—without a good reason for doing so—we enter an area mined by potential linguistic disasters. Although there may be instances in which a person's sex, for example, is germane ("A recent study showed that female patients do not object to being cared for by male nurses"), most of the time it is not. Nor is mentioning a person's race, sexual orientation, disability, age, or belief system usually germane.

20   Bias can be overt or subtle. Jean Gaddy Wilson (in Brooks and Pinson, *Working with Words*) says, "Following one simple rule of writing or speaking will eliminate most biases. Ask yourself: Would you say the same thing about an affluent, white man?"

Inclusive/Exclusive

21 Inclusive language includes everyone; exclusive language excludes some people. The following quotation is inclusive: "The greatest revolution of our generation is the discovery that human beings, by changing the inner attitudes of their minds, can change the outer aspects of their lives" (William James). It is clear that James is speaking of all of us.

22   Examples of sex-exclusive writing fill most quotation books: "Man is the measure of all things" (Protagoras). "The People, though we think of a great entity when we use the word, means nothing more than so many millions of individual men" (James Bryce). "Man is nature's sole mistake" (W. S. Gilbert).

Sexist/Nonsexist

23 Sexist language promotes and maintains attitudes that stereotype people according to gender while assuming that the male is the norm—the significant gender. Nonsexist language treats all people equally and either does not refer to a person's sex at all when it is irrelevant or refers to men and women in symmetrical ways.

24   "A society in which women are taught anything but the management of a family, the care of men, and the creation of the future generation is a society which is on the way out" (L. Ron Hubbard). "Behind every successful man is a woman—with nothing to wear" (L. Grant Glickman). "Nothing makes a man and wife feel

closer, these days, than a joint tax return" (Gil Stern). These quotations display various characteristics of sexist writing: (1) stereotyping an entire sex by what might be appropriate for some of it; (2) assuming male superiority; (3) using unparallel terms (*man and wife* should be either *wife and husband/husband and wife* or *woman and man/man and woman*).

25   The following quotations clearly refer to all people: "It's really hard to be roommates with people if your suitcases are much better than theirs" (J. D. Salinger). "If people don't want to come out to the ball park, nobody's going to stop them" (Yogi Berra). "If men and women of capacity refuse to take part in politics and government, they condemn themselves, as well as the people, to the punishment of living under bad government" (Senator Sam J. Ervin). "I studied the lives of great men and famous women, and I found that the men and women who got to the top were those who did the jobs they had in hand, with everything they had of energy and enthusiasm and hard work" (Harry S Truman).

Gender-Free/Gender-Fair/Gender-Specific

26 Gender-free terms do not indicate sex and can be used for either women/girls or men/boys (e.g., *teacher, bureaucrat, employee, hiker, operations manager, child, clerk, sales rep, hospital patient, student, grandparent, chief executive officer*).

27   Writing or speech that is gender-fair involves the symmetrical use of gender-specific words (e.g., *Ms. Leinwohl/Mr. Kelly, councilwoman/councilman, young man/young woman*) and promotes fairness to both sexes in the larger context. To ensure gender-fairness, ask yourself often: Would I write the same thing in the same way about a person of the opposite sex? Would I mind if this were said of me?

28   If you are describing the behavior of children on the playground, to be gender-fair you will refer to girls and boys an approximately equal number of times, and you will carefully observe what the children do, and not just assume that only the boys will climb to the top of the jungle gym and that only the girls will play quiet games.

29   Researchers studying the same baby described its cries as "anger" when they were told it was a boy and as "fear" when they were told it was a girl (cited in Cheris Kramarae, *The Voices and Words of Women and Men*). We are all victims of our unconscious and most deeply held biases.

30   Gender-specific words (for example, *alderwoman, businessman, altar girl*) are neither good nor bad in themselves. However, they need to be used gender-fairly; terms for women and terms for men should be used an approximately equal number of times in contexts that do not discriminate against either of them. One problem with gender-specific words is that they identify and even emphasize a person's sex when it is not necessary (and is sometimes even objectionable) to do so. Another problem is that they are so seldom used gender-fairly.

31   Although gender-free terms are generally preferable, sometimes gender-neutral language obscures the reality of women's or men's oppression. *Battered spouse* implies that men and women are equally battered; this is far from true. *Parent* is too often taken to mean *mother* and obscures the fact that more and more fathers are very much involved in parenting; it is better here to use the gender-specific *fathers and mothers or mothers and fathers* than the gender-neutral *parents*.

Generic/Pseudogeneric

32 A generic is an all-purpose word that includes everybody (e.g., *workers, people, voters, civilians, elementary school students*). Generic pronouns include: *we, you, they.*

33   A pseudogeneric is a word that is used as though it included all people, but that in reality does not. *Mankind, forefathers, brotherhood*, and *alumni* are not generic because they leave out women. When used about Americans, *immigrants* leaves out all those who were here long before the first immigrants. "What a christian thing to do!" uses *christian* as a pseudogeneric for *kind* or *good-hearted* and leaves out all kind, good-hearted people who are not Christians.

34   Although some speakers and writers say that when they use *man* or *mankind* they mean everybody, their listeners and readers do not perceive the word that way and these terms are thus pseudogenerics. The pronoun *he* when used to mean *he and she* is another pseudogeneric.

35   Certain generic nouns are often assumed to refer only to men, for example, *politicians, physicians, lawyers, voters, legislators, clergy, farmers, colonists, immigrants, slaves, pioneers, settlers, members of the armed forces, judges, taxpayers.* References to "settlers, their wives, and children," or "those clergy permitted to have wives" are pseudogeneric.

36   In historical context it is particularly damaging for young people to read about settlers and explorers and pioneers as though they were all white men. Our language should describe the accomplishments of the human race in terms of all those who contributed to them.

Sex and Gender

37 An understanding of the difference between sex and gender is critical to the use of bias-free language.

38   Sex is biological: people with male genitals are male, and people with female genitals are female.

39   Gender is cultural: our notions of "masculine" tell us how we expect men to behave and our notions of "feminine" tell us how we expect women to behave. Words like *womanly/manly, tomboy/sissy, unfeminine/unmasculine* have nothing to do with the person's sex; they are culturally acquired, subjective concepts about character traits and expected behaviors that vary from one place to another, from one individual to another.

40   It is biologically impossible for a woman to be a sperm donor. It may be culturally unusual for a man to be a secretary, but it is not biologically impossible. To say "the secretary . . . she" assumes all secretaries are women and is sexist because the issue is gender, not sex. Gender describes an individual's personal, legal, and social status without reference to genetic sex; gender is a subjective cultural attitude. Sex is an objective biological fact. Gender varies according to the culture. Sex is a constant.

41   The difference between sex and gender is important because much sexist language arises from cultural determinations of what a woman or man "ought" to be. Once a society decides, for example, that to be a man means to hide one's emotions,

bring home a paycheck, and be able to discuss football standings while to be a woman means to be soft-spoken, love shopping, babies, and recipes, and "never have anything to wear," much of the population becomes a contradiction in terms— unmanly men and unwomanly women. Crying, nagging, gossiping, and shrieking are assumed to be women's lot; rough-housing, drinking beer, telling dirty jokes, and being unable to find one's socks and keys are laid at men's collective door. Lists of stereotypes appear silly because very few people fit them. The best way to ensure unbiased writing and speaking is to describe people as individuals, not as members of a set.

Gender Role Words

42 Certain sex-linked words depend for their meanings on cultural stereotypes: *feminine/masculine, manly/womanly, boyish/girlish, husbandly/wifely, fatherly/ motherly, unfeminine/unmasculine, unmanly/unwomanly*, etc. What a person understands by these words will vary from culture to culture and even within a culture. Because the words depend for their meanings on interpretations of stereotypical behavior or characteristics, they may be grossly inaccurate when applied to individuals. Somewhere, sometime, men and women have said, thought, or done everything the other sex has said, thought, or done except for a very few sex-linked biological activities (e.g., only women can give birth or nurse a baby, only a man can donate sperm or impregnate a woman). To describe a woman as unwomanly is a contradiction in terms; if a woman is doing it, saying it, wearing it, thinking it, it must be— by definition—womanly.

43   F. Scott Fitzgerald did not use "feminine" to describe the unforgettable Daisy in *The Great Gatsby.* He wrote instead, "She laughed again, as if she said something very witty, and held my hand for a moment, looking up into my face, promising that there was no one in the world she so much wanted to see. That was a way she had." Daisy's charm did not belong to Woman: it was uniquely hers. Replacing vague sex-linked descriptors with thoughtful words that describe an individual instead of a member of a set can lead to language that touches people's minds and hearts.

Naming

44 Naming is power, which is why the issue of naming is one of the most important in bias-free language.

Self-Definition

45 People decide what they want to be called. The correct names for individuals and groups are always those by which they refer to themselves. This "tradition" is not always unchallenged. Haig Bosmajian (*The Language of Oppression*) says, "It isn't strange that those persons who insist on defining themselves, who insist on this elemental privilege of self-naming, self-definition, and self-identity encounter vigorous resistance. Predictably, the resistance usually comes from the oppressor or would-be oppressor and is a result of the fact that he or she does not want to relinquish the power which comes from the ability to define others."

46   Dr. Ian Hancock uses the term *exonym* for a name applied to a group by outsiders. For example, Romani peoples object to being called by the exonym *Gypsies*. They do not call themselves Gypsies. Among the many other exonyms are: the elderly, colored people, homosexuals, pagans, adolescents, Eskimos, pygmies, savages. The test for an exonym is whether people describe themselves as "red-men," "illegal aliens," "holy rollers," etc., or whether only outsiders describe them that way.

47   There is a very small but visible element today demanding that gay men "give back" the word *gay*—a good example of denying people the right to name themselves. A late-night radio caller said several times that gay men had "stolen" this word from "our" language. It was not clear what language gay men spoke.

48   A woman nicknamed "Betty" early in life had always preferred her full name, "Elizabeth." On her fortieth birthday, she reverted to Elizabeth. An acquaintance who heard about the change said sharply, "I'll call her Betty if I like!"

49   We can call them Betty if we like, but it's arrogant, insensitive, and uninformed: the only rule we have in this area says we call people what they want to be called.

"Insider/Outsider" Rule

50 A related rule says that insiders may describe themselves in ways that outsiders may not. "Crip" appears in *The Disability Rag*; this does not mean that the word is available to anyone who wants to use it. "Big Fag" is printed on a gay man's T-shirt. He may use that expression; a non-gay may not so label him. One junior-high student yells to another, "Hey, nigger!" This would be highly offensive and inflammatory if the speaker were not African American. A group of women talk about "going out with the girls," but a co-worker should not refer to them as "girls." When questioned about just such a situation, Miss Manners replied that "people are allowed more leeway in what they call themselves than in what they call others."

"People First" Rule

51 Haim Ginott taught us that labels are disabling; intuitively most of us recognize this and resist being labeled. The disability movement originated the "people first" rule, which says we don't call someone a "diabetic" but rather "a person with diabetes." Saying someone is "an AIDS victim" reduces the person to a disease, a label, a statistic; use instead "a person with/who has/living with AIDS." The 1990 Americans with Disabilities Act is a good example of correct wording. Name the person as a person first, and let qualifiers (age, sex, disability, race) follow, but (and this is crucial) only if they are relevant. Readers of a magazine aimed at an older audience were asked what they wanted to be called (elderly? senior citizens? seniors? golden agers?). They rejected all the terms; one said, "How about 'people'?" When high school students rejected labels like kids, teens, teenagers, youth, adolescents, and juveniles, and were asked in exasperation just what they would like to be called, they said, "Could we just be people?"

Women as Separate People

52 One of the most sexist maneuvers in the language has been the identification of women by their connections to husband, son, or father—often even after he is dead. Women are commonly identified as someone's widow while men are never referred to as anyone's widower. Marie Marvingt, a Frenchwoman who lived around the turn of the century, was an inventor, adventurer, stunt woman, superathlete, aviator, and all-around scholar. She chose to be affianced to neither man (as a wife) nor God (as a religious), but it was not long before an uneasy male press found her a fit partner. She is still known today by the revealing label "the Fiancée of Danger." If a connection is relevant, make it mutual. Instead of "Frieda, his wife of seventeen years," write "Frieda and Eric, married for seventeen years."

53   It is difficult for some people to watch women doing unconventional things with their names. For years the etiquette books were able to tell us precisely how to address a single woman, a married woman, a divorced woman, or a widowed woman (there was no similar etiquette on men because they have always been just men and we have never had a code to signal their marital status). But now some women are Ms. and some are Mrs., some are married but keeping their birth names, others are hyphenating their last name with their husband's, and still others have constructed new names for themselves. Some women—including African American women who were denied this right earlier in our history—take great pride in using their husband's name. All these forms are correct. The same rule of self-definition applies here: call the woman what she wants to be called.

THINKING CRITICALLY

1. Maggio begins her article with a discussion of the ways language has real effects on people's attitudes and actions. What are some of the examples she supplies? How does language create desirable or undesirable consequences?

2. What are the four excuses people make to avoid using unbiased language? How does Maggio counter those excuses? What additional counterargument does she supply in defense of nonbiased language?

3. What main idea links all the different ways in which bias can occur (see paragraph 19)? Does biased language refer to individuals or to groups of people? Would the following statement be an example of biased (or stereotyped) language? "Mary is wearing her hair in a French braid today, so she'll no doubt wear it that way tomorrow."

4. What are the categories Maggio specifically names as subject to biased language? Can you supply additional categories?

5. Maggio uses the term *symmetrical* several times (e.g., paragraphs 23 and 27). What does this term mean? Does Maggio want to encourage or discourage the use of symmetrical language? Does *symmetry* refer only to gender bias, or can it refer to other kinds of bias too?

6. What is the difference between gender-free, gender-fair, and gender-specific language in paragraphs 26 through 31? What examples does Maggio supply for each one? When is each kind of nonbiased language appropriate?

7. What does Maggio mean by a "generic" word? A "pseudogeneric" word? How might pseudogeneric references harm people?

8. What is an *exonym*? Are exonyms ever appropriate, according to Maggio's discussion? Did you recognize all the words Maggio lists in paragraph 46 as exonyms? Can you supply substitutes for all the exonyms? If not, what problems did you encounter? Can you supply examples of other exonyms from your own experience?

9. Why do you think Maggio considers naming "one of the most important [issues] in bias-free language" (paragraph 44)? What is so important about the ability to choose a name? What do you think the woman in paragraph 48 is communicating by choosing to be called Elizabeth? Why do you think Maggio links this announcement to the woman's fortieth birthday celebration?

10. What did the high school student in paragraph 8 really mean to say? Why do you think Maggio includes this statement? What point is she trying to make? Do you think that this student was male or female? Would it make a difference? Why doesn't Maggio specify?

WRITING ASSIGNMENTS

1. Locate an article in a contemporary newspaper that you think displays one or more of the biases Maggio describes. In a letter to the editor (no more than 500 words), persuade the newspaper editors to avoid such biased language in future articles. Remember that your writing will be more effective if you write in a calm, reasonable tone, use specific examples, and explain clearly the benefits of unbiased language.

2. Look back at Susanne K. Langer's essay, "Language and Thought" in Chapter 1. How is Maggio's understanding of biased language, and the harm it can create, based on an understanding of language as "symbol" (as Langer uses that term)? What are the distinguishing features of language as symbol that biased language uses? Pay special attention to Maggio's treatment of naming, because Langer claims that "names are the essence of language" (in Langer's paragraph 19).

3. How would you go about designing an advertising campaign for the magazine that Maggio says is "aimed at an older audience"? What words would you use to avoid offensive labeling and to avoid the vagueness of the broadly generic noun "people" (which is the same term the high school students ask to be designated by)?

The Word Police
Michiko Kakutani

Not everybody applauds the efforts of those hoping to rid the language of offensive terms. To detractors, all such linguistic sensitivity is no more than a symptom of political correctness—a kind of be-sensitive-or-else campaign. They complain that unlike standard dictionaries, which are meant to help people use words, the so-called *cautionary* guides warn people against using them. Such is the complaint of Michiko Kakutani, who specifically targets Rosalie Maggio's *The Bias-Free Word Finder* as an example of the menace of hypersensitivity. She complains that in the name of the "politics of inclusion," proponents hunt down users of "inappropriate" language like the thought police from George Orwell's *1984*. And, claims Kakutani, they fill the English language with sloppy, pious euphemisms.

Michiko Kakutani is literary critic for the *New York Times*, where this article first appeared in January 1993. She won a Pulitzer Prize in 1998 for her work as a literary critic.

1   This month's inaugural festivities, with their celebration, in Maya Angelou's words, of "humankind"—"the Asian, the Hispanic, the Jew/ The African, the Native American, the Sioux,/ The Catholic, the Muslim, the French, the Greek/ The Irish, the Rabbi, the Priest, the Sheik,/ The Gay, the Straight, the Preacher,/ The privileged, the homeless, the Teacher"—constituted a kind of official embrace of multiculturalism and a new politics of inclusion.

2   The mood of political correctness, however, has already made firm inroads into popular culture. Washington boasts a store called Politically Correct that sells pro-whale, anti-meat, ban-the-bomb T-shirts, bumper stickers and buttons, as well as a local cable television show called "Politically Correct Cooking" that features interviews in the kitchen with representatives from groups like People for the Ethical Treatment of Animals.

3   The Coppertone suntan lotion people are planning to give their longtime cover girl, Little Miss (Ms?) Coppertone, a male equivalent, Little Mr. Coppertone. And even Superman (Super-person?) is rumored to be returning this spring, reincarnated as four ethnically diverse clones: an African-American, an Asian, a Caucasian and a Latino.

4   Nowhere is this P.C. mood more striking than in the increasingly noisy debate over language that has moved from university campuses to the country at large—a development that both underscores Americans' puritanical zeal for reform and their unwavering faith in the talismanic power of words.

5   Certainly no decent person can quarrel with the underlying impulse behind political correctness: a vision of a more just, inclusive society in which racism, sexism and prejudice of all sorts have been erased. But the methods and fervor of the self-appointed language police can lead to a rigid orthodoxy—and unintentional self-parody—opening the movement to the scorn of conservative opponents and the mockery of cartoonists and late-night television hosts.

6   It's hard to imagine women earning points for political correctness by saying "ovarimony" instead of "testimony"—as one participant at the recent Modern Language Association convention was overheard to suggest. It's equally hard to imagine people wanting to flaunt their lack of prejudice by giving up such words and phrases as "bull market," "kaiser roll," "Lazy Susan," and "charley horse."

7   Several books on bias-free language have already appeared, and the 1991 edition of the Random House *Webster's College Dictionary* boasts an appendix titled "Avoiding Sexist Language." The dictionary also includes such linguistic mutations as "womyn" (women, "used as an alternative spelling to avoid the suggestion of sexism perceived in the sequence m-e-n") and "waitron" (a gender-blind term for waiter or waitress).

8   Many of these dictionaries and guides not only warn the reader against offensive racial and sexual slurs, but also try to establish and enforce a whole new set of usage rules. Take, for instance, *The Bias-Free Word Finder: A Dictionary of Nondiscriminatory Language* by Rosalie Maggio (Beacon Press)—a volume often indistinguishable, in its meticulous solemnity, from the tongue-in-cheek *Official*

Politically Correct Dictionary and Handbook put out last year by Henry Beard and Christopher Cerf (Villard Books). Ms. Maggio's book supplies the reader intent on using kinder, gentler language with writing guidelines as well as a detailed listing of more than 5,000 "biased words and phrases."

9   Whom are these guidelines for? Somehow one has a tough time picturing them replacing Fowler's *Modern English Usage* in the classroom, or being adopted by the average man (sorry, individual) in the street.

10   The "pseudogeneric 'he,'" we learn from Ms. Maggio, is to be avoided like the plague, as is the use of the word "man" to refer to humanity. "Fellow," "king," "lord" and "master" are bad because they're "male-oriented words," and "king," "lord" and "master" are especially bad because they're also "hierarchical, dominator society terms." The politically correct lion becomes the "monarch of the jungle," new-age children play "someone on the top of the heap," and the "Mona Lisa" goes down in history as Leonardo's "acme of perfection."

11   As for the word "black," Ms. Maggio says it should be excised from terms with a negative spin: she recommends substituting words like "mouse" for "black eye," "ostracize" for "blackball," "payola" for "blackmail" and "outcast" for "black sheep." Clearly, some of these substitutions work better than others: somehow the "sinister humor" of Kurt Vonnegut or "Saturday Night Live" doesn't quite make it; nor does the "denouncing" of the Hollywood 10.

12   For the dedicated user of politically correct language, all these rules can make for some messy moral dilemmas. Whereas "battered wife" is a gender-biased term, the gender-free term "battered spouse," Ms. Maggio notes, incorrectly implies "that men and women are equally battered."

13   On one hand, say Francine Wattman Frank and Paula A. Treichler in their book *Language, Gender, and Professional Writing* (Modern Language Association), "he or she" is an appropriate construction for talking about an individual (like a jockey, say) who belongs to a profession that's predominantly male—it's a way of emphasizing "that such occupations are not barred to women or that women's concerns need to be kept in mind." On the other hand, they add, using masculine pronouns rhetorically can underscore ongoing male dominance in those fields, implying the need for change.

14   And what about the speech codes adopted by some universities in recent years? Although they were designed to prohibit students from uttering sexist and racist slurs, they would extend, by logic, to blacks who want to use the word "nigger" to strip the term of its racist connotations, or homosexuals who want to use the word "queer" to reclaim it from bigots.

15   In her book, Ms. Maggio recommends applying bias-free usage retroactively: she suggests paraphrasing politically incorrect quotations, or replacing "the sexist words or phrases with ellipsis dots and/or bracketed substitutes," or using "sic" "to show that the sexist words come from the original quotation and to call attention to the fact that they are incorrect."

16   Which leads the skeptical reader of *The Bias-Free Word Finder* to wonder whether *All the King's Men* should be retitled *All The Ruler's People; Pet cemetery, Animal Companion Graves; Birdman of Alcatraz, Birdperson of Alcatraz;* and *The Iceman Cometh, The Ice Route Driver Cometh?*

17   Will making such changes remove the prejudice in people's minds? Should we really spend time trying to come up with non-male-based alternatives to "Midas touch," "Achilles' heel," and "Montezuma's revenge"? Will tossing out Santa Claus—whom Ms. Maggio accuses of reinforcing "the cultural male-as-norm system"—in favor of Belfana, his Italian female alter ego, truly help banish sexism? Can the avoidance of "violent expressions and metaphors" like "kill two birds with one stone," "sock it to 'em" or "kick an idea around" actually promote a more harmonious world?

18   The point isn't that the excesses of the word police are comical. The point is that their intolerance (in the name of tolerance) has disturbing implications. In the first place, getting upset by phrases like "bullish on America" or "the City of Brotherly Love" tends to distract attention from the real problems of prejudice and injustice that exist in society at large, turning them into mere questions of semantics. Indeed, the emphasis currently put on politically correct usage has uncanny parallels with the academic movement of deconstruction—a method of textual analysis that focuses on language and linguistic pyrotechnics—which has become firmly established on university campuses.

19   In both cases, attention is focused on surfaces, on words and metaphors; in both cases, signs and symbols are accorded more importance than content. Hence, the attempt by some radical advocates to remove the *Adventures of Huckleberry Finn* from curriculums on the grounds that Twain's use of the word "nigger" makes the book a racist text—never mind the fact that this American classic (written in 1884) depicts the spiritual kinship achieved between a white boy and a runaway slave, never mind the fact that the "nigger" Jim emerges as the novel's most honorable, decent character.

20   Ironically enough, the P.C. movement's obsession with language is accompanied by a strange Orwellian willingness to warp the meaning of words by placing them under a high-powered ideological lens. For instance, the "Dictionary of Cautionary Words and Phrases"—a pamphlet issued by the University of Missouri's Multicultural Management Program to help turn "today's journalists into tomorrow's multicultural newsroom managers"—warns that using the word "articulate" to describe members of a minority group can suggest the opposite, "that 'those people' are not considered well educated, articulate and the like."

21   The pamphlet patronizes minority groups, by cautioning the reader against using the words "lazy" and "burly" to describe any member of such groups; and it issues a similar warning against using words like "gorgeous" and "petite" to describe women.

22   As euphemism proliferates with the rise of political correctness, there is a spread of the sort of sloppy, abstract language that Orwell said is "designed to make lies sound truthful and murder respectable, and to give an appearance of solidity to pure wind." "Fat" becomes "big boned" or "differently sized"; "stupid" becomes "exceptional"; "stoned" becomes "chemically inconvenienced."

23   Wait a minute here! Aren't such phrases eerily reminiscent of the euphemisms coined by the Government during Vietnam and Watergate? Remember how the military used to speak of "pacification," or how President Richard M. Nixon's press secretary, Ronald L. Ziegler, tried to get away with calling a lie an "inoperative statement"?

24   Calling the homeless "the underhoused" doesn't give them a place to live; calling the poor "the economically marginalized" doesn't help them pay the bills. Rather, by playing down their plight, such language might even make it easier to shrug off the seriousness of their situation.

25   Instead of allowing free discussion and debate to occur, many gung-ho advocates of politically correct language seem to think that simple suppression of a word or concept will magically make the problem disappear. In the *Bias-Free Word Finder*, Ms. Maggio entreats the reader not to perpetuate the negative stereotype of Eve. "Be extremely cautious in referring to the biblical Eve," she writes; "this story has profoundly contributed to negative attitudes toward women throughout history, largely because of misogynistic and patriarchal interpretations that labeled her evil, inferior, and seductive."

26   The story of Bluebeard, the rake (whoops!—the libertine) who killed his seven wives, she says, is also to be avoided, as is the biblical story of Jezebel. Of Jesus Christ, Ms. Maggio writes: "There have been few individuals in history as completely androgynous as Christ, and it does his message a disservice to overinsist on his maleness." She doesn't give the reader any hints on how this might be accomplished; presumably, one is supposed to avoid describing him as the Son of God.

27   Of course the P.C. police aren't the only ones who want to proscribe what people should say or give them guidelines for how they may use an idea; Jesse Helms and his supporters are up to exactly the same thing when they propose to patrol the boundaries of the permissible in art. In each case, the would-be censor aspires to suppress what he or she finds distasteful—all, of course, in the name of the public good.

28   In the case of the politically correct, the prohibition of certain words, phrases and ideas is advanced in the cause of building a brave new world free of racism and hate, but this vision of harmony clashes with the very ideals of diversity and inclusion that the multi-cultural movement holds dear, and it's purchased at the cost of freedom of expression and freedom of speech.

29   In fact, the utopian world envisioned by the language police would be bought at the expense of the ideals of individualism and democracy articulated in "The Gettysburg Address." "Fourscore and seven years ago our forefathers brought forth on this continent a new nation, conceived in liberty and dedicated to the proposition that all men are created equal."

30   Of course, the P.C. police have already found Lincoln's words hopelessly "phallocentric." No doubt they would rewrite the passage: "Fourscore and seven years ago our foremothers and forefathers brought forth on this continent a new nation, formulated with liberty, and dedicated to the proposition that all humankind is created equal."

THINKING CRITICALLY

1. What kinds of people are mentioned in the lines of Maya Angelou's inauguration poem? What do these people symbolize, according to Kakutani? How many of these groups are represented in your classroom right now?

2. What specific substitutions of words does Kakutani complain about in paragraph 10? Can you supply the "biased" term that the "politically correct" phrase has replaced in the second half of the paragraph?

3. What are the three "messy moral dilemmas" Kakutani points out in paragraphs 12–14? Why does she tag the examples she cites as *dilemmas*? Why does she object to following politically correct guidelines in each case?

4. What is wrong, according to Kakutani in paragraphs 15 and 16, with Maggio's recommendation that unbiased language be applied retroactively? Rewrite one or two of the titles using Maggio's suggestions as quoted by Kakutani in paragraph 15—that is, use ellipses, brackets, and so on. How well do these suggestions work?

5. What examples of euphemism does Kakutani provide in paragraphs 22–24? What objections does she raise about these euphemisms? Why does she compare the new politically correct terms with terms from Watergate?

6. Describe the tone in the first three paragraphs of the article. Based on these paragraphs, did you think this piece was going to be serious, playful, or sarcastic? Upon what evidence did you base your response?

7. Look closely at the wording of Kakutani's first sentence in paragraph 22. Why doesn't she say outright that political correctness causes "sloppy, abstract language"? What do you think Maggio would say about the cause-and-effect relationship of political correctness and language?

8. Kakutani interrupts herself twice to insert a "correction"—to substitute a politically correct term for an incorrect term she has inadvertently let slip. These appear in paragraphs 9 and 26. What's going on here—didn't she have enough time to edit her article?

WRITING ASSIGNMENTS

1. Compare the views about language of Rosalie Maggio in "Bias-Free Language" and Kakutani in this article. What powers does each author believe language has? What power does language not have? Cite specific evidence from each author for your comparison.

2. Despite Kakutani's attack on Maggio's book, she agrees with at least some of Maggio's underlying assumptions—for example, about language and power, about the need to end prejudice, and other points. Identify and discuss at least three assumptions or values that both authors would agree on; then, discuss why they believe that different actions are appropriate.

3. Examine some samples of your own writing from earlier in the term, or from previous terms. Where have you struggled with politically correct language use? Have you always been successful in using it? What substitutions or changes did you try that, on rereading, seem less than satisfactory?

Crimes Against Humanity
Ward Churchill

As this chapter illustrates, many racial stereotypes are unfortunately built into American popular culture. To Ward Churchill, a man of Creek and Cherokee blood, none has been so damning as those regarding Native Americans. In this essay, Churchill argues that professional sports teams that take Indian names or use Indian cultural images and symbols as mascots, as logos, and for advertising, ultimately defame Native Americans. In fact, he argues that such seemingly innocent practices perpetuate the crimes committed against Native Americans.

> Ward Churchill is co-director of the Colorado chapter of the American Indian Movement and vice chair of the American Indian Anti-Defamation Council. He is the author of several books on Native Americans including *Fantasies of the Master Race: Literature, Cinema, and the Colonization of American Indians* (1992), *Indians Are Us* (1993), and *From a Native Son: Selected Essays on Indigenism, 1985–1995* (1996). This essay originally appeared in *Z Magazine* in March 1993.

1 During the past couple of seasons, there has been an increasing wave of controversy regarding the names of professional sports teams like the Atlanta "Braves," Cleveland "Indians," Washington "Redskins," and Kansas City "Chiefs." The issue extends to the names of college teams like Florida State University "Seminoles," University of Illinois "Fighting Illini," and so on, right on down to high school outfits like the Lama (Colorado) "Savages." Also involved have been team adoption of "mascots" replete with feathers, buckskins, beads, spears and "warpaint" (some fans have opted to adorn themselves in the same fashion), and nifty little "pep" gestures like the "Indian Chant" and "Tomahawk Chop."

2   A substantial number of American Indians have protested that use of native names, images and symbols as sports team mascots and the like is, by definition, a virulently racist practice. Given the historical relationship between Indians and non-Indians during what has been called the "Conquest of America," American Indian Movement leader (and American Indian Anti-Defamation Council founder) Russell Means has compared the practice to contemporary Germans naming their soccer team the "Jews," "Hebrews," and "Yids," while adorning their uniforms with grotesque caricatures of Jewish faces taken from the Nazis' anti-Semitic propaganda of the 1930s. Numerous demonstrations have occurred in conjunction with games—most notably during the November 15, 1992 match-up between the Chiefs and Redskins in Kansas City—by angry Indians and their supporters.

3   In response, a number of players—especially African Americans and other minority athletes—have been trotted out by professional team owners like Ted Turner, as well as university and public school officials, to announce that they mean not to insult but to honor native people. They have been joined by the television networks and most major newspapers, all of which have editorialized that Indian discomfort with the situation is "no big deal," insisting that the whole thing is just "good, clean fun." The country needs more such fun, they've argued, and "a few disgruntled Native Americans" have no right to undermine the nation's enjoyment of its leisure time by complaining. This is especially the case, some have argued, "in hard times like these." It has even been contended that Indian outrage at being systematically degraded—rather than the degradation itself—creates "a serious barrier to the sort of intergroup communication so necessary in a multicultural society such as ours."

4   Okay, let's communicate. We are frankly dubious that those advancing such positions really believe their own rhetoric, but, just for the sake of argument, let's accept the premise that they are sincere. If what they say is true, then isn't it time we spread such "inoffensiveness" and "good cheer" around among *all* groups so that *everybody* can participate *equally* in fostering the round of national laughs they call for? Sure it is—the country can't have too much fun or "intergroup involvement"—so the more, the merrier. Simple consistency demands that anyone who

thinks the Tomahawk Chop is a swell pastime must be just as hearty in his or her endorsement of the following ideas. The same logic used to defend the defamation of American Indians should help us all start yukking it up.

5   First, as a counterpart to the Redskins, we need an NFL team called "Niggers" to honor Afro-Americans. Half-time festivities for fans might include a simulated stewing of the opposing coach in a large pot while players and cheerleaders dance around it, garbed in leopard skins and wearing fake bones in their noses. This concept obviously goes along with the kind of gaiety attending the Chop, but also with the actions of the Kansas City Chiefs, whose team members—prominently including black members—lately appeared on a poster looking "fierce" and "savage" by way of wearing Indian regalia. Just a bit of harmless "morale boosting," says the Chiefs' front office. You bet.

6   So that the newly-formed Niggers sports club won't end up too out of sync while expressing the "spirit" and "identity" of Afro-Americans in the above fashion, a baseball franchise—let's call this one the "Sambos"—should be formed. How about a basketball team called the "Spearchuckers"? A hockey team called the "Jungle Bunnies"? Maybe the "essence" of these teams could be depicted by images of tiny black faces adorned with huge pairs of lips. The players could appear on TV every week or so gnawing on chicken legs and spitting watermelon seeds at one another. Catchy, eh? Well, there's "nothing to be upset about," according to those who love wearing "war bonnets" to the Super Bowl or having "Chief Illiniwik" dance around the sports arenas of Urbana, Illinois.

7   And why stop there? There are plenty of other groups to include. Hispanics? They can be "represented" by the Galveston "Greasers" and San Diego "Spics," at least until the Wisconsin "Wetbacks" and Baltimore "Beaners" get off the ground. Asian Americans? How about the "Slopes," "Dinks," "Gooks," and "Zipperheads"? Owners of the latter teams might get their logo ideas from editorial page cartoons printed in the nation's newspapers during World War II: slant-eyes, buck teeth, big glasses, but nothing racially insulting or derogatory, according to editors and artists involved at the time. Indeed, this Second World War–vintage stuff can be seen as just another barrel of laughs, at least by what current editors say are their "local standards" concerning American Indians.

8   Let's see. Who's been left out? Teams like the Kansas City "Kikes," Hanover "Honkies," San Leandro "Shylocks," Daytona "Dagos," and Pittsburgh "Polacks" will fill a certain social void among white folk. Have a religious belief? Let's all go for the gusto and gear the Milwaukee "Mackerel Snappers" and Hollywood "Holy Rollers." The Fighting Irish of Notre Dame can be rechristened the "Drunken Irish" or "Papist Pigs." Issues of gender and sexual preference can be addressed through creation of teams like the St. Louis "Sluts," Boston "Bimbos," Detroit "Dykes," and the Fresno "Fags." How about the Gainesville "Gimps" and Richmond "Retards," so the physically and mentally impaired won't be excluded from our fun and games?

9   Now, don't go getting "overly sensitive" out there. None of this is demeaning or insulting, at least not when it's being done to Indians. Just ask the folks who are doing it, or their apologists like Andy Rooney in the national media. They'll tell you— as in fact they *have* been telling you—that there's been no harm done, regardless of

what their victims think, feel, or say. The situation is exactly the same as when those with precisely the same mentality used to insist that Step 'n' Fetchit was okay, or Rochester, on the Jack Benny Show, or Amos and Andy, Charlie Chan, the Frito Bandito, or any of the other cutesy symbols making up the lexicon of American racism. Have we communicated yet?

10   Let's get just a little bit real here. The notion of "fun" embodied in rituals like the Tomahawk Chop must be understood for what it is. There's not a single non-Indian example used above which can be considered socially acceptable in even the most marginal sense. The reasons are obvious enough. So why is it different where American Indians are concerned? One can only conclude that, in contrast to the other groups at issue, Indians are (falsely) perceived as being too few, and therefore too weak, to defend themselves effectively against racist and otherwise offensive behavior.

11   Fortunately, there are some glimmers of hope. A few teams and their fans have gotten the message and have responded appropriately. Stanford University, which opted to drop the name "Indians" from Stanford, has experienced no resulting drop-off in attendance. Meanwhile, the local newspaper in Portland, Oregon recently decided its long-standing editorial policy prohibiting use of racial epithets should include derogatory team names. The Redskins, for instance, are now referred to as "the Washington team," and will continue to be described in this way until the franchise adopts an inoffensive moniker (newspaper sales in Portland have suffered no decline as a result).

12   Such examples are to be applauded and encouraged. They stand as figurative beacons in the night, proving beyond all doubt that it is quite possible to indulge in the pleasure of athletics without accepting blatant racism into the bargain.

13   On October 16, 1946, a man named Julius Streicher mounted the steps of a gallows. Moments later he was dead, the sentence of an international tribunal composed of representatives of the United States, France, Great Britain, and the Soviet Union having been imposed. Streicher's body was then cremated, and—so horrendous were his crimes thought to have been—his ashes dumped into an unspecified German river so that "no one should ever know a particular place to go for reasons of mourning his memory."

14   Julius Streicher had been convicted at Nuremberg, Germany of what were termed "Crimes Against Humanity." The lead prosecutor in his case—Justice Robert Jackson of the United States Supreme Court—had not argued that the defendant had killed anyone, nor that he had personally committed any especially violent act. Nor was it contended that Streicher had held any particularly important position in the German government during the period in which the so-called Third Reich had exterminated some 6,000,000 Jews, as well as several million Gypsies, Poles, Slavs, homosexuals, and other untermenschen (subhumans).

15   The sole offense for which the accused was ordered put to death was in having served as publisher/editor of a Bavarian tabloid entitled *Der Sturmer* during the early-to-mid 1930s, years before the Nazi genocide actually began. In this capacity, he had penned a long series of virulently anti-Semitic editorials and "news" stories, usually accompanied by cartoons and other images graphically depicting Jews in extraordinary derogatory fashion. This, the prosecution asserted, had done much to

"dehumanize" the targets of his distortion in the mind of the German public. In turn, such dehumanization had made it possible—or at least easier—for average Germans to later indulge in the outright liquidation of Jewish "vermin." The tribunal agreed, holding that Streicher was therefore complicit in genocide and deserving of death by hanging.

16   During his remarks to the Nuremberg tribunal, Justice Jackson observed that, in implementing its sentences, the participating powers were morally and legally binding themselves to adhere forever after to the same standards of conduct that were being applied to Streicher and the other Nazi leaders. In the alternative, he said, the victorious allies would have committed "pure murder" at Nuremburg— no different in substance from that carried out by those presumed to judge— rather than establishing the "permanent bench-mark for justice" which was intended.

17   Yet in the United States of Robert Jackson, the indigenous American Indian population had already been reduced, in a process which is ongoing to this day, from perhaps 12.5 million in the year 1500 to fewer than 250,000 by the beginning of the 20th century. This was accomplished, according to official sources, "largely through the cruelty of [Euro-American] settlers," and an informal but clear governmental policy which had made it an articulated goal to "exterminate these red vermin," or at least whole segments of them.

18   Bounties had been placed on the scalps of Indians—any Indians—in places as diverse as Georgia, Kentucky, Texas, the Dakotas, Oregon, and California, and had been maintained until resident Indian populations were decimated or disappeared altogether. Entire peoples such as the Cherokee had been reduced to half their size through a policy of forced removal from their homelands east of the Mississippi River to what were then considered less preferable areas in the West.

19   Others, such as the Navajo, suffered the same fate while under military guard for years on end. The United States Army had also perpetrated a long series of wholesale massacres of Indians at places like Horseshoe Bend, Bear River, Sand Creek, the Washita River, the Marias River, Camp Robinson, and Wounded Knee.

20   Through it all, hundreds of popular novels—each competing with the next to make Indians appear more grotesque, menacing, and inhumane—were sold in the tens of millions of copies in the U.S. Plainly, the Euro-American public was being conditioned to see Indians in such a way as to allow their eradication to continue. And continue it did until the Manifest Destiny of the U.S.—a direct precursor to what Hitler would subsequently call Lebensraumpolitik (the politics of living space)—was consummated.

21   By 1900, the national project of "clearing" Native Americans from their land and replacing them with "superior" Anglo-American settlers was complete; the indigenous population had been reduced by as much as 98 percent while approximately 97.5 percent of their original territory had "passed" to the invaders. The survivors had been concentrated, out of sight and mind of the public, on scattered "reservations," all of them under the self-assigned "plenary" (full) power of the federal government. There was, of course, no Nuremberg-style tribunal passing judgment on those who had fostered such circumstances in North America. No U.S. official or private citizen was ever imprisoned—never mind hanged—for implementing propagandizing what

had been done. Nor had the process of genocide afflicting Indians been completed. Instead, it merely changed form.

22   Between the 1880s and the 1980s, nearly half of all Native American children were coercively transferred from their own families, communities, and cultures to those of the conquering society. This was done through compulsory attendance at remote boarding schools, often hundreds of miles from their homes, where native children were kept for years on end while being systematically "deculturated" (indoctrinated to think and act in the manner of Euro-Americans rather than as Indians). It was also accomplished through a pervasive foster home and adoption program—including "blind" adoptions, where children would be permanently denied information as to who they were/are and where they'd come from—placing native youths in non-Indian homes.

23   The express purpose of all this was to facilitate a U.S. governmental policy to bring about the "assimilation" (dissolution) of indigenous societies. In other words, Indian cultures as such were to be caused to disappear. Such policy objectives are directly contrary to the United Nations 1948 Convention on Punishment and Prevention of the Crime of Genocide, an element of international laws arising from the Nuremberg proceedings. The forced "transfer of the children" of a targeted "racial, ethnical, or religious group" is explicitly prohibited as a genocidal activity under the Convention's second article.

24   Article II of the Genocide Convention also expressly prohibits involuntary sterilization as a means of "preventing births among" a targeted population. Yet, in 1975, it was conceded by the U.S. government that its Indian Health Service (IHS), then a subpart of the Bureau of Indian Affairs (BIA), was even then conducting a secret program of involuntary sterilization that had affected approximately 40 percent of all Indian women. The program was allegedly discontinued, and the IHS was transferred to the Public Health Service, but no one was punished. In 1990, it came out that the IHS was inoculating Inuit children in Alaska with Hepatitis-B vaccine. The vaccine had already been banned by the World Health Organization as having a demonstrated correlation with the HIV-Syndrome which is itself correlated to AIDS. As this is written, a "field test" of Hepatitis-A vaccine, also HIV-correlated, is being conducted on Indian reservations in the northern plains region.

25   The Genocide Convention makes it a "crime against humanity" to create conditions leading to the destruction of an identifiable human group, as such. Yet the BIA has utilized the government's plenary prerogatives to negotiate mineral leases "on behalf of" Indian peoples paying a fraction of standard royalty rates. The result has been "super profits" for a number of preferred U.S. corporations. Meanwhile, Indians, whose reservations ironically turned out to be in some of the most mineral-rich areas of North America, which makes us, the nominally wealthiest segment of the continent's population, live in dire poverty.

26   By the government's own data in the mid–1980s, Indians received the lowest annual and lifetime per capita incomes of any aggregate population group in the United States. Concomitantly, we suffer the highest rate of infant mortality, death by exposure and malnutrition, disease, and the like. Under such circumstances, alcoholism and other escapist forms of substance abuse are endemic in the Indian

community, a situation which leads both to a general physical debilitation of the population and a catastrophic accident rate. Teen suicide among Indians is several times the national average.

27   The average life expectancy of a reservation-based Native American man is barely 45 years; women can expect to live less than three years longer.

28   Such itemizations could be continued at great length, including matters like the radioactive contamination of large portions of contemporary Indian Country, the forced relocation of traditional Navajos, and so on. But the point should be made: Genocide, as defined in international law, is a continuing fact of day-to-day life (and death) for North America's native peoples. Yet there has been—and is—only the barest flicker of public concern about, or even consciousness of, this reality. Absent any serious expression of public outrage, no one is punished and the process continues.

29   A salient reason for public acquiescence before the ongoing holocaust in Native North America has been a continuation of the popular legacy, often through more effective media. Since 1925, Hollywood has released more than 2,000 films, many of them rerun frequently on television, portraying Indians as strange, perverted, ridiculous, and often dangerous things of the past. Moreover, we are habitually presented to mass audiences one-dimensionally, devoid of recognizable human motivations and emotions; Indians thus serve as props, little more. We have thus been thoroughly and systematically dehumanized.

30   Nor is this extent of it. Everywhere, we are used as logos, as mascots, as jokes: "Big Chief" writing tablets, "Red Man" chewing tobacco, "Winnebago" campers, "Navajo" and "Cherokee" and "Pontiac" and "Cadillac" pickups and automobiles. There are the Cleveland "Indians," the Kansas City "Chiefs," the Atlanta "Braves" and the Washington "Redskins" professional sports teams—not to mention those in thousands of colleges, high schools, and elementary schools across the country— each with their own degrading caricatures and parodies of Indians and/or things Indian. Pop fiction continues in the same vein, including an unending stream of New Age manuals purporting to expose the inner works of indigenous spirituality in everything from pseudo-philosophical to do-it-yourself styles. Blond yuppies from Beverly Hills amble about the country claiming to be reincarnated 17th century Cheyenne Ushamans ready to perform previously secret ceremonies.

31   In effect, a concerted, sustained, and in some ways accelerating effort has gone into making Indians unreal. It is thus of obvious importance that the American public begin to think about the implications of such things the next time they witness a gaggle of face-painted and war-bonneted buffoons doing the "Tomahawk Chop" at a baseball or football game. It is necessary that they think about the implications of the grade-school teacher adorning their child in turkey features to commemorate Thanksgiving. Think about the significance of John Wayne or Charleton Heston killing a dozen "savages" with a single bullet the next time a western comes on TV. Think about why Land-o-Lakes finds it appropriate to market its butter with the stereotyped image of an "Indian princess" on the wrapper. Think about what it means when non-Indian academics profess—as they often do—to "know more about Indians than Indians do themselves." Think about the significance of charlatans like Carlos Castaneda and Jamake Highwater and Mary Summer Rain and

Lynn Andrews churning out "Indian" bestsellers, one after the other, while Indians typically can't get into print.

32   Think about the real situation of American Indians. Think about Julius Streicher. Remember Justice Jackson's admonition. Understand that the treatment of Indians in American popular culture is not "cute" or "amusing" or just "good, clean fun."

33   Know that it causes real pain and real suffering to real people. Know that it threatens our very survival. And know that this is just as much a crime against humanity as anything the Nazis ever did. It is likely that the indigenous people of the United States will never demand that those guilty of such criminal activity be punished for their deeds. But the least we have the right to expect—indeed, to demand—is that such practices finally be brought to a halt.

THINKING CRITICALLY

1. How did the press react to the protests by Native Americans of their degradation by professional sports teams? How might the media's reaction have been more appropriate? Does Churchill supply any examples of suitable responses?

2. To make his point, Churchill suggests other racial and ethnic groups for sports teams' names and halftime activities. What specific racial stereotypes does he offer for different groups? What is the tone of his suggestions? Would you say his analogies are an effective part of his argument? Explain.

3. In paragraph 13, Churchill mentions Julius Streicher. Who was Streicher? How did Streicher's trial and execution serve as a "permanent benchmark for justice" (paragraph 16)? What point does Churchill make by placing this historical information immediately after his satire of team names?

4. According to Churchill, why has society gotten away with offensive stereotypes of Native Americans but not with stereotypes of other groups?

5. How well does the title of the essay fit the discussion? Explain, citing details from the text.

6. Beginning in paragraph 17, Churchill offers a brief historical survey of the crimes against Native Americans. Did you find this too much of a digression from the rest of his argument? Or do you think it was necessary for Churchill to bolster his argument regarding the cultural denigration of Native Americans by names for teams and products? Explain.

WRITING ASSIGNMENTS

1. Before you read this essay, did you feel that the use of Native American names, mascots, and symbols by sports teams and car manufacturers was denigrating and insulting to Native Americans? Did this essay change your way of thinking? Explain your answer.

2. Do you agree with Churchill's argument that the use of Native American names, images, caricatures, symbols, and so on for sports teams perpetuates crimes against this segment of humanity? Explain.

Exploring the Language of **VISUALS**

Depictions of the Cleveland Indians' Mascot Chief Wahoo

Chief Wahoo is the official mascot of the Cleveland Indians. The team's history states that their name honors a Native American named Louis Sockalexis, who briefly played for the team from 1897 to 1899. Many Native Americans have disputed this claim, calling it "revisionist history." The image of Chief Wahoo, which first appeared in 1915 when the team changed its name from the Naps to the Indians, has been bitterly disputed by many Native Americans who consider him a highly racist and unflattering stereotype. The team and its fans, however, argue that Chief Wahoo is an icon, whose image and name does not insult Native Americans.

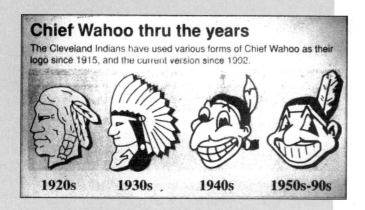

Chief Wahoo thru the years

The Cleveland Indians have used various forms of Chief Wahoo as their logo since 1915, and the current version since 1992.

| 1920s | 1930s | 1940s | 1950s-90s |

THINKING CRITICALLY

1. What does Chief Wahoo's name mean? Research his history online. In what ways could this mascot be considered offensive to Native Americans? What image does the mascot project?

2. What do you think Ward Churchill would say about the evolution (or devolution) of the Chief Wahoo image? Do you think he would find any of the depictions acceptable? Why or why not?

3. How has the image of Chief Wahoo changed over the last hundred years? Why do you think the image changed so much?

4. Could other ethnic groups represent a sports team without incident? Why or why not?

5. In your opinion, can the disagreement over the Cleveland Indians' official mascot be resolved? How would you mediate this controversy?

"Nigger": The Meaning of a Word

Gloria Naylor

Context can be everything when it comes to the meaning of a word, even a word recognized as an ugly epithet. As Gloria Naylor explains, when she was a little girl, the word *nigger* was spoken comfortably in front of her by relatives and family friends. She had heard it dozens of times, viewing it as a term of endearment. But she really didn't "hear" the term until it was "spit out" of the mouth of a white boy in her third-grade class.

Gloria Naylor, a native of New York City, is an accomplished writer whose first novel, *The Women of Brewster Place* (1982), won an American Book Award. She is also the author of *Linden Hills* (1985), *Mama Day* (1988), and *Bailey's Cafe* (1992). Her most recent book is *1996* (2005). This essay first appeared in the *New York Times* in February 1986.

1 Language is the subject. It is the written form with which I've managed to keep the wolf away from the door and, in diaries, to keep my sanity. In spite of this, I consider the written word inferior to the spoken, and much of the frustration experienced by novelists is the awareness that whatever we manage to capture in even the most transcendent passages falls far short of the richness of life. Dialogue achieves its power in the dynamics of a fleeting moment of sight, sound, smell and touch.

2 I'm not going to enter the debate here about whether it is language that shapes reality or vice versa. That battle is doomed to be waged whenever we seek intermittent reprieve from the chicken and egg dispute. I will simply take the position that the spoken word, like the written word, amounts to a nonsensical arrangement of sounds or letters without a consensus that assigns "meaning." And building from the meanings of what we hear, we order reality. Words themselves are innocuous; it is the consensus that gives them true power.

3 I remember the first time I heard the word nigger. In my third-grade class, our math tests were being passed down the rows, and as I handed the papers to a little boy in back of me, I remarked that once again he had received a much lower mark than I did. He snatched his test from me and spit out that word. Had he called me a nymphomaniac or a necrophiliac, I couldn't have been more puzzled. I didn't know what a nigger was, but I knew that whatever it meant, it was something he shouldn't have called me. This was verified when I raised my hand, and in a loud voice repeated what he had said and watched the teacher scold him for using a "bad" word. I was later to go home and ask the inevitable question that every black parent must face—"Mommy, what does 'nigger' mean?"

4 And what exactly did it mean? Thinking back, I realize that this could not have been the first time the word was used in my presence. I was part of a large extended family that had migrated from the rural South after World War II and formed a close-knit network that gravitated around my maternal grandparents. Their ground-floor apartment in one of the buildings they owned in Harlem was a weekend mecca for my immediate family, along with countless aunts, uncles and cousins who brought along assorted friends. It was a bustling and open house with assorted neighbors and tenants popping in and out to exchange bits of gossip, pick up an old

quarrel or referee the ongoing checkers game in which my grandmother cheated shamelessly. They were all there to let down their hair and put up their feet after a week of labor in the factories, laundries and shipyards of New York.

5 Amid the clamor, which could reach deafening proportions—two or three conversations going on simultaneously, punctuated by the sound of a baby's crying somewhere in the back rooms or out on the street—there was still a rigid set of rules about what was said and how. Older children were sent out of the living room when it was time to get into the juicy details about "you-know-who" up on the third floor who had gone and gotten herself "p-r-e-g-n-a-n-t!" But my parents, knowing that I could spell well beyond my years, always demanded that I follow the others out to play. Beyond sexual misconduct and death, everything else was considered harmless for our young ears. And so among the anecdotes of the triumphs and disappointments in the various workings of their lives, the word nigger was used in my presence, but it was set within contexts and inflections that caused it to register in my mind as something else.

6 In the singular, the word was always applied to a man who had distinguished himself in some situation that brought their approval for his strength, intelligence or drive:

7 "Did Johnny *really* do that?"

8 "I'm telling you, that nigger pulled in $6,000 of overtime last year. Said he got enough for a down payment on a house."

9 When used with a possessive adjective by a woman—"my nigger"—it became a term of endearment for husband or boyfriend. But it could be more than just a term applied to a man. In their mouths it became the pure essence of manhood—a disembodied force that channeled their past history of struggle and present survival against the odds into a victorious statement of being: "Yeah, that old foreman found out quick enough—you don't mess with a nigger."

10 In the plural, it became a description of some group within the community that have overstepped the bounds of decency as my family defined it: Parents who neglected their children, a drunken couple who fought in public, people who simply refused to look for work, those with excessively dirty mouths or unkempt households were all "trifling niggers." This particular circle could forgive hard times, unemployment, the occasional bout of depression—they had gone through all of that themselves—but the unforgivable sin was a lack of self-respect.

11 A woman could never be a "nigger" in the singular, with its connotation of confirming worth. The noun girl was its closest equivalent in that sense, but only when used in direct address and regardless of the gender doing the addressing. "Girl" was a token of respect for a woman. The one-syllable word was drawn out to sound like three in recognition of the extra ounce of wit, nerve or daring that the woman had shown in the situation under discussion.

12 "G-i-r-l, stop. You mean you said that to his face?"

13 But if the word was used in a third-person reference or shortened so that it almost snapped out of the mouth, it always involved some element of communal disapproval. And age became an important factor in these exchanges. It was only between individuals of the same generation, or from an older person to a younger (but never the other way around), that "girl" would be considered a compliment.

14   I don't agree with the argument that use of the word nigger at this social stratum of the black community was an internalization of racism. The dynamics were the exact opposite: the people in my grandmother's living room took a word that whites used to signify worthlessness or degradation and rendered it impotent. Gathering there together, they transformed "nigger" to signify the varied and complex human beings they knew themselves to be. If the word was to disappear totally from the mouths of even the most liberal of white society, no one in that room was naïve enough to believe it would disappear from white minds. Meeting the word head-on, they proved it had absolutely nothing to do with the way they were determined to live their lives.

15   So there must have been dozens of times that the "nigger" was spoken in front of me before I reached the third grade. But I didn't "hear" it until it was said by a small pair of lips that had already learned it could be a way to humiliate me. That was the word I went home and asked my mother about. And since she knew that I had to grow up in America, she took me in her lap and explained.

THINKING CRITICALLY

1. Does Naylor think that written or spoken words are more powerful? Why? What does she mean when she says that it is "consensus that gives [words] true power"?

2. What did Naylor do as a response to hearing the word *nigger*? In your judgment, were her actions appropriate and effective ways of handling the situation?

3. List four different meanings that Naylor says she has heard adults apply to the word *nigger*. How are these four meanings different from what she believed the boy in her class meant? Are all four meanings positive?

4. Why can't a woman be referred to as a *nigger*? What other term is used for a woman that achieves meaning similar to the term *nigger* for a man?

5. Naylor relates in some detail the circumstances surrounding the first time she heard the word *nigger*. Why does she paint such an elaborate picture? Why doesn't she simply list her age and the fact that she heard it used as an insult? What do you think prompted the boy to use this word?

6. Why does Naylor compare the word *nigger* specifically to *nymphomaniac* and *necrophiliac*? Why these words? How are they similar? How different? (Look them up in your dictionary if you are not sure what they mean.)

WRITING ASSIGNMENTS

1. In paragraphs 4 and 5, Naylor provides a detailed discussion of her extended family: where they lived, how they were related, what kind of atmosphere these people created, and what kinds of discussion children were permitted to eavesdrop on, etc. How is this information related to the subject of Naylor's essay, the meaning of the word *nigger*? Can you think of any words or expressions that are used by your own circle—family, friends, etc.—that would be inappropriate for outsiders to use, but acceptable by intimates? Explain.

2. Does Naylor approve of her family and friends' use of the word *nigger*? Why or why not? Does she approve of other people using the word? Why or why not?

3. Visit the Abolish the "N" word Web site at www.abolishthenword.com—a Web site that is committed to putting an end to all references to the word "nigger." After visiting the Web site, write an essay in which you agree or disagree with the points made by the site's authors that "The "N" word is not a term of endearment. It cannot be reappropriated. We cannot redefine the 'N' word or re-spell it to make it positive. . . ." How do you think Naylor would respond to the movement the Web site is promoting? Explain.

MAKING CONNECTIONS

1. How can the principles of gender-free, gender-fair, and gender-specific language be applied to language that is biased about handicap, religion, race, age, or other group characteristics? Supply one example for each principle and include a phrase that contains biased language and a revision resolving the problem.

2. Rosalie Maggio, Michiko Kakutani, and Ward Churchill take strong positions on the issue of "politically correct" language, while Robin Tomach Lakoff takes a more neutral position. Create a conversation between two or more of these authors that discusses the issues of language use. (Your conversation will be more effective if you focus on a particular topic/issue—perhaps choose a controversy in the news, a controversial TV program or movie, or anything to do with your school's speech/behavior codes.)

3. The issues of hate speech and stereotypical language seem to be deeply intertwined. Write an essay in which you explore the connection between the two and likely outcomes for the future. Are we moving toward a culture where more sensitive forms of speech become the norm? Will hate speech become a thing of the past if speech codes preventing it are instituted and enforced? Why or why not?

4. When did you first become aware of the word *nigger,* or of some other powerfully charged, racist or hateful word used to demean or diminish a person or a group of people? Were your recognitions gradual, or can you trace your recognition to a specific time and place? What did you do to try to understand the word or the problem? Write a personal narrative describing your memory of how racist language or hate speech could be used to hurt.

5. Almost everyone has been exposed to some form of ethnic, sexist, or racial insults. Write an essay discussing how the media—movies, television, books, and music—contribute to the growth of prejudicial language.

6. Several of the authors in this section examine the issue of epithets and how context affects their meaning. Choose an epithet and research its denotation and connotation. First explore various source books—standard dictionaries (the *Oxford English Dictionary* provides the etymology of words), slang dictionaries, encyclopedias, and so forth. Then interview class members about how they define these words. Do you find a difference between how the books define the words versus how your classmates define them? Organize your findings and report them to the class.

7. All of the authors in this unit have strong opinions about the nature of prejudice and stereotypes, opinions that you may or may not agree with. For this assignment, play devil's advocate and write a critique of one of the essays in this section. Be sure to refer to the writer's text when drafting your essay so that you can be specific about where you disagree.

CASE STUDY: CENSORSHIP AND FREE SPEECH ON CAMPUS

The Betrayal of Liberty on America's Campuses
Alan Charles Kors

> In the following essay, Alan Charles Kors argues that instituting sanctions on speech is a direct violation of students' right to free expression. Exactly where should the line be drawn as to what constitutes "hate speech"? The ambiguity of many university codes, says Kors, leads to sanctioning students for ridiculous and outrageous reasons. When students must consider every word they say, and even how they say it, they are prevented from engaging in honest intellectual inquiry, debate, and dialogue.
>
> Alan Charles Kors is a professor of history at the University of Pennsylvania. He is the co-author with Harvey Silverglate of *The Shadow University: The Betrayal of Liberty on America's Campuses* (1998). Together with Silverglate he founded The Foundation for Individual Rights in Education (FIRE), a nonprofit organization that addresses individual liberty and rights issues on campuses. The following essay was a feature of the Bradley Lecture Series of the American Enterprise Institute for Public Policy Research in October 1998.

1 Those things that threaten free and open debate and those things that threaten academic freedom are the direct enemy of liberty. Such threats exist most dangerously at universities not in curriculum and scholarship, but in the new university *in loco parentis* (the university standing in the place of parents), where our nation's colleges and universities, across the board, are teaching contempt for liberty and its components: freedom of expression and inquiry; individual rights and responsibilities over group rights and entitlements; equal justice under law; and the rights of private conscience. *That* assault upon liberty is occurring not in the sunlight of open decisions and advertised agendas, but in the shadows of an unaccountable middle-administration that has been given coercive authority over the lives, speech, consciences, and voluntary individuation and association of students.

2 Almost all colleges and universities, for example, have "harassment" policies that prohibit selective "verbal behavior" or "verbal conduct," but almost none has the honesty to call these "speech codes." These policies, adopted from employment law and catastrophic for universities, are applied to faculty and students, the latter not even being employees of a university, but, in fact, its clients. The core of these codes is the prohibition of the creation of "a hostile or offensive environment," with the remarkable variations and embellishments that follow from Hobbes's observation that to the learned it is given to be learnedly foolish. Within very recent times, Bowdoin College chose to outlaw jokes and ways of telling stories "experienced by others as harassing." Brown University banned verbal behavior that produced "feelings of impotence . . . anger . . . or disenfranchisement . . . [whether] intentional or unintentional." Colby prohibited speech that caused loss of "self-esteem." The University of Connecticut prohibited "inconsiderate jokes," "stereotyping," and

even "inappropriately directed laughter." Indeed, a student at Sarah Lawrence College recently was convicted of laughing at something that someone else said, and was ordered as a condition of remaining in the college, for his laughter, to read a book entitled *Homophobia on Campus*, see a movie about "homophobia," and write a paper about "homophobia." Rutgers University included within the forbidden and "heinous act" of harassment, "communication" that is "in any manner likely to cause annoyance or alarm," which causes *me* a great deal of annoyance *and* alarm. The University of Maryland–College Park outlaws not only "idle chatter of a sexual nature" and "comments or questions about the sensuality of a person," but pointedly explains that these verbal behaviors "do not necessarily have to be specifically directed at an individual to constitute sexual harassment." Expression goes well beyond the verbal, however, because the University of Maryland also prohibits "gestures . . . that are expressive of an idea, opinion, or emotion," including "sexual looks such as leering and ogling with suggestive overtones; licking lips or teeth; holding or eating food provocatively."

3   At Carnegie Mellon University, a student called his female opponent in an election for the Graduate Student Organization a "megalomaniac." He was charged with sexual harassment. The Dean of Students explained the deeper meaning of calling a woman a megalomaniac, citing a vast body of what he termed feminist "victim theory" on the plaintiff's behalf, and the associate provost submitted a brief that stated, "I have no doubt that this has created a hostile environment which impacts Lara's productivity as a student leader and as a graduate student."

4   Many universities, such as Berkeley itself, no less, adopted speech codes that outlawed "fighting words." That term is taken from the U.S. Supreme Court decision of the 1940s, *Chaplinsky v. New Hampshire* (a decision surely mooted by later Supreme Court decisions), in which, leftists take note, the unprotected fighting word was, of all things, "fascist." Many universities also leave the determination of whether something was a fighting word or created a hostile environment to the plaintiff. Thus, the University of Puget Sound states that harassment "depends on the point of view of the person to whom the conduct is unwelcome." The City University of New York warns that "sexual harassment is not defined by intentions, but by its impact on the subject." "No one," Bowdoin College warns, "is entitled to engage in behavior that is experienced by others as harassing." At the University of Connecticut, criticizing someone's limits of tolerance toward the speech of others is itself harassment: its code bans "attributing objections to any of the above [instances of harassment] to 'hypersensitivity' of the targeted individual or group."

5   West Virginia University prohibited, among many other things, "insults, humor, jokes, and anecdotes that belittle or demean an individual's or a group's sexuality or sex," and, try this one on for vagueness, "inappropriate displays of sexually suggestive objects or pictures which may include but are not limited to posters, pin-ups, and calendars." If applied equally, of course, such a policy would leave no sex or race safe in its conversations or humor, let alone in its artistic taste, but such policies never are applied equally. Thus, students at West Virginia received the official policies of the "Executive Officer for Social Justice," who stated the institutional orthodoxy about "homophobia" and "sexism." The Officer of Social Justice warned that "feelings" about gays and lesbians could not become

"attitudes": "Regardless of how a person feels about others, negative actions or attitudes based on misconceptions and/or ignorance constitute prejudice, which contradicts everything for which an institution of higher learning stands." Among those prejudices it listed "heterosexism . . . the assumption that everyone is het- erosexual, or, if they aren't, they should be." This, of course, outlawed specific re- ligious inner convictions about sexuality. Because everyone had the right to be free from "harassment," the policy specified "behaviors to avoid." These prohibitions affected speech and voluntary associations based upon beliefs. Thus, "DO NOT [in capital letters] tolerate 'jokes' which are potentially injurious to gays, lesbians and bisexuals. . . . DO NOT determine whether you will interact with someone by virtue of his or her sexual orientation." The policy also commanded specific pre- scriptions: "value alternate lifestyles . . . challenge homophobic remarks . . . [and] use language that is not gender specific. . . . Instead of referring to anyone's romantic partner as 'girlfriend' or 'boyfriend,' use positive generic terms such as a 'friend,' 'lover,' or 'partner.' Speak of your own romantic partner similarly." The "homophobia" policy ended with the warning that "harassment" or "discrim- ination" based on sexual preference was subject to penalties that ranged "from reprimand . . . to expulsion and termination, and including public service and edu- cational remediation." "Educational remediation," note well, is an academic euphemism for thought reform. Made aware of what their own university was doing, a coalition of faculty members threatened to expose West Virginia University for its obvious violations of the state and federal constitutions, and to sue the administration if need be. As I talk, the University has removed the offending codes from its freshmen orientation packages and from its website. We shall see if it has removed them from its operational policies.

6   When federal courts struck down two codes restricting "verbal behavior" at public universities and colleges, namely, at the University of Michigan and the University of Wisconsin, other public colleges and universities—even in those jurisdictions where codes had been declared unconstitutional—did not seek to abol- ish their policies. Thus, Central Michigan University, after the University of Michigan code had been struck down, maintained a policy whose prohibitions included "any intentional, unintentional, physical, verbal, or nonverbal behavior that subjects an individual to an intimidating, hostile or offensive educational . . . environment by demeaning or slurring individuals through . . . written literature because of their racial or ethnic affiliation or using symbols, epitaphs [sic, we hope] or slogans that infer [sic] negative connotations about an individual's racial or ethnic affiliation."

7   In 1993, this policy was challenged, successfully, in Federal District Court. The Court noted that the code applied to "all possible human conduct," and, citing internal University documents, ruled that Central Michigan intended to apply it to speech "which a person 'feels' has affronted him or some group, predicated on race or ethnicity." The Court ruled that if the policy's words had meaning, it banned, pre- cisely, protected speech. If someone's "treatise, term paper or even . . . cafeteria bull session" about the Middle East, the Court observed, blamed one group more than another on the basis of "some ancient ethnic traditions which give rise to barbarian combativeness or . . . inability to compromise," such speech, the Court found,

"would seem to be a good fit with the policy language." In fact, the Court ruled, "Any behavior, even unintentional, that offends any individual is to be prohibited under the policy. . . . If the speech gives offense it is prohibited." When the President of Central Michigan University offered assurances that the policy was not intended to be enforced in such a way as to "interfere impermissibly with individuals' rights to free speech," the Court declared itself "emphatically unimpressed" by such a savings clause, and it observed: "The university . . . says in essence, 'trust us; we may interfere, but not impermissibly.' The Court is not willing to entrust . . . the First Amendment to the tender mercies of this institution's discriminatory harassment/affirmative action enforcer."

8   Many in the academy insist that the entire phenomenon labeled "political correctness" is the mythical fabrication of opponents of "progressive" change. The authors of an American Association of University Professors' special committee report, the "Statement on the 'Political Correctness' Controversy" (1991), insisted, without irony, that claims of "political correctness" were merely smokescreens to hide the true agenda of such critics—a racist and sexist desire to thwart the aspirations of minorities and women in the academic enterprise.

9   It is, in fact, almost inconceivable that anyone of good faith could live on a college campus unaware of the repression, legal inequality, intrusions into private conscience, and malignant double standards that hold sway there. In the Left's history of McCarthyism, the firing or dismissal of one professor or student, the inquisition into the private beliefs of one individual, let alone the demands for a demonstration of fealty to community standards stand out as intolerable oppressions that coerced people into silence, hypocrisy, betrayal, and tyranny.

10   In fact, in today's assault on liberty on college campuses, there is not a small number of cases, speech codes, nor apparatuses of repression and thought reform. Number aside, however, a climate of repression succeeds not by statistical frequency, but by sapping the courage, autonomy, and conscience of individuals who otherwise might remember or revive what liberty could be.

11   Most students respect disagreement and difference, and they do not bring charges of harassment against those whose opinions or expressions "offend" them. The universities themselves, however, encourage such charges to be brought. At almost every college and university, students deemed members of "historically oppressed groups"—above all, women, blacks, gays, and Hispanics—are informed during orientations that their campuses are teeming with illegal or intolerable violations of their "right" not to be offended. To believe many new-student orientations would be to believe that there was a racial or sexual bigot, to borrow the mocking phrase of McCarthy's critics, "under every bed." At almost every college and university, students are presented with lists of a vast array of places to which they should submit charges of such verbal "harassment," and they are promised "victim support," "confidentiality," and sympathetic understanding when they file such complaints.

12   What an astonishing expectation to give to students: the belief that, if they belong to a protected category and have the correct beliefs, they have a right to four years of never being offended. What an extraordinary power to give to administrative tribunals: the prerogative to punish the free speech and expression of people to

whom they assign the stains of historical oppression, while being free, themselves, to use whatever rhetoric they wish against the bearers of such stains. While the world looks at issues of curriculum and scholarship, above all, to analyze and evaluate American colleges and universities, it is, in fact, the silencing and punishment of belief, expression, and individuality that ought to concern yet more deeply those who care about what universities are and could be. Most cases never reach the public, because most individuals accused of "verbal" harassment sadly (but understandably) accept plea-bargains that diminish their freedom but spare them Draconian penalties, including expulsion. Those settlements almost invariably involve "sensitivity training," an appalling term, "training," to hear in matters of the human mind and spirit. Even so, the files on prosecutions under speech codes are, alas, overflowing.

13   "Settlements," by the way, are one of the best-kept and most frightening secrets of American academic life, almost always assigned with an insistence upon confidentiality. They are nothing less than an American version of thought reform from benighted offender into a politically correct bearer, in fact or in appearance, of an ideology that is the regnant orthodoxy of our universities *in loco parentis*.

14   From this perspective, American history is a tale of the oppression of all "others" by white, heterosexual, Eurocentric males, punctuated by the struggles of the oppressed. "Beneficiaries" see their lives as good and as natural, and falsely view America as a boon to humankind. Worse, most "victims" of "oppression" accept the values of their oppressors. A central task of education, then, is to "demystify" such arbitrary power. Whites, males, and heterosexuals must recognize and renounce the injustice of their "privilege." Nonwhites, women, gays, and lesbians must recognize and struggle against their victimization, both in their beliefs and in their behaviors.

15   Such "demystification" has found a welcome home in a large number of courses in the humanities and social sciences, but for the true believers, this is insufficient, because most courses remain optional, many professors resist the temptation to proselytize, and students, for the most part, choose majors that take them far from oppression studies.

16   Indeed, students forever disappoint the ideologues. Men and women generally see themselves neither as oppressor nor oppressed, and, far from engaging in class warfare, often quite love each other. Most women refuse to identify themselves as "feminists." Group-identity centers—although they can rally support at moments of crisis—attract few students overall, because invitees busily go about the business of learning, making friends, pursuing interests, and seeking love—all the things that 18- to 22-year-olds have done from time immemorial. Attendance at group-identity organizations is often miniscule as a percentage of the intended population, and militant leaders complain endlessly about "apathy." Whites don't feel particularly guilty about being white, and almost no designated "victims" adopt truly radical politics. Most undergraduates unabashedly seek their portion of American freedom, legal equality, and bounty. What to do with such benighted students? Increasingly, the answer to that question is to use the *in loco parentis* apparatus of the university to reform their private consciences and minds. For the generation that once said, "Don't trust anyone *over* 30," the motto now is "Don't trust anyone *under* 30." Increasingly, Offices of Student Life, Residence Offices, and residence advisors

have become agencies of progressive social engineering whose mission is to bring students to mandatory political enlightenment.

17   Such practices violate more than honest education. Recognition of the sanctity of conscience is the single most essential respect given to individual autonomy. There are purely practical arguments for the right to avoid self-incrimination or to choose religious (or other) creeds, but there is none deeper than restraining power from intruding upon the privacy of the self. Universities and colleges that commit the scandal of sentencing students (and faculty) to "sensitivity therapy" do not even permit individuals to choose their therapists. The Christian may not consult his or her chosen counselor, but most follow the regime of the social worker selected by the Women's Center or by the Office of Student Life. . . .

18   Imagine a campus on which being denounced for "irreligous bigotry" or "un-Americanism" carried the same stigma that being denounced for "racism," "sexism," and "homophobia" now carries in the academic world, so that in such hearings or trials, the burden of proof invariably fell upon the "offender." The common sign at pro-choice rallies, "Keep your rosaries off our ovaries," would be prima facie evidence of language used as a weapon to degrade and marginalize, and the common term of abuse, "born-again bigot," would be compelling evidence of the choice to create a hostile environment for evangelicals. What panegyrics to liberty and free expression we would hear in opposition to any proposed code to protect the "religious" or the "patriotic" from "offense" and "incivility." Yet what deafening silence we have heard, in these times, in the campus acceptance of the speech provisions of so-called harassment codes.

19   The goal of a speech code, then, is to suppress speech one doesn't like. The goal of liberty and equal justice is to permit us to live in a complex but peaceful world of difference, disagreement, debate, moral witness, and efforts of persuasion—without coercion and violence. Liberty and legal equality are hard-won, precious, and, indeed—because the social world is often discomforting—profoundly complex and troublesome ways of being human. They require, for their sustenance, men and women who would abhor their own power of censorship and their own special legal privileges as much as they abhor those of others. In enacting and enforcing speech codes, universities, for their own partisan reasons, have chosen to betray the human vision of freedom and legal equality. It was malignant to impose or permit such speech codes; to deny their oppressive effects while living in the midst of those effects is beyond the moral pale.

20   On virtually any college campus, for all of its rules of "civility" and all of its prohibitions of "hostile environment," assimilationist black men and women live daily with the terms "Uncle Tom" and "Oreo" said with impunity, while their tormenters live with special protections from offense. White students daily hear themselves, their friends, and their parents denounced as "racists" and "oppressors," while their tormenters live with special protections from offense. Believing Christians hear their beliefs ridiculed and see their sacred symbols traduced—virtually nothing, in the name of freedom, may not be said against them in the classroom, at rallies, and in personal encounters—while their tormenters live with special protection from offense. Men hear their sex abused, find themselves blamed for all the evils of the world, and enter classrooms whose very goal is to make them feel discomfort, while their tormenters live with special protections from "a hostile environment."

21   It is our liberty, above all else, that defines us as human beings, capable of ethics and responsibility. The struggle for liberty on American campuses is one of the defining struggles of the age in which we find ourselves. A nation that does not educate in freedom will not survive in freedom, and will not even know when it has lost it. Individuals too often convince themselves that they are caught up in moments of history that they cannot affect. That history, however, is made by their will and moral choices. There is a moral crisis in higher education. It will not be resolved unless we choose and act to resolve it.

22   It is easy, however, to identify the vulnerabilities of the bearers of this worst and, at the time, most marginal legacy of the '60s: they loathe the society that they believe should support them generously in their authority over its offspring; they are detached from the values of individual liberty, legal equality, privacy, and the sanctity of conscience toward which Americans essentially are drawn; and, for both those reasons, they cannot bear the light of public scrutiny. Let the sunlight in.

THINKING CRITICALLY

1. Why does Kors believe racist and inflammatory speech should be protected by the First Amendment? What examples does he use to prove his point? Do you agree? Can you think of circumstances in which racist speech should not be protected? Explain.

2. How has this article affected your thinking on the subject of free speech and censorship? Has it changed your mind about the use of racially or sexually abusive language? Explain your perspective.

3. How are colleges and university administrators dealing with incidents of verbal abuse on American campuses? What is Kors's reaction to their handling of such problems? According to Kors, how are students being manipulated by university censorship rules?

4. Explain what Kors means when he says, "Many in the academy insist that the entire phenomenon labeled 'political correctness' is the mythical fabrication of opponents of 'progressive' change" (paragraph 8). Do you agree with this view?

5. Consider the author's voice in this essay. What sense do you get of Kors as an individual? Write a paragraph characterizing the author. Take into consideration his stand in the essay, his style and tone of writing, and the examples he uses to support his view and how he presents them.

Regulating Racist Speech on Campus
Charles R. Lawrence, III

Recent years have witnessed a disturbing rise in racist and sexist language on college campuses. Some administrations have dealt with the problem by banning outright offensive language on the grounds that racial slurs are violent verbal assaults that interfere with students' rights to an education. Others fear that placing sanctions on racist speech violates the First Amendment guarantee of free expression. In the following essay, law professor Charles R. Lawrence, III argues for the restriction of free speech by citing the U.S. Supreme Court's landmark decision in the case of *Brown v. Board of Education.*

Charles R. Lawrence teaches law at Georgetown University. He is the co-author of *We Won't Go Back: Making the Case for Affirmative Action* (1997), written with his wife and fellow Georgetown professor Mari J. Matsuda. Lawrence is best known for his work in antidiscrimination law, equal protection, and critical race theory. He is also a former president of the Society of American Law Teachers.

1   I have spent the better part of my life as a dissenter. As a high-school student, I was threatened with suspension for my refusal to participate in a civil-defense drill, and I have been a conspicuous consumer of my First Amendment liberties ever since. There are very strong reasons for protecting even racist speech. Perhaps the most important of these is that such protection reinforces our society's commitment to tolerance as a value, and that by protecting bad speech from government regulation, we will be forced to combat it as a community.

2   But I also have a deeply felt apprehension about the resurgence of racial violence and the corresponding rise in the incidence of verbal and symbolic assault and harassment to which blacks and other traditionally subjugated and excluded groups are subjected. I am troubled by the way the debate has been framed in response to the recent surge of racist incidents on college and university campuses and in response to some universities' attempts to regulate harassing speech. The problem has been framed as one in which the liberty of free speech is in conflict with the elimination of racism. I believe this has placed the bigot on the moral high ground and fanned the rising flames of racism.

3   Above all, I am troubled that we have not listened to the real victims, that we have shown so little understanding of their injury, and that we have abandoned those whose race, gender, or sexual preference continues to make them second-class citizens. It seems to me a very sad irony that the first instinct of civil libertarians has been to challenge even the smallest, most narrowly framed efforts by universities to provide black and other minority students with the protection the Constitution guarantees them.

4   The landmark case of *Brown v. Board of Education* is not a case that we normally think of as a case about speech. But *Brown* can be broadly read as articulating the principle of equal citizenship. *Brown* held that segregated schools were inherently unequal because of the *message* that segregation conveyed—that black children were an untouchable caste, unfit to go to school with white children. If we understand the necessity of eliminating the system of signs and symbols that signal the inferiority of blacks, then we should hesitate before proclaiming that all racist speech that stops short of physical violence must be defended.

5   University officials who have formulated policies to respond to incidents of racial harassment have been characterized in the press as "thought police," but such policies generally do nothing more than impose sanctions against intentional face-to-face insults. When racist speech takes the form of face-to-face insults, catcalls, or other assaultive speech aimed at an individual or small group of persons, it falls directly within the "fighting words" exception to First Amendment protection. The Supreme Court has held that words which "by their very utterance inflict injury or tend to incite an immediate breach of the peace" are not protected by the First Amendment.

6   If the purpose of the First Amendment is to foster the greatest amount of speech, racial insults disserve that purpose. Assaultive racist speech functions as a preemptive strike. The invective is experienced as a blow, not as a proffered idea, and once the blow is struck, it is unlikely that a dialogue will follow. Racial insults are particularly undeserving of First Amendment protection because the perpetrator's intention is not to discover truth or initiate dialogue but to injure the victim. In most situations, members of minority groups realize that they are likely to lose if they respond to epithets by fighting and are forced to remain silent and submissive.

7   Courts have held that offensive speech may not be regulated in public forums such as streets where the listener may avoid the speech by moving on, but the regulation of otherwise protected speech has been permitted when the speech invades the privacy of the unwilling listener's home or when the unwilling listener cannot avoid the speech. Racist posters, fliers, and graffiti in dormitories, bathrooms, and other common living spaces would seem to clearly fall within the reasoning of these cases. Minority students should not be required to remain in their rooms in order to avoid racial assault. Minimally, they should find a safe haven in their dorms and in all other common rooms that are a part of their daily routine.

8   I would also argue that the university's responsibility for insuring that these students receive an equal educational opportunity provides a compelling justification for regulations that insure them safe passage in all common areas. A minority student should not have to risk becoming the target of racially assaulting speech every time he or she chooses to walk across campus. Regulating vilifying speech that cannot be anticipated or avoided would not preclude announced speeches and rallies—situations that would give minority-group members and their allies the chance to organize counter-demonstrations or avoid the speech altogether.

9   The most commonly advanced argument against the regulation of racist speech proceeds something like this: we recognize that minority groups suffer pain and injury as the result of racist speech, but we must allow this hate mongering for the benefit of society as a whole. Freedom of speech is the lifeblood of our democratic system. It is especially important for minorities because often it is their only vehicle for rallying support for the redress of their grievances. It will be impossible to formulate a prohibition so precise that it will prevent the racist speech you want to suppress without catching in the same net all kinds of speech that it would be unconscionable for a democratic society to suppress.

10   Whenever we make such arguments, we are striking a balance on the one hand between our concern for the continued free flow of ideas and the democratic process dependent on that flow, and, on the other, our desire to further the cause of equality. There can be no meaningful discussion of how we should reconcile our commitment to equality and our commitment to free speech until it is acknowledged that there is real harm inflicted by racist speech and that this harm is far from trivial.

11   To engage in a debate about the First Amendment and racist speech without a full understanding of the nature and extent of that harm is to risk making the First Amendment an instrument of domination rather than a vehicle of liberation. We have not known the experience of victimization by racist, misogynist, and homophobic speech, nor do we equally share the burden of the societal harm it inflicts. We are often quick to say that we have heard the cry of the victims when we have not.

12   The *Brown* case is again instructive because it speaks directly to the psychic injury inflicted by racist speech by noting that the symbolic message of segregation affected "the hearts and minds" of Negro children "in a way unlikely ever to be undone." Racial epithets and harassment often cause deep emotional scarring and feelings of anxiety and fear that pervade every aspect of a victim's life.

13   *Brown* also recognized that black children did not have an equal opportunity to learn and participate in the school community if they bore the additional burden of being subjected to the humiliation and psychic assault contained in the message of segregation. University students bear an analogous burden when they are forced to live and work in an environment where at any moment they may be subjected to denigrating verbal harassment and assault. The same injury was addressed by the Supreme Court when it held that sexual harassment that creates a hostile or abusive work environment violates the ban on sex discrimination in employment of Title VII of the Civil Rights Act of 1964.

14   Carefully drafted university regulations would bar the use of words as assault weapons and leave unregulated even the most heinous of ideas when those ideas are presented at times and places and in manners that provide an opportunity for reasoned rebuttal or escape from immediate injury. The history of the development of the right to free speech has been one of carefully evaluating the importance of free expression and its effects on other important societal interests. We have drawn the line between protected and unprotected speech before without dire results. (Courts have, for example, exempted from the protection of the First Amendment obscene speech and speech that disseminates official secrets, that defames or libels another person, or that is used to form a conspiracy or monopoly.)

15   Blacks and other people of color are skeptical about the argument that even the most injurious speech must remain unregulated because, in an unregulated marketplace of ideas, the best ones will rise to the top and gain acceptance. Our experience tells us quite the opposite. We have seen too many good liberal politicians shy away from the issues that might brand them as being too closely allied with us.

16   Whenever we decide that racist speech must be tolerated because of the importance of maintaining societal tolerance for all unpopular speech, we are asking blacks and other subordinated groups to bear the burden for the good of all. We must be careful that the ease with which we strike the balance against the regulation of racist speech is in no way influenced by the fact that the cost will be borne by others. We must be certain that those who will pay that price are fairly represented in our deliberations and that they are heard.

17   At the core of the argument that we should resist all government regulation of speech is the ideal that the best cure for bad speech is good, that ideas that affirm equality and the worth of all individuals will ultimately prevail. This is an empty ideal unless those of us who would fight racism are vigilant and unequivocal in that fight. We must look for ways to offer assistance and support to students whose speech and political participation are chilled in a climate of racial harassment.

18   Civil rights lawyers might consider suing on behalf of blacks whose right to an equal education is denied by a university's failure to insure a nondiscriminatory educational climate or conditions of employment. We must embark upon the development of a First Amendment jurisprudence grounded in the reality of our history and our contemporary experience. We must think hard about how best to launch legal

attacks against the most indefensible forms of hate speech. Good lawyers can create exceptions and narrow interpretations that limit the harm of hate speech without opening the floodgates of censorship.

19   Everyone concerned with these issues must find ways to engage actively in actions that resist and counter the racist ideas that we would have the First Amendment protect. If we fail in this, the victims of hate speech must rightly assume that we are on the oppressors' side.

THINKING CRITICALLY

1. What reasons does Lawrence offer for protecting racist speech from governmental restrictions? Do you agree? How are university restrictions different from those imposed by the government?

2. According to the author, how in the debate over racist language does the fight against racism conflict with the fight for free speech? What fundamental problem does Lawrence have with this conflict? Are his reasons convincing?

3. Why, according to Lawrence, is racist speech "undeserving of First Amendment protection" (paragraph 6)? Do you agree? If not, why not? If so, can you think of any circumstances when racist speech should be protected?

4. Have you ever been the victim of abusive speech—speech that victimized you because of your race, gender, religion, ethnicity, or sexual preference? Do you agree with Lawrence's argument regarding "psychic injury" (paragraph 12)? Explain.

5. How convincingly does Lawrence argue that racist speech should not be protected by the First Amendment? What is the logic of his argument? What evidence does he offer as support?

6. Select one of Lawrence's arguments that you think is especially strong or especially weak, and explain why you think so.

7. Lawrence opens his essay saying that he has a long history as a "dissenter." What is his strategy? What assumptions does he make about his audience? What does his refusal to participate in a civil-defense drill have to do with the essay's central issues?

There's No Such Thing as Free Speech, and It's a Good Thing, Too
Stanley Fish

The two previous readings present different points of view regarding campus speech codes and free speech. In the next essay, academic and law professor Stanley Fish argues that there really is no such thing as free speech. Free speech is, he explains, "just the name we give to verbal behavior that serves the substantive agendas we wish to advance." Free speech is, in his opinion, simply a "political prize." As a social construct, free speech has always had "qualifiers" depending on who wielded power. And Fish thinks that the liberal left should realize that this reality isn't such a bad thing.

Stanley Fish is a professor of law at Florida International University. His many academic works include *Is There a Text in This Class?* (1984), *Professional Correctness: Literary and Political Change* (1995), and most recently, *How Milton Works* (2001). The following essay first appeared in the *Boston Review* and was later republished in his book of the same title, *There's No Such Thing as Free Speech, and It's a Good Thing, Too* (1994).

1 Lately, many on the liberal and progressive left have been disconcerted to find that words, phrases, and concepts thought to be their property and generative of their politics have been appropriated by the forces of neoconservatism. This is particularly true of the concept of free speech, for in recent years First Amendment rhetoric has been used to justify policies and actions the left finds problematical if not abhorrent: pornography, sexist language, campus hate speech. How has this happened? The answer I shall give in this essay is that abstract concepts like free speech do not have any "natural" content but are filled with whatever content and direction one can manage to put into them. "Free speech" is just the name we give to verbal behavior that serves the substantive agendas we wish to advance; and we give our preferred verbal behaviors *that* name when we can, when we have the power to do so, because in the rhetoric of American life, the label "free speech" is the one you want your favorites to wear. Free speech, in short, is not an independent value but a political prize, and if that prize has been captured by a politics opposed to yours, it can no longer be invoked in ways that further your purposes, for it is now an obstacle to those purposes. This is something that the liberal left has yet to understand, and what follows is an attempt to pry its members loose from a vocabulary that may now be a disservice to them.

2   Not far from the end of his *Areopagitica*, and after having celebrated the virtues of toleration and unregulated publication in passages that find their way into every discussion of free speech and the First Amendment, John Milton catches himself up short and says, of course I didn't mean Catholics, them we exterminate:

> I mean not tolerated popery, and open superstition, which as it extirpates all religious and civil supremacies, so itself should be extirpate . . . that also which is impious or evil absolutely against faith or manners no law can possibly permit that intends not to unlaw itself.

3   Notice that Milton is not simply stipulating a single exception to a rule generally in place; the kinds of utterance that might be regulated and even prohibited on pain of trial and punishment constitute an open set; popery is named only as a particularly perspicuous instance of the advocacy that cannot be tolerated. No doubt there are other forms of speech and action that might be categorized as "open superstitions" or as subversive of piety, faith, and manners, and presumably these too would be candidates for "extirpation." Nor would Milton think himself culpable for having failed to provide a list of unprotected utterances. The list will fill itself out as utterances are put to the test implied by his formulation: would this form of speech or advocacy, if permitted to flourish, tend to undermine the very purposes for which our society is constituted? One cannot answer this question with respect to a particular utterance in advance of its emergence on the world's stage; rather,

510 ■ Chapter 7 / Censorship and Free Speech

one must wait and ask the question in the full context of its production and (possible) dissemination. It might appear that the result would be ad hoc and unprincipled, but for Milton the principle inheres in the core values in whose name individuals of like mind came together in the first place. Those values, which include the search for truth and the promotion of virtue, are capacious enough to accommodate a diversity of views. But at some point—again impossible of advance specification—capaciousness will threaten to become shapelessness, and at that point fidelity to the original values will demand acts of extirpation.

4   I want to say that all affirmations of freedom of expression are like Milton's, dependent for their force on an exception that literally carves out the space in which expression can then emerge. I do not mean that expression (saying something) is a realm whose integrity is sometimes compromised by certain restrictions but that restriction, in the form of an underlying articulation of the world that necessarily (if silently) negates alternatively possible articulations, is constitutive of expression. Without restriction, without an inbuilt sense of what it would be meaningless to say or wrong to say, there could be no assertion and no reason for asserting it. The exception to unregulated expression is not a negative restriction but a positive hollowing out of value—we are for *this*, which means we are against *that*—in relation to which meaningful assertion can then occur. It is in reference to that value—constituted as all values are by an act of exclusion—that some forms of speech will be heard as (quite literally) intolerable. Speech, in short, is never a value in and of itself but is always produced within the precincts of some assumed conception of the good to which it must yield in the event of conflict. When the pinch comes (and sooner or later it will always come) and the institution (be it church, state, or university) is confronted by behavior subversive of its core rationale, it will respond by declaring "of course we mean not tolerated —————, that we extirpate," not because an exception to a general freedom has suddenly and contradictorily been announced, but because the freedom has never been general and has always been understood against the background of an originary exclusion that gives it meaning.

5   This is a large thesis, but before tackling it directly I want to buttress my case with an example taken from the charter and case law of Canada. Canadian thinking about freedom of expression departs from the line usually taken in the United States [in ways that bring that country very close to the *Areopagitica* as I have expounded it.] The differences are fully on display in a recent landmark case, *R. v. Keegstra*. James Keegstra was a high school teacher in Alberta who, it was established by evidence, "systematically denigrated Jews and Judaism in his classes." He described Jews as treacherous, subversive, sadistic, money loving, power hungry, and child killers. He declared them "responsible for depressions, anarchy, chaos, wars and revolution" and required his students "to regurgitate these notions in essays and examinations." Keegstra was indicted under Section 319(2) of the Criminal Code and convicted. The Court of Appeal reversed, and the Crown appealed to the Supreme Court, which reinstated the lower court's verdict.

6   Section 319(2) reads in part, "Every one who, by communicating statements other than in private conversation, willfully promotes hatred against any identifiable group is guilty of . . . an indictable offense and is liable to imprisonment for a term not exceeding two years." In the United States, this provision of the code

would almost certainly be struck down because, under the First Amendment, restrictions on speech are apparently prohibited without qualification. To be sure, the Canadian charter has its own version of the First Amendment, in Section 2(b): "Everyone has the following fundamental freedoms . . . (b) freedom of thought, belief, opinion, and expression, including freedom of the press and other media of communication." But Section 2(b), like every other section of the charter, is qualified by Section 1: "The Canadian Charter of Rights and Freedoms guarantees the rights and freedoms set out in it subject only to such reasonable limits prescribed by law as can be demonstrably justified in a free and democratic society." Or in other words, every right and freedom herein granted can be trumped if its exercise is found to be in conflict with the principles that underwrite the society.

7   This is what happens in *Keegstra* as the majority finds that Section 319(2) of the Criminal Code does in fact violate the right of freedom of expression guaranteed by the charter but is nevertheless a *permissible* restriction because it accords with the principles proclaimed in Section 1. There is, of course, a dissent that reaches the conclusion that would have been reached by most, if not all, U.S. courts; but even in dissent the minority is faithful to Canadian ways of reasoning. "The question," it declares, "is always one of balance," and thus even when a particular infringement of the charter's Section 2(b) has been declared unconstitutional, as it would have been by the minority, the question remains open with respect to the next case. In the United States the question is presumed closed and can only be pried open by special tools. In our legal culture as it is now constituted, if one yells "free speech" in a crowded courtroom and makes it stick, the case is over.

8   Of course, it is not that simple. Despite the apparent absoluteness of the First Amendment, there are any number of ways of getting around it, ways that are known to every student of the law. In general, the preferred strategy is to manipulate the distinction, essential to First Amendment jurisprudence, between speech and action. The distinction is essential because no one would think to frame a First Amendment that began "Congress shall make no law abridging freedom of action," for that would amount to saying "Congress shall make no law," which would amount to saying "There shall be no law," only actions uninhibited and unregulated. If the First Amendment is to make any sense, have any bite, speech must be declared not to be a species of action, or to be a special form of action lacking the aspects of action that cause it to be the object of regulation. The latter strategy is the favored one and usually involves the separation of speech from consequences. This is what Archibald Cox does when he assigns to the First Amendment the job of protecting "expressions separable from conduct harmful to other individuals and the community." The difficulty of managing this segregation is well known: speech always seems to be crossing the line into action, where it becomes, at least potentially, consequential. In the face of this categorical instability, First Amendment theorists and jurists fashion a distinction within the speech/action distinction: some forms of speech are not really speech because their purpose is to incite violence or because they are, as the court declares in *Chaplinsky v. New Hampshire (1942)*, "fighting words," words "likely to provoke the average person to retaliation, and thereby cause a breach of the peace."

9   The trouble with this definition is that it distinguishes not between fighting words and words that remain safely and merely expressive but between words that are provocative to one group (the group that falls under the rubric "average person") and words that might be provocative to other groups, groups of persons not now considered average. And if you ask what words are likely to be provocative to those nonaverage groups, what are likely to be *their* fighting words, the answer is anything and everything, for as Justice Holmes said long ago (in *Gitlow v. New York*), every idea is an incitement to somebody, and since ideas come packaged in sentences, in words, every sentence is potentially, in some situation that might occur tomorrow, a fighting word and therefore a candidate for regulation.

10   This insight cuts two ways. One could conclude from it that the fighting words exception is a bad idea because there is no way to prevent clever and unscrupulous advocates from shoveling so many forms of speech into the excepted category that the zone of constitutionally protected speech shrinks to nothing and is finally without inhabitants. Or, alternatively, one could conclude that there was never anything in the zone in the first place and that the difficulty of limiting the fighting words exception is merely a particular instance of the general difficulty of separating speech from action. And if one opts for this second conclusion, as I do, then a further conclusion is inescapable; insofar as the point of the First Amendment is to identify speech separable from conduct and from the consequences that come in conduct's wake, there is no such speech and therefore nothing for the First Amendment to protect. Or, to make the point from the other direction, when a court invalidates legislation because it infringes on protected speech, it is not because the speech in question is without consequences but because the consequences have been discounted in relation to a good that is judged to outweigh them. Despite what they say, courts are never in the business of protecting speech per se, "mere" speech (a nonexistent animal); rather, they are in the business of classifying speech (as protected or regulatable) in relation to a value—the health of the republic, the vigor of the economy, the maintenance of the status quo, the undoing of the status quo—that is the true, if unacknowledged, object of their protection.

11   But if this is the case, a First Amendment purist might reply, why not drop the charade along with the malleable distinctions that make it possible, and declare up front that total freedom of speech is our primary value and trumps anything else, no matter what? The answer is that freedom of expression would only be a primary value if it didn't matter what was said, didn't matter in the sense that no one gave a damn but just liked to hear talk. There are contexts like that, a Hyde Park corner or a call-in talk show where people get to sound off for the sheer fun of it. These, however, are special contexts, artificially bounded spaces designed to assure that talking is not taken seriously. In ordinary contexts, talk is produced with the goal of trying to move the world in one direction rather than another. In these contexts— the contexts of everyday life—you go to the trouble of asserting that X is Y only because you suspect that some people are wrongly asserting that X is Z or that X doesn't exist. You assert, in short, because you give a damn, not about assertion— as if it were a value in and of itself—but about what your assertion is about. It may seem paradoxical, but free expression could only be a primary value if what you are valuing is the right to make noise; but if you are engaged in some purposive activity

in the course of which speech happens to be produced, sooner or later you will come to a point when you decide that some forms of speech do not further but endanger that purpose.

12   Take the case of universities and colleges. Could it be the purpose of such places to encourage free expression? If the answer were "yes," it would be hard to say why there would be any need for classes, or examinations, or departments, or disciplines, or libraries, since freedom of expression requires nothing but a soapbox or an open telephone line. The very fact of the university's machinery—of the events, rituals, and procedures that fill its calendar—argues for some other, more substantive purpose. In relation to that purpose (which will be realized differently in different kinds of institutions), the flourishing of free expression will in almost all circumstances be an obvious good; but in some circumstances, freedom of expression may pose a threat to that purpose, and at that point it may be necessary to discipline or regulate speech, lest, to paraphrase Milton, the institution sacrifice itself to one of its *accidental* features.

13   Interestingly enough, the same conclusion is reached (inadvertently) by Congressman Henry Hyde, who addressed these very issues in an offered amendment to Title VI of the Civil Rights Act. The first section of the amendment states its purpose, to protect "the free speech rights of college students" by prohibiting private as well as public educational institutions from "subjecting any student to disciplinary sanctions solely on the basis of conduct that is speech." The second section enumerates the remedies available to students whose speech rights may have been abridged; and the third, which is to my mind the nub of the matter, declares as an exception to the amendment's jurisdiction any "educational institution that is controlled by a religious organization," on the reasoning that the application of the amendment to such institutions "would not be consistent with the religious tenets of such organizations." In effect, what Congressman Hyde is saying is that at the heart of these colleges and universities is a set of beliefs, and it would be wrong to require them to tolerate behavior, including speech behavior, inimical to those beliefs. But insofar as this logic is persuasive, it applies across the board, for all educational institutions rest on some set of beliefs—no institution is "just there" independent of any purpose—and it is hard to see why the rights of an institution to protect and preserve its basic "tenets" should be restricted only to those that are religiously controlled. Read strongly, the third section of the amendment undoes sections one and two—the exception becomes, as it always was, the rule—and points us to a balancing test very much like that employed in Canadian law: given that any college or university is informed by a core rationale, an administrator faced with complaints about offensive speech should ask whether damage to the core would be greater if the speech were tolerated or regulated.

14   The objection to this line of reasoning is well known and was reformulated by Benno Schmidt, former president of Yale University. According to Schmidt, speech codes on campuses constitute "well intentioned but misguided efforts to give values of community and harmony a higher place than freedom" (*Wall Street Journal*, May 6, 1991). "When the goals of harmony collide with freedom of expression," he continues, "freedom must be the paramount obligation of an academic community." The flaw in this logic is on display in the phrase "academic community," for the

phrase recognizes what Schmidt would deny, that expression only occurs in communities—if not in an academic community, then in a shopping mall community or a dinner party community or an airplane ride community or an office community. In these communities and in any others that could be imagined (with the possible exception of a community of major league baseball fans), limitations on speech in relation to a defining and deeply assumed purpose are inseparable from community membership.

15   Indeed, "limitations" is the wrong word because it suggests that expression, as an activity and a value, has a pure form that is always in danger of being compromised by the urgings of special interest communities; but independently of a community context informed by interest (that is, purpose), expression would be at once inconceivable and unintelligible. Rather than being a value that is threatened by limitations and constraints, expression, in any form worth worrying about, is a *product* of limitations and constraints, of the already-in-place presuppositions that give assertions their very particular point. Indeed, the very act of thinking of something to say (whether or not it is subsequently regulated) is already constrained—rendered impure, and because impure, communicable—by the background context within which the thought takes its shape. (The analysis holds too for "freedom," which in Schmidt's vision is an entirely empty concept referring to an urge without direction. But like expression, freedom is a coherent notion only in relation to a goal or good that limits and, by limiting, shapes its exercise.)

16   Arguments like Schmidt's only get their purchase by first imagining speech as occurring in no context whatsoever, and then stripping particular speech acts of the properties conferred on them by contexts. The trick is nicely illustrated when Schmidt urges protection for speech "no matter how obnoxious in content." "Obnoxious" at once acknowledges the reality of speech-related harms and trivializes them by suggesting that they are *surface* injuries that any large-minded ("liberated and humane") person should be able to bear. The possibility that speech-related injuries may be grievous and *deeply* wounding is carefully kept out of sight, and because it is kept out of sight, the fiction of a world of weightless verbal exchange can be maintained, at least within the confines of Schmidt's carefully denatured discourse.

17   To this Schmidt would no doubt reply, as he does in his essay, that harmful speech should be answered not by regulation but by more speech; but that would make sense only if the effects of speech could be canceled out by additional speech, only if the pain and humiliation caused by racial or religious epithets could be ameliorated by saying something like "So's your old man." What Schmidt fails to realize at every level of his argument is that expression is more than a matter of proffering and receiving propositions, that words do work in the world of a kind that cannot be confined to a purely cognitive realm of "mere" ideas.

18   It could be said, however, that I myself mistake the nature of the work done by freely tolerated speech because I am too focused on short-run outcomes and fail to understand that the good effects of speech will be realized, not in the present, but in a future whose emergence regulation could only inhibit. This line of reasoning would also weaken one of my key points, that speech in and of itself cannot be a value and is only worth worrying about if it is in the service of something with

which it cannot be identical. My mistake, one could argue, is to equate the something in whose service speech is with some locally espoused value (e.g., the end of racism, the empowerment of disadvantaged minorities), whereas in fact we should think of that something as a now-inchoate shape that will be given firm lines only by time's pencil. That is why the shape now receives such indeterminate characterizations (e.g., true self-fulfillment, a more perfect polity, a more capable citizenry, a less partial truth); we cannot now know it, and therefore we must not prematurely fix it in ways that will bind successive generations to error.

19   This forward-looking view of what the First Amendment protects has a great appeal, in part because it continues in a secular form the Puritan celebration of millenarian hopes, but it imposes a requirement so severe that one would except more justification for it than is usually provided. The requirement is that we endure whatever pain racist and hate speech inflicts for the sake of a future whose emer- gence we can only take on faith. In a specifically religious vision like Milton's, this makes perfect sense (it is indeed the whole of Christianity), but in the context of a politics that puts its trust in the world and not in the Holy Spirit, it raises more ques- tions than it answers and could be seen as the second of two strategies designed to delegitimize the complaints of victimized groups. The first strategy, as I have noted, is to define speech in such a way as to render it inconsequential (on the model of "sticks and stones will break my bones, but . . ."); the second strategy is to acknowl- edge the (often grievous) consequences of speech but declare that we must suffer them in the name of something that cannot be named. The two strategies are denials from slightly different directions of the *present* effects of racist speech; one con- fines those effects to a closed and safe realm of pure mental activity; the other imagines the effects of speech spilling over into the world but only in an ever- receding future for whose sake we must forever defer taking action.

20   I find both strategies unpersuasive, but my own skepticism concerning them is less important than the fact that in general they seem to have worked; in the par- lance of the marketplace (a parlance First Amendment commentators love), many in the society seemed to have bought them. Why? The answer, I think, is that peo- ple cling to First Amendment pieties because they do not wish to face what they correctly take to be the alternative. That alternative is *politics*, the realization (at which I have already hinted) that decisions about what is and is not protected in the realm of expression will rest not on principle or firm doctrine but on the ability of some persons to interpret—recharacterize or rewrite—principle and doctrine in ways that lead to the protection of speech they want heard and the regulation of speech they want heard and the regulation of speech they want silenced. (That is how George Bush can argue *for* flag-burning statutes and *against* campus hate- speech codes.) When the First Amendment is successfully invoked, the result is not a victory for free speech in the face of a challenge from politics but a *political victory* won by the party that has managed to wrap its agenda in the mantle of free speech.

21   It is from just such a conclusion—a conclusion that would put politics *inside* the First Amendment—that commentators recoil, saying things like "This could render the First Amendment a dead letter," or "This would leave us with no norma- tive guidance in determining when and what speech to protect," or "This effaces the

distinction between speech and action," or "This is incompatible with any viable notion of freedom of expression." To these statements (culled more or less at random from recent law review pieces) I would reply that the First Amendment has always been a dead letter if one understood its "liveness" to depend on the identification and protection of a realm of "mere" expression distinct from the realm of regulatable conduct; the distinction between speech and action has always been effaced in principle, although in practice it can take whatever form the prevailing political conditions mandate; we have never had any normative guidance for marking off protected from unprotected speech; rather, the guidance we have has been fashioned (and refashioned) in the very political struggles over which it then (for a time) presides. In short, the name of the game has always been politics, even when (indeed, especially when) it is played by stigmatizing politics as the area to be avoided.

22   In saying this, I would not be heard as arguing either for or against regulation and speech codes as a matter of general principle. Instead my argument turns away from general principle to the pragmatic (anti)principle of considering each situation as it emerges. The question of whether or not to regulate will always be a local one, and we can not rely on abstractions that are either empty of content or filled with the content of some partisan agenda to generate a "principled" answer. Instead we must consider in every case what is at stake and what are the risks and gains of alternative courses of action. In the course of this consideration many things will be of help, but among them will not be phrases like "freedom of speech" or "the right of individual expression," because, as they are used now, these phrases tend to obscure rather than clarify our dilemmas. Once they are deprived of their talismanic force, once it is no longer strategically effective simply to invoke them in the act of walking away from a problem, the conversation could continue in directions that are now blocked by a First Amendment absolutism that has only been honored in the breach anyway. To the student reporter who complains that in the wake of the promulgation of a speech code at the University of Wisconsin there is now something in the back of his mind as he writes, one could reply, "There was always something in the back of your mind, and perhaps it might be better to have this code in the back of your mind than whatever was in there before." And when someone warns about the slippery slope and predicts mournfully that if you restrict one form of speech, you never know what will be restricted next, one could reply. "Some form of speech is always being restricted, else there could be no meaningful assertion; we have always and already slid down the slippery slope; someone is always going to be restricted next, and it is your job to make sure that the someone is not you." And when someone observes, as someone surely will, that antiharassment codes chill speech, one could reply that since speech only becomes intelligible against the background of what isn't being said, the background of what has already been silenced, the only question is the political one of which speech is going to be chilled, and, all things considered, it seems a good thing to chill speech like "nigger," "cunt," "kike," and "faggot." And if someone then says, "But what happened to free-speech principles?" one could say what I have now said a dozen times, free-speech principles don't exist except as a component in a bad argument in which such principles are invoked to mask motives that would not withstand close scrutiny.

23   An example of a wolf wrapped in First Amendment clothing is an advertisement that ran in the Duke University student newspaper, the *Chronicle*. Signed by Bradley R. Smith, well known as a purveyor of anti-Semitic neo-Nazi propaganda, the ad is packaged as a scholarly treatise: four densely packed columns complete with "learned" references, undocumented statistics, and an array of so-called authorities. The message of the ad is that the Holocaust never occurred and that the German state never "had a policy to exterminate the Jewish people (or anyone else) by putting them to death in gas chambers." In a spectacular instance of the increasingly popular "blame the victim" strategy, the Holocaust "story" or "myth" is said to have been fabricated in order "to drum up world sympathy for Jewish causes." The "evidence" supporting these assertions is a slick blend of supposedly probative facts—"not a single autopsied body has been shown to be gassed"—and sly insinuations of a kind familiar to readers of *Mein Kampf* and *The Protocols of the Elders of Zion.* The slickest thing of all, however, is the presentation of the argument as an exercise in free speech—the ad is subtitled "The Case for Open Debate"—that could be objected to only by "thought police" and censors. This strategy bore immediate fruit in the decision of the newspaper staff to accept the ad despite a long-standing (and historically honored) policy of refusing materials that contain ethnic and racial slurs or are otherwise offensive. The reasoning of the staff (explained by the editor in a special column) was that under the First Amendment advertisers have the "right" to be published. "American newspapers are built on the principles of free speech and free press, so how can a newspaper deny these rights to anyone?" The answer to this question is that an advertiser is not denied his rights simply because a single media organ declines his copy so long as other avenues of publication are available and there has been no state suppression of his views. This is not to say that there could not be a case for printing the ad, only that the case cannot rest on a supposed First Amendment obligation. One might argue, for example, that printing the ad would foster healthy debate, or that lies are more likely to be shown up for what they are if they are brought to the light of day, but these are precisely the arguments the editor *disclaims* in her eagerness to take a "principled" free-speech stand.

24   What I find most distressing about this incident is not that the ad was printed but that it was printed by persons who believed it to be a lie and a distortion. If the editor and her staff were in agreement with Smith's views or harbored serious doubts about the reality of the Holocaust, I would still have a quarrel with them, but it would be a different quarrel; it would be a quarrel about evidence, credibility, documentation. But since on these matters the editors and I are in agreement, my quarrel is with the reasoning that led them to act in opposition to what they believed to be true. That reasoning, as I understand it, goes as follows: although we ourselves are certain that the Holocaust was a fact, facts are notoriously interpretable and disputable; therefore nothing is ever really settled, and we have no right to reject something just because we regard it as pernicious and false. But the fact—if I can use that word—that settled truths can always be upset, at least theoretically, does not mean that we cannot affirm and rely on truths that according to our present lights seem indisputable; rather, it means exactly the opposite: in the absence of absolute certainty of the kind that can only be provided by revelation (something I do not rule out but have not yet experienced), we must act on the basis of the certainty

we have so far achieved. Truth may, as Milton said, always be in the course of emerging, and we must always be on guard against being so beguiled by its present shape that we ignore contrary evidence; but, by the same token, when it happens that the present shape of truth is compelling beyond a reasonable doubt, it is our moral obligation to act on it and not defer action in the name of an interpretative future that may never arrive. By running the First Amendment up the nearest flagpole and rushing to salute it, the student editors defaulted on that obligation and gave over their responsibility to a so-called principle that was not even to the point.

25   Let me be clear. I am not saying that First Amendment principles are inherently bad (they are *inherently* nothing), only that they are not always the appropriate reference point for situations involving the production of speech, and that even when they are the appropriate reference point, they do not constitute a politics-free perspective because the shape in which they are invoked will always be political, will always, that is, be the result of having drawn the relevant line (between speech and action, or between high-value speech and low-value speech, or between words essential to the expression of ideas and fighting words) in a way that is favorable to some interests and indifferent or hostile to others. This having been said, the moral is not that First Amendment talk should be abandoned, for even if the standard First Amendment formulas do not and could not perform the function expected of them (the elimination of political considerations in decisions about speech), they still serve a function that is not at all negligible: they slow down outcomes in an area in which the fear of overhasty outcomes is justified by a long record of abuses of power. It is often said that history shows (itself a formula) that even a minimal restriction on the right of expression too easily leads to ever-larger restrictions; and to the extent that this is an empirical fact (and it is a question one could debate), there is some comfort and protection to be found in a procedure that requires you to jump through hoops—do a lot of argumentative work—before a speech regulation will be allowed to stand.

26   I would not be misunderstood as offering the notion of "jumping through hoops" as a new version of the First Amendment claim to neutrality. A hoop must have a shape—in this case the shape of whatever binary distinction is representing First Amendment "interests"—and the shape of the hoop one is asked to jump through will in part determine what kinds of jumps can be regularly made. Even if they are only mechanisms for slowing down outcomes, First Amendment formulas by virtue of their substantive content (and it is impossible that they be without content) will slow down some outcomes more easily than others, and that means that the form they happen to have at the present moment will favor some interests more than others. Therefore, even with a reduced sense of the effectivity of First Amendment rhetoric (it can not assure any particular result), the counsel with which I began remains relevant: so long as so-called free-speech principles have been fashioned by your enemy (so long as it is *his* hoops you have to jump through), contest their relevance to the issue at hand; but if you manage to refashion them in line with your purposes, urge them with a vengeance.

27   It is a counsel that follows from the thesis that there is no such thing as free speech, which is not, after all, a thesis as startling or corrosive as may first have

seemed. It merely says that there is no class of utterances separable from the world of conduct and that therefore the identification of some utterances as members of that nonexistent class will always be evidence that a political line has been drawn rather than a line that denies politics entry into the forum of public discourse. It is the job of the First Amendment to mark out an area in which competing views can be considered without state interference; but if the very marking out of that area is itself an interference (as it always will be), First Amendment jurisprudence is inevitably self-defeating and subversive of its own aspirations. That's the bad news. The good news is that precisely *because* speech is never "free" in the two senses required—free of consequences and free from state pressure—speech always matters, is always doing work; because everything we say impinges on the world in ways indistinguishable from the effects of physical action, we must take responsibility for our verbal performances—*all* of them—and not assume that they are being taken care of by a clause in the Constitution. Of course, with responsibility comes risks, but they have always been our risks, and no doctrine of free speech has ever insulated us from them. They are the risks, respectively, of permitting speech that does obvious harm and of shutting off speech in ways that might deny us the benefit of Joyce's *Ulysses* or Lawrence's *Lady Chatterly's Lover* or Titian's paintings. Nothing, I repeat, can insulate us from those risks. (If there is no normative guidance in determining when and what speech to protect, there is no normative guidance in determining what is art—like free speech a category that includes everything and nothing—and what is obscenity.) Moreover, nothing can provide us with a principle for deciding which risk in the long run is the best to take. I am persuaded that at the present moment, right now, the risk of not attending to hate speech is greater than the risk that by regulating it we will deprive ourselves of valuable voices and insights or slide down the slippery slope toward tyranny. This is a judgment for which I can offer reasons but no guarantees. All I am saying is that the judgments of those who would come down on the other side carry no guarantees either. They urge us to put our faith in apolitical abstractions, but the abstractions they invoke—the marketplace of ideas, speech alone, speech itself—only come in political guises, and therefore in trusting to them we fall (unwittingly) under the sway of the very forces we wish to keep at bay. It is not that there are no choices to make or means of making them; it is just that the choices as well as the means are inextricable from the din and confusion of partisan struggle. There is no safe place.

THINKING CRITICALLY

1. How does Fish establish his thesis in his opening paragraphs? Why does he assert that there really isn't such a thing as "free speech"? Explain.

2. In his first paragraph, Fish explains that his essay is an attempt to "pry" the liberal left "loose from a vocabulary that may now be a disservice to them." What is the "vocabulary" of the argument in support of free speech? Why does he feel that the liberal left's defense of free speech may be a "disservice"?

3. How does Fish's example of *R. v. Keegstra* in Canada support his argument? How does he feel about the Canadian interpretation of free speech? What is your own opinion of it? Explain.

4. In paragraph 9, Fish explains that one way lawyers circumvent the First Amendment is to manipulate the distinction between speech and action. What role does language play in this distinction? Explain.

5. What are "fighting words"? What is the author's position on "fighting words"? What complications do "fighting words" lend to the First Amendment's protections?

6. Evaluate Fish's argument regarding the role of colleges and universities and free speech. What is the purpose of higher education? How does free speech connect to this purpose, or does it?

7. Fish asserts that arguments in support of absolute free speech occur "in no context whatsoever." He makes a distinction between theoretical free speech and the real world. Respond to this part of his argument in your own words.

8. Fish cites an example of "a wolf wrapped in First Amendment clothing" in which neo-Nazi propagandist Bradley R. Smith manipulated student newspapers into printing an ad on the Holocaust that was "patently false" under the guise that he was asserting his right to free speech. What is Fish's position on publishing this material? Why does he feel that it shouldn't be protected by the First Amendment? In your opinion, were student newspapers manipulated? Should they have published the ad? Why or why not?

Who's Undermining Freedom of Speech on Campus Now

David Beito, Robert "K.C." Johnson, and Ralph E. Luker

In an effort to curtail criticism of campus speech codes, some colleges and universities have adopted speech codes that outline acceptable speech. Critics of such codes argue that they curtail campus discourse and the very foundation of a college education, posing a dangerous threat to ideals of free speech. Speech code advocates counter that certain types of language can create uncomfortable situations for some students, that this interferes with learning and the right to pursue an education without fear of intimidation. But who decides what is acceptable speech? Are campus speech codes going too far?

David Beito is an associate professor of history at the University of Alabama and the founding member of HNN blog: Liberty and Power. K. C. Johnson is a professor of history at Brooklyn College and the CUNY Graduate Center. Ralph Luker is an associate professor of history at Antioch College and co-editor of the first two volumes of *The Papers of Martin Luther King* (1994). This essay appeared online on George Mason University's History News Network (HNN) on April 11, 2005.

1   Freedom of speech is crucial both to a healthy democracy and the life of the mind. The First Amendment to the United States Constitution prohibits Congress from any act that would abridge it and the charters of most of our colleges and universities recognize that freedom of thought and speech are essential to a healthy academic community. Yet, freedom of speech has been a contested value since the birth of the Republic, most commonly in periods of war, from the Alien and Sedition Acts of 1798 through the USA PATRIOT Act of 2001.

2   It isn't surprising, then, that freedom of speech is now under siege. What is new in our academic communities is that it is threatened both from within and from outside them. The internal threat to free speech in academia is posed by "speech codes." They take many forms and vary from one college to the next university. After the 1960s, when American colleges and universities ceased to operate in *loco parentis*, campus speech codes emerged on one campus after another as a means of securing a "safe space" for some students who were offended by certain kinds of speech. On one campus or another, speech that is discomforting, embarrassing, flirtatious, gender specific, inappropriate, inconsiderate, harassing, intimidating, offensive, ridiculing or threatens a loss of "self-esteem" is banned by speech codes. Too often, they target student critics of academic bureaucracy.

3   Taken literally, speech codes would ban healthy jeering at a visiting sports team. Wouldn't want to intimidate those Aggies! More importantly, teachers have to be able to urge students to consider perspectives that they had not previously considered, without fear of being accused of being "offensive." Ultimately, speech codes are problematic because they vest final authority in the subjectivity of the offended. Whether it is "intentional or unintentional," for example, Brown University bans all "verbal behavior" that may cause "feelings of impotence, anger, or disenfranchisement." The nation's Founders, who did not mind offending British authorities, would have been ill-educated by such constrictions on free speech.

4   The problem with speech codes is that speech that should be self-governed by good manners and humility is prescripted by inflexible legal codification. Fortunately, however, Philadelphia's Foundation for Individual Rights in Education has fought and won a series of legal battles that have curtailed the prevalence of speech codes in public higher education. In private colleges and universities, where First Amendment rights do not necessarily prevail, the struggle continues on an institution by institution basis.

5   Just when there is good news to report about the unconstitutionality of speech codes on public campuses, however, new threats to free speech arise from outside the academic community. They come from the Center for the Study of Popular Culture in Los Angeles. The Center and its legal arm, the Individual Rights Foundation, are led by David Horowitz. A militant activist on the left in the 1960s, Horowitz abandoned it 25 years ago to become a militant activist on the right. Most recently, he has campaigned for enactment of an "Academic Bill of Rights."

6   Like campus speech codes, Horowitz's Academic Bill of Rights appears well intentioned. Insisting that academic communities must be more responsive to outside criticism, it adopts a form of the American Association of University Professors' 1915 "General Report of the Committee on Academic Freedom and Tenure." It holds that political and religious beliefs should not influence the hiring and tenuring of faculty or the evaluation of students, that curricular and extra-curricular activities should expose students to the variety of perspectives about academic matters and public issues, and that institutions must not tolerate obstructions to free debate nor, themselves, become vehicles of partisan advocacy. Who could oppose such commitments? They are already features of the professorate's assumed values.

7   Yet, the American Association of University Professors and the American Civil Liberties Union criticize Horowitz's "Academic Bill of Rights" as an effort to

"proscribe and prescribe activities in classrooms and on college campuses." One has only to look at the legislative progress of Horowitz's political campaign to understand why. His Academic Bill of Rights has been introduced in Congress by Representative Jack Kingston (R-GA), but it's had greater promotion in the state legislatures of California, Colorado, Florida, Georgia, Indiana, Maine, Massachusetts, Ohio, Tennessee, and Washington.

8   Instead of being the even-handed vehicle it claims to be, everywhere it is a function of right-wing attacks on academic communities. In Florida, for example, Representative Dennis Baxley says that the bill he introduced will give students legal standing to sue professors who do not teach "intelligent design" as an acceptable alternate to the theory of evolution. His critics respond that it could give students who are holocaust deniers or who oppose birth control and modern medicine legal standing to sue their professors.

9   Beyond the governing authority of Florida's public colleges and universities and in the name of free thought and free speech, it would encode in state law restrictions against those values.

10   The Founders, who recalled their own exercise of free speech and free thought, when they challenged British governing authority, wrote guarantees protecting them from constricting government action. In academic communities, we need an alliance across ideological divides to support free speech by abolishing "speech codes" and to fight the "Academic Bill of Rights" in state legislatures and the Congress because it is a Trojan Horse that intends the opposite of what it claims on its face.

THINKING CRITICALLY

1. In paragraph 3, the authors assert that "Ultimately, speech codes are problematic because they vest final authority in the subjectivity of the offended." What does this statement mean? Do you agree with the authors' position? Why or why not?

2. The authors note that the Academic Bill of Rights could be used by students who oppose birth control or deny the Holocaust the grounds to sue professors. Review the Academic Bill of Rights (following this essay) and explain why you agree or disagree that this is a valid concern.

3. Research the arguments for and against campus speech codes as expressed in university publications available online for at least four colleges or universities. How are the codes similar and how are they different? Are they open for interpretation? In your opinion, do they unfairly restrict freedom of speech on campus? Discuss your research with the class. If your own campus has a speech code, include it in your discussion.

4. The authors argue that Horowitz's "Academic Bill of Rights" is "a Trojan Horse that intends the opposite of what it claims on its face." What is a Trojan Horse? How does the term apply to the point the authors are making in this essay? Explain.

Academic Bill of Rights

David Horowitz

I. The Mission of the University

The central purposes of a University are the pursuit of truth, the discovery of new knowledge through scholarship and research, the study and reasoned criticism of intellectual and cultural traditions, the teaching and general development of students to help them become creative individuals and productive citizens of a pluralistic democracy, and the transmission of knowledge and learning to a society at large. Free inquiry and free speech within the academic community are indispensable to the achievement of these goals. The freedom to teach and to learn depend upon the creation of appropriate conditions and opportunities on the campus as a whole as well as in the classrooms and lecture halls. These purposes reflect the values— pluralism, diversity, opportunity, critical intelligence, openness and fairness—that are the cornerstones of American society.

II. Academic Freedom

1. The Concept. Academic freedom and intellectual diversity are values indispensable to the American university. From its first formulation in the General Report of the Committee on Academic Freedom and Tenure of the American Association of University Professors, the concept of academic freedom has been premised on the idea that human knowledge is a never-ending pursuit of the truth, that there is no humanly accessible truth that is not in principle open to challenge, and that no party or intellectual faction has a monopoly on wisdom. Therefore, academic freedom is most likely to thrive in an environment of intellectual diversity that protects and fosters independence of thought and speech. In the words of the General Report, it is vital to protect "as the first condition of progress, [a] complete and unlimited freedom to pursue inquiry and publish its results."

Because free inquiry and its fruits are crucial to the democratic enterprise itself, academic freedom is a national value as well. In a historic 1967 decision (Keyishian v. Board of Regents of the University of the State of New York) the Supreme Court of the United States overturned a New York State loyalty provision for teachers with these words: "Our Nation is deeply committed to safeguarding academic freedom, [a] transcendent value to all of us and not merely to the teachers concerned." In Sweezy v. New Hampshire, (1957) the Court observed that the "essentiality of freedom in the community of American universities [was] almost self-evident."

2. The Practice. Academic freedom consists in protecting the intellectual independence of professors, researchers and students in the pursuit of knowledge and the expression of ideas from interference by legislators or authorities within the institution itself. This means that no political, ideological or religious orthodoxy will be imposed on professors and researchers through the hiring or tenure or termination process, or through any other administrative means by the academic institution. Nor shall legislatures impose any such orthodoxy through their control of the university budget.

This protection includes students. From the first statement on academic freedom, it has been recognized that intellectual independence means the protection of students—as well as faculty—from the imposition of any orthodoxy of a political, religious or ideological nature. The 1915 General Report admonished faculty to avoid "taking unfair advantage of the student's immaturity by indoctrinating him with the teacher's own opinions before the student has had an opportunity fairly to examine other opinions upon the matters in question, and before he has sufficient knowledge and ripeness of judgment to be entitled to form any definitive opinion of his own." In 1967, the AAUP's Joint Statement on Rights and Freedoms of Students reinforced and amplified this injunction by affirming the inseparability of "the freedom to teach and freedom to learn." In the words of the report, "Students should be free to take reasoned exception to the data or views offered in any course of study and to reserve judgment about matters of opinion."

Therefore, to secure the intellectual independence of faculty and students and to protect the principle of intellectual diversity, the following principles and procedures shall be observed.

These principles fully apply only to public universities and to private universities that present themselves as bound by the canons of academic freedom. Private institutions choosing to restrict academic freedom on the basis of creed have an obligation to be as explicit as is possible about the scope and nature of these restrictions.

1. All faculty shall be hired, fired, promoted and granted tenure on the basis of their competence and appropriate knowledge in the field of their expertise and, in the humanities, the social sciences, and the arts, with a view toward fostering a plurality of methodologies and perspectives. No faculty shall be hired or fired or denied promotion or tenure on the basis of his or her political or religious beliefs.

2. No faculty member will be excluded from tenure, search and hiring committees on the basis of their political or religious beliefs.

3. Students will be graded solely on the basis of their reasoned answers and appropriate knowledge of the subjects and disciplines they study, not on the basis of their political or religious beliefs.

4. Curricula and reading lists in the humanities and social sciences should reflect the uncertainty and unsettled character of all human knowledge in these areas by providing students with dissenting sources and viewpoints where appropriate. While teachers are and should be free to pursue their own findings and perspectives in presenting their views, they should consider and make their

students aware of other viewpoints. Academic disciplines should welcome a diversity of approaches to unsettled questions.

5. Exposing students to the spectrum of significant scholarly viewpoints on the subjects examined in their courses is a major responsibility of faculty. Faculty will not use their courses for the purpose of political, ideological, religious or anti-religious indoctrination.

6. Selection of speakers, allocation of funds for speakers programs and other student activities will observe the principles of academic freedom and promote intellectual pluralism.

7. An environment conducive to the civil exchange of ideas being an essential component of a free university, the obstruction of invited campus speakers, destruction of campus literature or other effort to obstruct this exchange will not be tolerated.

8. Knowledge advances when individual scholars are left free to reach their own conclusions about which methods, facts, and theories have been validated by research. Academic institutions and professional societies formed to advance knowledge within an area of research, maintain the integrity of the research process, and organize the professional lives of related researchers serve as indispensable venues within which scholars circulate research findings and debate their interpretation. To perform these functions adequately, academic institutions and professional societies should maintain a posture of organizational neutrality with respect to the substantive disagreements that divide researchers on questions within, or outside, their fields of inquiry.

THINKING CRITICALLY

1. In the previous essay, David Beito, Robert "K. C." Johnson, and Ralph E. Luker explain that David Horowitz's Academic Bill of Rights has been the basis of great debate on college campuses and even Congress. Outline the arguments that both supporters and opponents might pose to this document.

2. The Academic Bill of Rights has been used as the basis of legislation in Congress and has been introduced on the state level to state governments. Write a letter to your state's representative explaining why you support or do not support the Academic Bill of Rights from the perspective of a college student.

3. Read Stanley Fish's response to the Academic Bill of Rights, " 'Intellectual Diversity': the Trojan Horse of a Dark Design" printed in the *Chronicle of Higher Education* on February 13, 2004 at http://chronicle.com/free/v50/i23/23b01301.htm (if the link is broken, search for the article by its title online.) Why does Fish object to the Academic Bill of Rights? What evidence does he provide the bill is flawed? Explain.

Exploring the Language of VISUALS

Free Speech Zone

Zachary Parker

THINKING CRITICALLY

1. What does the language on the sign mean? What is the cartoonist trying to say in this cartoon? Based on the cartoon, what is his position on the issue of free speech zones? Explain.

2. What is the shape of the sign on which the words appear? What is the meaning of the sign and what does it convey?

3. Have you ever participated in or witnessed a demonstration on campus? Was the demonstration restricted to a particular area? Could the participants speak freely, or were they restricted in what they could say?

4. In your opinion, should leaders of controversial groups—for example, people with extremist views, such as from the Ku Klux Klan or Hamas—be allowed to speak on campus? What about staunchly pro-life and pro-choice groups? Anti-war demonstrators? Who decides what is extremist? students? administration? What do you think?

MAKING CONNECTIONS

1. Suppose that a leader of a known hate group were invited to your campus—someone certain to speak in inflammatory racist language. Would you defend that person's right to address the student body? Why or why not? Should the person be protected under the First Amendment? Why or why not?

2. Write a letter to the editor of your school newspaper advocating restricted or unlimited speech on campus. In your letter, explain your viewpoint and provide supporting material. How do you think your letter would be received by the student body? Explain.

3. Imagine that a condition of acceptance to your school was signing an agreement that you would refrain from using racist, sexist, or otherwise abusive language on campus. Weighing the social benefits of such a measure against the restrictions on freedom of expression, write a paper in which you explain why you would or would not sign such an agreement.

4. Some of the essays in this section discuss censorship codes limiting racist or hate speech on campus. Write a code to be implemented at your college or university. Consider students' rights to free speech, what constitutes hate speech, and what limits can be placed on hate speech. Write a prologue to your code explaining and supporting its tenets.

5. In 1996, Robert B. Chatelle, co-chair of the Political Issues Committee National Writers Union, wrote a letter to Wesleyan University President Douglas Bennet to express concern about a Wesleyan student who had been suspended by the university's student judicial board for violating the Wesleyan speech code. Read Chatelle's argument at http://users.rcn.com/kyp/schools/bennet2.html. After identifying both sides of the conflict, write your own views in an essay. As support, use information from the readings in this section, as well as from your own personal experience.

6. In a January 2003 article in *Boston Magazine*, "The Thought Police," Boston lawyer Harvey Silverglate stated that the First Amendment should protect your right to say what you wish, but that you are not immune to what happens after that. You may be subjected to angry retorts, public shunning, and social pressure, but you should not be officially punished for your language. Write a response to Silverglate expressing your own opinion on this assessment of the First Amendment. We saw Margaret Sanger gagged in Chapter 2. Here, an artist uses the same gag imagery and a symbol of liberty to make a point about free speech in America. Just what are the limits of our First Amendment rights?

8 The English Language Debate

■ Is there such a thing as an American language? Is the United States becoming a multi-lingual country? Should it be?

Ours is a nation of immigrants—of people with different racial origins, ethnic identities, religions, and languages. Our national motto, *e pluribus unum* ("one out of many"), bespeaks the pride we feel in our multicultural heritage. Our unity is predicated on like-minded moral values, political and economic self-interest, and perhaps, a common language. What exactly is the language of the American people? Is it the rigid, rule-laden language of our grade-school grammar books? Is it the language we use at home, at work, or within our peer groups? Or is it even a form of English at all? This chapter focuses on issues concerning language and our nation—on how we define the language of the American people.

What Is "Standard" English?

The section opens with an exploration of American English by Robert MacNeil in "Do You Speak American?" MacNeil sets out to understand why the English spoken in one part of the country can differ so much from that in another. Even common words and expressions can be vastly different, begging the question, what exactly is "American English"? Richard Lederer continues the discussion in "All-American Dialects." John Simon, one of America's most famous and formidable language guardians, argues that good English is a serious social and personal issue in his essay, "Why Good English Is Good for You." His essay is followed by a poem by Taylor Mali, "Totally like whatever, you know?" that presents a tongue-in-cheek viewpoint of how teens are losing the ability to express their convictions because their very language is failing them. Linguist John Esling explores the way accents influence our perceptions of others and ourselves in "Everyone Has an Accent but Me." Then student Lilly Gonzales explains why a new language spoken primarily by the children of Spanish-speaking immigrants, "Spanglish," can be a blessing and a curse. The section concludes with an engaging discussion by Bill Bryson on just what is "good" and "bad" English.

Should English Be the Official Language of the USA?

It might come as a surprise to some people to learn that English is not the official language of the United States. Nowhere in the Constitution is there such a provision. The founders of our nation were apparently more concerned with establishing a common political philosophy than a common tongue. A growing number of Americans feel that English should be declared the national language. At stake in the controversy are the competing American traditions of multicultural tolerance and national unity. Proponents of the "English-only" movement argue that bilingualism creates cultural division and hinders assimilation and successful integration. Opponents contend that such attitudes deny non-English-speaking Americans their cultural heritage, encourage xenophobic attitudes, violate civil rights, and inflame prejudice against immigrants. This section examines the different sides to this still unsettled issue.

The section opens with an essay supporting English as a national language for the United States by the late S. I. Hayakawa, "English Should Be the Only Language." His viewpoint is seconded by Mauro E. Mujica, a Chilean immigrant who explains why he feels it is vitally important that the United States adopt English as its official language in "Why the U.S. Needs an Official Language." The idea of English as the official language of the nation is certainly nothing new. Over two hundred years ago, U.S. President and Revolutionary War patriot John Adams proposed an American Language Academy for the preservation of American English. Writer Julia Ortiz Cofer then explores the difficulties nonnative speakers face in a country where English is the language of power. Gregory Rodriguez ends the section with "The Overwhelming Allure of English" in which he explains that while Spanish may be the unofficial second language of the United States, the power of English—in politics, the media, and the arts—ensures that it remains number one.

WHAT IS "STANDARD" ENGLISH?

Do You Speak American?
Robert MacNeil

"Hoagie," "grinder," "bomb," "spukie," "po-boy," or "hero"—so many different names for pretty much the same thing, depending on where you place your order for a sub-sandwich. While politicians may argue for or against the idea of a standard, national language, English-speaking Americans across the country are busy keeping the language vibrant and diverse. Robert MacNeil sets out to discover "why is the English spoken by Maine lobstermen so different from that spoken by cowboys in Texas?" How are regionalized words created? MacNeil traveled across the nation to try and find answers to these questions and to better understand the evolving and colorful language that is "American English."

Robert MacNeil is the former co-anchor of PBS's Emmy Award-winning *MacNeil/Lehrer NewsHour*. He is the author of several books including *Do You Speak American?* (2004) and *The Story of English* (1986). This article first appeared in the January 2005 issue of *USA Today Magazine*. MacNeil wrote this essay as a companion piece to his PBS documentary, co-written by Bill Cran, "Do You Speak American?" which explores the country's linguistic diversity.

1 On Columbus Avenue in New York, a young waitress approaches our table and asks, "How are you guys doin'?" My wife and I are old enough to be her grandparents, but we are "you guys" to her. Today, in American English, guys can be guys, girls, or grandmothers. Girls call themselves guys, even dudes. For a while, young women scorned the word girls, but that is cool again, probably because African-American women use it and it can be real cool—even empowering—to whites to borrow black talk, like the word cool. It is empowering to gay men to call themselves queer, once a hated homophobic term, but now used to satirize the whole

shifting scene of gender attitudes in the TV reality show, "Queer Eye for the Straight Guy." As society changes, so does language, and American society has changed enormously in recent decades. Moreover, when new norms are resented or feared, language often is the target of that fear or resentment.

2   How we use the English language became a hot topic during the 1960s, and it remains so today—a charged ingredient in the culture wars, as intensely studied and disputed as any other part of our society. That is appropriate because nothing is more central to our identity and sense of who we are and where we belong. "Aside from a person's physical appearance, the first thing someone will be judged by is how he or she talks," maintains linguist Dennis Baron.

3   Many feel that the growing informality of American life, the retreat from fixed standards, ("the march of casualization," *The New York Times* recently called it)— in clothing, manners, sexual mores—is reflected in our language and is corrupting it. They see schools lax about teaching grammar and hear nonstandard forms accepted in broadcasting, newspapers, politics, and advertising. They believe the slogan "Winston tastes good like a cigarette should" is so embedded in the national psyche that few Americans would now balk at the use of "like" (instead of "as") because that usage is fast becoming the new standard. They hate such changes in the language and they despair for our culture.

4   Others, however, believe language is thriving—as inventive and vigorous as English was in the time of the Elizabethans—and they see American English as the engine driving what is now a global language.

5   The controversies, issues, anxieties, and assumptions swirling around language today [can be] highly emotional and political. Why are black and white Americans speaking less and less like each other? Does Hispanic immigration threaten the English language? Is our exposure to national media wiping out regional differences and causing us all to speak the same? Is the language really in serious decline? Well, we have quite a debate about that.

6   The people who believe so are known as prescriptivists: those who want us to obey prescribed rules of grammar. They do not mind being called curmudgeons and they alternate between pleasure and despair—pleasure in correcting their fellow citizens: despair that they cannot stop the language from going to hell in our generation.

The Prince of Prescriptivists

7 One of the leading curmudgeons of our time—he has been called the Prince of Prescriptivists—is John Simon, theater critic for *New York Magazine*, and he comes to do battle in "Do You Speak American?" Simon sees the language today as "unhealthy, poor, sad, depressing, and probably fairly hopeless." In the foreword to a new book, *The Dictionary of Disagreeable English*, he writes: "No damsel was ever in such distress, no drayhorse more flogged, no defenseless child more drunkenly abused than the English language today."

8   The enemies for Simon are the descriptivists, those content to describe language as it actually is used. They include the editors of great dictionaries who, Simon charges, have grown dangerously permissive, abandoning advice on what is correct and what is not. He calls descriptivist linguists "a curse on their race."

9   One such individual is Jesse Sheidlower, American editor of the august *Oxford English Dictionary*. Does he believe the language is being mined by the great informality of American life? "No, it is not being ruined at all," he replies. Sheidlower believes that Simon and other language conservatives actually are complaining that linguists and dictionary writers no longer are focused on the language of the elite. They look at the old days and say. "Well, everything used to be very proper, and now we have all these bad words and people are being careless, and so forth." In fact, he insists people always have spoken that way. "It's just that you didn't hear them because the media would only report on the language of the educated upper middle class," Sheidlower points out. "Nowadays . . . we see the language of other groups, of other social groups, of other income levels, in a way that we never used to.

10   "Language change happens and there's nothing you can do about it." To which Simon replies, "Maybe change is inevitable—maybe. Maybe dying from cancer is also inevitable, but I don't think we should help it along."

11   Helping it along, to Simon, would mean surrendering to the word "hopefully," one of his pet peeves. "To say, 'Hopefully it won't rain tomorrow'—who, or what, is filled with hope? Nothing. So you have to say, 'I hope it won't rain tomorrow.' But you can say, 'I enter a room hopefully,' because you are the vessel for that hopefulness."

12   Sheidlower replies that modern computer databases make it possible to check texts back over the centuries: "We see that 'hopefully' is not in fact very new . . . . It goes back hundreds of years, and it has been very common even in highly educated speech for much of the time."

13   This battle—the stuff of angry skirmishes in books, magazines, and seminars—is only one part of what makes our language news today. Other findings may surprise many people because they challenge widely held popular conceptions, or misconceptions, about the language. . . .

14   While computers, information technology, globalization, digital communications, and satellites have revolutionized how we work, equally potent revolutions have occurred concerning the home, family structure and marriage, sexual mores, the role of women, race relations, and the rise of teenagers as a major consumer and marketing force. With this has come alterations in our public manners, eating habits, clothing, and tolerance of different lifestyles—all of which have been swept by a tide of informality.

Linguists Spring into Action

15   Observing how these rapid social changes have altered our language have been the linguists, whose new branch of the social sciences really came into its own in the 1960s, followed more recently by sociolinguistics, the study of how language and society interact. They have produced a body of fascinating research that usually is couched in technical language difficult for nonlinguists to understand. Dozens of linguists have lent their skills to help us translate their findings, and marry their scholarship to our sampling of the actual speech of ordinary Americans in all its variety, vitality, and humor, drawn from the widest social spectrum. They include

waitresses, cowboys, hip-hop artists, Marine drill sergeants, Border Patrol agents, Mexican immigrants, Cajun musicians, African-American and Hispanic broadcasters, and Silicon Valley techies (who try to make computers talk like real people), as well as writers and editors, teachers and teenagers, surfers and snowboarders, actors and screenwriters, and presidents and politicians.

16   Did they all sound the same? One of the most common assumptions is that our total immersion in the same mass media is making us all speak in a similar manner. Not true, claim the linguists. We are not talking more alike, but less.

17   One of the enduring themes in American life is the pull of national against regional interests and regret for local distinctiveness erased in the relentless march of uniformity. It surfaced in the song "Little Boxes" by Pete Seeger, about people put into little boxes of identical houses made of "ticky tacky" and who all come out the same. Today, with more and more national franchising of basic elements—food, mobile homes, clothing, hotels, recreation—the U.S. can seem like one giant theme park endlessly reduplicated, the triumph of the cookie cutter culture and its distinctive art form, the national TV commercial.

18   Paradoxically, however, language is one fundamental aspect of our cultural identity in which growing homogenization is a myth. While some national trends are apparent, regional speech differences not only thrive, in some places they are becoming more distinctive. Local differences, pride, and identity with place are asserting themselves strongly, perhaps as instinctive resistance to the homogenizing forces of globalization. One remarkable example is the speech of urban African-Americans, which is diverging from standard mainstream English. After decades of progress in civil rights, and the growth of a large and successful black middle class, African-American speech in our big cities dramatically is going its own way.

19   Two linguists, Guy Bailey, provost of the University of Texas at San Antonio, and Patricia Cukor-Avila of the University of North Texas at Denton have documented this. For 18 years, they have studied a small community in East Central Texas they named "Springville," which appears to live in a time warp from a century ago, when it was the center for local cotton sharecroppers, black and white. Little remains now but the original general store. During the late 1930s, the Works Progress Administration recorded the voices of elderly blacks, some former slaves, some the children of slaves.

20   One of them, Laura Smalley, was born to a slave mother. She was nine at the time of Emancipation in 1863. She told how the slave owner kept them ignorant of Lincoln's Proclamation for six months. "An' I thought ol' master was dead, but he wash'. . . . He'd been off to the war an' come back. All the niggers gathered aroun' to see ol' master again. You know, an' ol' master didn' tell, you know, they was free. . . . They worked there, I think now they say they worked them six months after that, six months. And turn them loose on the 19th of June. That's why, you know, they celebrate that day. Colored folks celebrates that day."

Black and White Dialects

21 Reviewing the speech of Smalley and others, the linguists were taken by how similar it was to the speech of rural whites of that time and place, but now dissimilar to the

speech of blacks today. Features characteristic of modern black speech, what linguists call African-American vernacular English—such as the invariant "be," as in "they 'be' working," or the deleted copular, leaving out the auxiliary verb in "they working"—were absent.

22   Here are samples of modern speech of African-Americans in large cities:

> "When the baby be sleep, and the othe' kids be at school, and my husband be at work, then . . . I might can finally sit down."

> "She told David they Mama had went to Chicago to see her sister and her sister's new baby."

These examples show the invariant "be," and the construction "had went." Bailey and Cukor-Avila say that these features did not exist in black speech before World War II. They conclude that, after the great migration to the North from World War I to the 1970s, blacks were segregated in urban ghettos, had less contact with whites than they had in places like Springville, and their speech began to develop new features, as all human speech does when people are separated culturally and have little communication.

23   This has serious consequences in efforts to reduce the school dropout rate among blacks. Not only white teachers, but many African-American instructors, despise the "street talk" or "slang" as they call it, and often treat the children as if they were stupid or uneducable. In 1979, a Federal judge in Detroit ruled that an Ann Arbor, Mich., school, ironically named after Martin Luther King, Jr., was discriminating against black kids because of their language and ordered the school to remedy it. Yet, the prejudice lives on elsewhere.

24   In 1997, Oakland schools tried to get black speech recognized not as a dialect of English but a separate language, Ebonics, to qualify for Federal money to teach English as a second language. That backfired amid furious protests nationally from black and white educators.

25   What is shocking to linguists is the manner in which many newspaper columnists excoriate black English, using terms such as "gibberish." In the linguistic community, black English is recognized as having its own internal consistency and grammatical forms. It certainly is not gibberish (which means something unintelligible) because it works effectively for communication within the urban community.

26   One of the first to give black English this measure of respect was William Labov of the University of Pennsylvania, who testified at a Senate hearing during the Ebonics furor in 1997: "This African-American vernacular English . . . is not a set of slang words, or a random set of grammatical mistakes, but a well-formed set of rules of grammar and pronunciation that is capable of conveying complex logic and reasoning."

27   To linguists, the fault lies not in a particular dialect, but in what attitudes others bring to it. Steve Harvey, an African-American who hosts the most popular morning radio show in Los Angeles, told us: "I speak good enough American. You know, I think there's variations of speaking American. I don't think there's any one set way, because America's so diverse." He added, "You do have to be bilingual in this country, which means you can be very adept at slang, but you also have to be adept at getting through the job interview."

28   Now, without fanfare, some Los Angeles schools have been trying a more sympathetic approach to help minority students become bilingual—by teaching them the differences between African-American Language, as they call it, and Mainstream American English. We visited PS 100 in Watts to watch fifth-graders play a "Jeopardy"-like game in which they won points for "translating" such sentences as "Last night we bake cookies."

> Teacher: "What language is it in?"
>
> Student: "AAL."
>
> Teacher: "It is in African-American Language. What linguistic feature is in AAL?"
>
> Student: "Past-tense marker-ed."
>
> Teacher: "Past-tense marker-ed. That's cool! And how do you code-switch it to Mainstream American English?"
>
> Student: "Last night we baked cookies."
>
> Teacher: "You got five hundred more points." Big cheers from the kids.

29   So, four decades after the passage of landmark legislation outlawing racial discrimination, the news is that it blatantly survives in language. Columnists would not dream of describing other attributes of being African-American with epithets like "gibberish." They could, however, get away with it in writing about black language, which remains a significant barrier to success in school and ultimately in the job market and housing—pathways to the American dream.

30   Ironically, as much as it is despised, black English is embraced and borrowed by whites, especially young whites in thrall to the appeal of hip hop music. There are divergences just as dramatic within the English of white Americans. Around the Great Lakes, people are making what Labov believes are "revolutionary changes in the pronunciation of short vowels that have remained relatively stable in the language for a thousand years."

31   Labov is director of an effort to determine the boundaries of different dialects within American speech. Traditionally, that was achieved by comparing distinctive local or regional words people used for every day things. One surviving example is the different terms for the long sandwich that contains cold cuts, cheese, and lettuce—a grinder in some parts of New England; a wedge in Rhode Island: a spuky in Boston; a hero in New York; a hoagie in Philadelphia; a submarine in Ohio and farther west. By drawing lines around places where each term is used, linguists can form maps of dialect areas. Many such regional terms are dying out because old craft skills are replaced by products marketed nationally. Labov leads a new method in which the different ways people pronounce words are recorded with colored dots on a map of the U.S. Connecting the dots produces the Atlas of North American English.

32   Labov and his colleagues found startling pronunciation changes in cities such as Chicago, Cleveland, and Detroit and New York State's Rochester and Syracuse. On a computer in his office in Philadelphia, we heard a woman say the word "black," then the complete phrase: "Old senior citizens living on one 'black,' " and

it was apparent that she was pronouncing "block" like "black." Similarly, another woman mentions what sounds like "bosses." The full sentence reveals she means "buses:" "I can vaguely remember when we had 'bosses' with the antennas on top."

33   When one vowel changes, so do the neighboring ones: "caught" shifts toward "cot," "cot" toward "cat," "cat" toward "kit" or "keeyat." Labov thinks these changes are quite important. "From our point of view as linguists, we want to understand why people should become more different from each other. We're all watching the same radio and television; we live side by side. And it's important to recognize that people don't always want to behave in the same way."

34   Labov has a theory that, behind changes like these, are women, the primary transmitters of language. Traditionally enjoying less economic power than men, women rely on the symbolic power offered by words. Labov believes women are more apt than men to adopt "prestige forms" of language and symbols of noncon-formism—new or "stigmatized forms" that can acquire a kind of "covert prestige." Labov writes that women are quicker and more forceful in employing the new social symbolism, whatever it may be. Working on his landmark study, "The Principles of Linguistic Change," he identifies a particular type of woman—working class, well-established in her community—who takes pleasure in being nonconformist and is strong enough to influence others. He sees parallels between leadership in fashion and language change. Most young women are alert to nov-elty in fashion; some have the confidence to embrace it and the natural authority to induce others to follow.

35   These are mysterious forces working on our language from underneath, as it were, and producing startling changes that, far from homogenizing our speech, actually create more diversity. Despite all the forces of global and national unifor-mity in products and trends, Americans clearly still want to do their own thing linguistically. An example is Pittsburgh, where the local dialect, or Pittsburghese, is celebrated, constantly talked about, and made a commodity. They know themselves as "Yinzers," from "yinz," the plural of "you," or "you ones." They use "slippy" for "slippery"; "red up" means to "tidy up"; and "anymore" as in "Anymore, there's so many new buildings you can't tell which is which." In downtown Pittsburgh—pronounced "dahntahn"—the question, "Did you eat yet?" sounds like "Jeet jet?" If you haven't, the response is, "No, 'jew?' "

36   Barbara Johnstone, a linguist from Pittsburgh, thinks the pride in their local speech is a way for Pittsburghers to talk about who they are and what it means to live there. People treasure their local accents, because where they come from, or where they feel they belong, still does matter. In the words of California linguist, Carmen Fought, "People want to talk like the people they want to be like." This contradicts the common assumption that media exposure is making everyone sound the same.

Local Accents Prevail

37 Yet, amusingly, people often are quite unaware of how their own speech sounds to others. Linguists we met were full of stories about people in Texas or coastal North Carolina with strong local accents who were convinced they sounded like Walter Cronkite. It happened to me. I grew up in the Canadian province of Nova Scotia, so fascinated with words that I called a memoir of my childhood *Wordstruck*. Even in

my own family, I often heard the same words said differently. My grandfather, from Nova Scotia's south shore, said "garridge" while his daughter, my mother, said "gar-aghe."

38   Until I first came to the U.S. in 1952, I was unaware how different my speech was even from that of neighboring New England. I was 21 and (briefly, thank God!) an aspiring actor, thrilled to be working in a summer theater in Massachusetts. The first time I stepped on to the stage and opened my mouth, the director said, "You can't talk like that." I was stunned, not knowing until that moment that I was pronouncing "out" to rhyme with "oat," and "about" with "aboat"—still the common Nova Scotian pronunciation. Anxious not to close any career doors, I immediately began trying to modify the "oat" sound, but 50 years later, when I am tired or back with my brothers in Canada, I still slip into the pronunciations I grew up with.

39   What appears to be the determining force in whether regional dialects survive or disappear is not media influence, but rather the movements of people. We talked to John Coffin, a lobsterman in South Freeport, Maine. Once a quiet fishing and ship-building harbor but now a bustling outlet shopping center, the town has attracted so many new visitors and residents that Coffin fears the Maine way of speaking—with its characteristic "ayeh" for "yes"—is disappearing: "I think in this area it's going to be a lost thing," and that makes him sad. "I'd like to think my children and grandchildren talk that way, whether people laugh at you, wherever we go—whatever." Do people laugh at his Maine accent? "Oh, yes, lots of times. When I was in the military, they made fun of me wicked." "Wicked" is a typical Maine word, meaning "very," as in " 'wicked' good."

40   This homogenizing trend is obvious on some of the islands, like Ocrakoke, off the coast of North Carolina, home of the Hoi Toiders, people who pronounce "high tide" as "hoi toid." These islands have become meccas for individuals from elsewhere building vacation homes, displacing locals and their dialect.

41   Still, the national media are having some effect: Labov notes two sound changes that have spread nationally, probably from California. One is the vowel in "do," which increasingly sounds like "dew." Labov calls it "oo-fronting"; the sound is produced more to the front of the mouth. You also hear it in the word "so," which sounds like "so-ew." Another trend, more noticeable among young women, but also some men, is a rising inflection at the ends of sentences, making statements such as "The bus station is around the corner" sound like a query. One of the regions where "oo-fronting" is common is the South, where there are changes just as dramatic as those in the North. Southern ghosts do not say "boo," but "bew."

42   The most prevalent shift is that Southerners increasingly are pronouncing the "r" at the ends of words such as father. In part, this is due to the large migration of Northerners to Southern cities. Partly it is the historic decline in influence of the coastal Southern areas that once boasted the great slave-holding plantation culture, and the kind of r-less pronunciation we associated with languid belles posing in hoop skirts on the porches of ante-bellum houses. This advancing "r" marks the growing prestige of what linguists call Inland Southern, the speech deriving from Appalachia. That pattern goes back to the earliest days of British settlement, when people from parts of England who did not pronounce "r" settled the coastal areas, while the Scots-Irish, settlers from Northern Ireland who spoke with a strong "r," moved into the hills of Appalachia because the easily-cultivated coastal land already was taken.

43   Their speech has been given a huge boost by the rise of country music, no longer a regional craze, but a national phenomenon. Those who "sing country," wherever they come from, "talk country" and "talkin' country" has become a kind of default way of speaking informal American. It is considered easygoing and friendly. President George W. Bush has made it his trademark, with no disadvantage politically because, like him, a great many Americans say, "Howya doin'? Doin' fine!" and they are not more particular than he is about making subject agree with verb in sentences such as, "There's no negotiations with North Korea."

44   The economic rise of the South has had another startling result. So many Americans have moved into the South and Southwest and happily adopted Southernisms—such as "y'all" and "fixin' to" and pronouncing "I" as "all," not the Northern "eye-ee"—that more Americans now speak some variety of Southern than any other dialect. That is the conclusion of linguist John Fought, who believes that, as the population shift to the Sun Belt continues, "In time, we should expect 'r-full' southern to become accepted as standard American speech."

45   That news will come as a shock to Northerners conditioned over generations to despise Southern talk, considering it evidence of stupidity and backwardness. In the film "Sweet Home Alabama," the good ol' boy played by Josh Lucas says to his Northernized wife, Reese Witherspoon, "Just because I talk slow, doesn't mean I'm stupid." The context leads the audience to believe him.

46   The comedian Jeff Foxworthy still fills huge theaters North and South with his hilarious routine ridiculing Southern speech and Northern attitudes towards it. He kills them with his list of Southern "words:"

> "May-o-naise. Man, a's a lotta people here tonight,"

> "Urinal. I told my brother, 'You're in a lotta trouble when Daddy gets home.'"

> "Wichadidja. Hey, you didn't bring your track with you, did you?"

47   Northern attitudes to Southerners may be ameliorating slightly, possibly because it no longer is uncool in Northern cities to like country music and the culture that goes with it. Yet, an ingrained sense of the prestige of some dialects and scorn for others is very much alive. Linguist Dennis Preston of Michigan State University has spent years studying the prejudices Americans have concerning speech different from their own. He joined us on a train west from Philadelphia, demonstrating his regular technique. Establishing quick rapport with other passengers. he got them to mark on a map of the U.S. where they thought people spoke differently. Almost without exception, they circled the South and New York to locate the worst English. Referring to New York, a Pennsylvania woman told Preston contemptuously, "They say waader!" Preston asked, "What do you say?" "Water!" she declared proudly.

A Distinct New York Voice

48 Preston, though, detects another emotion creeping in beneath the scorn, and that is pleasure. People may think Southern or New York speech is not good, but they find them charming, and that must be partly an effect of media exposure, for instance, to

the sympathetic New York characters in the TV series "Law and Order." Linguists believe that broadcasting and the movies help all Americans understand different dialects, perhaps appreciating the diversity in our culture. Moreover, no matter how they themselves speak, Americans learn to understand the language of network broadcasters, which is the closest thing to an overall American standard. That standard coincides with the speech that Preston's subjects inevitably identify as the best American speech—that of the Midwest—because it has the fewest regional features.

49   That Midwest standard is relevant to the cutting edge of computer research in Silicon Valley. There is heavy investment in efforts to make computers speak like us and understand us. The researchers believe they will achieve that in 10 to 15 years but it is an incredible challenge.

50   What these efforts demonstrate is how infinitely complex our language and understanding of it is, how meaning turns on the subtlest changes in intonation, how vast any computer data base must be to catch all the nuances we take for granted. How do you program a computer to avoid those charming errors in context which foreigners make in perfectly grammatical sentences? For instance, a sign in an Egyptian hotel states: "Patrons need have no anxiety about the water. It has all been passed by the management." Or, this in a Swiss hotel: "Due to the impropriety of entertaining guests of the opposite sex in the bedrooms, it is suggested that the lobby be used for this purpose."

51   The effort to make computers understand speech raises other questions about the future of language. Will the technology, and the business imperatives behind it, create an irresistible drive toward more standard speech? If so, which accents or varieties of American speech will that leave out? Whom will it disenfranchise because of their dialect—African-Americans, Hispanics, Cajuns in Louisiana? A couple of years ago, the police chief of Shreveport, La., complained that the computer voice-recognition system used to route nonemergency calls did not understand the local accent. Researchers point out, however, that if you speak like someone from the Midwest, computers will understand you.

52   The emerging technology is irresistible for business. When United Airlines introduced a computerized voice-recognition system for flight information-replacing live bodies—it saved a reported $25,000,000. As these systems become more sophisticated, a lot of companies will want them to replace expensive warm bodies. Inevitably, more and more of our lives will involve talking to and being understood by computers. Being understood will be increasingly important. Will the technology work to reinforce existing linguistic stereotypes—about your Tex. race, ethnicity, gender, or where you live—or help to break them down? Will we have to talk as computers would like us to in order for them to obey us?

53   During the California portion of filming "Do You Speak American?" I drove a car equipped with an elaborate voice-recognition system. I speak a version of standard broadcast American English, and I tried to enunciate clearly. Occasionally, it worked, but often it did not and the car kept saying, "Pardon me? Pardon me?" and I gave it up.

54   Everything in the American experience, each new frontier encountered—geographical, spiritual, technological—has altered our language. What kind of a frontier are we crossing by teaching computers our most fundamental human skill, that of the spoken word?

THINKING CRITICALLY

1. In paragraph 2, linguist Dennis Baron comments, "Aside from a person's physical appearance, the first thing someone will be judged by is how he or she talks." Do you judge people on how they speak? What assumptions do you make about people who have certain accents? How they use standard grammar? What judgments do you think people make about you based on how you talk? Explain.

2. What is the difference between prescriptive and descriptive linguistics? Where do the prescriptivists and the descriptivists stand on the current state of American English? With which viewpoint do you agree?

3. To prepare for his documentary, MacNeil interviewed many people, including "waitresses, cowboys, hip-hop artists, Marine drill sergeants, Border Patrol agents, Mexican immigrants, Cajun musicians, African-American and Hispanic broadcasters, and Silicon Valley techies . . . writers and editors, teachers and teenagers, surfers and snowboarders, actors and screenwriters, and presidents and politicians." Why do you think he chose these people to represent the linguistic trends of American English? Do you think he chose an accurate cross-section of people? What linguistic patterns would you expect from this group? Explain.

4. MacNeil notes that "one of the most common assumptions is that our total immersion in the same mass media is making us all speak in a similar manner." How could the mass media influence the way we speak? Has the mass media been successful in creating a standard form of American English? Explain.

5. What is Ebonics? Why did it backfire in 1997 in Oakland, California? What replaced the Ebonic concept, and why?

6. Linguist William Labov theorizes that regional linguistic trends are primarily transmitted by women. Review his ideas and explain why you agree or disagree, in whole or in part, with his theory.

7. MacNeil wonders what will happen if computers are able to speak and understand speech. In your own words, respond to his concerns. What do you think will happen to American English, and why?

WRITING ASSIGNMENTS

1. MacNeil notes that some dialects and speech patterns are considered more "correct" than others. Review the results of his research and take the quiz he describes in his essay on PBS's "*Do You Speak American?*" Web site: www.pbs.org/speak/speech/mapping/map.html. What do your results tell you about your own language biases?

2. In his essay, MacNeil observes that rather than sounding more alike, Americans are more linguistically different than ever before. Listen to some local dialects on PBS's "Do You Speak American?" Web site and review its "Myths and Realities" section at www.pbs.org/speak/seatosea/americanvarieties. Before reading MacNeil's results, did you accept as true any of the myths he debunks?

3. Write an essay in which you explain why it is better to support a descriptive or prescriptive position regarding American English.

All-American Dialects

Richard Lederer

Richard Lederer is the author of countless articles about language and humor, as well as many books on language, including *Anguished English* (1989) and *The Bride of Anguished English* (2002). His syndicated column, "Looking at Language", appears in newspapers and magazines throughout the United States. He is also a language commentator on Public Radio, with his weekly program, *A Way with Words.* This essay appeared in the May 2003 issue of *The Vocabula Review.*

1   I have tongue and will travel, so I run around the country speaking to groups of teachers, students, librarians, women's clubbers, guild professionals, and corporate clients. These good people go to all the trouble of putting together meetings and conferences, and I walk in, share my thoughts about language in their lives, and imbibe their collective energy and synergy. I will go anywhere to spread the word about words, and in going anywhere from California to the New York Island, from the redwood forest to the Gulf Stream waters, I hear America singing. We are teeming nations within a nation, a nation that is like a world. We talk in melodies of infinite variety; we dance to their sundry measures and lyrics.

2   Midway through John Steinbeck's epic novel *The Grapes of Wrath* young Ivy observes, "Ever'body says words different. Arkansas folks says 'em different, and Oklahomy folks says 'em different. And we seen a lady from Massachusetts, an' she said 'em differentest of all. Couldn't hardly make out what she was sayin'."

3   One aspect of American rugged individualism is that not all of us say the same word in the same way. Sometimes we don't even use the same name for the same object.

4   I was born and grew up in Philadelphia a coon's age, a blue moon, and a month of Sundays ago—when Hector was a pup. *Phillufia,* or *Philly,* which is what we kids called the city, was where the epicurean delight made with cold cuts, cheese, tomatoes, pickles, and onions stuffed into a long, hard-crusted Italian bread loaf was invented.

5   The creation of that sandwich took place in the Italian pushcart section of the city, known as Hog Island. Some linguists contend that it was but a short leap from *Hog Island* to *hoagie,* while others claim that the label *hoagie* arose because only a hog had the appetite or the technique to eat one properly.

6   As a young adult I moved to northern New England (*N'Hampsha,* to be specific), where the same sandwich designed to be a meal in itself is called a grinder—because you need a good set of grinders to chew them. But my travels around the United States have revealed that the hoagie or grinder is called at least a dozen other names—a bomber, Garibaldi (after the Italian liberator), hero, Italian sandwich, rocket, sub, submarine (which is what they call it in California, where I now live), torpedo, wedge, wedgie, and, in the deep South, a poor-boy (usually pronounced *poh-boy*).

7   In Philadelphia, we washed our hoagies down with soda. In New England, we did it with tonic, and by that word I don't mean medicine. Soda and tonic in other parts are known as pop, soda pop, a soft drink, Coke, and quinine.

8   In northern New England, they take the term *milk shake* quite literally. To many residing in that little corner of the country, a milk shake consists of milk mixed with flavored syrup—and nothing more—shaken until foamy. If you live in Rhode Island or in southern Massachusetts and you want ice cream in your milk drink, you ask for a cabinet (named after the square wooden cabinet in which the mixer was encased). If you live farther north, you order a velvet or a frappe (from the French *frapper,* to ice).

9   Clear—or is it clean?—or is it plumb?—across the nation, Americans sure do talk "different."

10   What do you call those flat, doughy things you often eat for breakfast—battercakes, flannel cakes, flapjacks, fritters, griddle cakes, or pancakes?

11   Is that simple strip of grass between the street and the sidewalk a berm, boulevard, boulevard strip, city strip, devil strip, green belt, the parking, the parking strip, parkway, sidewalk plot, strip, swale, tree bank, or tree lawn?

12   Is the part of the highway that separates the northbound lanes from the southbound lanes the centerline, center strip, mall, medial strip, median strip, medium strip, or neutral ground?

13   Is it a cock horse, dandle, hicky horse, horse, horse tilt, ridy horse, seesaw, teeter, teeterboard, teetering board, teetering horse, teeter-totter, tilt, tilting board, tinter, tinter board, or tippity bounce?

14   Do fisherpersons employ an angledog, angleworm, baitworm, earthworm, eaceworm, fishworm, mudworm, rainworm, or redworm? Is a larger worm a dew worm, night crawler, night walker, or town worm?

15   Is it a crabfish, clawfish, craw, crawdab, crawdad, crawdaddy, crawfish, crawler, crayfish, creekcrab, crowfish, freshwater lobster, ghost shrimp, mudbug, spiny lobster, or yabby?

16   Depends where you live and who or whom it is you're talking to.

17   I figger, figure, guess, imagine, opine, reckon, and suspect that my being bullheaded, contrary, headstrong, muley, mulish, ornery, otsny, pigheaded, set, sot, stubborn, or utsy about this whole matter of dialects makes you sick to, in, or at your stomach.

18   But I assure you that, when it comes to American dialects, I'm not speaking fahdoodle, flumaddiddle, flummydiddle, or flurriddiddle—translation: nonsense. I'm no all-thumbs-and-no-fingers, all-knees-and-elbows, all-left-feet, antigoddling, bumfuzzled, discombobulated, flusterated, or foozled bumpkin, clodhopper, country jake, hayseed, hick, hillbilly, hoosier, jackpine savage, mossback, mountain-boomer, pumpkin-husker, rail-splitter, rube, sodbuster, stump farmer, swamp angel, yahoo, or yokel.

19   The biblical book of Judges (12:4-6) tells us how one group of speakers used the word *shibboleth,* Hebrew for "stream," as a military password. The Gileadites had defeated the Ephraimites in battle and were holding some narrow places on the Jordan River that the fleeing Ephraimites had to cross to get home. In those days,

it was hard to tell one kind of soldier from another because soldiers didn't wear uniforms.

20   The Gileadites knew that the Ephraimites spoke a slightly different dialect of Hebrew and could be recognized by their inability to pronounce an initial *sh* sound. Thus, each time a soldier wanted to cross the river:

> The men of Gilead said unto him, Art thou an Ephraimite? If he said, Nay, then they said unto him, Say now Shibboleth: and he said Shibboleth: for he could not frame to pronounce it right. Then they took him and slew him at the passages of Jordan: and there fell at that time of the Ephraimites forty and two thousand.

21   During World War II, some American officers adapted the strategy of the Old Testament Gileadites. Knowing that many Japanese have difficulty pronouncing the letter *l,* these officers instructed their sentries to use only passwords that had *l*'s in them, such as *lallapalooza.* The closest the Japanese got to the sentries was *rarraparooza.* These days English speakers don't get slaughtered for pronouncing their words differently from other English speakers, but the way those words sound can be labeled "funny" or "quaint" or "out of touch." In George Bernard Shaw's play *Pygmalion,* Professor Henry Higgins rails at Liza Doolittle and her cockney accent:

> A woman who utters such depressing and disgusting sounds has no right to be anywhere—no right to live. Remember that you are a human being with a soul and the divine gift of articulate speech: that your native language is the language of Shakespeare and Milton and The Bible; and don't sit there crooning like a bilious pigeon!

22   Most of us are aware that large numbers of people in the United States speak very differently than we do. Most of us tend to feel that the way "we" talk is right, and the way "they" talk is funny. "They," of course, refers to anyone who differs from "us."

23   If you ask most adults what a dialect is, they will tell you it is what somebody else in another region passes off as English. These regions tend to be exotic places like Mississippi or Texas—or Brooklyn, where *oil* is a rank of nobility, and *earl* is a black, sticky substance.

24   It is reported that many southerners reacted to the elections of Jimmy Carter and Bill Clinton by saying, "Well, at last we have a president who talks without an accent." Actually, southerners, like everyone else, do speak with an accent, as witness these tongue-in-cheek entries in our *Dictionary of Southernisms*:

ah: organ for seeing
are: sixty minutes
arn: ferrous metal
ass: frozen water
ast: questioned
bane: small, kidney-shaped vegetable

bar: seek and receive a loan; grizzly
bold: heated in water
card: one who lacks courage
farst: a lot of trees
fur: distance
har: to employ
hep: to assist
hire yew: a greeting
paw tree: verse
rat: opposite of lef
reckanize: to see
tarred: exhausted
t'mar: day following t'day
thang: item
thank: to cogitate

25   Any glossary of Southernspeak would be incomplete without "*yawl*: a bunch of you's." When I visited Alexandria, Louisiana, a local pastor offered me proof that *y'all* has biblical origins, especially in the letters of the apostle Paul: "We give thanks to God always for you all, making mention of you in our prayers" (First Epistle to the Thessalonians, 1:2), and "First, I thank my God through Jesus Christ for you all" (First Epistle to the Romans, 1:8). "Obviously," the good reverend told me, "Saint Paul was a Southerner." Then he added, "Thank you, Yankee visitor, for appreciating our beloved Southernspeak. We couldn't talk without it!"

26   An anonymous poem that I came upon in Louisville, Kentucky, clarifies the plural use of the one-syllable pronoun *y'all*:

Y'all gather 'round from far and near,
Both city folk and rural,
And listen while I tell you this:
The pronoun y'all is plural.

If I should utter, "Y'all come down,
Or we-all shall be lonely,"
I mean at least a couple folks,
And not one person only.

If I should say to Hiram Jones,
"I think that y'all are lazy,"
Or "Will y'all let me use y'all's knife?"
He'd think that I was crazy.

Don't think I mean to criticize
Or that I'm full of gall,
But when we speak of one alone,
We all say "you," not "y'all."

27   If the truth about dialects be told, we all have accents. Many New Englanders drop the *r* in *cart* and *farm* and say *caht* and *fahm*. Thus, the midwesterner's "park the car in Harvard Yard" becomes the New Englander's "pahk the cah in Hahvahd

Yahd." But those *r*'s aren't lost. A number of upper northeasterners, including the famous Kennedy family of Massachusetts, add *r*'s to words, such as *idear* and *Cuber* when those words come before a vowel or at the end of a sentence.

28   When an amnesia victim appeared at a truck stop in Missouri in the fall of 1987, authorities tried in vain to help her discover her identity. Even after three months, police "ran into a brick wall," according to the *Columbia Daily Tribune.* Then, linguist Donald Lance of the University of Missouri–Columbia was called in to analyze her speech. After only a few sentences, Lance recognized the woman's West Pennsylvania dialect, and, within one month, police in Pittsburgh located the woman's family.

29   Among the clues used to pinpoint the woman's origin was the West-Pennsylvanian use of *greezy,* instead of *greasy,* and *teeter-totter,* rather than *seesaw.* Dialectologists know that people who pronounce the word as *greezy* usually live south of a line that wiggles across the northern parts of New Jersey, Pennsylvania, Ohio, Indiana, and Illinois.

30   Linguist Roger Shuy writes about the reactions of Illinois residents in a 1962 survey of regional pronunciations, including the soundings of *greasy*:

> The northern Illinois informants felt the southern pronunciation was crude and ugly; it made them think of a very messy, dirty, sticky, smelly frying pan. To the southern and midland speakers, however, the northern pronunciation con-noted a messy, dirty, sticky, smelly skillet.

31   Using the tools of his trade, Shuy was able to accurately profile Ted Kaczynski, the elusive Unabomber who terrorized the nation through the 1990s. Culling lin-guistic evidence from Kaczynski's "Manifesto," published in the *New York Times,* and the notes and letters accompanying the bombs, Shuy deduced the Unabomber's geographical origin, religious background, age, and education level.

32   Among the clues were the Unabomber's use of *sierras* to mean "mountains," an indication that the writer had spent some time living in northern California. In his "Manifesto," Kaczynski used expressions common to a person who was a young adult in the 1960s—*Holy Robots, working stiff,* and *playing footsy.* His use of soci-ological terms, such as *other directed,* and his many references to individual *drives* suggested an acquaintance with the sociology in vogue during the sixties, particu-larly that of David Reisman. The complexity of Kaczynski's sentence structure, in-cluding the subjunctive mood, and the learnedness of his vocabulary, such as the words *surrogate, sublimate, overspecialization,* and *tautology,* pointed to someone highly educated.

33   All these conclusions were verified when Kaczynski was captured. He was in his early fifties, he had grown up in Chicago, he had lived for a time in northern California, and he was well educated, having once been a university professor.

34   Now is the time to face the fact that you speak a dialect. When you learned language, you learned it as a dialect; if you don't speak a dialect, you don't speak. *Dialect* isn't a label for careless, unlettered, nonstandard speech. A dialect isn't something to be avoided or cured.

35   Each language is a great pie. Each slice of that pie is a dialect, and no single slice is the language. Don't try to change your language into the kind of English that nobody really speaks. Be proud of your slice of the pie.

36   In the early 1960s, Steinbeck decided to rediscover America in a camper with his French poodle Charlie. The writer reported his observations in a book called *Travels with Charlie* and included these thoughts on American dialects:

> I can remember a time when I could almost pinpoint a man's place of origin by his speech. That is growing more difficult now and will in some foreseeable future become impossible. It is a rare house or building that is not rigged with spiky combers of the air. Radio and television speech becomes standardized, perhaps better English than we have ever used. Just as our bread, mixed and baked, packaged and sold without benefit of accident or human frailty, is uniformly good and uniformly tasteless, so will our speech become one speech.

37   Forty years have passed since Steinbeck made that observation, and the hum and buzz of electronic voices have since permeated almost every home across our nation. Formerly, the psalmist tells us, "the voice of the turtle was heard in the land," but now it is the voice of the broadcaster, with his or her immaculately groomed diction. I hope that American English does not turn into a bland, homogenized, pasteurized, assembly-line product. May our bodacious American English remain tasty and nourishing—full of flavor, variety, and local ingredients.

THINKING CRITICALLY

1. In paragraph 5–16, Lederer cites the many different words different regions of the country use for the same item. Identify the "standard" word for each item (for example, submarine sandwich) as well as the word you would probably use for it.

2. How have dialects been used historically to identify different groups of people? Explain.

3. Lederer comments, "Now is the time to face the fact that you speak a dialect. When you learned language, you learned it as a dialect; if you don't speak a dialect, you don't speak." How would you describe your personal dialect? Can you detect it? Ask someone else, from another part of the country, to describe your dialect. Does their assessment surprise you? Why or why not?

4. Phonetically spell out how you would pronounce Lederer's list of "Southernisms." As a class, share your pronunciations as part of a group discussion on different dialects.

eye	*boiled*	*poetry*
hour	*coward*	*right and left*
iron	*forest*	*recognize*
ice	*far*	*tired*
asked	*hire*	*tomorrow and today*
bean	*help*	*thing*
bear	*how are you?*	*think*

WRITING ASSIGNMENTS

1. Interview and record at least four students from different parts of the country and ask them to read a short passage from a literary work or a local newspaper. What differences do you notice? Do some students sound more "educated" based on pronunciation? Have the students in your study listen to the recordings

of the other participants and ask them to try to identify what region of the country the speakers are from and which dialects sound more or less "sophisticated." Summarize your results in a short essay, following the concepts outlined in Lederer's essay.

2. American slang expressions color regional dialects and make language unique. Visit *Alpha Dictionary*'s Web site on American slang at www.alphadictionary.com/slang and look up some common slang expressions you may use in your own speech (or common words in current "teenspeak," such as *sick, bait, bling, chill, fly, phat, sweet*, and *word*). How do the slang expressions differ from the words' original meanings? As part of a broader study, ask an older adult to identify some slang expressions from their youth. Do you have any slang words in common? Write a short essay exploring the role of slang in today's youth culture, and how it influences local language.

Why Good English Is Good for You

John Simon

Is rule-based grammar going the way of the dinosaur? Does it hinder the creative voice and individual style? The author of the next essay, a staunch "prescriptivist," argues that grammatical rules keep language vibrant. "Language remains alive," explains John Simon, "because each speaker (or writer) can and must, within the framework of accepted grammar, syntax, and pronunciation, produce a style that is his very own." The next essay is not just a wry and incisive look at the way American English is abused; it is an argument in favor of using "good" English—an effort that improves not only communication but also memory and thinking.

John Simon served as a theatre critic at *New York Magazine* for nearly 40 years. A renowned critic of the arts and of what he views as the shoddy language of Americans, for years he wrote a regular language column for *Esquire*, from which some essays, including the one below, were published in a collection about the decline of literacy, *Paradigms Lost* (1980).

1 What's good English to you that . . . you should grieve for it? What good is correct speech and writing, you may ask, in an age in which hardly anyone seems to know, and no one seems to care? Why shouldn't you just fling bloopers riotously with the throng, and not stick out from the rest like a sore thumb by using the language correctly? Isn't grammar really a thing of the past, and isn't the new idea to communicate in *any* way as long as you can make yourself understood?

2 The usual, basic defense of good English (and here, again, let us not worry about nomenclature—for all I care, you may call it "Standard English," "correct American," or anything else) is that it helps communication, that it is perhaps even a *sine qua non* of mutual understanding. Although this is a crude truth of sorts, it strikes me as, in some ways, both more and less than the truth. Suppose you say, "Everyone in their right mind would cross on the green light" or "Hopefully, it won't rain tomorrow," chances are very good that the person you say this to will understand you, even though you are committing obvious solecisms or creating needless ambiguities. Similarly, if you write in a letter, "The baby has finally

ceased its howling" (spelling *its* as *it's*), the recipient will be able to figure out what was meant. But "figuring out" is precisely what a listener or reader should not have to do. There is, of course, the fundamental matter of courtesy to the other person, but it goes beyond that: why waste time on unscrambling simple meaning when there are more complex questions that should receive our undivided attention? If the many cooks had to worry first about which out of a large number of pots had no leak in it, the broth, whether spoiled or not, would take forever to be ready.

3   It is, I repeat, only initially a matter of clarity. It is also a matter of concision. Space today is as limited as time. If you have only a thousand words in which to convey an important message it helps to know that "overcomplicated" is correct and "overly complicated" is incorrect. Never mind the grammatical explanations; the two extra characters and one space between words are reason enough. But what about the more advanced forms of wordmongering that hold sway nowadays? Take redundancy, like the "hopes and aspirations" of Jimmy Carter, quoted by Edwin Newman as having "a deeply profound religious experience"; or elaborate jargon, as when Charles G. Walcutt, a graduate professor of English at CUNY, writes (again as quoted by Newman): "The colleges, trying to remediate increasing numbers of . . . illiterates up to college levels, are being highschoolized"; or just obfuscatory verbiage of the pretentious sort, such as this fragment from a letter I received: "It is my impression that effective in*ter* personal verbal communication depends on prior effective in*tra*-personal verbal communication." What this means is that if you think clearly, you can speak and write clearly—except if you are a "certified speech and language pathologist," like the writer of the letter I quote. (By the way, she adds the letters Ph.D. after her name, though she is not even from Germany, where *Herr* and *Frau Doktor* are in common, not to say vulgar, use.)

4   But except for her ghastly verbiage, our certified language pathologist (whatever that means) is perfectly right: there is a close connection between the ability to think and the ability to use English correctly. After all, we think in words, we conceptualize in words, we work out our problems inwardly with words, and using them correctly is comparable to a craftsman's treating his tools with care, keeping his materials in good shape. Would you trust a weaver who hangs her wet laundry on her loom, or lets her cats bed down in her yarn? The person who does not respect words and their proper relationships cannot have much respect for ideas—very possibly cannot have ideas at all. My quarrel is not so much with minor errors that we all fall into from time to time even if we know better as it is with basic sloppiness or ignorance or defiance of good English.

5   Training yourself to speak and write correctly—and I say "training yourself" because nowadays, unfortunately, you cannot depend on other people or on institutions to give you the proper training, for reasons I shall discuss later—training yourself, then, in language, means developing at the very least two extremely useful faculties: your sense of discipline and your memory. Discipline because language is with us always, as nothing else is: it follows us much as, in the old morality play, Good Deeds followed Everyman, all the way to the grave; and, if the language is written, even beyond. Let me explain: if you keep an orderly apartment, if you can see to it that your correspondence and bill-paying are attended to

regularly, if your diet and wardrobe are maintained with the necessary care—good enough; you are a disciplined person.

6   But the preliminary discipline underlying all others is nevertheless your speech: the words that come out of you almost as frequently and—if you are tidy— as regularly as your breath. I would go so far as to say that, immediately after your bodily functions, language is first, unless you happen to be an ascetic, an anchorite, or a stylite; but unless you are a sty*lite*, you had better be a styl*ist*.

7   Most of us—almost all—must take in and give out language as we do breath, and we had better consider the seriousness of language pollution as second only to air pollution. For the linguistically disciplined, to misuse or mispronounce a word is an unnecessary and unhealthy contribution to the surrounding smog. To have taught ourselves not to do this, or—being human and thus also imperfect—to do it as little as possible, means deriving from every speaking moment the satisfaction we get from a cap that snaps on to a container perfectly, an elevator that stops flush with the landing, a roulette ball that comes to rest exactly on the number on which we have placed our bet. It gives us the pleasure of hearing or seeing our words—because they are abiding by the rules—snapping, sliding, falling precisely into place, expressing with perfect lucidity and symmetry just what we wanted them to express. This is comparable to the satisfaction of the athlete or ballet dancer or pianist finding his body or legs or fingers doing his bidding with unimpeachable accuracy.

8   And if someone now says that "in George Eliot's lesser novels, she is not completely in command" is perfectly comprehensible even if it is ungrammatical, the "she" having no antecedent in the nominative (*Eliot's* is a genitive), I say, "Comprehensible, perhaps, but lopsided," for the civilized and orderly mind does not feel comfortable with that "she"—does not hear that desired and satisfying click of correctness—unless the sentence is restructured as "George Eliot, in her lesser novels, is not . . ." or in some similar way. In fact, the fully literate ear can be thrown by this error in syntax; it may look for the antecedent of that "she" else-where than in the preceding possessive case. Be that as it may, playing without rules and winning—in this instance, managing to communicate without using good English—is no more satisfactory than winning in a sport or game by accident or by disregarding the rules: which is really cheating.

9   The second faculty good speech develops is, as I have mentioned before, our memory. Grammar and syntax are partly logical—and to that extent they are also good exercisers and developers of our logical faculty—but they are also partly arbitrary, conventional, irrational. For example, the correct "compared to" and "contrasted with" could, from the logical point of view, just as well be "contrasted to" and "compared with" ("compared with," of course, is correct, but in a different sense from the one that concerns us here, namely, the antithesis of "contrasted with"). And, apropos *different*, logic would have to strain desperately to explain the exclusive correctness of "different from," given the exclusive correctness of "other than," which would seem to justify "different than," jarring though that is to the cultivated ear.

10   But there it is: some things are so because tradition, usage, the best speakers and writers, the grammar books and dictionaries have made them so. There may

even exist some hidden historical explanation: something, perhaps, in the Sanskrit, Greek, Latin, or other origins of a word or construction that you and I may very easily never know. We can, however, memorize; and memorization can be a wonderfully useful thing—surely the Greeks were right to consider Mnemosyne (memory) the mother of the Muses, for without her there would be no art and no science. And what better place to practice one's mnemonic skills than in the study of one's language?

11   There is something particularly useful about speaking correctly and precisely because language is always there as a foundation—or, if you prefer a more fluid image, an undercurrent—beneath what is going on. Now, it seems to me that the great difficulty of life lies in the fact that we must almost always do two things at a time. If, for example, we are walking and conversing, we must keep our mouths as well as feet from stumbling. If we are driving while listening to music, we must not allow the siren song of the cassette to prevent us from watching the road and the speedometer (otherwise the less endearing siren of the police car or the ambulance will follow apace). Well, it is just this sort of bifurcation of attention that care for precise, clear expression fosters in us. By learning early in life to pay attention both to what we are saying and to how we are saying it, we develop the much-needed life skill of doing two things simultaneously.

12   Put another way, we foster our awareness of, and ability to deal with, form and content. If there is any verity that modern criticism has fought for, it is the recognition of the indissolubility of content and form. Criticism won the battle, won it so resoundingly that this oneness has become a contemporary commonplace. And shall the fact that form *is* content be a platitude in all the arts but go unrecognized in the art of self-expression, whether in conversation or correspondence, or whatever form of spoken or written utterance a human being resorts to? Accordingly, you are going to be judged, whether you like it or not, by the correctness of your English as much as by the correctness of your thinking; there are some people to whose bad English is as offensive as gibberish, or as your picking your nose in public would be to their eyes and stomachs. The fact that people of linguistic sensibilities may be a dying breed does not mean that they are wholly extinct, and it is best not to take any unnecessary chances.

13   To be sure, if you are a member of a currently favored minority, many of your linguistic failings may be forgiven you—whether rightly or wrongly is not my concern here. But if you cannot change your sex or color to the one that is getting preferential treatment—Bakke case or no Bakke case—you might as well learn good English and profit by it in your career, your social relations, perhaps even in your basic self-confidence. That, if you will, is the ultimate practical application of good English; but now let me tell you about the ultimate impractical one, which strikes me as being possibly even more important.

14   Somewhere in the prose writings of Charles Péguy, who was a very fine poet and prose writer—and, what is perhaps even more remarkable, as good a human being as he was an artist—somewhere in those writings is a passage about the decline of pride in workmanship among French artisans, which, as you can deduce, set in even before World War I, wherein Péguy was killed. In the passage I refer to, Péguy

bemoans the fact that cabinet-makers no longer finish the backs of furniture—the sides that go against the wall—in the same way as they do the exposed sides. What is not seen was just as important to the old artisans as what is seen—it was a moral issue with them. And so, I think, it ought to be with language. Even if no one else notices the niceties, the precision, the impeccable sense of grammar and syntax you deploy in your utterances, you yourself should be aware of them and take pride in them as in pieces of work well done.

15   Now, I realize that there are two possible reactions among you to what I have said up to this point. Some of you will say to yourselves: what utter nonsense! Language is a flexible, changing, living organism that belongs to the people who speak it. It has always been changed according to the ways in which people chose to speak it, and the dictionaries and books on grammar had to, and will have to, adjust themselves to the people and not the other way around. For isn't it the glory of language that it keeps throwing up new inventions as surf tosses our differently polished pebbles and bits of bottle glass onto the shore, and that in this inexhaustible variety, in this refusal to kowtow to dry-as-dust scholars, lies its vitality, its beauty?

16   Others among you, perhaps fewer in number, will say to yourselves: quite so, there is such a thing as Standard English, or purity of speech, or correctness of expression—something worth safeguarding and fostering; but how the devil is one to accomplish that under the prevailing conditions: in a democratic society full of minorities that have their own dialects or linguistic preferences, and in a world in which television, advertising, and other mass media manage daily to corrupt the language a little further? Let me try to answer the first group first, and then come back to the questions of the second.

17   Of course language is, and must be, a living organism to the extent that new inventions, discoveries, ideas enter the scene and clamor rightfully for designations. Political, social, and psychological changes may also affect our mode of expression, and new words or phrases may have to be found to reflect what we might call historical changes. It is also quite natural for slang terms to be invented, become popular, and in some cases, remain permanently in the language. It is perhaps equally inevitable (though here we are on more speculative ground) for certain words to become obsolescent and obsolete, and drop out of the language. But does that mean that grammar and syntax have to keep changing, that pronunciations and meanings of words must shift, that more complex or elegant forms are obliged to yield to simpler or cruder ones that often are not fully synonymous with them and not capable of expressing certain fine distinctions? Should, for instance, "terrestrial" disappear entirely in favor of "earthly," or are there shades of meaning involved that need to remain available to us? Must we sacrifice "notwithstanding" because we have "in spite of" or "despite"? Need we forfeit "jettison" just because we have "throw overboard"? And what about "disinterested," which is becoming a synonym for "uninterested," even though that means something else, and though we have no other word for "disinterested"?

18   "Language has *always* changed," say these people, and they might with equal justice say that there has always been war or sickness or insanity. But the truth is that some sicknesses that formerly killed millions have been eliminated, that some

so-called insanity can today be treated, and that just because there have always been wars does not mean that someday a cure cannot be found even for that scourge. And if it cannot, it is only by striving to put an absolute end to war, by pretending that it can be licked, that we can at least partly control it. Without such assumptions and efforts, the evil would be so widespread that, given our current weaponry, we would no longer be here to worry about the future of language.

19   But we are here, and having evolved linguistically this far, and having the means—books of grammar, dictionaries, education for all—to arrest unnecessary change, why not endeavor with might and mind to arrest it? Certain cataclysms cannot be prevented: earthquakes and droughts, for example, can scarcely, if at all, be controlled; but we can prevent floods, for which purpose we have invented dams. And dams are precisely what we can construct to prevent floods of ignorance from eroding our language, and, beyond that, to provide irrigation for areas that would otherwise remain linguistically arid.

20   For consider that what some people are pleased to call linguistic evolution was almost always a matter of ignorance prevailing over knowledge. There is no valid reason, for example, for the word *nice* to have changed its meanings so many times—except ignorance of its exact definition. Had the change never occurred, or had it been stopped at any intermediate stage, we would have had just as good a word as we have now and saved some people a heap of confusion along the way. But if *nice* means what it does today—and it has two principal meanings, one of them, as in "nice distinction," alas, obsolescent—let us, for heaven's sake, keep it where it is, now that we have the means with which to hold it there.

21   If, for instance, we lose the accusative case *whom*—and we are in great danger of losing it—our language will be the poorer for it. Obviously, "The man, whom I had never known, was a thief" means something other than "The man who I had never known was a thief." Now, you can object that it would be just as easy in the first instance to use some other construction; but what happens if *this* one is used incorrectly? Ambiguity and confusion. And why should we lose this useful distinction? Just because a million or ten million or a billion people less educated than we are cannot master the difference? Surely it behooves us to try to educate the ignorant up to our level rather than to stultify ourselves down to theirs. Yes, you say, but suppose they refuse to or are unable to learn? In that case, I say, there is a doubly good reason for not going along with them. Ah, you reply, but they are the majority, and we must accept their way or, if the revolution is merely linguistic, lose our "credibility" (as the current parlance, rather confusingly, has it) or, if the revolution is political, lose our heads. Well, I consider a sufficient number of people to be educable enough to be capable of using *who* and *whom* correctly, and to derive satisfaction from this capability—a sufficient number, I mean, to enable us to preserve *whom*, and not to have to ask "for who the bell tolls."

22   The main problem with education, actually, is not those who need it and cannot get it, but those who should impart it and, for various reasons, do not. In short, the enemies of education are the educators themselves: miseducated, underpaid, overburdened, and intimidated teachers (frightened because, though the pen is supposed to be mightier than the sword, the switchblade is surely more powerful than the

ferrule), and professors who—because they are structural linguists, democratic respecters of alleged minority rights, or otherwise misguided folk—believe in the sacrosanct privilege of any culturally underprivileged minority or majority to dictate its ignorance to the rest of the world. For, I submit, an English improvised by slaves and other strangers to the culture—to whom my heart goes out in every human way—under dreadfully deprived conditions can nowise equal an English that the best literary and linguistic talents have, over the centuries, perceptively and painstakingly brought to a high level of excellence.

23   So my answer to the scoffers in this or any audience is, in simplest terms, the following: contrary to popular misconception, language does not belong to the people, or at least not in the sense in which *belong* is usually construed. For things can rightfully belong only to those who invent or earn them. But we do not know who invented language: is it the people who first made up the words for *father* and *mother*, for *I* and *thou*, for *hand* and *foot*; or is it the people who evolved the subtler shadings of language, its poetic variety and suggestiveness, but also its unambiguousness, its accurate and telling details? Those are two very different groups of people and two very different languages, and I, as you must have guessed by now, consider the latter group at least as important as the former. As for *earning* language, it has surely been earned by those who have striven to learn it properly, and here even economic and social circumstances are but an imperfect excuse for bad usage; history is full of examples of people rising from humble origins to learn, against all kinds of odds, to speak and write correctly—even brilliantly.

24   *Belong*, then, should be construed in the sense that parks, national forests, monuments, and public utilities are said to belong to the people: available for properly respectful use but not for defacement and destruction. And all that we propose to teach is how to use and enjoy the gardens of language to their utmost aesthetic and salubrious potential. Still, I must now address myself to the group that, while agreeing with my aims, despairs of finding practical methods for their implementation.

25   True enough, after a certain age speakers not aware of Standard English or not exceptionally gifted will find it hard or impossible to change their ways. Nevertheless, if there were available funds for advanced methods in teaching; if teachers themselves were better trained and paid, and had smaller classes and more assistants; if, furthermore, college entrance requirements were heightened and the motivation of students accordingly strengthened; if there were no structural linguists and National Councils of Teachers of English filling instructors' heads with notions about "Students' Rights to Their Own Language" (they have every right to it as a *second* language, but none as a *first*); if teachers in all disciplines, including the sciences and social sciences, graded on English usage as well as on specific proficiencies; if aptitude tests for various jobs stressed good English more than they do; and, above all, if parents were better educated and more aware of the need to set a good example to their children, and to encourage them to learn correct usage, the situation could improve enormously.

26   Clearly, to expect all this to come to pass is utopian; some of it, however, is well within the realm of possibility. For example, even if parents do not speak very

good English, many of them at least can manage an English that is good enough to correct a very young child's mistakes; in other words, most adults can speak a good enough four-year-old's idiom. They would thus start kids out on the right path; the rest could be done by the schools.

27   But the problem is what to do in the most underprivileged homes: those of blacks, Hispanics, immigrants from various Asian and European countries. This is where day-care centers could come in. If the fathers and mothers could be gainfully employed, their small children would be looked after by day-care centers where— is this asking too much?—good English could be inculcated in them. The difficulty, of course, is what to do about the discrepancy the little ones would note between the speech of the day-care people and that of their parents. Now, it seems to me that small children have a far greater ability to learn things, including languages, than some people give them credit for. Much of it is indeed rote learning, but, where languages are concerned, that is one of the basic learning methods even for adults. There is no reason for not teaching kids another language, to wit, Standard English, and turning this, if desirable, into a game: "At home you speak one way; here we have another language," at which point the instructor can make up names and explanations for Standard English that would appeal to pupils of that particular place, time, and background.

28   At this stage of the game, as well as later on in school, care should be exercised to avoid insulting the language spoken in the youngsters' homes. There must be ways to convey that both home and school languages have their validity and uses and that knowing both enables one to accomplish more in life. This would be hard to achieve if the children's parents were, say, militant blacks of the Geneva Smitherman sort, who execrate Standard English as a weapon of capitalist oppression against the poor of all races, colors, and religions. But, happily, there is evidence that most black, Hispanic, and other non-Standard English-speaking parents want their children to learn correct English so as to get ahead in the world.

29   Yet how do we defend ourselves against the charge that we are old fogeys who cannot emotionally adjust to the new directions an ever-living and changing language must inevitably take? Here I would want to redefine or, at any rate, clarify, what "living and changing" means, and also explain where we old fogeys stand. Misinformed attacks on Old Fogeydom, I have noticed, invariably represent us as people who shudder at a split infinitive and would sooner kill or be killed than tolerate a sentence that ends with a preposition. Actually, despite all my travels through Old Fogeydom, I have yet to meet one inhabitant who would not stick a preposition onto the tail of a sentence; as for splitting infinitives, most of us O.F.'s are perfectly willing to do that, too, but tactfully and sparingly, where it feels right. There is no earthly reason, for example, for saying "to dangerously live," when "to live dangerously" sounds so much better; but it does seem right to say (and write) "What a delight to sweetly breathe in your sleeping lover's breath"; that sounds smoother, indeed sweeter, than to "breathe in sweetly" or "sweetly to breathe in." But infinitives begging to be split are relatively rare; a sensitive ear, a good eye for shades of meaning will alert you whenever the need to split arises; without that ear and eye, you had better stick to the rules.

30   About the sense in which language is, and must be, alive, let me speak while donning another of my several hats—actually it is not a hat but a cap, for there exists in Greenwich Village an inscription on a factory that reads "CRITIC CAPS." So with my drama critic's cap on, let me present you with an analogy. The world theater today is full of directors who wreak havoc on classic plays to demonstrate their own ingenuity, their superiority, as it were, to the author. These directors—aborted playwrights, for the most part—will stage productions of *Hamlet* in which the prince is a woman, a flaming homosexual, or a one-eyed hunchback.

31   Well, it seems to me that the same spirit prevails in our approach to linguistics, with every newfangled, ill-informed, know-nothing construction, definition, pronunciation enshrined by the joint efforts of structural linguists, permissive dictionaries, and allegedly democratic but actually demagogic educators. What really makes a production of, say, *Hamlet* different, and therefore alive, is that the director, while trying to get as faithfully as possible at Shakespeare's meanings, nevertheless ends up stressing things in the play that strike him most forcefully; and the same individuality in production design and performances (the Hamlet of Gielgud versus the Hamlet of Olivier, for instance—what a world of difference!) further differentiates one production from another, and bestows on each its particular vitality. So, too, language remains alive because each speaker (or writer) can and must, *within the framework of accepted grammar, syntax, and pronunciation,* produce a style that is his very own, that is as personal as his posture, way of walking, mode of dress, and so on. It is such stylistic differences that make a person's—or a nation's—language flavorous, pungent, alive, and all this without having to play fast and loose with the existing rules.

32   But to have this, we need, among other things, good teachers and, beyond them, enlightened educators. I shudder when I read in the *Birmingham* (Alabama) *Post-Herald* of October 6, 1978, an account of a talk given to eight hundred English teachers by Dr. Alan C. Purves, vice-president of the National Council of Teachers of English. Dr. Purves is quoted as saying things like "We are in a situation with respect to reading where . . . ," and culminating in the following truly horrifying sentence: "I am going to suggest that when we go back to the basics, I think what we should be dealing with is our charge to help students to be more proficient in producing meaningful language—language that says what it means." Notice all the deadwood, the tautology, the anacoluthon in the first part of that sentence; but notice especially the absurdity of the latter part, in which the dubious word "meaningful"—a poor relation of "significant"—is thought to require explaining to an audience of English teachers.

33   Given such leadership from the N.C.T.E., the time must be at hand when we shall hear—not just "Don't ask for who the bell rings" (*as not* and *tolls* being, of course, archaic, elitist language), but also "It rings for you and I."

THINKING CRITICALLY

1. In your own words, why is good English good for you?
2. Consider the two examples Simon gives in paragraph 2: "Everyone in their right mind would cross on the green light" and "Hopefully, it won't rain tomorrow."

If they communicate perfectly well, why haggle over the minor grammatical errors?

3. How does Simon justify so strong a statement as that in paragraph 7: "Language pollution . . . [is] second only to air pollution"? Do you agree? Can you think of circumstances in which bad language might be a threat to health—mental or otherwise?

4. Simon argues that good speech develops memory. How does he explain that? Can you substantiate that based on your own experience and practice?

5. One counter-response to Simon's call for upholding the standards of correct English is the assertion: "Language is a flexible, changing, living organism that belongs to the people who speak it." (This statement is nearly identical to Bill Bryson's claim in a following essay.) How does Simon answer that charge? Can the language have rigid standards and still allow natural changes to occur? If so, give examples.

6. Simon singles out the word *nice* as one of the many victims of too much change. What are some of the current meanings of *nice*? Can you think of other words that have suffered too much change? What about the words *awful, terrific, wonderful,* and *fantastic*? What changes have they undergone since their original meanings?

7. Simon claims that "the enemies of education are the educators themselves" (paragraph 22). How does he justify such an assertion? Do you agree, given your own educational experience?

8. According to Simon, who are linguistically "the most underprivileged" children? What suggestions does Simon make for dealing with them?

9. From the tone and attitude of this essay, what kind of man would you say Simon is? Does he sound cranky and pedantic or snobbish and elitist? Or does he sound reasonable and friendly? Cite passages to substantiate your answer.

WRITING ASSIGNMENTS

1. Simon asserts that "you are going to be judged, whether you like it or not, by the correctness of your English as much as by the correctness of your thinking." Write an essay about an occasion when you judged people on the basis of their English—or an occasion when you were judged on that basis. Describe how the language used by others prejudiced you for or against them—or how such prejudices might have operated for or against you.

2. Simon criticizes parents strongly for not setting good language examples for their children. Write a paper describing the quality of language training in your own home. Did your parents encourage you to learn correct usage? Were they strict with you about it? Do you feel adequately trained in English usage, or handicapped because of your upbringing?

3. This essay by Simon was originally an address to a college audience. Imagine yourself addressing an audience on the same subject: "Why Good English Is Good for You." This time you are addressing not Simon's college audience, but a group of people who speak nonstandard, "uneducated" English. Write a speech that they might benefit from in language that they would understand and not be repelled by.

Totally Like Whatever, You Know?

Taylor Mali

In case you hadn't noticed,
it has somehow become uncool
to sound like you know what you're talking about?
Or believe strongly in what you're saying?
Invisible question marks and parenthetical (you know?)'s
have been attaching themselves to the ends of our sentences?
Even when those sentences aren't, like, questions? You know?

Declarative sentences—so-called
Because they used to, like, DECLARE things to be true
as opposed to other things which were, like, not—
have been infected by a totally hip
and tragically cool interrogative tone? You know?
Like, don't think I'm uncool just because I've noticed this;
this is just like the word on the street, you know?
It's like what I've heard?
I have nothing personally invested in my own opinions, okay?
I'm just inviting you to join me in my uncertainty?

What has happened to our conviction?
Where are the limbs out on which we once walked?
Have they been, like, chopped down
with the rest of the rain forest?
Or do we have, like, nothing to say?
Has society become so, like, totally . . .
I mean absolutely . . . You know?
That we've just gotten to the point where it's just, like . . .
whatever!

And so actually our disarticulation . . . ness
is just a clever sort of . . . thing
to disguise the fact that we've become
the most aggressively inarticulate generation
to come along since . . .
you know, a long, long time ago!

I entreat you, I implore you, I exhort you,
I challenge you: To speak with conviction.
To say what you believe in a manner that bespeaks
the determination with which you believe it.
Because contrary to the wisdom of the bumper sticker,
It is not enough these day to simply QUESTION AUTHORITY
You have to speak with it, too.

THINKING CRITICALLY

1. What point is Mali trying to make in this poem? Who do you think Mali is trying to inspire? Explain, referring to specific lines or words in the poem in your response.

2. In the first part of the poem, Mali asks readers whether they have noticed that it is "uncool" to sound intelligent, or to speak with conviction. Do you agree with Mali's observation?

3. Who is the target audience for this poem?

4. Do you, or any of your friends use the language Mali notes in your daily conversations? End sentences in a "upnote"? Use the words *like, whatever,* and *you know*? If so, do you think this speech style undermines your ability to speak with conviction? Why or why not?

5. How does the first part of Mali's poem contrast with the end of it? How does the language change? the tone? Explain.

Everyone Has an Accent but Me
John Esling

Everybody has an accent. Accent is the way we speak, pronounce our words, intone sounds, and inflect voice. From listening to others speak, we make judgements about their background, education, culture, nationality, and social status. In fact, we are far more likely to judge a person by his or her accent than by how they dress or carry themselves, or with whom they socialize. As John Esling explains in the next essay, we all have an accent, even if we think we don't.

John Esling is a professor of linguistics at the University of Victoria in British Columbia. He is also secretary of the International Phonetic Association, and author of the *University of Victoria Phonetic Database.* This essay first appeared in the book, *Language Myths* (1999), edited by Laurie Bauer and Peter Trudgill.

1 "I don't have an accent!" wails the friend indignantly. And we are all amused because the pronunciation of the utterance itself demonstrates to our ears that the claim is false. The speaker who voices this common refrain believes absolutely that his or her speech is devoid of any distinguishing characteristics that set it apart from the speech of those around them. We listeners who hear it are for our part equally convinced that the speaker's accent differs in some significant respect from our own. The key to understanding this difference of opinion is not so much in the differences in speech sounds that the speakers use but in the nature of "own-ness"— what does it mean to be "one of us" and to sound like it? It all comes down to a question of belonging. Accent defines and communicates who we are. Accent is the map which listeners perceive through their ears rather than through their eyes to "read" where the speaker was born and raised, what gender they are, how old they are, where they might have moved during their life, where they went to school, what occupation they have taken up, and even how short or tall they are, how much they might weigh, or whether they are feeling well or ill at the moment.

2   The fact is that everyone has an accent. It tells other people who we are because it reflects the places we have been and the things we have done. But the construct of accent, like so many other things, is relative. We may only realize that others think we have an accent when we leave the place we came from and find ourselves among people who share a different background from our own, or when a newcomer to our local area stands out as having a distinctly different pronunciation from most of those in our group—that is, relative to us. The closer we are to our native place and the more people that are there who grew up like us, the more likely we are to sound like those people when we talk. In other words, we share their local accent.

3   Some countries have one accent which is accepted as "standard" and which enjoys higher social prestige than any other. This is true of RP (Received Pronunciation) in the UK, of standard French in France and of many countries that have evolved a broadcast standard for radio and television. We may feel that this national standard is accentless and that non-standard speakers, by contrast, have accents. Nevertheless, it has to be recognized that standards that have evolved in the broadcast industry have their roots in language varieties that already exist in distinct social groups and their institutions. To use one particular group's accent in broadcasting is to give that accent a wider reach than perhaps it had before, but the accent itself is no "less" of an accent than any other, although it may represent groups and institutions with more political and economic power than groups whose members use another accent.

4   Our perceptions and production of speech also change with time. If we were to leave our native place for an extended period, our perception that the new accents around us were strange would only be temporary. Gradually, depending on our age, what job we are doing and how many different sorts of folks with different types of accents surround us, we will lose the sense that others have an accent and we will begin to fit in—to accommodate our speech patterns to the new norm. Not all people do this to the same degree. Some remain intensely proud of their original accent and dialect words, phrases and gestures, while others accommodate rapidly to a new environment by changing, among other things, their speech habits, so that they no longer "stand out in the crowd". Whether they do this consciously or not is open to debate and may differ from individual to individual, but like most processes that have to do with language, the change probably happens before we are aware of it and probably couldn't happen if we were.

5   So when we say, "I don't have an accent," we really mean, "You wouldn't think I had an accent if you knew who I was and knew where I'd been." It has more to do with acceptance—agreeing to stop listening to the other as "other"—than with absolute differences in the vowels, consonants or intonation patterns that a speaker uses. At the most basic level, we acknowledge that every individual will always have some speech characteristics that distinguish him or her from everyone else, even in our local community. This is the essence of recognition—we can learn to pick a friend's voice out of the crowd even though we consider everyone in our local crowd to have the same "accent" compared to outsiders. So what we call accent is relative not only to experience but also to the number of speech features we wish to distinguish at a time.

6   Human perception is categorical. When it comes to placing an accent, we listen and categorize according to accents we have heard before. We have a hard time placing an accent that we have never heard before, at least until we find out what to associate that accent with. Our experience of perceiving the sounds of human speech is very much a question of "agreeing" with others to construct certain categories and then to place the sounds that we hear into them. In contemporary constructivist psychology, this process is called the "co-construction of reality," in which differences can be said not to exist until we construct them. One result of these principles is that we can become quite attuned to stereotypical accents that we have heard only occasionally and don't know very well, while we become "insensitive" to the common accents we hear all around us every day. The speech of our colleagues seems "normal" to our ears, while the speech of a stranger stands out as different from that norm. So we feel that we don't have an accent because of the weight of experience that tells us that we are the best possible example of the "norm."

7   Details of pronunciation conjure up stereotypes. A few consonants and vowels or the briefest of intonation melodies cause us to search our memories for a pattern that matches what we have just heard. This is how we place speakers according to dialect or language group. It is also how we predict what the rest of their consonants and vowels and intonational phrasing will be like. Sometimes we are wrong, but usually we make good guesses based on limited evidence, especially if we've heard the accent before. Because we are used to the word order and common expressions of our language, a stranger's exotic pronunciation of a word which we recognize and understand can be catalogued as foreign, and we may ascribe it to one familiar stereotype or another and predict what the speaker's pronunciation of other words will be like. In this way, we see others as having an accent—because we take ourselves as the norm or reference to compare and measure others' speech.

8   It is interesting for the student of phonetics to observe the various ways in which one person's accent can differ from another's. There are three "strands" of accent which Professor David Abercrombie of the Department of Linguistics of the University of Edinburgh for many years taught his students to distinguish: the very short consonant and vowel sounds which alternate in rapid succession; the longer waves of rhythmic and melodic groupings, which we call rhythm and intonation; and the longest-term, persistent features that change very little in a given individual's voice, which we call voice quality.

9   Consonants and vowels are the building blocks of linguistic meaning, and slight changes in their quality inherently carry large differences in meaning, which we detect immediately. *Bought, bat, bet, bait* is a four-way distinction for an English speaker, but may only be a two-way distinction for a Spanish or Japanese speaker. Differences in vowels can make dialects of English incomprehensible even to each other at first. An American pronunciation of "John" can sound like "Jan" to a Scot; and a Scots pronunciation of "John" can sound like "Joan" to an American. Consonants are also critical in deciding the meaning of a word. The American who asked if she could clear away some "bottles" was understood by the pub owner in Scotland to have said "barrels," not only because of the vowel but also because the d-like pronunciation of the t-sound is almost exactly like the d-like pronunciation of the rolled r in Scots. Again, it is the speaker generating the utterance who thinks

primarily in terms of meaning and not in terms of the sounds being used to transmit that meaning. It is the hearer who must translate the incoming speech sounds into new, meaningful units (which we usually call words) and who cannot help but notice that the signals coming in are patterned differently from the hearer's own system of speech sounds. Confusion over the meaning of a word can only highlight these differences, making the translation of meaning more difficult and making each participant in the conversation feel that the other has an accent. The impression is therefore mutual.

10   Another meaningful component of accent is intonation or the "melody" of speech. Differences in the rises and falls of intonation patterns, and the rhythmic beat that accompanies them, can be as significant as differences in the melodies of tunes that we recognize or in the beat of a waltz compared to a jig. One of the characteristics of the American comedian Richard Pryor's ability to switch from "white talk" to "black talk" is the control of the height and of the rising and falling of the pitch of the voice. Even more rapid timing of these rises and falls is an indication of languages such as Swedish and languages such as Chinese which have different tones, that is, pitches that distinguish word meanings from each other. Pitch can have the greatest effect on our impression of an accent or on our ability to recognize a voice. Our mood—whether we are excited or angry or sad—can change the sound of our voice, as the tempo of our speech also speeds up or slows down, so that we may sound like a different person.

11   Voice quality is the ensemble of more or less permanent elements that appear to remain constant in a person's speech. This is how we recognize a friend's voice on the telephone even if they only utter a syllable. Some voices are nasal; others low and resonant; others breathy; and still others higher pitched and squeaky. Presumably, the better we know a person, the less we feel they have a noticeable accent. Naturally, however, if they didn't have a distinguishable ensemble of accent features, we couldn't tell their voice apart from other people's. Travelers to a foreign country often experience an inability to tell individual speakers of a foreign language apart. As it once did in our native language, this ability comes with practice, that is, with exposure. The reason is that we need time to distinguish, first, to which strand of accent each particular speech gesture belongs and, second, which speech details are common to most speakers of that language and which belong only to the individual. Unless the individual's speech stands out in some remarkable way, we are likely to perceive the collection of common, group traits first.

12   Much of our perception of accent could actually be visual. Hand and facial gestures which accompany speech could cue a listener that the speaker comes from a different place, so that we expect the person to sound different from our norm. If we expect to hear an accent, we probably will. Sooner or later, wherever they live, most people encounter someone from another place. A stranger from out of town, a foreigner, even a person who had moved away and returned. But even in the same community, people from different social groups or of different ages can be distinguished on the basis of their speech. One of the intriguing linguistic aspects of police work is to locate and identify suspects on the basis of their accent. Often, this technique comes down to the skill of being able to notice details of speech that other observers overlook. Sometimes, an academic approach such as broadcasting a voice to a large number of "judges" over the radio or on television is necessitated.

In this case, an anonymous suspect can often be narrowed down as coming from a particular area or even identified outright. Computer programs are also having moderate success at verifying individual speakers on the basis of their accent. These techniques are sometimes called "voiceprints," implying that each individual is unique, but as with human listeners, success may depend on how much speech from the individual can be heard and in how many contexts.

13   One of the most popular characterizations of the notion of accent modification has been George Bernard Shaw's *Pygmalion*, revived on stage and screen as *My Fair Lady*. The phonetician, Professor Higgins, is renowned for tracing the course of people's lives from their accents, and Eliza Doolittle, at the opposite extreme, while probably aware of different accents and able to identify them to some degree, appears at first quite unable to produce speech in anything other than her local-dialect accent. The transformation of Eliza, explained in sociolinguistic terms, is the apparent result of her accommodation to a new social milieu and her acceptance of a new role for herself. In terms of constructivist psychology, she co-constructed a new reality—a new story—for her life and left the old story behind. The transformation had its physical effect (she was no longer recognized in her former neighborhood) as well as its linguistic realization (her accent changed to suit her new surroundings). We all leave parts of the speaking style of our early years behind, while we adopt new patterns more suited to our later years. Whether we change a lot or a little depends on individual choices within a web of social circumstance.

THINKING CRITICALLY

1. What do we mean when we say that someone doesn't have an accent? Is there a type of English that we seem to recognize as "accentless"? Why, according to the author, is such a determination false?

2. Consider the title of Esling's essay. How does it connect to his essay's thesis? Why do so many people feel that they don't have an accent? Explain.

3. Before reading this essay, how would you have described your accent? Would you have said you had one? After responding to this question, ask a friend or classmate from a different part of the country if they would agree with your assessment.

4. What stereotypes are associated with accents? Try to identify as many accents as you can think of and what stereotypes you associate with them.

5. Have you ever made presumptions about a person based on his or her accent? How did the phonetic elements Esling describes, such as intonation, pronunciation of consonants and vowels, and voice quality influence your judgment? Why do we use these phonetic cues to form opinions about other people?

6. According to the author, what makes it possible for us to distinguish accents? Why can't we distinguish our own?

WRITING ASSIGNMENTS

1. In his opening paragraph, Esling comments that accent serves as a "map" that tells others many things about us, including where we come from, our age, gender, education, and background. Write an essay in which you explore the relationship between accent and how we judge others. Do you judge people by how

they speak? Is it automatic? Have you ever been wrong? Why do we tend to judge people by their accents?

2. At the end of his essay, Esling refers to George Bernard Shaw's play, *Pygmalion*. Read the preface Shaw wrote regarding the subject matter and the social commentary behind his story at www.bartleby.com/138/0.html, in which he notes, "it is impossible for an Englishman to open his mouth without making some other Englishman hate or despise him." What did Shaw mean by this statement? Does his observation hold any truth for Americans today? Why or why not? Explain.

Viva Spanglish!

Lilly Gonzales

Spanglish is a combining of Spanish and English words or parts of words that some people say is becoming a language itself. It is spoken primarlily in areas of the United States immersed in both English and Spanish, such as the U.S.-Mexico border, and in bilingual communities in Southern California, Texas, Miami, Florida, and New York City. Spanglish authority Ilan Stavans, the author of *The Sounds of Spanglish: The Making of a New American Language* (2003), notes that it is spoken by many of the approximately 35 million people of Hispanic descent in the United States. He attributes criticism of Spanglish to the status quo's fear of an "overall hispanización of society" in which Spanish is infiltrating English. In this next essay, Lilly Gonzales explains how her "hybrid language" of English and Spanish may get her "critical glares" or even pity, but she has no intentions of giving up what she considers her native tongue.

Lilly Gonzales grew up on the Texas-Mexico border. This editorial first appeared in the October 2001 issue of *Texas Monthly*.

1 It was 1985 and I was in a pre-kindergarten class at Palmer Elementary in the small South Texas town of Pharr. My teacher, Mrs. Herrera, thought I didn't know any English, and I had no plans to let her know I did (thanks to my eldest sister, who had made sure I knew English before I entered school). All the other kids in my class spoke only Spanish; I didn't want to be the conceited one who spoke in English. Then one day Mrs. Herrera stumped me with a question I couldn't answer in Spanish. I was forced to say it in English—and just like that, my secret was out. When my Spanish-speaking mother wanted to know why I had refused to speak English in school, I was stumped again. The Spanish word for "embarrassed" (avergonzada) wouldn't come to me, so I tried a translation based on phonetics and told her I had been too embarazada. I thought she'd understand my little Spanglish invention, but she just burst out laughing. I, her four-year-old daughter, had just told her I was too pregnant to speak English.

2 And that was my first experience with Spanglish, a hybrid of English and Spanish used by U.S. Latinos who live between two coexisting worlds (Mexican Americans, for example). It wouldn't be the last time Spanglish backfired on me. In fact, every time I'm surrounded by native Spanish speakers, I pray that my Spanglish doesn't intrude into the conversation. But it usually does, and the Spanish pros either

smile at me with a pitying look that says I've lost touch with my heritage or glare critically at me as if I've just raped their language.

3   Strangers usually give me the pity smile. At Mexican restaurants, if my server is Latino and my Spanish sounds less than perfect, I'm rewarded with it. God forbid I should ask for el menu de lonche (Spanglish for "lunch menu") instead of the proper menu de almuerzo. I encountered the pity smile when I met my boyfriend's mother for the first time. She speaks flawless Spanish, so naturally I was terrified. Around my third Spanish sentence, my Spanglish popped out. "Nunca hay donde parquear (There's never anywhere to park)," I said, wincing as soon as I had said that last word. Parquear is Spanglish for the Spanish estacionar. She gave me the pity smile.

4   Those who know me better give me the critical glare. I hate the critical glare. Every time my family heads to Mexico to visit relatives, I dread the inevitable. I'll be talking with my cousins and my Spanglish will trickle into my otherwise fluent Spanish. They'll call me pocha, which means "sellout." In my Spanish literature classes at Northwestern University, near Chicago, there's added pressure to speak perfect Spanish. Professors jeer when I speak up in class and Spanglish flows out of my mouth.

5   Don't they understand that Spanglish is my native tongue? I grew up on the Texas-Mexico border with both Spanish and English, and my Spanglish is the product of that. I spoke Spanish with my parents, Spanglish with my siblings and friends, and English with everyone else. My thoughts are in Spanglish.

6   I left Texas to go to Northwestern in 1998, but every time I hear Spanglish, I feel I'm home again. There's no better icebreaker than discovering that you and a stranger both speak it. It carries an implicit understanding of each other's background (immigrant parents, bilingual environment) and plight (trying to make it in a country where Latinos are still a minority). Suddenly, you're amigos, and you're dancing effortlessly between the two languages. At Latino nightclubs, Spanglish wins me friends in the ladies' room. Wherever the employees are Spanglish-speaking Latinos, it gets me perks. And at Northwestern, it has given me my best friends. I was in a dorm hallway my freshman year when I heard them speaking Spanglish, and I impulsively poked my head in their room and joined their conversation. They didn't mind—Spanglish speakers embrace other Spanglish speakers. It's an unwritten law.

7   And that's why I refuse to give it up, despite the pity smile and the critical glare. I've had a lifetime love affair with Spanglish, embarazada or not.

THINKING CRITICALLY

1. According to Gonzales, who speaks "Spanglish" and why?

2. How did Spanglish evolve for Gonzales? What happens when she speaks it to "flawless" Spanish speakers? How does she feel about her use of Spanglish?

3. Gonzales explains that "Spanglish is my native tongue" and that even her "thoughts are in Spanglish." Think for a moment about the language of your thoughts—are they in a particular language? A version of English? Another language entirely? Explain.

WRITING ASSIGNMENTS

1. The author explains that Spanglish is an icebreaker that allows two people who both speak it to instantly understand each other's background and history. What does your language reveal about you and your background? Have you ever traveled and heard someone speak with the same accent as you or use words or expressions unique to your own cultural background? How did you feel? Explain.

2. Gonzales comments that her Spanish relatives call her a "sellout" for speaking Spanglish? What does she mean? Is such pressure to withstand the influence of English surprising? Write an essay in which you explore the importance of language to one's cultural heritage and identity.

Good English and Bad
Bill Bryson

More than one billion people in the world speak English, and much of the rest of the world is attempting to. But as Paul Roberts explains in his essay in Chapter 1, the English language, with its various historical influences, is deceptively complex. Even language authorities will stumble over its idiosyncrasies. And the reason is simple: In an effort to establish criteria for *good* English for generations to come, seventeenth-century grammarians wrote rules of English modeled on those of Latin, which, though dead, was considered the most admirable and purest tongue. But as Bill Bryson explains, imposing Latin rules on English is like asking people to play baseball according to the rules of football. They don't go together; likewise, ancient standards of usage don't always describe how the language works today. In this lively and engaging discussion, Bryson explains how the distinction of *good* English from *bad* English is mostly a matter of conditioning and prejudice.

Bill Bryson is an American journalist living in England. He has worked for the *Times* of London and the *Independent* also of London, and has written articles for the *New York Times, Esquire, GQ,* and other magazines. His books include *A Dictionary of Troublesome Words* (2004), *The Lost Continent: Travels in Small Town America* (1989), and the highly acclaimed *The Mother Tongue* (1990), from which this essay comes. His most recent book is the critically acclaimed *A Short History of Nearly Everything* (2003).

1 Consider the parts of speech. In Latin, the verb has up to 120 inflections. In English it never has more than five (e.g., *see, sees, saw, seeing, seen*) and often it gets by with just three (*hit, hits, hitting*). Instead of using loads of different verb forms, we use just a few forms but employ them in loads of ways. We need just five inflections to deal with the act of propelling a car—*drive, drives, drove, driving*, and *driven*—yet with these we can express quite complex and subtle variations of tense: "I drive to work every day," "I have been driving since I was sixteen," "I will have driven 20,000 miles by the end of this year." This system, for all its ease of use, makes labeling difficult. According to any textbook, the present tense of the verb *drive* is *drive*. Every junior high school pupil knows that. Yet if we say, "I used to drive to

work but now I don't," we are clearly using the present tense *drive* in a past tense sense. Equally if we say, "I will drive you to work tomorrow," we are using it in a future sense. And if we say, "I would drive if I could afford to," we are using it in a conditional sense. In fact, almost the only form of sentence in which we cannot use the present tense form of *drive* is, yes, the present tense. When we need to indicate an action going on right now, we must use the participial form *driving*. We don't say, "I drive the car now," but rather "I'm driving the car now." Not to put too fine a point on it, the labels are largely meaningless.

2   We seldom stop to think about it, but some of the most basic concepts in English are naggingly difficult to define. What, for instance, is a sentence? Most dictionaries define it broadly as a group of words constituting a full thought and containing, at a minimum, a subject (basically a noun) and predicate (basically a verb). Yet if I inform you that I have just crashed your car and you reply, "What!" or "Where?" or "How!" you have clearly expressed a complete thought, uttered a sentence. But where are the subject and predicate? Where are the noun and verb, not to mention the prepositions, conjunctions, articles, and other components that we normally expect to find in a sentence? To get around this problem, grammarians pretend that such sentences contain words that aren't there. "What!" they would say, really means "What are you telling me—you crashed my car?" while "Where?" is a shorthand rendering of "Where did you crash it?" and "How?" translates as "How on earth did you manage to do that, you old devil you?" or words to that effect. The process is called *ellipsis* and is certainly very nifty. Would that I could do the same with my bank account. Yet the inescapable fact is that it is possible to make such sentences conform to grammatical precepts only by bending the rules. When I was growing up we called that cheating.

3   In English, in short, we possess a language in which the parts of speech are almost entirely notional. A noun is a noun and a verb is a verb largely because the grammarians say they are. In the sentence "I am suffering terribly" *suffering* is a verb, but in "My suffering is terrible," it is a noun. Yet both sentences use precisely the same word to express precisely the same idea. *Quickly* and *sleepily* are adverbs but *sickly* and *deadly* are adjectives. *Breaking* is a present tense participle, but as often as not it is used in a past tense sense ("He was breaking the window when I saw him"). *Broken*, on the other hand, is a past tense participle but as often as not it is employed in a present tense sense ("I think I've just broken my toe") or even future tense sense ("If he wins the next race, he'll have broken the school record"). To deal with all the anomalies, the parts of speech must be so broadly defined as to be almost meaningless. A noun, for example, is generally said to be a word that denotes a person, place, thing, action, or quality. That would seem to cover almost everything, yet clearly most actions are verbs and many words that denote qualities—*brave, foolish, good*—are adjectives.

4   The complexities of English are such that the authorities themselves often stumble. Each of the following, penned by an expert, contains a usage that at least some of his colleagues would consider quite wrong.

> "Prestige is one of the few words that has had an experience opposite to that described in 'Worsened Words.'" (H. W. Fowler, *A Dictionary of*

Modern English Usage, second edition) It should be "one of the few words that *have* had."

"Each of the variants indicated in boldface type count as an entry." (*The Harper Dictionary of Contemporary Usage*) It should be "each . . . *counts.*"

"It is of interest to speculate about the amount of dislocation to the spelling system that would occur if English dictionaries were either proscribed or (as when Malory or Sir Philip Sidney were writing) did not exist." (Robert Burchfield, *The English Language*) Make it "*was* writing."

"A range of sentences forming statements, commands, questions and exclamations cause us to draw on a more sophisticated battery of orderings and arrangements." (Robert Burchfield, *The English Language*) It should be *causes.*

"The prevalence of incorrect instances of the use of the apostrophe . . . together with the abandonment of it by many business firms . . . suggest that the time is close at hand when this moderately useful device should be abandoned." (Robert Burchfield, *The English Language*) The verb should be *suggests.*

"If a lot of the available dialect data is obsolete or almost so, a lot more of it is far too sparse to support any sort of reliable conclusion." (Robert Claiborne, *Our Marvelous Native Tongue*) *Data* is a plural.

"His system of citing examples of the best authorities, of indicating etymology, and pronunciation, are still followed by lexicographers." (Philip Howard, *The State of the Language*) His system *are*?

"When his fellowship expired he was offered a rectorship at Boxworth . . . on condition that he married the deceased rector's daughter." (Robert McCrum, et al., *The Story of English*) A misuse of the subjunctive: It should be "on condition that he marry."

5   English grammar is so complex and confusing for the one very simple reason that its rules and terminology are based on Latin—a language with which it has precious little in common. In Latin, to take one example, it is not possible to split an infinitive. So in English, the early authorities decided, it should not be possible to split an infinitive either. But there is no reason why we shouldn't, any more than we should forsake instant coffee and air travel because they weren't available to the Romans. Making English grammar conform to Latin rules is like asking people to play baseball using the rules of football. It is a patent absurdity. But once this insane notion became established grammarians found themselves having to draw up ever more complicated and circular arguments to accommodate the inconsistencies. As Burchfield notes in *The English Language,* one authority. F. Th. Visser, found it necessary to devote 200 pages to discussing just one aspect of the present participle. That is as crazy as it is amazing.

6   The early authorities not only used Latin grammar as their model, but actually went to the almost farcical length of writing English grammars in that language,

as with Sir Thomas Smith's *De Recta et Emendata Linguae Anglicae Scriptione Dialogus* (1568), Alexander Gil's *Logonomia Anglica* (1619), and John Wallis's *Grammatica Linguae Anglicanae* of 1653 (though even he accepted that the grammar of Latin was ill-suited to English). For the longest time it was taken entirely for granted that the classical languages *must* serve as models. Dryden spoke for an age when he boasted that he often translated his sentences into Latin to help him decide how best to express them in English.

7   In 1660, Dryden complained that English had "not so much as a tolerable dictionary or a grammar; so our language is in a manner barbarous." He believed there should be an academy to regulate English usage, and for the next two centuries many others would echo his view. In 1664, The Royal Society for the Advancement of Experimental Philosophy formed a committee "to improve the English tongue," though nothing lasting seems to have come of it. Thirty-three years later in his *Essay Upon Projects*, Daniel Defoe was calling for an academy to oversee the language. In 1712, Jonathan Swift joined the chorus with a *Proposal for Correcting, Improving and Ascertaining the English Tongue.* Some indication of the strength of feeling attached to these matters is given by the fact that in 1780, in the midst of the American Revolution, John Adams wrote to the president of Congress appealing to him to set up an academy for the purpose of "refining, correcting, improving and ascertaining the English language" (a title that closely echoes, not to say plagiarizes, Swift's pamphlet of sixty-eight years before). In 1806, the American Congress considered a bill to institute a national academy and in 1820 an American Academy of Language and Belles Lettres, presided over by John Quincy Adams, was formed, though again without any resounding perpetual benefits to users of the language. And there were many other such proposals and assemblies.

8   The model for all these was the Académie Française, founded by Cardinal Richelieu in 1635. In its youth, the academy was an ambitious motivator of change. In 1762, after many years of work, it published a dictionary that regularized the spellings of some 5,000 words—almost a quarter of the words then in common use. It took the *s* out of words like *estre* and *fenestre*, making them *[ace]tre* and *fen[ace]tre*, and it turned *roy* and *loy* into *roi* and *loi*. In recent decades, however, the academy has been associated with an almost ayatollah-like conservatism. When in December 1988 over 90 percent of French schoolteachers voted in favor of a proposal to introduce the sort of spelling reforms the academy itself had introduced 200 years earlier, the forty venerable members of the academy were, to quote the London Sunday *Times*, "up in apoplectic arms" at the thought of tampering with something as sacred as French spelling. Such is the way of the world. Among the changes the teachers wanted and the academicians did not were the removal of the circumflex on *[ace]tre, fen[ace]tre*, and other such words, and taking the -*x* off plurals such as *bureaux, chevaux*, and *chateaux* and replacing it with an -*s*.

9   Such actions underline the one almost inevitable shortcoming of national academies. However progressive and far-seeing they may be to begin with, they almost always exert over time a depressive effect on change. So it is probably fortunate that the English-speaking world never saddled itself such a body, largely because as many influential users of English were opposed to academies as favored them.

Samuel Johnson doubted the prospects of arresting change and Thomas Jefferson thought it in any case undesirable. In declining an offer to be the first honorary president of the Academy of Language and Belles Lettres, he noted that had such a body been formed in the days of the Anglo-Saxons English would now be unable to describe the modern world. Joseph Priestley, the English scientist, grammarian, and theologian, spoke perhaps most eloquently against the formation of an academy when he said in 1761 that it was "unsuitable to the genius of a free nation. . . . We need make no doubt but that the best forms of speech will, in time, establish themselves by their own superior excellence: and in all controversies, it is better to wait the decisions of time, which are slow and sure, than to take those of synods, which are often hasty and injudicious." [Quoted by Baugh and Cable, page 269]

10   English is often commended by outsiders for its lack of a stultifying authority. Otto Jespersen as long ago as 1905 was praising English for its lack of rigidity, its happy air of casualness. Likening French to the severe and formal gardens of Louis XIV, he contrasted it with English, which he said was "laid out seemingly without any definite plan, and in which you are allowed to walk everywhere according to your own fancy without having to fear a stern keeper enforcing rigorous regulations." [*Growth and Structure of the English Language*, page 16]

11   Without an official academy to guide us, the English-speaking world has long relied on self-appointed authorities such as the brothers H. W. and F. G. Fowler and Sir Ernest Gowers in Britain and Theodore Bernstein and William Safire in America, and of course countless others. These figures write books, give lectures, and otherwise do what they can (i.e., next to nothing) to try to stanch (not staunch) the perceived decline of the language. They point out that there is a useful distinction to be observed between *uninterested* and *disinterested*, between *imply* and *infer, flaunt* and *flout, fortunate* and *fortuitous, forgo* and *forego*, and *discomfort* and *discomfit* (not forgetting *stanch* and *staunch*). They point out that *fulsome*, properly used, is a term of abuse, not praise, that *peruse* actually means to read thoroughly, not glance through, that *data* and *media* are plurals. And from the highest offices in the land they are ignored.

12   In the late 1970s, President Jimmy Carter betrayed a flaw in his linguistic armory when he said: "The government of Iran must realize that it cannot flaunt, with impunity, the expressed will and law of the world community." *Flaunt* means to show off; he meant *flout*. The day after he was elected president in 1988, George Bush told a television reporter he couldn't believe the enormity of what had happened. Had President-elect Bush known that the primary meaning of *enormity* is wickedness or evilness, he would doubtless have selected a more apt term.

13   When this process of change can be seen happening in our lifetimes, it is almost always greeted with cries of despair and alarm. Yet such change is both continuous and inevitable. Few acts are more salutary than looking at the writings of language authorities from recent decades and seeing the usages that heightened their hackles. In 1931, H. W. Fowler was tutting over *racial*, which he called "an ugly word, the strangeness of which is due to our instinctive feeling that the termination -al has no business at the end of a word that is not obviously Latin." (For similar reasons he disliked *television* and *speedometer*.) Other authorities have variously—and sometimes

hotly—attacked *enthuse, commentate, emote, prestigious, contact* as a verb, *chair* as a verb, and scores of others. But of course these are nothing more than opinions, and, as is the way with other people's opinions, they are generally ignored.

14   So if there are no officially appointed guardians for the English language, who sets down all those rules that we all know about from childhood—the idea that we must never end a sentence with a preposition or begin one with a conjunction, that we must use *each other* for two things and *one another* for more than two, and that we must never use *hopefully* in an absolute sense, such as "Hopefully it will not rain tomorrow"? The answer, surprisingly often, is that no one does, that when you look into the background of these "rules" there is often little basis for them.

15   Consider the curiously persistent notion that sentences should not end with a preposition. The source of this stricture, and several other equally dubious ones, was one Robert Lowth, an eighteenth-century clergyman and amateur grammarian whose *A Short Introduction to English Grammar,* published in 1762, enjoyed a long and distressingly influential life both in his native England and abroad. It is to Lowth we can trace many a pedant's most treasured notions: the belief that you must say *different from* rather than than *different to* or *different than*, the idea that two negatives make a positive, the rule that you must not say "the heaviest of the two objects," but rather "the heavier," the distinction between *shall* and *will*, and the clearly nonsensical belief that *between* can apply only to two things and *among* to more than two. (By this reasoning, it would not be possible to say that St. Louis is between New York, Los Angeles, and Chicago, but rather that it is among them, which would impart a quite different sense.) Perhaps the most remarkable and curiously enduring of Lowth's many beliefs was the conviction that sentences ought not to end with a preposition. But even he was not didactic about it. He recognized that ending a sentence with a preposition was idiomatic and common in both speech and informal writing. He suggested only that he thought it generally better and more graceful, not crucial, to place the preposition before its relative "in solemn and elevated" writing. Within a hundred years this had been converted from a piece of questionable advice into an immutable rule. In a remarkable outburst of literal-mindedness, nineteenth-century academics took it as read that the very name *pre-position* meant it must come before something— anything.

16   But then this was a period of the most resplendent silliness, when grammarians and scholars seemed to be climbing over one another (or each other; it doesn't really matter) in a mad scramble to come up with fresh absurdities. This was the age when, it was gravely insisted, Shakespeare's *laughable* ought to be changed to *laugh-at-able* and *reliable* should be made into *relionable*. Dozens of seemingly unexceptional words—*lengthy, standpoint, international, colonial, brash*—were attacked with venom because of some supposed etymological deficiency or other. Thomas de Quincey, in between bouts of opium taking, found time to attack the expression *what on earth*. Some people wrote *mooned* for *lunatic* and *foresayer* for *prophet* on the grounds that the new words were Anglo-Saxon and thus somehow more pure. They roundly castigated those ignoramuses who impurely combined

Greek and Latin roots into new words like *petroleum* (Latin *petro* + Greek *oleum*). In doing so, they failed to note that the very word with which they described themselves, *grammarians*, is itself a hybrid made of Greek and Latin roots, as are many other words that have lived unexceptionably in English for centuries. They even attacked *handbook* as an ugly Germanic compound when it dared to show its face in the nineteenth century, failing to notice that it was a good Old English word that had simply fallen out of use. It is one of the felicities of English that we can take pieces of words from all over and fuse them into new constructions—like *trusteeship*, which consists of a Nordic stem (*trust*), combined with a French affix (*ee*), married to an Old English root (*ship*). Other languages cannot do this. We should be proud of ourselves for our ingenuity and yet even now authorities commonly attack almost any new construction as ugly or barbaric.

17   Today in England you can still find authorities attacking the construction *different than* as a regrettable Americanism, insisting that a sentence such as "How different things appear in Washington than in London" is ungrammatical and should be changed to "How different things appear in Washington from how they appear in London." Yet *different than* has been common in England for centuries and used by such exalted writers as Defoe, Addison, Steele, Dickens, Coleridge, and Thackeray, among others. Other authorities, in both Britain and America, continue to deride the absolute use of *hopefully. The New York Times Manual of Style and Usage* flatly forbids it. Its writers must not say, "Hopefully the sun will come out soon," but rather are instructed to resort to a clumsily passive and periphrastic construction such as "It is to be hoped that the sun will come out soon." The reason? The authorities maintain that *hopefully* in the first sentence is a misplaced modal auxiliary—that it doesn't belong to any other part of the sentence. Yet they raise no objection to dozens of other words being used in precisely the same unattached way—*admittedly, mercifully, happily, curiously*, and so on. The reason *hopefully* is not allowed is because, well, because somebody at the *New York Times* once had a boss who wouldn't allow it because his professor had forbidden it, because *his* father thought it was ugly and inelegant, because *he* had been told so by his uncle who was a man of great learning . . . and so on.

18   Considerations of what makes for good English or bad English are to an uncomfortably large extent matters of prejudice and conditioning. Until the eighteenth century it was correct to say "you was" if you were referring to one person. It sounds odd today, but the logic is impeccable. *Was* is a singular verb and *were* a plural one. Why should *you* take a plural verb when the sense is clearly singular? The answer—surprise, surprise—is that Robert Lowth didn't like it. "I'm hurrying, are I not?" is hopelessly ungrammatical, but "I'm hurrying, aren't I?"—merely a contraction of the same words—is perfect English. *Many* is almost always a plural (as in "Many people were there"), but not when it is followed by *a,* as in "Many a man was there." There's no inherent reason why these things should be so. They are not defensible in terms of grammar. They are because they are.

19   Nothing illustrates the scope of prejudice in English between than the issue of the split infinitive. Some people feel ridiculously strong about it. When the British Conservative politician Jock Bruce-Gardyne was economic secretary to

the Treasury in the early 1980s, he returned unread any departmental correspondence containing a split infinitive. (It should perhaps be pointed out that a split
infinitive is one in which an adverb comes between *to* and a verb, as in *to quickly
look*.) I can think of two very good reasons for not splitting an infinitive.

1. Because you feel that the rulers of English ought to conform to the grammatical
   precepts of a language that died a thousand years ago.

2. Because you wish to cling to a pointless affectation of usage that is without the
   support of any recognized authority of the last 200 years, even at the cost of
   composing sentences that are ambiguous, inelegant, and patently contorted.

20   It is exceedingly difficult to find any authority who condemns the split infinitive—Theodore Bernstein, H. W. Fowler, Ernest Gowers, Eric Partridge, Rudolph
Flesch, Wilson Follett, Roy H. Copperud, and others too tedious to enumerate here
all agree that there is no logical reason not to split an infinitive. Otto Jespersen even
suggests that, strictly speaking, it isn't actually possible to split an infinitive. As
he puts it: "'To' . . . is no more an essential part of an infinitive than the definite
article is an essential part of a nominative, and no one would think of calling 'the
good man' a split nominative." [*Growth and Structure of the English Language,*
page 222]

21   Lacking an academy as we do, we might expect dictionaries to take up the
banner of defenders of the language, but in recent years they have increasingly
shied away from the role. A perennial argument with dictionary makers is whether
they should be *prescriptive* (that is, whether they should prescribe how language
should be used) or *descriptive* (that is, merely describe how it is used without
taking a position). The most notorious example of the descriptive school was the
1961 *Webster's Third New International Dictionary* (popularly called *Webster's
Unabridged*), whose editor, Philip Gove, believed that distinctions of usage were
elitist and artificial. As a result, usages such as *imply* as a synonym for *infer* and
flout being used in the sense of *flaunt* were included without comment. The dictionary provoked further antagonism, particularly among members of the U.S. Trademark Association, by refusing to capitalize trademarked words. But what really
excited outrage was its remarkable contention that *ain't* was "used orally in most
parts of the U.S. by many cultivated speakers."

22   So disgusted was the *New York Times* with the new dictionary that it announced
it would not use it but would continue with the 1934 edition, prompting the language authority Bergen Evans to write: "Anyone who solemnly announces in the
year 1962 that he will be guided in matters of English usage by a dictionary published in 1934 is talking ignorant and pretentious nonsense," and he pointed out that
the issue of the *Times* announcing the decision contained nineteen words condemned by the *Second International.*

23   Since then, other dictionaries have been divided on the matter. *The American
Heritage Dictionary,* first published in 1969, instituted a usage panel of distinguished commentators to rule on contentious points of usage, which are discussed,
often at some length, in the text. But others have been more equivocal (or prudent

or spineless depending on how you view it). The revised *Random House Dictionary of the English Language*, published in 1987, accepts the looser meaning for most words, though often noting that the newer usage is frowned on "by many"—a curiously timid approach that at once acknowledges the existence of expert opinion and yet constantly places it at a distance. Among the looser meanings it accepts are *disinterested* to mean *uninterested* and *infer* to mean *imply*. It even accepts the existence of *kudo* as a singular—prompting a reviewer from *Time Magazine* to ask if one instance of pathos should now be a patho.

24   It's a fine issue. One of the undoubted virtues of English is that it is a fluid and democratic language in which meanings shift and change in response to the pressures of common usage rather than the dictates of committees. It is a natural process that has been going on for centuries. To interfere with that process is arguably both arrogant and futile, since clearly the weight of usage will push new meanings into currency no matter how many authorities hurl themselves into the path of change.

25   But at the same time, it seems to me, there is a case for resisting change—at least slapdash change. Even the most liberal descriptivist would accept that there must be *some* conventions of usage. WE must agree to spell *cat* c-a-t and not e-l-e-p-h-a-n-t, and we must agree that by that word we mean a small furry quadruped that goes *meow* and sits comfortably on one's lap and not a large lumbering beast that grows tusks and is exceedingly difficult to housebreak. In precisely the same way, clarity is generally better served if we agree to observe a distinction between *imply* and *infer, forego* and *forgo, fortuitous* and *fortunate, uninterested* and *disinterested*, and many others. As John Ciardi observed, resistance may in the end prove futile, but at least it tests the changes and makes them prove their worth.

26   Perhaps for our last words on the subject of usage we should turn to the last words of the venerable French grammarian Dominique Bonhours, who proved on his deathbed that a grammarian's work is never done when he turned to those gathered loyally around him and whispered: "I am about to—or I am going to—die; either expression is used."

THINKING CRITICALLY

1. How did early grammarians help shape the rules of current usage? According to Bryson, how did they contribute to some of the idiosyncrasies of English rules? Give some examples of rules formulated by early grammarians that do not work.

2. Given all the anomalies in the English language, what is the author suggesting about standards of usage? How does his discussion make you feel about your own lapses in grammar?

3. What, according to Bryson, is the difference between "good English" and "bad English"? What is his basis of distinction? Do you agree with his views?

4. Bryson reports that for centuries grammarians called for the official regulation of English usage. What fundamental attitudes about language did these proposals underscore? What about the attitudes of Thomas Jefferson and Joseph Priestley? Where does Bryson stand on the issue of regulation?

5. What kind of personality does Bryson project in this essay? In other words, based on his tone, word choice, his style, the examples he chooses, his comments, and so on, how would you describe him?

6. What examples of Bryson's sense of humor can you point to? How does his humor contribute to the essay? Is this a strategy you might employ in your writing?

7. How would you evaluate Bryson's own use of English? How might Bryson respond to the criticism that while defending nonstandard usage, his own writing strictly obeys the rules of traditional usage?

WRITING ASSIGNMENTS

1. Do you think that dictionaries should be prescriptive instead of descriptive—that is, should they take a position on the traditional rules of proper grammar, usage, and spelling? Write a letter to Bill Bryson explaining how you feel about this and give three specific reasons.

2. Have you ever been bothered by someone's poor grammar or usage? If so, describe in a brief essay your experience and your feelings. Has this essay affected your attitude at all? Explain.

3. If you heard the president or some other official make grammatical and usage errors in an interview, would that affect your view of that person? Would it make him or her seem less deserving of your respect or seem more down-to-earth? Write out your thoughts in an essay, perhaps citing some examples of faulty presidential usage you've found on your own.

MAKING CONNECTIONS

1. As best you can, try to describe your own English usage. Do you think that you speak "good English"? How would the various authors from this section respond to your form of usage? Explain.

2. Now that you have read the different perspectives concerning "standard English," write an essay on where you stand on the issue. Do you think we need language guardians such as John Simon? Is English a changing and malleable medium to which we must adapt according to popular opinion? Do you think we have a right to use whatever form of English we choose?

3. Consider the English language education you received in school. Was it prescriptive, or did it allow for more flexibility? Did you learn the rules of grammar and sentence structure? Has this instruction helped you in your daily life? Was your academic language useful to you as a writer and thinker, or has it proven largely unnecessary? Explain.

4. What is the difference between "good English" and "real English"? In your opinion, should one be used in certain cases and not in others? Explain.

5. Do you think you have an accent? Can you hear yourself speak it? Do you know anyone who claims not to have an accent? What do they mean? Are they accurate in their assessment of their speech? Write an essay in which you explore the concept of the accent in your local area and the way people react to speech. Is one way of speaking considered more educated or intelligent than another?

SHOULD ENGLISH BE THE OFFICIAL LANGUAGE OF THE USA?

Bilingualism in America: English Should Be the Only Language

S. I. Hayakawa

The late S. I. Hayakawa was a leading advocate of the English-only movement. A former U.S. senator from California and a professor of linguistics who published several books on language, Hayakawa was born in Vancouver, British Columbia, to Japanese parents. Hayakawa served as honorary chairman of U.S. English, a public-interest organization based in Washington, D.C., that is working to establish English as the nation's only official language.

In this essay, Hayakawa explains why he feels that English must be the only recognized official language of the United States. This article originally appeared in *USA Today* magazine in July of 1989, by which time English had been made the official language in 17 states.

1 During the dark days of World War II, Chinese immigrants in California wore badges proclaiming their original nationality so they would not be mistaken for Japanese. In fact, these two immigrant groups long had been at odds with each other. However, as new English-speaking generations came along, the Chinese and Japanese began to communicate with one another. They found they had much in common and began to socialize. Today, they get together and form Asian-American societies.

2 Such are the amicable results of sharing the English language. English unites us as Americans—immigrants and native-born alike. Communicating with each other in a single, common tongue encourages trust, while reducing racial hostility and bigotry.

3 My appreciation of English has led me to devote my retirement years to championing it. Several years ago, I helped to establish U.S. English, a Washington, D.C.–based public interest group that seeks an amendment to the U.S. Constitution declaring English our official language, regardless of what other languages we may use unofficially.

4 As an immigrant to this nation, I am keenly aware of the things that bind us as Americans and unite us as a single people. Foremost among these unifying forces is the common language we share. While it is certainly true that our love of freedom and devotion to democratic principles help to unite and give as a mutual purpose, it is English, our common language, that enables us to discuss our views and allows us to maintain a well-informed electorate, the cornerstone of democratic government.

5 Because we are a nation of immigrants, we do not share the characteristics of race, religion, ethnicity, or native language which form the common bonds of

society in other countries. However, by agreeing to learn and use a single, universally spoken language, we have been able to forge a unified people from an incredibly diverse population.

6   Although our 200-year history should be enough to convince any skeptic of the powerful unifying effects of a common language, some still advocate the official recognition of other languages. They argue that a knowledge of English is not part of the formula for responsible citizenship in this country.

7   Some contemporary political leaders, like the former mayor of Miami, Maurice Ferre, maintain that "Language is not necessary to the system. Nowhere does our Constitution say that English is our language." He also told the *Tampa Tribune* that, "Within ten years there will not be a single word of English spoken [in Miami]—English is not Miami's official language—[and] one day residents will have to learn Spanish or leave."

8   The U.S. Department of Education also reported that countless speakers at a conference on bilingual education "expounded at length on the need for and eventually of, a multilingual, multicultural United States of America with a national language policy citing English and Spanish as the two 'legal languages.'"

9   As a former resident of California, I am completely familiar with a system that uses two official languages, and I would not advise any nation to move in such a direction unless forced to do so. While it is true that India functions with ten official languages, I haven't heard anyone suggest that it functions particularly well because of its multilingualism. In fact, most Indians will concede that the situation is a chaotic mess which has led to countless problems in the government's efforts to manage the nation's business. Out of necessity, English still is used extensively in India as a common language.

10   Belgium is another clear example of the diverse effects of two officially recognized languages in the same nation. Linguistic differences between Dutch- and French-speaking citizens have resulted in chronic political instability. Consequently, in the aftermath of the most recent government collapse, legislators are working on a plan to turn over most of its powers and responsibilities to the various regions, a clear recognition of the diverse effects of linguistic separateness.

11   There are other problems. Bilingualism is a costly and confusing bureaucratic nightmare. The Canadian government has estimated its bilingual costs to be nearly $400,000,000 per year. It is almost certain that these expenses will increase as a result of a massive expansion of bilingual services approved by the Canadian Parliament in 1988. In the United States, which has ten times the population of Canada, the cost of similar bilingual services easily would be in the billions.

12   We first should consider how politically infeasible it is that our nation ever could recognize Spanish as a second official language without opening the floodgates for official recognition of the more than 100 languages spoken in this country. How long would it take, under such an arrangement, before the United States started to make India look like a model of efficiency?

13   Even if we can agree that multilingualism would be a mistake, some would suggest that official recognition of English is not needed. After all, our nation has existed for over 200 years without this, and English as our common language has continued to flourish.

14   I could agree with this sentiment had government continued to adhere to its time-honored practice of operating in English and encouraging newcomers to learn the language. However, this is not the case. Over the last few decades, government has been edging slowly towards policies that place other languages on a par with English.

15   In reaction to the cultural consciousness movement of the 1960s and 1970s, government has been increasingly reluctant to press immigrants to learn the English language, lest it be accused of "cultural imperialism." Rather than insisting that it is the immigrant's duty to learn the language of this country, the government has acted instead as if it has a duty to accommodate an immigrant in his native language.

16   A prime example of this can be found in the continuing debate over Federal and state policies relating to bilingual education. At times, these have come danger-ously close to making the main goal of this program the maintenance of the immi-grant child's native language, rather than the early acquisition of English.

17   As a former U.S. senator from California, where we spend more on bilingual education programs than any other state, I am very familiar with both the rhetoric and reality that lie behind the current debate on bilingual education. My experience has convinced me that many of these programs are shortchanging immigrant chil-dren in their quest to learn English.

18   To set the record straight from the start, I do not oppose bilingual education *if it is truly bilingual.* Employing a child's native language to teach him (or her) English is entirely appropriate. What is not appropriate is continuing to use the children of Hispanic and other immigrant groups as guinea pigs in an unproven program that fails to teach English efficiently and perpetuates their dependency on their native language.

19   Under the dominant method of bilingual education used throughout this coun-try, non-English-speaking students are taught all academic subjects such as math, science, and history exclusively in their native language. English is taught as a sep-arate subject. The problem with this method is that there is no objective way to measure whether a child has learned enough English to be placed in classes where academic instruction is entirely in English. As a result, some children have been kept in native language classes for six years.

20   Some bilingual education advocates, who are more concerned with maintain-ing the child's use of their native language, may not see any problem with such a situation. However, those who feel that the most important goal of this program is to get children functioning quickly in English appropriately are alarmed.

21   In the Newhall School District in California, some Hispanic parents are raising their voices in criticism of its bilingual education program, which relies on native language instruction. Their children complain of systematically being segregated from their English-speaking peers. Now in high school, these students cite the fail-ure of the program to teach them English first as the reason for being years behind their classmates.

22   Even more alarming is the Berkeley (Calif.) Unified School District, where educators have recognized that all-native-language instruction would be an inade-quate response to the needs of their non-English-speaking pupils. Challenged by a student body that spoke more than four different languages and by budgetary

constraints, teachers and administrators responded with innovative language programs that utilized many methods of teaching English. That school district is now in court answering charges that the education they provided was inadequate because it did not provide transitional bilingual education for every non-English speaker. What was introduced 20 years ago as an experimental project has become— despite inconclusive research evidence—the only acceptable method of teaching for bilingual education advocates.

23   When one considers the nearly 50 percent dropout rate among Hispanic students (the largest group receiving this type of instruction), one wonders about their ability to function in the English-speaking mainstream of this country. The school system may have succeeded wonderfully in maintaining their native language, but if it failed to help them to master the English language fully, what is the benefit?

Alternatives

24 If this method of bilingual education is not the answer, are we forced to return to the old, discredited, sink-or-swim approach? No, we are not, since, as shown in Berkeley and other school districts, there are a number of alternative methods that have been proven effective, while avoiding the problems of all-native-language instruction.

25   Sheltered English and English as a Second Language (ESL) are just two pro-grams that have helped to get children quickly proficient in English. Yet, political recognition of the viability of alternate methods has been slow in coming. In 1988, we witnessed the first crack in the monolithic hold that native language instruction has had on bilingual education funds at the Federal level. In its reauthorization of Federal bilingual education, Congress voted to increase the percentage of funds available for alternate methods from four to 25 percent of the total. This is a great breakthrough, but we should not be satisfied until 100 percent of the funds are available for any program that effectively and quickly can get children functioning in English, regardless of the amount of native language instruction it uses.

26   My goal as a student of language and a former educator is to see all students succeed academically, no matter what language is spoken in their homes. I want to see immigrant students finish their high school education and be able to compete for college scholarships. To help achieve this goal, instruction in English should start as early as possible. Students should be moved into English mainstream classes in one or, at the very most, two years. They should not continue to be segre-gated year after year from their English-speaking peers.

27   Another highly visible shift in Federal policy that I feel demonstrates quite clearly the eroding support of government for our common language is the require-ment for bilingual voting ballots. Little evidence ever has been presented to show the need for ballots in other languages. Even prominent Hispanic organizations acknowledge that more than 90 percent of native-born Hispanics currently are fluent in English and more than half of that population is English monolingual.

28   Furthermore, if the proponents of bilingual ballots are correct when they claim that the absence of native language ballots prevents non-English-speaking citizens from exercising their right to vote, then current requirements are clearly unfair

because they provide assistance to certain groups of voters while ignoring others. Under current Federal law, native language ballots are required only for certain groups: those speaking Spanish, Asian, or Native American languages. European or African immigrants are not provided ballots in their native language, even in jurisdictions covered by the Voting Rights Act.

29   As sensitive as Americans have been to racism, especially since the days of the Civil Rights Movement, no one seems to have noticed the profound racism expressed in the amendment that created the "bilingual ballot." Brown people, like Mexicans and Puerto Ricans; red people, like American Indians; and yellow people, like the Japanese and Chinese, are assumed not to be smart enough to learn English. No provision is made, however, for non-English-speaking French-Canadians in Maine or Vermont, or Yiddish-speaking Hassidic Jews in Brooklyn, who are white and thus presumed to be able to learn English without difficulty.

30   Voters in San Francisco encountered ballots in Spanish and Chinese for the first time in the elections of 1980, much to their surprise, since authorizing legislation had been passed by Congress with almost no debate, roll-call vote, or public discussion. Naturalized Americans, who had taken the trouble to learn English to become citizens, were especially angry and remain so. While native language ballots may be a convenience to some voters, the use of English ballots does not deprive citizens of their right to vote. Under current voting law, non-English-speaking voters are permitted to bring a friend or family member to the polls to assist them in casting their ballots. Absentee ballots could provide another method that would allow a voter to receive this help at home.

31   Congress should be looking for other methods to create greater access to the ballot box for the currently small number of citizens who cannot understand an English ballot, without resorting to the expense of requiring ballots in foreign languages. We cannot continue to overlook the message we are sending to immigrants about the connection between English language ability and citizenship when we print ballots in other languages. The ballot is the primary symbol of civic duty. When we tell immigrants that they should learn English—yet offer them full voting participation in their native language—I fear our actions will speak louder than our words.

32   If we are to prevent the expansion of policies such as these, moving us further along the multilingual path, we need to make a strong statement that our political leaders will understand. We must let them know that we do not choose to reside in a "Tower of Babel." Making English our nation's official language *by law* will send the proper signal to newcomers about the importance of learning English and provide the necessary guidance to legislators to preserve our traditional policy of a common language.

THINKING CRITICALLY

1. Why does Hayakawa feel it is particularly important for a nation of immigrants to communicate in a single, common tongue? Does the fact that he is an immigrant himself lend credence to his argument? Do you agree with this viewpoint? Why or why not?

2. What is Hayakawa's assessment of countries that recognize two or more official languages? From what you know of multilingual countries, do you tend to agree or disagree with his assessment?

3. How does Hayakawa define bilingual education? What does he feel is its biggest flaw? Drawing from your own experience, do you agree with him? Explain your answer.

4. What alternative to current bilingual education does Hayakawa suggest? Do his alternatives seem like reasonable and feasible solutions?

WRITING ASSIGNMENTS

1. Have you ever been in a place where you did not speak the language? What if you were a child entering a school in which you did not speak the local language? With your classmates, discuss what this experience might be like. If you have been in a similar situation, discuss how your experience influences your opinion about bilingual education.

2. Research the bilingual policy in your state. (If your state does not have a bilingual policy, find out if any legislation is currently under review for either a bilingual policy or to adopt English as the official language of the state.) What is the demographic profile of your state's immigrant population? How does your state provide for non-native speakers in terms of education and social policy?

Why the U.S. Needs an Official Language
Mauro E. Mujica

The question of whether America should have an official language is highly controversial. The English-only movement is particularly troubling for many Spanish-speaking areas of the country, such as California, the Southwest, and Florida. Opponents to the movement fear that laws forbidding the use of Spanish could violate their civil liberties. English-only proponents insist that linguistic divisions prevent national unity, isolate ethnic groups, and reinforce the economic disparagement between the haves and the have-nots. It may surprise Americans that outside the United States, many people believe the United States should adopt an official language: English. In the next essay, Mauro Mujica explains that Americans seem to be the last people to recognize the need for an official language, and why that language should be English.

Mauro E. Mujica is chairman and CEO of U.S. English Inc., the nation's oldest and largest citizens' action group dedicated to preserving the unifying role of the English language. Mujica, who was born in Chile and immigrated to the United States in 1965, has appeared on many television and radio programs including *Today*, *Good Morning America*, and *60 Minutes*. This essay was printed online in 2003 by *The World & I*, a publication that seeks to present a broad range of thought-provoking readings in politics, science, culture, and humanity.

1 In June 2003, the Pew Research Center announced the results of an extensive survey on global trends such as the spread of democracy, globalization, and technology.

Titled "Views of a Changing World," it was conducted from 2001 to 2003 and polled 66,000 people from 50 countries. The survey received some publicity in the United States, mainly because it showed that anti-American sentiments were on the up-swing around the world. Less publicized was the fact that there is a now a global consensus on the need to learn English.

2   One question in the Pew survey asked respondents to agree or disagree with the statement "Children need to learn English to succeed in the world today." Many nations showed almost unanimous agreement on the importance of learning English. Examples include Vietnam, 98 percent; Indonesia, 96 percent; Germany and South Africa, 95 percent; India, 93 percent; China and the Philippines, 92 percent; Honduras, Japan, Nigeria, and Uganda, 91 percent; and France, Mexico, and Ukraine, 90 percent.

3   To an immigrant like myself (from Chile), these results come as no surprise. Parents around the world know that English is the global language and that their children need to learn it to succeed. English is the language of business, higher ed-ucation, diplomacy, aviation, the Internet, science, popular music, entertainment, and international travel. All signs point to its continued acceptance across the planet.

4   Given the globalization of English, one might be tempted to ask why the United States would need to declare English its official language. Why codify something that is happening naturally and without government involvement?

The Retreat of English

5 In fact, even as it spreads across the globe, English is on the retreat in vast sections of the United States. Our government makes it easy for immigrants to function in their native languages through bilingual education, multilingual ballots and driver's license exams, and government-funded translators in schools and hospitals. Providing most essential services to immigrants in their native languages is expensive for American taxpayers and also keeps immigrants linguistically isolated.

6   Historically, the need to speak and understand English has served as an impor-tant incentive for immigrants to learn the language and assimilate into the main-stream of American society. For the last 30 years, this idea has been turned on its head. Expecting immigrants to learn English has been called "racist." Marta Jimenez, an attorney for the Mexican American Legal Defense and Educational Fund, speaks of "the historical use of English in the United States as a tool of oppression."

7   Groups such as the National Association for Bilingual Education complain about the "restrictive goal" of having immigrant children learn in English. The for-mer mayor of Miami, Maurice Ferre, dismissed the idea of even a bilingual future for his city. "We're talking about Spanish as a main form of communication, as an official language," he averred. "Not on the way to English."

8   Perhaps this change is best illustrated in the evolving views of the League of United Latin American Citizens (LULAC). Started in 1929, the group was origi-nally pro-English and pro-assimilation. One of the founding aims and purposes of LULAC was "to foster the acquisition and facile use of the Official Language of

our country that we may hereby equip ourselves and our families for the fullest enjoyment of our rights and privileges and the efficient discharge of our duties and obligations to this, our country." By the 1980s the executive director of LULAC, Arnoldo Torres, could proudly proclaim, "We cannot assimilate and we won't!"

9   The result of this is that the United States has a rapidly growing population of people—often native born—who are not proficient in English. The 2000 Census found that 21.3 million Americans (8 percent of the population) are classified as "limited English proficient," a 52 percent increase from 1990 and more than double the 1980 total. More than 5 million of these people were born in the United States.

10   Citing census statistics gives an idea of how far English is slipping in America, but it does not show how this is played out in everyday life. Consider the following examples:

- The *New York Times* reports that Hispanics account for over 40 percent of the population of Hartford, Connecticut, and that the city is becoming "Latinized." Last year, Eddie Perez became Hartford's first Hispanic mayor. The city Web page is bilingual, and after-hours callers to the mayor's office are greeted by a message in Spanish. Half of Hartford's Hispanics do not speak English. According to Freddy Ortiz, who owns a bakery in the city, "In the bank, they speak Spanish; at the hospital, they speak Spanish; my bakery suppliers are starting to speak Spanish. Even at the post office, they are Americans, but they speak Spanish." Even Mayor Perez notes that "we've become a Latin city, so to speak. It's a sign of things to come."
- In May, about 20 percent of the students at Miami Senior High School, where 88 percent of the students speak English as a second language, failed the annual Florida Comprehensive Assessment Test (FCAT) exam, which is required for graduation. The poor results prompted protests and demands for the test to be given in Spanish as well as English. Over 200 students and teachers gathered outside the school waving signs and chanting "No FCAT." A state senator from Miami introduced a bill that would allow the FCAT to be given in Spanish.
- Just a day before the Pew survey was released, Gwinnett County in Georgia announced it will provide its own staff translators for parents of students who speak Spanish, Korean, and Vietnamese. The school board approved $138,000 for the new translators despite a tight budget. Donna Robertson, a principal at an elementary school in the county, claimed the translators are only a short-term solution. The real solution, she claims, is a multilingual school staff. There are 46 languages spoken among students in Gwinnett County.
- In May, a poll taken by NBC News and the *Sun-Sentinel* newspaper of Fort Lauderdale, Florida, found 83 percent of Hispanics in south Florida agreeing that "it is easy to get along day in and day out without speaking English well/at all."

The Costs of Multilingualism

11 Multilingual government is not cheap. Bilingual education alone is estimated to cost taxpayers billions of dollars per year. The federal government has spent over $100 million to study the effectiveness of bilingual education, only to discover that it is less effective at teaching English than English immersion programs are. Much

of the cost for court and school translators, multilingual voting ballots, and multiple document translations is picked up at the local level. Even during good economic times, this is a burden. In lean years it is a budget breaker, taking funds away from education, health care, transportation, and police and fire services.

12   For example, Los Angeles County spent $3.3 million, 15 percent of the entire election budget, to print election ballots in seven languages and hire multilingual poll workers for the March 2002 primary. The county also spends $265 per day for each of 420 full-time court interpreters. San Francisco spends $350,000 per each language that documents must be translated into under its bilingual government ordinance. Financial officials in Washington, D.C., estimate that a proposed language access would cost $7.74 million to implement. The bill would require all city agencies to hire translators and translate official documents for any language spoken by over 500 non-English-speaking people in the city.

13   The health-care industry, already reeling from a shortage of nurses and the costs of treating the uninsured, was dealt another blow by President Clinton. Executive Order 13166 was signed into law on August 11, 2000. The order requires private physicians, clinics, and hospitals that accept Medicare and Medicaid to provide, at their own expense, translators for any language spoken by any patient. The cost of an interpreter can exceed the reimbursement of a Medicare or Medicaid visit by 13 times—costing doctors as much as $500 per translator.

14   Of course, there are also nonmonetary costs associated with a multilingual America. These expenses often have a human cost.

15   A 22-year-old immigrant won a $71 million settlement because a group of paramedics and doctors misdiagnosed a blood clot in his brain. The man's relatives used the Spanish word intoxicado to describe his ailment. They meant he was nauseated, but the translator interpreted the word to mean intoxicated.

16   Six children were killed when a loose tailgate from a tractor trailer fell off on a Milwaukee highway. The driver of the family's SUV could not avoid the tailgate, which punctured the gas tank and caused the vehicle to explode. An investigation found that other truckers had tried to warn the driver of the tractor trailer about his loose tailgate, but the driver did not understand English.

17   An immigrant in Orange County, California, died from a fall into a 175-degree vat of chemicals at an Anaheim metal-plating shop. Though the company's instructions clearly forbade walking on the five-inch rail between tanks, they were printed in English, a language that the worker did not understand. An inquiry into the accident found that many of the recent hires were not proficient in English.

18   Hispanics accounted for nearly one-third of Georgia's workplace deaths in 2000, despite making up only 5.3 percent of the state's population. The National Institute for Occupational Safety and Health, a branch of the U.S. Centers for Disease Control and Prevention, blamed "misunderstandings arising from language barriers" for the deaths and said they "could be prevented and don't have to happen."

The Dis-United States

19 We need only look to Canada to see the problems a multilingual society can bring. America's northern neighbor faces a severe constitutional crisis over the issue of language. In 1995, the predominately French-speaking province of Quebec came

within a few thousand votes of seceding from Canada. The secessionist Parti
Québécois ruled the province until this year. The national government must cater to
Quebec to preserve order and maintain a cohesive government. This has spurred
secessionist movements in English-speaking western Canada on the grounds that
the Canadian government favors French speakers.

20   Of course, battles over language rage across the globe, but since Canada is so
similar, it offers the most instructive warning for the United States. While the policy of official multilingualism has led to disunity, resentment, and near-secession, it
is also very costly. Canada's dual-language requirement costs approximately
$260 million each year. Canada has one-tenth the population of the United States
and spent that amount accommodating only two languages. A similar language
policy would cost the United States much more than $4 billion annually, as we have
a greater population and many more languages to accommodate.

21   Unless the United States changes course, it is clearly on the road to a Canadian-
style system of linguistic enclaves, wasteful government expenses, language battles
that fuel ethnic resentments, and, in the long run, serious ethnic and linguistic sepa-
ratist movements.

22   What is at stake here is the unity of our nation. Creating an American-style
Quebec in the Southwest as well as "linguistic islands" in other parts of the United
States will be a disaster far exceeding the Canadian problem. Now, over 8 percent
of the population cannot speak English proficiently. What happens when that number turns to 10 percent, 20 percent, or more?

23   The American assimilation process, often called the melting pot, is clearly not
working. Declaring English to be our official language would bring back the
incentive to learn it. Specifically, this step would require that all laws, public
proceedings, regulations, publications, orders, actions, programs, and policies are
conducted in the English language. There would be some commonsense exceptions
in the areas of public health and safety, national security, tourism, and commerce.

24   Of course, declaring English the official language would only apply to government. People can still speak whatever language they choose at home and in private
life. Official English legislation should also be combined with provisions for more
English classes for non-English speakers. This can be paid for with a fraction of the
money saved by ending multilingual government.

25   A bill in Congress would make this a reality. . . . If it passes, we can start to
rebuild the American assimilation process and lessen the amount of linguistic separation in the United States. If it fails, we might have lost the last best chance for a
sensible and cohesive language policy in this country. If that happens we can say
"hasta la vista" to the "United" States and "adelante" to Canadian-style discord
over the issues of language and ethnicity.

THINKING CRITICALLY

1. The Pew study reported that many people outside of the United States strongly
   feel that knowledge of English is necessary for success. What is the basis for
   this sentiment? Does it surprise you? Why or why not?

2. In paragraph 4, Mujica postulates, "one might be tempted to ask why the United
   States would need to declare English its official language. Why codify something

that is happening naturally and without government involvement?" Evaluate his argument as to why it is indeed important that the United States adopt English as its official language.

3. What is the irony of the "retreat" of English in the United States? Explain.

4. According to Mujica, what are the costs of multilingualism? Include in your answer the cultural, political, intellectual, social, and economic ramifications of a nation that does not adopt an official language.

5. Other countries such as France, England, and Brazil are not deemed "racist" (paragraph 6) for having national languages. Is the United States different from other countries that have official languages? Why or why not? In your opinion, do you think that adopting English as the official language of the United States would be racist?

6. According to Mujica, what are the social issues behind opposition to English as the official language?

WRITING ASSIGNMENTS

1. Interview a number of people who had to learn English as a second language. How did they do it? What difficulties did they encounter? What assistance were they given as they learned English? How did learning English affect their lives? Encourage your interviewees to share stories of success as well as of failure.

2. An argument in favor of bilingual education is that mother-tongue instruction increases cultural and ethnic pride in the heritage of the mother country. Immigrant children are allowed to take pride in their home culture, while learning in their native tongue. Do you think denying them this heritage and forcing English upon people is, as Marta Jimenez asserts, an attorney for the Mexican American Legal Defense and Educational Fund, "a tool of oppression"? Write a paper in which you explore your feelings on this pro-bilingual perspective.

Proposal for an American Language Academy
John Adams

John Adams was the first (1789–1797) vice president of the United States and the second president of the United States. As an author, Adams helped define and outline the principles of American values and the core of legislature and government. In 1780, Adams, recognizing the unifying nature of language, lobbied Congress to institute an American Language Academy, to "correct and improve" the English language in the newly formed United States. Perhaps inspired by the illustrious L'Académie Française, which was created to preserve and refine the French language, Adams forsaw that English was "destined to be more generally the language of the world." His proposal to Congress, written while on a mission to Europe during the Revolutionary War, appears below.

1 As eloquence is cultivated with more care in free republics than in other governments, it has been found by constant experience that such republics have produced the greatest purity, copiousness, and perfection of language. It is not to be disputed that the form of government has an influence upon language, and language in its

turn influences not only the form of government, but the temper, the sentiments, and manners of the people. The admirable models which have been transmitted through the world, and continued down to these days, so as to form an essential part of the education of mankind from generation to generation, by those two ancient towns, Athens and Rome, would be sufficient, without any other argument, to show the United States the importance to their liberty, prosperity, and glory, of an early attention to the subject of eloquence and language.

2   Most of the nations of Europe have thought it necessary to establish by public authority institutions for fixing and improving their proper languages. I need not mention the academies in France, Spain, and Italy, their learned labors, nor their great success. But it is very remarkable, that although many learned and ingenious men in England have from age to age projected similar institutions for correcting and improving the English tongue, yet the government have never found time to interpose in any manner; so that to this day there is no grammar nor dictionary extant of the English language which has the least public authority; and it is only very lately, that a tolerable dictionary has been published, even by a private person, and there is not yet a passable grammar enterprised by any individual.

3   The honor of forming the first public institution for refining, correcting, improving, and ascertaining the English language, I hope is reserved for congress; they have every motive than can possibly influence a public assembly to undertake it. It will have a happy effect upon the union of the States to have a public standard for all persons in every part of the continent to appeal to, both for the signification and pronunciation of the language. The constitutions of all the States in the Union are so democratical that eloquence will become the instrument for recommending men to their fellow-citizens, and the principal means of advancement through the various ranks and offices of society.

4   In the last century, Latin was the universal language of Europe. Correspondence among the learned, and indeed among merchants and men of business, and the conversation of strangers and travellers, was generally carried on in that dead language. In the present century, Latin has been generally laid aside, and French has been substituted in its place, but has not yet become universally established, and, according to present appearances, it is not probable that it will. English is destined to be the next and succeeding centuries more generally the language of the world than Latin was in the last or French is in the present age. The reason of this is obvious, because the increasing population in America, and their universal connection and correspondence with all nations will, aided by the influence of England in the world, whether great or small, force their language into general use, in spite of all the obstacles that may be thrown in their way, if any such there should be.

5   It is not necessary to enlarge further, to show the motives which the people of America have to turn their thoughts early to this subject; they will naturally occur to congress in a much greater detail than I have time to hint at. I would therefore submit to the consideration of congress the expediency and policy of erecting by their authority a society under the name of "the American Academy for refining, improving, and ascertaining the English Language." The authority of congress is necessary to give such a society reputation, influence, and authority through all the States and with other nations. The number of members of which it

shall consist, the manner of appointing those members, whether each State shall have a certain number of members and the power of appointing them, or whether congress shall have a certain number of members and the power of appointing them, or whether congress shall appoint them, whether after the first appointment the society itself shall fill up vacancies, these and other questions will easily be determined by congress.

6   It will be necessary that the society should have a library consisting of a complete collection of all writings concerning languages of every sort, ancient and modern. They must have some officers and some other expenses which will make some small funds indispensably necessary. Upon a recommendations from congress, there is no doubt but the legislature of every State in the confederation would readily pass a law making such a society a body politic, enable it to sue and be sued, and to hold an estate, real or personal, of a limited value in that State.

THINKING CRITICALLY

1. In paragraph 4, Adams predicts that English, like Latin and French before it, will become the "language of the world." In your own words, explain why Adams was correct or incorrect. To support your response, research the influence and prevalence of English in the international realms of commerce, education, science, and politics.

2. Do you think an American Language Academy is a good idea? Why or why not?

3. How do you think Congress would receive Adams's proposal today? Explain.

4. Based on his proposal, do you think that Adams is a descriptivist or a prescriptivist? Would he support the idea of English as the official language of the United States? Do you think he would be surprised to learn that this is such a political issue?

And May He Be Bilingual
Julia Ortiz Cofer

A native of Puerto Rico, Julia Ortiz Cofer moved to the United States when she was a young girl. Educated at both American and British universities, she is the author of several books, including the novel *The Line of the Sun* (1989), for which she was nominated for a Pulitzer Prize, a collection of essays, *The Latin Deli* (1993), and *Silent Dancing: A Partial Remembrance of a Puerto Rican Childhood* (1998). Ortiz Cofer teaches literature and writing at the University of Georgia at Athens. This essay was first published in her 2000 book, *Woman in Front of the Sun: On Becoming a Writer.*

Latin Women Pray
In incense churches
They pray in Spanish to an Anglo God
With Jewish heritage.
And this Great White Father

> Impertubable in his marble pedestal
> Looks down upon his brown daughters
> Votive candles shinning like lust
> In his all seeing eyes
> Unmoved by their persistent prayers.
>
> Yet year after year
> Before his image they kneel
> Margarita Josefina Maria and Isabel
> All fervently hoping
> That if not omnipotent
> At least he be bilingual.

1 In this early poem I express the sense of powerlessness I felt as a nonnative speaker of English in the United States. Nonnative. Nonparticipant in the mainstream culture. *Non*, as in no, not, nothing. This little poem is about the non-ness of the non-speakers of the ruling language making a pilgrimage to the only One who can help, hopeful in their faith that someone is listening, yet still suspicious that even He doesn't understand their language. I grew up in the tight little world of the Puerto Rican community in Paterson, New Jersey, and later moved to August, Georgia, where my "native" universe shrank even further to a tiny group of us who were brought to the Deep South through the military channels our fathers had chosen out of economic necessity. I wrote this ironic poem years ago, out of a need to explore the loneliness, the almost hopelessness, I had felt and observed in the other nonnative speakers, many my own relatives, who would never master the English language well enough to be able to connect with the native speakers in as significant ways as I did.

2 Having come to age within the boundaries of language exiles, and making only brief forays out in the vast and often frightening landscape called *the mainstream*, it's easy for the newcomer to become ethnocentric. That's what Little Italy, Little Korea, Little Havana, Chinatown, and barrios are, centers of ethnic concerns. After all, it's a natural human response to believe that there is safety only within the walls around the circle of others who look likes us, speak like us, behave like us: it is the animal kingdom's basic rule of survival—if whatever is coming toward you does not look like you or your kin, either fight or fly.

3 It is this primal fear of the unfamiliar that I have conquered through education, travel, and my art. I am an English teacher by profession and a writer by vocation. I have written several books of prose and poetry based mainly on my experiences in growing up Latina in the United States. Until a few years ago, when multiculturalism became part of the American political agenda, no one seemed to notice my work; suddenly I find myself a Puerto Rican/American (Latina)/Woman writer. Not only am I supposed to share my particular vision of American life, but I am also supposed to be a role model for a new generation of Latino students who expect me to teach them how to get a piece of the proverbial English language pie. I actually enjoy both of these public roles, in moderation. I love teaching literature. Not my own work, but the work of my literary ancestors in English and American literature—my

field, that is, the main source of my models as a writer. I also like going into my classrooms at the University of Georgia, where my English classes at this point are still composed mainly of white American students, with a sprinkling of African American and Asian American, and only occasionally a Latino, and sharing my bi-cultural, bilingual views with them. It is a fresh audience. I am not always speaking to converts.

4   I teach American literature as an outsider in love with the Word—whatever language it is written in. They, at least some of them, come to understand that my main criterion when I teach is excellence and that I will talk to them about so-called minority writers whom I admire in the same terms as I will the old standards they know they are supposed to honor and study. I will show them why they should admire them, not blindly, but with a critical eye. I speak English with my Spanish accent to these native speakers. I tell them about my passion for the genius of humankind, demonstrated through literature: the power of language to affect, to enrich, or to diminish and destroy lives, its potential to empower someone like me, someone like them. The fact that English is my second language does not seem to matter beyond the first few lectures, when the students sometimes look askance at one another, perhaps wondering whether they have walked into the wrong class-room and at any moment this obviously "Spanish" professor will ask them to start conjugating regular and irregular verbs. They can't possibly know this about me: in my classes, everyone is safe from Spanish grammar recitation. Because almost all of my formal education has been in English, I avoid all possible risk of falling into a discussion of the uses of the conditional or the merits of the subjunctive tense in the Spanish language. Hey, I just *do* Spanish, I don't explain it.

5   Likewise, when I *do* use my Spanish and allude to my Puerto Rican heritage, it comes from deep inside me where my imagination and memory reside, and I do it through my writing. My poetry, my stories, and my essays concern themselves with the coalescing of languages and cultures into a vision that has meaning first of all for me; then, if I am served well by my craft and the transformation occurs, it will also have meaning for others as art.

6   My life as a child and teenager was one of constant dislocation. My father was in the U.S. Navy, and we moved back to Puerto Rico during his long tours of duty abroad. On the Island, my brother and I attended a Catholic school run by American nuns. Then it was back to Paterson, New Jersey, to try to catch up, and sometimes we did, academically, but socially it was a different story altogether. We were the perennial new kids on the block. Yet when I write about these gypsy days, I con-struct a continuity that allows me to see my life as equal to any other, with its share of chaos, with its own system of order. This is what I have learned from writing as a minority person in America that I can teach my students: Literature is the human search for meaning. It is as simple and as profound as that. And we are all, if we are thinking people, involved in the process. It is both a privilege and a burden.

7   Although as a child I often felt resentful of my rootlessness, deprived of a stable home, lasting friendships, the security of one house, one country, I now real-ize that these same circumstances taught me some skills that I use today to adapt in a constantly changing world, a place where you can remain in one spot for years and still wake up every day to strangeness wrought by technology and politics.

We can stand still and find ourselves in a different nation created overnight by decisions we did not participate in making. I submit that we are all becoming more like the immigrant and can learn from her experiences as a stranger in a strange land. I know I am a survivor in language. I learned early that possessing the secret of words was to buy my passport into mainstream life. Notice I did not say "assimilation" into mainstream life. This is a word that has come to mean the acceptance of loss of native culture. Although I know for a fact that to survive everyone "assimilates" what they need out of many different cultures, especially in America, I prefer to use the term "adapt" instead. Just as I acquired the skills to adapt to American life, I have now come to terms with a high-tech world. It is not that different. I learned English to communicate, but now I know computer language. I have been greedy in my grasping and hoarding of words. I own enough stock in English to feel secure in almost any situation where my language skills have to serve me; and I have claimed my rich Puerto Rican culture to give scope and depth to my personal search for meaning.

8   As I travel around this country I am constantly surprised by the diversity of its peoples and cultures. It is like a huge, colorful puzzle. And the beauty is in its complexity. Yet here are some things that transcend the obvious differences: great literature, great ideas, and great idealists, for example. I find Don Quixote plays almost universal; after all, who among does not have an Impossible Dream? Shakespeare's wisdom is planetary in its appeal; Ghandi's and King's message is basic to the survival of our civilization, and most people know it; and other voices that are like a human racial memory speak in a language that can almost always be translated into meaning.

9   And genius doesn't come in only one package. The Bard happened to be a white gentleman from England, but what about our timid Emily Dickinson? Would we call on her in our class, that mousy little girl in the back of the room squinting at the chalkboard and blushing at everything? We almost lost her art to neglect. Thank God poetry is stronger than time and prejudices.

10   This is where my idealism as a teacher kicks in: I ask myself, who is to say that at this very moment there isn't a Native American teenager gazing dreamily at the desert outside her window as she works on today's assignment, seeing the universe in a grain of sand, preparing herself to share her unique vision with the world. It may all depend on the next words she hears, which may come out of my mouth, or yours. And what about the African American boy in a rural high school in Georgia who showed me he could rhyme for as long as I let him talk, His teachers had not been able to get him to respond to literature. Now they listened in respectful silence as he composed an ode to his girl and his car extemporaneously, in a form so tight and right (contagious too) that when we discuss the exalted Alexander Pope's oeuvre, we call it heroic couplets. But he was intimidated by the manner in which Pope and his worthy comrades in the canon had been presented to him and his classmates, as gods from Mount Olympus, inimitable and incomprehensible to mere mortals like himself. He was in turn surprised to see, when it was finally brought to his attention, that Alexander Pope and he shared a good ear.

11   What I'm trying to say is that the phenomenon we call culture in a society is organic, not manufactured. It grows where we plant it. Culture is our garden, and

we may neglect it, trample on it, or we may choose to cultivate it. In America we are dealing with varieties we have imported, grafted, cross-pollinated. I can only hope the experts who say that the land is replenished in this way are right. It is the ongoing American experiment, and it has to take root in the classroom first. If it doesn't succeed, then we will be back to praying and hoping that at least He be bilingual.

THINKING CRITICALLY

1. Why did Ortiz Cofer feel "powerless" as a nonnative speaker of English in the United States? How did she reconcile this feeling as an adult? Explain.

2. Why does Ortiz Cofer object to the word "assimilate"? What word does she use instead? Do you think she makes a valid point?

3. Based on her essay, do you think Ortiz Cofer agrees or disagrees that English should be the official language of the United States? Explain.

4. How does Ortiz Cofer's poem connect to the points she makes in her essay? Do you think her sharing this early poem makes her essay stronger? Why or why not?

5. Why does Ortiz Cofer point out that she does not favor Latino or minority writers over the more traditional writers? Why does she want her readers to know this?

6. What is the point of Ortiz Cofer's essay? Identify her thesis, and summarize each paragraph as it connects back to her main point.

WRITING ASSIGNMENTS

1. Write an essay analyzing Ortiz Cofer's opening poem. In what ways is the poem autobiographical? How does tone, irony, and imagery work to convey meaning in the poem? Explain.

2. Ortiz Cofer relates the story of one student who came to appreciate literature after she nurtured his ability to rhyme (paragraph 10). Write a personal narrative describing your own appreciation of literature and/or writing, such as a time when a teacher inspired you, or a moment when you connected to the theme or ideas expressed in a poem, story, or play.

The Overwhelming Allure of English
Gregory Rodriguez

Mexican-Americans comprise the second largest immigrant population in American history and they are poised to become America's largest minority group. Influences of Latino culture are pervading mainstream society, from style and architecture, to music and language. In the next piece, Gregory Rodriguez explains that although Latino culture and Spanish make an impact on American society, English still prevails. While Spanish may be the "unofficial" second language of the United States, its influence on individuals speaking Spanish fades within a generation or two.

Rodriguez is a senior fellow at the New America Foundation, a nonpartisan public policy institute "dedicated to bringing exceptionally promising new voices and ideas to the fore of the nation's public discourse." He is a contributing editor to the opinion section of the *Los Angeles Times* and a political analyst for *MSNBC*. This article was published in the *New York Times* on April 7, 2002.

1   A generation of large-scale Latin American immigration has turned Spanish into the unofficial second language of the United States.

2   In March [of 2002], Texas held the nation's first-ever gubernatorial debate in Spanish. President Bush never misses an opportunity to show that he, too, can speak the language of Cervantes. Meanwhile, with the press of a button, most automated teller machines can communicate with customers in digital Spanish. From the streets of Miami to Los Angeles, it sometimes feels as if Spanish is giving English a run for its money.

3   But even with this proliferation of Spanish, the United States is still, in the words of one prominent sociologist, a country that is a "language graveyard" for foreign tongues. While many Americans fret over the state of their nation's primary language, there are signs everywhere that English is triumphant both at home and abroad.

4   As the United States strengthens its position as the world's economic superpower, the global reach of its popular culture—and accompanying English language—only grows. By mid-century, half the planet is expected to be more or less proficient in English, compared to roughly 12 percent now. Why should the American-born children of immigrants be somehow immune to the rising power of the international language of diplomacy and commerce?

5   Still, there is a growing concern that the rise of Spanish threatens the pre-eminence of English in America. [In March of 2002] Iowa became the 27th state to declare English its official language—the 10th since 1995. While *The Des Moines Register* dismissed the act as "an embarrassment" perpetrated by a "bunch of yahoos in the Legislature," four out of five Iowans supported it.

6   To be sure, the United States' proximity to Latin America combined with the sheer size and continuous nature of Latino migration has changed the nation's cultural landscape. Mass media, modern transportation and the Internet all nurture Spanish in the United States in a way inconceivable to earlier waves of immigrants. And unlike those who came before, today's immigrants can hear their native tongue on morning drive-time radio and watch soap operas from their homeland in the evening. Over the last decade, Spanish-language TV and radio boomed in the nation's largest media markets.

7   But while immigration has powered the rise of Spanish-language media, a new demographic trend is already shifting the balance in favor of English—even in the heaviest immigrant media markets in America. In Los Angeles, home to the nation's largest Latino immigrant population, Spanish-language radio stations routinely topped the charts for most of the 1990's. But the growth of Spanish-language radio leveled off in the last few years. For the past nine months, KROQ, an alternative, youth-oriented rock station, has snagged the region's highest overall ratings. It is the first time since 1991 that an English-language station has remained

No. 1 for three consecutive ratings periods. A fragmented Spanish-language radio market helped KROQ, but the station has a fundamental trend on its side.

8   "The Hispanic share of our listenership has increased gradually over the past 10 years," says Trip Reeb, KROQ's general manager. Without actively seeking to broaden its ethnic appeal, the station, long considered "white," now has a 40 percent Latino audience. In fact, a growing number of mainstream English-language radio stations find themselves with sizable Latino audiences. "Right when everyone is discovering the importance of using Spanish, we're seeing Latinos become the backbone of the English-language audience," said Patricia Suarez, president of Suarez/Frommer & Associates, an advertising firm in Pasadena, Calif.

9   Sometime in the 1990's, demographers say, the foreign-born portion of the Latino population reached its peak. In other words, on the basis of current projections, from now on the immigrant or first generation will be a smaller percentage of Hispanic America. According to Barry Edmonston, the head of the Population Research Center at Portland State University, the fastest-growing segment of the Latino population is the third generation, which is projected to triple by 2040. The second generation is expected to double. "In every immigrant experience, there is a shift from immigrant culture to ethnic American culture," said Mr. Edmonston. "Hispanics are in the middle of that shift right now."

10   As American Latinos now become less an immigrant market and more an ethnic market, the equation of Latinos with Spanish is beginning to fade. While slower to make the shift than other immigrant groups, Latino linguistic assimilation is not entirely unlike that of immigrants at the turn of the 20th century. According to the 1990 Census, fully two-thirds of third-generation Latino children spoke only English. And while bilingualism does persist longer within Latino families, particularly along the border region, there is no indication this precludes the use of English as the primary language.

11   As in past waves of immigration, the first generation tends to learn only enough English to get by; the second is bilingual; and the third tends to be English-dominant if not monolingual.

12   "The big picture is that bilingualism is very difficult to maintain in the U.S., and by the third generation it is extraordinarily difficult to maintain," said Richard Alba, a sociology professor at the State University of New York at Albany. "This is because English is so dominant and so highly rewarded."

13   It makes sense that the shift to English is being felt first in the youth entertainment market. A two-year-old study by Nielsen Media Research shows that even in households where the adults speak Spanish, younger Latinos prefer to watch television in English. In fact, the preference for English over Spanish becomes more lopsided the younger the demographic. Nickelodeon, the children's cable network, has embraced mainstream Latino characters more than any other network.

14   Two years ago, the Walt Disney Company failed in the first large-scale effort by a Hollywood studio to broaden its domestic Latino base. But after simultaneously releasing an English and Spanish-language version of the animated film "The Emperor's New Groove" in 16 theaters, the studio pulled the dubbed version for lack of interest. "The Latino audience clearly came out for the movie, but that

audience definitely preferred to see it in English," said Richard W. Cook, chairman of Walt Disney Motion Pictures Group.

15   Similarly, even as the Latino population exploded, Spanish-language movie theaters in Southern California were closing. In the last half of the 1990's, a company that screens foreign and dubbed films cut the number of its movie houses dedicated to Spanish-speaking audiences by more than half. Like Americans at large, the average Latino moviegoer is a teenager. And the average Latino teenager is American-born and more eager to see a contemporary English-language action film than the art-house fare from contemporary Latin America. In fact, a recent study of the children of immigrants found that by the end of high school 9 in 10 preferred to speak English and 98 percent spoke it proficiently.

16   At the same time, Spanish is certainly not going away in the regions of the country that serve as gateways to new immigrants. American-born Latinos can enjoy Latin-American soap operas or old-fashioned boleros on the radio. But like children of immigrants in the past, the descendants of today's newcomers will negotiate their work lives and create art and music in the language in which they are schooled. While bilingual education is often blamed for the persistence of Spanish in the United States, most such programs are designed to shift the child into English-speaking classes within three or four years. In addition, a few elementary school years in Spanish do not give students adult-level proficiency. Even in Miami, the nation's quintessential bilingual city, international corporations complain of a shortage of fully bilingual workers to conduct business with Latin Americans in professional Spanish.

17   Thus, despite the obvious benefits of bilingualism in a globalizing world, English still overwhelms the languages that immigrants bring to these shores. Not unlike previous large waves of immigrants, Latinos are introducing words and phrases of their native language into mainstream English. But within generations of arriving in America, Latinos eager to read the classic works of Cervantes or Gabriel García Márquez will most likely do so through English translations.

THINKING CRITICALLY

1. In what ways is the United States a "language graveyard"? Explain.

2. According to Rodriguez, what is the "overwhelming allure of English"? What examples does he give to support his argument that English prevails even when attempts to preserve multilingualism are made?

3. What is the author's position on the issue of English as the official language of the United States? Identify passages from his essay that reveal his position. Is his argument biased? balanced? Explain.

4. Think about your own family's experience in the United States. Did they need to learn a new language? Did it take them long to be accepted? If so, how quickly did they learn English? Did it require generations to complete? Or is the process of learning English still a daily reality for your family? Explain.

5. Rodriguez observes that in 2002, a gubernatorial debate (in Texas) was held in Spanish. Do you think this is an indication that Spanish is gaining wider acceptance? Why or why not?

WRITING ASSIGNMENTS

1. Rodriguez ends his essay with the observation "Not unlike previous large waves of immigrants, Latinos are introducing words and phrases of their native language into mainstream English." How does Spanish influence American English? Write a paper assessing the influence of Spanish on mainstream English in the United States.

2. If Mauro E. Mujica, Julia Ortiz Cofer, and Gregory Rodriguez were to engage in a debate on the issue of language assimilation, especially as it relates to the Latino population, how do you think each would respond to the others? As a first step in this exercise, summarize each writer's argument. Does one author develop a stronger case? Explain.

MAKING CONNECTIONS

1. Write an essay supporting or opposing an amendment to the United States Constitution making English the official language.

2. A national language is the language of public discourse, control, and power. Do you think that English instruction for non-English-speaking children should be left to chance or be approached by early, intensive instruction in school? Write a paper in which you explore your thoughts on this question. Consider in your discussion the effects of home language and culture on personal pride.

3. One argument against bilingual education is that language-minority children cannot be separated from language-majority speakers if they are to enjoy the maximum benefits of public school education. The argument further maintains that if children are taught separately, they will never properly integrate into blended classrooms and later the professional community. Write a paper in which you take a stand for or against this argument.

4. Have you ever been in a place where you did not speak the language? At a social gathering? traveling in a non-English speaking region or country? in an educational setting? With your classmates, discuss these situations. If you have been in one of these situation, discuss how your experience influences your opinion about bilingual education.

5. Consider how information is distributed in your community. Do you live in a multilingual area? Do signs feature other languages in addition to English? What about access to television programming or medical services? If so, how does this multilingual environment affect your own social and linguistic experience, if at all? Explain.

6. Many of the essays in this section refer to the concept of "mainstream" society, and how English is the language of "mainstream" society. Write an essay in which you identify and describe mainstream society. Who is part of it, and how do they belong in it? Who decides what is "mainstream" and what is not? Or if you wish, you may argue that such an entity does not exist in modern America.

Credits

Image Credits

Page 23: www.rften.org. **Page 25:** AKG Images. **Page 26:** Kavaler/Art Resource, NY. **Page 27:** Snark/Art Resource, NY. **Page 49:** Bil Keane, Inc. King Features Syndicate. **Page 90:** UNESCO. **Page 93:** AP Wideworld Photos. **Page 130:** Reza/Webistan, Paris. **Page 133:** Bettman/CORBIS. **Page 152:** Bettman/CORBIS. **Page 154:** Bill Aron/PhotoEdit. **Page 196:** Getty Images. **Page 236:** AP Wideworld Photos. **Page 237:** AP Wideworld Photos. **Page 259:** Courtesy of the Arab American Institute. **Page 290:** AP Wideworld Photos. **Page 297:** PureStock/Jupiter Images. **Page 336:** © The New Yorker Collection 1997 Roz Chast from cartoonbank.com. All Rights Reserved. **Page 367:** Lee Snider/The Image Works. **Page 433:** The Advertising Archives. **Page 434:** Copyright © 2006 by Escort Inc. All Rights Reserved. **Page 436:** Courtesy of Visa. **Page 438:** The Advertising Archives. **Page 440:** Lowe Worldwide, Inc. as agent for National Fluid Milk Processor Promotion Board. **Page 443:** © 2000 Rohan Van Twest/Stone/Getty Images. **Page 454:** Reprinted with permission of the American Library Association. **Page 458:** The Adventures of Huckleberry Finn, by Mark Twain, © 1988 The Mark Twain Foundation. Published by the University of California Press. **Page 526:** Zachary Parker/www.zacharyparker.com. **Page 528:** Michael Newman/PhotoEdit.

Text Credits

John Leo, "The Thought Police Keep Marching West," by John Leo. First appeared on Townhall.com, March 5, 2006. Reprinted by permission.

Michael C. Corballis, *From Hand to Mouth*. Copyright © 2002 by Princeton University Press. Reprinted by permission of Princeton University Press.

Susanne K. Langer, "Language and Thought," *Fortune*, 1944. Reprinted by permission.

Paul Roberts, "A Brief History of English," *Understanding English*. Copyrighted © 1958 by Paul Roberts. Copyright renewed. Reprinted by permission of Longman Publishers.

Stephen Pinker, "Horton Heard a Who," as it appeared in *Time Magazine* November 1, 1999. Reprinted by permission of the author.

Margalit Fox, "Another Language for the Deaf," Copyright © 2002 by The New York Times Co. Reprinted by permission.

James Geary, "Speaking in Tongues," © 1997 Time, Inc., July 7, 1997. Reprinted by permission.

Soo Ji Min, "Lost in Translation," from *Science and Spirit*; November/December 2004; pages 36-41. Reprinted by permission of the Helen Dwight Reid Educational Foundation. Published by Heldref Publications, 1319 Eighteenth St. NW, Washington, DC 20036-1802. Copyright © 2004.

Index of Authors and Titles